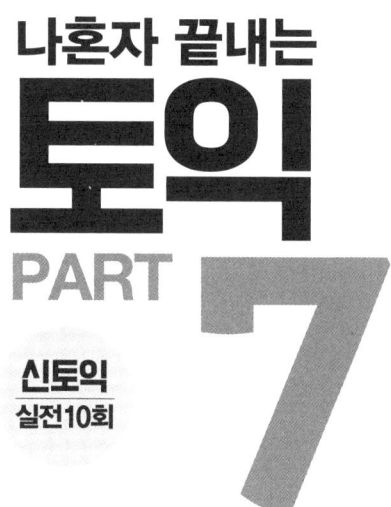

나혼자 끝내는

토익

PART 7

신토익
실전10회

나혼자 끝내는 토익 PART 7

신토익 실전 10회

지은이 이미영, 박선영
펴낸이 임상진
펴낸곳 (주)넥서스

초판 1쇄 인쇄 2017년 7월 25일
초판 1쇄 발행 2017년 7월 30일

출판신고 1992년 4월 3일 제311-2002-2호
10880 경기도 파주시 지목로 5
Tel (02)330-5500 Fax (02)330-5555

ISBN 979-11-6165-080-7 13740

www.nexusbook.com

나혼자 끝내는
토익
PART 7

이미영·박선영 지음

신토익
실전10회

넥서스

PREFACE

TOEIC 분야에 몸담은 지 벌써 10년 차가 되어 갑니다. 시간이 지나면서, 시험의 경향과 유형도 바뀌고, 공부하는 학생들의 성향과 공부 방법조차 많이 바뀌었습니다. 그러나 딱 한 가지 변하지 않는 것이 있는데, 바로 TOEIC을 공부하는 학생들의 '고득점에 대한 바람'입니다. 모든 건 바뀌어도 원하는 점수를 받거나 고득점을 꿈꾸는 학생들의 마음은 변함이 없습니다. 하지만 이는 말처럼 쉬운 일도, 단기간에 가능한 일도 아닐 것입니다.

특히, 신토익이 시행된 이후 상대적으로 점수가 잘 오르지 않는 RC에서 어려움을 느끼는 학생들이 많이 있습니다. RC에서 점수 획득의 중요한 요소는 무엇보다도 '시간 관리 및 문제 해결 능력'입니다. 주어진 시간 안에 문제 해결 능력을 발휘해서 좋은 점수를 받는다는 것은 굉장한 훈련과 노력을 요합니다. 그중 PART 7은 긴 지문과 선택지로 이루어져 있기 때문에 시간이 부족한 경우가 많습니다. 결국 RC에서 시간 정복의 핵심 열쇠는 PART 7의 문제 해결 능력이라고 해도 과언이 아니겠지요.

하나, TOEIC 시험은 매달 새로운 문제로 구성됩니다. 〈나혼자 끝내는 토익 PART 7〉은 최신 기출 문제들의 '주제와 형식, 문제의 경향' 등을 모두 분석하고 종합하여 실전 난이도와 가장 유사하게 만들었습니다.

둘, PART 7에 자주 출제되는 지문뿐만 아니라 특수한 지문, 빈출 유형 및 특수 유형 문제를 골고루 배치해서 실전에서 실력을 가장 잘 발휘할 수 있도록 설계되었습니다.

셋, 상세한 해석과 해설, 어휘를 담았습니다. 내용이 잘 이해되지 않거나 해설 및 어휘가 불충분한 책이 많이 있습니다만, 이 책은 분명 다르다는 것을 아시게 될 겁니다.

오늘도 많은 학생들이 단 몇 점이라도 더 올리기 위해 구슬땀을 흘리고 있습니다. 이런 학생들에게 이 책이 보다 효과적으로 목표 점수를 받는 데 많은 보탬이 되기를 바랍니다.

이미영

정말 시간 부족이 문제일까요? 토익 시험을 치른 후 대부분의 수험생들은 한결같이 시간이 부족했다고 합니다. 특히 新토익 개정 이후 PART 7의 늘어난 문항 수와 새로워진 유형으로 인해 시간 내에 풀기가 여간 힘들어진 것이 아닙니다. 그래서인지 일부 수험생들은 시험 시간을 왜 더 늘려주지 않는가에 대해 불만을 토로하기도 합니다. 하지만 반대로 생각해 봅시다. 예를 들어 PART 7을 하루 24시간을 투자하여 충분히 풀어 본다면, 모든 문제의 정답을 찾을 수 있을까요? 아마도 이 또한 만만치 않을 것입니다. 따라서 주어진 시간 내에 정확한 풀이를 위해서는 더욱 전략적인 독해의 방법이 필요한 때입니다.

독해는 번역이 아닙니다! 즉, 독해 지문을 우리말로 일일이 바꾼다고 하여 글을 정확히 이해할 수 없습니다. 영어로 된 문장을 읽는 것이 불편하다고 무턱대고 우리말로 바꾸는 데만 치중하면, 지문이 전달하려는 메시지를 전혀 파악할 수 없게 됩니다. 번역을 하게 되면 기억해야 할 정보량이 늘어나게 되므로 시간도 오래 걸릴 뿐만 아니라 문제 풀이를 위한 메시지의 파악을 명확하게 할 수 없습니다.

독해는 의사소통입니다! 지문은 하나의 메시지를 전달하기 위한 여러 문장들의 집합체라고 볼 수 있습니다. 지문의 주요한 메시지가 정해지면, 그 이후부터는 모든 문장들이 이것과 같은 뜻의 다른 표현(paraphrasing)으로 설득력 있는 추가적인 정보를 제공합니다. 그러므로 지문이 말하려는 메시지가 무엇인지 파악해야 하지, 단순히 우리말로 번역해서는 안 됩니다. PART 7은 독해를 통하여 지문이 전달하려는 메시지를 정확히 파악하는, 수험생의 의사소통 능력을 평가하는 시험이라는 것을 명심하세요.

본 교재는 수험생들의 독해에 대한 오해를 바로잡고, 정확한 전략을 구사할 수 있도록 철저한 계산하에 제작되었습니다. 주어진 시간 내에 지문 내용 이해과 정확한 의사소통을 해낼 수 있도록 실제 토익과 유사한 메시지(topic sentence)와 말 바꾸기 표현(paraphrasing), 그리고 오답 선택지로 구성하였습니다. 본 교재를 접한 수험생들만큼은 부디 가장 효과적인 전략을 통하여 속 시원하게 고득점을 성취하기를 열렬히 응원합니다.

박선영

CONTENTS

FEATURES

1 Part 7 신유형
완전 분석 & 반영

더욱 까다로워진 신토익 PART 7 경향을 파악하여 출제
원리와 어휘를 완전히 분석하고 반영하였다.

2 문제+정답+번역+해설+어휘
한 권에 수록

저자의 핵심 노하우와 패러프레이징을 정리한 알짜 해설을
수록하여 추가 해설집 구매 없이 한 권으로 끝낼 수 있다.

3 저자 직강 PART 7 공략법
음성 강의

저자 직강 음성 강의로 PART 7 가장 궁금했던 사항을 말끔히
해결할 수 있다. 저자만의 신토익 고득점 노하우에 대한 팁을
얻을 수 있다. (QR 코드 또는 www.nexusbook.com
다운로드)

4 나혼토 1:1 저자 코칭

궁금한 것은 바로바로 해결하는 나만의 1:1 토익 코치로 궁금한
사항을 저자에게 직접 질문하고 답변을 받을 수 있다.

저자 이미영 (1, 3, 5, 7, 9회 집필)
다음 카페(http://cafe.daum.net/speedytoeic)
≫ [나혼토 1 : 1 코칭] 게시판 이용

저자 박선영 (2, 4, 6, 8, 10회 집필)
카카오톡 ID로 찾기(ID: matrix20)
≫ 친구 추가 후 1:1 채팅

5 빈출 어휘 리스트 및 테스트지

교재 전체에 등장한 모든 어휘를 언제든지 편리하게 활용하며
테스트지를 통해 최종 점검을 할 수 있다.
(QR 코드 또는 www.nexusbook.com 다운로드)

신토익 핵심 정보

2016년 5월 29일 정기시험부터 현재의 영어 사용 환경을 반영한 신(新)토익이 시행되었습니다. 전체 문항 수와 시험 시간은 동일하지만 각 파트별로 문항 수는 변화가 있으며 그동안 출제되지 않았던 그래프와 문자 메시지, 채팅, 삼중 지문 등 새로운 지문 유형과 문제가 출제됩니다.

🔍 신토익 시험의 구성

구성	Part	Part별 내용	문항수	시간	배점
Listening Comprehension	1	사진 묘사	6	45분	495점
	2	질의 응답	25		
	3	짧은 대화	39		
	4	설명문	30		
Reading Comprehension	5	단문 공란 채우기	30	75분	495점
	6	장문 공란 채우기	16		
	7	단일 지문	29		
		이중 지문	10		
		삼중 지문	15		
Total		7 Parts	200문제	120분	990점

🔍 신토익 이후 달라진 부분

❶ **Part 1** 문항 10개에서 6개로 감소
❷ **Part 2** 문항 30개에서 25개로 감소
❸ **Part 3** 문항 30개에서 39개로 증가, 〈3인 대화〉, 〈5턴 이상의 대화〉, 〈의도 파악, 시각 정보 연계 문제〉 추가
❹ **Part 4** 문항 30개로 기존과 동일, 〈의도 파악 문제〉, 〈시각 정보 연계 문제〉 추가
❺ **Part 5** 문항 40개에서 30개로 감소
❻ **Part 6** 문항 12개에서 16개로 증가, 〈알맞은 문장 고르기〉 추가
❼ **Part 7** 문항 48개에서 54개로 증가, 〈문자 메시지·온라인 채팅 지문〉, 〈의도 파악, 문장 삽입 문제〉, 〈삼중 지문〉 추가

🔍 신토익 핵심 정보

Part 3	화자의 의도 파악 문제	2~3문항	• 대화문에서 화자가 한 말의 의도를 묻는 유형
	시각 정보 연계 문제	2~3문항	• 대화문과 시각 정보(도표, 그래픽 등)간 연관 관계를 파악하는 유형
	3인 대화	대화 지문 1~2개	• 일부 대화문에서 세 명 이상의 화자가 등장함
	5턴 이상의 대화		• 주고 받는 대화가 5턴 이상으로 늘어난 대화 유형
Part 4	화자의 의도 파악 문제	2~3문항	• 담화문에서 화자가 한 말의 의도를 묻는 유형
	시각 정보 연계 문제	2~3문항	• 담화문과 시각 정보(도표, 그래픽 등)간 연관 관계를 파악하는 유형
Part 6	알맞은 문장 고르기	4문항 (지문당 1문항)	• 지문의 흐름상 빈칸에 들어갈 알맞은 문장 고르기 • 선택지가 모두 문장으로 제시되며 문맥 파악이 필수
★ Part 7	문장 삽입 문제	2문항 (지문당 1문항)	• 주어진 문장을 삽입할 수 있는 적절한 위치 고르기
	문자 메시지·온라인 채팅	각각 지문 1개	• 2명이 대화하는 문자 메시지, 다수가 참여하는 온라인 채팅
	의도 파악 문제	2문항 (지문당 1문항)	• 화자가 말한 말의 의도를 묻는 문제 • 문자 메시지, 온라인 채팅 지문에서 출제
	삼중 지문	지문 3개	• 세 개의 연계 지문에 대한 이해도를 묻는 문제

나혼토 학습 스케줄

초급 수험자 독해 실력이 부족해서 평균 10문제 이상은 그냥 찍고 나와요.

아직은 독해 실력이 부족한 때입니다. 특히 실제 토익 시험을 보면서 시간이 부족한 경우가 많은데 이는 평소에 실전처럼 시간을 기록하며 연습을 하는 것이 중요합니다. 또한 어휘 실력이 부족한 시기이므로 온라인으로 제공되는 어휘테스트도 활용해 보세요.
(www.nexusbook.com에서 어휘리스트, 어휘테스트 제공)

1~2일차	3~4일차	5~6일차	7~8일차	9~10일차	11~12일차
Actual Test 1 문제 풀이 & 해설	Actual Test 2 문제 풀이 & 해설	Actual Test 3 문제 풀이 & 해설	Actual Test 4 문제 풀이 & 해설	Actual Test 5 문제 풀이 & 해설	Actual Test 6 문제 풀이 & 해설

13~14일차	15~16일차	17~18일차	19~20일차
Actual Test 7 문제 풀이 & 해설	Actual Test 8 문제 풀이 & 해설	Actual Test 9 문제 풀이 & 해설	Actual Test 10 문제 풀이 & 해설

중급 수험자 해석은 다 했는데 정답을 잘 못 고르겠어요.

지문의 내용을 다 파악했다고 해서 문제의 정답을 고를 수 있는 것은 아닙니다. 문제에서 원하는 핵심 포인트를 파악하고 지문에서 이에 대한 단서를 찾는 연습이 필요합니다. 실전 문제 풀이를 통해서 실전 감각을 키우는 것이 중요한 때입니다.

1일차	2일차	3일차	4일차	5일차	6일차
Actual Test 1 문제 풀이 & 해설	Actual Test 2 문제 풀이 & 해설	Actual Test 3 문제 풀이 & 해설	Actual Test 4 문제 풀이 & 해설	Actual Test 5 문제 풀이 & 해설	Actual Test 6 문제 풀이 & 해설

7일차	8일차	9일차	10일차
Actual Test 7 문제 풀이 & 해설	Actual Test 8 문제 풀이 & 해설	Actual Test 9 문제 풀이 & 해설	Actual Test 10 문제 풀이 & 해설

고급 수험자 다 맞았다고 생각했지만 꼭 3~4문제는 틀려요.

가끔은 정말 시험을 잘 봤다고 생각하지만 예상치 못한 곳에서 틀리는 문제가 있는 경우입니다. 추론과 같은 문제는 정답의 힌트가 예상하지 못한 곳에서도 나올 수 있으므로 틀린 문제 위주로 다시 복습하는 것이 중요합니다.

1일차	2일차	3일차	4일차	5일차
Actual Test 1, 2 문제 풀이 & 해설	Actual Test 3, 4 문제 풀이 & 해설	Actual Test 5, 6 문제 풀이 & 해설	Actual Test 7, 8 문제 풀이 & 해설	Actual Test 9, 10 문제 풀이 & 해설

나혼토 실력 점검

테스트가 끝난 후 각 테스트별로 점검해 보세요. 테스트별로 맞은 개수를 확인하며 실력이 향상됨을 체크해 보세요.

	테스트 날짜	맞은 개수	체감 난이도		
Actual Test 01			상	중	하
Actual Test 02			상	중	하
Actual Test 03			상	중	하
Actual Test 04			상	중	하
Actual Test 05			상	중	하
Actual Test 06			상	중	하
Actual Test 07			상	중	하
Actual Test 08			상	중	하
Actual Test 09			상	중	하
Actual Test 10			상	중	하

본책 활용법

각 실전 문제를 시작하기 전에 시작 시간과 종료 시간을 기록할 수 있습니다. 권장 풀이 시간은 55분이니 반드시 시간을 기록하여 시간 내에 풀 수 있도록 해야 합니다. 그리고 본책 뒤에 있는 OMR 카드(가위로 잘라서 사용 가능)를 활용하여 실제 시험에서처럼 정답을 입력하며 풀 수 있도록 훈련하세요.

정답 및 해설 활용법

정답 및 해설집에는 문제, 해석 및 해설이 자세하게 나와 있습니다. 정답의 힌트가 되는 부분에는 문제 번호와 함께 밑줄로 표시하였습니다. 틀린 문제는 정확하고 상세한 해설을 읽은 후, 왜 틀렸는지 꼭 다시 확인해 보세요.

잠깐!!
시작 전 **꼭** 확인하세요!

☑ 실제 시험과 같이
책상을 정리하고
마음의 준비를 하세요.

☑ 핸드폰은 잠깐 끄고
대신 아날로그 시계를
활용해 보세요.

☑ 권장 풀이 시간은 55분입니다.
시간을 꼭 지켜주세요.

☑ 어렵다고 넘어가지 마세요.
가능하면 차례대로 풀어 보세요.

Actual Test

01

시작 시간   :

종료 시간   :

PART 7

Directions: In this part you will read a selection of texts, such as magazine and newspaper articles, e-mails, and instant messages. Each text or set of texts is followed by several questions. Select the best answer for each question and mark the letter (A), (B), (C), or (D) on your answer sheet.

Questions 147-148 refer to the following letter.

Derek Manning

48 Frost Lane

Greenville, Vermont

Dear Mr. Manning:

I am writing in response to the letter you sent to our customer service department, dated July 11. Let me start by extending my sincere apologies for the negative experience you had with one of our products, the Kitchen Pro Indoor Grill.

Upon examination of the item you returned, it was determined to be defective. As you clearly stated that you do not wish to exchange the product for a functioning unit, I have authorized a full refund. I would also like to take this opportunity to send you a gift certificate for $50.

Once again, please accept my apologies. I know this must have been a disappointing experience as a first-time customer. However, I hope you choose to give Kitchen Pro products a second chance.

Sincerely,

Nancy Schofield

Director of Customer Services

Kitchen Pro Corporation

147 What is the purpose of the letter?

(A) To explain the product's new functions

(B) To compensate the customer for a delay in exchanging an item

(C) To promote a special online sale

(D) To apologize for a faulty product

148 What is indicated about the recipient of the letter?

(A) He is interested in working in customer service.

(B) He has never purchased anything from Kitchen Pro before.

(C) He wants to exchange an item with another one.

(D) He originally purchased the indoor grill as a gift.

Questions 149-150 refer to the following text message chain.

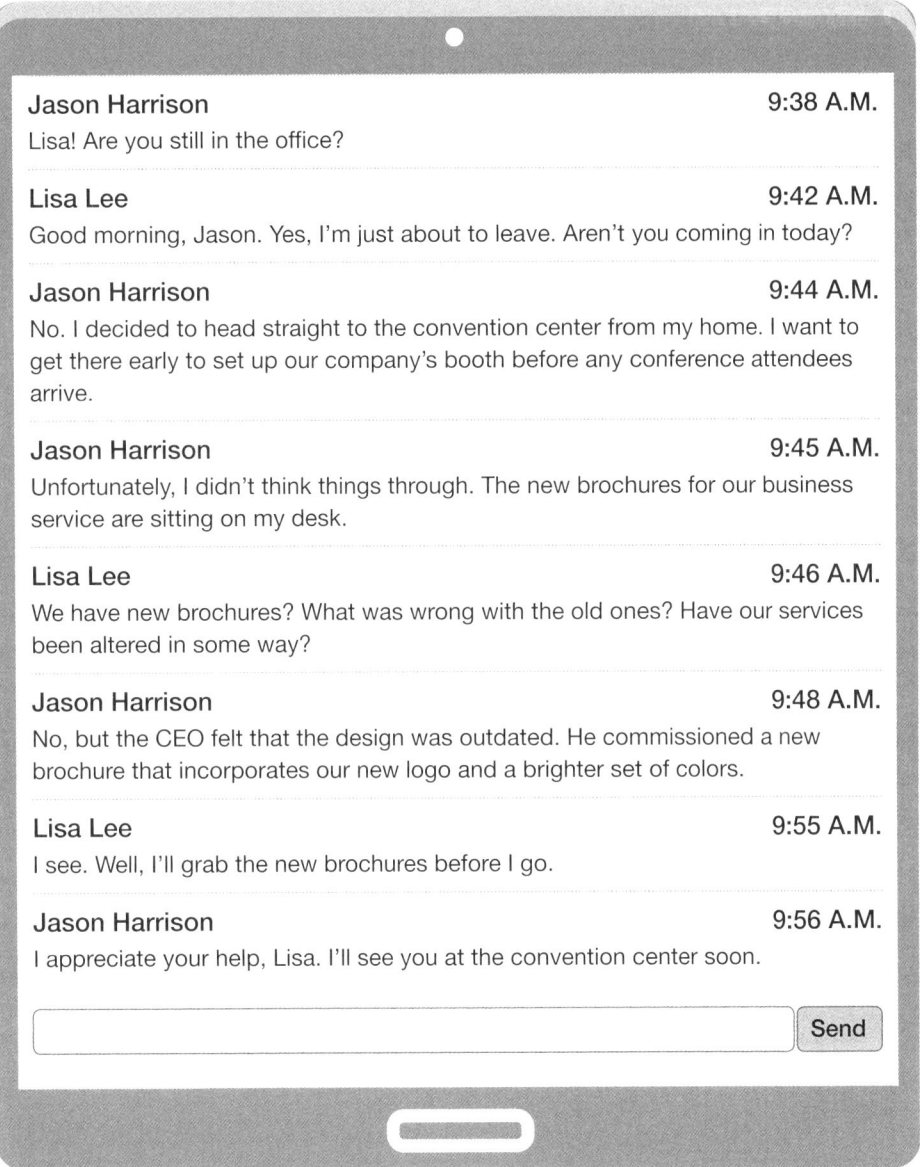

Jason Harrison   9:38 A.M.
Lisa! Are you still in the office?

Lisa Lee   9:42 A.M.
Good morning, Jason. Yes, I'm just about to leave. Aren't you coming in today?

Jason Harrison   9:44 A.M.
No. I decided to head straight to the convention center from my home. I want to get there early to set up our company's booth before any conference attendees arrive.

Jason Harrison   9:45 A.M.
Unfortunately, I didn't think things through. The new brochures for our business service are sitting on my desk.

Lisa Lee   9:46 A.M.
We have new brochures? What was wrong with the old ones? Have our services been altered in some way?

Jason Harrison   9:48 A.M.
No, but the CEO felt that the design was outdated. He commissioned a new brochure that incorporates our new logo and a brighter set of colors.

Lisa Lee   9:55 A.M.
I see. Well, I'll grab the new brochures before I go.

Jason Harrison   9:56 A.M.
I appreciate your help, Lisa. I'll see you at the convention center soon.

Send

149 What is indicated about the old business service brochures?

(A) They contained incorrect information.
(B) They were designed by the CEO.
(C) They do not have a modern appearance.
(D) They were delivered to the wrong location.

150 At 9:45 A.M., what does Mr. Harrison mean when he writes, "I didn't think things through"?

(A) He underestimated an amount.
(B) He typed something incorrectly.
(C) He misunderstood Ms. Lee.
(D) He made a poor decision.

GO ON TO THE NEXT PAGE

Northshore Business News

The Green Sky Coffee Corporation has released plans for a new branch to be located in the Northshore business district. This will be the 25th Green Sky coffee shop nationwide and the first in the state. Northshore's mayor, Jan Brown, released the following statement: "Northshore is proud to welcome the Green Sky brand to our newly revitalized business district."

Green Sky is one of the fastest-growing coffee companies in the USA. Along with its retail stores, the company supplies several major fast-food chains and two international airlines with coffee and coffee-related products. The Northshore store will be located in the Main Street Mall, which was recently re-opened as part of an effort to attract more stores to the town's struggling commercial area.

151 What is the purpose of the article?

(A) To announce the future opening of a store
(B) To describe the details of a mayor's speech
(C) To discuss the problems faced by a town
(D) To explain a company's plans to diversify

152 What is mentioned about Northshore's business district?

(A) It is the home of the Green Sky headquarters.
(B) Several fast-food restaurants have opened there.
(C) Attempts are being made to improve it.
(D) It suffered due to the opening of the Main Street Mall.

Questions 153-155 refer to the following letter.

Lisa Cavanaugh
1140 East 15th Street, Apartment 12B
Forest Hills, New York

Dear Ms. Cavanaugh:

Enclosed are the items from the order you placed on March 3 via our Web site. However, I regret to inform you that this is only a partial shipment, as two of the items were unexpectedly found to be out of stock.

In this package, you will find the following:
  - one Povar ZX 14-inch laptop
  - one leather laptop carrying case
  - one wireless mouse and mouse pad

The missing items are the Redgate external hard drive and the Povar travel charger. – [1] –. We have placed an order for these items with our overseas supplier and are currently awaiting shipment. We estimate you will receive them by the end of next week. – [2] –. Please accept my sincere apologies if this causes you any inconvenience.

If you do not wish to wait and prefer to cancel the undelivered portion of your order, just let me know. However, if you do so, I must request that you inform me of your decision within 48 hours. – [3] –. If we do not, we will proceed with the shipment of the remainder of your order. – [4] –. Again, I apologize for the unexpected delay and hope you will not let it prevent you from continuing your patronage of our Web site.

Sincerely,

Jasmine Cho
Discount Cybermall

---

153 What is the purpose of the letter?

(A) To place an order for laptop accessories
(B) To seek clarification of an order's details
(C) To request payment of delivery fees
(D) To inform a customer of a partial order shipping delay

154 What is NOT included in the package?

(A) Povar ZX 14-inch laptop
(B) Povar travel charger
(C) Leather laptop carrying case
(D) Wireless mouse and mouse pad

155 In which of the positions marked [1], [2], [3], and [4] does the following sentence best fit?

"Due to the situation, we will waive our usual cancellation fee if we hear from you within this period."

(A) [1]
(B) [2]
(C) [3]
(D) [4]

GO ON TO THE NEXT PAGE

Questions 156-158 refer to the following Web page.

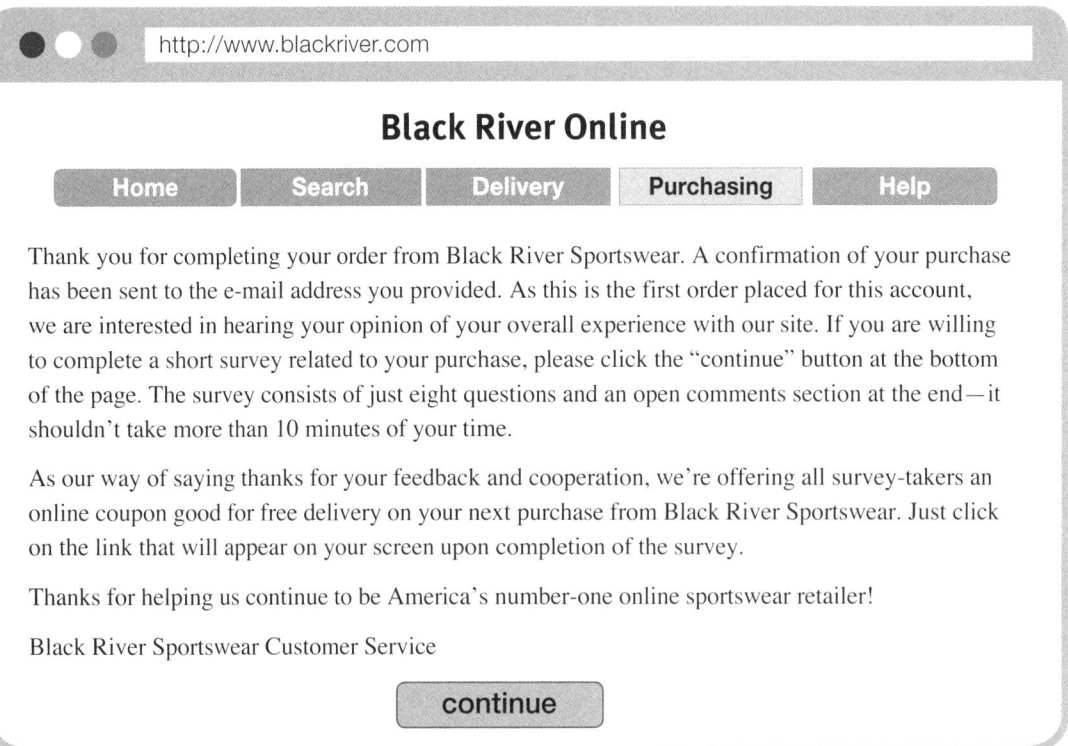

http://www.blackriver.com

Black River Online

| Home | Search | Delivery | **Purchasing** | Help |

Thank you for completing your order from Black River Sportswear. A confirmation of your purchase has been sent to the e-mail address you provided. As this is the first order placed for this account, we are interested in hearing your opinion of your overall experience with our site. If you are willing to complete a short survey related to your purchase, please click the "continue" button at the bottom of the page. The survey consists of just eight questions and an open comments section at the end—it shouldn't take more than 10 minutes of your time.

As our way of saying thanks for your feedback and cooperation, we're offering all survey-takers an online coupon good for free delivery on your next purchase from Black River Sportswear. Just click on the link that will appear on your screen upon completion of the survey.

Thanks for helping us continue to be America's number-one online sportswear retailer!

Black River Sportswear Customer Service

continue

---

156 What is indicated about the user?

(A) The user made a purchase from the site for the first time.
(B) The user failed to provide all of the required information.
(C) The user has submitted a letter of complaint about the site.
(D) The user has elected to delete the account with the company.

157 What is the user being asked to do?

(A) Resubmit some personal information
(B) Explain the reasons for a comment
(C) Answer questions about a transaction
(D) Confirm the given delivery address

158 What is being offered to the user?

(A) Ten percent off on this purchase
(B) A free selection of sportswear items
(C) A full refund for the damaged goods
(D) Complimentary delivery on a future order

BRIGHTER WORLD INC. (PRODUCT #3351A)

Step-by-step Assembly

1. Remove all parts from their plastic packaging.
2. Affix the lampshade firmly to the lamp arm using the enclosed screws.
3. Put the plastic covering atop the base and exert pressure until it clicks into place.
4. Slide the lamp arm into the slot on the top of the lamp base.
5. Rotate the arm clockwise to tighten.

Caution

· The desk lamp must not be plugged in until it has been fully assembled.
· This product's small parts present a swallowing hazard. Keep them away from small children.
· Be sure to always keep this product on a dry, flat surface.
· The desk lampshade may become hot after extended use. Adjust the lamp by gripping the arm.

Notes

· Brighter World light bulbs are sold separately.
· The on/off switch is located on the side of the lamp base.

---

159 What do the instructions explain how to do?

(A) Pack a lamp for delivery
(B) Replace a lamp's light bulb
(C) Repair a damaged desk lamp
(D) Put together the parts of a lamp

160 What is NOT found in the package?

(A) Screws
(B) A light bulb
(C) A lamp base
(D) A lampshade

161 What should be done before inserting the arm into the base?

(A) The lamp should be plugged into an electrical socket.
(B) The switch should be slid into the "on" position.
(C) The lamp arm should be twisted until it is tight.
(D) The plastic covering should be affixed to the base.

162 Why are users advised to adjust the lamp by the arm?

(A) To keep from burning themselves
(B) To avoid breaking the light bulb
(C) To make sure the shade is tight
(D) To ensure it is on a flat surface

GO ON TO THE NEXT PAGE

Actual Test 01   19

Local Artist Returns with Free Exhibition

The Lorimer Gallery has announced an upcoming exhibition of the work of Remington-born artist Charles Ramirez. The exhibition will last for one week, from August 14th to the 20th, and will feature more than 50 watercolor paintings and original sketches by the artist. The gallery has further announced that there will be no admission fee for this special exhibition.

Mr. Ramirez grew up in the Hillside section of Remington and received a degree in commercial design from Remington State College. After relocating to Berlin, he began to paint scenes of the city using watercolors. Named one of Europe's "promising young artists" by Pallet Magazine, Mr. Ramirez now has paintings in more than 25 major museums around the world. One of his works recently sold for $350,000 to an anonymous bidder. Next month's exhibition marks his first return to his hometown since departing in 2014.

"I wanted to give something back to the community that raised me," Mr. Ramirez said in a recent interview with WRTV, "so I arranged a free showing of my paintings with the folks at the Lorimer Gallery." The artist will be on hand at the opening of the exhibition, giving a welcoming speech and signing limited-edition prints.

163 What is suggested about Remington State College?

(A) It owns the Lorimer Gallery.
(B) It is the site of an art exhibition.
(C) It is the school Mr. Ramirez attended.
(D) It has branches in Remington and Berlin.

164 What will Mr. Ramirez do on August 14?

(A) Accept an award from a magazine
(B) Auction off a watercolor painting
(C) Give a lecture at an art school
(D) Autograph copies of his artwork

Test 01

NOTICE

Due to damage caused by last summer's flooding, the resident parking lot of the River Mill Building will be repaved during the week of April 3 – 7. Along with the repaving, the lot will be relined in order to accommodate three additional handicapped spaces.

The project will take place in two stages: On Monday and Tuesday, April 3 and 4, the north end of the parking lot (spaces 1 - 34) will be closed to residents. – [1] –. On these days, all cars must be moved from these spaces to the guest parking lot or parked on the street. – [2] –. If parking on the street, please pay attention to all signage to avoid a parking ticket. – [3] –. The south end of the lot (spaces 35 - 50) will be repaved on Wednesday and relined on Thursday. Therefore, all cars must be cleared from this section during those two days. – [4] –. We apologize for any inconvenience this may cause. Any questions or concerns should be directed to the apartment manager's office.

165 What is the purpose of the notice?

(A) To announce the reopening of an improved facility
(B) To warn drivers about unpaid parking tickets
(C) To inform apartment residents of a project
(D) To apologize for flood damage to a building

166 What is mentioned about the handicapped parking spaces?

(A) People have been using them illegally.
(B) There will be more added to the parking lot.
(C) They will be unavailable in the month of April.
(D) They have been moved to a new part of the parking lot.

167 In which of the positions marked [1], [2], [3], and [4] does the following sentence best fit?

"The lot won't be fully functional until Friday."

(A) [1]
(B) [2]
(C) [3]
(D) [4]

GO ON TO THE NEXT PAGE

Questions 168-171 refer to the following online chat discussion.

Denzel Smith [3:13 P.M.]		I'd like to start by discussing a possible expansion opportunity. Is everyone familiar with the Hartsville Mall?
Charlotte Cooney [3:13 P.M.]		It's located on Highway 15, isn't it? I read about the plans for it last year, but I didn't realize that it had opened for business already.
Eric Kim [3:14 P.M.]		Actually, it hasn't. Construction is complete, but the grand opening has been pushed back several times. Apparently they're having difficulty securing retail tenants. Word on the street is that they're struggling with a 50% vacancy rate.
Charlotte Cooney [3:16 P.M.]		And you want to open a new branch there? Doesn't that seem like a big risk?
Denzel Smith [3:17 P.M.]		It is a risk, but it might also be a great opportunity. Their property management team is getting desperate. They've lowered their rental fees by nearly 30%. What do you think, Eric?
Eric Kim [3:19 P.M.]		It's worth looking into. Do you know why they can't find tenants?
Denzel Smith [3:20 P.M.]		Not really. It could be related to the slowdown in the economy, I guess.
Eric Kim [3:21 P.M.]		We need to ascertain the reason before we make any moves. There could be problems with the location or possibly with the structure itself.
Charlotte Cooney [3:22 P.M.]		I'll contact the property manager and ask to see some of their retail spaces.
Eric Kim [3:22 P.M.]		Excellent. Let us know what you find.

	Send

168 What type of business does Mr. Smith most likely work for?

(A) Retail sales
(B) Construction
(C) Property management
(D) Risk assessment

169 Why does Mr. Smith suggest opening a branch in the Hartsville Mall?

(A) The mall is located near a major highway.
(B) The leasing terms have been improved.
(C) There are few new malls in the area.
(D) There is an unexpected vacancy.

170 At 3:19 P.M., what does Mr. Kim mean when he writes, "It's worth looking into"?

(A) The team needs to make plans in advance.
(B) The mall looks good but has many problems.
(C) The business is too valuable to be risked.
(D) The proposal is good enough to consider.

171 What is NOT mentioned as a possible reason for the mall's problem?

(A) An economic downturn
(B) Competition from online malls
(C) A poorly chosen location
(D) Structural flaws in the building

City News Briefs

On Thursday, construction of the Heather Meadows housing development was officially approved by the city council by a vote of 7 to 4. The construction will take place on the former site of Riverview Park, which was closed by the city last summer due to security concerns.

Over the past several weeks the city council had been debating a proposal to replace the park with low-income housing. Some local residents were unhappy to have lost their park. "I'm not sure why this decision was made," said Eric Murphy, a father of three who lives across the street from the former park. "The park wasn't perfect. Sometimes teenagers gathered there and made noise. But it was nice to have a green space nearby."

However, the city council had a different view, calling the defunct park "a magnet for illegal activities." City council chairperson Lauren Miura praised the housing project, calling it a victory in the city's long fight against homelessness. "Once the people in the neighborhood see the architect's beautiful plans for the housing development," she explained, "they'll be as excited as we are." The mayor was not available for comment, but his office released a statement reaffirming his continued support of the council. Construction of Heather Meadows is scheduled to be completed in May of next year.

172 Why was this article written?

(A) To complain about a city council decision
(B) To explain why a popular city park was closed
(C) To invite citizens to attend the next city council meeting
(D) To announce the approval of a housing development project

173 Which of the following most likely describes Heather Meadows?

(A) A wilderness area near a city park
(B) A planned residence for low-income tenants
(C) A new park proposed by the city council
(D) An urban neighborhood with high crime rates

174 What is indicated about Riverview Park?

(A) It is near Heather Meadows.
(B) It is now being renovated.
(C) It was the site of a meeting.
(D) It has been shut down.

175 The word "released" in paragraph 3, line 10, is closest in meaning to

(A) asked
(B) issued
(C) rejected
(D) accepted

GO ON TO THE NEXT PAGE

House for Rent – Rosehill Heights

A beautiful, two-story house is available for rent in the city's exclusive Rosehill Heights neighborhood. Due to high demand, houses in this neighborhood rarely come available, so don't miss this chance.

This three-bedroom, two-bathroom home features a small backyard and a full, unfinished basement suitable for storage. It will be available on June 1, and the landlord is seeking a lease agreement of two years or longer. All applicants must provide references from previous landlords.

Rent is $2,400 per month and includes water, snow removal, trash removal and off-street parking for two vehicles. The tenant is responsible for electricity and gas. Indoor pets are permitted with a refundable $500 deposit per animal.

The house will be rented unfurnished, but the current tenant is willing to sell some furniture. There will be an open house on May 14. To arrange a private showing before that date, please contact Ed Marino, the property manager, at marinohomes@freenet.com.

To:	Dara Westwood <soccermom33@fastmail.com>
From:	Ed Marino <marinohomes@freenet.com>
Date:	May 20
Subject:	Re: Rosehill Heights House

Thanks for your e-mail. I do remember meeting you and your husband on May 14. In response to your question about outdoor pets, I'm sorry to say that they are not permitted at all. Having seen the house, you surely understand that the yard is too small for an outdoor dog. I'm sorry I didn't make that clear. If you are still interested in the house, please let me know.

Best wishes,

Ed Marino

176 What is indicated about Rosehill Heights?

(A) It is known for its homes with large yards.
(B) It is located in a low-income district.
(C) It is a place where many people want to live.
(D) It is difficult for most people to get to.

177 What is NOT indicated about the house for rent?

(A) It has space for two cars on the property.
(B) It contains more bedrooms than bathrooms.
(C) It has a lower level where things can be stored.
(D) It currently doesn't have any furniture in it.

178 What is a deposit required for?

(A) Renting the home's furniture
(B) Establishing electrical service
(C) Parking off the street
(D) Keeping a pet indoors

179 How does Mr. Marino most likely know Ms. Westwood?

(A) He gave her a private tour of the home.
(B) He lives in an apartment next to her home.
(C) He met her at an open-house event.
(D) He is a former coworker of her husband.

180 What information was communicated unclearly between Mr. Marino and Ms. Westwood?

(A) The rules regarding pets
(B) The size of the house's yard
(C) The date of their appointment
(D) The location of the neighborhood

GO ON TO THE NEXT PAGE

Questions 181-185 refer to the following letter and e-mail.

Sarah Nordstrom
Hiring Director
Van Buren Publishing
Carolton Plaza, Suite 113
Kirkville, NY

Dear Ms. Nordstrom:

Please accept this cover letter and attached résumé in application for the position of editorial assistant as advertised in the September 1 edition of the Kirkville Daily Journal. I am a recent graduate of Olympic Business College with an associate degree in business administration, and I am seeking an entry-level position with a respected company. I have heard many good things about Van Buren Publishing and would be eager to join your company.

Although I have no formal work experience, I assisted in the office of the Cybercell Corporation as a summer intern in 2017. I also volunteered at the Newton Homeless Shelter in 2016, serving as a kitchen manager.

I have also included a letter of reference from my supervisor at the homeless shelter and can provide a transcript from my college. If possible, I would love to come in for an interview and tell you more about myself. I look forward to your response.

Sincerely yours,

Rebecca Wilson

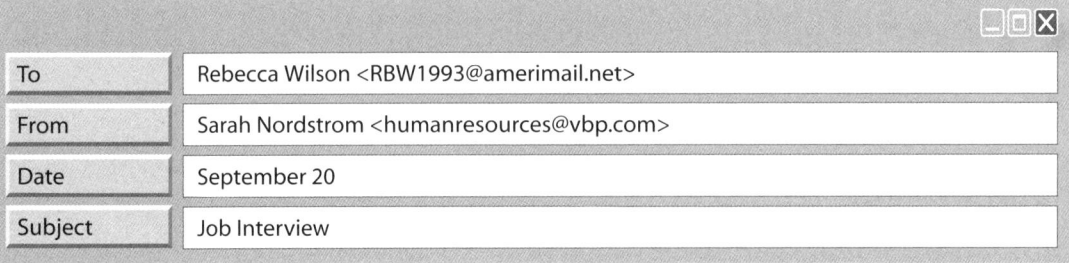

To	Rebecca Wilson <RBW1993@amerimail.net>
From	Sarah Nordstrom <humanresources@vbp.com>
Date	September 20
Subject	Job Interview

Dear Rebecca:

Thank you for visiting our offices last week for an interview. It was a pleasure to meet such a bright young woman with a promising future in business. We were also impressed by Robert Miller's enthusiastic letter praising your organizational abilities.

Unfortunately, we have decided to hire another candidate for this position. This decision was based on his past experience in the field. We will keep your résumé on file and contact you if we have any future openings that suit your abilities. Thank you for your time, and best of luck with your continued job search.

Sarah Nordstrom

181 According to the letter, what is Ms. Wilson's current work situation?

(A) She is unemployed.
(B) She teaches at a business college.
(C) She works for the Cybercell Corporation.
(D) She was recently fired from Van Buren Publishing.

182 Where did Ms. Wilson do office work?

(A) Van Buren Publishing
(B) Cybercell Corporation
(C) Olympic Business College
(D) Newton Homeless Shelter

183 Who most likely is Robert Miller?

(A) An intern at Cybercell Corporation
(B) A professor at Olympic Business College
(C) A supervisor at the Newton Homeless Shelter
(D) A human resources manager at Van Buren Publishing

184 What does Ms. Nordstrom say about Ms. Wilson's résumé?

(A) It was unprofessional.
(B) It was not received on time.
(C) It will be retained by the company.
(D) It has been submitted to the hiring director.

185 In the e-mail, the word "suit" in paragraph 2, line 3, is closest in meaning to

(A) share
(B) match
(C) improve
(D) overlook

GO ON TO THE NEXT PAGE

Questions 186-190 refer to the following advertisement, online Web page, and e-mail.

Spring Savings for Your Summer Wardrobe!

Spring is already here, and that means summer is just around the corner. Get ready for the hot weather with sizzling Internet-only deals from Zenith Fashions! Mix and match any three tops with any three pairs of shorts, and we'll give you 25% off your entire order, along with free shipping if you pay with a Zenith credit card. This offer is available exclusively through our Zenith Online Web site, which has recently been renovated for enhanced usability, and includes all of our available shirts and shorts. The sale only lasts until the end of the month, so don't wait! Visit www.shopzenith.com and stock up on stylish shorts and summery tops.

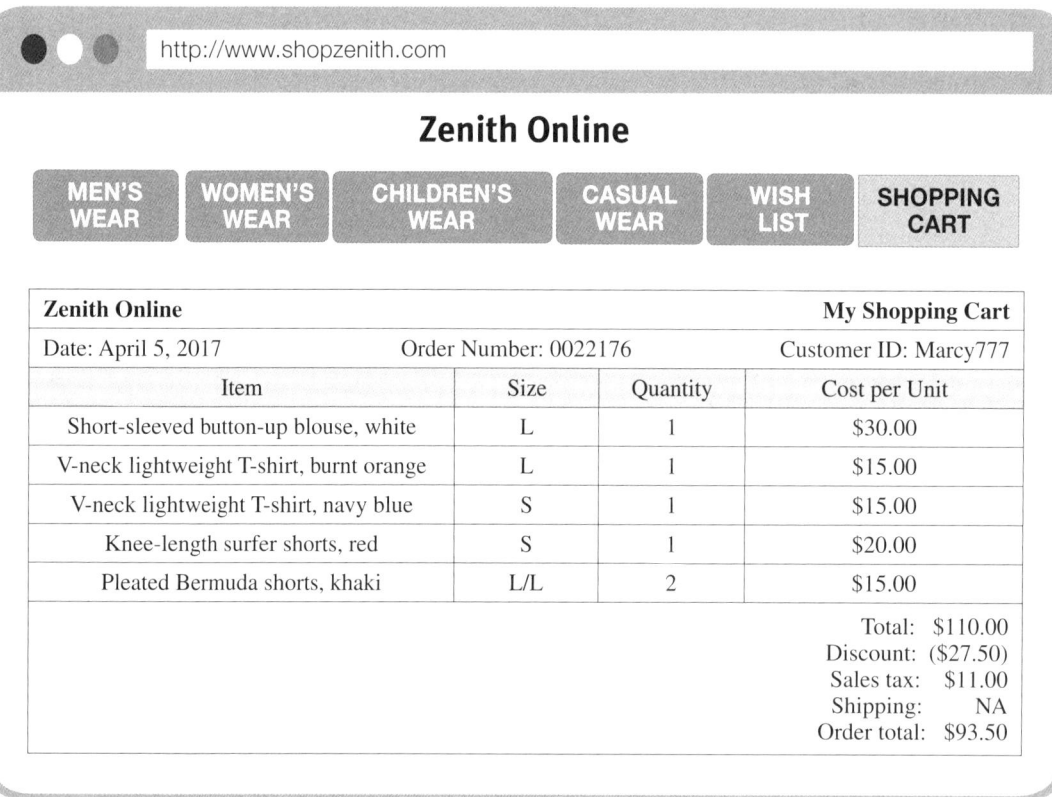

http://www.shopzenith.com

Zenith Online

| MEN'S WEAR | WOMEN'S WEAR | CHILDREN'S WEAR | CASUAL WEAR | WISH LIST | SHOPPING CART |

Zenith Online — **My Shopping Cart**

Date: April 5, 2017   Order Number: 0022176   Customer ID: Marcy777

Item	Size	Quantity	Cost per Unit
Short-sleeved button-up blouse, white	L	1	$30.00
V-neck lightweight T-shirt, burnt orange	L	1	$15.00
V-neck lightweight T-shirt, navy blue	S	1	$15.00
Knee-length surfer shorts, red	S	1	$20.00
Pleated Bermuda shorts, khaki	L/L	2	$15.00

Total: $110.00
Discount: ($27.50)
Sales tax: $11.00
Shipping: NA
Order total: $93.50

To: customerservice@zenithcorp.com
From: marcy777@usemail.com
Date: April 10
Subject: Order Number 0022176

Good morning.

I'd like to bring your attention to a mistake in an order I placed on April 5. I ordered three tops and three pairs of shorts, taking advantage of your spring sale. Although the 25% discount was correctly applied and my items were shipped free of charge, there was a mix-up with the shirt sizes. I requested a large short-sleeved blouse, a large T-shirt, and a small T-shirt. Instead, I received two large T-shirts and a large blouse.

Having had personal experience correcting these kinds of mistakes, I know how frustrating it can be when customers demand immediate attention. However, the mis-sized item was intended as a birthday gift for my daughter. Therefore, I would really appreciate if you can have the correct item sent to me before April 15, as that's her birthday. If this is not possible, please contact me at 617-555-2891 at your earliest convenience.

Marcy Mason

186 What is mentioned about the Zenith Fashions Web site?

(A) It offers a limited selection.
(B) It was recently updated.
(C) It is for members only.
(D) It has won awards.

187 Which is suggested about Ms. Mason's order?

(A) It was placed in the last week of April.
(B) It includes several out-of-stock items.
(C) She paid for it with a Zenith credit card.
(D) A sales tax was added to it in error.

188 What is Ms. Mason's complaint about her order?

(A) One of the items was delivered late.
(B) One of the items was damaged.
(C) One of the items was not included.
(D) One of the items was the wrong size.

189 What is implied about Ms. Mason?

(A) She has poor computer skills.
(B) She is a longtime Zenith customer.
(C) She is unaware of the spring sale.
(D) She has worked in customer service.

190 Which item did Ms. Mason purchase as a gift?

(A) A white blouse
(B) A navy blue T-shirt
(C) An orange T-shirt
(D) Khaki shorts

GO ON TO THE NEXT PAGE

Delivering Food and Smiles to Senior Citizens

by Mary Ono

Like many elderly residents of Bridgefield, Victoria Elgin doesn't have any family living nearby. And she stopped driving five years ago, when she could no longer easily read the road signs. This has made it difficult to buy groceries. "I used to walk to the supermarket down the road every Monday," she says, "but I just don't have the energy anymore.

That's where Helping Hands Express (HHE) comes in. It's a nonprofit organization that delivers groceries and fresh produce to senior citizens who are unable to shop for themselves due to mobility issues. Bridgefield sisters Doris and Kelly Ingram gave up promising legal careers to start HHE last year.

Food and other essential items are picked up and delivered on a weekly basis. Local businesses have contributed to the effort by donating items for those seniors living on a low budget. "The whole community has chipped in," says Doris Ingram. "It's really been a rewarding experience for everyone involved."

Homestyle Cooking Comes to Downtown Bridgefield

At first glance, Bloom's Diner—a new eatery recently opened on South High Street—doesn't look like anything special. But its unassuming exterior and overly familiar décor are quickly forgotten once you open the menu. Owner and head chef Domenic Patel definitely has a vision that sets Bloom's Diner apart from its competition—everything on the menu is comfort food your mom likely made when you were a kid. I ordered the macaroni and cheese with chunks of ham, a bowl of tomato soup and a side of sautéed green beans. While the green beans were uninspired, the tomato soup was packed with peppery flavor. And the macaroni and cheese was perfect. It transported me back in time 20 years to my mother's kitchen. Other popular menu items include Chef Patel's wide selection of desserts. His apple pie won first prize at the county fair earlier this year, and his pound cake and walnut brownies are delicious too.

Sally's Rating: ★★★★☆

Sally Matthews is the food and wine editor for the Bridgefield Telegram.

March 16, 2017

Doris Ingram
Helping Hands Express
2801 East Pleasant Street
Bridgefield, CA 90087

Dear Ms. Ingram:

Please forgive me for sending an unsolicited letter. I was given your address by the reporter who wrote the article about your organization in the Bridgefield Telegram.

I actually know the elderly woman featured in the article, or at least I knew her when I was a kid. She used to give me piano lessons after school. Reading about her problems and how your organization is helping her really opened my eyes to the challenges faced by older people in our community and moved me to take action.

As the owner of a small local restaurant, I'd like to get involved. Desserts are my specialty, and I have an award-winning item that I'd like to donate to be included in your weekly deliveries. I know desserts are not an essential part of anyone's diet, but we all deserve a sweet treat once in a while, don't we?

If you're interested, please stop by Bloom's Diner on South High Street any evening. I'll treat you to a complimentary dinner and we can discuss details.

Sincerely,
Domenic Patel

191 What is suggested about Ms. Elgin?

(A) Her eyesight is failing.
(B) She doesn't have any money.
(C) She doesn't have an education.
(D) Her family visits her often.

192 What is implied about Doris Ingram?

(A) She was formerly an attorney.
(B) She takes care of her older sister.
(C) She is experiencing financial problems.
(D) She owns a local supermarket.

193 In the letter, the word "unsolicited" in paragraph 1, line 1, is closest in meaning to

(A) not brief
(B) not polite
(C) not interesting
(D) not requested

194 Who did Chef Patel learn piano from as a child?

(A) Mary Ono
(B) Victoria Elgin
(C) Doris Ingram
(D) Kelly Ingram

195 What does Chef Patel want donate to HHE?

(A) Macaroni and cheese
(B) Apple pies
(C) Pound cake
(D) Walnut brownies

GO ON TO THE NEXT PAGE

https://www.visitgreenisland.com

Green Island: Your Vacation Home by the Sea!

Accommodation

Hotel Paradiso – 67 Hill Highway, Green Island Village – The oldest hotel on the island, the Paradiso is known for the beautiful antique furniture found in its rooms. Its popular restaurant offers delicious meals at affordable prices.

The Laughing Rabbit Hotel – 14 Beach Road, Green Island Village – This budget option is popular with visiting families, due to its large swimming pool and friendly staff. Rooms on the east side of the building feature ocean views.

The Sunset Resort – 719 Cliffside Boulevard, Port West – A high-end resort on the west side of the island, the Sunset is located just north of sleepy Port West. It offers luxury rooms and gourmet dining in a romantic setting.

The Ocean View Inn – 13 Beach Road, Green Island Village – Located on the south end of the village, just across the street from the Laughing Rabbit, this mid-range option is known for its fantastic views. Ask for a room on the top floor.

Check It Out! Real People, Real Reviews

The Laughing Rabbit Hotel

I stayed at this hotel for three nights on a weekend visit to Green Island this past July. I originally booked a room at the place across the street, but they couldn't accommodate me when my dates unexpectedly changed. I made a reservation at the Laughing Rabbit at their suggestion, with mixed results. My room was spacious, with a king-sized bed and an ocean view, and the front desk clerk was very helpful. She happily helped me decide which sites to visit and where to eat. Unfortunately, the hotel was full of screaming kids. I was looking forward to relaxing by their pool, but the noise level was unbearable. The price was right, so booking here is definitely an option if you're on a budget. But if you do, be sure to bring earplugs.

Luis Guerrero

To	luisg47@fabco.com
From	manager@lrh.net
Date	August 5
Re	My Stay at Your Hotel

Dear Mr. Guerrero:

Thank you for your review. We really appreciate your kind words regarding Mary Walker, our front desk clerk. She's been with us for years and is a great worker. As for your complaints about the noise level, allow me to extend a sincere apology on behalf of the entire hotel. There was a large family reunion at the hotel during your stay, and I'm afraid some of the children got a bit unruly. As compensation for the inconvenience you experienced during your holiday, I'd like to offer you the attached coupon for a free night's stay. Hopefully, you'll come back to our little island soon and give the Laughing Rabbit a second chance.

Sincerely,

Keira Rousch
Hotel Manager

196 What is suggested about the Sunset Resort?

(A) It is located downtown.
(B) It is newly built.
(C) It is popular.
(D) It is expensive.

197 Where did Mr. Guerrero originally plan to stay?

(A) Hotel Paradiso
(B) The Laughing Rabbit Hotel
(C) The Sunset Resort
(D) The Ocean View Inn

198 Which direction did Mr. Guerrero's room face?

(A) North
(B) South
(C) East
(D) West

199 What did Ms. Walker do for Mr. Guerrero?

(A) She gave him a hotel coupon.
(B) She moved him to a quieter room.
(C) She helped him plan his itinerary.
(D) She changed his reservation.

200 What is indicated as the cause of the high noise levels during Mr. Guerrero's stay?

(A) Construction works
(B) A family gathering
(C) A local holiday
(D) Musical concerts

잠깐!!
시작 전 꼭 확인하세요!

☑ 실제 시험과 같이
책상을 정리하고
마음의 준비를 하세요.

☑ 핸드폰은 잠깐 끄고
대신 아날로그 시계를
활용해 보세요.

☑ 권장 풀이 시간은 55분입니다.
시간을 꼭 지켜주세요.

☑ 어렵다고 넘어가지 마세요.
가능하면 차례대로 풀어 보세요.

Actual Test

02

시작 시간   :

종료 시간   :

PART 7

Directions: In this part you will read a selection of texts, such as magazine and newspaper articles, e-mails, and instant messages. Each text or set of texts is followed by several questions. Select the best answer for each question and mark the letter (A), (B), (C), or (D) on your answer sheet.

Questions 147-148 refer to the following notice.

WINTER IS COMING!

Every winter, there are lots of troubles caused by temperature drop and heavy snow.

Here are some things you should check to stay warm and comfortable in winter:

- When the temperature goes below -7 degrees Celsius, make sure that you turn your heaters on. If you are going out, leave the heater on as low as you can. This will prevent pipes from freezing and bursting.
- Let all faucets drip to block freezing.
- Cover the water meter with warm blankets.
- After snow falls, it is best to remove it around door entrances as soon as possible. The snow might turn into ice after some time.

So remember that being cautious and quick can prevent you from freezing at your own home waiting for repair. Keep warm and have happy holidays!

147 What information is provided?

(A) How to escape from an avalanche
(B) How to get through the cold winter
(C) How to enhance water flow
(D) How to install new pipes

148 According to the notice, what are the residents asked to do?

(A) Check the temperature every 7 hours
(B) Close all windows and doors
(C) Turn the heater off when going out
(D) Keep the faucets running with a steady stream of water

Questions 149-150 refer to the following e-mail.

To:	Gordon Shirks <shirks76@hotmail.uk>
From:	Customer Service <customerservice@topsneakers.com>
Date:	August 3
Subject:	Original Canvas 1961

Dear Mr. Shirks:

I am very pleased to inform you that our store is in possession of the "Original Canvas 1961" from the brand Hollis. In the past, I told you that this particular model had been discontinued and that it would be hard to find it in any of our stores. However, Hollis has decided to make a limited sale on the original model for its 40th anniversary! When I heard that, I remembered that you left your e-mail address in case we had one in stock. So I'm happy to tell you that your long-awaited "Original Canvas 1961" is now available. If you are still interested in purchasing this model, please return this e-mail or call our store at 021-555-6751. We are willing to wait for your answer for a week before we put it out for a normal sale. I'll be waiting for your call.

Sincerely,

Bob Truman

149 Why was the e-mail sent to Mr. Shirks?
  (A) To let him know that he left his purchase at the store
  (B) To ask him to design sneakers for an anniversary
  (C) To ask whether he will give up his sneaker model for an auction
  (D) To ask him to make a decision

150 What does Mr. Truman offer to Mr. Shirks?
  (A) Giving a discount coupon for his next purchase
  (B) Holding onto the product for a limited period
  (C) Providing free delivery since he waited a long time
  (D) Sending a poster of all the Hollis models

GO ON TO THE NEXT PAGE

Quilting in Fall

Instructors: Nancy Gibbons & Melisa Donovan
First session registration: September 1, 15 people
Second session registration: October 1, 15 people
Location: Nana & Mel's Traditional Quilts, 15 Oakwood St.

Our quilting shop is opening up seasonal lessons. Participants of all levels are welcome to come to our shop. Beginners can learn to make purses and coasters. Those who have a little bit of experience can learn to make dolls, quilting bags and more. Those with advanced skills can learn to make quilts for their families. Talented quilters can also come just to use the space and materials.

Material fees will vary according to types and sizes of the fabrics and buttons, but we guarantee you that we provide you with the lowest cost in the neighborhood. If you have your own fabric, the fees will be waived.

Once you register, you can come at any time or as often as you want during our business hours, which are 10 A.M. – 5 P.M. How many times a week you come to our shop is also up to you. But we want to limit the class to 15, so make sure you don't miss the registration dates.

151 What is the purpose of the information?

(A) To tell people about the renovation of a shop
(B) To promote sales of craft materials
(C) To advertise the opening of a class
(D) To request a new location for the shop

152 What is NOT stated about the quilting shop?

(A) Students of any level are welcome to join.
(B) Students with their own materials don't have to pay.
(C) It provides materials of the best qualities.
(D) The class has a limitation on the number of students.

Questions 153-154 refer to the following text message chain.

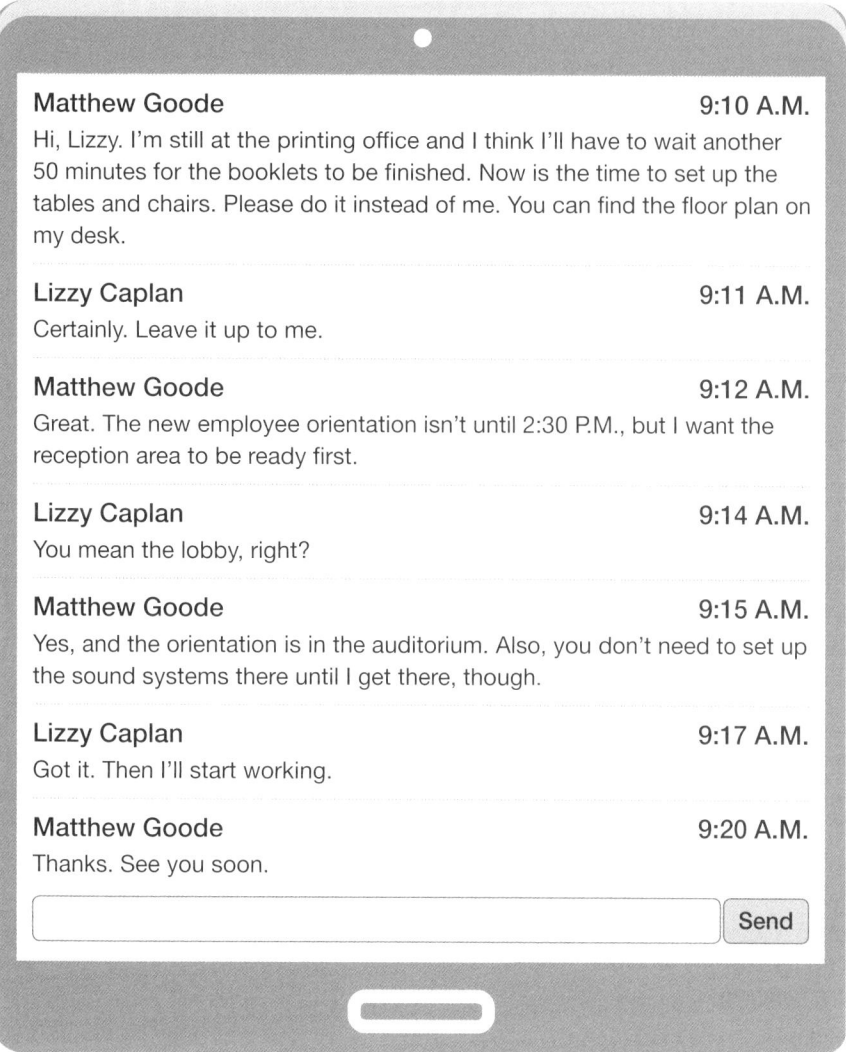

Matthew Goode   9:10 A.M.

Hi, Lizzy. I'm still at the printing office and I think I'll have to wait another 50 minutes for the booklets to be finished. Now is the time to set up the tables and chairs. Please do it instead of me. You can find the floor plan on my desk.

Lizzy Caplan   9:11 A.M.

Certainly. Leave it up to me.

Matthew Goode   9:12 A.M.

Great. The new employee orientation isn't until 2:30 P.M., but I want the reception area to be ready first.

Lizzy Caplan   9:14 A.M.

You mean the lobby, right?

Matthew Goode   9:15 A.M.

Yes, and the orientation is in the auditorium. Also, you don't need to set up the sound systems there until I get there, though.

Lizzy Caplan   9:17 A.M.

Got it. Then I'll start working.

Matthew Goode   9:20 A.M.

Thanks. See you soon.

| Send |

153 At 9:11 A.M., what does Ms. Caplan most likely mean when she writes, "Leave it up to me"?

(A) She is positive that a booklet is on each table.
(B) She is sure that Mr. Goode chose the right pamphlets.
(C) She is confirming the order for tables.
(D) She will help Mr. Goode.

154 Where most likely is Ms. Caplan going next?

(A) To an audience room
(B) To a printing shop
(C) To a lobby
(D) To a supply room

GO ON TO THE NEXT PAGE

Mitsui Will Launch a New Smartphone in May

While all the cutting-edge phone companies have strived for releasing smartphones, Mitsui seemed to have given up on the high-technology race. – [1] –. Mitsui has announced that it will be launching a smartphone that will be more than just a competitor.

The new model name for Mitsui's smartphone is "Invincible," since the company hopes it will be undefeated in the industry for some time. – [2] –. The company promises that the model has Internet access speed faster than computers. It comes equipped with dual rear cameras and Quad DAC chip for high-quality sound that resembles a live opera performance.

The response of other smartphone companies such as Ace and Nautics seems to be anticipatory as well as anxious. – [3] –. The air was tense around the staff members of the other smartphone companies, when they saw the yet-to-be-launched model. Consumers are also excited about the new model, but there are concerns about the price of the smartphones getting too high. – [4] –.

155 What is indicated about "Invincible"?

(A) It has a 12-megapixel camera.
(B) MP3 player feature is not installed.
(C) It is named after a company's motto.
(D) It has great Internet speed.

156 The word "strived" in paragraph 1, line 2, is closest in meaning to

(A) triggered
(B) rushed
(C) attempted
(D) decided

157 In which of the positions marked [1], [2], [3], and [4] does the following sentence best belong?

"But now that seems to be a bit of a hasty conclusion."

(A) [1]
(B) [2]
(C) [3]
(D) [4]

DON'T MISS THIS CHANCE
TO SPEND THE HOLIDAYS WITH YOUR LOVED ONES!

The Residence Resort is making you an offer you just cannot refuse! Our resort is on one of the most beautiful islands of Hawaii. So come on to this gorgeous island and have a dream vacation at an unbelievable price!

If you make a reservation for next month within this week, you can be accompanied by one person for free! So treat yourself and another lucky person to a relaxing experience at our resort by the beach. However, the ticket purchaser must match the owner of the credit card and is required to pay in full at the time of purchase.

The benefits do not end there. This event also includes a morning buffet at the Triumph Restaurant on the ground floor. So make your reservations this week for a fantastic holiday next month!

Please note: The benefits will be applied to only weekday reservations.

16575 PAOAKALANI AVE.
HONOLULU, HI 98615
USA

158 What is being advertised?

(A) Lunch at a hotel
(B) A family trip
(C) A resort experience
(D) A weekend spa

159 According to the advertisement, what is mentioned about the benefits?

(A) The reservation has to be made next month.
(B) The companion gets to stay for free.
(C) The morning buffet will be provided at half price.
(D) Rooms with an ocean view are available.

160 To get the benefits, by when does a person need to make a reservation?

(A) Today
(B) This week
(C) Next month
(D) In the summer

GO ON TO THE NEXT PAGE

Community Health Center
We have moved to a new location!

Visit us at:
824 Merina Avenue
Stoneybrook County

Gym Hours
Monday-Friday: 7:00 A.M. – 10:00 P.M.
Saturday & Sunday: 9:00 A.M. – 6:00 P.M.

* The sauna will open and close at the same time as the gym. No additional fees will be charged for the sauna.
(The sauna is for people who use the gym. That is, patrons who use the sauna must also use the gym.)
* We are not open on national holidays.

To celebrate our moving to a larger place, everyone gets a chance to experience our gym for free this week. From Monday (April 1) to Sunday (April 7), anyone can come in and enjoy our equipment and facilities. Just bring your ID card and let us know that you are from the neighborhood.

Those who have a membership may also come and check out the new facilities. Then we'll be selling new memberships starting next week.

Three-month Membership Fee: $120.00
Six-month Membership Fee: $220.00
One-year Membership Fee: $410.00

Try out the free gym first and decide on your membership!

161 What is the purpose of this notice?

(A) To announce a change
(B) To give out free coupons
(C) To notify a membership fee increase
(D) To inform residents of a free membership

162 What is NOT true about the health center?

(A) It is on Merina Avenue.
(B) It has a sauna.
(C) It will reopen next week.
(D) It closes on legal holidays.

163 What can be inferred about the center?

(A) The sauna opens every day.
(B) There is no discount for the membership fee.
(C) Additional costs for the sauna are incurred.
(D) The original building was less spacious than it is now.

Questions 164-167 refer to the following memo.

To: All staff members
From: Mario Panchonaz
Date: January 12
Subject: Sabrina Gilligan

I'm delighted to announce that the board of directors has appointed Sabrina Gilligan to the position of Marketing Manager. – [1] –. She will be in charge of directing staff members and planning new strategies for the marketing team. This change will be effective starting tomorrow.

– [2] –. She was highly recommended and transferred to our headquarters in Chicago. She is known for being punctual and honest. And even though she is strict with herself, she has a big heart to all workers. She has been a role model to all staff members and even to executives. – [3] –. So the position of Marketing Manager is just a new title for what she is already doing now.

I believe that her splendid experience and outstanding leadership will be a great new foundation for our company. – [4] –. I hope that all of you will give her your warmest congratulations. As the goal for our company is to improve every day, I believe this change will give us another step forward. Keep up the good work!

Mario Panchonaz
CEO

164 Why was the memo written?

(A) To inform workers about a staff party
(B) To appoint a new board
(C) To share this year's strategies
(D) To announce an employee change

165 What is Ms. Gilligan's responsibility?

(A) Recommending talented employees
(B) Supervising all branches
(C) Making new strategies for her team
(D) Teaching leadership to the staff

166 In which city would Ms. Gilligan most likely be working?

(A) New York
(B) Chicago
(C) Boston
(D) Washington

167 In which of the positions marked [1], [2], [3], and [4] does the following sentence best belong?

"Ms. Gilligan joined our company in Boston in 2012 and was promoted to Junior Marketing Manager in 2016."

(A) [1]
(B) [2]
(C) [3]
(D) [4]

GO ON TO THE NEXT PAGE

Questions 168-171 refer to the following online chat discussion.

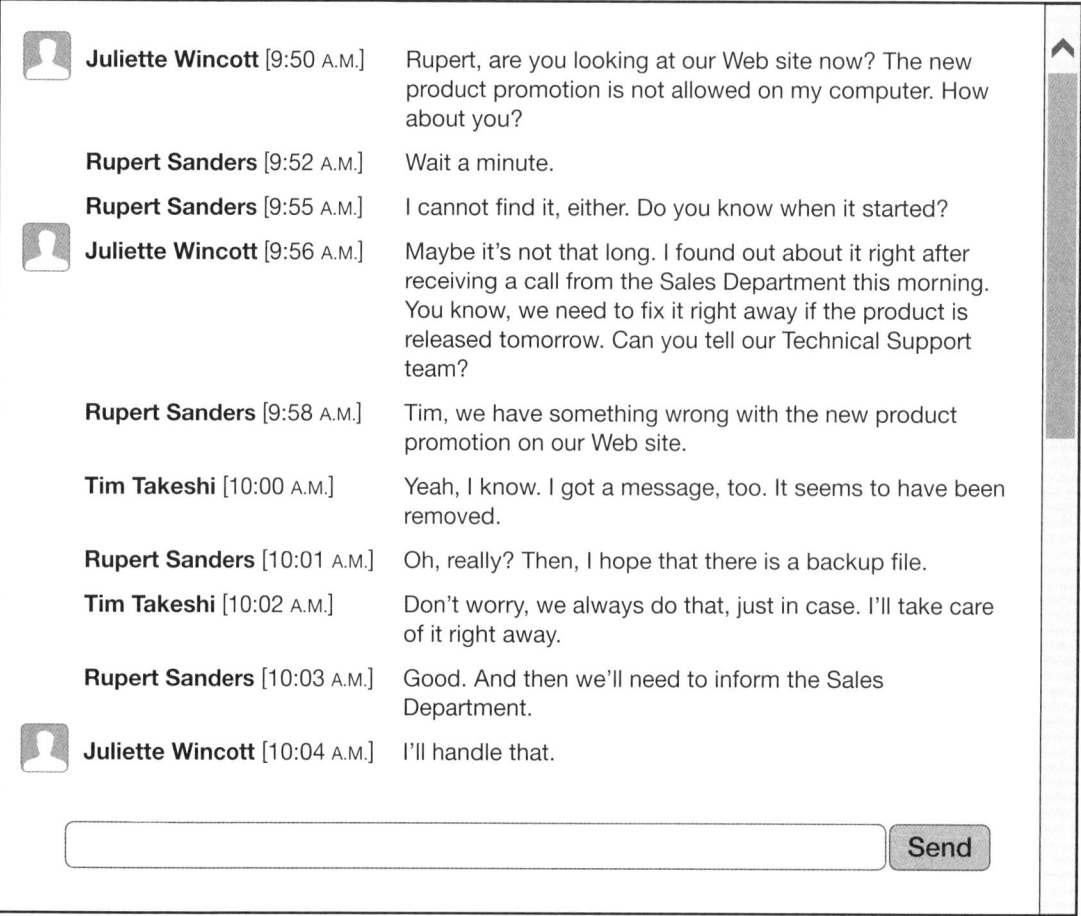

Juliette Wincott [9:50 A.M.]	Rupert, are you looking at our Web site now? The new product promotion is not allowed on my computer. How about you?
Rupert Sanders [9:52 A.M.]	Wait a minute.
Rupert Sanders [9:55 A.M.]	I cannot find it, either. Do you know when it started?
Juliette Wincott [9:56 A.M.]	Maybe it's not that long. I found out about it right after receiving a call from the Sales Department this morning. You know, we need to fix it right away if the product is released tomorrow. Can you tell our Technical Support team?
Rupert Sanders [9:58 A.M.]	Tim, we have something wrong with the new product promotion on our Web site.
Tim Takeshi [10:00 A.M.]	Yeah, I know. I got a message, too. It seems to have been removed.
Rupert Sanders [10:01 A.M.]	Oh, really? Then, I hope that there is a backup file.
Tim Takeshi [10:02 A.M.]	Don't worry, we always do that, just in case. I'll take care of it right away.
Rupert Sanders [10:03 A.M.]	Good. And then we'll need to inform the Sales Department.
Juliette Wincott [10:04 A.M.]	I'll handle that.

Send

---

168 What does Ms. Wincott report?

(A) Placing orders cannot be processed in the stores.
(B) The wrong contact information is listed online.
(C) The company's Web site cannot be opened.
(D) Some information is not displayed online.

169 From whom did Ms. Wincott learn about the problem?

(A) A customer
(B) A sales associate
(C) A technical supporter
(D) A store manager

170 At 10:01 A.M., what does Mr. Sanders most likely mean when he writes, "Then, I hope that there is a backup file"?

(A) He worries about the store's promotion.
(B) He wants Mr. Takeshi to explain the procedures.
(C) He would like to restrict access to the online stores.
(D) He wants some information to be returned online.

171 What will Ms. Wincott most likely do next?

(A) Update company policies
(B) Post a notice on bulletin boards
(C) Contact the Sales team
(D) Promote the new product

To	Elli Tannenbaum <ellitan@ifxmotors.com>
From	Human Resources <human@ifxmotors.com>
Date	March 22
Subject	Evaluation

Dear Ms. Tannenbaum:

This e-mail is sent out from the Human Resources team, and you are obliged to adhere to its confidentiality. For a fair evaluation of our staff members, we on the Human Resources team randomly select a staff member with a relatively low position to evaluate the higher position of his or her team. It is important that you follow the guidelines given below and submit the evaluation sheet by the end of this week by e-mail.

- Do not let anyone see you make your evaluations.
- You may do the evaluations after work and at any convenient place.
- You are not authorized to send the form to anyone else.
- The evaluation form is in seven pages with five criteria.
- Do not skip any questions.
- Essay form questions do not have to be long, but we ask you to describe specific incidents.

We trust your honesty and fairness for a truthful evaluation. We promise you secrecy. We also appreciate your time and effort in doing this evaluation and will use the data wisely.

If you have any questions regarding the evaluation, please send your e-mail to or call anyone on the Human Resources team.

Thank you for your cooperation.

Human Resources

---

172 What is the purpose of the e-mail?

(A) To remind Elli of an upcoming evaluation
(B) To ask for cooperation on the evaluation
(C) To ask for suggestions on making forms
(D) To recommend Elli for a promotion

173 What is NOT indicated about the evaluation?

(A) No question can be left unanswered.
(B) It consists of five criteria.
(C) The participant will receive a gift certificate after the evaluation.
(D) The participant cannot send the form to another person.

174 The word "incidents" in paragraph 2, line 6, is closest in meaning to

(A) traumas
(B) happenings
(C) disturbances
(D) sequels

175 What is implied about Elli?

(A) She has a high position on her team.
(B) She volunteered to do the evaluation.
(C) She is a member of the Human Resources team.
(D) She has to evaluate a senior staff member.

GO ON TO THE NEXT PAGE

The most important thing is to have a good relationship.

Are you looking for a way to lead your business more smoothly and effectively? If so, all you need is Relationloop Consulting.

We at Relationloop Consulting have been working for the prosperity of our local companies for over a decade. We are offering consulting services and training to make good relationships with your clients and staff. Don't hesitate to try it right now. We will be a great partner for your business. Please visit our Web site and achieve massive success!

www.relationloop.com

Hank Shirman
Relationloop Consulting
339 Wilson Ave.
Toronto, Ontario

Dear Mr. Shirman,

I just wanted to thank you again for helping our company run more smoothly. Your consulting on relationships at the offce has helped our employees understand each other more and communicate more efficiently. This was my first year running the company after my father passed away. I had a rough time with the loss of my father and had to run the whole company. Thanks to you, my staff members have much more faith in me than a year ago. Also, I have learned a lot with your group sessions. I came to understand the staff's anxiety of getting a new boss. And I learned that this anxiety turned into hostility, in order for the staff members to defend themselves in a new environment. Now I have these sessions regularly. These days, the staff members seem to be comfortable around me enough to joke with me and share honest complaints.

Thank you so much. You have not just saved my company, but all of us. Please let me know if you ever need a written recommendation from us. I'll be happy to provide it to you.

Best of luck in all your endeavors.

Sincerely,

Wilhelmina Untermyer
CEO, Lipsmackin Syrups

176 For whom is the advertisement intended?

(A) Consulting companies
(B) Staff
(C) An educational institute
(D) Owners of local businesses

177 What is the purpose of the letter?

(A) To demand a refund
(B) To apply for a job
(C) To show appreciation for work done
(D) To suggest a business plan

178 What can be inferred about Relationloop Consulting?

(A) The company started operations 20 years ago.
(B) Mr. Shirman has hired the company several times.
(C) The company and Lipsmackin Syrups are in Toronto.
(D) The company is an advertising agency.

179 According to the letter, what is the outcome of Mr. Shirman's efforts?

(A) Better quality in products
(B) Effective communication between workers
(C) Increase in the number of employees
(D) More efficient work by staff members

180 What does Ms. Untermyer offer to do for Mr. Shirman?

(A) Hold a meeting
(B) Open a job position
(C) Have dinner in Toronto
(D) Provide a recommendation

GO ON TO THE NEXT PAGE

Can You Act or Dance or Sing in an Auditorium Full of People?

Even if you think not, give it a try! You might find that you have talent you never knew about.

The Stevens Point Young Thespians Club is getting ready for its 13th year of fun. It is looking for new members to take part in its activities in the fall and spring semesters.

It is an ambitious club, and its tentative schedule this year includes some drama, tragedy, comedy, and even romance. Last year, this club staged *A Midsummer Night's Dream*, *Annie Get Your Gun*, *The Lion King*, *Mamma Mia*, and *West Side Story*. If you are sure you can't get up on stage, you can serve in one of its support roles. You can serve as a stagehand, a ticket taker, a camera operator or a set designer. The Stevens Point Young Thespians Club welcomes all people aged 18 and younger to join. You can have the experience of a lifetime, helping the club put on these productions in the city's Thompson Theater.

The club will hold its first meeting next Wednesday at 5:30 P.M. For more information, contact its volunteer and sponsor, Tina Jones, at 177 Main Street #137.

September 3
Tina Jones
177 Main Street #137
Stevens Point, Wisconsin

Dear Ms. Jones:

I saw the news about your club yesterday and I was intrigued. I am new to the city and a bit shy, but maybe I could join and help.

I have some experience acting when my family lived in Caldwell, where I was a student for the past two years. I was in two plays (*Phantom of the Opera* and *Billy Elliot*), but the parts I played were fairly small. I have also taken private dance classes since I was 11 years old, so I might be able to dance in some of the Young Thespians Club shows. I have been singing in my church's choir for the past several years although I don't think my voice is very good. Do you think I would be able to join the Stevens Point Young Thespians Club?

Sincerely,

Sarah McDonald

181 What is the purpose of the article?

(A) To seek donations for the club
(B) To celebrate the club's annual event
(C) To recruit new members of the club
(D) To announce ticket prices for *Annie Get Your Gun*

182 What is mentioned about the Stevens Point Young Thespians Club?

(A) It started business over a decade ago.
(B) It is limited to 18 students.
(C) Only proven actors are welcome.
(D) It is searching for a new faculty supervisor.

183 In the letter, the word "intrigued" in paragraph 1, line 1, is closest in meaning to

(A) preferred
(B) planned
(C) participated
(D) interested

184 What would Sarah most likely do if she joins the club?

(A) Serve as a stagehand
(B) Help publicize the club
(C) Be the secretary of the club
(D) Sing, dance, and act on stage

185 What can be inferred about Sarah?

(A) She is self-confident.
(B) She knows little about how theatrical productions are staged.
(C) She is probably over 18 years old.
(D) She has several experiences related to theater.

GO ON TO THE NEXT PAGE

Questions 186-190 refer to the following e-mails and form.

To	Stephanie Chase <dreamchaser@mochinosh.com>
From	Max Orwell <maxpw@officesupplies.com>
Date	July 10
Subject	Request
Attachment	Sample photos and order form.zip

Dear Ms. Chase:

Thank you for using Success Office Supplies. Before the products are manufactured, please check the ordered items and the samples from the attached photographs and the order form.

As soon as you confirm the samples and the numbers of the items, we'll send the samples off to the factory. After that, you will not be able to get any refund on the confirmed parts. However, if the products are damaged during delivery or are different from the samples, you will receive a full refund.

The whole manufacturing and delivery period will take five to seven business days. After the products have left our factory to be delivered, you will be charged by your credit card. Please note that once the orders are sent to the factory they cannot be canceled or adjusted.

If you have any questions, please contact us by telephone or by e-mail.

Sincerely,

Max Orwell
Success Office Supplies

SUCCESS OFFICE SUPPLIES ORDER FORM

Name: Stephanie Chase at Mochinosh
The date of the order: July 9

Item	Count
Canvas bag with company logo	2,500
Ballpoint pen with company logo	3,000
Coffee mug with company logo	3,000

* If you see any errors on this form or have any questions, please feel free to call or e-mail us immediately. Thank you for your order.

* Contact information
  821-555-8678
  customerservice@officesupplies.com

To:	Max Orwell <maxpw@officesupplies.com>
From:	Stephanie Chase <dreamchaser@mochinosh.com>
Date:	July 11
Subject:	Re: Request

I have checked the attached samples and they all look good. The logos are vivid, and there seem to be no smudges around the edges as you said when we talked on the phone.

However, I would like to make a few changes in the number of canvas bags to 4,000 although your summary is correct. That will be all for the order.

Just one more thing. Can I be informed when the items have been made and they leave your factory? Also, I would like to get the delivery number and the name of the delivery service.

Thanks.

Stephanie Chase
Mochinosh Technology
Brooklyn, NY

---

186 What is the purpose of the first e-mail?

(A) To inform Ms. Chase about unavailable services
(B) To notify Ms. Chase that a catalogue has been sent
(C) To request a confirmation on an order
(D) To ask for samples to be sent

187 What is indicated about refunds in the first e-mail?

(A) Partial refunds are given for damaged products.
(B) A refund is impossible on confirmed parts.
(C) Cups are nonrefundable.
(D) A refund takes about a week.

188 In the second e-mail, the word "smudges" in paragraph 1, line 2, is closest in meaning to

(A) blinks
(B) smears
(C) grins
(D) glitters

189 Why did Ms. Chase send the e-mail?

(A) To cancel some items
(B) To request a quick delivery
(C) To increase the number of an item
(D) To change the location of the company logo

190 According to the second e-mail, what is NOT true about Ms. Chase?

(A) She wants to be notified when the items are sent.
(B) She looked at the sample photos.
(C) She wants to recommend a delivery company.
(D) She spoke with Mr. Orwell on the phone.

GO ON TO THE NEXT PAGE

Questions 191-195 refer to the following advertisement, e-mail, and résumé.

JOB OPPORTUNITY

Tycoon Banks is seeking an ambitious and motivated individual to fill a vacancy in its local office.

The position we are trying to fill requires a candidate with outstanding communication skills who is people-friendly. We are also looking for a person eager to learn all aspects of the financial services industry through our comprehensive training program. Sales representatives receive competitive salaries as well as incentives for big sales.

Applicants with prior sales experience will be given preference, but that is not required. If you are interested in working for a company that is an industry leader, we look forward to hearing from you. Qualified applicants should send their résumés to the Human Resources Manager, Clara Hamilton, at clarahamilton@tycoonbanks.co.ca.

To	Clara Hamilton <clarahamilton@tycoonbanks.co.ca>
From	Daniel Kinsley <dkinsley@jmail.net >
Date	February 10
Subject	Applying for Sales Representative
Attachment	Résumé_Daniel Kinsley.doc

Dear Ms. Hamilton:

I'm writing to apply for the advertised position. With this e-mail I am attaching my résumé.

I am confident that I meet all the requirements for the job. I grew up in a rather large family of two brothers and three sisters. So I am a natural people person. I am an excellent team player and weekend volunteer worker at the Montreal Community Center.

I am sure that I will be able to bring enthusiasm to your company. I would greatly appreciate an opportunity for an interview.

Thank you.

Daniel Kinsley

RÉSUMÉ

1. PERSONAL DETAILS
- Name: Daniel Kinsley
- Address: 2030 Yung St., Suite 4514, Montreal, Quebec
- Phone number: 821-555-8521
- E-mail: dkinsley@jmail.net

2. OBJECTIVE
A position as a representative in Sales Department

3. EDUCATION
Mar. 2010 – Feb. 2015 Montreal University
Bachelor of Arts in Business Administration with a minor in Psychology

4. EXPERIENCE
- Date of employment: Feb. 2015 – Jan. 2017
- Name: ABC Insurance Company
- Position held: the sales staff

191 According to the advertisement, what position is most likely being offered?

(A) Sales Representative
(B) Human Resources Manager
(C) Financial Consultant
(D) Training Assistant

192 What is NOT indicated as a benefit offered by the company?

(A) Regular vacation
(B) High salary
(C) Performance-related pay
(D) Training program

193 What qualification is required by Tycoon Banks?

(A) Personal connections
(B) Enthusiasm to learn
(C) Ability to assist the CEO
(D) Job experience

194 Why did Daniel send the e-mail?

(A) To ask for details about the position
(B) To express appreciation
(C) To send an application
(D) To confirm an interview

195 What is indicated about Daniel?

(A) He lives near the company.
(B) He will be preferred for the job.
(C) He has few siblings.
(D) He is applying for a job for the first time.

GO ON TO THE NEXT PAGE

Dieting has never been so easy!

It is so hard to part with foods that we love. Yes, we all know that eating healthy is the key to a great diet. However, the thoughts of dessert refuse to go away. But not anymore! Dr. Fielder and Delicioso Bakery have come up with diet meals made of desserts! Too good to be true? But it is true!

Dr. Fielder has studied diabetes for 25 years. He himself comes from a family with a long history of diabetes. All his life he had to say no to dessert or nibble on carrot sticks while his friends bit into birthday cakes. Then three years ago, he put aside the research on seeking a cure for diabetes and decided to make desserts for diabetic people. So he contacted the ever-so-popular dessert company, Delicioso Bakery. Since its founding in 1972, it has been the best place for desserts in the city.

Dr. Fielder and the staff of Delicioso Bakery came up with varieties of cookies, cakes and muffins that actually have no sugar and butter in them. Though these desserts were made for diabetic people, the test groups of both diabetics and non-diabetics have lost a considerable amount of weight. So this became the Delicioso's Delight Plan! If you buy any of Delicioso's Delight products, there will be a "How to Diet" instruction in the box. It's as simple as replacing your desserts and meal breads with Delicioso's Delight.

Our products are not just fulfilling and healthy, they are delicious!

HOW TO DIET #3
Are you really hungry?
Think carefully before eating.

In fact, people continue to eat for various reasons, such as stress and hormonal abnormality, even though they are not hungry. Therefore, you must check whether you are hungry before eating something, considering when and how much you ate.

Delicioso's Delight products are rich in fiber which fills you up easily, and can prevent overeating. Dieting is not difficult now.

Stay tuned for our next diet tips!

Delicioso's Delight
398 Pitt Street
Cornwall-on-Hudson, NY 12520

Dear Delicioso Bakery and even Dr. Fielder:

I have seen your ad and at first I was very skeptical. I mean, how can cookies and cakes be a diet? So I bought a box of Delicioso's Delight cookies and some breads to prove that you were wrong. But you were right!

The cookies were delicious, but the fibers made me feel full after the third cookie. I took the muffins for breakfast. Usually I would eat four pancakes with lots of syrup and bacon. But with your muffins, one is enough for the morning. It is quite a large muffin and tastes good, too. So I have to admit your products really work, and I feel grateful.

Anyway, I have lost fifteen pounds in a month. I am a pretty heavy guy so I have a long way to go, but I think I can do it with your products!

Thank you so much.

Ken Erickson

196 What is being advertised?

(A) Diabetic pills
(B) Homemade desserts
(C) Diet food
(D) Replacement for sugar

197 In the advertisement, the word "considerable" in paragraph 3, line 3, is closest in meaning to

(A) careful
(B) large
(C) steady
(D) thoughtful

198 According to the advertisement, what is NOT true about Delicioso Bakery?

(A) It conducted a joint research.
(B) It is a famous company.
(C) It was established 25 years ago.
(D) It sells diet meals with instructions.

199 Why was the letter written?

(A) To show appreciation
(B) To make a complaint
(C) To request a new menu
(D) To make an order for the product

200 Which product most likely contains instruction number 3?

(A) Pancake
(B) Bacon
(C) Cookie
(D) Sandwich

잠깐!!
시작 전 꼭 확인하세요!

☑ 실제 시험과 같이
   책상을 정리하고
   마음의 준비를 하세요.

☑ 핸드폰은 잠깐 끄고
   대신 아날로그 시계를
   활용해 보세요.

☑ 권장 풀이 시간은 55분입니다.
   시간을 꼭 지켜주세요.

☑ 어렵다고 넘어가지 마세요.
   가능하면 차례대로 풀어 보세요.

Actual Test

03

시작 시간   :

종료 시간   :

PART 7

Directions: In this part you will read a selection of texts, such as magazine and newspaper articles, e-mails, and instant messages. Each text or set of texts is followed by several questions. Select the best answer for each question and mark the letter (A), (B), (C), or (D) on your answer sheet.

Questions 147-148 refer to the following memo.

MEMO

This is a reminder to all department supervisors that the three-day Christmas holiday later this month will cause an adjustment in our standard payroll schedule. The payday that would fall on Friday the 26th has been pushed forward by three days and will now fall on Tuesday the 23rd. Moreover, our traditional year-end bonuses will be included in this paycheck. As a consequence of this shift in the schedule, the deadline for overtime and expense payment requests has also been moved ahead. Normally these requests are accepted up until Monday afternoon; this month they are due by the end of the day on Friday the 19th. Please be sure that your entire staff is aware of this modified schedule and encourage them to direct any questions or concerns to my office.

147 What is the purpose of the memo?

(A) To apologize for a paycheck mix-up
(B) To change the dates of a holiday
(C) To announce a new year-end bonus
(D) To give the details of an altered schedule

148 When will workers be receiving their bonuses?

(A) Friday the 19th
(B) Monday the 22nd
(C) Tuesday the 23rd
(D) Friday the 26th

Questions 149-150 refer to the following text message chain.

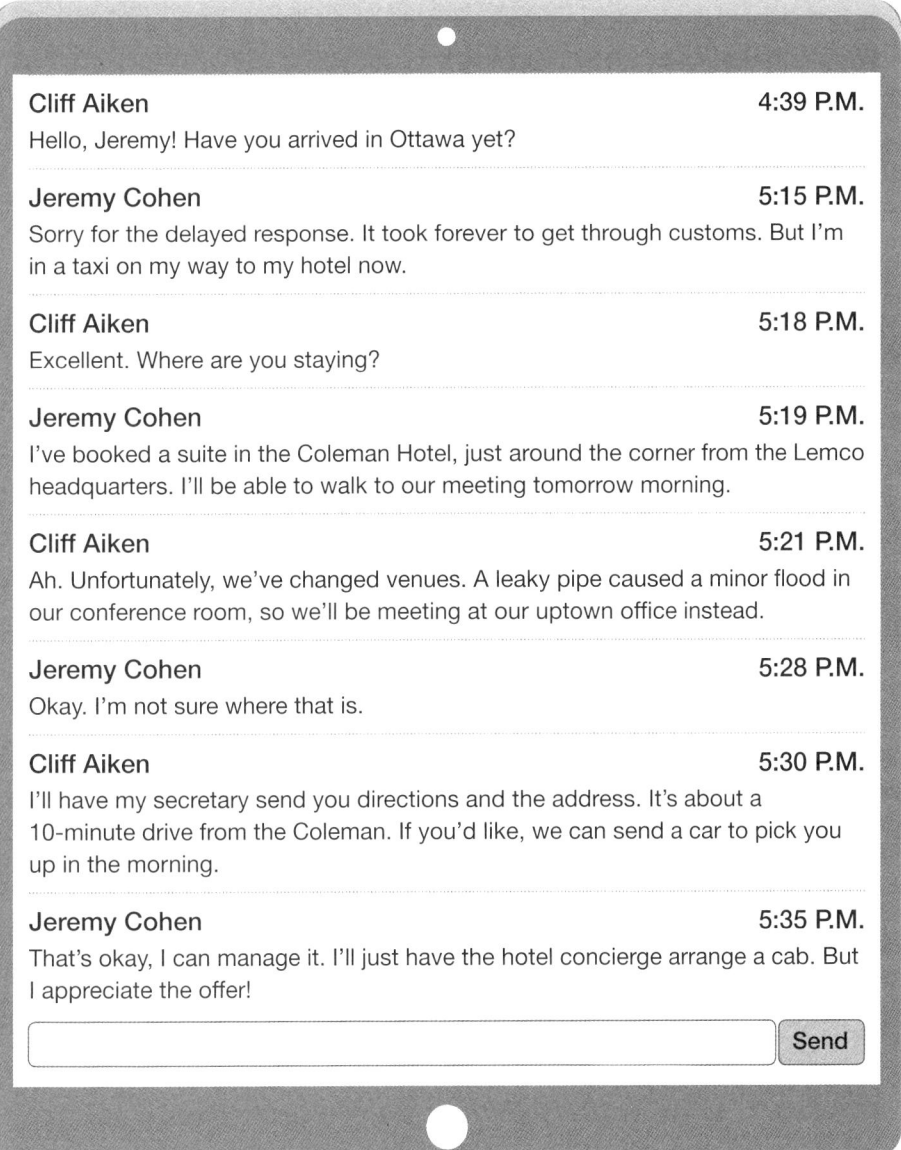

Cliff Aiken	**4:39 P.M.**
Hello, Jeremy! Have you arrived in Ottawa yet?	
Jeremy Cohen	**5:15 P.M.**
Sorry for the delayed response. It took forever to get through customs. But I'm in a taxi on my way to my hotel now.	
Cliff Aiken	**5:18 P.M.**
Excellent. Where are you staying?	
Jeremy Cohen	**5:19 P.M.**
I've booked a suite in the Coleman Hotel, just around the corner from the Lemco headquarters. I'll be able to walk to our meeting tomorrow morning.	
Cliff Aiken	**5:21 P.M.**
Ah. Unfortunately, we've changed venues. A leaky pipe caused a minor flood in our conference room, so we'll be meeting at our uptown office instead.	
Jeremy Cohen	**5:28 P.M.**
Okay. I'm not sure where that is.	
Cliff Aiken	**5:30 P.M.**
I'll have my secretary send you directions and the address. It's about a 10-minute drive from the Coleman. If you'd like, we can send a car to pick you up in the morning.	
Jeremy Cohen	**5:35 P.M.**
That's okay, I can manage it. I'll just have the hotel concierge arrange a cab. But I appreciate the offer!	

Send

149 What is indicated about Lemco?

(A) It has more than one office.
(B) It is a manufacturer of automobiles.
(C) It does not employ a large number of workers.
(D) It is no longer located near the Coleman Hotel.

150 At 5:35 P.M., what does Mr. Cohen mean when he writes, "That's okay, I can manage it"?

(A) He thinks an office manager will come soon.
(B) He can speak with his supervisor by himself.
(C) He believes Lemco's proposal is acceptable.
(D) He can handle the situation without assistance.

GO ON TO THE NEXT PAGE

Questions 151-152 refer to the following schedule.

The 11th Annual Triboro International Film Festival

West Street Cinema Schedule

The West Street Cinema is proud to be taking part in the Triboro International Film Festival for the first time. Holders of festival passes, which can be purchased online for $30 each, will be admitted to all films at no charge. For all others, tickets are $10 for adults and $5 for children under 12. Please refer to the following show times:

Film	Date	Show times
Silent Mode (drama, Germany)	Friday, March 7	5 P.M. / 9 P.M.
The Horrible Words (documentary, USA)	Friday, March 7	7 P.M. / 11 P.M.
Policeman (drama, Poland)	Saturday, March 8	2 P.M. / 6 P.M. / 10 P.M.
Out of the Light (comedy, Korea)	Saturday, March 8	4 P.M. / 8 P.M. / 12 A.M.
In Your Dreams (comedy, Canada)	Sunday, March 9	12 P.M. / 5 P.M.
Looking for New York (drama, Russia)	Sunday, March 9	8 P.M.

151 What is indicated about festival passes?

(A) Their cost for adults is twice as much as their cost for kids.
(B) They can only be used for admittance on Friday and Saturday.
(C) People who have them will be entitled to free entry.
(D) They can be purchased at the West Street Cinema.

152 Which drama can be viewed on Saturday afternoon?

(A) *Silent Mode*
(B) *Policeman*
(C) *Out of the Light*
(D) *Looking for New York*

Questions 153-154 refer to the following online chat discussion.

Annie Lopez [4:52 P.M.]		Yesterday's meeting seemed to go well. I think our clients were satisfied with our proposed design.
Henry Lin [4:53 P.M.]		Do you? They didn't have anything bad to say, but they seemed unimpressed. I think we blew it.
Paul Green [4:55 P.M.]		I have to agree with Henry on this one. I interpreted their silence as disappointment. But I'm not sure what we did wrong.
Henry Lin [4:56 P.M.]		In my opinion, we didn't provide them with enough technical details. By trying to keep our presentation brief, we sacrificed a lot of crucial information.
Paul Green [4:58 P.M.]		Do you think we should put together a revised presentation with added components and send it to them?
Annie Lopez [4:59 P.M.]		Wait a minute, guys! You're moving too fast. The clients might be perfectly happy with what we showed them.
Paul Green [5:02 P.M.]		I suppose we can contact them and find out.
Annie Lopez [5:03 P.M.]		They'll get in touch with us if they need more information. We should just wait.
Paul Green [5:05 P.M.]		Okay. But I'm going to start revising the presentation, just in case.
Henry Lin [5:06 P.M.]		Good idea, Paul. It's better to be safe than sorry. If they feel our original presentation was weak, we can have an improved version ready to go.

Test 03

Send

153 At 4:53 P.M., what does Mr. Lin mean when he writes, "I think we blew it"?

(A) He feels they made their presentation too quickly.
(B) He believes their proposal was a failure.
(C) He suspects they missed a call from the clients.
(D) He thinks that his team gave their best effort.

154 What does Ms. Lopez suggest?

(A) Making adjustments to the presentation
(B) Shortening the length of the meetings
(C) Adding more details to the designs
(D) Allowing the clients to make contact first

GO ON TO THE NEXT PAGE

To: Britney Lacasse <brit88@memail.com>
From: William Albert <walbert@familyfeast.com>
Date: October 6
Subject: Overcharge

Dear Ms. Lacasse,

I was recently made aware of your complaint regarding the price you were charged for a delivery order placed with Family Feast's Riverview restaurant on October 3 of this year. – [1] –. Specifically, you are requesting a full refund for your meal because you were charged $32 rather than $26. – [2] –. You placed an order with our Riverview restaurant using a menu from our Jamestown restaurant. – [3] –. As a restaurant chain, the prices of our food can vary from franchise to franchise in certain circumstances. – [4] –. I have authorized the manager of our Riverview restaurant to compensate you for the difference of $6, but your specific request is not possible considering the circumstances.

Sincerely,

William Albert
Customer Relations Director
Family Feast Restaurants, Inc.

155 Why is the e-mail written?

(A) To reject a request for a full refund
(B) To apologize for a mistake in a bill
(C) To complain about a restaurant's prices
(D) To explain why an order was delivered late

156 What is indicated about the Jamestown Family Feast franchise?

(A) It has received several complaints from customers.
(B) Its employees aren't satisfied with the work conditions.
(C) It won't be open for business until the first week of October.
(D) Its prices are lower than those of the Riverview franchise.

157 In which of the positions marked [1], [2], [3], and [4] does the following sentence best fit?

"Unfortunately, I feel that this was caused by a mistake on your part rather than on the part of the restaurant."

(A) [1]
(B) [2]
(C) [3]
(D) [4]

Customer Satisfaction Questionnaire

Thank you for choosing to stay with Hospitality Suites. Before you check out, please take a few minutes to fill out the following customer satisfaction questionnaire. All guests who complete a form will be automatically entered in our monthly drawing for a free night's stay in any of our hotels nationwide.

1. Please indicate at which hotel location you stayed. _____

2. What was the purpose of your stay? _____

3. Please indicate your satisfaction level, with 1 representing "unsatisfied" and 5 representing "completely satisfied."

Check-in process	1	2	3	4	5
Room cleanliness	1	2	3	4	5
Staff friendliness	1	2	3	4	5
Staff helpfulness	1	2	3	4	5
Breakfast buffet	1	2	3	4	5

You may give any additional comments in the box below

Please include your name and e-mail address or mobile phone number here. These will only be used for the purpose of selecting and notifying a winner of our monthly drawing. The information in this questionnaire will be kept strictly anonymous.

158 What will guests receive for completing the questionnaire?

(A) A preferred customer VIP card
(B) A discount on their monthly bill
(C) A chance to win a free night in a hotel
(D) A letter of thanks from the hotel manager

159 What is NOT included as a category on the form?

(A) How easy it was to make a reservation
(B) How well the room had been cleaned
(C) How helpful the hotel's employees were
(D) How good the food served for breakfast was

160 What is indicated about the information in the questionnaire?

(A) It must be confirmed by phone or e-mail.
(B) It should be provided after checking out.
(C) It may be used to promote the hotel online.
(D) It will not be linked to the guest's name.

GO ON TO THE NEXT PAGE

NOTICE

The Harmon Free Clinic was temporarily shut down after a fire destroyed its James Street facilities in September. After a two-month hiatus, the clinic will be reopening its doors in a new location. The new facility is less than three blocks away, in the Fresh Market shopping center across the street from Central Plaza. Patients who have been redirected the New City Medical Center in Lennox are invited to return to our convenient Amity location. The clinic's official reopening will be on Monday, November 19, but our phone lines will be open for scheduling appointments beginning on Wednesday the 14th. Our entire original staff of highly qualified doctors and nurses will return, along with a new addition: Dr. Maria Bell, a specialist in childhood nutrition issues. For directions, more information, and a sneak peek at some photos of our new offices, please visit our Web site at www.harmon-fc.org.

161 What is the purpose of the notice?

(A) To direct a doctor's patients to the new office
(B) To announce a partnership between two businesses
(C) To inform people that a closed business will reopen
(D) To explain the circumstances behind a clinic's closure

162 Where is the new location of the Harmon Free Clinic?

(A) On James Street in Amity
(B) Around the corner from Central Plaza
(C) In the Fresh Market shopping center
(D) In the New City Medical Center in Lennox

163 What can customers do starting on November 14?

(A) Schedule appointments by phone
(B) Look at photos of the new office
(C) Visit the Harmon Free Clinic
(D) Choose a new medical facility

164 Who is Maria Bell?

(A) A guest lecturer at a medical school's event
(B) A new member of the Harmon Free Clinic's staff
(C) The person in charge of scheduling appointments
(D) The head doctor at the New City Medical Center

YOU ARE INVITED TO A PARTY!

Where: Eastside Park
When: Saturday, May 11 from 2 P.M. to 7 P.M.
Why: To learn more about the GSBA

The Greenport Small Business Association (GSBA) is hosting a barbecue party! – [1] –. You will also have a chance to meet with current members in order to expand your personal business network and establish useful connections. – [2] –.

This invitation includes up to five family members, and small children are more than welcome. Along with delicious food, there will be performances, fun games and live music. Party attendees will be under no obligation to join the GSBA. Just come and have fun with your neighbors! – [3] –.

RSVP: Please respond by calling GSBA's event coordinator Harriet Lin at 555-1132 and letting her know how many people will be attending. – [4] –. We look forward to meeting you!

---

165 What is NOT an activity at the party?

(A) Meeting GSBA members
(B) Enjoying exciting games
(C) Listening to live music
(D) Winning fun prizes

166 The word "establish" in paragraph 1, line 3, is closest in meaning to

(A) turn on
(B) give in
(C) put off
(D) set up

167 In which of the positions marked [1], [2], [3], and [4] does the following sentence best fit?

"Its purpose is to allow small business owners who have not yet joined the association to learn more about the benefits and privileges of membership."

(A) [1]
(B) [2]
(C) [3]
(D) [4]

168 What information does Ms. Lin require?

(A) The name of the small business
(B) The name of the GSBA member
(C) The business owner's membership number
(D) The number of people coming to the party

GO ON TO THE NEXT PAGE

IT STAFFING SOLUTIONS

Tired of placing ad after ad on online job sites? Worried about the high turnover rates in your IT department? Sick of wasting time and resources poring over hundreds of résumés? IT Staffing Solutions (ISS) is here to help!

We supply businesses in the Detroit metropolitan area with highly qualified IT professionals on a temporary basis. Take a look at the following benefits:

- · We carefully interview each candidate so you don't have to.
- · You're not required to add ISS workers to your benefits plan.
- · Our workers can fill in for sick employees for six months or a single afternoon.
- · You can hire our technicians as permanent employees with no strings attached.

In addition, we take care of all payroll issues. Once your company contracts with ISS, you simply need to pay a monthly service fee. We do the rest. To learn more about hiring temporary technicians, schedule an appointment to meet with one of our representatives by calling us at 882-555-9014.

169 What is being advertised?

(A) A service that provides temporary employees
(B) A Web site that finds jobs for IT professionals
(C) A business looking to provide technology services
(D) A position in a company's IT department

170 Which of the following is indicated as a benefit of ISS employees?

(A) They telecommute from their own homes.
(B) They are paid less than permanent employees.
(C) They have gone through a rigorous training program.
(D) They can work for as short or long a time as needed.

171 What is an additional advantage of contracting with ISS?

(A) Permanent workers are available for a small fee.
(B) The service includes handling employee payments.
(C) The company can save money with tax deductions.
(D) There are weekly meetings with an ISS representative.

Questions 172-175 refer to the following warranty.

Corvex LCD Television Limited Warranty

■ **Coverage** For a period of 12 months from the date of purchase, Corvex will reimburse the consumer in full for any parts and labor required to repair defects in the television. These repairs must be performed at a certified Corvex service center. In the event that the television cannot be repaired, Corvex will provide the consumer with an equal or updated model at no charge. Corvex will not be responsible for repairs performed by non-certified technicians.

■ **Assistance** For assistance in locating a certified Corvex service center in the USA, please call us toll-free at 1-888-555-2923. For a list of certified Corvex service centers outside of the USA, please visit our Web site at www.corvex.com and click on "International Repairs."

■ **Exceptions** This limited warranty does not cover the following:
  - Damage due to user neglect or misuse
  - Damage due to exposure to the elements, including moisture and salt
  - Damage caused by natural disasters, including floods and earthquakes
  - Damage caused by unmoving images left on the screen for prolonged periods

This warranty only applies to products purchased for personal use and will be automatically voided if the product is used for commercial purposes.

172 For whom is this warranty most likely intended?

(A) Retailers who specialize in home electronics
(B) Manufacturers who produce LCD screens
(C) Consumers who purchase televisions for their homes
(D) Shop owners who order parts for Corvex products

173 What will happen if a defective product cannot be repaired?

(A) It will be sent to a non-certified technician overseas.
(B) The customer must return it to the place it was purchased.
(C) The certified service center will offer a full refund.
(D) It will be replaced with the same model or a better one.

174 How would a consumer in Canada locate a certified service center?

(A) By visiting a Web site
(B) By e-mailing a service agent
(C) By calling a toll-free number
(D) By asking a local Corvex retailer

175 Which of the following actions would void the warranty?

(A) Moving the television outside of the USA
(B) Using the television for business functions
(C) Shipping the television through a non-certified carrier
(D) Purchasing the television directly from the manufacturer

GO ON TO THE NEXT PAGE

Gary Lee
Accounting Manager
Progress Industries
301 School Street
Newark, NJ

Dear Mr. Lee,

Please accept this letter as my official resignation from the position of credit coordinator. As I am giving you two weeks' notice, my final day with Progress Industries will be Friday, October 22.

As per our earlier discussions, the problem centers on the company's inability to offer flexible work hours. With two young children at home and a third due in January, I am simply unable to meet the company's 9-to-6 requirements on a consistent basis. I sincerely regret the situation, as I have enjoyed my four years with Progress Industries, but I need to put my family first. If you would like to meet to discuss the details of my departure, please let me know.

Yours truly,

Bradley Sullinger

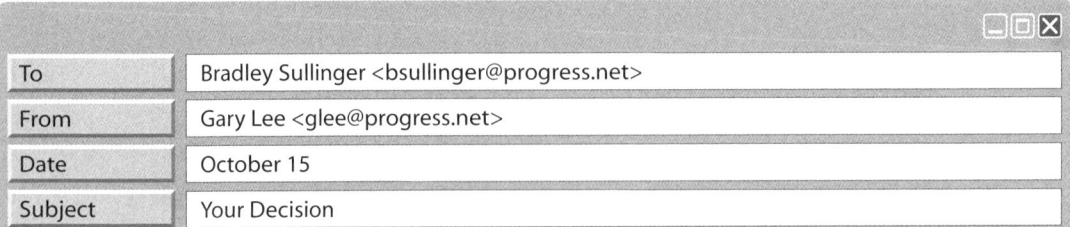

To	Bradley Sullinger <bsullinger@progress.net>
From	Gary Lee <glee@progress.net>
Date	October 15
Subject	Your Decision

I'm glad to hear you've reconsidered your resignation and have decided to stay on with us in a part-time position. I truly feel that this is the best solution for everyone involved. Furthermore, I've spoken with Human Resources, and they've prepared the paperwork for your upcoming paternity leave. You should stop by their office on the 8th floor when you have a chance. Also, I think you and I should meet on the 18th of this month to go over our expectations for your new role with the department. Let me know if you have some free time on that day.

Gary

176 What is the purpose of Mr. Sullinger's letter?

(A) To accept a position with the company
(B) To complain about his overtime hours
(C) To respond to a business proposal
(D) To inform the company that he is quitting

177 Why does Mr. Sullinger mention his family?

(A) To stress the importance of his salary
(B) To show how much he enjoys his job
(C) To explain the delay in his response
(D) To give the reason for his decision

178 When will Mr. Sullinger likely be taking time off?

(A) In two weeks
(B) Sometime in January
(C) Before the start of October
(D) From October 18th to the 22nd

179 What most likely happened before Mr. Lee sent the e-mail to Mr. Sullinger?

(A) Mr. Lee allowed Mr. Sullinger to transfer to Human Resources.
(B) Mr. Sullinger resigned from his job in the Accounting Department.
(C) Mr. Lee moved to a new office on the building's 8th floor.
(D) Mr. Sullinger changed his position from full-time to part-time.

180 What does Mr. Lee want to discuss on October 18th?

(A) The company's new regulations
(B) The problem of high employee turnover
(C) A staff shortage in Human Resources
(D) Mr. Sullinger's new duties

GO ON TO THE NEXT PAGE

Recycling Controversy

by Heather Beck, Business Reporter

Albert's Soda, a local beverage firm, is facing unexpected opposition after recently opening a new manufacturing center in East Pottsville. According to the international environmental group Be Green, the new East Pottsville plant will not be using recycled glass to make the bottles for Albert's popular brand of Pop Cola soda. Kara Page, the spokesperson for the local chapter of Be Green, says the organization is urging consumers to boycott all of Albert's Soda products until their demands are met. Specifically, Be Green is asking Albert's Soda to resume its past practice of using recycled glass for all its beverage products and to open up its plant to independent environmental inspectors. The company has issued a press release with a statement from Albert's Soda president Kevin Carter explaining that the situation at the East Pottsville plant is currently under review.

The Newburgh Standard
Editorial Department
PO Box 1172
Newburgh, NE

To the Editor:

I am writing in reference to your article on the Albert's Soda boycott. While I was quite pleased that you chose to include an article on this important issue in your Business Briefs section, it contained a couple of factual errors by the reporter that I feel I must correct. I am actually the spokesperson for the local branch of Be Green. The person you misidentified is the head of media relations of the international organization itself. Also, we are not calling for a boycott of all of Albert's products — just Pop Cola. Although we have been informed that the company is reconsidering its recycling policy, nothing has been done at this point. We therefore ask all consumers to help us protect the environment by not purchasing Pop Cola.

Sincerely,

Eric Aikawa

181 What is true about the new manufacturing center?

(A) It is next to a recycling center.
(B) It has been closed by protests.
(C) It is located in East Pottsville.
(D) It is creating water pollution.

182 What is indicated about Pop Cola?

(A) It is a brand aimed at environmentalists.
(B) It will be exported to countries around the world.
(C) It used to be packaged in recycled glass bottles.
(D) It is the most popular cola brand in the nation.

183 What is the purpose of the letter?

(A) To praise the writing of a journalist
(B) To point out some mistakes in an article
(C) To accuse a company's president of lying
(D) To complain about a threat to the environment

184 Who is Be Green's head of media relations?

(A) Heather Beck
(B) Eric Aikawa
(C) Kevin Carter
(D) Kara Page

185 What does Mr. Aikawa say about the current situation?

(A) It is getting worse.
(B) It has been misrepresented.
(C) It is slowly improving.
(D) It has not changed.

GO ON TO THE NEXT PAGE

● ● ●

To	Lawrence Markowitz <lawrencem@plainview.gov>
From	Matthew Dexter <matthewd@plainview.gov>
Date	March 5
Subject	Town Festival

Good morning, Lawrence.

It's that time of year again! We need to start planning for the annual town festival. The director asked me to put you in charge of gathering the support and participation of local businesses. I know you don't have any experience with this, but you did such a good job organizing the festival equipment rentals last year that I know you can handle it. We need to encourage businesses to either donate $100 to our general fund or sponsor one of the planned events. For donating $500, sponsors get free advertising in all of the festival's marketing material. And if they donate $2,000, the name of their business will be included in the event's name. We also offer full sponsorship of the entire festival for $10,000, but no one has ever taken us up on that. Let's get together soon, and I'll let you know more about the city's protocol for soliciting donations so you can avoid making any mistakes.

Matt

March 16, 2017

Pet World
32 East Main Street
Plainview, KS 71203

Dear Ms. Becker,

I'd like to express my sincere appreciation for your participation in this year's town festival as an event sponsor. As per our telephone discussion on March 13, Pet World will be the sole sponsor of the children's scavenger hunt, which will be renamed the Pet World Prize Hunt. This is one of our most popular events, so I'm sure it will bring a lot of favorable attention to your store. We are currently putting together our marketing material and would appreciate if you could email a GIF image of your store's logo, along with any copy you want included, to kdaniels@plainview.gov at your earliest convenience. As for remittance of your sponsorship donation, you can contact Mary Bradley in our finance department at 555-8101 to make arrangements.

Sincerely,

Lawrence Markowitz
Event Coordinator
Plainview Town Council

The 27th Annual Plainview Town Festival

Event	Location	Starting Time
Opening Parade	Main Street	10 A.M.
The Plainview Times 5-K Fun Run	Start: Town Hall Finish: Plainview High School	12 P.M.
Afternoon Concert – The Blue Sky Band	Upper Fairgrounds	2 P.M.
The Pet World Prize Hunt	Lower Fairgrounds	3 P.M.
Evening Concert and Dance	Upper Fairgrounds	5 P.M.

186 What is suggested about Lawrence Markowitz?

(A) He is a friend with the owner of Pet World.
(B) He was recently hired by the city government.
(C) He has experience sponsoring festival events.
(D) He took part in preparing last year's festival.

187 In the e-mail, the word "protocol" in paragraph 1, line 9, is closest in meaning to

(A) cooperation
(B) approval
(C) etiquette
(D) atmosphere

188 How much money will Pet World likely donate to the festival?

(A) $100
(B) $500
(C) $2,000
(D) $10,000

189 Where can festival attendees enjoy a daytime musical performance?

(A) Plainview High School
(B) Town Hall
(C) The Upper Fairgrounds
(D) The Lower Fairgrounds

190 What is NOT included as a festival event?

(A) A foot race
(B) A town picnic
(C) A children's game
(D) A couple of concerts

GO ON TO THE NEXT PAGE

ATTENTION!

Prodigy Laboratories is seeking summer interns to work in our Chicago and East Chicago computer research centers. Anyone with an interest in technological innovation and experience in computer programming is welcome to apply. The experience can be in the workplace or the classroom, but all applicants must be proficient in either C, C++ or Java. Qualified applicants will be required to submit a reference from either a current professor or supervisor—references from personal acquaintances, coworkers or classmates will not be accepted. The internships run from the beginning of July to the end of August and include a weekly stipend. Interested parties should submit their résumé in person at our administrative offices on Twelfth Street or mail it to our corporate headquarters in the Burnside Tower.

To	Susan Paladino <suziep@mymail.com>
From	Danielle Lachapelle <lachapelle@prodigylabs.com>
Date	June 15
Subject	Re: Summer Internship

Thank you for your interest in our summer intern program. After reviewing your résumé, I'd like to invite you to officially apply for the program by filling out and returning the attached form. As I mentioned when you stopped by to submit your résumé, only qualified applicants will be asked to fill out an application form. While this doesn't assure your acceptance into the program, we anticipate offering an internship position to all our official applicants barring any red flags that may come up during the review process. You can email the completed form, along with a letter of reference, to this e-mail address. However, before filling out the form, please give me a call so I can fill you in on the requirements for the letter of reference.

Danielle Lachapelle
HR associate
847-555-0228

Prodigy Laboratories – Internship Application Form

Name: Susan Paladino

Sex: Female

Age: 23

Current occupation: Part-time programmer

Current address: 43 Mayflower Avenue, Gary, Indiana

Programming experience: Firestorm Games, two years

Check the programming languages in which you are proficient:

Java ☑   C ☑   C++ ☑

Reason for applying (50 words or less): I'm currently working part-time for a small gaming company, but have been planning to apply to graduate school. Before doing so, I would love a chance to expand my skills working for a large company like Prodigy Labs, even if it is just on a short-term basis.

Reference letter from: Steven Jacobs

191 What is the purpose of Ms. Lachapelle's e-mail?

(A) To accept an applicant into an internship program

(B) To answer an applicant's question about a form

(C) To request a letter of reference from an applicant

(D) To supply an applicant with an application form

192 Where did Ms. Paladino most likely submit her résumé?

(A) The Chicago computer research center

(B) The East Chicago computer research center

(C) The company's administrative offices

(D) The corporate headquarters

193 According to the e-mail, what is Ms. Paladino most likely to do next?

(A) Request a letter of reference

(B) Fill out the application form

(C) Contact Ms. Lachapelle by phone

(D) Stop by the administrative offices

194 According to the form, what is probably true about Ms. Paladino?

(A) She is interested in obtaining a master's degree.

(B) She has worked for Prodigy Laboratories before.

(C) She does not know any programming languages.

(D) She emailed her résumé to the wrong address.

195 Who most likely is Mr. Jacobs?

(A) A Prodigy Laboratories employee

(B) A Firestorm Games employee

(C) A friend of Ms. Paladino

(D) A university professor

GO ON TO THE NEXT PAGE

Mobius Computers Taking a New Direction

Struggling independent computer manufacturer Mobius Computers has announced a dramatic change in its business plan. All of the company's popular Mobius Stores across the nation will be closing their doors by the end of next month. In their place, the company will be turning to a purely online business model, with the entire purchasing process taking place online. This startling announcement coincides with their hiring of Oswald Brown, former CEO of the successful startup FastFlow, as their vice-president of operations, replacing the much-admired Seth Moon. Said Mobius CEO Alberto Cruz, "Oswald has helped us realize that by shedding unneeded brick-and-mortar assets and streamlining the purchasing process, Mobius will be better equipped to meet our customers' needs in the fast and efficient manner today's consumers have come to expect from a cutting-edge company." Customers who have previously made in-store purchases from Mobius are being offered a special 20% discount on online purchases in an effort to ease the transition process.

 https://www.you-review.com

User: Marcia Conway
Business: Mobius Online
What I purchased: Mobius ProPad 2000
My rating: One star

My experience: I wasn't really planning on upgrading to a ProPad 2000, but when I received an e-mail offering me a 20% discount, I decided to go ahead and get one. The one catch was that I had to buy it online, as the company is apparently closing all of their physical stores. Sadly, the days of the friendly and helpful Mobius salesperson are apparently over as well. They've all been replaced by customer service representatives who respond to even the most important query by cutting-and-pasting a template answer into an e-mail. The ProPad itself is all right, but hardware was never Mobius's strongpoint—it was their excellent customer service and support, both pre- and post-purchase. Without it, there just aren't enough reasons to buy one of their middle-of-the-road products.

March 16, 2017

Elyse Northrup
Chairperson of the Board of Directors
Mobius Computers
PO Box 1182
Los Angeles, CA 90011

Dear Ms. Northrup,

Please accept my resignation as vice-president of operations, effective immediately.

I sincerely regret that the situation has come to this so quickly. I was determined to stick with my plan through the inevitable rough period, but it has become clear that I no longer have the full support of the board of directors. After conferring with my esteemed predecessor, I have decided that it is in the best interest of the company that I step down rather than engage in a prolonged battle with the board. Clearly, our transition away from the philosophy of having an overstaffed store in every major city had its fair share of detractors. However, with my previous company, I proved that a purely online business model can succeed in the apparel industry. I am convinced that the same would have held true in the computer manufacturing industry if I had been given enough time.

Unfortunately, that was not the case. Please contact my secretary to make arrangements for a meeting to discuss my severance plan and other details of my departure.

Sincerely,

Oswald Brown

196 What is the article mainly about?

(A) A computer manufacturer's hiring of a new executive
(B) A surprise merger between two struggling companies
(C) Financial difficulties faced by the computer industry
(D) Unexpected modifications in a company's business model

197 What is Ms. Conway's primary complaint?

(A) Poor customer service
(B) Failure to receive a discount
(C) Difficulty finding a store
(D) Low quality hardware

198 What is suggested about Ms. Conway?

(A) She previously purchased a computer at a Mobius Store.
(B) She prefers the old ProPad to the most recent model.
(C) She had a bad experience with the staff at a Mobius Store.
(D) She is impressed by the low cost of the ProPad 2000.

199 What kind of products did FastFlow most likely sell?

(A) Computers
(B) Software
(C) Automobiles
(D) Clothing

200 Who did Mr. Brown consult with before making his decision to resign?

(A) Elyse Northrup
(B) Seth Moon
(C) Marcia Conway
(D) Alberto Cruz

잠깐!!
시작 전 꼭 확인하세요!

☑ 실제 시험과 같이
　책상을 정리하고
　마음의 준비를 하세요.

☑ 핸드폰은 잠깐 끄고
　대신 아날로그 시계를
　활용해 보세요.

☑ 권장 풀이 시간은 55분입니다.
　시간을 꼭 지켜주세요.

☑ 어렵다고 넘어가지 마세요.
　가능하면 차례대로 풀어 보세요.

Actual Test

04

시작 시간   :

종료 시간   :

PART 7

Directions: In this part you will read a selection of texts, such as magazine and newspaper articles, e-mails, and instant messages. Each text or set of texts is followed by several questions. Select the best answer for each question and mark the letter (A), (B), (C), or (D) on your answer sheet.

Questions 147-148 refer to the following notice.

SMALL-BUSINESS SEMINAR SLATED FOR NOVEMBER 3!

Noted author Jimmy Thompson has agreed to host a seminar entitled "How to Set Up Your Own Small Business" here at the Seven Oceans Hotel. It will be from 7 to 9 P.M. on Wednesday, November 3. If you have long wanted to be your own boss, this seminar will tell all you need to start turning your plans into action.

The California-born Mr. Thompson, who has written three best-selling books on this topic, will be here to guide you through the process of planning your own small business. By following his precepts, you can be successful as a small businessman or -woman. Numerous people have done so with impressive results, including Janet Graham of Lexington, Kentucky. She took Mr. Thompson's seminar in 2015, started her own business (a travel agency) in 2016 and is now earning a net income of $35,000 per year.

The cost of the seminar is $75, which is well worth it since that includes 35 pages of handouts. A certificate of completion will be sent to your home later, engraved with your name. Mr. Thompson's seminars usually sell out, so it is a good idea to sign up early.

147 For whom is this notice most likely intended?

(A) Authors
(B) Future business owners
(C) Government officials
(D) Travelers

148 What are readers of the notice recommended to do?

(A) Enroll in the seminar quickly
(B) Book a room at the Seven Oceans Hotel
(C) Buy one of Jimmy Thompson's books
(D) Make a donation to Mr. Thompson's foundation

Questions 149-150 refer to the following letter.

January 24
Thomas Ullom, CEO
California High-Tech Corporation
Palo Alto, CA

Dear Mr. Ullom:

I have known Teresa Smith for the two years during which she worked as an Accounting Assistant in the Design Department at General Motors Corporation. I have always been impressed by Teresa's attitude towards her work as well as her performance on the job. Her interpersonal and communication skills are superb and have allowed her to have positive working relationships with both our staff and our clients.

Teresa has the listening and interviewing skills needed to gather information from clientele in her performance of financial assessments. Teresa also possesses fine writing skills which have enabled her to compose quality business letters. She has the analytical skills to diagnose problems and come up with viable solutions. Her ability to remain calm during frenzied periods proves that she can work well under pressure.

I do not doubt that she has a bright future in the accounting profession. I believe she deserves to be in charge of a department of her own. I recommend her for employment without hesitation. Please let me know if you need further information.

Ruprecht Jones
General Motors Corporation
Detroit, Michigan
(896) 555-9532
rj@gm.com

149 What is the purpose of this letter?
   (A) To issue a complaint about a car made by General Motors
   (B) To recommend a person for employment
   (C) To ask for a discount for a large number of cars purchased
   (D) To look for a talented person

150 Which of the following skills of Ms. Smith was NOT mentioned?
   (A) Interpersonal and communication skills
   (B) Ability to design automobiles
   (C) Problem solving skills
   (D) Ability to stay calm under pressure

GO ON TO THE NEXT PAGE

Questions 151-152 refer to the following text message chain.

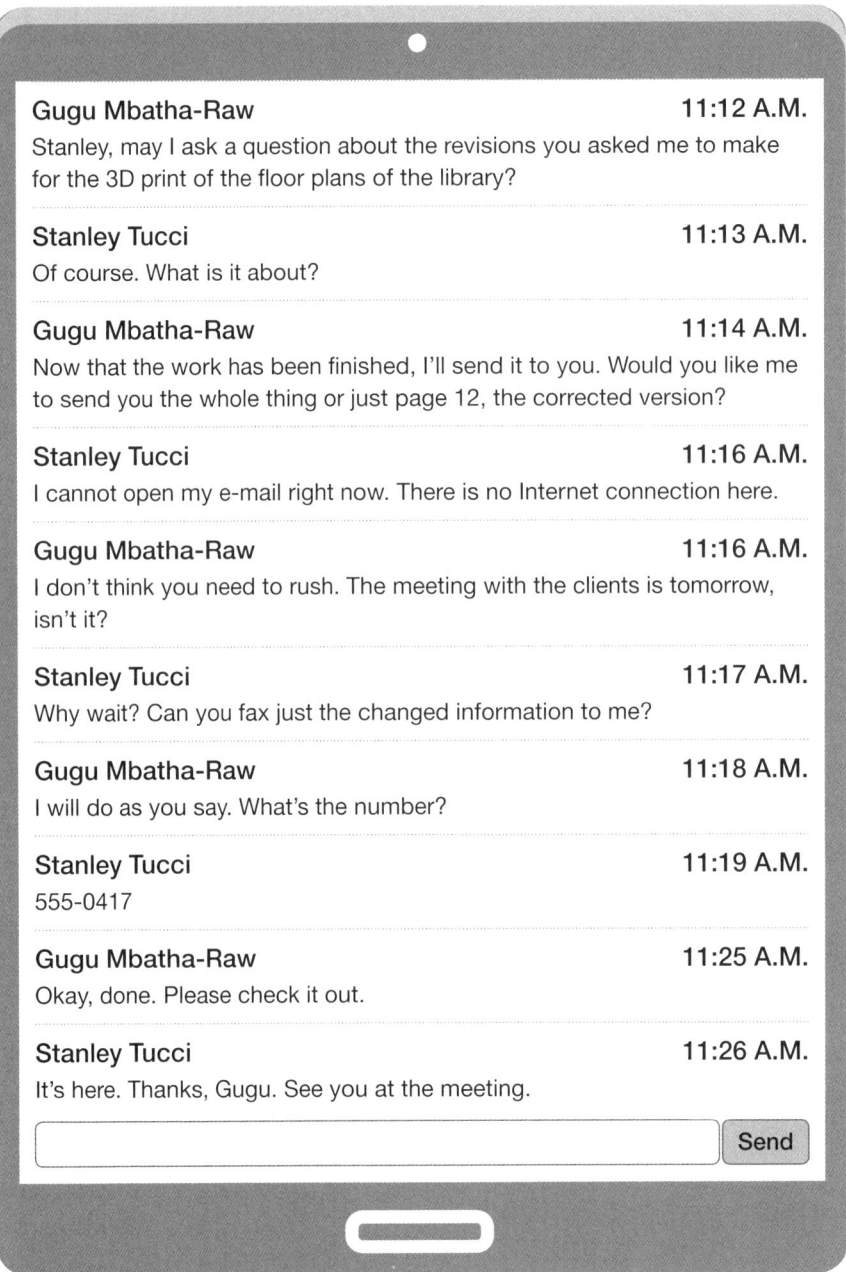

Gugu Mbatha-Raw	11:12 A.M.
Stanley, may I ask a question about the revisions you asked me to make for the 3D print of the floor plans of the library?	
Stanley Tucci	11:13 A.M.
Of course. What is it about?	
Gugu Mbatha-Raw	11:14 A.M.
Now that the work has been finished, I'll send it to you. Would you like me to send you the whole thing or just page 12, the corrected version?	
Stanley Tucci	11:16 A.M.
I cannot open my e-mail right now. There is no Internet connection here.	
Gugu Mbatha-Raw	11:16 A.M.
I don't think you need to rush. The meeting with the clients is tomorrow, isn't it?	
Stanley Tucci	11:17 A.M.
Why wait? Can you fax just the changed information to me?	
Gugu Mbatha-Raw	11:18 A.M.
I will do as you say. What's the number?	
Stanley Tucci	11:19 A.M.
555-0417	
Gugu Mbatha-Raw	11:25 A.M.
Okay, done. Please check it out.	
Stanley Tucci	11:26 A.M.
It's here. Thanks, Gugu. See you at the meeting.	

Send

151 Who most likely is Ms. Mbatha-Raw?

(A) A receptionist
(B) A computer technician
(C) An architect
(D) A library clerk

152 At 11:17 A.M., what does Mr. Tucci most likely mean when he writes, "Why wait"?

(A) He wants to make a phone call.
(B) He wants to receive a document immediately.
(C) He wants his team to meet him at once.
(D) He wants to postpone the meeting.

Opportunity in Montreal!

Our moderately sized private school in Montreal, Canada has an opening for an English teacher beginning in July. You will be teaching elementary and middle-school students, using our tried-and-true curriculum. Your salary will be $1,800 per month, which is well above the average for such positions. You will teach 30 hours per week from 2 until 8 P.M., Monday through Friday. You will be provided with a furnished apartment just 10 minutes away from our school. We are looking for a native English speaker, keeping in mind that Montreal is a city where French is mostly used.

To be hired here, you must have at least a bachelor's degree (in any field) from an accredited university. If you have teaching experience, that is a plus but it is not absolutely necessary. You must be able to prove that you do not have a criminal background, however.

All of the other teachers at our school are friendly and willing to help you "learn the ropes." Sometimes two teachers plan lessons and work together to teach students, which facilitates our students' learning of English. We carefully screen students before we enroll them so you can be assured no loud or belligerent kids will disrupt your educational efforts.

Contact Jean François at 82-2-555-3371.

153 What is the purpose of this advertisement?

(A) To publicize an educational institute throughout Canada
(B) To recruit overseas students to the academy
(C) To emphasize the importance of English
(D) To hire a person to teach at an English academy

154 What is indicated about the students?

(A) They are loud and rude.
(B) They have no interest whatsoever in learning English.
(C) They are respectful of the teachers.
(D) They come from poor, lower class families.

GO ON TO THE NEXT PAGE

San Antonio (Jul 3) — The San Antonio Express (SAE) filed for bankruptcy protection in a federal court in Texas on Monday, as it struggled to cope with growing debt and falling ad revenue. – [1] –.

The Express, which was acquired in 2008 by media investor Jimmy Patrick, had hired bankruptcy advisers and law firms in recent months as it sought to negotiate with creditors.

It is only the latest sign of trouble for the American newspaper industry. – [2] –. Patrick's holding company, SAE Corporation, has reduced the newsrooms of many of its papers and sold off some of them entirely.

Patrick issued a statement saying, "Over the last year, we have tried to find solutions to our financial problems and will continue to do so.

We still hope to revive this proud newspaper, which first began publishing in the 1930s. But our creditors need to realize that some factors are beyond our control."

In a court filing, SAE Corporation said it had nearly $4 billion in debt, compared with $1.6 billion in assets. – [3] –. Most of that debt was taken on when Patrick acquired the newspaper — a deal he struck using mostly borrowed money.

The main creditors listed by SAE in its court filing include big banks like JP Morgan Chase and Merrill Lynch. – [4] –. Some analysts contend that the corporation will not be able to avoid defaulting on its debts by the third quarter of this year.

155 What is this article about?

(A) The resignation of a newspaper's chief editor

(B) The newspaper's plans to add a new section

(C) A newspaper declaring bankruptcy

(D) Jimmy Patrick's decision to retire from the media business

156 How did Mr. Patrick come to own the San Antonio Express?

(A) By taking out loans to buy it

(B) By selling off some of his other properties

(C) By using his vast inheritance

(D) By merging it with another newspaper in San Antonio

157 In which of the positions marked [1], [2], [3], and [4] does the following sentence best belong?

"Several newspaper companies are coping with declining revenues and mounting debts."

(A) [1]

(B) [2]

(C) [3]

(D) [4]

Questions 158-160 refer to the following e-mail.

To	Terry Litrada <terryl@hotmail.com>
From	Celina Mounts <celinamounts@gmail.com>
Date	December 13
Subject	While Shopping in our Store

Dear Ms. Litrada:

This is in response to your e-mail of December 12. You stated that you had an unpleasant experience while shopping in our store, Julia's Boutique. If in fact one of our sales associates (Ann Steinburg) followed you around and acted as though you were a shoplifter, I truly apologize. You said that Ms. Steinburg was giving you the "evil eye," but I do not know what that means. Was she staring at you somehow or just looking at you and standing ready to help? I hope it was the latter because that is how I train all my employees here at Julia's Boutique.

I have spoken with Ms. Steinburg, and she denies that any such incident happened. She insists that she would never try to make a customer feel uncomfortable. Perhaps you misunderstood her intentions.

I would remind you that our employees have the duty to watch out for shoplifters. My store suffered losses of more than $2,500 in theft in 2016, and we really can't afford to have customers steal. So please forgive us if we made a mistake in your case. Come back to Julia's Boutique and let us show how much we appreciate our customers.

Sincerely,

Celina Mounts, Store Manager

158 Why did Ms. Litrada most likely write to Ms. Mounts?

(A) To complain about a worker at the store
(B) To praise the quality of dresses on sale at Julia's Boutique
(C) To ask why certain items were not on sale
(D) To inquire about the store's opening and closing hours

159 According to Ms. Mounts, what might be the source of the problem?

(A) Ms. Steinburg was having a bad day.
(B) Ms. Steinburg was merely watching and eager to help Ms. Litrada.
(C) Ms. Litrada resembled a suspected shoplifter.
(D) Ms. Litrada is using her e-mail as a way to get a discount on clothes at the store.

160 What is indicated about Ms. Mounts?

(A) She is seeking to resolve a matter between an employee and a customer.
(B) She doesn't accept Ms. Steinburg's excuse.
(C) She needs to hire some new sales associates at Julia's Boutique.
(D) She thinks Ms. Litrada complains too much.

GO ON TO THE NEXT PAGE

From: Max Gibbons
31 Town Lake Street
Kansas City, MO 66421
E-mail: maxieg@email.com

To: Cindy Probst
Chief Executive Officer
Probst Design Studios
88 Brackenridge Avenue
Kansas City, MO 66432

Dear Ms. Probst:

Please accept this letter as formal notification of my resignation at Probst Design Studios. I have been offered a job at a start-up company in Florida. It is with considerable sorrow that I leave a job where I have worked with such a great team. I have truly enjoyed the variety of projects and challenges at your firm and have learned a lot about the fashion design industry.

As called for in my employment contract, I am giving one month's notice. This means my last day at PDS will be on August 3. I still have two major projects — one for Givenchy and the other for the Gap — and I will ensure that they are completed before that day.

Let me express my gratitude to you, Denise Antoine, Blake Johnson, Troy McDaniels and the rest of the management team for all you have done for me over the last four years. You taught me how to design attractive and affordable clothes for teenagers and skills I will retain throughout my professional career.

Please feel free to get in touch should you require information after I have left.

Yours sincerely,

Max Gibbons

161 Why is Max Gibbons leaving Probst Design Studios?

    (A) He plans to run his own business.
    (B) He has found a different job.
    (C) He is moving overseas with his family.
    (D) He must stay home and take care of his ailing mother.

162 What is suggested about Mr. Gibbons?

    (A) He started as an intern.
    (B) He was poorly paid.
    (C) He worked on designing clothes for young people.
    (D) He once had a conflict with Troy McDaniels.

163 When was this letter written?

    (A) In July
    (B) In August
    (C) In September
    (D) In October

GO ON TO THE NEXT PAGE

Questions 164-167 refer to the following letter.

June 22

Ken Houseman

Eggleston Insurance Agency

Seattle, Washington

Dear Mr. Houseman:

I am writing in reference to my life insurance policy (No. 339-478992). It was issued in 2015 by a different agent, Margo Adams. – [1] –. Ms. Adams has since left the Eggleston Insurance Agency, from what I have been told, and you have taken her place.

The premiums for my life insurance policy have been automatically deducted from my bank account on a monthly basis. But I got my bank account statement recently, and was somewhat surprised to find that the premiums have gone up from $34 a month to $88. – [2] –. Furthermore, why was I not notified about such an increase? Honestly, I am not sure I would have continued with the policy had I known the premiums would go up so sharply.

I read in the Seattle Times about a company that offers life insurance for just $47 per month, and the rates are guaranteed not to go up for at least five years. – [3] –. I am seriously considering switching to that company if you do not offer a satisfactory explanation about this dramatic rise in the premiums.

I am not angry, but I just want to know why I am now paying so much for life insurance. Do you think I should continue with the policy? – [4] –.

Sincerely,

Jenny Rivers

164 Why did Ms. Rivers write to Mr. Houseman?

(A) To change the beneficiary of her life insurance policy
(B) To tell him she wants another insurance policy
(C) To track down Margo Adams
(D) To ask about a rise in monthly life insurance premiums

165 Who most likely is Margo Adams?

(A) Ms. Rivers' next-door neighbor
(B) An editorial writer for the Seattle Times
(C) Mr. Houseman's predecessor at the Eggleston Insurance Agency
(D) The director of the Eggleston Insurance Agency

166 In the letter, the word "switching" in paragraph 3, line 3, is closest in meaning to

(A) buttoning
(B) turning
(C) changing
(D) examining

167 In which of the positions marked [1], [2], [3], and [4] does the following sentence best belong?

"This is a big jump, and I wish to know why."

(A) [1]
(B) [2]
(C) [3]
(D) [4]

Questions 168-171 refer to the following online chat discussion.

👤	**Janelle Monae** [11:29 A.M.]	Hi, Jim. I want to know the inventory status. Do you have a minute?
	Jim Parsons [11:30 A.M.]	Sure!
👤	**Janelle Monae** [11:31 A.M.]	The database indicates that we only have 4 cases of ADFC Color Toner (30 ink cartridges per case) left. We've recently been delivering a lot. Why don't we order more?
	Jim Parsons [11:32 A.M.]	No, we don't have to. To offer a cheaper brand to our customers, we've already signed up with another supplier. Last week while you were out, I ordered 50 cases from the supplier. They are not delivered yet.
👤	**Janelle Monae** [11:33 A.M.]	Good job!
	Jim Parsons [11:35 A.M.]	Also, on Monday, I notified print shops of the change so they are already aware of it.
👤	**Janelle Monae** [11:37 A.M.]	Thanks again!

Send

168 At 11:30 A.M., what does Mr. Parsons most likely mean when he writes, "Sure"?

(A) He has time to report to Ms. Monae.
(B) He knew what was ordered by Ms. Monae.
(C) He agrees to be with Ms. Monae
(D) He permitted Ms. Monae to work on a project.

169 What is suggested about Ms. Monae?

(A) She created a database.
(B) She received an order today.
(C) She will place an order tomorrow.
(D) She has recently been on a business trip.

170 What type of business do Mr. Parsons and Ms. Monae work for?

(A) A print shop
(B) A retailer
(C) A manufacturer
(D) A distributor

171 What did Mr. Parsons do earlier in the week?

(A) He revised an order form.
(B) He trained a new employee.
(C) He informed customers of the new product.
(D) He assisted Ms. Monae financially.

GO ON TO THE NEXT PAGE

Invoice #T987246

October 14

To: Archie Drakeson
Dynamic Software Inc.
15 Madison Ave.
Chicago, IL 44293

From: Best Western Hotel
154 Grand St.
Miami, FL 73401

This invoice is issued for the services below:

Accommodation services:	
One single room $150 (10% tax included) / night * 3	$450.00
Room services:	
Breakfast buffet $35 (10% tax included) / meal * 2	$70.00
Mini-bar: mini-liquor ($25/ bottle) * 2	$50.00
fun size snack ($15/ bag) * 3	$45.00
--	
Total:	$615.00

Please have a look at this invoice and return it with your check. The invoice is payable fifteen days after the date of issue. If you need an additional receipt to present at your company, please contact me in person, by e-mail or by phone.

We hope you had a wonderful time with us. See you again soon!

Jennifer Trudy

Reception Manager
E-mail: jennifer_t@bestwestern.com
Tel: 412-555-5280

172 What is the invoice about?

    (A) Food and shelter
    (B) International calls
    (C) Dry cleaning services
    (D) Upgrading room type

173 When is the payment due?

    (A) October 14
    (B) October 29
    (C) November 3
    (D) November 8

174 What is the total amount for accommodations?

    (A) $45.00
    (B) $70.00
    (C) $450.00
    (D) $615.00

175 What is NOT given among the ways to contact Jennifer Trudy?

    (A) In person
    (B) Through the Internet
    (C) By phone
    (D) By fax

GO ON TO THE NEXT PAGE

Test 04

Memo

To: All employees
From: Wallace Judson
Date: January 3
Subject: Urgent Measures

As you know, the national and international economic recession has had an effect on the financial performance at Wallace Judson Law Firm. Given this distressing fact, I find it necessary to implement some cost-cutting measures in order to ensure our long-term viability.

The information related to these actions is available in our latest online newsletter.

I hope that all employees understand the need for the measures and will cooperate fully in helping to implement them. The department heads, specifically Jerry Robertson, Don Meredith and Janis Brandeberry, have the responsibility to ensure that these measures are followed.

WALLACE JUDSON LAW FIRM

Cost-cutting Measures

1. Please operate air conditioners only in the summer months (June, July and August) from 8:30 A.M. to 5:30 P.M. They must be turned off after that.

2. Unless urgent work has to be completed, all employees must leave the office by 8 P.M. at the latest. If they must stay until a later time, they should inform their immediate supervisors or my assistant, Marijo Guerrero.

3. I ask you to use office supplies sparingly. If new supplies are needed, please inform Mr. Robertson, Mr. Meredith or Ms. Brandeberry and sign in the logbook for monitoring purposes.

176 Why was this memo written?

(A) To instruct all staff members about new policies

(B) To announce the economic recession

(C) To ask workers to donate money

(D) To solicit opinions on the company's expansion

177 In the memo, the word "distressing" in paragraph 1, line 2, is closest in meaning to

(A) distracted

(B) relieved

(C) painful

(D) surprising

178 What is indicated about office supplies?

(A) Workers are now required to bring in their own.

(B) Workers should keep records of use.

(C) A new supplier has been hired to bring them to the office.

(D) They will be stored in a supply cabinet.

179 What are workers asked to do by 8 P.M.?

(A) Turn off the air conditioners

(B) Clean their cubicles and empty the trash cans

(C) Stop sending international faxes and e-mails

(D) Be out of the office

180 What is implied about the law firm?

(A) Employees have to do over night work.

(B) The company will continue to be in a difficult financial situation.

(C) Use of stationery should be reported to the department heads.

(D) Monitoring software will be brought in as early as possible.

GO ON TO THE NEXT PAGE

Questions 181-185 refer to the following e-mails.

To	Eliot Abrams <eliot@gmail.com>
From	Eleanor Moore <emoore@tri-state.com>
Date	February 3
Subject	Refer Clients to Us

Dear Mr. Abrams:

Since you are a business broker, you probably realize that hundreds of seller-financed business notes come into existence annually when businesses are bought and sold. That is a great opportunity for extra profits.

Tri-State Investments is Alabama's largest buyer of business notes. We pay out referral fees every week to business brokers like you. Such people, by referring clients to us, help those clients get a lump sum of cash for business notes. You can perform a valuable service by showing your clients how to get cash for their business. In the process, you earn our referral fees and increase your commissions by facilitating sales that were in doubt over the issue of cash.

Unlike other companies, we buy only business notes. We are members of the American Association of Business Brokers, the Southern Business Opportunity Council and the Better Business Bureau. I would be happy to answer any questions you might have. Please note that there is no cost for you to pay a personal visit to our office, which is located at 115 Main Street in Birmingham. I would be glad to outline the available options for a specific business-note situation, or find how we may work together. I look forward to hearing from you.

Sincerely,

Eleanor Moore, Associate
Tri-State Investments

To: Eleanor Moore <emoore@tri-state.com>
From: Eliot Abrams <eliot@gmail.com>
Date: February 4
Subject: Re: Refer Clients to Us

Dear Ms. Moore:

I am in receipt of your e-mail dated February 3, and I must say I read it with interest. I have been a business broker for the past decade. During that time, I have sought to help many clients in situations much like what you described. Had they known of the chance of getting a lump sum of cash for their business notes, they would have been greatly pleased.

I have no doubt that we can work together. Let me tell you about a particular client that may need this service soon. It is a used-car dealership in Tuscaloosa named Cal's Auto Credit. I anticipate there will soon be a change of ownership there, and the prospective owner will almost certainly be short of funds after the dealership changes hands. Please tell me – how would you quantify the size of the lump-sum payment for this small company? It did approximately $400,000 in sales last year, which is fairly typical. Furthermore, what would be my referral fee if you do this vital financial service for Cal's Auto Credit? I hope it would be no less than $5,000.

I would like to discuss the chance of us having an ongoing business relationship. I have several other clients who are worthy of such a referral.

Sincerely,

Eliot Abrams

181 What is the purpose of the first e-mail?

(A) To give notice of a late payment
(B) To order office supplies
(C) To offer a business service
(D) To advertise about a new product

182 In the first e-mail, the word "notes" in paragraph 1, line 2, is closest in meaning to

(A) records
(B) certificates
(C) bills
(D) currencies

183 What is suggested about Mr. Abrams?

(A) He is Ms. Moore's supervisor.
(B) He bought a used-car recently.
(C) He is a member of the American Association of Business Brokers.
(D) He will go to Birmingham in the near future.

184 What kind of company may Mr. Abrams refer to Ms. Moore?

(A) One that sells paper products
(B) One that makes door-to-door deliveries
(C) One that sells used automobiles
(D) One that makes arrangements for trip

185 According to the second e-mail, what issue does Mr. Abrams want Ms. Moore to address?

(A) The amount of referral fee
(B) The legitimacy of Tri-State Investments
(C) The distance from Tuscaloosa to Birmingham
(D) The legal document before making any agreement

GO ON TO THE NEXT PAGE

THE JEFFERSON CLASSIC BUILDING

As you may be aware, this building is one of the oldest in our district in Phoenix. Therefore, the elevators are old and rather slow. We have gotten numerous complaints about the elevators in recent years.

Of course, we want to keep our building up to date as much as possible. However, our options regarding the elevators are somewhat limited. To install new ones would be expensive, disrupt nearly all of our occupants and take a long time. We wish to make the right decision about this very important matter.

Thus, we are asking occupants and workers of the Jefferson Classic Building to write us about this issue. Please take time to send a letter to me, Chuck Harley, at the address below. Tell me honestly what you think the problems are, and feel free to make suggestions on how to fix them. I promise you that we will take your feedback seriously.

Chuck Harley
Building Supervisor
Jefferson Classic Building, Room 100
Phoenix, Arizona

Chuck Harley
Jefferson Classic Building, Room 100
Phoenix, Arizona

Dear Mr. Harley:

I work for C&C Communications on the seventh floor of the Jefferson Classic Building. My job at this company began three years ago, and I can tell you that the problems with the elevators are serious and worse than ever. Sometimes a large group of people stands in the first-floor lobby waiting for an elevator for as long as five minutes. As you know, we are all quite busy, and that is valuable time we are losing. Also, the elevators are not dependable. One of them broke down just last week and remains out of order. When will it be fixed? Until you have it repaired, we are left with just three functioning elevators—one on the west side and two on the east.

Since you asked for suggestions, I will offer mine. I really think all of the elevators at the Jefferson Classic Building need to be replaced with modern, high-speed ones. There would be some disruption and it would not be cheap, but I recommend having the two on the west side (including the one that is now inoperative) taken out and replaced. That is, do not repair the old ones but install new ones. After those have been done, you could turn your attention to the two on the east side. I think most of the tenants would be grateful for this change, and in the long run it will ensure the viability of this building.

Sincerely,

Tammy Josephson
C&C Communications

Notice

To: All tenants
From: Maintenance department, Jefferson Classic Building
Subject: Building Improvement Project

DO NOT use one of the western elevators which is in need of replacement of major parts. We'll repair it as soon as possible. Sorry for your inconvenience.

After that, continue using the existing elevators for a while. Six months later, one elevator in the west and east will be replaced by state-of-the-art models.

Thank you for your proposals to improve this building. Now and forever, we'll try to offer you better facilities and environment.

186 What is indicated about the elevators?

(A) There are five elevators.
(B) Another elevator is being installed.
(C) They have been remodeled recently.
(D) They are slow and undependable.

187 What option does Mr. Harley wish to avoid?

(A) Replacing the old elevators with new ones
(B) Renovation of the current elevators
(C) Repair of the inoperative elevator
(D) Closing the elevators permanently

188 What is NOT mentioned as a possible problem if new elevators are installed?

(A) It would not be done quickly.
(B) It would cost a lot of money.
(C) It would be a violation of local policy.
(D) It would cause many problems for tenants.

189 What is suggested about Ms. Josephson?

(A) She has been in the Jefferson Classic Building for five years.
(B) She agrees to Mr. Harley's suggestion.
(C) She thinks that people are wasting valuable time because of an elevator.
(D) She assures that none of the occupants will leave the building.

190 What can be inferred about the Jefferson Classic Building?

(A) An occupant's proposal was partially accepted.
(B) It is desperate for new tenants.
(C) Some tenants have already left.
(D) It is the most prestigious building in Phoenix.

Questions 191-195 refer to the following notice, form, and e-mail.

10th National Auditing Forum Convention

July 10, Hyatt Hotel

Rose Harper, Program Manager

The schedule for the convention is as follows:

- ◇ **9:00** Opening speech (Samuel Banks, President of the Auditing Association)
- ◇ **9:30** Presentation of new equipment to enhance auditing
  (Tanya Coops, Marketing Manager of High Tech Inc.)
- ◇ **11:00** Notification of changes in auditing regulations
  (Mark Hoverbens, Junior Associate of the Auditing Association)
- ◇ **12:00** Lunch break
- ◇ **14:00** Presentation on upgraded software for auditing
  (Charles Isenberg, Sales Manager of Techron Co.)
- ◇ **16:00** Mini-group experience on new technologies & FAQs
- ◇ **17:00** Closing speech (Samuel Banks, President of the Auditing Association)

Feedback Form

Name Hilary Spencer

Which session did you find most helpful? Why?

The presentation that Mr. Isenberg made was the most helpful. His software was very innovative, and improved on the actual working environment. It was also very useful and impressive that the presenter demonstrated how the program works in detail.

How could the convention be improved?

I think the time for group activities was too short. I wish I had enough time to experience and discuss newly introduced products.

To :   Charles Isenberg <charles@hotmail.com>
From: Hilary Spencer <HS@hotmail.com>
Date: July 15
Subject: Auditing Software

Dear Mr. Isenberg,

Your presentation at the 10th National Auditing Forum Convention was very impressive.

I have introduced your software to our company's executives. They were greatly interested in your auditing software and asked me to contact you.

So I would like to schedule a meeting to discuss future matters. Please let me know a convenient time for you. I look forward to hearing from you soon.

Sincerely,

Hilary Spencer
Audit Commissioner of London

191 What is the purpose of the notice?

(A) To give profiles of the speakers
(B) To let the guests know about the menus
(C) To give a detailed schedule
(D) To invite people to an event

192 According to the notice, what most likely happened at 16:50?

(A) Participants asked some questions.
(B) Small snacks were handed out.
(C) A presentation on new software was done.
(D) Participants heard a closing speech.

193 Which speaker was Ms. Spencer satisfied with?

(A) President of the Auditing Association
(B) Sales Manager of Techron Co.
(C) Marketing Manager of High Tech Inc.
(D) Audit Commissioner of London

194 Why was the e-mail sent?

(A) To request a sample
(B) To arrange another presentation
(C) To ask for a meeting
(D) To inform a person about the location of the firm

195 What does Hilary Spencer want Charles Isenberg to do?

(A) Let her know when he will be available
(B) Come to her office and set up new supplies
(C) Prepare a project proposal for her executives
(D) Make plans for joint research on auditing

GO ON TO THE NEXT PAGE

Questions 196-200 refer to the following letter, text message, and e-mail.

April 27
Anthony Sandow
WV Transportation Ltd.
87 Tecumseh Road
Hatfield, West Virginia 08065

Dear Mr. Sandow:

I wish to apply for the programmer position advertised in the Hatfield Union. Enclosed with this letter you will find my résumé and four references, along with their letters of recommendation.

The job described in this listing is very interesting, and I really think my strong technical background and education should make me a competitive candidate. The primary strengths I possess for this position are that I have successfully designed, developed and supported a variety of applications. As my résumé indicates, I have a bachelor's degree in Computer Programming from West Virginia University. In addition, I fully understand the life cycle of a software development project. I have four years of experience in learning and developing new technologies.

I can be reached any time via e-mail at pc@email.com or my cell phone, 214-555-9842. Thank you for your time and consideration.

Sincerely,

Pam Cantrell
330 Millmar Drive
Charleston, West Virginia 08642

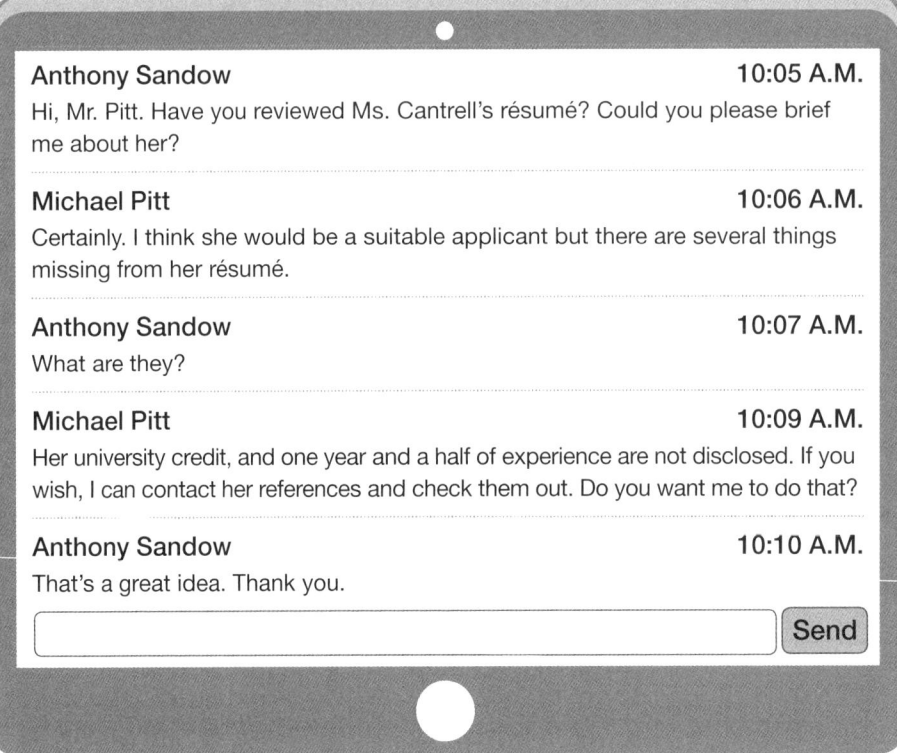

Anthony Sandow	10:05 A.M.
Hi, Mr. Pitt. Have you reviewed Ms. Cantrell's résumé? Could you please brief me about her?	

Michael Pitt	10:06 A.M.
Certainly. I think she would be a suitable applicant but there are several things missing from her résumé.	

Anthony Sandow	10:07 A.M.
What are they?	

Michael Pitt	10:09 A.M.
Her university credit, and one year and a half of experience are not disclosed. If you wish, I can contact her references and check them out. Do you want me to do that?	

Anthony Sandow	10:10 A.M.
That's a great idea. Thank you.	

Send

To	▼	Pam Cantrell <pc@email.com>
From	▼	Anthony Sandow <Anthony@wvtransport.com>
Date	▼	May 25
Subject	▼	About your Application

Dear Ms. Cantrell:

First of all, I apologize for the delay in responding to your letter. I was out of town for three weeks due to an urgent business matter in South Carolina. And as soon as I got back to Hatfield, we had a management seminar that lasted five business days. So please do not misconstrue this for lack of interest.

I reviewed carefully your résumé and have a couple of questions about it. First of all, you did not state what your grade point average was while at West Virginia University. We do not hire people who did not graduate with at least a 3.5 GPA (out of a possible 4.0). Second, there seems to be a gap of 18 months after your graduation and your first job. What were you doing during that time?

My collegue attempted to contact all four of your references, but three of them — George Anderson of Cincinnati, Eileen Brown of Lexington and Evelyn Perkins of Tucson — were not available. The fourth, Ronald Jones of Atlanta, said you only stayed at his company for two months before moving on to another job. Frankly speaking, this is not very encouraging. Perhaps you can explain these various issues. I am willing to offer you such an opportunity. Please come to my office for an interview at 3:00 P.M. on Tuesday, June 2.

Sincerely,
Anthony Sandow

196 What position did Ms. Cantrell apply for?

(A) A computer programmer
(B) A secretary
(C) A customer service representative
(D) An assistant in the human resources department

197 In the e-mail, the word "misconstrue" in paragraph 1, line 3, is closest in meaning to

(A) blame
(B) maintain
(C) cheat
(D) misunderstand

198 Why did Mr. Sandow take nearly a month to respond to Ms. Cantrell's letter?

(A) Her application got lost on his desk.
(B) He had to deal with a family emergency.
(C) He had other urgent business matters to attend to.
(D) He was interviewing other applicants.

199 From whom did Mr. Pitt get the information about Ms. Cantrell?

(A) George Anderson
(B) Eileen Brown
(C) Evelyn Perkins
(D) Ronald Jones

200 What is indicated about Mr. Sandow?

(A) He was notified of the missing information from Ms. Cantrell's reference.
(B) He will not hire Ms. Cantrell under any circumstance.
(C) He is dubious but willing to give Ms. Cantrell a chance.
(D) He thinks Ms. Cantrell is a fine candidate but plans to hire another person.

잠깐!!
시작 전 꼭 확인하세요!

☑ 실제 시험과 같이
　책상을 정리하고
　마음의 준비를 하세요.

☑ 핸드폰은 잠깐 끄고
　대신 아날로그 시계를
　활용해 보세요.

☑ 권장 풀이 시간은 55분입니다.
　시간을 꼭 지켜주세요.

☑ 어렵다고 넘어가지 마세요.
　가능하면 차례대로 풀어 보세요.

Actual Test

05

시작 시간　　　　　:

종료 시간　　　　　:

PART 7

Directions: In this part you will read a selection of texts, such as magazine and newspaper articles, e-mails, and instant messages. Each text or set of texts is followed by several questions. Select the best answer for each question and mark the letter (A), (B), (C), or (D) on your answer sheet.

Questions 147-148 refer to the following Web page.

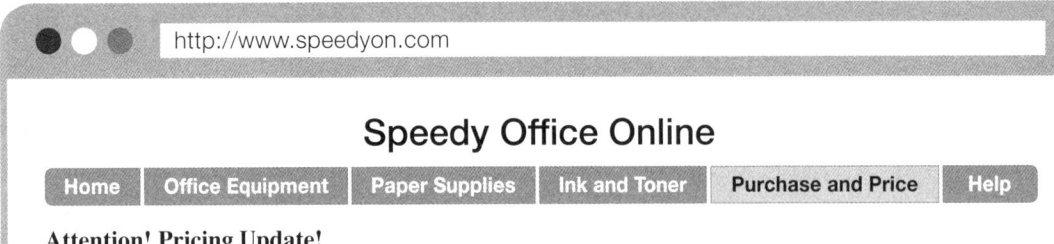

http://www.speedyon.com

Speedy Office Online

| Home | Office Equipment | Paper Supplies | Ink and Toner | Purchase and Price | Help |

Attention! Pricing Update!

The following updates to our prices will be effective for all orders placed on or after December 16, 2017. These changes were unavoidable due to one of our long-time suppliers going out of business. The price increases only pertain to the below listed products. Any products not included on this list will still be available at their usual low prices, and there is no change to our affordable delivery fees.

Item	Old Price	New Price
A4 copy paper (sheets)	$25.50/carton	$28.00/carton
Fax paper (rolls)*	$16.00/carton	$36.00/carton
Fax toner cartridges	$85.00/each	$99.00/each
Ballpoint pens	$2.50/pack	$3.00/pack
Plain business envelopes	$29.00/carton	$32.50/carton

*Our fax paper is no longer available in cartons of 6 rolls. All cartons now contain 12 rolls. If you have any questions or concerns, you can contact us at any time.

147 What is stated about the company's delivery service?

(A) It is no longer being offered.
(B) It has undergone a rate increase.
(C) It is not affected by the price changes.
(D) It has been outsourced to another company.

148 What does the Web page indicate about paper for fax machines?

(A) Its price has more than doubled per carton.
(B) It is no longer being sold by Speedy Office Online.
(C) It can be purchased either as sheets or rolls.
(D) It is now available in cartons of six rolls each.

Questions 149-151 refer to the following e-mail.

To: Oliver Yao <oyao@redhouse.com>
From: Julia Wooden <jwooden@redhouse.com>
Date: February 2
Subject: Monitors

Hello, Oliver.

This is Julia from the IT department. We received a shipment of new 27-inch desktop monitors on Monday, and the CEO has instructed me to replace all of the 23-inch monitors currently in use. Since you're the head of Research and Development, I'd like you to do a quick survey of your team when you get a chance. It doesn't have to be today, but I need to hear back from you by Friday. Just find out who has smaller monitors and whether or not they want to upgrade to larger ones. And don't worry—to prevent any disruption of team schedules, we won't be replacing monitors until the weekend. I look forward to hearing from you soon.

Julia

149 What is the purpose of the e-mail?

(A) To place an order for office equipment
(B) To inform a client about a delivery delay
(C) To request information from a coworker
(D) To apologize for a change in schedule

150 Why won't the IT team install new monitors until the weekend?

(A) Their schedule is very full.
(B) The monitor shipment was delayed.
(C) The CEO needs to approve the project.
(D) They don't want to interfere with work.

151 What will Mr. Yao probably do after receiving this e-mail?

(A) Start replacing some outdated computers
(B) Explain a computer problem to the CEO
(C) Place an order for 27-inch computer monitors
(D) Ask the workers on his team some questions

GO ON TO THE NEXT PAGE

Questions **152-153** refer to the following conference schedule.

17th Annual Ethical Journalism Conference
Saturday, June 3 - Schedule of Speakers

Main Hall	Room A	Room B
11 A.M. to 1 P.M. Jen Carrington, president, Organization for Ethical Journalism Opening Remarks and Welcoming Activities	No scheduled events	No scheduled events
Lunch Break	Lunch Break	Lunch Break
2 P.M. to 3 P.M. Wallace Meeks, reporter, New York News Images of War: Responsible Photojournalism	2 P.M. to 3 P.M. Eunjin Kim, journalism professor, University of Pennsylvania Journalism in the Classroom: Educating the Next Generation	2 P.M. to 3 P.M. Jen Carrington, president, Organization for Ethical Journalism Open Forum
3 P.M. to 4 P.M. Frank O'Reilly, CEO, UniNews Corp. Free News: Protecting Newspapers from the Internet	3 P.M. to 4 P.M. Karen Suarez, chief editor, Montreal Press Political Perils: Avoiding Bias in the News	No scheduled events

152 Who is the host of the free discussion event?

(A) Jen Carrington
(B) Wallace Meeks
(C) Frank O'Reilly
(D) Eunjin Kim

153 What is NOT indicated as a lecture topic at the conference?

(A) Teaching journalism to students
(B) Staying neutral on political issues
(C) Taking photographs on the battlefield
(D) Promoting online newspapers

Questions 154-155 refer to the following text message chain.

Madison Ono	1:52 P.M.

It's nearly 2 P.M., and the hard copies of the contracts still haven't arrived.

Emily Smith	1:56 P.M.

Are you sure? The courier service guaranteed they would be delivered by noon today.

Madison Ono	2:03 P.M.

I just checked again with the front desk. All packages have to be dropped off there. They haven't gotten anything.

Emily Smith	2:04 P.M.

I'll get to the bottom of this. Hold on while I call the courier and get some answers.

Emily Smith	2:15 P.M.

We have a problem. Apparently, their delivery truck broke down. They sent another truck to pick up the parcels, but they don't think the contracts will get to you for another hour or so.

Madison Ono	2:18 P.M.

I am not happy about this. Our partners from Lightman, Inc. will be here in 15 minutes to sign the contracts.

Emily Smith	2:19 P.M.

I can fax you copies right now. Let the Lightman people go over the copies first. By the time they're finished checking them, the originals will have arrived.

Madison Ono	2:21 P.M.

I suppose that will work.

[Send]

Test 05

154 At 2:04 P.M., what does Ms. Smith mean when she writes, "I'll get to the bottom of this"?
(A) She will take responsibility for the mistake.
(B) She is worried that she will lose her job.
(C) She is working hard to make things better.
(D) She will identify the cause of the problem.

155 What is indicated as the cause of the delivery delay?
(A) A broken fax machine
(B) A stalled vehicle
(C) A wrong address
(D) A missed phone call

GO ON TO THE NEXT PAGE

Patterson High School will be holding its annual Career Day on Saturday, April 3 in the school's new gymnasium. This is a mandatory event for all seniors, presented with the goal of guiding our graduating students to make wise career choices. Each year, as part of the event, several parents of Patterson High School students volunteer to give short talks about their own work experience. If you would like to share some time and professional knowledge with our students, please send a short e-mail to Karl Grayson, the school's career counselor, at kgrayson@phs.ok.edu. Please include a brief description of your occupation and a daytime phone number we can reach you at. Thank you for your cooperation!

156 What is the purpose of the announcement?

(A) To encourage seniors to attend an event
(B) To solicit volunteers to give brief speeches
(C) To inform parents of a change in schedule
(D) To announce an open job position at a school

157 What information should be included in the e-mail?

(A) A description of the student's career goals
(B) A confirmation of event attendance
(C) A short summary of the parent's profession
(D) A list of the names of graduating seniors

Green River Natural Cereal Corporation

LOGO DESIGN CONTEST
OFFICIAL SUBMISSION FORM

Green River needs a fresh look, so we're turning to our customers for help with designing a new logo. We want something that says: "Green River cereal is healthy, natural and simply delicious!" The ten best designs will be selected by our board of directors and posted on the Green River Web site, where our customers can vote for their favorite. The designer of the winning logo will receive a check for $10,000, and the nine runners-up will be given a one-year supply of delicious Green River products.

To enter, simply fill in the information below and then attach your logo design in the space provided. Logos may be hand-drawn or computer-created images.

Name	
Date of birth	
Address	

I certify that the above design is my own creation and does not violate any existing copyrights. I further certify that I am not now nor have ever been an employee of the Green River Natural Cereal Corporation (GRNCC) or any of its subsidiaries, nor are any of my immediate family members. I understand that by entering this contest, I am granting GRNCC full permission to use my design in promotional material and packaging.

Name (print clearly)	
Signature	
Date	

158 What is indicated as part of the process of choosing a logo?

(A) Online voting
(B) A panel discussion
(C) A random drawing
(D) Live presentations

159 What is NOT something contest entrants must confirm?

(A) They have not copied someone else's work.
(B) They designed the logo without help from others.
(C) They have never been employed by GRNCC.
(D) They agree to allow the company to use their design.

160 What will the winner of the contest receive?

(A) A trip to the Green River factory
(B) Free products for twelve months
(C) A position on the board of directors
(D) A certain amount of money

GO ON TO THE NEXT PAGE

Test 05

Questions 161-163 refer to the following online chat discussion.

Rich Kumar [11:01 A.M.]	How are the interviews for the open sales representative position going?
Alison Agee [11:02 A.M.]	Actually, Justin is handling those, Mr. Kumar. I screened the résumés and identified the top five candidates. I left it to Justin to schedule and conduct the interviews.
Rich Kumar [11:04 A.M.]	I see. Justin, are you there?
Justin Farrell [11:07 A.M.]	Yeah, I am. But I haven't gotten around to scheduling the interviews yet. I've just got too much on my plate at the moment.
Alison Agee [11:08 A.M.]	Are you serious, Justin? I expected those interviews to be underway by now.
Rich Kumar [11:09 A.M.]	To be honest, I think you're the one who dropped the ball here, Alison. You're the hiring supervisor. These interviews are your responsibility.
Alison Agee [11:11 A.M.]	You're right, Mr. Kumar. I should have done a better job delegating the work.
Rich Kumar [11:13 A.M.]	Don't worry, there's still plenty of time. But someone needs to get those interviews scheduled as soon as possible.
Justin Farrell [11:14 A.M.]	I can do it this afternoon. But maybe you can get someone else to conduct the actual interviews.
Alison Agee [11:15 A.M.]	All right. Just get me that schedule by the end of the day, and I'll take care of it from there.

Send

161 What reason does Mr. Farrell give for not scheduling the interviews?

(A) He is not qualified to interview applicants.
(B) He was never asked to schedule them.
(C) He doesn't think the applicants are qualified.
(D) He has been too busy with other work.

162 At 11:09 A.M., what does Mr. Kumar mean when he writes, "I think you're the one who dropped the ball here"?

(A) He is worried that Ms. Agee is getting upset.
(B) He feels that the problem is Ms. Agee's fault.
(C) He believes that Ms. Agee is telling the truth.
(D) He thinks that Ms. Agee has found a solution.

163 What is Mr. Farrell most likely to do next?

(A) Contact the most qualified applicants
(B) Reschedule the upcoming interviews
(C) Review the submitted résumés
(D) Place a new help-wanted ad

Questions 164-167 refer to the following flyer.

Why don't you join us?

Are you a woman between the ages of 18 and 36 who has lost 20 or more kilograms in the past year? – [1] –. If so, you may be qualified to take part in a paid study at the University of Tacoma's Health and Nutrition Center. You must be in good health, live in the greater Tacoma area and be able to devote approximately 30 minutes a night to the study, which will last for a total of four months. – [2] –. Responsibilities include logging your daily calorie intake and recording changes in your weight on a weekly basis. – [3] –. Participants will receive $35 per week throughout the study with a $250 bonus for successful completion of the entire four-month program. Prospective applicants should visit the main administrative office of the Health and Nutrition Center between 10 A.M. and 4 P.M. Monday through Friday. – [4] –.

164 What is NOT stated as a requirement for participating in the study?

(A) Being female
(B) Living in a certain area
(C) Weighing a certain amount
(D) Being in a certain age range

165 In which of the positions marked [1], [2], [3], and [4] does the following sentence best fit?

"This can be done online, but short visits to the Health and Nutrition Center are required twice a month."

(A) [1]
(B) [2]
(C) [3]
(D) [4]

166 What is indicated as part of the compensation for participants?

(A) A daily allowance
(B) Weekly payments
(C) Monthly bonuses
(D) An annual salary

167 How should interested parties apply to participate in the study?

(A) By going to the center in person
(B) By visiting the center's Web site
(C) By sending an e-mail to the center
(D) By filling out an application form

GO ON TO THE NEXT PAGE

Overtime Work

It has come to our attention that there is some confusion among our recent hires regarding the proper process for reporting overtime work. Please note that all overtime work must first be approved by either your immediate supervisor or the department manager. The total hours of your approved overtime work should then be recorded on a twice-monthly basis on the company's official overtime reporting forms. These forms are no longer available at the Human Resources office—they must be printed out from the company Web site. The due date for these forms is at the close of business on the 14th and 28th days of each month. Once these forms have been received by your supervisor and processed by the Payroll department, your payment will be included in the following month's paycheck. If you have any questions, please contact Human Resources. Thank you.

---

168 What is the purpose of the notice?

(A) To clarify a procedure
(B) To propose a policy change
(C) To request overtime work
(D) To announce a job opening

169 Who is this notice intended for?

(A) Department managers
(B) Company clients
(C) New employees
(D) Payroll workers

170 How often are overtime forms accepted?

(A) Once a week
(B) Every weekday
(C) Two times a month
(D) Every two months

171 Where can the overtime forms be obtained?

(A) On the Internet
(B) From department managers
(C) In the Payroll department
(D) At the Human Resources office

The Harrisville city government's film commission has announced that it has reached an agreement with Starmount Studios to allow director Harrison Jackson to film several scenes for his latest movie within the city limits. According to the press release, the movie, *Victory's End*, tells the story of three former soldiers who decide to rob a bank. – [1] –.

The exact locations of the shooting have not yet been released, nor have the names of the cast members. However, former wrestling legend Paul Engleton is rumored to have been offered the starring role. – [2] –. This is the culmination of nearly six months of efforts by the newly appointed film commission to attract major film projects to Harrisville as a means of boosting the local economy. – [3] –.

A local civic group, the Harrisville Citizen's Network, has expressed public safety concerns over the filming of a car chase on city streets, but Eric Jacobson, a spokesperson for the Harrisville police department, has assured the public that measures will be taken to ensure that strict safety guidelines are observed. – [4] –.

Test 05

172 Why was this article written?

(A) To describe an accident that took place on a movie set

(B) To announce the establishment of a new film commission

(C) To explain that parts of a movie will be filmed locally

(D) To notify fans of a famous director's upcoming film

173 In which of the positions marked [1], [2], [3], and [4] does the following sentence best fit?

"Along with the bank robbery scene, a car chase and a fight in a café between the main character and a police officer will be filmed in Harrisville."

(A) [1]
(B) [2]
(C) [3]
(D) [4]

174 What is indicated as the main advantage of having the movie filmed in Harrisville?

(A) Local businesses will be featured.
(B) The city will benefit financially.
(C) It will attract tourists to the city.
(D) City residents can meet celebrities.

175 In paragraph 3, line 6, the word "measures" is closest in meaning to

(A) actions
(B) suggestions
(C) protests
(D) analyses

GO ON TO THE NEXT PAGE

Return to Madrid Is Now Available!

Blue Horizon publishing is pleased to announce the release of *Return to Madrid*, the latest work by acclaimed writer Michelle Park. A work of non-fiction, the book tells the story of Park's return to the city she first visited as a language exchange student nearly 20 years ago. She visits her favorite places and meets people she knew during her student days, including a local folk singer, who is now a popular recording artist. Large sections of the book detail his work on an upcoming album. Written with humor and insight, the book is a delight to read. Local radio station WEZD will be doing a feature on the book, with the station manager reading the opening chapter. If you are interested in Spain or just like good writing in general, please tune in to morning DJ Marcella Rose's show on Sunday, April 11, at 10 A.M. The book itself is now on sale and can be purchased online or from any major bookseller.

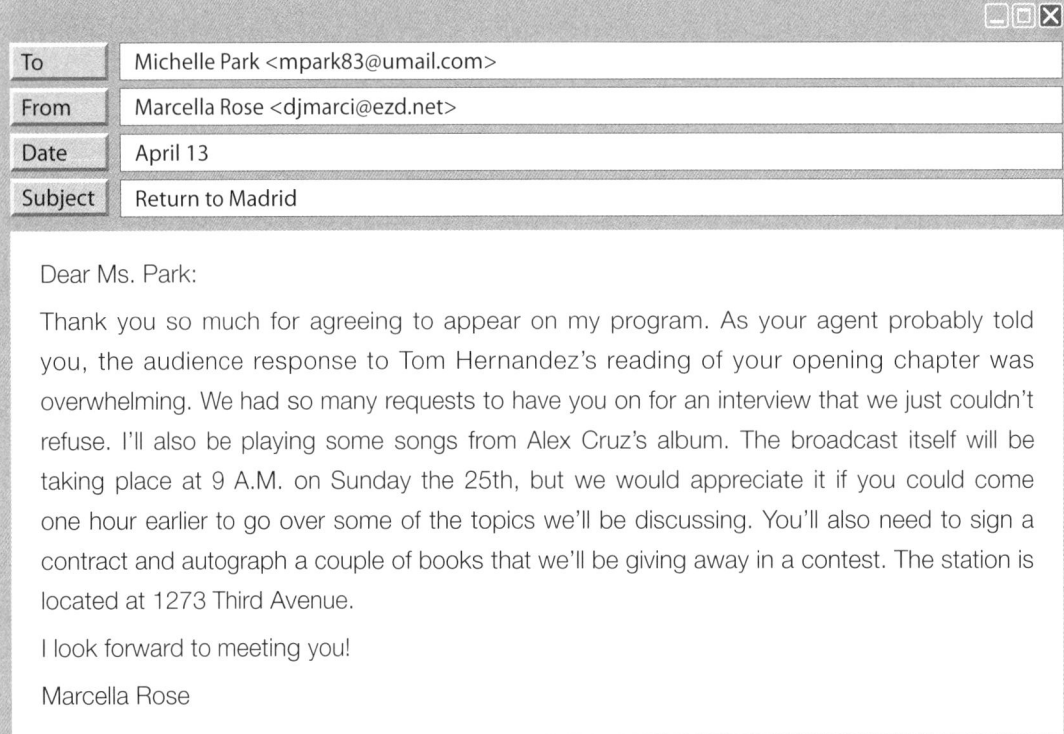

To	Michelle Park <mpark83@umail.com>
From	Marcella Rose <djmarci@ezd.net>
Date	April 13
Subject	Return to Madrid

Dear Ms. Park:

Thank you so much for agreeing to appear on my program. As your agent probably told you, the audience response to Tom Hernandez's reading of your opening chapter was overwhelming. We had so many requests to have you on for an interview that we just couldn't refuse. I'll also be playing some songs from Alex Cruz's album. The broadcast itself will be taking place at 9 A.M. on Sunday the 25th, but we would appreciate it if you could come one hour earlier to go over some of the topics we'll be discussing. You'll also need to sign a contract and autograph a couple of books that we'll be giving away in a contest. The station is located at 1273 Third Avenue.

I look forward to meeting you!

Marcella Rose

176 Why did Ms. Park visit Madrid 20 years ago?

(A) To research a book
(B) To record an album
(C) To study Spanish
(D) To visit friends

177 What is mentioned about the book?

(A) It is the author's first novel.
(B) It is a work of fiction.
(C) It will be released soon.
(D) It is amusing to read.

178 Who is Tom Hernandez?

(A) Ms. Park's agent
(B) The station manager
(C) A Spanish folk singer
(D) A morning DJ

179 What will be done with the autographed books?

(A) They will be auctioned to listeners.
(B) They will be donated to charity.
(C) They will be given to the DJs.
(D) They will be used as contest prizes.

180 What is NOT something Ms. Park will be doing on the day of the broadcast?

(A) Being interviewed
(B) Signing a contract
(C) Singing some songs
(D) Reviewing discussion topics

GO ON TO THE NEXT PAGE

Notice of Failed Delivery

Dear Postal Customer:

Your local mail carrier attempted to deliver a package to **_40 Haverston Lane at 10 A.M. on 4/14/2017_**. This was our second attempt to deliver this package. However, no one was present at the above address. The sender has marked this parcel as "signature required," so we cannot leave it at your doorstep. We will attempt redelivery tomorrow morning at approximately the same time. If no one is expected to be available to sign for the package, please mark one of the boxes below and reattach this notice to your door.

Thank you.

The US Postal Service

☐   I will pick up my package at the 74th Street Post Office.

☑   Please leave my package with my neighbor at 42 Haverston Lane.

Postmaster
South Lake Post Office
South Lake, MN 55924

Dear Sir or Madam:

I was recently sent a package from my brother in Los Angeles. As it contained valuable documents, I was required to sign for it. Unfortunately, I was at work at the time. Since I would be in the office the next day as well, I indicated on the form left by the postman that the package should be left with my neighbor across the street, who is a close friend of mine.

The next day my friend called me at my office and said she had not received the package. When I called the post office, I was told that the package had been received and signed for by John Murphy, a name I did not recognize. Only after some time did I realize that this person was my new next-door neighbor, a man I had never met.

He graciously brought me the package when I returned home, but the carelessness of the postman involved caused me great distress. To make matters worse, he has yet to extend an apology. I am seeking your assurance that this type of situation will not happen again.

Sincerely,

Oscar Alvarez

181 Where was this notice most likely found?

(A) On a package containing documents
(B) At Mr. Alvarez's new neighbor's house
(C) On the front door of Mr. Alvarez's house
(D) At the 74th Street Post Office

182 What is probably true about Mr. Alvarez?

(A) He is employed by the post office.
(B) He recently moved to a new address.
(C) He refused to pay the delivery charges.
(D) He works during the daytime.

183 Who lives at 42 Haverston Lane?

(A) The local mail carrier
(B) Mr. Alvarez's friend
(C) Mr. Alvarez's brother
(D) John Murphy

184 What is the purpose of the letter?

(A) To report a missing package
(B) To complain about a delivery error
(C) To accuse a neighbor of postal theft
(D) To seek reimbursement for lost documents

185 In the letter, the word "extend" in paragraph 3, line 2, is closest in meaning to

(A) emphasize
(B) offer
(C) expand
(D) retract

GO ON TO THE NEXT PAGE

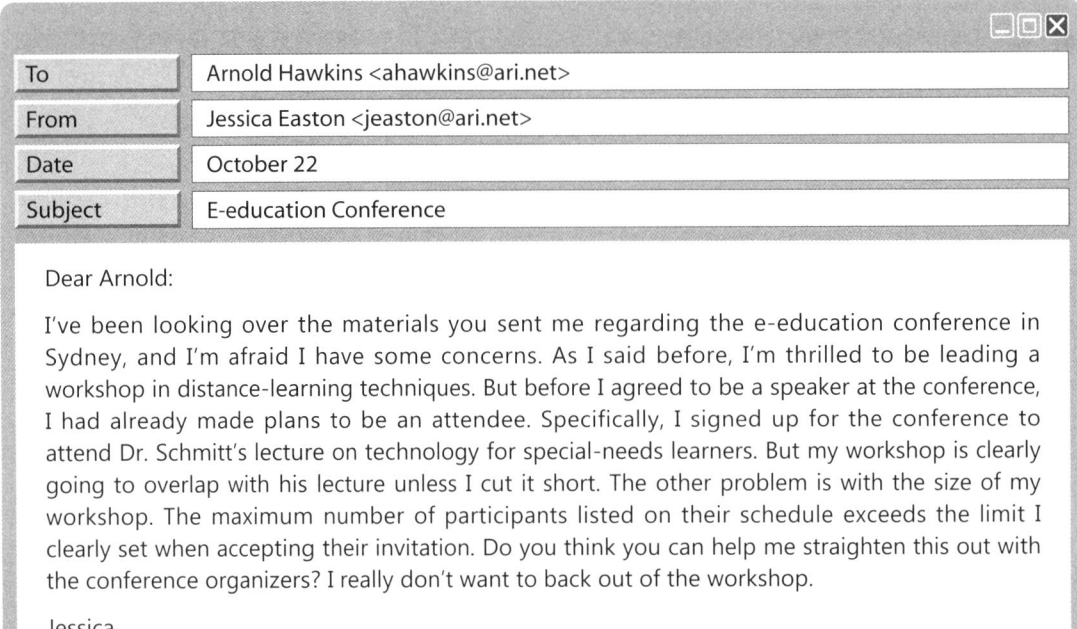

To	Arnold Hawkins <ahawkins@ari.net>
From	Jessica Easton <jeaston@ari.net>
Date	October 22
Subject	E-education Conference

Dear Arnold:

I've been looking over the materials you sent me regarding the e-education conference in Sydney, and I'm afraid I have some concerns. As I said before, I'm thrilled to be leading a workshop in distance-learning techniques. But before I agreed to be a speaker at the conference, I had already made plans to be an attendee. Specifically, I signed up for the conference to attend Dr. Schmitt's lecture on technology for special-needs learners. But my workshop is clearly going to overlap with his lecture unless I cut it short. The other problem is with the size of my workshop. The maximum number of participants listed on their schedule exceeds the limit I clearly set when accepting their invitation. Do you think you can help me straighten this out with the conference organizers? I really don't want to back out of the workshop.

Jessica

October 22, 2017

Edu-Tech Conference Committee
GPO Box 7091
Bankstown, NSW 2200

Dear Committee Members:

I'm writing on behalf of my manager at Academic Research Incorporated, Jessica Easton. As you are well aware, Jessica has agreed to conduct a workshop at your upcoming conference. However, after reviewing the promotional materials you sent her, she has two requests that she wants you to consider. The first is to start her workshop one hour earlier, so that she — along with the workshop participants — can attend Dr. Schmitt's lecture, which, due to his stature and popularity, is clearly anticipated to be one of the conference's highlights. The second is to reduce the maximum number of participants in her workshop listed on your current schedule by 20 people. She fears that a failure to do so will have an adverse effect on her ability to effectively interact with the participants.

If you are unable or unwilling to meet these requests, please contact me at your earliest possible convenience so that we can discuss the matter further.

Sincerely,

Arnold Hawkins
Assistant Office Manager
Academic Research Incorporated

Edu-Tech 2017
Amended Schedule

Workshops			Main Hall	
Workshop Topic	**Time**	**Max. Size**	**Event**	**Time**
Virtual reality in the classroom	**New** 9 A.M. to 11 A.M.	50 participants	Lecturer: Dr. Amy Chang Topic: Teaching Technology to Teachers	10:30 A.M. to 11:30 A.M.
Distance-learning techniques	**New** 11 A.M. to 1 P.M.	**New** 30 participants		
Dealing with hardware issues	2 P.M. to 4 P.M.	40 participants	Lecturer: Dr. Otto Schmitt Topic: Technology for Special-Needs Learners	1:30 P.M. to 2:30 P.M.
Online lesson planning	4 P.M. to 6 P.M.	50 participants		

186 What is the purpose of the e-mail?

(A) To approve a schedule
(B) To request assistance
(C) To propose a workshop
(D) To praise a conference

187 What is suggested about Dr. Schmitt?

(A) He is an employee of Academic Research Incorporated.
(B) He is an esteemed figure in his field.
(C) He will participate in Ms. Easton's workshop.
(D) He will not be attending the conference.

188 What is NOT true about Ms. Easton?

(A) She is Mr. Hawkins' manager.
(B) She will be leading a workshop.
(C) She will be attending a lecture.
(D) She is in charge of the conference.

189 What did the original schedule list as the maximum number of participants in Ms. Easton's workshop?

(A) 20
(B) 30
(C) 40
(D) 50

190 What is the final event of the Edu-Tech conference?

(A) A workshop on fixing broken machines
(B) A lecture on students with learning disabilities
(C) A workshop on creating lessons on the Internet
(D) A lecture on training teachers in technology

GO ON TO THE NEXT PAGE

Effective July 28th

This is a notice for all users of the Pleasanton public transportation system. Due to an adjustment in city bus routes, bus number 49-1 will no longer be stopping at the following two intersections: 45th Street and Second Avenue; and 45th Street and Fourth Avenue. This change will take place beginning on July 28, 2017. From that date forward, the two aforementioned stops will remain in place, but they will only be serviced by the airport express shuttle, also known as bus number 323-A. We appreciate your understanding and thank you for riding the city's buses.

To: Customer Service <customerservice@bellevuedpt.gov>
From: Josh Fizer <fizz97@allonline.com>
Date: July 29th
Subject: Change in Bus Routes

It has recently come to my attention that the 49-1 bus will no longer be stopping in front of the Newside Shopping Arcade on the corner of 45th and Fourth. I find this decision hard to understand, as that is one of the most popular stops on the route. In my case, I'm a salesclerk at Eagle Stereo, located inside the arcade, and have recently bought an annual bus pass, as I use the 49-1 for my daily commute. Now, however, the $600 pass is completely useless to me. Normally, I take the train into the city and catch the 49-1 from the station.

You can also take the 62-1 or the 84 bus from the station, but neither stops near the arcade. Only the airport bus does now, and it doesn't go anywhere near the train station. So now I have to find a new way to get to work. Although the pass is clearly marked as non-refundable and non-transferable, I'd like to request an exception to this policy due to the fact that my dilemma was caused by your department's decision to change the route. If a full refund is not possible, I'd like to request a prorated refund for the months that are left on the pass.

Josh Fizer

Department of Public Transportation – Reimbursement Form

Name: Josh Fizer

Address: 46 Mill Street, Pleasanton, NC 27013

Mobile: 704-555-2018

E-mail: fizz97@allonline.com

Amount Requested: $500

Reason for Request:

I'm requesting a partial refund for my annual bus pass. I can no longer use the pass due to your change in the 49-1 bus route. I previously discussed this situation with Melanie Anderson, who approved my request. She said I should reference case #22914.

Preferred Method of Reimbursement (if approved)

☒ Personal check

☐ Cashier's check

☐ Cash

☐ Direct deposit (include bank information on the back of this form)

Please fill out this form completely and return it by mail to:

Bellevue Department of Transportation

392 Lakeside Industrial Park

Bellevue, NC 83212

191 What is the purpose of the announcement?

(A) To explain the reason for a bus delay

(B) To invite comments on the city bus service

(C) To warn residents about a traffic problem

(D) To inform passengers of a route change

192 What is indicated about Mr. Fizer?

(A) He had a dispute with a bus driver.

(B) He is employed in retail sales.

(C) He lives near the airport.

(D) He is looking for a job.

193 Who most likely is Melanie Andersen?

(A) A bus driver

(B) Mr. Fizer's friend

(C) Mr. Fizer's boss

(D) A city employee

194 Which bus does not stop at the train station?

(A) The 49-1

(B) The 62-1

(C) The 84

(D) The 323-A

195 How many months are left on Mr. Fizer's annual bus pass?

(A) Six

(B) Eight

(C) Ten

(D) Twelve

GO ON TO THE NEXT PAGE

Important Airline Policy Update

North Pacific Air has initiated a change in its checked-baggage policy for international flights effective immediately. Specifically, the checked baggage allowance per international traveler has been increased from one piece of luggage to two pieces. Additionally, the weight limit for each bag has been raised from 20 to 25 kilograms, and the penalty for overweight bags has been lowered from $100 to $50 per bag. The charge for each additional checked bag above the two-piece allowance, however, remains $25 per bag for up to four additional bags. Please note that these changes do not affect our domestic flight policies in any way—the same policy of one free bag, a 20-kilogram limit and a $100 penalty for overweight bags currently remains in effect. If you have questions, please address them to a staff member at our check-in counter.

Thank you.

Wings.com Airline Passenger Online Review

I recently took advantage of one of North Pacific Air's new direct flights, flying from Tokyo to my hometown of San Francisco. Overall, the flight experience was satisfactory. NPA exists somewhere between a budget airline and a standard international carrier—its prices are low, and you get what you pay for. I was quite pleased, however, to discover that I would not be charged for my second checked bag. Apparently this is a new change, and it's a very welcome one.

However, a friend who recently flew from LA to New York on NPA informed me that their old one-bag policy remains in effect for domestic flights, which I find very disappointing. I hope the airline considers expanding their new baggage policy to cover all of their flights.

To:	Eric Sundstrom <travelguy@jazzco.com>
From:	Kyrie Lopez <lopezk@npa.com>
Date:	December 10
Subject:	Your Review

Thank you for taking the time to review your recent flight with North Pacific Air on the Wings.com Web site. We're happy to hear that you're as excited as we are about our new, traveler-friendly baggage policy. The consumer response has been overwhelmingly positive, which is extremely gratifying. As for your suggestion regarding expanding the policy to our domestic flights, I'm sorry to say we are unable to do so due to restrictions imposed by the Federal Aviation Administration. However, we will be cutting the overweight baggage penalty for domestic passengers by 25% starting in 2018. We will also continue to search for ways to raise the quality of our domestic service to the level that our international customers have come to expect.

Sincerely,

Kyrie Lopez
North Pacific Airlines

196 How many bags can each passenger now check for free on international flights?

(A) One
(B) Two
(C) Three
(D) Four

197 What is Mr. Sundstrom's general opinion of the airline?

(A) It is cheap but treats its passengers poorly.
(B) It is better than most international airlines.
(C) It is a good value considering its low prices.
(D) It is fast and convenient but overpriced.

198 In the e-mail, the word "gratifying" in paragraph 1, line 4, is closest in meaning to

(A) satisfying
(B) frightening
(C) embarrassing
(D) startling

199 How much money did Mr. Sundstrom save due to the new policy?

(A) $25
(B) $50
(C) $75
(D) $100

200 What will the overweight bag penalty for domestic passengers be in 2018?

(A) Nothing
(B) $10
(C) $50
(D) $75

잠깐!!
시작 전 꼭 확인하세요!

☑ 실제 시험과 같이
책상을 정리하고
마음의 준비를 하세요.

☑ 핸드폰은 잠깐 끄고
대신 아날로그 시계를
활용해 보세요.

☑ 권장 풀이 시간은 55분입니다.
시간을 꼭 지켜주세요.

☑ 어렵다고 넘어가지 마세요.
가능하면 차례대로 풀어 보세요.

Actual Test

06

시작 시간   :

종료 시간   :

PART 7

Directions: In this part you will read a selection of texts, such as magazine and newspaper articles, e-mails, and instant messages. Each text or set of texts is followed by several questions. Select the best answer for each question and mark the letter (A), (B), (C), or (D) on your answer sheet.

Questions 147-148 refer to the following advertisement.

ARE YOU LOOKING FOR AN EXCITING NEW EXPERIENCE?

Do you have experience in developing and maintaining sales proposals? Are you experienced in supervising the production of marketing materials? Are you well organized? Are you a people person?

If you answered yes to each of those questions, then you may have the qualifications to be the new marketing coordinator at Samick Davis Corporation. This new position entails managing a wide range of marketing processes and projects. These include interactions with sales, product development and customer service departments. The job of the marketing coordinator is to ensure collaboration between departments.

Requirements for this position will include:
> ▶ Computer proficiency with Microsoft Office, Web design, etc.
> ▶ Ability to operate under pressure and meet tight deadlines
> ▶ A solid understanding of marketing principles
> ▶ A bachelor's degree in business, marketing or organizational development

If you meet the requirements and you are interested in entering into an exciting, fast-paced job, contact Samick Davis. You can send a letter of interest and résumé to Samick Davis via e-mail at samadavis@hotmail.com.

147 What is NOT a requirement for this job?
- (A) A master's degree
- (B) Ability to work under pressure
- (C) Knowledge of marketing principles
- (D) Previous work experience

148 How can applicants contact the company about this job?
- (A) By phone
- (B) By letter
- (C) By e-mail
- (D) In person

NOTICE

Subject: 4th Annual Retreat
To: All staff members

Welcome, everyone, to the 4th annual Bradford Publishing Press retreat. I would like everyone to give special thanks to our wonderful CEO John Bradford for his choice in having the retreat in the beautiful Catskill Mountains. I hope everyone made it here with no trouble and has settled in. I know you are really ready to relax, but I have to make some announcements for the weekend. First on the list, tomorrow morning at nine A.M. Sue Ettan will hold a workshop on how to deal with customer phone calls properly. At two o'clock, there will be a four-hour hike to the short peak on Eagle Ridge. If you don't want to join the hike, you have many other choices—just ask one of the employees about this fabulous resort. After dinner at eight o'clock, we will be holding a year-end sales report and yearly awards in the new auditorium.

149 What is the announcement about?

(A) What is going to happen during the weekend
(B) How to deal with customer phone calls
(C) Who won a sales award
(D) The life of John Bradford

150 What is implied about Sue Ettan?

(A) She is going hiking.
(B) She is making a reservation.
(C) She will give out the sales report.
(D) She works in the customer service department.

GO ON TO THE NEXT PAGE

Questions 151-152 refer to the following text message chain.

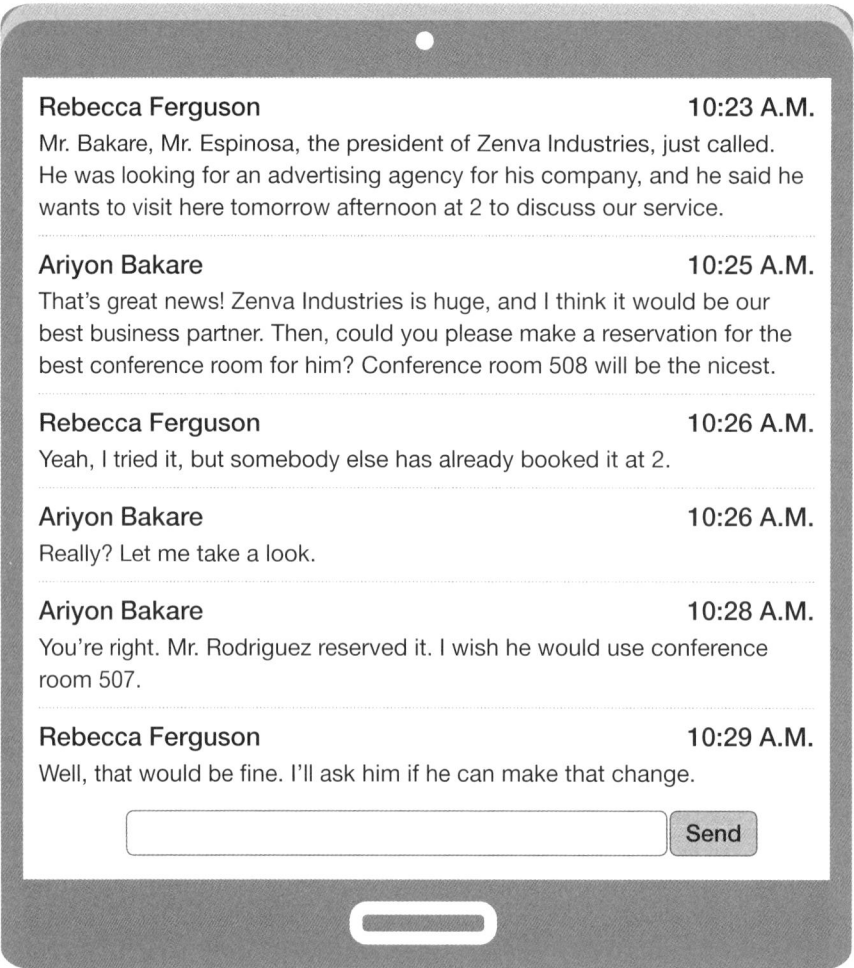

Rebecca Ferguson   10:23 A.M.

Mr. Bakare, Mr. Espinosa, the president of Zenva Industries, just called. He was looking for an advertising agency for his company, and he said he wants to visit here tomorrow afternoon at 2 to discuss our service.

Ariyon Bakare   10:25 A.M.

That's great news! Zenva Industries is huge, and I think it would be our best business partner. Then, could you please make a reservation for the best conference room for him? Conference room 508 will be the nicest.

Rebecca Ferguson   10:26 A.M.

Yeah, I tried it, but somebody else has already booked it at 2.

Ariyon Bakare   10:26 A.M.

Really? Let me take a look.

Ariyon Bakare   10:28 A.M.

You're right. Mr. Rodriguez reserved it. I wish he would use conference room 507.

Rebecca Ferguson   10:29 A.M.

Well, that would be fine. I'll ask him if he can make that change.

Send

151 Where do Mr. Bakare and Ms. Ferguson most likely work?

(A) At a law firm
(B) At a advertising company
(C) At a entertainment company
(D) At a publishing house

152 At 10:29 A.M., what does Ms. Ferguson most likely mean when she writes, "Well, that would be fine"?

(A) She wants Mr. Bakare to reserve the location.
(B) She needs to call her coworker.
(C) She wants Mr. Rodriguez to accept the change.
(D) She needs to change a schedule for a meeting.

New Science World

Sign up for a subscription for another year, and you will continue to enjoy the wonder of discoveries made in the sciences throughout the year. As you renew your subscription, you will gain insightful information not found in your common everyday magazine. *New Science World* will bring the best of the sciences to your door every month. Do not be left out. If you renew your subscription this month, you will have the choice of three different discount plans.

1 year	~~$35.00~~ → $29.99
2 years	~~$57.00~~ → $49.99
5 years	~~$145.00~~ → $129.99

In addition, you don't want to miss out on our yearly collector's edition. This year, the collector's edition will feature Isaac Newton, the father of modern physics and mathematics. We will show how he still has many things to teach modern scientists. Read how he still is influencing the sciences.

153 What is the main purpose of the advertisement?

(A) To inform readers of some new policies
(B) To tell readers of the new magazine
(C) To urge readers to sign up this month for a magazine
(D) To report to readers about the addition of a collector's edition

154 What is NOT implied about the magazine?

(A) The reader of the magazine already has a subscription.
(B) The collector's edition is only for those who subscribed for 5 years.
(C) The magazine is issued monthly.
(D) Lots of new discoveries can be found in the magazine.

GO ON TO THE NEXT PAGE

Memo

TO: Marketing and Publicity Team
FROM: Michael Johnson
DATE: November 14, 2017
SUBJECT: New Proposal

The new 2017 market and research analysis has been completed. – [1] –. The new data show that the marketing team needs to perform a new survey of customer demographics. The marketing strategy used for the last two years is not performing up to our standards. In addition, the sales department is suggesting that sales have dropped by about 2.1% in the last four months. – [2] –.

I would like to propose first that a new survey of customer demographics be done for the new line of summer clothing. Through the new knowledge attained, the company can target different demographics with more precise marketing. Second, the marketing team needs to expand its advertising. – [3] –. The new IT age has opened the door to many new possibilities for marketing. The marketing team has started advertising via only the Internet, but I believe that the advertisement needs to be more expansive.

In January, the marketing team will be holding a meeting; the date is not fixed yet. – [4] –. At this meeting, all employees will be encouraged to bring forth any new ideas for advertising and thoughts on how to target our demographics.

Michael Johnson
Management

155 What is going to happen in January?

(A) A new marketing plan will start.
(B) Advertising will expand to new demographics.
(C) The marketing team will hold discussions.
(D) Advertising via the Internet will start.

156 What can be inferred from this memo?

(A) The survey helps many companies establish marketing strategies.
(B) The marketing team uses various ways of advertising.
(C) Employees in the marketing team have more new ideas.
(D) Sales have dropped because of obsolete advertising.

157 In which of the positions marked [1], [2], [3], and [4] does the following sentence best belong?

"What this figures suggests is that swift action needs to be taken."

(A) [1]
(B) [2]
(C) [3]
(D) [4]

GO ON TO THE NEXT PAGE

Questions 158-160 refer to the following e-mail.

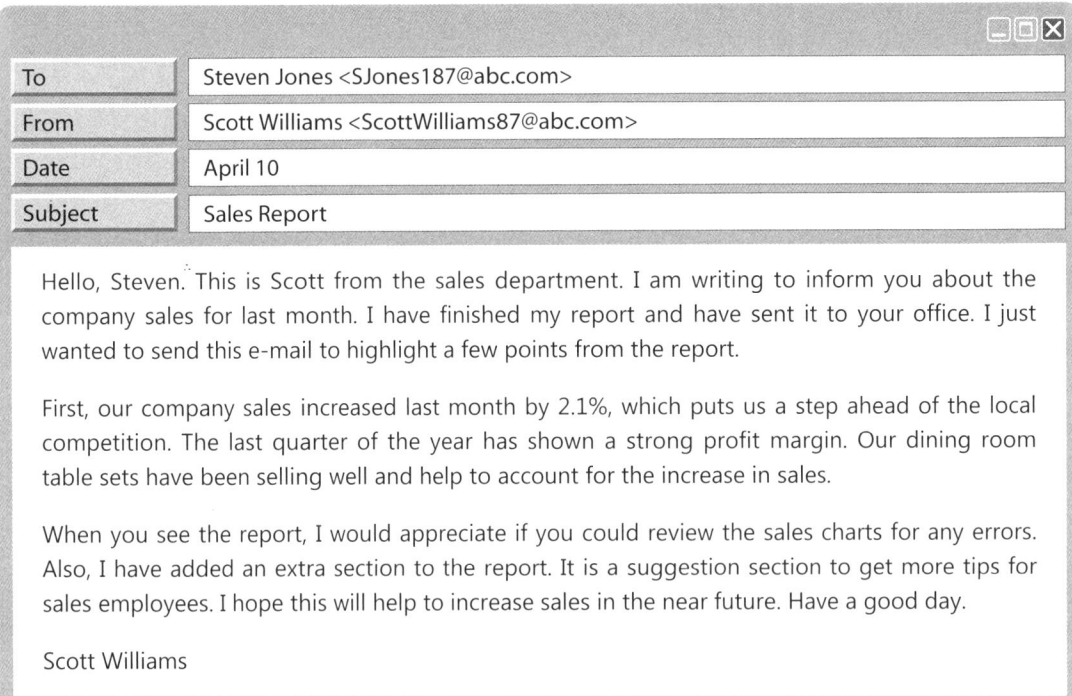

To: Steven Jones <SJones187@abc.com>

From: Scott Williams <ScottWilliams87@abc.com>

Date: April 10

Subject: Sales Report

Hello, Steven. This is Scott from the sales department. I am writing to inform you about the company sales for last month. I have finished my report and have sent it to your office. I just wanted to send this e-mail to highlight a few points from the report.

First, our company sales increased last month by 2.1%, which puts us a step ahead of the local competition. The last quarter of the year has shown a strong profit margin. Our dining room table sets have been selling well and help to account for the increase in sales.

When you see the report, I would appreciate if you could review the sales charts for any errors. Also, I have added an extra section to the report. It is a suggestion section to get more tips for sales employees. I hope this will help to increase sales in the near future. Have a good day.

Scott Williams

---

158 What is the purpose of the e-mail?

(A) To report the results of last month's performance
(B) To point out errors in the report
(C) To boost the sales of table sets
(D) To inform staff members that Mr. Williams sent an e-mail

159 What does Mr. Williams point out in his e-mail?

(A) The errors of the report
(B) The increased sales of last month
(C) The suggestions for customer service employees
(D) The size of dining room table sets

160 The word "highlight" in paragraph 1, line 3, is closest in meaning to

(A) emphasize
(B) intensify
(C) hide
(D) increase

Notice

Greetings to all employees of Hansol Phone Company. This week the company will be closed for the coming holiday on Friday. With this notice I would like to wish you a happy holiday.

Now because of the coming holiday, the company will make some adjustments to the weekly schedule. First, this Wednesday and Thursday the company will close an hour earlier. Second, the company will need our factory workers and sales personnel to put in an extra two hours of work this week which they will be able to split over two days. They will be given a choice of what day or days they would like to complete their hours. Please review the new schedule for this week. If you have any questions, please contact your manager.

Monday	Tuesday	Wednesday	Thursday	Friday
Open: 9:00	Open: 9:00	Open: 9:00	Open: 9:00	
Lunch: 12:00-12:50	Lunch: 12:00-12:50	Lunch: 12:00-12:30	Lunch: 12:00-12:30	Holiday
Close: 17:00	Close: 17:00	Close: 16:00	Close: 16:00	

Robert Jordan
Management Department

161 What is the purpose of the notice?

(A) To announce a new work schedule
(B) To promote a new product
(C) To encourage the employees
(D) To increase sales

162 When will be the company close an hour early?

(A) Monday and Tuesday
(B) Tuesday and Wednesday
(C) Wednesday and Thursday
(D) Tuesday and Thursday

163 What is mentioned in the notice?

(A) All the employees have to work more hours than usual.
(B) There is no change in lunch time.
(C) Only certain employees have to work two extra hours.
(D) The company will not be closed on the holiday.

GO ON TO THE NEXT PAGE

Memo

TO: All Phancy Shoes Employees
FROM: Management
SUBJECT: Mandatory Workshops

The company will be holding mandatory workshops every Saturday for the next 3 weeks. These workshops must be attended for reason of occupational safety. Recent events have been brought to the attention of management. It seems that some employees do not have a clear understanding of the procedures in receiving shipments, taking inventory, and safety in the workplace.

The first workshop will deal with the procedures to receive shipments. The second workshop will deal with how to properly take inventory. These workshops will demonstrate correct procedures, and employees will practice taking inventory. The presenter will demonstrate two methods of taking inventory. The third workshop will deal with safety in the work place. Safety in the work place is extremely important for this company. Management hopes each employee will take this workshop seriously. Safety in the workplace encompasses many aspects of daily work.

Remember that these workshops are mandatory, and they will be held on Saturday, September 3rd, 10th, and 17th. Each workshop will start at 9:00 A.M., so be sure to be on time.

Robert Brown
Management

164 What is the purpose of the memo?

(A) To stress the importance of the workshops
(B) To give a speech to employees
(C) To express satisfaction with the workshops
(D) To inform employees of several workshops

165 Why is the company holding the workshops?

(A) Because there was an accident.
(B) Because management wants employees to be safe.
(C) Because employees should demonstrate how to manage inventory.
(D) Because communication with employees is important.

166 How many days are the workshops being held?

(A) Three days
(B) Three weeks
(C) Every weekend
(D) All day this Saturday

167 The word "mandatory" in paragraph 1, line 1, is closest in meaning to

(A) obligatory
(B) fixed
(C) important
(D) serious

GO ON TO THE NEXT PAGE

Test 06

Questions 168-171 refer to the following online chat discussion.

John Walker [3:31 P.M.]	Good afternoon. I want everyone to talk about the opinions of staff members at your branch after the announcement of the restructuring.
Rose Samberg [3:33 P.M.]	Right after the initial announcement, they felt uncomfortable, but seemed to gradually calm down. They are keeping a close eye on future changes.
Ronda Black [3:34 P.M.]	Staff members here expect that the restructuring will involve some staff arrangements and massive layoffs. Due to the severe economic recession, employees are worried about any changes that might happen.
Sung Kang [3:35 P.M.]	I'm careful to say something about this issue to my employees. I have nothing to say to them without further information.
John Walker [3:36 P.M.]	We're working on it. After the decisions are made roughly in June through a meeting of department heads, I'll consult in more detail with you.
Ronda Black [3:37 P.M.]	In July, some of our offices might be filled with moving boxes. I have mixed feelings.
John Walker [3:38 P.M.]	Until the restructuring is complete, your cooperation is greatly needed. If you have any other questions, please feel free to contact me.

Send

168 Why did Mr. Walker send the message?

(A) To schedule a meeting
(B) To announce possible plans
(C) To find out employees' opinions
(D) To confirm schedules for office relocation

169 At 3:36 P.M., what does Mr. Walker most likely mean when he writes, "We're working on it"?

(A) The work hours has been extended significantly.
(B) Several offices will be closed soon.
(C) He meets regularly with CEOs.
(D) The managers are gathering more detailed information.

170 When will the branches receive an update?

(A) In May
(B) In June
(C) In July
(D) In August

171 What are the branch managers expected to do?

(A) Hire new employees
(B) Ask questions at any time
(C) Provide new identification cards
(D) Order office equipment

Questions 172-175 refer to the following letter.

Jim Thomas
980 Alm Street
Denver, CO 80247

Dear Mr. Thomas:

I have booked the date for my arrival at the Colorado Nova Factory. – [1] –. I will be arriving at Denver International Airport on Monday, October 24 at 4:00 P.M. You do not need to worry about a place for me to stay. I have booked a room at the local Holiday Motel.

I am looking forward to walking the floor of the factory. Also, I am interested in viewing the health records and the safety records of the employees. – [2] –. We will be instigating a new safety program in the workplace at the beginning of next year. I am also excited about seeing the factory's new fluorescent lights product line. – [3] –. I believe that this is a great product for the new market that will be opening overseas in the coming years as countries develop.

As always, I am looking forward to seeing you again. I will see you on the 24th. – [4] –.

Sincerely,

Arthur Clark

172 What is the letter about?

(A) Mr. Clark's visit to the Colorado Nova Factory
(B) Mr. Clark's visit to corporate headquarters
(C) The new production of fluorescent lights
(D) The new market opening overseas

173 What will the company do early next year?

(A) Check health records
(B) Start a safety program in the workplace
(C) Produce fluorescent lights
(D) Fire some employees

174 In which of the positions marked [1], [2], [3], and [4] does the following sentence best belong?

"There has been concern at corporate headquarters that safety in the workplace is in need of improvement."

(A) [1]
(B) [2]
(C) [3]
(D) [4]

175 What is NOT mentioned in the letter?

(A) How long Mr. Clark is staying
(B) When Mr. Clark is arriving
(C) New markets opening overseas
(D) Where Mr. Clark is staying

GO ON TO THE NEXT PAGE

Questions 176-180 refer to the following advertisement and contract.

For Sale: 2016 PanAmerican 4-door sedan

I purchased the sedan a year ago and I've been driving this car without any accident. However, I am planning to change my car to an SUV because of my children. If interested, please contact me at the mobile phone number below and I can arrange a time for you to come by to look at the car.

Samuel Davis

023-555-8403

Seller's Information

Name: Samuel Davis

Address: 3544 Main Street

City: Jamestown

State: Virginia

Zip Code: 32095

Buyer's Information

Name: Bob Scofield

Address: 257 Newman Road

City: Newman

State: Virginia

Zip Code: 32083

Description of Vehicle Being Sold

Year: <u>2016</u>

Body Style: <u>4-Door Sedan</u>
       (2-Dr., 4-Dr., etc.)

Odometer reading: <u>18,000 Miles</u>

Maker: <u>PanAmerican</u>

VIN#: <u>39470662394</u>

(Vehicle ID Number)

Color: <u>dark blue</u>

Disclosure & Warranty

The seller certifies that the odometer reading of this vehicle is correct to his/her knowledge, and that the seller has not modified the odometer, disconnected it, or rolled back the mileage during ownership.

This vehicle is being sold "as is," meaning there is no warranty for any defects, and all repairs are the responsibility of the BUYER unless the SELLER indicates any repairs for which he/she will pay for here:

<u>NO other repairs are to be paid for by the SELLER. The BUYER hereby assumes all financial responsibility</u>.

Payment

The SELLER certifies to the BUYER that the SELLER has the authority to sell this vehicle and transfer the title to the BUYER. The SELLER further certifies that the title is free of liens.

Selling Price of Vehicle: <u>$5,350.00</u>

Signatures

The SELLER and the BUYER agree that to the best of their knowledge, all the information on this Bill of Sale is correct. The SELLER has received payment from the BUYER and hereby transfers ownership of this vehicle to the BUYER.

176 Why was the contract written?

(A) To complain about the service
(B) To upgrade the vehicle being sold
(C) To describe the sale of a vehicle
(D) To report a change of information

177 According to the contract, who sold the car?

(A) Isaac Newton
(B) Samuel Davis
(C) Bob Scofield
(D) PanAmerican

178 What type of car was purchased?

(A) 2016 PanAmerican dark blue, 4-door car
(B) 2016 PanAmerican blue, 2-door car
(C) 2017 PanAmerican dark blue, 4-door car
(D) 2017 PanAmerican blue car

179 What is NOT true about the contract?

(A) The buyer is responsible for all repairs unindicated by the seller.
(B) The selling price is indicated.
(C) The buyer has the ownership by the contract.
(D) The seller has modified the vehicle to sell at good price.

180 What is suggested about the vehicle?

(A) It has accident history.
(B) It is for the children of Mr. Scofield.
(C) Mr. Scofield took it for a test drive in Jamestown.
(D) Its second owner is Mr. Davis.

GO ON TO THE NEXT PAGE

Questions 181-185 refer to the following e-mails.

To	Dr. Benway <BenWy@hotmail.com>
From	Randy Smith <RandyS@hotmail.com>
Date	February 1
Subject	Request for Graduate Research

Dear Dr. Benway:

I am a graduate student at the University of Georgia. I am currently conducting research on the archaeological remains of Frodo Site 34AJ24. I am interested in examining oyster shells and soil samples from this site to compare them with other sites along the coast of Georgia and South Carolina. My hope is to collect data from many sites to aid in a general estimation of the age of the many Shell Mounds.

I have contacted Sue Jones, the Laboratory Coordinator about the hours at the archaeology lab. Sue said that she might be able to give me time for research for a week in February. She recommended that I work with you. I am hoping that as the Principal Investigator of the excavation you can be of help in my research.

If you are available from February 20th to 25th, I would like to do the research during this time, but I can change the date if need be. I would also like to discuss with you the data that I have collected from other sites. My hope is that you may be able to help with my data collection. I would appreciate any help with my estimation of the age of the mounds. You can contact me through my e-mail address at RandyS@hotmail.com. I hope to hear from you soon.

Sincerely,

Randy Smith

To:	Randy Smith <RandyS@hotmail.com>
From:	Dr. Benway <BenWy@hotmail.com>
Date:	February 2
Subject:	Re: Request for Graduate Research

Dear Mr. Smith:

I would like to thank you for contacting me. I believe I may be of assistance since I conducted similar research in that area when I was working on my Ph.D. at the University of Maryland. I congratulate you for choosing the age of Shell Mounds as a topic because that is a matter of great relevance in our scientific field.

Please note that I will not be available on February 20th, due to a speech I must give in Boston on that day. But other than that day, I will be fine. I would like to review the data you have collected so far and would like to discuss it with you in detail. In particular, I wish to know more about your research methodologies. Perhaps when you finish your studies at the University of Georgia we will be able to collaborate by doing more in-depth research.

At any rate, I look forward to seeing you on the 21st.

Sincerely,

Dr. Benway

181 What is the purpose of the first e-mail?

(A) To estimate the age of shell mounds
(B) To ask for some assistance for research
(C) To conduct research on the Frodo Site
(D) To collect data from Ms. Jones

182 In the first e-mail, the word "estimation" in paragraph 1, line 4, is closest in meaning to

(A) figure
(B) decision
(C) confirmation
(D) assumption

183 When will Mr. Smith be with Dr. Benway?

(A) March 20th to 25th
(B) February 20th to 25th
(C) February 21st to 25th
(D) February 19th

184 What is the topic that Mr. Smith is researching?

(A) The Frodo Site
(B) Oyster shells
(C) The age of Shell Mounds
(D) Archaeology

185 According to the e-mails, which of the following is NOT true?

(A) Ms. Jones is the laboratory coordinator.
(B) Dr. Benway is an expert archaeologist.
(C) Mr. Smith wants to discuss his research.
(D) Dr. Benway is a professor at the University of Maryland.

GO ON TO THE NEXT PAGE

Blue Chateau Resort

Our conference rooms, located amid the comfort of the majestic Catskill Mountains, offer the perfect get-away from the office congestion. Here at Blue Chateau Resort, your company's employees can relax in open space and the fresh air. Along with the grand view of the Catskill Mountains come many hiking trails, a sports complex and a spa to offer many different ways to relieve stress.

The Blue Chateau Resort offers many services for small and big business meetings. We have 4 conference rooms open for year-round use, and a brand-new auditorium supplied with a top-of-the-line audio system, video projectors and newly installed high-speed wireless Internet service. Hence you are in the wilderness but have all the connections of a major city. As for the concern of a place to stay, the Blue Chateau Resort has wonderful traditional Catskill log cabins. Our resort has both singles and doubles furnished with cable TV, fast Internet service, kitchenette and beautiful views of the Catskills.

For more information, contact us via
Telephone: 740-555-0356
Our new Web site: http://www.bluechateauresort.com
E-mail: bluechateauresort@netmail.com (for the attention of Sam Davis)

Don't hesitate to make your company's reservation today!

http://www.bluechateauresort.com/services/prices

| Meetings & Events | Accommodations | Services | Q&A |

Conference room
- Standard: $280 per day during the week / $350 per day on weekends
- Auditorium: $600 per day during the week / $680 per day on weekends
  (It can accommodate up to 100 people at one time.)

Equipment
- Audio system: $30 per day
- Video projector: $45 per day
  (The auditorium is equipped with all audiovisual equipment which is available free of charge. Also, you can use wireless Internet anywhere in the resort.)

Accommodation
- Log cabin: Single $45 per night during the week / $50 per night on the weekends
             Double $50 per night during the week / $55 per night on the weekends

If you have any questions, call or e-mail us without a moment's hesitation.
Thank you.

E-mail: bluechateauresort@netmail.com

To: Sam Davis <bluechateauresort@netmail.com>
From: John Bradford <JohnBradford908@bradfordpublishing.com>
Date: March 5
Subject: Blue Chateau Resort Information

Dear Mr. Davis:

Hello, sir. This is John Bradford, the CEO of Bradford Press. I am responding to your advertisement in the New York Times. I have been looking for a nice get-away for my employees that also has an auditorium. The Blue Chateau resort seems to hold some promise, but I have a few questions.

I would like to know if there are any company package prices for one weekend. Also does the resort offer any seasonal price discounts? My last question is about the availability of rooms during the month of April. Thank you for your time.

Sincerely,

John Bradford

186 What is the advertisement about?

(A) A publishing company
(B) A travel agency
(C) A new auditorium
(D) A company retreat

187 What is indicated about Blue Chateau Resort?

(A) It requires payment in advance.
(B) It is known for its restaurant.
(C) It is located in the Catskill Mountains.
(D) It was once owned by Mr. Davis.

188 According to the e-mail, what kinds of information does Mr. Bradford seek?

(A) Reduced prices and room availability
(B) Beverages to be served
(C) Directions to the resort
(D) Details about the sports complex

189 What is NOT mentioned in the advertisement?

(A) An auditorium with video projectors
(B) Log cabins with grand views
(C) A conference room for business meetings
(D) Seasonal price discount

190 What can be inferred about Mr. Bradford?

(A) He recently founded a company.
(B) He needs to train new employees and security guards.
(C) He is interested in investing in the resort.
(D) He can have maximal 100 staff participate in the upcoming event.

GO ON TO THE NEXT PAGE

August 2017 Issue of British Consumer Reports
Problem Persists with ProCinema's New Home Theater System

Consumers and blog writers seem to be in agreement that ProCinema has made a faulty product in its 7-Channel Home Theater SKS-3020. That system was put on the market, to much fanfare, last year. It was supposed to replace and improve upon the 5-Channel Home Theater SKS-2020, which was a big money-maker for ProCinema over the past four years.

A wiring problem in the rear speakers has bedeviled the new product and those who bought it. Many have complained loudly to ProCinema, and sales have dropped week by week. Sales are now off 40% in comparison to the 5-Channel Home Theater SKS-2020, and some people are even asking that it be brought back and the 7-Channel Home Theater SKS-3020 be junked.

This is an especially unwelcome matter for ProCinema which has built its reputation on satisfying customers with quality products. If the wiring problem in the new system is not fixed quickly, the Liverpool-based company is going to lose market share and that is never easy to make up.

To	David Brown <DBrown@ProCinema.com>
From	Kimberly Johnson <KJohnson@ProCinema.com>
Subject	7-Channel Home Theater SKS-3020
Attachment	Problem Persists with ProCinema's New Home Theater System.doc

Dear David:

Please take a look at the enclosed article from British Consumer Reports. As it makes painfully clear, we have a serious problem with one of our key products, the 7-Channel Home Theater SKS-3020. Since you are in charge of quality control at ProCinema, I ask you to get your best people to work on this immediately. If the wiring problem is not cleared up, we will have to issue a recall. That is something no company likes to do since it hurts in terms of money and public relations.

I can tell you that Tom Ibbotson, chairman of the Board of Directors of ProCinema, is already advocating a recall. The company president, Kathleen Monte, is holding off on any such plans until we hear back from you. I need a definitive answer about the wiring problem with the 7-Channel Home Theater SKS-3020 by Friday at the latest.

Sincerely,

Kim Johnson
Management

ProCinema will recall SKS-3020

Due to a serious wiring problem in its rear speakers, we made a final decision to recall the 7-Channel Home Theater SKS-3020.

All customers who recently purchased this new product can send it to our home appliance store for three months beginning on July 21. We'll take care of it immediately and completely.

We, ProCinema, are quite sorry for your inconvenience. We promise to offer you better products and services in the future.

191 What is the main point in the article?

(A) The president of ProCinema is retiring.
(B) Sales of the 5-Channel Home Theater SKS-2020 are up.
(C) There is a wiring problem with the 7-Channel Home Theater SKS-3020.
(D) Blog writers are praising the 7-Channel Home Theater SKS-3020.

192 What are some customers suggesting?

(A) That the 7-Channel Home Theater SKS-3020 be replaced by an earlier model.
(B) That the 7-Channel Home Theater SKS-3020 is ProCinema's greatest product yet.
(C) That Procinema's reputation is better than ever.
(D) That ProCinema is making a lot of money with the new system.

193 What is true about Mr. Brown?

(A) He lives in Liverpool.
(B) He has recently hired Ms. Johnson.
(C) He will be on a business trip on July 21.
(D) He is responsible for quality control.

194 What does Tom Ibbotson want to do?

(A) Call a meeting of the Board of Directors
(B) Recall the 7-Channel Home Theater SKS-3020
(C) Bring back the 5-Channel Home Theater SKS-2020
(D) Fire David Brown

195 What is suggested about ProCinema?

(A) President Kathleen Monte has made up her mind.
(B) Ms. Johnson needs an answer from customers by Friday.
(C) ProCinema's profits may increase gradually.
(D) The 5-Channel Home Theater SKS-2020 may be junked.

GO ON TO THE NEXT PAGE

Questions 196-200 refer to the following e-mails and text message.

To	Richard Dervish <Richard_D@southeastelectrical.com>
From	Shirley Austin <S_Austin@hotmail.com>
Date	April 5
Subject	Response to Job Advertisement in hotjobs.com

Dear Mr. Dervish:

I am responding to the advertisement you placed on behalf of Southeast Electrical Corporation in the job search engine hotjobs.com. First, please allow me to state my experience in the field of electrical engineering (EE). I hold a master's degree in EE from North Carolina College of Technology. During my years as an undergraduate student, I worked as a laboratory assistant under Dr. Catherine Forbes.

I earned a doctoral degree at Duke University in 2017. During that time, I had an internship in the research and development department at North Carolina Power Company. I stayed there after getting my Ph.D. and believe I have made some solid contributions, but I am open to new opportunities—hence my interest in working for Southeast Electrical Corporation. I specialize in the construction of electrical circuit boards, primarily for large power generators. As my attached résumé and three reference letters attest, I am a reliable and energetic employee.

Please give my application serious consideration. I hope to hear from you soon.

Sincerely,

Shirley Austin

To:	Shirley Austin <S_Austin@hotmail.com>
From:	Richard Dervish <Richard_D@southeastelectrical.com>
Date:	April 15
Subject:	Re: Response to Job Advertisement in hotjobs.com

Dear Dr. Austin:

Thank you for your interest in Southeast Electrical Corporation. I have reviewed your résumé along with three reference letters. There seems to be little doubt that you have a strong educational pedigree. You clearly have all the qualities we are looking for in an electrical engineer.

However, there is one aspect of your résumé that I wish to clear up. You stated that you have experience in building electrical circuit boards for large power generators, but what kind of generators are you speaking of? There are steam turbine generators, radioisotope thermoelectric generators, nuclear generators and other kinds as well.

Please respond to this e-mail with more specific information about the variety of generators you have designed in your career. Once we have these pertinent facts in hand, we will be able to decide whether to bring you in for an interview. Thank you for your time.

Sincerely,

Richard Dervish

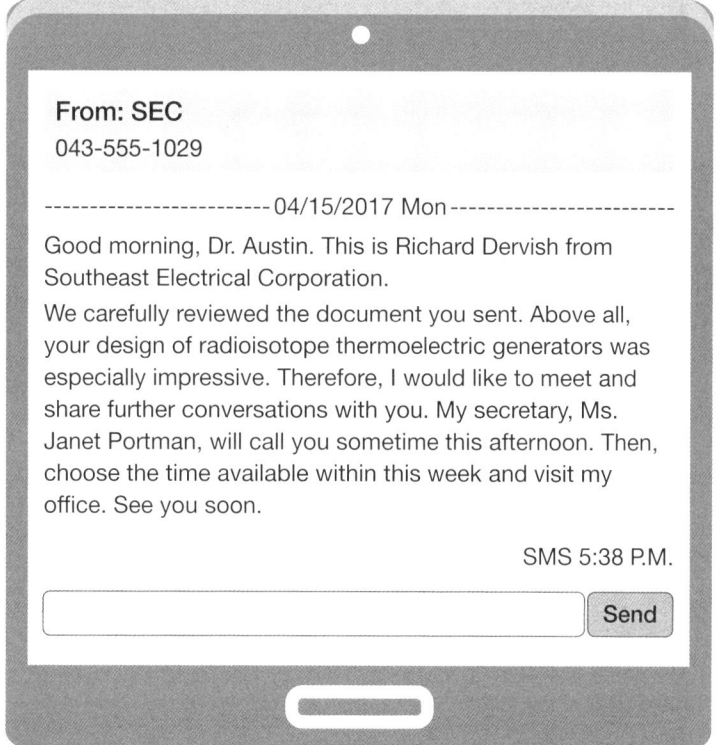

From: SEC
043-555-1029

------------------------- 04/15/2017 Mon -------------------------
Good morning, Dr. Austin. This is Richard Dervish from Southeast Electrical Corporation.
We carefully reviewed the document you sent. Above all, your design of radioisotope thermoelectric generators was especially impressive. Therefore, I would like to meet and share further conversations with you. My secretary, Ms. Janet Portman, will call you sometime this afternoon. Then, choose the time available within this week and visit my office. See you soon.

SMS 5:38 P.M.

[   ] Send

196 Who is Richard Dervish?

(A) A student at North Carolina College of Technology
(B) A worker at North Carolina Power Company
(C) An agent at hotjobs.com
(D) An employee at Southeast Electrical Corporation

197 What does Dr. Austin specialize in?

(A) Public relations
(B) Assisting Dr. Forbes
(C) Teaching graduate students
(D) Designing electrical circuit boards

198 What specific information does Mr. Dervish ask for?

(A) When Dr. Austin may come in for an interview
(B) The topic of Dr. Austin's Ph.D. dissertation
(C) Dr. Austin's educational background
(D) Information about electrical generators

199 What is suggested by the text message?

(A) Mr. Dervish has worked with Dr. Austin many times.
(B) Southeast Electrical Corporation will launch a new product in April.
(C) Dr. Austin sent an e-mail to Mr. Dervish on April 15.
(D) Mr. Dervish has recently been hired as a manager.

200 What can be inferred about Dr. Austin?

(A) She works at North Carolina Power Company permanently.
(B) She submitted a résumé and application form to hotjobs.com.
(C) She received a great deal of help from the classified ads.
(D) She will talk with Ms. Portman on the phone.

잠깐!!
시작 전 꼭 확인하세요!

☑ 실제 시험과 같이
   책상을 정리하고
   마음의 준비를 하세요.

☑ 핸드폰은 잠깐 끄고
   대신 아날로그 시계를
   활용해 보세요.

☑ 권장 풀이 시간은 55분입니다.
   시간을 꼭 지켜주세요.

☑ 어렵다고 넘어가지 마세요.
   가능하면 차례대로 풀어 보세요.

Actual Test

07

시작 시간   :

종료 시간   :

PART 7

Directions: In this part you will read a selection of texts, such as magazine and newspaper articles, e-mails, and instant messages. Each text or set of texts is followed by several questions. Select the best answer for each question and mark the letter (A), (B), (C), or (D) on your answer sheet.

Questions 147-148 refer to the following e-mail.

To: All employees
From: Harold Kahn <Kahnh@krontel.com>
Date: July 4

Hello, everyone.

The past few months have been eventful ones for Krontel Industries. I know you're all curious about our company's status, so here's a quick update. Our planned merger with HVC Corporation fell through due to an inability to agree on certain terms during the latest round of negotiations. However, our board of directors has voted to resume our talks with HVC in the new year, so nothing is confirmed at this point. Also, you may have heard that Hillary Trong, our corporate vice president, has decided to retire. I just want to assure you that this has nothing to do with the HVC situation. She's stepping down for personal reasons. Finally, I'd just like to thank everyone for your continued hard work and for making Krontel a great place to work.

Harold Kahn
CEO, Krontel Industries

147 Why did Mr. Khan send this e-mail?

(A) To propose a merger between two companies
(B) To announce a new corporate vice president
(C) To inform employees about recent events
(D) To explain why he is leaving the company

148 What is indicated about the Krontel board of directors?

(A) It has elected a new chairperson.
(B) It has accepted a proposal from HVC.
(C) It has demanded that Mr. Kahn resign.
(D) It has chosen to continue negotiations.

Memo

To: All Ludwig Building employees

From: Jonathan Pace, IT Manager

Beginning next Monday, the building's new phone system will be fully operational. The primary change from the old system will be the addition of a personal voice mailbox for each individual. You will be able to access your new mailbox on Monday simply by hitting the pound key on your desk phone and following the step-by-step instructions. The other change is that it will now be necessary to press 9 before making any external phone calls. And in order to reach your coworkers by phone, you'll need to press 1, followed by their extension number. I expect the transition to the new system to be seamless, but the IT team will be available to help you with any problems you may encounter.

149 What is the purpose of the memo?
(A) To remind employees of the office passcodes
(B) To explain changes caused by a new system
(C) To inform workers of a stoppage of service
(D) To enforce a policy on personal phone calls

150 What is indicated as the reason an employee would press the pound key?
(A) To delete a message
(B) To contact the IT team
(C) To end a telephone call
(D) To initiate a process

GO ON TO THE NEXT PAGE

Questions 151-152 refer to the following text message chain.

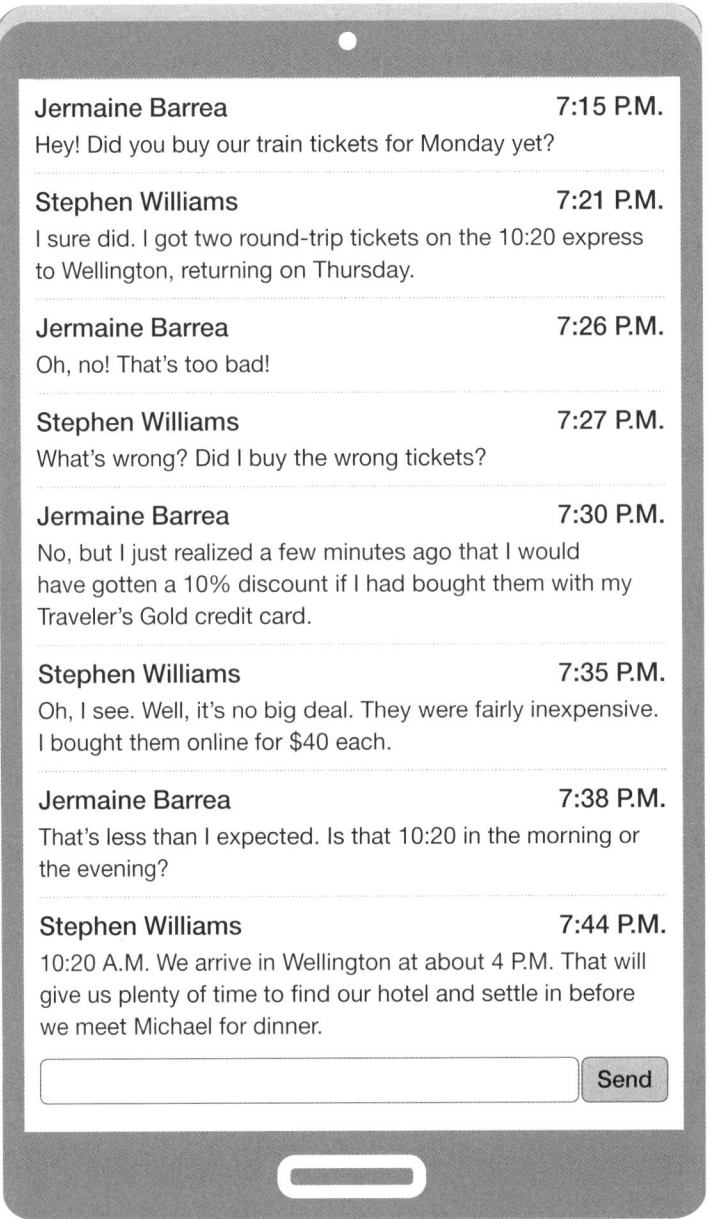

Jermaine Barrea   7:15 P.M.
Hey! Did you buy our train tickets for Monday yet?

Stephen Williams   7:21 P.M.
I sure did. I got two round-trip tickets on the 10:20 express to Wellington, returning on Thursday.

Jermaine Barrea   7:26 P.M.
Oh, no! That's too bad!

Stephen Williams   7:27 P.M.
What's wrong? Did I buy the wrong tickets?

Jermaine Barrea   7:30 P.M.
No, but I just realized a few minutes ago that I would have gotten a 10% discount if I had bought them with my Traveler's Gold credit card.

Stephen Williams   7:35 P.M.
Oh, I see. Well, it's no big deal. They were fairly inexpensive. I bought them online for $40 each.

Jermaine Barrea   7:38 P.M.
That's less than I expected. Is that 10:20 in the morning or the evening?

Stephen Williams   7:44 P.M.
10:20 A.M. We arrive in Wellington at about 4 P.M. That will give us plenty of time to find our hotel and settle in before we meet Michael for dinner.

Send

151 What is NOT suggested about Mr. Barrea and Mr. Williams?

(A) Their train tickets cost a total of $80.
(B) Their destination is Wellington.
(C) They will arrive in the afternoon.
(D) They will stay for one week.

152 At 7:35 P.M., what does Mr. Williams mean when he writes, "It's no big deal"?

(A) The ticket price seems too high.
(B) The problem is not significant.
(C) The credit card was not accepted.
(D) The trip is not important.

Questions 153-155 refer to the following instructions.

Westland Docupro 2000

Operating Instructions

1. Slide the power switch to the on position, indicated by the "l" symbol. The green LED light at the front of the machine will illuminate when the machine is properly activated. If the green light does not appear, make sure the machine's door is firmly shut.

2. Position the unwanted documents on the paper feeder tray and press them gently forward. The machine will automatically begin cutting up the paper once it has crossed its feeder sensors.

3. When you have finished, wait for the machine to automatically deactivate. This will occur approximately five seconds after the last document has been completely destroyed. The green LED light will go off, and the red one will glow steadily.

4. If a blinking red light appears, a paper jam has occurred. Gently pull any visible documents out of the feeder tray. Please note that you should never place your fingers inside the machine, as the blades can cause serious injuries even when deactivated.

5. Open the front door and check the plastic waste bag. If it is full, slide the entire frame out of the machine, and then remove the bag for disposal.

Test 07

153 What most likely is the Docupro 2000?

(A) A paper shredder
(B) A computer printer
(C) A copy machine
(D) A digital scanner

154 Which of the following will prevent the machine from working?

(A) Failing to close the door properly
(B) Activating the feeder sensors
(C) Installing a plastic waste bag
(D) Placing documents on the tray

155 According to the instructions, what does a flashing light indicate?

(A) The machine is on.
(B) The paper is stuck.
(C) The door is open.
(D) The waste bag is full.

GO ON TO THE NEXT PAGE

Questions 156-158 refer to the following Web page.

London City University

| Home | STUDY | LIFE | CONTACT US |

Looking for a place to stay this summer? I have a two-bedroom apartment less than two kilometers from the campus that I'm looking to sublet from the beginning of June through the end of August. This is a legal sublet, so, even though you wouldn't need to sign a contract, you would need to be approved by the landlord. He's pretty easygoing, though! I will be studying overseas as part of an exchange program during those three months, so you could move right in and use my stuff - no need to buy furniture, kitchenware or towels! It's the perfect situation for a visiting student or professor, or just someone looking for a place to spend the summer. There is a double bed in the main bedroom and a single bed in the other, which I use as a study. There is a bathtub and separate shower in the bathroom, as well as a washer and dryer. If you're interested, please send me an e-mail telling me a bit about yourself, and I'll get back to you as soon as possible.

156 Who most likely posted the notice on this Web page?

(A) A real estate agent
(B) A building owner
(C) A professor
(D) A student

157 What is indicated about the landlord?

(A) He does not know about the sublet.
(B) He requires a signed contract.
(C) He is not a strict person.
(D) He lives in the building.

158 Which is NOT stated as being included with the apartment?

(A) Two beds
(B) A dishwasher
(C) Pots and pans
(D) A clothes washer

Questions 159-160 refer to the following online chat discussion.

Jon Rose [4:41 P.M.]		Good afternoon, guys. I need someone to get me out of a jam. I had an unexpected schedule change and need a volunteer to pick up Dr. Van Dyke at the airport tomorrow afternoon.
Brandon Cho [4:42 P.M.]		I'd be happy to go get her, Mr. Rose. I have a light schedule tomorrow.
Debbie Wade [4:42 P.M.]		I can do it. Would I be able to use the company car?
Jon Rose [4:47 P.M.]		That's the problem. I need the company car to get to an out-of-town conference tomorrow. Do either of you have your own vehicle?
Debbie Wade [4:48 P.M.]		Sorry, but I don't.
Brandon Cho [4:49 P.M.]		I have an SUV. But if you'd prefer that Debbie pick her up, she's welcome to borrow it.
Jon Rose [4:51 P.M.]		Thanks, Brandon, but I'm sure you can handle it on your own.
Brandon Cho [4:53 P.M.]		Sure, no problem. What time does she arrive? Do you have her flight number?
Jon Rose [4:54 P.M.]		It slipped my mind, actually. Go see my secretary. She'll fill you in on all of the details.
Brandon Cho [4:55 P.M.]		All right. I'll talk to her.

Send

159 What will Mr. Cho most likely do next?

(A) Obtain the flight information
(B) Drive his SUV to the airport
(C) Contact Dr. Van Dyke
(D) Return to his home

160 At 4:41 P.M., what does Mr. Rose mean when he writes, "I need someone to get me out of a jam"?

(A) He is stuck in traffic.
(B) He wants some data.
(C) He requires assistance.
(D) He is worried about a project.

GO ON TO THE NEXT PAGE

Questions 161-164 refer to the following letter.

Joseph Kidman
Acquisitions Department
Reingold Accounting
19188 6th Avenue
Detroit, MI 48207

Dear Mr. Kidman:

It was a pleasure to meet with you and your staff at your Detroit office last Friday. As per our discussion about providing security equipment and monitoring services to your company, I'm sending you a formal price estimate that has been approved by our CEO. – [1] –. Although the scale of the services we would be providing to your company fail to meet the threshold for this discount, our CEO has agreed to extend it in anticipation of your company's forecasted growth. – [2] –. If you agree to these terms, the discount will be in place for one year from the signing of the contract. – [3] –. After this period has expired, we will only continue to offer the bulk discount if your company's required services have met or surpassed our standard minimum. – [4] –. Please review the attached estimate and get back to me at your earliest convenience.

Sincerely,

Patrick Jensen
Houseman Security Services

161 What is the purpose of this letter?

(A) To follow up on a meeting
(B) To introduce a new service
(C) To reject a proposal
(D) To request a confirmation

162 What is suggested as being included with this letter?

(A) A letter of introduction
(B) A cost approximation
(C) A revised contract
(D) A product list

163 In which of the positions marked [1], [2], [3], and [4] does the following sentence best fit?

"These prices reflect the 15% bulk discount we offer to our larger customers."

(A) [1]
(B) [2]
(C) [3]
(D) [4]

164 What will happen after one year if an agreement is reached?

(A) The bulk discount will be increased.
(B) The contract will be automatically renewed.
(C) The CEO will request another meeting.
(D) The contract's terms will be reassessed.

SMART STUFF CUSTOMIZED PHONE CASES

ONLINE ORDER FORM

Full Name	
Mailing Address	
Phone Number	

Select a case type:

☐ Hard $14.99   ☐ Soft (plastic) $9.99   ☐ Soft (leather) $29.99

Choose a case color:

☐ White   ☐ Black   ☐ Green   ☐ Red   ☐ Dark Blue   ☐ Light Blue

Select a texture:

☐ Smooth   ☐ Rough

Add an inscription. Inscriptions must not exceed 30 characters in length, including spaces, and may only include letters, numbers and punctuation ($5 extra).

Add a photo. Photos must be attached as a JPG image and may not exceed 2.5 MB in size ($15 extra).

Add $7 for three-day express shipping or $3 for standard delivery. Free domestic shipping on all orders exceeding $19.99. Special rates are available for orders of 15 cases or more. A 10% discount on the total price of the order will be provided. For more information, please contact us at 516-555-9927.

---

165 What is NOT stated as being a customizable option?

(A) Size
(B) Color
(C) Texture
(D) Material

166 What is indicated about inscriptions?

(A) They come in different colors.
(B) There is a choice of fonts.
(C) They are free of charge.
(D) There is a length limit.

167 How can customers have their delivery charges waived?

(A) By ordering over the telephone
(B) By selecting a slower shipping option
(C) By exceeding a certain dollar amount
(D) By ordering a large number of cases

168 Which of the following would qualify for a special discount?

(A) Charges for express shipping
(B) A particular number of products ordered
(C) A sales item purchased before a special date
(D) The purchase of an inscribed case

GO ON TO THE NEXT PAGE

Questions 169-171 refer to the following advertisement.

JL Mistmaker

The JL Mistmaker is the perfect desktop companion for people confined to a dry office all day. This state-of-the-art ultrasonic humidifier features a 1.5-liter water tank that can provide you with more than 10 hours of continuous moisture. Because of its compact size and nearly silent ultrasonic motor, the Mistmaker is the number one choice of office workers across the nation.

The water tank is removable for easy refilling, and there is no inconvenient filter to clean. And if you forget to turn your Mistmaker off at the end of a busy day, don't worry! The system automatically switches off once the water tank is empty.

Doctors recommend the use of humidifiers to help ease cold and flu symptoms, including sore throats, coughs and nasal congestion. They're also an excellent way to prevent dry skin and soothe tired, itchy eyes.

The JL Mistmaker comes in four vibrant colors and is not available in any stores. To order yours today for the low price of $39.99, call JL Electronics toll-free at 1-888-555-7822.

169 What is stated as a safety feature of the JL Mistmaker?

(A) Double filtering
(B) Automated shutdown
(C) Temperature regulation
(D) Waterproof casing

170 What is NOT mentioned as a benefit of humidifiers?

(A) Reducing stress
(B) Moistening skin
(C) Comforting eyes
(D) Easing coughs

171 How can a JL Mistmaker be purchased?

(A) On the Internet
(B) From wholesalers
(C) At department stores
(D) Over the phone

Questions 172-175 refer to the following notice.

Important Notification

Polk-Mathias Bank (PMB) will be undertaking its regularly scheduled weekend system maintenance beginning Friday, March 2 at 10 P.M. and finishing on Sunday, March 4 at 2 P.M. During this time, our ATMs will be functioning, but not all of their features will be available. – [1] –. It will not be possible to make ATM deposits during the entire period, and ATM balance inquiries may be periodically unavailable. – [2] –. The PMB Cyber Banking Web site will be offline briefly, from 12 A.M. to 3 A.M., in the early morning hours of Saturday, March 3. At all other times, it will be online and all of its features will be available. – [3] –. However, all PMB Mobile Banking services will be unavailable for the entire period. Finally, all types of debit card and credit card transactions will be available as usual, but balance payments will not be accepted. Polk-Mathias Bank schedules regular system maintenance in order to ensure that our customers enjoy the most secure electronic services available. – [4] –. We apologize for any inconvenience this may cause. If you have any questions, you can contact us during normal banking hours at 602-555-9542.

172 What is suggested about the maintenance?

(A) It is an unexpected event.
(B) Its pace will be accelerated.
(C) It occurs on a fixed schedule.
(D) Its starting date has been delayed.

173 What is indicated about depositing money via ATMs?

(A) It will not be affected by the maintenance.
(B) It is only permitted for a short time on March 2.
(C) It may or may not be possible over the weekend.
(D) It cannot be done during the maintenance period.

174 In which of the positions marked [1], [2], [3], and [4] does the following sentence best fit?

"However, ATM withdrawals will not be affected by the maintenance."

(A) [1]
(B) [2]
(C) [3]
(D) [4]

175 What is indicated as a limitation for credit card users?

(A) They can't pay their bills.
(B) They can't make purchases.
(C) They can't check their balances.
(D) They can't call customer service.

GO ON TO THE NEXT PAGE

Test 07

Announcement

As part of our recent acquisition of West Coast Industries, we're happy to announce that all of our full-time employees are eligible for 50% off on membership at any West Coast Health World fitness center. When registering with the health club, either online or in person, simply use the following code: BVC115. You'll find the space for this code at the bottom of the registration form. Immediate family members are also entitled to this discount, with a limit of three family members per employee. They will need to use a slightly different code: BVC115F.

Our part-time employees can enjoy a 20% discount by using BVC112, and contract workers can get 10% off on a membership by using BVC111. However, family members of part-time and contract workers are not eligible for any discounts. Please note that all application forms using these codes will be reviewed by our payroll department for approval, and we urge you not to abuse these codes. Also, the discount doesn't apply to existing memberships, but it is available upon renewal.

West Coast Health World
Registration Form

Name: Natalie Linn

Gender: Female

Age: 27

E-mail address: soccerfan97@goldpro.com
(Requested for updates and promotional material only. Will not be sold to or shared with any third parties.)

☑ New Member
☐ Renewal

Please select a membership plan.

☐ Gold Membership ($90 per month): Offers all the features of our Full Membership along with daily consultations with a personal trainer and full access to our VIP lounge.

☑ Full Membership ($50 per month): Features full access to all of our facilities, along with a free parking sticker, a gym locker and complimentary West Coast workout clothes (T-shirt and shorts).

☐ Economy Membership ($30 per month): A budget plan with access to all facilities excluding the swimming pool and sauna. Does not include locker, parking sticker or workout clothes.

☐ Pool Membership ($12 per month): Unlimited access to our Olympic-sized pool and attached changing room only.

Discount Code (if applicable): BVC115F

Date: September 8, 2017

Signature: *Natalie Linn*

176 What is the purpose of the announcement?

(A) To advertise a fitness center
(B) To clarify a registration process
(C) To announce a corporate merger
(D) To offer an employee discount

177 What is mentioned about the payroll department?

(A) It can offer more information.
(B) It has an open job position.
(C) It is moving to a new location.
(D) It will check the application forms.

178 How much will Ms. Linn pay per month for her membership?

(A) $50
(B) $45
(C) $30
(D) $25

179 What is indicated about the applicant's e-mail address?

(A) It is not a required field to fill in.
(B) It will only be used by the fitness center.
(C) It must be verified by the management.
(D) It can be replaced by a mobile phone number.

180 What is indicated as a benefit of a Gold Membership?

(A) One-on-one training advice
(B) A special discount on gym products
(C) 24-hour access to the center
(D) A VIP space in the parking lot

GO ON TO THE NEXT PAGE

GOT THE TAX BLUES?

Even under the best circumstances, filing taxes can be difficult. But sometimes it can seem as impossible as a maze without an exit. That's why Oldham, Smith, Farrell and DeSantos is now offering special consultation services. You'll get a direct one-on-one consultation with one of our tax attorneys, with unlimited post-consultation advice by phone or e-mail from our highly qualified staff, for a one-time low fee.

Wayne Oldham - Specializing in tax delinquency

Haven't been paying your taxes? We can help you rectify the situation with a minimum of penalties. Strict confidentiality guaranteed!

Lisa Smith - Specializing in small businesses

New business owners already have enough on their hands. Let us show you how to file your taxes quickly and efficiently.

Charles Farrell - Specializing in immigration issues

New arrivals to our country face special challenges when it comes to taxes. We offer translation services in Spanish, French, Korean and Japanese.

Eric DeSantos - Specializing in recent college graduates

No longer a dependent of your parents? Come to us for clear and simple guidance on how to file on your own taxes.

To get started, visit our Web site at www.osfd-law.com today!

Customer Satisfaction Survey

Please fill out the form below to let us know about your experience with Oldham, Smith, Farrell and DeSantos. There's no need to include your name, so feel free to be open and honest. This card can be mailed to our office or placed in the comment box located in our waiting room.

Was our attorney prompt, professional and polite at your initial consultation?

Yes, my meeting with your attorney went quite well. I was actually 10 minutes late for our appointment, but he assured me that it wasn't a problem.

Were all of your questions answered?

Yes. Having arrived here midway through the tax year, I wasn't sure how to report my earnings from my home country. Your attorney explained the situation clearly and provided me with the proper forms.

What was your experience with our post-consultation services?

I subsequently called your office twice for additional information, but the woman I spoke to wasn't nearly as helpful as the attorney.

Would you engage our services again in the future?

Probably not, as I now feel confident that I can handle my tax filing on my own. However, I would recommend your services to friends and colleagues.

181 What is indicated as a feature of the service?

(A) A single payment
(B) 24-hour phone lines
(C) Online conferencing
(D) A membership card

182 What does the firm promise people who have failed to pay their taxes?

(A) Zero penalties
(B) Free advice
(C) Partial refunds
(D) Total privacy

183 With whom did the client in the survey most likely meet?

(A) Wayne Oldham
(B) Lisa Smith
(C) Charles Farrell
(D) Eric DeSantos

184 What aspect of the service was the client dissatisfied with?

(A) The promptness of the attorney
(B) The procurement of needed documents
(C) The response to the follow-up questions
(D) The overall cost of the service

185 Which of the following is NOT information requested on the form?

(A) The demeanor of the attorney
(B) Whether the client's queries were answered
(C) How the client heard about the service
(D) The likelihood of using the service again

GO ON TO THE NEXT PAGE

Questions 186-190 refer to the following announcement, e-mail, and form.

Attention All Employees

Due to the unavoidable deadline extensions on the Guttenberg project that management announced last week, Human Resources is implementing a vacation blackout for the last two weeks. With the revamped project schedule, it will probably be completed by March 1. As we cannot afford another delay, we will need all hands in the office during this vital period. Normal vacation scheduling through the established channels will resume in March. We apologize for any inconvenience this may cause, and the CEO personally wishes to convey his appreciation of everyone's hard work as we strive to successfully complete this important project. If you have any questions, you may address them directly to Harold Borgia, the head of HR, at habor@JIVC.org.

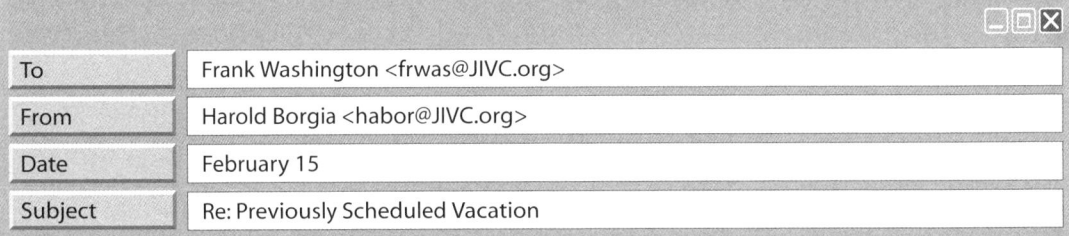

To	Frank Washington <frwas@JIVC.org>
From	Harold Borgia <habor@JIVC.org>
Date	February 15
Subject	Re: Previously Scheduled Vacation

Hello, Frank.

Thank you for bringing your situation to my attention. However, after a lengthy discussion with your supervisor, I'm afraid that I must disagree with your assertion that you are non-essential personnel in regards to the Guttenberg project.

Your programming skills are expected to play a key part in the final testing of the Web platform. I also understand that you planned your vacation quite a bit in advance and have already made some substantial non-refundable payments for travel and accommodation.

Therefore, if you can find one of your colleagues willing to take your place on the testing team, I will grant you an exception to the vacation blackout. Please note that you must resubmit your request for leave once your proposed replacement has been approved by your supervisor. I hope this compromise is to your satisfaction.

Harold Borgia
HR Director, JIVC

JIVC Vacation Request Form

Employee Name:	Frank Washington
Title and Department:	Associate Programmer, IT dept.
Extension:	ext 62
E-mail:	frwas@JIVC.org
Dates Requested:	February 17 - 21

Please check the appropriate box below:

☑ Paid leave
☐ Unpaid leave
☐ Bereavement leave
☐ Maternity/Paternity leave

Additional Comments

As per my discussion with Mr. Borgia, I'm requesting an exception to the vacation blackout. My replacement has been approved by Marcia Lopez. Thank you!

Employee Signature: *Frank Washington*

Please print out this form and return it in person to the HR office.

---

186 What is indicated as the cause of the vacation blackout?

(A) A financial crisis
(B) A new partnership
(C) A communication error
(D) An unexpected delay

187 In the e-mail, the word "note" in paragraph 3, line 2, is closest in meaning to

(A) write down
(B) count on
(C) be aware of
(D) turn off

188 What is Mr. Washington's role in the Guttenberg project?

(A) Data entry
(B) Online testing
(C) Deadline scheduling
(D) Software procurement

189 Why did Mr. Washington request an exemption to the vacation blackout?

(A) He has completed his part of the project.
(B) He was never informed of the blackout.
(C) He already paid for his planned vacation.
(D) He wants to telecommute from home.

190 Who most likely is Marcia Lopez?

(A) A human resources employee
(B) Mr. Washington's replacement
(C) Mr. Washington's supervisor
(D) The company's CEO

GO ON TO THE NEXT PAGE

Grant Automotive Strikes Deal with Lyssa

Local parts manufacturer Grant Automotive today announced a landmark deal with Lyssa Motors to supply the Italian car manufacturer with keyless ignition systems for both the Regal sedan and the SX5—the latest in their line of luxury SUVs, which will replace the popular Starion model. The contract is estimated to be valued in the millions and will likely have a favorable effect on the local economy by generating new jobs and subcontracting opportunities. The initial agreement is for one year, with an option for three six-month extensions. Grant Automotive was established in 1965, originally supplying automobile manufacturers with metal parts before branching out into electronics and computer systems. Lyssa is the fifth-largest automobile manufacturer in Europe, and is known for its powerful engines and attention to detail.

CAR WORLD – AUTOMOBILE REVIEWS IN BRIEF

Make: Lyssa

Model: SX5

Verdict: Luxurious but Problematic

The SX5 is Lyssa's latest high-end SUV offering, and as you would expect from a company with a reputation for unbridled luxury, the vehicle is packed with the kind of nifty gadgets and welcome conveniences that make driving a special experience, while also offering decent gas mileage. Featuring the same voice-activated climate control system and adjustable cup holders as the sporty V15 model, the SX5 is clearly designed with both drivers and passengers in mind. It is not, however, without its flaws. The unconventional L5 suspension system, first introduced last year with the SX5's predecessor, makes for a bumpy ride, and the electronic ignition system is less dependable than one would hope, often requiring several attempts before the engine actually starts. Considering the SX5's eyebrow-raising price tag, you would expect better.

March 24, 2017

Richard Lewis
CEO, Grant Automotive
1771 Industrial Avenue
Watertown, WI 53094

Dear Mr. Lewis:

This letter is to inform you of the decision of Lyssa Motors Ltd. to officially decline the second and third options to extend our contract for the provision of electronic ignition systems. In short, we are not fully satisfied with the performance of your product, and neither are consumers, based on the results of our intensive customer surveys. This information has repeatedly been conveyed to your staff, most recently in a video conference call with your sales representatives, but we have had no indication that any changes have been made on your end to address our concerns. Although we will continue to uphold our end of the deal for the remainder of the original contract and upcoming option, I have instructed our procurement department to begin the process of finding a new supplier.

Sincerely,

Marianne Pellegrino
Chief Operating Officer
Lyssa Motors Ltd.

191 What is the article mainly about?

(A) The opening of a new manufacturing plant
(B) The purchase of a fleet of automobiles
(C) A lucrative deal for a local company
(D) An international business merger

192 Which model was the first to use the L5 suspension system?

(A) The SX5
(B) The V15
(C) The Regal
(D) The Starion

193 What is NOT a criticism of the SX5 in the review?

(A) It costs too much.
(B) It does not start reliably.
(C) It does not drive smoothly.
(D) It consumes too much gas.

194 According to the letter, what is indicated as the source of Lyssa's dissatisfaction?

(A) The terms of the original contract
(B) The cost of shipping and handling
(C) The quality of the purchased part
(D) The number of parts provided

195 How long will the Grant-Lyssa contract have lasted when it is terminated?

(A) 6 months
(B) 12 months
(C) 18 months
(D) 24 months

GO ON TO THE NEXT PAGE

Questions 196-200 refer to the following e-mail, letter, and schedule.

To:	Langston Cole <langston@alpine.net>
From:	Ian McDonald <ian_mcdonald@chc.com>
Date:	November 12
Subject:	Proposed Schedule

Hello, Langston.

It looks like we've run into a bit of a snag. We received your proposed construction schedule for the Fairview development, and management is not satisfied with it. Either my manager, Tom Gustin, or one of our project coordinators will be formally contacting your boss in a day or so, but I just wanted to give you a heads-up about the specific problems.

The first is the long delay between the scheduled delivery of the plumbing and wiring components and the beginning of the installation process. They want to know what kind of storage will be in place to prevent potential weather damage during the ten days between delivery and installation. The second is the weeklong break in the middle of the project, which was neither previously mentioned nor approved. And finally, the opening ceremony is meant to occur on the first of August, but your final day of construction is scheduled later than that. I hope your company is flexible with the schedule so that we can find some middle ground.

Ian

November 18, 2017

Kimberly Adams
Colorado Housing Corporation
61 White Creek Lane
Liston, CO 80013

Dear Ms. Adams:

In response to your letter dated November 13 regarding the Fairview housing development, I can offer the following solutions. First of all, accommodating your plans to hold the opening ceremony on August 1 is not a problem. We can simply condense our final inspection process from six to three days. As for the plumbing and wiring components, there are no on-site storage facilities— materials waiting to be used are simply covered by waterproof tarps. While we are unable to alter the scheduled installation starting date of July 1 for the components in question, we can, with your approval, change their delivery date. Finally, the mid-project break is non-negotiable. It is union mandated and set to coincide with the time required for the concrete foundations to dry and set.

Sincerely,

Salvatore Underwood
Alpine Construction

Fairview Housing Development – Final Construction Schedule

Date	Task	Date	Task
3/18 to 4/19	Leveling and preparation of the site	6/28	Delivery of plumbing and wiring components
4/20 to 4/22	Application of concrete for foundations	7/1 to 7/15	Installation of plumbing and wiring components
4/23 to 4/30	Break period	7/15 to 7/28	Interior and exterior finishing touches
5/1 to 6/30	General construction of building frames	7/29 to 7/31	Final inspection

196 What is the purpose of the e-mail?

(A) To apologize for a delay in a schedule
(B) To notify someone of an upcoming ceremony
(C) To complain about faulty construction
(D) To warn someone about a potential problem

197 Who most likely is Kimberly Adams?

(A) Ian McDonald's manager
(B) Tom Gustin's boss
(C) A building inspector
(D) A project coordinator

198 What was the delivery date for plumbing and wiring components in the original schedule?

(A) June 1
(B) June 21
(C) June 30
(D) July 1

199 What does Mr. Underwood say about the weeklong break?

(A) It will be shortened.
(B) It will be pushed back.
(C) It cannot be changed.
(D) It does not apply to this project.

200 What was the final date of construction in the original schedule?

(A) July 29
(B) July 30
(C) August 2
(D) August 3

잠깐!!
시작 전 꼭 확인하세요!

☑ 실제 시험과 같이
   책상을 정리하고
   마음의 준비를 하세요.

☑ 핸드폰은 잠깐 끄고
   대신 아날로그 시계를
   활용해 보세요.

☑ 권장 풀이 시간은 55분입니다.
   시간을 꼭 지켜주세요.

☑ 어렵다고 넘어가지 마세요.
   가능하면 차례대로 풀어 보세요.

Actual Test

08

시작 시간   :

종료 시간   :

PART 7

Directions: In this part you will read a selection of texts, such as magazine and newspaper articles, e-mails, and instant messages. Each text or set of texts is followed by several questions. Select the best answer for each question and mark the letter (A), (B), (C), or (D) on your answer sheet.

Questions 147-148 refer to the following Web page.

www.realtimeedu.com

| HOME | CURRICULA | NOTICE | REGISTRATION |

Real-time lectures for the hearing-impaired are now available online. Those who are hard of hearing will be able to read what the professor is saying on their notebook computers. Classroom helpers will type what the professors are saying during the lecture so you can read their words. Moreover, the actual lecturing scene will be shown next to the real-time lecture scripts, so you will be getting the same content of lectures as the rest of your classmates. Just follow the directions below to access the real-time lecture note Web page.

1. Go to the university's main Web site.
2. Click on "Real-Time Lectures."
3. To access our online archives, you need to log in by
   a. Typing in your student ID.
   b. Entering your specified password.
4. Click the title of your course, and enjoy studying with your classmates.

147 Who is this information intended for?

(A) Applicants for classroom helpers
(B) Web designers
(C) Students with disabilities
(D) Professors who teach online

148 What is implied about the "Real-Time Lectures?"

(A) They are for students who are sick at home.
(B) The lectures can be stored on computers.
(C) Printed scripts are handed out right after class.
(D) Logging in is necessary for access.

PARTY MANIACS!

PARTY LIKE THERE IS NO TOMORROW!

Party Maniacs takes pride in providing our customers with the best atmosphere for all kinds of anniversaries with just the right setting that you have been dreaming of. We specialize in making and creating customized decorations and settings which will suit your event. Whether it is for a member of your family, a friend or a coworker, or even just for the sake of making a boring day into an exciting one, we will be there to set the tone.

That is not all! We are also capable of putting on elegant events and can add some fun to those events as well with great bands and customized ice sculptures. Any party can have a swan or an angel sculpture, but we can make any shape of your choice with class.

To organize a party with us, please call 201-555-9645. We are open from 9 A.M. to 7 P.M., Monday to Friday. On Saturdays, we are open from 9 A.M. to 3 P.M.

149 What kind of company most likely is Party Maniacs?

(A) A hotel
(B) A veterinary hospital
(C) A catering service
(D) An event management company

150 According to the advertisement, what can customers be offered?

(A) Party food for pets
(B) Traditional food
(C) Personalized items
(D) Group discounts

GO ON TO THE NEXT PAGE

City Bikers
Pedal across Washington!

City Bikers is happy to announce that the 11th annual Cross-State Bike Race is set to begin on April 17th. The starting point will be Seattle, and the destination will be Pullman.

- Participants must submit their registration fees by April 1st.
- Since it is such a long race, certification of health is required.
- Escorting cars and safety agents will be provided.
- Temporary accommodations will be available every evening.
- The entrance fee is $200. Sleeping bags, drinking water, and snacks as well as accommodations are included in the fee.
- Returning participants from last year are eligible for a $35 rebate after the event.
- Prizes will be given to the first five arriving participants. Other participants will also receive medals.

City Bikers is proud to announce that there have been no big accidents for the last decade, and we would like to keep the record as it is. Moreover, 11% of the entrance fee will be donated to the Heart-to-Heart Children's Foundation, so join a refreshing spring bike ride for a good cause.

151 What is the notice about?

(A) Motor insurance
(B) An annual competition
(C) Attracting sponsors
(D) Bike sales

152 What is NOT indicated about the event?

(A) Refunds are not possible after registration.
(B) The final destination is Pullman.
(C) Some of the money raised will be donated to a charitable organization.
(D) Water and snacks are included in the fee.

Questions 153-154 refer to the following text message chain.

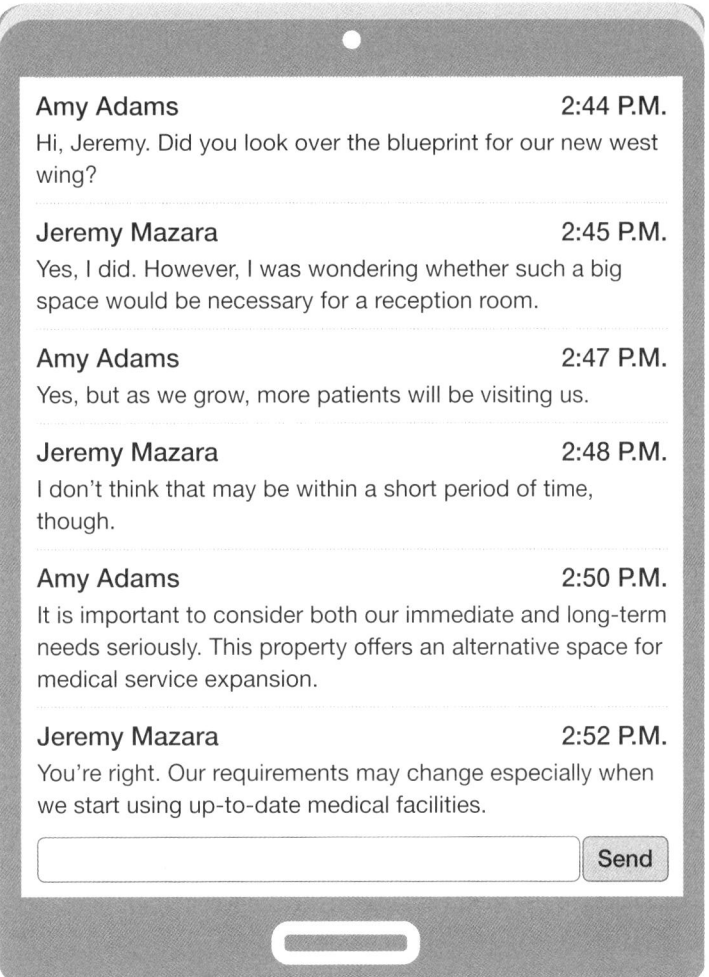

Amy Adams   2:44 P.M.

Hi, Jeremy. Did you look over the blueprint for our new west wing?

Jeremy Mazara   2:45 P.M.

Yes, I did. However, I was wondering whether such a big space would be necessary for a reception room.

Amy Adams   2:47 P.M.

Yes, but as we grow, more patients will be visiting us.

Jeremy Mazara   2:48 P.M.

I don't think that may be within a short period of time, though.

Amy Adams   2:50 P.M.

It is important to consider both our immediate and long-term needs seriously. This property offers an alternative space for medical service expansion.

Jeremy Mazara   2:52 P.M.

You're right. Our requirements may change especially when we start using up-to-date medical facilities.

Send

153 At what kind of business does Ms. Adams most likely work?

(A) A medical clinic
(B) A construction company
(C) A real estate agency
(D) A local manufacturer

154 At 2:52 P.M., what does Mr. Mazara most likely mean when he writes, "You're right"?

(A) Medical equipment should be rented.
(B) A new service will be too expensive.
(C) The property may suit the future needs.
(D) The building needs structural renovations.

GO ON TO THE NEXT PAGE

Pamela Reeves
298 Eastwood Avenue
Kansas City, KS 66104

Dear Ms. Reeves:

We would like to show you our appreciation for choosing AllWays Telecom as your mobile telephone service provider for the next 24 months. We promise you the clearest quality and the most current technology in the country. This letter is meant to validate your contract with us. – [1] –. Your personal identification number and a copy of the contract are enclosed with this letter.

As a part of AllWays Telecom's services, we provide you a membership card. The moment you have signed your contract, a membership is automatically issued. – [2] –. If you wish to receive the membership card more quickly, you can register online and pick it up at any of our stores. Benefits of the membership card are written in detail on the back of this letter.

Along with the membership benefits, you can enjoy a variety of convenient features such as caller ID, spam message reports, and roaming services without any extra charges. – [3] –. We also provides premium services such as navigation with real-time traffic reports, ringtones, and Internet access.

We are committed to providing our customers with the best service, anytime and anywhere. To contact our 24-hour customer service department, please call 1-800-555-0058. – [4] –. To make adjustments to any of your information, you can use the online services or call the service call center.

Sincerely,

Tom Bradshaw
Manager of Customer Relations

155 What is indicated as a benefit that AllWays Telecom provides?

(A) It supports fees when changing your phone number.
(B) Internet access is free for the first three months.
(C) A customer can get a discount on a membership card.
(D) Caller ID services are free of charge.

156 What is suggested about the customer service call center?

(A) Calls from other countries are free.
(B) It provides real-time traffic reports.
(C) It is always open.
(D) It has offline stores.

157 In which of the positions marked [1], [2], [3], and [4] does the following sentence best belong?

"However, it takes about two weeks for it to get processed and will be sent to you by mail."

(A) [1]
(B) [2]
(C) [3]
(D) [4]

GO ON TO THE NEXT PAGE

Questions 158-160 refer to the following information.

WESTSIDE MEDIA ASSOCIATION
THE INTERNATIONAL EXHIBITION CENTER
SAN JOSE

Date: December 20

Place: Jefferson Hall

Time: 10 A.M. – 4 P.M.

The information of the seminars is as followed. Seminars also offer information and application forms for internships.

Alice Cooper San Jose News	**What makes a station work** Alice Cooper has been the morning news anchor at the San Jose News for three years. She also served as a reporter at the San Jose News for five years before she became an anchor.
Sam Gladwell CNC 10 Radio	**Being "the" person** Sam Gladwell joined CNC 10 Radio in 2007, and prior to that he was a producer of CNC's hit morning show, "How Are You This Morning?" for ten years. He is now general manager of the country's most popular radio station.
Nicole Park ABN Media	**How to put ideas on TV** Nicole Park has worked her way up from a writer to a main producer at ABN Media. She is also known as an innovative producer who makes original programs and sells them all over the world.
Sandra Fernandes Monterey Media	**More types of jobs that you didn't know of** Sandra Fernandes is the CEO of Monterey Media and has helped launch one of the most popular local radio stations, Party FM 106.9.

---

158 What is indicated in the information?

(A) The capacity of Jefferson Hall

(B) The location of the application forms

(C) Topics of the seminars

(D) Representative programs of the San Jose News

159 Which speaker has experience as a writer?

(A) Alice Cooper

(B) Sam Gladwell

(C) Nicole Park

(D) Sandra Fernandes

160 Which job position do Sam and Nicole have in common?

(A) Anchor

(B) CEO

(C) Reporter

(D) Producer

Hermes's Delivery Service (HDS)

Hermes's Delivery Service is now equipped with a nationwide network. We have made a contract with Eagle Airlines and Global Airlines, making it possible to reach every nation in one day. The outcome of this contract will definitely put HDS at the top of the competition not only in the U.S., but globally. We have increased our speed, but other strengths such as our computerized system, safe packaging, and reliable delivery services are still with us. Moreover, we will provide all deliveries at a special fee.

To use our services, please call our central number, 1-800-555-8767. Our operators will connect you to the nearest branch. You can also place an order online at our Web site, www.hds.com. Whether by phone or online, orders received before noon are guaranteed to be delivered the very day. Orders received after 5 P.M. are guaranteed to be picked up on that very day and delivered the next day.

Compensations: HDS promises to make all deliveries within 24 hours. Furthermore, we will do our best to deliver the contents as safely as possible. If our services have not fulfilled your expectations, we will willingly compensate you for any inconvenience. However, delivery delay and package damage by natural disasters will not be subject to compensation.

161 Why was the notice written?

(A) To declare a bankruptcy
(B) To notify customers of a new service
(C) To announce a new contract
(D) To explain the process of usage

162 What is NOT mentioned as one of HDS's advantages?

(A) Online order discounts
(B) Worldwide network
(C) High-tech system
(D) Careful packaging

163 What is indicated about HDS's compensation policy?

(A) Package damage from storms will be fully refunded.
(B) Compensation should be paid within 24 hours.
(C) Complaints are accepted only online.
(D) Late deliveries will be subject to compensation.

GO ON TO THE NEXT PAGE

The Daily Economist

SLU Steels Quarterly Financial Report

London (April 19) — Luke Fisher, the CFO of SLU Steels, reported today that the firm's earnings for the year's first quarter have preceded last year's earning rate by 7%. This is a shocking outcome considering the current state of the market. – [1] –. Mr. Fisher has also applied the company's balance sheet showing the graph of the red arrow slowly but steadily going up. This result is an expected result from the alliance of SLU Steels with Rockport Steels (USA) last December. – [2] –. By creating a closer alliance, the two companies aim to strengthen their business of supplying high-grade products to automakers and shipbuilders.

Mr. Fisher told the press that SLU Steels will seek other ways to keep the red arrow from coming down. SLU Steels has been a driving force in England's economic growth since the 1970s as a key supplier of basic industries. – [3] –. It has gone beyond strengthening the basis, and is now going a step further with its focus shifted to new technology development for the purpose of leading the rapidly changing global steel industry.

Mr. Fisher declared that for the next few years, the company will concentrate mainly on technology and product diversification. There are only a few steelmakers in the world, including SLU Steels, but that doesn't mean the competition is any weaker than in other markets. – [4] –. Mr. Fisher mentioned that SLU Steels still seeks the top spot in the steel industry and will pull up the nation's economy.

---

164 What is the purpose of this article?

(A) To state the firm's financial performance
(B) To announce a merger
(C) To introduce the firm's new product
(D) To accuse a firm for an illegal act

165 In which of the positions marked [1], [2], [3], and [4] does the following sentence best belong?

"Both companies have made a deal to buy additional shares in each other to counterbalance challenges stemming from consolidation in the steel industry."

(A) [1]
(B) [2]
(C) [3]
(D) [4]

166 What has boosted the growth of SLU Steels?

(A) Development of a new material
(B) Increase in market share
(C) Good investment in stocks
(D) Union with another company

167 What is NOT suggested about SLU Steels?

(A) Its earning rate is going up.
(B) It plans to respond to changes in the industry.
(C) It is now the most powerful steel company in the world.
(D) It has taken a leading role in economic growth since the 1970s.

Questions 168-171 refer to the following online chat discussion.

Nathaly Thibault [11:15 A.M.]   Hi, all. Thanks for participating in the online discussion. Before our next meeting, I would like to share some information about how the preparation for the event is going. Michael, is there something new?

Michael Stuhlbarg [11:16 A.M.]   Yes, I have great news. The local Chamber of Commerce finally allowed us to hold the job fair at City Hall!

Bo-Hee Park [11:17 A.M.]   How amazing!

Kenneth Valade [11:18 A.M.]   That's great news! I was worried about it.

Michael Stuhlbarg [11:19 A.M.]   I informed them that we planned to give local companies priorities to participate in the event. That convinced them.

Nathaly Thibault [11:20 A.M.]   Oh, great! Any other news?

Bo-Hee Park [11:21 A.M.]   King Steel Industries has already agreed to set up 3 booths at the fair. I am also making several calls to other local companies. I will try to have responses from other entries by Friday at the latest.

Kenneth Valade [11:22 A.M.]   I'm still getting more suitable lecturers for workshops we are planning in the event. Shawn Levy has tentatively agreed to lead a lecture, "How to Interact."

Nathaly Thibault [11:23 A.M.]   That would be great. I know that he is a famous professional in this field.

Send

---

168 What are the writers discussing?

(A) A local company
(B) An exposition
(C) A lecture
(D) A public institution

169 At 11:18 A.M., what does Mr. Valade most likely mean when he writes, "I was worried about it"?

(A) He did not think the proposal would be approved.
(B) He did not think the institution would attend the event.
(C) He thought the meeting would be canceled.
(D) He thought the local entrepreneur would be left out.

170 What is Ms. Park expecting?

(A) A notice about a permit
(B) A response from a lecturer
(C) Changes in the plan
(D) Replies from several businesses

171 Who most likely is Mr. Levy?

(A) A new official
(B) A speaker
(C) An event organizer
(D) A panelist

GO ON TO THE NEXT PAGE

Emily Mills
Chief Executive Officer
PSI International Co.

Dear Ms. Mills:

We would like to show sincere gratitude for your company's generous donations to our organization over the past several years in which you have regularly supported us both materially and morally.

At the beginning of the fundraising, many of our staff members felt that we had set the goal too high, at $1,000,000. But as I have mentioned to you before, this goal is not just a number that has come up in my mind, but the actual amount of money needed to construct a hospital for premature babies and their mothers along with providing them with basic needs such as nutrition and vaccinations. But to our surprise, many have given attention to our cause and have helped us reach that goal.

What adds more to our appreciation is the enthusiasm of your employees. We were deeply touched as we saw the 2,000 hand-knitted hats that your employees had sent us. The hats are still being sent to our headquarters, and we can never thank you enough. Moreover, the clothes and sneakers that your employees have gathered from your own charity fair for us have been sent to the children of Ethiopia. We have received pictures and video clips of the Ethiopian children showing their joy about these gifts. I'll email them to you soon.

More than 50 companies have devoted their time and resources to this fundraiser, making it possible for us to reach the goal and more. This has shown us that we can hope for a brighter future.

We will keep updating you on how you have helped to make this world a better place.

Sincerely,

Samuel Tucker
Fundraising Chair
No More Tears in Africa (NMTA)

172 Why did Mr. Tucker send this letter to Ms. Mills?

(A) To request the date for a fundraiser
(B) To apply for a loan
(C) To ask for a donation
(D) To express appreciation for support

173 What does the NMTA intend to use the money for?

(A) Giving scholarships to children
(B) Building a facility
(C) Buying hats
(D) Renting a place for a fundraiser

174 What was sent to the children of Ethiopia?

(A) Schoolbags
(B) Badges
(C) Caps
(D) Shoes

175 What is NOT true about the fundraiser?

(A) More than 50 companies have participated in it.
(B) Donations of $1 million have been made.
(C) It received goods from PSI International.
(D) It was not able to raise funds to match the initial projection.

GO ON TO THE NEXT PAGE

Web Designer Positions Open at Dreamwebs

June 23rd

Dreamwebs is a newly emerging but fast-growing company. We offer a wide selection of professional Web designs. We have a short history but a long list of satisfied customers, and we expect to continue to give our best to our clients.

We are currently expanding our office in order to meet the rising demands for our services. As a result, we are seeking an experienced or a very talented Web designer. A Web designer is mainly responsible for making our customers satisfied by providing them with a high-quality Web site. So Web designers are expected to be competent to fulfill the needs of clients as well as be sensitive and willing to listen to them. For more specific information about this job position, please visit our Web site.

Interested parties should forward to our company via email a portfolio, a résumé, and a cover letter explaining their interest, highlighting their Web-designing experience and outlining their expectations of job conditions. Online home pages will also be accepted as a portfolio. However, we cannot respond to every application submitted. Those who pass the initial screening process will be contacted approximately a week before the interview. If you have any questions, please contact our Human Resources department.

www.dreamwebsdesign.com/news/jobopening

| Home | Service | News | Q&A |

We are looking for outstanding individuals working together.

Tasks for the position include but are not limited to:
- Creating portfolios and designs for clients' selection.
- Working as a team player on big projects.
- Close adherence to clients' needs and creating professional Web sites.
- Being in charge of communicating with clients and offering the best design that satisfies the clients and the designer him/herself.
- Venturing new design ideas for future business projects.

This position is open to anyone who possesses a bachelor of arts degree in computer design or a related field. At least three years of prior experience is preferred but those who believe they are especially talented may also apply. Interested candidates should be able to come up with a sketch in a reasonable time and be able to plan a timetable and uphold that schedule in executing that sketch to a full design. Excellent communication skills are also needed to guide customers to see your vision.

* If you need more information, you can get in touch with the hiring manager, Mr. Gray, at 403-555-0132.

176 What is indicated about Dreamwebs?

(A) It is the top designing company in the market.
(B) It is relocating to a new location.
(C) Its customer base is increasing.
(D) It has recently lost a lot of designers.

177 What are those interested in the position guided to do?

(A) Submit a cover letter stressing their job experiences
(B) Upload résumés on their home pages
(C) Create a Web design for the company and upload it
(D) Wait one month until an interview can be arranged

178 What is NOT a responsibility of the advertised position?

(A) Cooperate with the colleagues
(B) Get the work done on time
(C) Draw up a variety of draft designs
(D) Manage the clients' data

179 In the Web page, the word "reasonable" in paragraph 2, line 4, is closest in meaning to

(A) irrational
(B) modern
(C) practical
(D) unfair

180 Which of the following can the applicants NOT use to apply for the job?

(A) Mail
(B) E-mail
(C) Web site
(D) Telephone

GO ON TO THE NEXT PAGE

Test 08

DAN'S OFFICE SUPPLIES

Don't miss this chance!

Work easier than others!

Try the Neo-Tech EZ77 Mouse!

And now it's on sale!

$79.99 → $36.99

Order now, and it ships to anywhere you are.

Plus, there is no need to pay all taxes, shipping, and handling costs!

It is an opportunity of a "work time"; this special offer is a one-time-only event, so take a closer look! The Neo-Tech EZ77 Mouse has been selling like hotcakes! We are so overwhelmed by the attention that we are giving back the love to you at a very low price. This revolutionary product is made from eco-friendly material and is customized to fit a natural human hand grip. It is available in a wide variety of colors, so hurry to get the color of your choice. To make an order, call 1-558-555-1346 or go to our Web site, http://www.dansofficesupplies.com, where you can get a 10% accumulated point when you register as a member.

To whom it may concern:

Hello. My name is Brandon Perry, and I recently purchased (on September 6/received: September 8) a Neo-Tech EZ77 Mouse. I have a question about the purchase fee. In your advertisement, it clearly stated that all taxes, shipping and handling costs will not be charged. However, when the product arrived, the receipt definitely included shipping fees ($7).

So on September 8, I made a call to your service center. After being put on hold for 15 minutes, I was finally connected to a staff member. I told the representative my problem, and she said that she would look into it and give me a call. So I left her my contact information. But I received no answer from anyone in your company. So, I made another call 2 days later, but the same thing had happened again! I had specifically told the service person that the previous person had forgotten to give me a call.

I would very much like an explanation about how this could happen, as well as how the shipping fee was unreasonably charged. If the problem is not solved within 3 days, I intend to report your business to the local Consumer Services Bureau. Moreover, I will upload this letter on your Web site.

Sincerely,

Brandon Perry

181 Why has the price of the mouse been reduced?

(A) The model has been upgraded.
(B) The manufacturing company has lowered the price.
(C) The mouse has given the company a great profit.
(D) The supplier has promoted a new technology.

182 In the advertisement, the word "available" in paragraph 1, line 5, is closest in meaning to

(A) useful
(B) free
(C) accessible
(D) familiar

183 What is the purpose of the letter?

(A) To request information
(B) To inquire about bulk purchases
(C) To express gratitude for quick service
(D) To ask about a staff member

184 How much was Mr. Perry charged?

(A) $36.99
(B) $43.99
(C) $79.99
(D) $86.99

185 What can NOT be inferred about Mr. Perry?

(A) On the day of delivery, he spoke to a staff member.
(B) He has seen the advertisement of the product before.
(C) Taxes have been charged to him.
(D) He made a call to the center on September 10 again.

GO ON TO THE NEXT PAGE

To: Universal Garden Spa
From: Amy Bates, Leisure Town Inc.
Date: December 7

Leisure Town Inc. is delighted to announce that our acquisition of Universal Garden Spa has been finalized. We have already taken over the management and are now fully responsible for everything related to Universal Garden Spa. We very much look forward to continuing a productive business relationship with all of our members. If you need some help, you can contact representatives listed on an enclosed sheet.

The following is a list of contacts for the significant people within our company:

Personnel Department
Human resources manager, Ms. Stella Stone <stellastone@leisuretown.com>

Service Maintenance
Maintenance supervisor, Mr. Nolan Dean <n_dean@leisuretown.com>

Facility Maintenance
Facility service coordinator, Mr. Lucas Barnes <lucasrepairs@leisuretown.com>

Technical Maintenance
Technical service coordinator, Mr. Dylan West <techdylan@leisuretown.com>

Office Management
Office operations manager, Ms. Amy Bates <abates@leisuretown.com>

Leisure Town Inc.
1-555-8520

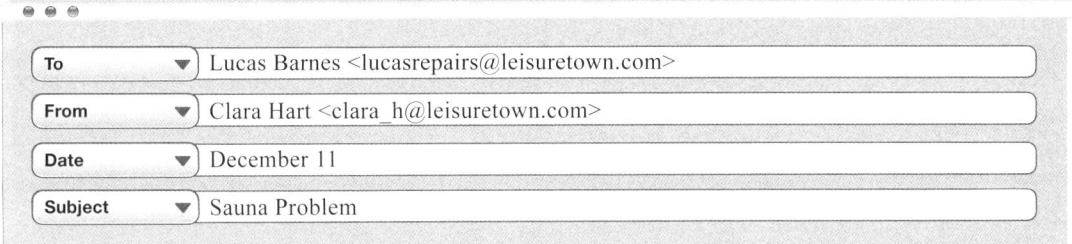

To ▼ Lucas Barnes <lucasrepairs@leisuretown.com>

From ▼ Clara Hart <clara_h@leisuretown.com>

Date ▼ December 11

Subject ▼ Sauna Problem

Hello. My name is Clara Hart, and I work at the front desk at the Japanese garden spa section of Universal Garden Spa. Lately I have been receiving complaints about one of the saunas in the spa. The customers have said that the temperature is not high enough but the humidity is too dense. I have checked the sauna, and the actual temperature doesn't go above 60 degrees Celsius, while the indicated temperature is 77 degrees Celsius. Also, one of the ventilating fans has stopped. I think that this is the cause of the density problem. The sauna is closed for now but it needs to be fixed fast because it is an essential facility for the spa. Please let me know when it can be fixed.

Sincerely,

Clara Hart

186 What kind of business is Leisure Town Incorporated in?

(A) It trains professional massage therapists.

(B) It provides consulting to companies.

(C) It introduces suitable people to open positions.

(D) It manages spa facilities.

187 What is stated in the memo?

(A) Universal Garden Spa will be raising its membership fees.

(B) Individuals of expertise may be contacted for aid.

(C) Universal Garden Spa will be put up for auction.

(D) Workforce reduction will be carried out soon.

188 Which department is Ms. Hart contacting?

(A) Facility Maintenance

(B) Personnel Department

(C) Office Management

(D) Technical Maintenance

189 Why did Ms. Hart write the e-mail?

(A) To apply for a job

(B) To inquire about the user charge for the spa

(C) To report a problem

(D) To conduct an inspection

190 In the e-mail, the word "dense" in paragraph 1, line 4, is closest in meaning to

(A) light

(B) rough

(C) thick

(D) loose

GO ON TO THE NEXT PAGE

Questions 191-195 refer to the following e-mail, memo, and guideline.

To	Lydia Holmes <lydiah@smithandgrant.com>
From	Jack Grant <jg1970@smithandgrant.com>
Date	June 8
Subject	E-mail Usage

Dear Lydia:

I believe that it is time to remind the employees of our company's protocol for the use of e-mail. While I do trust that the employees use e-mail properly most of the time, I also think that e-mails are not only used for business.

So to refresh the memories of our original staff members and enlighten new employees, an announcement of the e-mail protocol is necessary. Smith & Grant Co. acknowledges that the use of e-mail is an essential tool for business. However, misuse of this tool can have a negative impact upon the reputation of the business.

While I want to make sure our staff members have a clear understanding of what kind of e-mail is appropriate or not, I do not want them to feel that they are being strictly regulated. So I would appreciate it if you would make a memo for the staff members to see on my behalf. Please complete it as soon as possible, and I hope the policy will be announced in about a week.

Thanks in advance.

Jack Grant
Smith & Grant Co.

Memo

Dear staff,

This is about our current e-mail use policy. Please take time to read and familiarize yourself with the protocol for e-mail usage, for our company's safety and yours.

Do not misunderstand this memo as a warning. Use of e-mail is affirmatively permitted and supported wherever such use holds the goals and objectives for the benefit of the business. However, we have a policy that we would like all employees to be aware of. Therefore, you should download guidelines for the policy on our website, display them on your desk and keep checking them.

Lydia Holmes

E-mail Use Policy

Make sure that your e-mails:
- follow the current legislation
- are used in a tolerable manner
- don't misuse the Internet

Unacceptable usage

1. Being in possession or spreading of images, text or materials that have the possibility of being indecent or illegal
2. Inserting any form of computer virus into the corporate network
3. Using e-mail and Internet for personal business
4. Using passwords or mailboxes that are not permitted
5. Violating copyright
6. Undertaking deliberate activities that can squander staff work or networked resources
7. Sending out unsolicited commercial or advertising material
8. Personal attacks or threats by sending offensive, discriminatory or abusive text

Monitoring

Please be aware that the company's e-mail resources are provided only for business purposes. Therefore, the company has the right to examine and inspect any data recorded in the system. In order to carry out this policy, Smith & Grant Co. also holds the right to use monitoring software to look into the use and content of e-mails. Such monitoring is for legitimate purposes only and will be implemented in accordance with a process agreed to by employees.

---

191 According to the e-mail, what does Mr. Grant want Ms. Holmes to do?

(A) Send out guidelines
(B) Find software that monitors e-mails
(C) Make a proposal for a policy
(D) Monitor compliance with a policy

192 In the e-mail, the word "enlighten" in paragraph 2, line 1, is closest in meaning to

(A) recruit
(B) instruct
(C) help
(D) illuminate

193 What is indicated about the e-mail use policy?

(A) It was attached to the memo sent by Ms. Holmes.
(B) It needs to be updated.
(C) Attachments will be limited to a certain volume.
(D) It was probably announced in the middle of June.

194 What is NOT considered a violation of e-mail use?

(A) Using e-mail for employees' personal purpose
(B) Sending racist text
(C) Spreading illegal images
(D) Exchanging files between coworkers

195 What is mentioned about e-mail monitoring?

(A) The company will perform a monthly inspection.
(B) The company has the authority to monitor e-mails.
(C) The inspection process will be done by the CEO.
(D) An employee with inappropriate data will be fired.

GO ON TO THE NEXT PAGE

Questions **196-200** refer to the following e-mails and information.

To	Dan Parker <d_parker@quadtech.com>
From	Lucy Morris <lucym@quadtech.com>
Date	June 19
Subject	Train Reservation
Attachment	Schedule.doc

Dear Dan:

Earlier today you told me that you would be going to New York by train. So I have attached the schedule for trains coming out of Maine to New York on July 2, and trains returning from New York to Maine on July 6. There's an option of an express train or a regular train. The "XAT" is speedier and more comfortable train, for as I have heard, it has a little more space between the seats. However, half of the seats for "XAT" are reversed, so if you are sensitive to the direction of your ride you might have to think about choosing this option, because the seats are randomly assigned. So give it some thought, check the departing times and let me know your choices at your earliest convenience. I will then set things up for you.

One more thing. Would Ms. Turner also be going to New York? I heard that she was thinking about going to the "World Traffic Forum" that you are attending, but she is currently on a business trip to India and cannot be reached. So I was wondering whether she had mentioned anything to you. Should I reserve train tickets for her for the same dates and times?

Sincerely,

Lucy Morris

Schedule

Date	July 2			
Train Number	X214 (XAT)	A5678 (Regular)	A9521 (Regular)	X271 (XAT)
Depart: Maine	10:15 A.M.	12:05 P.M.	2:30 P.M.	4:50 P.M.
Arrive: New York	12:35 P.M.	3:35 P.M.	6:00 P.M.	7:10 P.M.

Date	July 6			
Train Number	A7412 (Regular)	X214 (XAT)	A5641 (Regular)	X804 (XAT)
Depart: New York	9:20 A.M.	11:55 A.M.	3:45 P.M.	6:20 P.M.
Arrive: Maine	12:50 P.M.	2:15 P.M.	7:15 P.M.	8:50 P.M.

* If you have any questions, feel free to email me anytime.

To:	Lucy Morris <lucym@quadtech.com>
From:	Dan Parker <d_parker@quadtech.com>
Date:	June 21
Subject:	Re: Train Reservation

Thank you for the attachment. I need to get to New York on July 2 because the forum begins on July 3. So I think I'll take the last train. I have no problem with carsickness so the direction does not matter. On July 6, the closing ceremony for the forum ends at 2 P.M., so the best option for me is probably the A5641 (Regular) 3:45 P.M. train. And yes, Lily Turner is to attend the forum with me so you should reserve her tickets as well. Just reserve the same tickets as mine.

I have one more favor to ask of you. Can you also reserve hotel rooms for me and Lily? We would like to stay at the Richmond Hotel, which is near the Jefferson Convention Center where the forum is held. Please reserve two single rooms for four nights. And also inform the hotel that we would be checking in late on July 2.

Thank you so much. I really appreciate your efforts.

Sincerely,

Dan Parker

196 Why did Ms. Morris send the e-mail to Mr. Parker?

(A) To suggest that he accompany her on his trip
(B) To request a changed schedule
(C) To introduce a more comfortable train
(D) To notify him of the transportation schedule

197 What is indicated about the "XAT" train?

(A) The seats are all backwards.
(B) The ticket prices are expensive.
(C) It offers extra space.
(D) The seats are selected by passengers.

198 Why does Ms. Morris ask Mr. Parker about Ms. Turner?

(A) Ms. Turner cannot be reached.
(B) Ms. Turner is Mr. Parker's assistant.
(C) Mr. Parker took a message from Ms. Turner.
(D) Ms. Turner is going to New York with Mr. Parker.

199 What does Mr. Parker want Ms. Morris to do?

(A) Give a speech at the forum
(B) Arrange a cab from the station to the hotel
(C) Send him the map to the Jefferson Convention Center
(D) Book transportation and accommodations

200 Which train on July 2 would Ms. Morris reserve for Ms. Turner?

(A) A5678
(B) X271
(C) X214
(D) A9521

잠깐!!

시작 전 꼭 확인하세요!

☑ 실제 시험과 같이
  책상을 정리하고
  마음의 준비를 하세요.

☑ 핸드폰은 잠깐 끄고
  대신 아날로그 시계를
  활용해 보세요.

☑ 권장 풀이 시간은 55분입니다.
  시간을 꼭 지켜주세요.

☑ 어렵다고 넘어가지 마세요.
  가능하면 차례대로 풀어 보세요.

Actual Test

09

시작 시간   :

종료 시간   :

PART 7

Directions: In this part you will read a selection of texts, such as magazine and newspaper articles, e-mails, and instant messages. Each text or set of texts is followed by several questions. Select the best answer for each question and mark the letter (A), (B), (C), or (D) on your answer sheet.

Questions 147-148 refer to the following form.

DALLAS PUBLIC LIBRARIES

INTERLIBRARY LOAN REQUEST

If the book you are looking for is not part of our collection, you may ask to borrow it from another public library within the state. Please note that recent releases and reference books are not available through the interlibrary loan system. Individuals are limited to four loan requests per month.

Name: Kyle Lofton

Submission Date: February 2

Contact phone number or e-mail: 469-555-7301

Library Card Number: 8882156a

Branch where the book will be picked up: Fifth Avenue Library

Book title: The Life and Times of Connor O'Brien

Author's name: Phillip Zhang

There is no guarantee that we can provide your requested book by a given date. Most requests take approximately two to three weeks to fill. After this form is received, you will be contacted with an estimated date of arrival.

---

147 What will the library most likely do after this form is submitted?

(A) Inform Mr. Lofton of the book's location
(B) Deliver the book to another library
(C) Purchase the book from a bookstore
(D) Tell Mr. Lofton when he will get the book

148 What is NOT included in the information requested on the form?

(A) How the person can be contacted
(B) Where the book should be sent
(C) When the book is needed
(D) What the name of the book is

Questions 149-150 refer to the following text message chain.

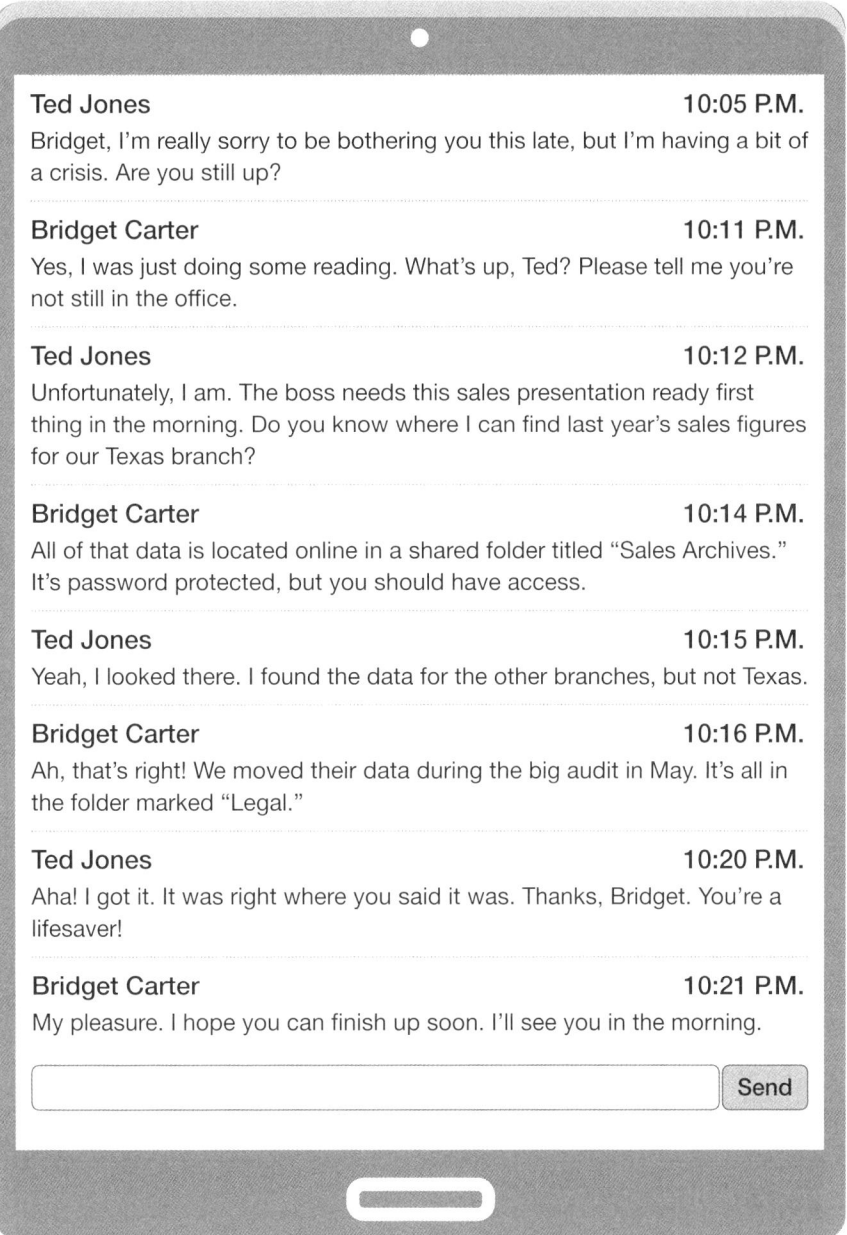

Ted Jones   10:05 P.M.

Bridget, I'm really sorry to be bothering you this late, but I'm having a bit of a crisis. Are you still up?

Bridget Carter   10:11 P.M.

Yes, I was just doing some reading. What's up, Ted? Please tell me you're not still in the office.

Ted Jones   10:12 P.M.

Unfortunately, I am. The boss needs this sales presentation ready first thing in the morning. Do you know where I can find last year's sales figures for our Texas branch?

Bridget Carter   10:14 P.M.

All of that data is located online in a shared folder titled "Sales Archives." It's password protected, but you should have access.

Ted Jones   10:15 P.M.

Yeah, I looked there. I found the data for the other branches, but not Texas.

Bridget Carter   10:16 P.M.

Ah, that's right! We moved their data during the big audit in May. It's all in the folder marked "Legal."

Ted Jones   10:20 P.M.

Aha! I got it. It was right where you said it was. Thanks, Bridget. You're a lifesaver!

Bridget Carter   10:21 P.M.

My pleasure. I hope you can finish up soon. I'll see you in the morning.

Send

149 What is indicated as Mr. Jones' problem?

(A) He is being audited.
(B) He misplaced a presentation.
(C) He cannot locate some data.
(D) He is being transferred to Texas.

150 At 10:20 P.M., what does Mr. Jones mean when he writes, "I got it"?

(A) He received her text message.
(B) He is the one who did the work.
(C) He understands the situation.
(D) He found what he was looking for.

GO ON TO THE NEXT PAGE

Questions 151-152 refer to the following e-mail.

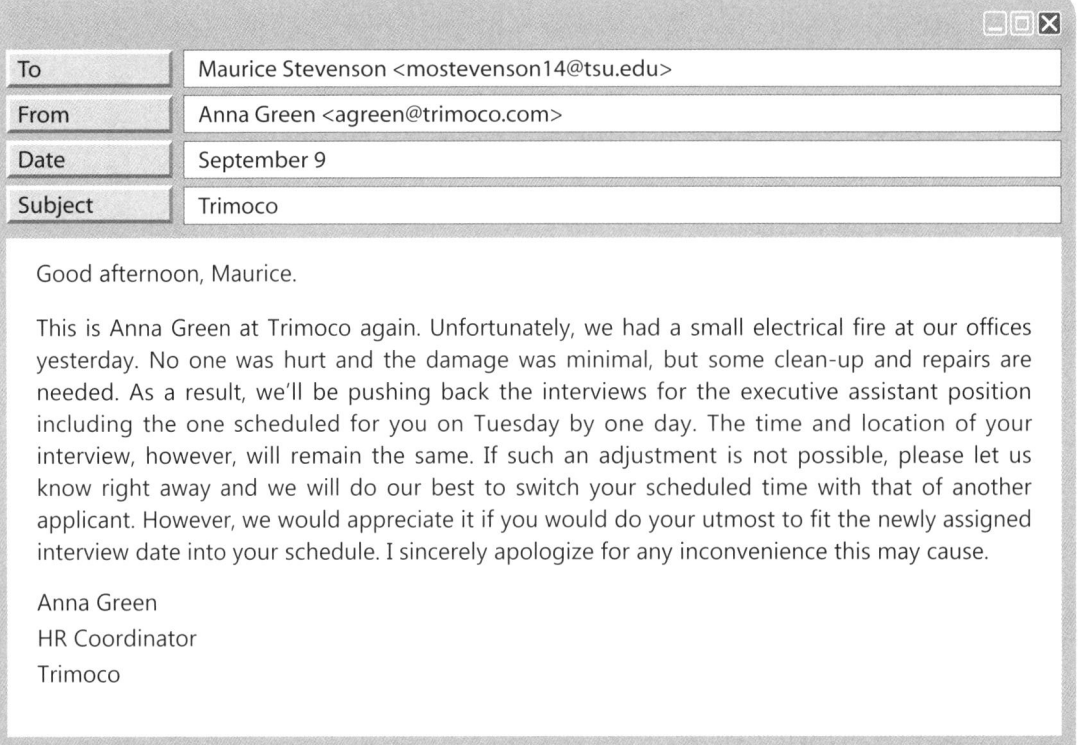

To	Maurice Stevenson <mostevenson14@tsu.edu>
From	Anna Green <agreen@trimoco.com>
Date	September 9
Subject	Trimoco

Good afternoon, Maurice.

This is Anna Green at Trimoco again. Unfortunately, we had a small electrical fire at our offices yesterday. No one was hurt and the damage was minimal, but some clean-up and repairs are needed. As a result, we'll be pushing back the interviews for the executive assistant position including the one scheduled for you on Tuesday by one day. The time and location of your interview, however, will remain the same. If such an adjustment is not possible, please let us know right away and we will do our best to switch your scheduled time with that of another applicant. However, we would appreciate it if you would do your utmost to fit the newly assigned interview date into your schedule. I sincerely apologize for any inconvenience this may cause.

Anna Green
HR Coordinator
Trimoco

151 What is the purpose of the e-mail?

(A) To change an interview date
(B) To apologize for a mistake
(C) To request a new office
(D) To reject a job applicant

152 What is suggested about Mr. Stevenson?

(A) He has previously worked with Trimoco.
(B) He was supposed to meet someone at Trimoco.
(C) He is an employee of Trimoco.
(D) He agrees to Ms. Green's suggestion.

Questions 153-154 refer to the following online chat discussion.

Damien Allen [2:05 P.M.] Has anyone been in touch with John O'Brien recently?

Charlene Mullin [2:06 P.M.] I spoke to him on the phone a few days ago. Is everything okay?

Amy Makowski [2:06 P.M.] I just saw him in the breakroom about 15 minutes ago. He was going over some papers. Is something wrong?

Damien Allen [2:07 P.M.] The breakroom? That's not good. I'm across town at a client meeting. He was supposed to be here five minutes ago, and he's not answering his phone.

Charlene Mullin [2:08 P.M.] Uh-oh. His battery may have died. Hold on. I'll see if I can track him down.

Damien Allen [2:09 P.M.] Thanks. I really don't want to handle this on my own. This is his client. I'm just here to help him out with some technical explanations.

Amy Makowski [2:10 P.M.] Well, hopefully he's on his way. You know John. He always leaves everything until the last minute.

Charlene Mullin [2:13 P.M.] He was still in the breakroom. He completely forgot about the meeting, but he's hopping in a cab right now. He said to give his apologies to the client and to tell her he'll be there in 15 minutes.

Damien Allen [2:14 P.M.] I hope there isn't any traffic. Well, thanks for your help, guys.

> [Send]

---

153 Where is Mr. Allen during the chat discussion?

(A) Out of the office
(B) In a breakroom
(C) In a taxi cab
(D) At his home

154 At 2:10 P.M., what does Ms. Makowski mean when she writes, "You know John"?

(A) You have met John previously.
(B) You should act more like John does.
(C) You are familiar with John's tendencies.
(D) You are responsible for John's behavior.

GO ON TO THE NEXT PAGE

Ride in Comfort on the Peninsula Shuttle

Getting to the airport is terribly inconvenient. Parking is too expensive, and state budget cuts have taken away our public transportation options. But Lincoln International Airport now has a new addition to its offering of private transportation services: the Peninsula Shuttle.

The Peninsula Shuttle serves all of the communities located on the peninsula, including Jackson, Bayside, North Farrington and Farrington Beach. Buses leave from Lighthouse Point at the top of each hour, starting at 6 A.M. and ending at 10 P.M. The first shuttle leaves the airport at 6:30 A.M. and the last at 10:30 P.M. There are five stops in between: the Jackson bus station, Main Street in Bayside, the Peninsula Mall, the North Farrington bus station, and the Farrington Beach post office.

One-way tickets can be purchased in advance for just $8.00 or for $10.00 from the driver. County transit cards are accepted, and senior citizens and students receive a 10% discount. For more information, visit our Web site at www.liashuttle.com.

155 What is suggested about Lincoln International Airport?

(A) It has several flights a day to the peninsula.
(B) Its last flight leaves around 8 in the evening.
(C) It cannot be reached by public transportation.
(D) It is located near a large urban area.

156 When does the last Peninsula Shuttle bus leave the airport?

(A) 6:00 P.M.
(B) 6:30 P.M.
(C) 10:00 P.M.
(D) 10:30 P.M.

157 How much would a student pay for a ticket purchased on the bus?

(A) $7.20
(B) $8.00
(C) $9.00
(D) $10.00

Full Moon Photography Supplies
Merchandise Return Form

Full Moon offers a 30-day return policy on all our merchandise, excluding products bought at a discount of 30% or more. We cover the delivery costs for all damaged items, but the customer is responsible for shipping and handling fees for all items being exchanged or returned for other reasons. An original receipt or invoice must be included with all product returns.

Name	Lucy Edwards
Shipping Address	15 Mercy Lane, Apt 2B, Darrington, Montana 59012

Service Requested:

☐ Exchange

☑ Cash Refund

☐ Store Credit

☐ Repair

Name of item being returned: Micron 17-mm SLR Zoom Lens

Reason for the return: I purchased this product after I accidentally dropped my original zoom lens while photographing wildlife on an assignment overseas. However, after trying this new lens out for a few days, I was not satisfied with the image quality. I've decided to have my original lens repaired instead.

158 What is indicated as a reason a customer would have to pay delivery charges?

(A) The product was bought on sale.
(B) The customer doesn't have a receipt.
(C) The returned item is undamaged.
(D) More than one month has passed.

159 Why is Ms. Edwards returning the item?

(A) It did not meet her expectations.
(B) It is not what she ordered.
(C) It was damaged in an accident.
(D) It was repaired improperly.

160 What is most likely true about Ms. Edwards?

(A) She is a professional photographer.
(B) She does not know the return policy.
(C) She has never purchased a zoom lens before.
(D) She has had previous problems with Full Moon.

Test 09

GO ON TO THE NEXT PAGE

Questions 161-164 refer to the following article.

Online and On the Road

– [1] –. In our continuing look at the hottest new technology, we're going to check out the latest trend in the automotive industry: Connected Cars. These vehicles are exactly what their name suggests—automobiles that are connected to the Internet. Basically, your car becomes a rolling hot spot, allowing you and your passengers to link all of your devices to the Internet through the car's connection.

But there's much more to it than that! – [2] –. For example, if you get into a serious accident, your car will automatically alert the traffic police and your insurance company. Other safety features include warnings about hazardous driving conditions and mechanical problems. – [3] –.

When your car is connected, there's no need for your keys. – [4] –. You can start your engine, turn on your heater, lock your doors and enable your car's alarm with your cell phone, no matter where you are. It seems like new features are added to these cars every month. Given the speed at which this technology is evolving, it won't be long before connected cars are able to drive themselves!

161 What is suggested about the article?

(A) It was written by an expert.
(B) It is part of an ongoing series.
(C) It is not based on facts.
(D) It has been published before.

162 What is NOT mentioned as a benefit of connected cars?

(A) They get help after an accident.
(B) They alert you to possible danger.
(C) They do not require the use of keys.
(D) They can make you a better driver.

163 In which of the positions marked [1], [2], [3], and [4] does the following sentence best fit?

"Since your car is constantly online, it can send and transmit important information."

(A) [1]
(B) [2]
(C) [3]
(D) [4]

164 Why does the writer mention cell phones?

(A) To point out the source of new technology
(B) To suggest they will no longer be a necessity
(C) To explain how connected cars can be controlled
(D) To show how quickly connected cars are changing

Questions 165-168 refer to the following instructions.

If your problem is related to your WiFi connection, please refer to the following troubleshooting instructions.

First, make sure your router software is up to date, all of your cables are securely plugged in and the new router is turned on. If this doesn't resolve your problem, choose the statement below that best describes your situation and follow the recommended solutions.

(A) I cannot connect to the Internet at all.

Make sure you are accessing the correct network. There may be several available networks with similar names.

(B) I can access the Internet, but the connection is unusually slow.

1) Close any programs that may be using a large amount of bandwidth, such as streaming movies or online games.

2) Check to see what other devices are connected to your network. Turning off unneeded devices may improve your connection speed.

(C) My Internet connection comes and goes.

Move your device closer to your router. Routers have a limited range and can be blocked by certain materials or other electronic devices.

---

165 Who would most likely be reading the instructions?

(A) Someone whose computer is infected with a virus
(B) Someone who wants to learn about WiFi
(C) Someone who owns an electronics store
(D) Someone who recently purchased a router

166 What is NOT suggested as a preliminary problem-solving step?

(A) Making sure you have the most recent software
(B) Turning off all other wireless devices
(C) Checking for improperly connected cables
(D) Ensuring that the router is switched on

167 What problem related to network names is mentioned?

(A) Forgetting a network name
(B) Mistaking several similar names
(C) Creating names that are too long
(D) Sharing a network name with others

168 What is suggested as a solution to an intermittent connection?

(A) Relocating the device to the router
(B) Closing down other programs
(C) Changing the network's name
(D) Updating all of the software

GO ON TO THE NEXT PAGE

Dear Club Members:

It is with my deepest regrets that I write to inform you that the Leeland Pines Tennis Club is going out of business on September 1. We've been one of the most popular tennis clubs in the state for more than 10 years, but the gentleman who owns the property on which the club is located has elected not to renew our lease. Apparently, he plans to convert the property into a gated residential community for senior citizens in the near future.

Although the situation is out of our hands, you can rest assured that you will be entitled to a prorated refund for the canceled portion of your membership. As an alternative, you will have the choice of transferring the remainder of your membership to Tennis World, a nearby tennis club that has graciously agreed to accept all former Leeland Pines members.

If you wish to transfer your membership, please let us know by August 31. If we don't hear from you by then, we will begin processing your refund.

Yours Truly,

Amanda Novichkov

169 What is the purpose of the letter?

(A) To offer refunds for inferior service
(B) To recruit members from rival clubs
(C) To inform customers of new benefits
(D) To announce the end of a business

170 What is indicated about the owner of the property?

(A) He will use the land in another way.
(B) He has been placed in a nursing home.
(C) He is demanding a higher monthly rent.
(D) He belongs to a different tennis club.

171 Why does the writer mention Tennis World?

(A) To explain her new job
(B) To give members an option
(C) To compare her club's benefits
(D) To blame them for her problems

Stratford Culinary Institute

More Than Just a Cooking School

At most cooking schools, you simply learn how to cook. But at Stratford, we teach you how to succeed.

A diploma from Stratford means something in the restaurant industry. – [1] –. That means that nine out of ten Stratford graduates are working in a professional kitchen soon after graduating.

– [2] –. Our secret is the largest number of career counselors of any culinary school in the country. Our Career Services department will be there for you, before and after you graduate, to make sure your culinary career starts smoothly. – [3] –. We also have a network of dedicated alumni who will be happy to offer advice once you begin your new job.

And, of course, no one can match the comprehensiveness of a Stratford education. Employers know that Stratford graduates come prepared to excel. – [4] –. You can choose from one of our three award-winning programs: Culinary Arts, International Cuisine, and Baking Arts. Not sure which is right for you? Call us at 212-555-1172.

---

172 Who would most likely respond to this advertisement flyer?

(A) Someone who works in a kitchen
(B) Someone who teaches cooking classes
(C) Someone who wants to become a chef
(D) Someone who owns a restaurant

173 What is indicated about institute graduates?

(A) Most of them find work quickly.
(B) Many of them recommend the institute.
(C) Some of them are now famous.
(D) Few of them work in kitchens.

174 What is NOT indicated as being a strong point of the institute?

(A) Numerous career counselors
(B) Helpful past graduates
(C) Affordable tuition costs
(D) A well-rounded education

175 In which of the positions marked [1], [2], [3], and [4] does the following sentence best fit?

"We have a post-graduation job placement rate of nearly 90%."

(A) [1]
(B) [2]
(C) [3]
(D) [4]

Test 09

GO ON TO THE NEXT PAGE

To: Evcorp Department Managers

From: Hanna Kwon

On November 15 we will be hosting four visitors from our sister company in Japan. The purpose of their visit is to exchange thoughts and information about our automated order processing systems. While most of their three-day stay will be taken up with meetings concerning order processing, they will have a free evening on the 16th.

We would love for some of our employees, especially those with Japanese language skills or a familiarity with Japanese culture, to take them out for a casual dinner and show them around our town. The four visitors will be accompanied by our business director, but we would like to have more people join them to ensure a more enjoyable and social atmosphere. If any of your staff members have free time that evening and would like to take part, please have them send me an e-mail or stop by my office before the end of the week. Thanks for your help!

To: Hanna Kwon <hannak@evcorp.net>

From: Lawrence Markowitz <lawrencem@evcorp.net>

Date: November 10

Subject: Visitors from Japan

Hello, Hanna.

I just heard from John Goodwin, my department manager, that you're looking for people to spend a little time with some of our colleagues from Japan. I was actually stationed near Tokyo for three years when I was in the Air Force, and although my skills are probably a bit rusty, I speak Japanese fairly well. I would like to help you out by showing them around the offices or taking them out on the town. Unfortunately, I'm scheduled to be in Evanston with Gus Rodgers on the 16th to give a presentation and probably won't be back until 8 or 9 P.M. However, if you need someone to help out in any way on one of the other days they'll be here, please let me know. I've also offered my services to our company's business director, Jody Cobb, but I haven't heard back from her yet.

Lawrence Markowitz

IT Coordinator

176 What is the purpose of the memo?

    (A) To recruit volunteers
    (B) To welcome visitors
    (C) To adjust a schedule
    (D) To ask for ideas

177 In the memo, the word "concerning" in paragraph 1, line 4, is closest in meaning to

    (A) worrying
    (B) protecting
    (C) involving
    (D) defining

178 Who will be with the Japanese visitors on the evening of November 16?

    (A) Jody Cobb
    (B) John Goodwin
    (C) Hanna Kwon
    (D) Gus Rodgers

179 What is suggested about Mr. Markowitz?

    (A) He is no longer employed by Evcorp.
    (B) He formerly served in the military.
    (C) He is currently away on vacation.
    (D) He has been promoted to manager.

180 Why can't Mr. Markowitz attend dinner on the 16th?

    (A) He will be on a business trip.
    (B) His Japanese isn't good enough.
    (C) He already has personal plans.
    (D) His manager won't allow it.

GO ON TO THE NEXT PAGE

Nothing Says "I Love You" Like Fresh Flowers!

Mercury Florists is a chain of more than 100 flower shops located up and down the East Coast. By having so many outlets, we can keep our delivery costs lower than those of our competitors. Even better, we can guarantee two-hour delivery to nearly any address from Maine to Florida.

The easiest way to order a Mercury bouquet is simply by calling us toll-free at 1-888-555-3559. Orders can also be placed online at our new Web site (www.mercuryflowers.com) or by stopping by any of our retail outlets.

APRIL INTERNET SPECIAL! Spring is here, and so are our famous Peruvian lilies. The bouquet comes with 25 stems, each of which contains 4 to 5 flowers. The lilies come in bud form, but will quickly open once the stems are placed in water. Soon you'll have 100 or more flowers in several different colors. Order your bouquet online during the month of April, and the cost will be slashed from $39.99 to just $19.99. You can also add a decorative vase for just $5 extra!

Mercury Florists
Customer Service Center
PO Box 77181
Durham, North Carolina 27703

Dear Sir or Madam:

On April 17, my niece gave birth to her first daughter. Due to my health issues, I couldn't be there to celebrate with her. Since I live in New York City and she lives in a rural area 500 miles away, I decided to have flowers delivered to her. A friend of mine recommended your company.

I went to your Web site, selected your Peruvian Lilies Special, and completed my order online. Unfortunately, I mistakenly entered the wrong street address—113 Blue Mountain Road rather than 311 Blue Mountain Road. According to my niece, your delivery driver drove up and down that country road until he found someone who recognized her name. He finally delivered a bouquet of beautiful flowers in a lovely green vase.

It is rare to see people put such a sincere effort into their jobs these days. My niece got the driver's name: Brandon Ware. So I just wanted to take a moment to commend his dedication to his job. Please pass this message on to his supervisor.

Sincerely,
Karen Kingsbury

181 What is indicated as an advantage of the company?

(A) Freshly cut flowers
(B) Convenient bulk sales
(C) Low delivery fees
(D) Wide variety of options

182 What is indicated as the simplest way to place an order?

(A) By fax
(B) By phone
(C) In person
(D) On the Internet

183 How much did Ms. Kingsbury most likely pay for her lilies?

(A) $14.99
(B) $19.99
(C) $24.99
(D) $39.99

184 What was Ms. Kingsbury's reason for writing the letter?

(A) To praise a deliveryman
(B) To request a partial refund
(C) To point out an error in an ad
(D) To complain about a late delivery

185 What is indicated as the reason for the driver's confusion?

(A) He was not from the area.
(B) He did not speak English well.
(C) He misread a customer's name.
(D) He was given incorrect information.

GO ON TO THE NEXT PAGE

Important Update for Apex Bank Customers

Our downtown branch located on Sixth Avenue will be closed for renovations from April 16th to May 12th. The two ATMs located in the lobby will still be accessible, but customers wishing to speak to a bank representative will have to visit our other downtown branch, which can be found on the corner of Second Avenue and Virginia Street. We regret the inconvenience but are pleased to announce that the Sixth Avenue branch will be updated into a state-of-the-art, customer-friendly facility, with sofas, conference tables and touch-screen information modules. This will result in a banking experience that is faster, more comfortable, and more enjoyable for all of our customers. At the same time, the branch will retain the classic traditional features of the century-old building in which it is located. You can find more details about our renovation plans on the Apex Bank Web site.

Instant Customer Reviews – Seattle – Banking and Finance

In case you haven't heard, the Apex Bank on Sixth Avenue has finally reopened, and I can tell you that it has undergone a complete transformation. It looks more like a breakroom at a tech start-up than a traditional bank. Although the new layout was off-putting at first, I quickly learned to love it. The old number-ticket dispensers have been replaced with touch screens, and the clerks are no longer hidden behind a big counter—they come right out and deal with you face to face. While the lobby ATMs are the same old models, there are three brand new ones inside the branch itself. There are even pastries and free coffee to indulge in while you wait. I was pretty frustrated when their renovations ran several weeks longer than they had announced, but it was worth the wait!

Fred Nichols – Apex Bank customer since 2014

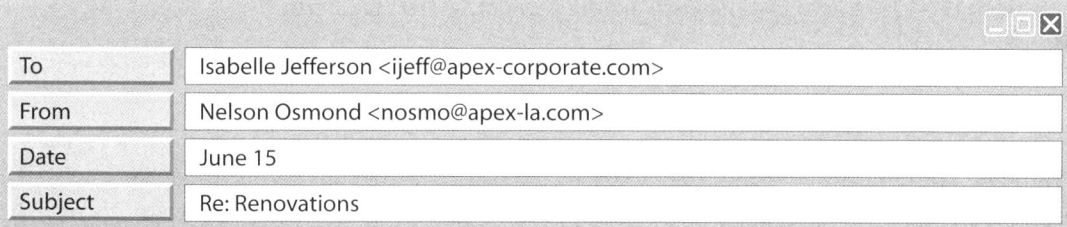

To	Isabelle Jefferson <ijeff@apex-corporate.com>
From	Nelson Osmond <nosmo@apex-la.com>
Date	June 15
Subject	Re: Renovations

Hello, Isabelle.

As someone who has strong opinions, I find it hard to admit when I'm wrong. But in this case, it's unavoidable. I know I strongly resisted your attempts to have the Los Angeles branch serve as the prototype for the new, lounge-style layout. It just seemed like too much of a change to attempt all at once. But I've just come back from visiting the Seattle branch, and I was blown away by the results. The new layout really does improve efficiency, and the customer satisfaction surveys that Helen Schmidt, the branch manager, showed me were impressive. Can we schedule a meeting to discuss the implementation of a similar renovation down here? Let me know at your earliest convenience.

Sincerely,

Nelson Osmond
Branch Manager
Apex Bank, LA

---

186 What is NOT indicated about the Apex Bank on Sixth Avenue?

(A) It was scheduled to reopen in May.
(B) It has a pair of ATMs in its lobby.
(C) It is moving to Second Avenue.
(D) It is located in an older building.

187 What does Mr. Nichols indicate as the cause of his annoyance?

(A) An unexpectedly lengthy closure
(B) A surprisingly rude bank staff
(C) A lack of new technology
(D) An inconvenient location

188 How many ATMs does the Sixth Avenue Apex Bank have after its renovation?

(A) None
(B) 2
(C) 3
(D) 5

189 What was Mr. Osmond's original opinion of the change to a new bank style?

(A) He was excited about it.
(B) He felt it was too extreme.
(C) He thought it cost too much.
(D) He was concerned about safety.

190 What does Mr. Osmond want Ms. Jefferson to do?

(A) Apologize for her rude behavior
(B) Take a tour of the Seattle branch
(C) Conduct a customer satisfaction survey
(D) Talk with him about renovating his branch

Test 09

GO ON TO THE NEXT PAGE

Attention! University Library Staff!

The third annual International Collegiate Library Association Conference has been scheduled for November 4 in Auckland, New Zealand. We are looking for three volunteers to represent our institution at this event. You will be required to spend three days in New Zealand, with two additional travel days, and, upon returning, you will be expected to make a variety of presentations related to the information you obtain at the conference. Round-trip air fare and a private room at the Plaza Hotel for two nights will be provided by the university. However, attendees must pay for their own food and drinks, and they will not be compensated for any additional expenses incurred. If you are interested in taking part or would like more information, please contact Gary Bronson at gbronson@uta.edu by this Friday at the latest.

To :	Gary Bronson <gbronson@uta.edu>
From:	Richard Collison <rcollison@uta.edu>
Date:	October 20
Subject:	ICLA Conference

Hello, Mr. Bronson.

I'm writing to express my interest in attending this year's ICLA conference on behalf of the university library. As you may remember, we attended the very first ICLA conference in Barcelona together, although I missed last year's Miami conference due to a schedule conflict. This year's event caught my eye, as I have family in Auckland. However, I do have a few special requests. First, I'd prefer to leave from Montreal rather than Ottawa. I don't believe this would affect the ticket price. Also, would it be possible to stay at the Harborside Hotel rather than the Plaza Hotel? The reason is that the Plaza is quite far from my grandparents' home, which I would like to visit. Finally, I would like to add three vacation days to the end of the trip, so I can spend more time with my family. I promise I would be prepared to make a presentation about the conference the following Monday. Thanks for considering my requests!

Richard Collison
Library Acquisitions Specialist

New Zealand Arrival Card

Name:	Richard Collison
Citizenship:	Canadian
Number of accompanying members:	0
Passport Number:	001163629
Length of stay:	six days
Main purpose of visit:	attending a conference
Address in New Zealand:	Plaza Hotel, Auckland
Port of Embarkation:	Montreal, Canada
Aircraft or vessel number:	Air New Zealand Flight 23

191 In the announcement, the word "compensated" in paragraph 1, line 8, is closest in meaning to

(A) paid back
(B) included in
(C) consulted on
(D) questioned about

192 What is indicated as a requirement of conference attendees?

(A) They must use their vacation time.
(B) They must share a hotel room.
(C) They must share what they learn.
(D) They must speak at the conference.

193 What is indicated about Mr. Collison?

(A) He attends the ICLA conference every year.
(B) He no longer works at the university library.
(C) He has previously met Mr. Bronson.
(D) He is a citizen of New Zealand.

194 Where was the second annual ICLA conference held?

(A) Auckland
(B) Barcelona
(C) Miami
(D) Montreal

195 Which of Mr. Collison's requests did Mr. Bronson deny?

(A) Attending the conference
(B) Switching to another hotel
(C) Taking additional days off
(D) Leaving from a different airport

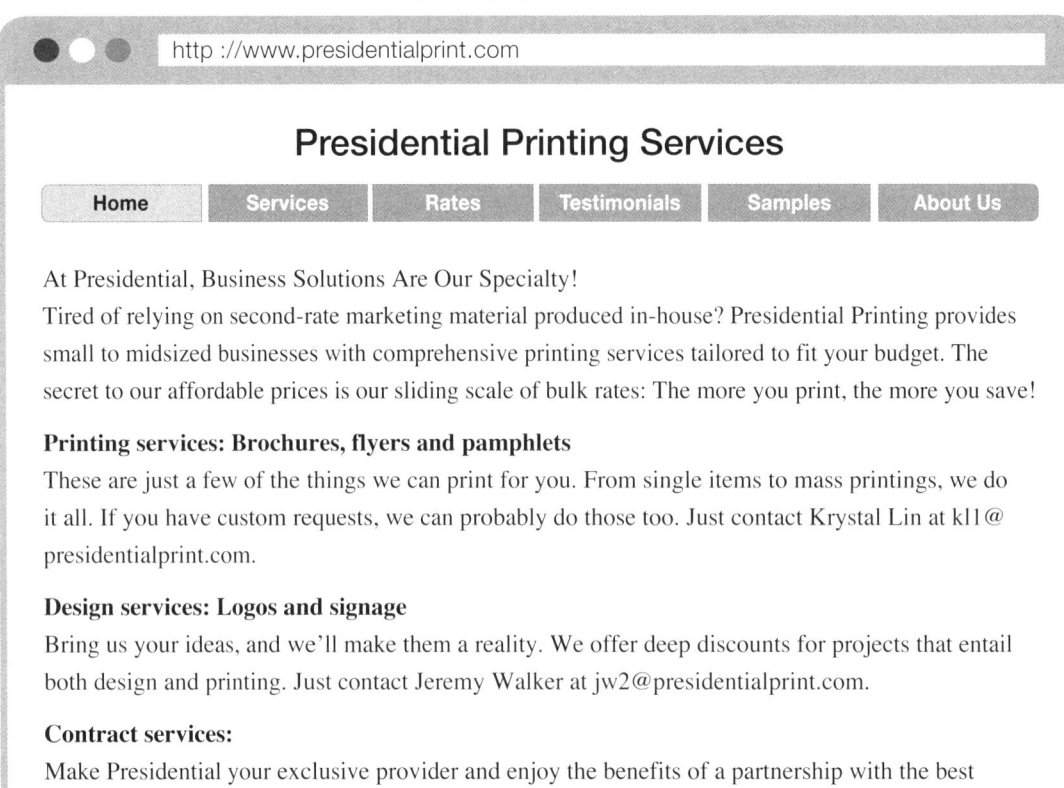

Presidential Printing Services

| Home | Services | Rates | Testimonials | Samples | About Us |

At Presidential, Business Solutions Are Our Specialty!

Tired of relying on second-rate marketing material produced in-house? Presidential Printing provides small to midsized businesses with comprehensive printing services tailored to fit your budget. The secret to our affordable prices is our sliding scale of bulk rates: The more you print, the more you save!

Printing services: Brochures, flyers and pamphlets

These are just a few of the things we can print for you. From single items to mass printings, we do it all. If you have custom requests, we can probably do those too. Just contact Krystal Lin at kl1@presidentialprint.com.

Design services: Logos and signage

Bring us your ideas, and we'll make them a reality. We offer deep discounts for projects that entail both design and printing. Just contact Jeremy Walker at jw2@presidentialprint.com.

Contract services:

Make Presidential your exclusive provider and enjoy the benefits of a partnership with the best printing service in the area. Just contact Ian Lee at il1@presidentialprint.com.

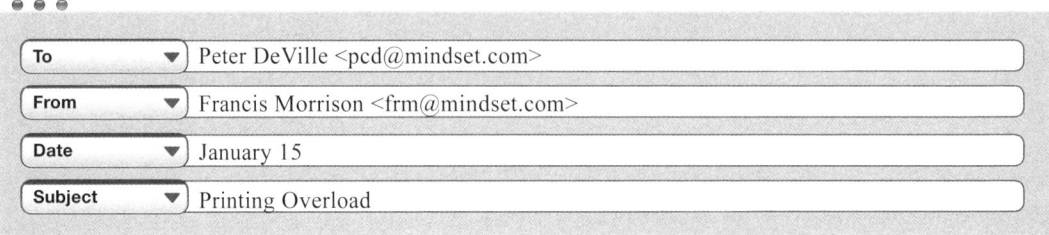

To	Peter DeVille <pcd@mindset.com>
From	Francis Morrison <frm@mindset.com>
Date	January 15
Subject	Printing Overload

Hello, Peter.

I've been thinking about what you said at last Thursday's management meeting about the drain on the IT department's resources from the amount of printed materials being requested by our sales teams. I know that as the IT manager you've made an investment in printing software and hardware, but I think it's time we considered outsourcing our printing needs. We can continue to utilize our equipment on a smaller, more specialized scale, while sending the bulk of our printing out-of-house. This way we could shift the responsibility away from your department and over to the administrative department. Take a look at this service when you get a chance: www.presidentialprint.com. I've been emailing back and forth with the person in charge of partnerships. They're local and affordable, so they might be the solution to our problem.

Francis

ANNOUNCEMENT REGARDING PRINT JOBS

Starting this upcoming Monday, requests for printing will be outsourced to a local provider, Presidential Printing Services. Our in-house printing equipment and technology will be reserved for executive use only. Exceptions to this rule are possible, but only with permission from the IT manager. New print job request forms are available on the employee intranet—just follow the link marked "forms and documents" on the main page. Please do not print out the forms or bring them to the human resources office. They must be filled in online and emailed to Jake Young at printing@mindset.com as an attachment. If you have any problems with the new service, please bring them to Jake rather than discussing them directly with our provider.

196 What is NOT a service offered by Presidential?

(A) Creating logos
(B) Printing pamphlets
(C) Designing Web sites
(D) Partnering with businesses

197 Who did Mr. Morrison most likely contact at Presidential?

(A) Ian Lee
(B) Krystal Lin
(C) Jeremy Walker
(D) Jake Young

198 Who can give employees permission to use the in-house printing equipment?

(A) Ian Lee
(B) Peter DeVille
(C) Francis Morrison
(D) Jake Young

199 Which part of the company does Mr. Young most likely work for?

(A) The administrative department
(B) The human resources department
(C) The IT department
(D) The sales department

200 How should print request forms be delivered?

(A) By e-mail
(B) In person
(C) By fax
(D) By mail

잠깐!!
시작 전 **꼭** 확인하세요!

- ☑ 실제 시험과 같이
  책상을 정리하고
  마음의 준비를 하세요.

- ☑ 핸드폰은 잠깐 끄고
  대신 아날로그 시계를
  활용해 보세요.

- ☑ 권장 풀이 시간은 55분입니다.
  시간을 꼭 지켜주세요.

- ☑ 어렵다고 넘어가지 마세요.
  가능하면 차례대로 풀어 보세요.

Actual Test

10

시작 시간	:	
종료 시간	:	

PART 7

Directions: In this part you will read a selection of texts, such as magazine and newspaper articles, e-mails, and instant messages. Each text or set of texts is followed by several questions. Select the best answer for each question and mark the letter (A), (B), (C), or (D) on your answer sheet.

Questions 147-148 refer to the following notice.

Customer Satisfaction Survey

High Park Mart wants to know what you think of us!

High Park Mart cares deeply about its customers. That is why we kindly ask you to participate in our satisfaction survey. A survey is the best way to give us your thoughts about our choice of products and services. The more we hear from you, the more we can give back. We are very interested in your needs and anxious to improve on what we may be doing wrong.

The survey is very brief, and it will take less than a minute to finish. The questions are mainly about our services and our products.

There are no mandatory questions, so you can skip some of them. Your answers will be kept confidential. Do not hesitate to notify us of our faults. Any small problem will get our attention. Do not feel any pressure and write your honest opinion.

Thank you for your cooperation.

147 What is the purpose of the notice?

(A) To hire new staff members
(B) To ask for cooperation
(C) To express thanks
(D) To announce holidays

148 What is stated about the survey?

(A) It takes a couple of minutes to finish.
(B) No question should be left unanswered.
(C) Gift certificates will be given to those who finish.
(D) The answers won't be revealed to the public.

Memo

To: All employees
From: Bella Pierce
Date: May 1
Subject: Customer Service

Mother's Day is just around the corner. So we are almost face to face with a hectic weekend. So I hope that all of you would gather your strength and make sure the satisfaction of customers is your top priority. Making a customer happy is the right and only way to meet our sales targets. Also, a happy face on our customers can be considered our natural vitamins. As you all know, happiness is contagious.

So after giving some thought to ways of improving customer service, the management team has come up with the "Best Service Award." We'll ask the customers for the best service they had and which department was the friendliest. The award-winning department will get an extra bonus on top of the regular holiday bonus. So let's all give our best efforts to make this Mother's Day the best weekend for all!

Thank you!

Bella Pierce
Sales Department

149 Why is the memo written?

(A) To ask for suggestions on improving customer service
(B) To encourage employees to offer better service
(C) To announce a vacation policy for holidays
(D) To request votes to pick the best department

150 What is implied about Bella?

(A) She thought up the "Best Service Award."
(B) She received a complaint from a customer.
(C) She is a sales manager.
(D) She gave people bonuses today.

Questions 151-152 refer to the following text message chain.

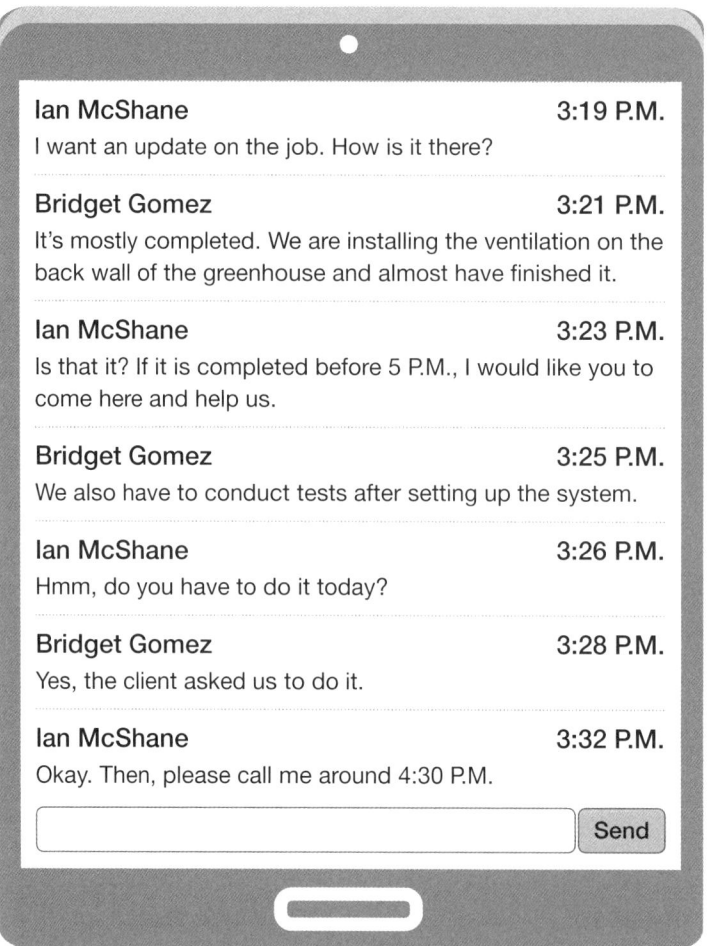

Ian McShane	3:19 P.M.
I want an update on the job. How is it there?	

Bridget Gomez	3:21 P.M.
It's mostly completed. We are installing the ventilation on the back wall of the greenhouse and almost have finished it.	

Ian McShane	3:23 P.M.
Is that it? If it is completed before 5 P.M., I would like you to come here and help us.	

Bridget Gomez	3:25 P.M.
We also have to conduct tests after setting up the system.	

Ian McShane	3:26 P.M.
Hmm, do you have to do it today?	

Bridget Gomez	3:28 P.M.
Yes, the client asked us to do it.	

Ian McShane	3:32 P.M.
Okay. Then, please call me around 4:30 P.M.	

Send

151 What type of business does Ms. Gomez most likely work in?

(A) A furniture company
(B) A construction company
(C) A sanitation company
(D) A design firm

152 At 3:23 P.M., what does Mr. McShane most likely mean when he writes, "Is that it"?

(A) He needs to confirm the reservation of a job.
(B) He wants to know how long it will take to complete the project.
(C) He should identify the cause of a problem.
(D) He asks if other services are needed.

Questions 153-154 refer to the following advertisement.

BOLLYWOOD MOVIE NIGHTS

Time: 7:00 – 9:30 P.M., every Thursday in July

Location: Milton Community Center, located next to the National Museum of Arts and History

Enjoy the Indian spirit with Bollywood movies on a hot summer night. We'll be showing you movies like *Bend it like Beckham*, *Dil Se*, *Lagaan: Once Upon a Time in India* and the most famous, *Slumdog Millionaire*. Not only can you enjoy the movies, but you can also try Indian snacks like Aloo Tikki (seasoned potatoes and chick peas), Samosa (a stuffed pastry), and Lassi (blended yogurt with water or milk and Indian spices). The snacks will be sold at a very reasonable price, and all the proceeds will be donated to a fund for building schools in India.

The movies will be shown for free, but the seats will be limited so we suggest that you come at least 15 minutes before the movie starts. Once the movie starts, we won't allow seating of additional audience members regardless of empty seats.

For more information, call 742-555-6502.

153 What is being advertised?

(A) Upcoming movie nights
(B) The opening of an Indian restaurant
(C) A charity foundation for children
(D) Class registration on Indian cooking

154 What is NOT indicated about the event?

(A) Seating is limited.
(B) Food will be complimentary.
(C) The event will be temporary.
(D) One of the movies is *Slumdog Millionaire*.

GO ON TO THE NEXT PAGE

Questions 155-157 refer to the following letter.

Kevin Dixon

987 Westwood Ave.

Vancouver, British Columbia

Dear Mr. Dixon:

Thank you for visiting Somerset Beach resort during your visit to Hawaii. I have read your urgent e-mail and checked the lost property office.

Our staff found your poster of Duke Kahanamoku on the same day that you accidentally left it behind. We are keeping it in a safe place where it won't be ruined. You have requested that we send the item to your address, and we are more than happy to do so. But before we send it to you, we wanted to confirm one thing. Since the resort is on an island, there is an extra shipping fee. The total delivery fee will be $30. Our concern is that the monetary value of the poster is less than $15. We understand that Duke Kahanamoku was a legendary surfer and that the particular poster you have purchased is only sold on our island. But we had to ask whether you realized there was an extra delivery fee when you asked us to send your poster. At any rate, $30 will be due upon delivery.

Please give us a reply and let us know your thoughts.

Sincerely,

Henry Fleming

Manager, Customer Relations

---

155 Why was the letter sent to Mr. Dixon?

(A) To ask for a confirmation
(B) To inform him about the new shipping policy
(C) To make an order
(D) To request a refund

156 What problem did Mr. Dixon have?

(A) His poster was ruined during room service.
(B) He forgot to reply to the letter.
(C) He left an item at a hotel after his visit.
(D) He couldn't meet Duke Kahanamoku.

157 What is mentioned about the poster?

(A) It is only sold in Hawaii.
(B) It has a mythical drawing on it.
(C) It costs more than $20.
(D) It was signed by Duke Kahanamoku.

Laundry Day

Attention, neighbors! The cold winter has finally been beaten down by the warmth of spring! – [1] –.

So gather up all your laundry because it is mega-sale time at Norton's Laundry! Yes, the neat and tidy Norton's is loosening up not on our work but our prices! What a way to start your spring cleaning, huh? – [2] –.

Beginning Monday next week (March 25th) to Saturday (March 30th), dry cleaning fees will drop down by 50%. So bring all of your winter coats, sweaters, jumpers, and more. There is no laundry we can't get the stains off! And this is by far the best bargain in the city! Get a fresh start on spring with less burden on your pocket book. – [3] –. Neatly cleaned and folded winter clothes will give you room for your spring ones!

Moreover, cleaning fees for shoes will also be 30% off! – [4] –. We'll turn them into shiny ones for you to use next year.

Don't miss this great chance! We'll be waiting for you and your laundry.

Norton's Laundry: 20 Elm Street
Business hours: 8:00 A.M. – 7:00 P.M. (Mon. – Fri.)   9:00 A.M. – 2:00 P.M. (Sat.)
Tel: 033-555-9785

---

158 How long does the sale last?

(A) For 4 days
(B) For 5 days
(C) For 6 days
(D) For 7 days

159 What is true about the advertisement?

(A) Delivery service is included in the fee.
(B) There will be a reduced fee for footwear.
(C) Norton's Laundry opens everyday.
(D) Norton's Laundry always opens at 8 A.M.

160 In which of the positions marked [1], [2], [3], and [4] does the following sentence best belong?

"Don't be shy, and bring your snow- and dirt-stained boots and sneakers."

(A) [1]
(B) [2]
(C) [3]
(D) [4]

GO ON TO THE NEXT PAGE

August 11
Julia Brooks
153 Veeno Ave.
Montreal, Quebec

Dear Ms. Brooks:

We thank you for your purchase of our new skin care set. We hope you are fully content with our product and service.

Your purchased product is our newest release, so we are enclosing a customer survey. Your feedback is really valuable to us. It is important for us to bring our services and products in line with our consumers' needs. It is a very brief survey consisting of the front and back of a piece of paper. If you decide to participate, you can mail it to us. Please use the provided envelope with our address on it which is enclosed with the survey for your convenience.

In lieu of mailing the survey, you can take it to one of our stores near you.

After we receive your survey, we'll send you a $120 gift certificate for a future purchase to show our appreciation. If you hand in the survey at one of our stores, you will be able to receive the certificate immediately.

If you have a complaint to file, do not wait for the mail to bring it to us. Instead, please give us a call right away.

Thank you for your cooperation.

Sincerely,

Kaylee Webb
Manager, Customer Service

161 What is the purpose of the letter?

(A) To introduce the launching of a new product

(B) To request the return of a document

(C) To apologize for a mistake in delivery

(D) To ask for a recommendation

162 The word "needs" in paragraph 2, line 3, is closest in meaning to

(A) attempts

(B) demands

(C) figures

(D) tests

163 What is enclosed with the letter?

(A) A gift certificate

(B) Cosmetics

(C) The map of a local store

(D) An envelope

GO ON TO THE NEXT PAGE

March 1

Globenet

Globenet is a satellite service that has 150 main channels and an additional 50 special channels. More than 200 million viewers of cable channels use Globenet as their service. The head office of Globenet which provides full equipment and support to all employees is looking for a decent, people-loving technician right now.

Job Description
The main responsibilities of TV satellite technicians involve setting satellite dishes and connecting cable networks to TVs. There are also relatively simpler works such as adding cable channels and adjusting the location of the installed satellite. Successful candidates can earn promotions to work as technician managers.

Qualifications
    * At least 1 year of experience handling electric wires
    * Driver's license
    * Excellent communication skills
    * Bright attitude to serve customers

Process of Selection
An application with a description of your job experience should be submitted to the e-mail address below by the 21st of March. We do not have a fixed form, so you can submit any type of application as long as it has your contact number on it. Chosen candidates will be individually contacted by phone, so make sure to include your phone number in your application. Submit your application to Joseph Mitchell at joseph_m@globenet.com.

164 According to the advertisement, what is NOT a job responsibility?

(A) Setting satellite dishes
(B) Attracting new customers
(C) Connecting cables to TVs
(D) Putting in additional cable channels

165 What is required to apply for the job position?

(A) More than a year of technical experience
(B) A college diploma
(C) Life insurance
(D) The ability to speak various languages

166 By when do the applicants have to send in an application?

(A) This week
(B) Next week
(C) Within three weeks
(D) Within four weeks

167 What is NOT indicated about the advertisement?

(A) When the candidates have to submit the documents
(B) What information should be entered in the applications
(C) When the candidates will be reached
(D) Where the applicants send the applications

GO ON TO THE NEXT PAGE

Questions 168-171 refer to the following online chat discussion.

Ken Moore [8:25 A.M.]		Hello, Brian. Where are you now?
Brian Howard [8:28 A.M.]		I'm in my offce, why?
Ken Moore [8:30 A.M.]		We are running out of sugar for the White Snow cakes in our branch. Can you find out how much is left in the warehouse? If not, I have to get some at a store around here.
Brian Howard [8:33 A.M.]		Amy is in the warehouse. Hmm, wait. I'm including her here. How much do you need?
Ken Moore [8:35 A.M.]		Maybe I think that twenty bags would cover it.
Amy Goodwin [8:38 A.M.]		Lucky you!
Ken Moore [8:39 A.M.]		Great. We'll need it by 11 A.M. at the latest.
Amy Goodwin [8:40 A.M.]		Actually, I will be loading some materials for other branches onto a truck. The amount you required should fit, too. I'll deliver it to you first.
Ken Moore [8:42 A.M.]		Thanks, you all. Would you list my name and the number of bags on the log?
Amy Goodwin [8:43 A.M.]		Sure.

Send

---

168 What type of business does Mr. Moore probably work for?

(A) A grocery store
(B) A delivery service
(C) A bakery company
(D) A warehouse

169 At 8:38 A.M., what does Ms. Goodwin most likely mean when she writes, "Lucky you"?

(A) The instructions are easy.
(B) She is free at 11 A.M.
(C) The money Mr. Howard required is available.
(D) The ingredient for a project is enough.

170 Where does Ms. Goodwin say she will go?

(A) To a warehouse
(B) To Mr. Moore's store
(C) To a grocery store
(D) To Mr. Howard's office

171 What does Mr. Moore ask Ms. Goodwin to do?

(A) Give directions to a destination
(B) Approve a request he made
(C) Fill out a document
(D) Calculate how much he needs

Questions 172-175 refer to the following article.

Chicago, Illinois – Local citizens enjoyed themselves at the Renaissance Hotel for the 11th annual Fundraiser for the Chicago Children's hospital. – [1] –. An amazing 2,100 people gathered for last night's event. The highlights of the evening were a parody act of comedians of several famous sitcoms. – [2] –. The last part of the event was partially hosted by three children who were sponsored by the Fund and have fully recovered. The children hosts were on the stage for 30 minutes, but it was more than enough to touch the hearts of the audience members.

The performers made donations to the Fundraiser as well as local businesses and Chicagoans. The Renaissance Hotel has supported the Fundraiser by hosting it free of charge. – [3] –. But the biggest donor was the same as last year, the Chicago City Bank. Mr. Ed Johnson, the president of the bank, made an even bigger donation than last year by giving $1.5 million. Though this event doesn't have a long history, more and more people are voluntarily participating. – [4] –. The Renaissance Hotel has already volunteered to host next year's event. This generous tradition takes place in May every year.

172 Where was the event held?

(A) At a hotel
(B) At a hospital
(C) At City Hall
(D) At a bank

173 Who was the biggest donator?

(A) A medical center
(B) Accommodation
(C) Performers
(D) A financial institution

174 What is indicated about the event?

(A) It happens every winter.
(B) The Renaissance Hotel hosted it for free.
(C) It raised a total of $1.5 million.
(D) It was fully hosted by children.

175 In which of the positions marked [1], [2], [3], and [4] does the following sentence best belong?

"There were also adorable acts from the children from the Chicago Children's Hospital."

(A) [1]
(B) [2]
(C) [3]
(D) [4]

GO ON TO THE NEXT PAGE

It takes a village to raise a child
Why not our village?

Many of you will be familiar with the expression, "It takes a village to raise a child." This sentence alone makes us think about the impacts of groups on a small individual and the efforts needed to give a child the environment he or she needs. But how much are we providing to the children in our town? We all think that we should, but how or where?

We have answers to those questions! The Oakville Town Youth Community Center is in need of volunteers to teach the youth this summer. We need classes to attract youth from hazards such as drugs and violence.

Whatever talent you've got, we're eager to open up a class for you. Just log onto our Web site (www.oakvilleyouth.com), put in your target age and what type of class yours will be. Any type of arts and craft such as pottery, quilting, and model planes can be a great idea for classes. All kinds of sports and book clubs are also possible. We want to discourage classes that require expensive equipment, such as photography and computer programming. The community center is raising funds for computers but it seems that it will take some time.

Please submit a quick draft of your class plan for 12 weeks, but you can change the contents of the plan after it is submitted. We'll go through your plans, and if the community center staff thinks it's educational, we'll contact you and assign you a classroom.

If you think 12 weeks is too much, you can volunteer for a one-day presentation on careers, health, CPR, and more.

Also you can volunteer to help the classes. There are so many ways you can make our town a better place. And now is the time!

Oakville Town Youth Community Center : 617 Perry Street
Tel: 612-555-9787

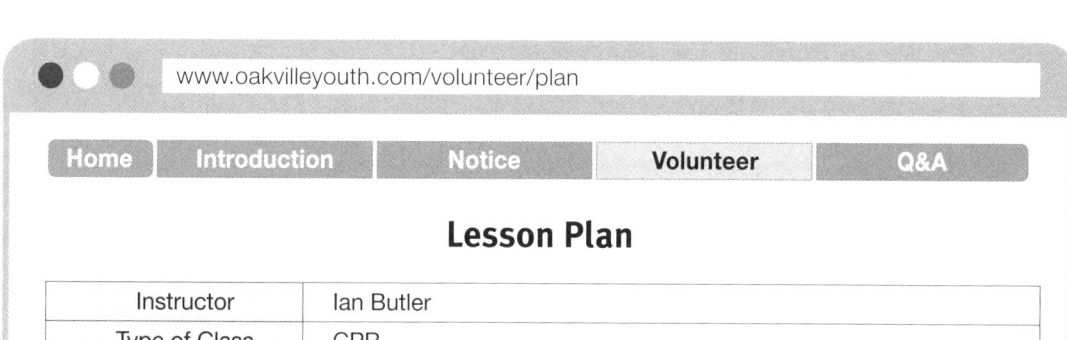

| Home | Introduction | Notice | **Volunteer** | Q&A |

Lesson Plan

Instructor	Ian Butler
Type of Class	CPR
Target Age	15~18 year olds
Location	Oakville Town Youth Community Center B102
Time	□ 12-week class (June 1 ~ August 31) ■ one-day presentation: Wed, July 23, 2017

Comments

I taught the students how to perform CPR on adults, children, and infants at your center B102 three years ago. I need about 30 students and 40 mats for this presentation. This is a tentative plan and I emphasize that it is flexible.

176 What is the announcement about?

(A) The need for volunteers
(B) How to prevent children from using drugs
(C) The request for a new school
(D) The closing of a youth center

177 When will the community center open new classes?

(A) In spring
(B) In summer
(C) In fall
(D) In winter

178 What does the center need to open a class?

(A) More than 3 helpers
(B) A rough course outline
(C) Materials and sports equipment
(D) New computers

179 What kind of class is NOT suggested?

(A) Photography
(B) Pottery
(C) Book reading
(D) Baseball

180 What is implied about Mr. Butler?

(A) It is his first time working with Oakville Town Youth Community Center.
(B) His plan for an event has been fixed.
(C) He does not need any equipment for his presentation.
(D) He considers a 12-week program too long.

Test 10

GO ON TO THE NEXT PAGE

Questions 181-185 refer to the following memo and e-mail.

To: All employees
From: John Gibson
October 4

Dear Colleagues:

Please join us on the evening of October 12 at the Grand Hall of the Palace Hotel for a celebration in honor of Rob Harper.

Rob is leaving Vintage Comics to accept an exciting opportunity to become a full-time animator. Rob has signed a contract to be the animation director of the new animation movie at Dreamjobs. We'll be able to see Rob's work at the movie theater with our families.

It is sad to say goodbye, but for this happy goodbye let's all wish Rob well. To show our appreciation, I am putting together a scrapbook as a gift. I'm going to use Rob's comic characters to say the messages that we want to say to him. So if you would like to leave a message to Rob, please send an e-mail to me. Any statement will be fine, but make sure it is not too long. One or two sentences will be fine. Also, please let me know if you will be able to come to the party.

Thank you very much. I hope to see many of you at this event!

Sincerely,

John Gibson
Assistant Manager

To	John Gibson <john_g@vintagecomics.com>
From	Tyler Miller <tylermiller@vintagecomics.com>
Date	October 8
Subject	Farewell Party

Dear John:

Rob has been my coworker for 5 years. It has been great to work with him, and I am sad to see him leave but truly excited for his success. Much as I would like to be at the party on October 12 to tell Rob how wonderful he has been, I will be out of town that week. I was asked to be the art director of our booth at the 2017 Comic Fair in New York. The Fair starts on the 10th and ends on the 13th, so I won't be able to see Rob go. I will personally have dinner with him, however.

Anyway, about your scrapbook, I would like my message to go in, too. Please use *Jack the Mushroom* character and write: "Wherever you are, I've got your back."

Thank you.

Tyler Miller

181 What is the intention of the memo?

(A) To inform people about the news article on Rob

(B) To request people to bring gifts

(C) To ask for a place for a party

(D) To invite people to an event

182 Why is Mr. Harper leaving Vintage Comics?

(A) He opened his own business.

(B) He wants to go back to his hometown.

(C) He got hired by another company.

(D) He has to be hospitalized.

183 What is mentioned about Mr. Harper?

(A) He served as a full-time worker.

(B) His work will air on TV.

(C) Tyler has been his friend for the past 5 years.

(D) One of his characters is *Jack the Mushroom*.

184 In the memo, the word "show" in paragraph 3, line 1, is closest in meaning to

(A) express

(B) perform

(C) release

(D) exhibit

185 How long will the 2017 Comic Fair last?

(A) For 2 days

(B) For 3 days

(C) For 4 days

(D) For 5 days

GO ON TO THE NEXT PAGE

Angels' Kitchen Catering Services

For your next event, put your worries aside and call Angel's Kitchen Catering Services to prepare gourmet food with a delicate presentation.

We offer you
- An expert coordinator to help you step by step to plan a perfect event
- Various menu options
- Trained and courteous servers
- A variety of tableware
- Decorating specialists

If you plan to host a huge event, you can use the enclosed special coupons. Please enjoy the incredible benefits within a limited period.

For further questions, please make a phone call at 043-555-8523, or send a fax to 043-555-8525 or visit our Web site at www.angelskitchen.com.

Angels' Kitchen Catering Services

Summer Special Discount Coupon

We are offering the best and perfect service to you!

Please cut out the coupon below and feel free to use it for your own needs.

15% discount	25% discount
on rates for events serving more than	on rates for events serving more than
150 people	**250 people**
July 1 ~ August 31	**July 1 ~ August 31**

To: Angels' Kitchen Catering Services
From: Ellie Lane
Date: June 20
Subject: Catering Estimates

I would like to host a 4th of July outing for my employees and their families. I have 50 employees, and if they bring all their family members, it will be around 160 to 200 people. A simple and classic type of 4th of July menu with BBQ, small sandwiches and finger foods would be nice.

Before I make a formal request, I would like to know about the approximate price and menu choices for the event I am planning. Also, is it possible to get a 20% discount if my guests go over the number of 200?

Please call me on my cell phone at 014-555-9632 and let me know.

Thank you very much.

Ellie Lane

---

186 What is NOT being offered by Angels' Kitchen Catering Services?

(A) Experts on decorations
(B) A wide choice of dishware
(C) Etiquette learning service
(D) Abundant menu choices

187 In the flyer, the word "delicate" in paragraph 1, line 2, is closest in meaning to

(A) bright
(B) graceful
(C) expensive
(D) weak

188 For whom is Ms. Lane planning an event?

(A) Her friends
(B) Her clients
(C) Her grandparents
(D) Her colleagues and their families

189 How much discount can Ms. Lane get for the event?

(A) 10%
(B) 15%
(C) 20%
(D) 25%

190 How does Ms. Lane want to be contacted by Angels' Kitchen Catering Services?

(A) By fax
(B) By phone
(C) By a visit to her office
(D) By e-mail

GO ON TO THE NEXT PAGE

Test 10

To: All branch managers
From: AmTop Bank, Headquarters
Date: February 1
Subject: Preparation for the Launching of Thunder Card

The Thunder Card is one of our bank's latest credit card services. It will go on the market on the 15th of this month.

For that matter, all bank personnel should be familiar with the terms and conditions related to the Thunder Card. Although these specifics are not prepared yet, you can check the final version of all the relevant information by tomorrow morning.

Furthermore, all branch managers are obligated to submit an evaluation report on the Thunder Card products after a month of its launching.

Thunder Card
Terms and Conditions

* All bank staff must be fully aware of the terms and conditions of the Thunder Card products.
  1) Clients must have an initial deposit of $300.
  2) Clients should fill out the application form TC 01.
  3) Product beneficiaries must also have an income at least $4,000 a month.
  4) Card recipients must present identification such as below:
     — Company identification card, driver's license, telephone bills (Mobile only), passport
* Clients interested in joining the service must be properly informed of the rules stated above.

To: All employees of branch

From: AmTop Bank, Washington, D.C. branch

Date: March 20

Subject: Thunder Card Update

Attention: Please secure a copy of this message for your reference. After the launching of the Thunder Card, we have experienced a couple of problems, such as:

1. Customers complaining of inoperative cards or the cards not being registered on the main system.
2. Minors requesting cards with driver's license. (Note: A driver's license can be obtained at the age of 16. However, credit cards are not available to clients until they are the age of 20.

We have learned valuable lessons from the past month and this will help us improve our plans for the future. We have to be more thorough and not make the same mistakes again. So we are planning to have a seminar and training on the Thunder Card products. We hope that this training can be the foundation for our need to provide high-quality service to our clients.

Mason Potter

Washington, D.C. branch

---

191 What is the intention of the memo?

(A) To tell employees to sell the new card product

(B) To request opinions about the Thunder Card

(C) To inquire about consumers' response to the new product

(D) To inform all branch managers of the near future plan

192 What is requested of the branch managers?

(A) Sell the new product on site to customers

(B) Submit the assessment of the new product

(C) Brainstorm a card design by the end of this month

(D) Attract more of the affiliating companies

193 What is NOT requested of a customer who wants Thunder Card products?

(A) Presentation of ID card

(B) An initial deposit

(C) Regular income

(D) Property asset

194 Which of the following is NOT identified about product launching?

(A) Some of the cards were not operating.

(B) The product was launched in early March.

(C) A workshop is scheduled after the launch of the product.

(D) Minors were requesting to be entitled to a card.

195 What is being suggested by Mr. Potter?

(A) That the employees attend a training session

(B) That the number of sales representatives be increased

(C) That the bank's closing time be adjusted

(D) That employees have as much experience as possible

GO ON TO THE NEXT PAGE

KDC Electronics

We greatly appreciate your purchase of our product!

We, KDC Electronics, are always trying to supply top-quality home appliances for you. We guarantee goods against any problems within 2 years from the date of your purchase.

Also, we are open to your comments, suggestions, and questions at any time. For us to respond to your messages, visit our website at www.kdcelectronics.com and don't forget to leave your **Name, E-mail address, Telephone number, and Country**.

---

www.kdcelectronics.com/contactus

KDC ELECTRONICS.COM

CONTACT US

| Name | Chloe Rice | Telephone | 312-555-4765 |
| E-mail | chloe1981@topmail.com | Country | U.K. |

Comments

Recently I purchased a refrigerator from one of your stores. The product was installed properly and it worked wonderfully. But this morning when I woke up, liquids were coming out of the refrigerator. When I opened the refrigerator, it was almost the same temperature as the room. The freezer was just slightly cooler than the fridge. I had to run to the store, get ice, and put some of the food in the ice box, but most of the food has gone bad or is starting to look bad. Can you come today to fix it? Also, I purchased this product less than a year ago, so I believe I don't have to pay the repair fees. Is that correct?

To	Chloe Rice <chloe1981@topmail.com>
From	Customer Service <customer@kdcelectronics.com>
Date	August 11
Subject	Customer Comment on August 11

We apologize for the inconvenience you have experienced with your KDC refrigerator. Despite the fact that each appliance is thoroughly tested before it leaves the warehouse, some units with minor defects do make it to local stores.

I will contact the service team to be at your residence today. So I recommend that all the contents of the refrigerator be removed. However, do not disconnect it from the power source.

Your appliance is covered with a standard two-year warranty, so our services will not cost you anything. I will arrange a service man to visit you today. However, if the service man seems to be late, contact him at 1-800-555-7412.

Please note that some KDC refrigerators are reported to have problems as follows.

The KDC-10 may have buzzing sounds, and the KDC-R2 may have an interior light problem. The KDC-GV has temperature problems. The KDC-Q5 has a problem of its freezers becoming too cold. The warranties for these models have been extended.

Sincerely,
Evan Lloyd
Customer Service representative
KDC Electronics

196 Which contact information is NOT necessary when contacting the company?

(A) Name
(B) Residential address
(C) E-mail address
(D) Telephone number

197 In the e-mail, the word "appliance" in paragraph 1, line 2, is closest in meaning to

(A) device
(B) facility
(C) privilege
(D) asset

198 According to the e-mail, what is Ms. Rice advised to do before the service man comes?

(A) Unplug her refrigerator
(B) Call the service center to confirm
(C) Empty the refrigerator
(D) Turn off the light in the refrigerator

199 According to the e-mail, what kind of refrigerator did Ms. Rice probably purchase?

(A) KDC-GV
(B) KDC-10
(C) KDC-R2
(D) KDC-Q5

200 What is suggested about Ms. Rice?

(A) She purchased the refrigerator over 12 months ago.
(B) She asked a home appliance manufacturer for a full refund.
(C) She has done business with KDC several times before.
(D) Her refrigerator will be fixed on the day she requested.

ANSWER SHEET

응시일자 :   년   월   일

수험번호

성 명	한글	
	한자	
	영자	

좌석번호

Ⓐ Ⓑ Ⓒ Ⓓ Ⓔ
① ② ③ ④ ⑤ ⑥ ⑦

Actual Test 1

READING (Part V~VI)

NO.	ANSWER	NO.	ANSWER
	A B C D		A B C D
141		161	
142		162	
143		163	
144		164	
145		165	
146		166	
147		167	
148		168	
149		169	
150		170	
151		171	
152		172	
153		173	
154		174	
155		175	
156		176	
157		177	
158		178	
159		179	
160		180	

NO.	ANSWER
	A B C D
181	
182	
183	
184	
185	
186	
187	
188	
189	
190	
191	
192	
193	
194	
195	
196	
197	
198	
199	
200	

Actual Test 2

READING (Part V~VI)

NO.	ANSWER	NO.	ANSWER	NO.	ANSWER
	A B C D		A B C D		A B C D
141		161		181	
142		162		182	
143		163		183	
144		164		184	
145		165		185	
146		166		186	
147		167		187	
148		168		188	
149		169		189	
150		170		190	
151		171		191	
152		172		192	
153		173		193	
154		174		194	
155		175		195	
156		176		196	
157		177		197	
158		178		198	
159		179		199	
160		180		200	

Actual Test 3

READING (Part V~VI)

NO.	ANSWER	NO.	ANSWER	NO.	ANSWER
	A B C D		A B C D		A B C D
141		161		181	
142		162		182	
143		163		183	
144		164		184	
145		165		185	
146		166		186	
147		167		187	
148		168		188	
149		169		189	
150		170		190	
151		171		191	
152		172		192	
153		173		193	
154		174		194	
155		175		195	
156		176		196	
157		177		197	
158		178		198	
159		179		199	
160		180		200	

1. 사용 필기구 : 컴퓨터용 연필(연필을 제외한 샤인펜, 볼펜 등은 사용 절대 불가)

2. 정못된 필기구 사용과 〈보기〉의 올바른 표기 이외의 정못된 표기로 한 경우에는 당 위원회의 OMR기기가
판독한 결과에 따르며 그 결과는 본인 책임입니다. 1개의 정답만 골라 아래의 올바른 표기대로 정확히 표기
하여야 합니다.
〈보기〉 올바른 표기 : ●   정못된 표기 : ◯ ◑ ◍

3. 답안지는 컴퓨터로 처리되므로 훼손하시면 안 되며, 상단의 타이밍마크(❚❚❚❚)부분을 찾거나, 낙서 등을
하면 본인에게 불이익이 발생할 수 있습니다.

4. 감독관의 확인이 없거나 시험 종료 후에 답안 작성을 계속할 경우 시험 무효 처리됩니다.

* 서약서 내용을 읽으시고 확인란에 반드시 서명하십시오.

본인은 TOEIC 시험 문제의 일부 또는 전부를 유출하거나 어떠한 형태로도 타인에게 누설 공개하
지 않을 것이며 인터넷 또는 인쇄물 등을 이용해 유포하거나 참고 자료로 활용하지 않을 것입니다.
또한 TOEIC 시험 부정 행위 처리 규정을 준수할 것을 서약합니다.

서	약	

확 인

확 인	

ANSWER SHEET

응시일자 : 년 월 일

수험번호

성 한글 영자
명 한자

좌석번호

ⒶⒷⒸⒹⒺ
①②③④⑤⑥⑦

확 인

Actual Test 4
READING (Part V~VI)

NO.	ANSWER	NO.	ANSWER	NO.	ANSWER
	A B C D		A B C D		A B C D
141	Ⓐ Ⓑ Ⓒ Ⓓ	161	Ⓐ Ⓑ Ⓒ Ⓓ	181	Ⓐ Ⓑ Ⓒ Ⓓ
142	Ⓐ Ⓑ Ⓒ Ⓓ	162	Ⓐ Ⓑ Ⓒ Ⓓ	182	Ⓐ Ⓑ Ⓒ Ⓓ
143	Ⓐ Ⓑ Ⓒ Ⓓ	163	Ⓐ Ⓑ Ⓒ Ⓓ	183	Ⓐ Ⓑ Ⓒ Ⓓ
144	Ⓐ Ⓑ Ⓒ Ⓓ	164	Ⓐ Ⓑ Ⓒ Ⓓ	184	Ⓐ Ⓑ Ⓒ Ⓓ
145	Ⓐ Ⓑ Ⓒ Ⓓ	165	Ⓐ Ⓑ Ⓒ Ⓓ	185	Ⓐ Ⓑ Ⓒ Ⓓ
146	Ⓐ Ⓑ Ⓒ Ⓓ	166	Ⓐ Ⓑ Ⓒ Ⓓ	186	Ⓐ Ⓑ Ⓒ Ⓓ
147	Ⓐ Ⓑ Ⓒ Ⓓ	167	Ⓐ Ⓑ Ⓒ Ⓓ	187	Ⓐ Ⓑ Ⓒ Ⓓ
148	Ⓐ Ⓑ Ⓒ Ⓓ	168	Ⓐ Ⓑ Ⓒ Ⓓ	188	Ⓐ Ⓑ Ⓒ Ⓓ
149	Ⓐ Ⓑ Ⓒ Ⓓ	169	Ⓐ Ⓑ Ⓒ Ⓓ	189	Ⓐ Ⓑ Ⓒ Ⓓ
150	Ⓐ Ⓑ Ⓒ Ⓓ	170	Ⓐ Ⓑ Ⓒ Ⓓ	190	Ⓐ Ⓑ Ⓒ Ⓓ
151	Ⓐ Ⓑ Ⓒ Ⓓ	171	Ⓐ Ⓑ Ⓒ Ⓓ	191	Ⓐ Ⓑ Ⓒ Ⓓ
152	Ⓐ Ⓑ Ⓒ Ⓓ	172	Ⓐ Ⓑ Ⓒ Ⓓ	192	Ⓐ Ⓑ Ⓒ Ⓓ
153	Ⓐ Ⓑ Ⓒ Ⓓ	173	Ⓐ Ⓑ Ⓒ Ⓓ	193	Ⓐ Ⓑ Ⓒ Ⓓ
154	Ⓐ Ⓑ Ⓒ Ⓓ	174	Ⓐ Ⓑ Ⓒ Ⓓ	194	Ⓐ Ⓑ Ⓒ Ⓓ
155	Ⓐ Ⓑ Ⓒ Ⓓ	175	Ⓐ Ⓑ Ⓒ Ⓓ	195	Ⓐ Ⓑ Ⓒ Ⓓ
156	Ⓐ Ⓑ Ⓒ Ⓓ	176	Ⓐ Ⓑ Ⓒ Ⓓ	196	Ⓐ Ⓑ Ⓒ Ⓓ
157	Ⓐ Ⓑ Ⓒ Ⓓ	177	Ⓐ Ⓑ Ⓒ Ⓓ	197	Ⓐ Ⓑ Ⓒ Ⓓ
158	Ⓐ Ⓑ Ⓒ Ⓓ	178	Ⓐ Ⓑ Ⓒ Ⓓ	198	Ⓐ Ⓑ Ⓒ Ⓓ
159	Ⓐ Ⓑ Ⓒ Ⓓ	179	Ⓐ Ⓑ Ⓒ Ⓓ	199	Ⓐ Ⓑ Ⓒ Ⓓ
160	Ⓐ Ⓑ Ⓒ Ⓓ	180	Ⓐ Ⓑ Ⓒ Ⓓ	200	Ⓐ Ⓑ Ⓒ Ⓓ

Actual Test 5
READING (Part V~VI)

NO.	ANSWER	NO.	ANSWER	NO.	ANSWER
	A B C D		A B C D		A B C D
141	Ⓐ Ⓑ Ⓒ Ⓓ	161	Ⓐ Ⓑ Ⓒ Ⓓ	181	Ⓐ Ⓑ Ⓒ Ⓓ
142	Ⓐ Ⓑ Ⓒ Ⓓ	162	Ⓐ Ⓑ Ⓒ Ⓓ	182	Ⓐ Ⓑ Ⓒ Ⓓ
143	Ⓐ Ⓑ Ⓒ Ⓓ	163	Ⓐ Ⓑ Ⓒ Ⓓ	183	Ⓐ Ⓑ Ⓒ Ⓓ
144	Ⓐ Ⓑ Ⓒ Ⓓ	164	Ⓐ Ⓑ Ⓒ Ⓓ	184	Ⓐ Ⓑ Ⓒ Ⓓ
145	Ⓐ Ⓑ Ⓒ Ⓓ	165	Ⓐ Ⓑ Ⓒ Ⓓ	185	Ⓐ Ⓑ Ⓒ Ⓓ
146	Ⓐ Ⓑ Ⓒ Ⓓ	166	Ⓐ Ⓑ Ⓒ Ⓓ	186	Ⓐ Ⓑ Ⓒ Ⓓ
147	Ⓐ Ⓑ Ⓒ Ⓓ	167	Ⓐ Ⓑ Ⓒ Ⓓ	187	Ⓐ Ⓑ Ⓒ Ⓓ
148	Ⓐ Ⓑ Ⓒ Ⓓ	168	Ⓐ Ⓑ Ⓒ Ⓓ	188	Ⓐ Ⓑ Ⓒ Ⓓ
149	Ⓐ Ⓑ Ⓒ Ⓓ	169	Ⓐ Ⓑ Ⓒ Ⓓ	189	Ⓐ Ⓑ Ⓒ Ⓓ
150	Ⓐ Ⓑ Ⓒ Ⓓ	170	Ⓐ Ⓑ Ⓒ Ⓓ	190	Ⓐ Ⓑ Ⓒ Ⓓ
151	Ⓐ Ⓑ Ⓒ Ⓓ	171	Ⓐ Ⓑ Ⓒ Ⓓ	191	Ⓐ Ⓑ Ⓒ Ⓓ
152	Ⓐ Ⓑ Ⓒ Ⓓ	172	Ⓐ Ⓑ Ⓒ Ⓓ	192	Ⓐ Ⓑ Ⓒ Ⓓ
153	Ⓐ Ⓑ Ⓒ Ⓓ	173	Ⓐ Ⓑ Ⓒ Ⓓ	193	Ⓐ Ⓑ Ⓒ Ⓓ
154	Ⓐ Ⓑ Ⓒ Ⓓ	174	Ⓐ Ⓑ Ⓒ Ⓓ	194	Ⓐ Ⓑ Ⓒ Ⓓ
155	Ⓐ Ⓑ Ⓒ Ⓓ	175	Ⓐ Ⓑ Ⓒ Ⓓ	195	Ⓐ Ⓑ Ⓒ Ⓓ
156	Ⓐ Ⓑ Ⓒ Ⓓ	176	Ⓐ Ⓑ Ⓒ Ⓓ	196	Ⓐ Ⓑ Ⓒ Ⓓ
157	Ⓐ Ⓑ Ⓒ Ⓓ	177	Ⓐ Ⓑ Ⓒ Ⓓ	197	Ⓐ Ⓑ Ⓒ Ⓓ
158	Ⓐ Ⓑ Ⓒ Ⓓ	178	Ⓐ Ⓑ Ⓒ Ⓓ	198	Ⓐ Ⓑ Ⓒ Ⓓ
159	Ⓐ Ⓑ Ⓒ Ⓓ	179	Ⓐ Ⓑ Ⓒ Ⓓ	199	Ⓐ Ⓑ Ⓒ Ⓓ
160	Ⓐ Ⓑ Ⓒ Ⓓ	180	Ⓐ Ⓑ Ⓒ Ⓓ	200	Ⓐ Ⓑ Ⓒ Ⓓ

Actual Test 6
READING (Part V~VI)

NO.	ANSWER	NO.	ANSWER	NO.	ANSWER
	A B C D		A B C D		A B C D
141	Ⓐ Ⓑ Ⓒ Ⓓ	161	Ⓐ Ⓑ Ⓒ Ⓓ	181	Ⓐ Ⓑ Ⓒ Ⓓ
142	Ⓐ Ⓑ Ⓒ Ⓓ	162	Ⓐ Ⓑ Ⓒ Ⓓ	182	Ⓐ Ⓑ Ⓒ Ⓓ
143	Ⓐ Ⓑ Ⓒ Ⓓ	163	Ⓐ Ⓑ Ⓒ Ⓓ	183	Ⓐ Ⓑ Ⓒ Ⓓ
144	Ⓐ Ⓑ Ⓒ Ⓓ	164	Ⓐ Ⓑ Ⓒ Ⓓ	184	Ⓐ Ⓑ Ⓒ Ⓓ
145	Ⓐ Ⓑ Ⓒ Ⓓ	165	Ⓐ Ⓑ Ⓒ Ⓓ	185	Ⓐ Ⓑ Ⓒ Ⓓ
146	Ⓐ Ⓑ Ⓒ Ⓓ	166	Ⓐ Ⓑ Ⓒ Ⓓ	186	Ⓐ Ⓑ Ⓒ Ⓓ
147	Ⓐ Ⓑ Ⓒ Ⓓ	167	Ⓐ Ⓑ Ⓒ Ⓓ	187	Ⓐ Ⓑ Ⓒ Ⓓ
148	Ⓐ Ⓑ Ⓒ Ⓓ	168	Ⓐ Ⓑ Ⓒ Ⓓ	188	Ⓐ Ⓑ Ⓒ Ⓓ
149	Ⓐ Ⓑ Ⓒ Ⓓ	169	Ⓐ Ⓑ Ⓒ Ⓓ	189	Ⓐ Ⓑ Ⓒ Ⓓ
150	Ⓐ Ⓑ Ⓒ Ⓓ	170	Ⓐ Ⓑ Ⓒ Ⓓ	190	Ⓐ Ⓑ Ⓒ Ⓓ
151	Ⓐ Ⓑ Ⓒ Ⓓ	171	Ⓐ Ⓑ Ⓒ Ⓓ	191	Ⓐ Ⓑ Ⓒ Ⓓ
152	Ⓐ Ⓑ Ⓒ Ⓓ	172	Ⓐ Ⓑ Ⓒ Ⓓ	192	Ⓐ Ⓑ Ⓒ Ⓓ
153	Ⓐ Ⓑ Ⓒ Ⓓ	173	Ⓐ Ⓑ Ⓒ Ⓓ	193	Ⓐ Ⓑ Ⓒ Ⓓ
154	Ⓐ Ⓑ Ⓒ Ⓓ	174	Ⓐ Ⓑ Ⓒ Ⓓ	194	Ⓐ Ⓑ Ⓒ Ⓓ
155	Ⓐ Ⓑ Ⓒ Ⓓ	175	Ⓐ Ⓑ Ⓒ Ⓓ	195	Ⓐ Ⓑ Ⓒ Ⓓ
156	Ⓐ Ⓑ Ⓒ Ⓓ	176	Ⓐ Ⓑ Ⓒ Ⓓ	196	Ⓐ Ⓑ Ⓒ Ⓓ
157	Ⓐ Ⓑ Ⓒ Ⓓ	177	Ⓐ Ⓑ Ⓒ Ⓓ	197	Ⓐ Ⓑ Ⓒ Ⓓ
158	Ⓐ Ⓑ Ⓒ Ⓓ	178	Ⓐ Ⓑ Ⓒ Ⓓ	198	Ⓐ Ⓑ Ⓒ Ⓓ
159	Ⓐ Ⓑ Ⓒ Ⓓ	179	Ⓐ Ⓑ Ⓒ Ⓓ	199	Ⓐ Ⓑ Ⓒ Ⓓ
160	Ⓐ Ⓑ Ⓒ Ⓓ	180	Ⓐ Ⓑ Ⓒ Ⓓ	200	Ⓐ Ⓑ Ⓒ Ⓓ

1. 사용 필기구 : 컴퓨터용 연필 (연필을 제외한 사인펜, 볼펜 등은 사용 절대 불가)

2. 정정된 필기구 사용과 〈보기〉의 올바른 표기 이외의 잘못된 표기로 한 경우에는 단 위원회의 OMR기기가 판독한 경우에 따르며 그 결과는 본인 책임입니다. 17개의 잘못된 골라 아래의 올바른 표기대로 정확히 표기 하여야 합니다.

〈보기〉 올바른 표기 : ● 잘못된 표기 : ◐◑

3. 답안지는 컴퓨터로 처리되므로 훼손하시면 안 되며, 상단의 타이밍마크(▮▮▮)부분을 찢거나, 낙서 등을 하면 본인에게 불이익이 발생할 수 있습니다.

4. 감독관의 확인이 없거나 시험 종료 후에 답안 작성을 계속할 경우 시험 무효 처리됩니다.

* 서약 내용을 읽으시고 확인란에 반드시 서명하십시오.

서 약

본인은 TOEIC 시험 문제의 일부 또는 전부를 유출하거나 어떠한 형태로든 타인에게 누설 공개하지 않을 것이며 인터넷 또는 이메일 등을 이용해 유포하거나 참고 자료로 활용하지 않을 것입니다. 또한 TOEIC 시험 부정 행위 처리 규정을 준수할 것을 서약합니다.

확 인

ANSWER SHEET

응시일자 : 　　년　　월　　일

수험번호

성명

성	한글	
명	한자	
	영자	

좌석번호

Ⓐ Ⓑ Ⓒ Ⓓ Ⓔ
① ② ③ ④ ⑤ ⑥ ⑦

확 인

Actual **Test 7**

READING (Part V~VI)

(answer bubbles for No. 141–200)

Actual **Test 8**

READING (Part V~VI)

(answer bubbles for No. 141–200)

Actual **Test 9**

READING (Part V~VI)

(answer bubbles for No. 141–200)

1. 사용 필기구 : 컴퓨터용 연필(연필을 제외한 사인펜, 볼펜 등은 사용 절대 불가)

2. 절못된 표기구 사용과 〈보기〉의 올바른 표기 이외의 잘못된 표기로 한 경우에는 당 위원회의 OMR기기가 판독할 결과에 따르며 그 결과는 본인 책임입니다. 1개의 정답만 골라 아래의 올바른 표기대로 정확히 표기하여야 합니다.

〈보기〉올바른 표기 : ●　　잘못된 표기 : ○ ◑ ◐ ⦿

3. 답안지는 컴퓨터로 처리되므로 훼손하거나 더럽히면 안 되며, 상단의 타이밍마크(▮▮▮▮)부분을 찢거나, 낙서 등을 하면 본인에게 불이익이 발생할 수 있습니다.

4. 감독관의 확인이 없거나 시험 종료 후에 답안 작성을 계속할 경우 시험 무효 처리됩니다.

※서약 내용을 읽으시고 확인란에 반드시 서명하십시오.

서 약

본인은 TOEIC 시험 문제의 일부 또는 전부를 유출하거나 어떠한 형태로든 타인에게 누설 공개하지 않을 것이며 인터넷 또는 인쇄물 등을 이용해 유포하거나 참고 자료로 활용하지 않을 것입니다. 또한 TOEIC 시험 부정행위 처리 규정을 준수할 것을 서약합니다.

Actual **Test 10**

READING (Part V~VI)

NO.	ANSWER A B C D	NO.	ANSWER A B C D	NO.	ANSWER A B C D
141	Ⓐ Ⓑ Ⓒ Ⓓ	161	Ⓐ Ⓑ Ⓒ Ⓓ	181	Ⓐ Ⓑ Ⓒ Ⓓ
142	Ⓐ Ⓑ Ⓒ Ⓓ	162	Ⓐ Ⓑ Ⓒ Ⓓ	182	Ⓐ Ⓑ Ⓒ Ⓓ
143	Ⓐ Ⓑ Ⓒ Ⓓ	163	Ⓐ Ⓑ Ⓒ Ⓓ	183	Ⓐ Ⓑ Ⓒ Ⓓ
144	Ⓐ Ⓑ Ⓒ Ⓓ	164	Ⓐ Ⓑ Ⓒ Ⓓ	184	Ⓐ Ⓑ Ⓒ Ⓓ
145	Ⓐ Ⓑ Ⓒ Ⓓ	165	Ⓐ Ⓑ Ⓒ Ⓓ	185	Ⓐ Ⓑ Ⓒ Ⓓ
146	Ⓐ Ⓑ Ⓒ Ⓓ	166	Ⓐ Ⓑ Ⓒ Ⓓ	186	Ⓐ Ⓑ Ⓒ Ⓓ
147	Ⓐ Ⓑ Ⓒ Ⓓ	167	Ⓐ Ⓑ Ⓒ Ⓓ	187	Ⓐ Ⓑ Ⓒ Ⓓ
148	Ⓐ Ⓑ Ⓒ Ⓓ	168	Ⓐ Ⓑ Ⓒ Ⓓ	188	Ⓐ Ⓑ Ⓒ Ⓓ
149	Ⓐ Ⓑ Ⓒ Ⓓ	169	Ⓐ Ⓑ Ⓒ Ⓓ	189	Ⓐ Ⓑ Ⓒ Ⓓ
150	Ⓐ Ⓑ Ⓒ Ⓓ	170	Ⓐ Ⓑ Ⓒ Ⓓ	190	Ⓐ Ⓑ Ⓒ Ⓓ
151	Ⓐ Ⓑ Ⓒ Ⓓ	171	Ⓐ Ⓑ Ⓒ Ⓓ	191	Ⓐ Ⓑ Ⓒ Ⓓ
152	Ⓐ Ⓑ Ⓒ Ⓓ	172	Ⓐ Ⓑ Ⓒ Ⓓ	192	Ⓐ Ⓑ Ⓒ Ⓓ
153	Ⓐ Ⓑ Ⓒ Ⓓ	173	Ⓐ Ⓑ Ⓒ Ⓓ	193	Ⓐ Ⓑ Ⓒ Ⓓ
154	Ⓐ Ⓑ Ⓒ Ⓓ	174	Ⓐ Ⓑ Ⓒ Ⓓ	194	Ⓐ Ⓑ Ⓒ Ⓓ
155	Ⓐ Ⓑ Ⓒ Ⓓ	175	Ⓐ Ⓑ Ⓒ Ⓓ	195	Ⓐ Ⓑ Ⓒ Ⓓ
156	Ⓐ Ⓑ Ⓒ Ⓓ	176	Ⓐ Ⓑ Ⓒ Ⓓ	196	Ⓐ Ⓑ Ⓒ Ⓓ
157	Ⓐ Ⓑ Ⓒ Ⓓ	177	Ⓐ Ⓑ Ⓒ Ⓓ	197	Ⓐ Ⓑ Ⓒ Ⓓ
158	Ⓐ Ⓑ Ⓒ Ⓓ	178	Ⓐ Ⓑ Ⓒ Ⓓ	198	Ⓐ Ⓑ Ⓒ Ⓓ
159	Ⓐ Ⓑ Ⓒ Ⓓ	179	Ⓐ Ⓑ Ⓒ Ⓓ	199	Ⓐ Ⓑ Ⓒ Ⓓ
160	Ⓐ Ⓑ Ⓒ Ⓓ	180	Ⓐ Ⓑ Ⓒ Ⓓ	200	Ⓐ Ⓑ Ⓒ Ⓓ

수험번호

Actual **Test**

READING (Part V~VI)

NO.	ANSWER A B C D	NO.	ANSWER A B C D	NO.	ANSWER A B C D
141	Ⓐ Ⓑ Ⓒ Ⓓ	161	Ⓐ Ⓑ Ⓒ Ⓓ	181	Ⓐ Ⓑ Ⓒ Ⓓ
142	Ⓐ Ⓑ Ⓒ Ⓓ	162	Ⓐ Ⓑ Ⓒ Ⓓ	182	Ⓐ Ⓑ Ⓒ Ⓓ
143	Ⓐ Ⓑ Ⓒ Ⓓ	163	Ⓐ Ⓑ Ⓒ Ⓓ	183	Ⓐ Ⓑ Ⓒ Ⓓ
144	Ⓐ Ⓑ Ⓒ Ⓓ	164	Ⓐ Ⓑ Ⓒ Ⓓ	184	Ⓐ Ⓑ Ⓒ Ⓓ
145	Ⓐ Ⓑ Ⓒ Ⓓ	165	Ⓐ Ⓑ Ⓒ Ⓓ	185	Ⓐ Ⓑ Ⓒ Ⓓ
146	Ⓐ Ⓑ Ⓒ Ⓓ	166	Ⓐ Ⓑ Ⓒ Ⓓ	186	Ⓐ Ⓑ Ⓒ Ⓓ
147	Ⓐ Ⓑ Ⓒ Ⓓ	167	Ⓐ Ⓑ Ⓒ Ⓓ	187	Ⓐ Ⓑ Ⓒ Ⓓ
148	Ⓐ Ⓑ Ⓒ Ⓓ	168	Ⓐ Ⓑ Ⓒ Ⓓ	188	Ⓐ Ⓑ Ⓒ Ⓓ
149	Ⓐ Ⓑ Ⓒ Ⓓ	169	Ⓐ Ⓑ Ⓒ Ⓓ	189	Ⓐ Ⓑ Ⓒ Ⓓ
150	Ⓐ Ⓑ Ⓒ Ⓓ	170	Ⓐ Ⓑ Ⓒ Ⓓ	190	Ⓐ Ⓑ Ⓒ Ⓓ
151	Ⓐ Ⓑ Ⓒ Ⓓ	171	Ⓐ Ⓑ Ⓒ Ⓓ	191	Ⓐ Ⓑ Ⓒ Ⓓ
152	Ⓐ Ⓑ Ⓒ Ⓓ	172	Ⓐ Ⓑ Ⓒ Ⓓ	192	Ⓐ Ⓑ Ⓒ Ⓓ
153	Ⓐ Ⓑ Ⓒ Ⓓ	173	Ⓐ Ⓑ Ⓒ Ⓓ	193	Ⓐ Ⓑ Ⓒ Ⓓ
154	Ⓐ Ⓑ Ⓒ Ⓓ	174	Ⓐ Ⓑ Ⓒ Ⓓ	194	Ⓐ Ⓑ Ⓒ Ⓓ
155	Ⓐ Ⓑ Ⓒ Ⓓ	175	Ⓐ Ⓑ Ⓒ Ⓓ	195	Ⓐ Ⓑ Ⓒ Ⓓ
156	Ⓐ Ⓑ Ⓒ Ⓓ	176	Ⓐ Ⓑ Ⓒ Ⓓ	196	Ⓐ Ⓑ Ⓒ Ⓓ
157	Ⓐ Ⓑ Ⓒ Ⓓ	177	Ⓐ Ⓑ Ⓒ Ⓓ	197	Ⓐ Ⓑ Ⓒ Ⓓ
158	Ⓐ Ⓑ Ⓒ Ⓓ	178	Ⓐ Ⓑ Ⓒ Ⓓ	198	Ⓐ Ⓑ Ⓒ Ⓓ
159	Ⓐ Ⓑ Ⓒ Ⓓ	179	Ⓐ Ⓑ Ⓒ Ⓓ	199	Ⓐ Ⓑ Ⓒ Ⓓ
160	Ⓐ Ⓑ Ⓒ Ⓓ	180	Ⓐ Ⓑ Ⓒ Ⓓ	200	Ⓐ Ⓑ Ⓒ Ⓓ

Actual **Test**

READING (Part V~VI)

NO.	ANSWER A B C D	NO.	ANSWER A B C D	NO.	ANSWER A B C D
141	Ⓐ Ⓑ Ⓒ Ⓓ	161	Ⓐ Ⓑ Ⓒ Ⓓ	181	Ⓐ Ⓑ Ⓒ Ⓓ
142	Ⓐ Ⓑ Ⓒ Ⓓ	162	Ⓐ Ⓑ Ⓒ Ⓓ	182	Ⓐ Ⓑ Ⓒ Ⓓ
143	Ⓐ Ⓑ Ⓒ Ⓓ	163	Ⓐ Ⓑ Ⓒ Ⓓ	183	Ⓐ Ⓑ Ⓒ Ⓓ
144	Ⓐ Ⓑ Ⓒ Ⓓ	164	Ⓐ Ⓑ Ⓒ Ⓓ	184	Ⓐ Ⓑ Ⓒ Ⓓ
145	Ⓐ Ⓑ Ⓒ Ⓓ	165	Ⓐ Ⓑ Ⓒ Ⓓ	185	Ⓐ Ⓑ Ⓒ Ⓓ
146	Ⓐ Ⓑ Ⓒ Ⓓ	166	Ⓐ Ⓑ Ⓒ Ⓓ	186	Ⓐ Ⓑ Ⓒ Ⓓ
147	Ⓐ Ⓑ Ⓒ Ⓓ	167	Ⓐ Ⓑ Ⓒ Ⓓ	187	Ⓐ Ⓑ Ⓒ Ⓓ
148	Ⓐ Ⓑ Ⓒ Ⓓ	168	Ⓐ Ⓑ Ⓒ Ⓓ	188	Ⓐ Ⓑ Ⓒ Ⓓ
149	Ⓐ Ⓑ Ⓒ Ⓓ	169	Ⓐ Ⓑ Ⓒ Ⓓ	189	Ⓐ Ⓑ Ⓒ Ⓓ
150	Ⓐ Ⓑ Ⓒ Ⓓ	170	Ⓐ Ⓑ Ⓒ Ⓓ	190	Ⓐ Ⓑ Ⓒ Ⓓ
151	Ⓐ Ⓑ Ⓒ Ⓓ	171	Ⓐ Ⓑ Ⓒ Ⓓ	191	Ⓐ Ⓑ Ⓒ Ⓓ
152	Ⓐ Ⓑ Ⓒ Ⓓ	172	Ⓐ Ⓑ Ⓒ Ⓓ	192	Ⓐ Ⓑ Ⓒ Ⓓ
153	Ⓐ Ⓑ Ⓒ Ⓓ	173	Ⓐ Ⓑ Ⓒ Ⓓ	193	Ⓐ Ⓑ Ⓒ Ⓓ
154	Ⓐ Ⓑ Ⓒ Ⓓ	174	Ⓐ Ⓑ Ⓒ Ⓓ	194	Ⓐ Ⓑ Ⓒ Ⓓ
155	Ⓐ Ⓑ Ⓒ Ⓓ	175	Ⓐ Ⓑ Ⓒ Ⓓ	195	Ⓐ Ⓑ Ⓒ Ⓓ
156	Ⓐ Ⓑ Ⓒ Ⓓ	176	Ⓐ Ⓑ Ⓒ Ⓓ	196	Ⓐ Ⓑ Ⓒ Ⓓ
157	Ⓐ Ⓑ Ⓒ Ⓓ	177	Ⓐ Ⓑ Ⓒ Ⓓ	197	Ⓐ Ⓑ Ⓒ Ⓓ
158	Ⓐ Ⓑ Ⓒ Ⓓ	178	Ⓐ Ⓑ Ⓒ Ⓓ	198	Ⓐ Ⓑ Ⓒ Ⓓ
159	Ⓐ Ⓑ Ⓒ Ⓓ	179	Ⓐ Ⓑ Ⓒ Ⓓ	199	Ⓐ Ⓑ Ⓒ Ⓓ
160	Ⓐ Ⓑ Ⓒ Ⓓ	180	Ⓐ Ⓑ Ⓒ Ⓓ	200	Ⓐ Ⓑ Ⓒ Ⓓ

성명	한글 한자 영자		좌석번호
			Ⓐ Ⓑ Ⓒ Ⓓ Ⓔ ① ② ③ ④ ⑤ ⑥ ⑦

서 약

확 인

이미영·박선영 지음

나혼자 끝내는 토익 PART 7

신토익 실전10회

신토익 고득점을 결정하는 PART 7 필수 정복 코스

| PART 7 실전 10회 문제집 | + | 핵심 패러프레이징을 수록한 해설집 | + | 나혼토 1:1 지자 코칭 |

정답 및 해설

넥서스

Actual Test

01

저자 이미영

다음 카페(http://cafe.daum.net/speedytoeic)
≫ [나혼토 1:1 코칭] 게시판 이용

본책 P12

📖 Reading Comprehension

PART 7

147 (D)	148 (B)	149 (C)	150 (D)	151 (A)	152 (C)	153 (D)	154 (B)	155 (C)
156 (A)	157 (C)	158 (D)	159 (D)	160 (B)	161 (D)	162 (A)	163 (C)	164 (D)
165 (C)	166 (B)	167 (D)	168 (A)	169 (B)	170 (D)	171 (B)	172 (D)	173 (B)
174 (D)	175 (B)	176 (C)	177 (D)	178 (D)	179 (C)	180 (A)	181 (A)	182 (B)
183 (C)	184 (C)	185 (B)	186 (B)	187 (C)	188 (D)	189 (D)	190 (B)	191 (A)
192 (A)	193 (D)	194 (B)	195 (B)	196 (D)	197 (D)	198 (C)	199 (C)	200 (B)

[147-148]

대러 매장

48 프로스트 레인

그린빌 버몬트

매닝 씨에게:

저는 귀하께서 7월 11일에 저희 고객 서비스 부서로 보낸 편지에 대한 담당자로서 이 편지를 쓰고 있습니다. **147** 먼저 귀하께서 저희 제품 중 하나인 키친 프로로 인해 경험하셨던 좋지 않은 경험에 대해서 진심 어린 사과를 드리고 싶습니다.

귀하께서 반품한 제품을 살펴본 결과, 그 제품에 결함이 있다는 것을 확인할 수 있었습니다. 귀하께서는 재대로 작동되는 제품으로 교환되기를 원하지 않는다고 분명히 말씀하셨으니, 전액 환불해 드리려고 했습니다. 저는 또한 이 기회를 빌려 귀하께서 50달러에 상응하는 상품권을 보내드리려고 합니다.

다시 한번, 저희 고객님, 사과를 받아주십시오. **148** 이번 일로 인한 모든 저희 제품을 처음 구매한 신 고객분으로서 실망스러운 경험이었을 것입니다. 그래서 저는 귀하가 저희 제품을 한 번 더 기회를 주기로 결정하시기를 바랍니다.

낸시 스캐필드 드림

고객 서비스 부장

키친 프로사

어휘 in response to ~에 답하여　extend one's apology 사과하다　upon ~하자마자　examination 조사　determine 알아내다, 밝히다　defective 결함이 있는　exchange A for B A를 B로 교환하다　functioning 기능하는　unit (전체·제품의) 한 세트, 한 개　authorize 하가하다　gift certificate 상품권　function 기능, 작동　compensate 보상하다　faulty product 불량품

147 편지의 목적은 무엇인가?

(A) 제품의 새로운 기능에 관해 설명하려고

(B) 상품 교환 지연에 대해 고객에게 보상하려고

(C) 온라인 할인 판매를 광고하려고

(D) 불량품에 대해 사과하려고

해설 주제나 목적 문제의 힌트는 보통 지문 앞쪽에 등장한다. 좋지 않았던 경험에 대해 진심으로 사과를 드리고 싶었다고 했으므로 정답은 (D)이다. 상품 결함이 있었던 것이지 제품을 교환하는 것이 지연된 것은 아니므로 (B)는 오답이다.

148 편지의 수령인에 관해 알 수 있는 것은 무엇인가?

(A) 고객 서비스 부서에서 일하는 것에 익숙하다.

(B) 전에 키친 프로에서 구입한 적이 없다.

(C) 그는 다른 상품으로 교환되기를 원한다.

(D) 완제 선물로 실내용 그림을 구매했다.

해설 편지 수령인이 매닝 씨가 제품을 처음 구입한 고객(first-time customer)이라고 했으므로, 매닝 씨가 전에 키친 프로에서 구입한 적이 없다는 것을 추론할 수 있다. 따라서 정답은 (B)이다. (A)는 지문에 자주 등장하는 customer service를 반복한 함정이다.

[149-150]

<table>
<tr><td colspan="2">제이슨 해리슨</td></tr>
<tr><td>리사, 아직 사무실에 있나요?</td><td>오전 9시 38분</td></tr>
<tr><td colspan="2">리사 리</td></tr>
<tr><td>안녕하세요, 제이슨. 네, 지금 막 나가려고 했어요. 오늘 오지 않나요?</td><td>오전 9시 42분</td></tr>
<tr><td colspan="2">제이슨 해리슨</td></tr>
<tr><td>아뇨. 저는 장례식 회의장으로 곧장 가기로 했어요. 모든 회의 참석자들이 도착하기 전에 우리 회사의 부스를 설치하기 위해 일찍 일찍 가고 싶어요.</td><td>오전 9시 44분</td></tr>
<tr><td colspan="2">제이슨 해리슨</td></tr>
<tr><td>**150** 안타깝게도, 제가 주의 깊지 못해서 우리 사업 서비스에 대한 새로운 책자들이 제 책상에 있어요.</td><td>오전 9시 45분</td></tr>
<tr><td colspan="2">리사 리</td></tr>
<tr><td>새로운 책자들이 있다고요? 이전 것들은 뭐가 문제였나요? 우리 서비스가 어떻게 바뀌었나요?</td><td>오전 9시 46분</td></tr>
<tr><td colspan="2">제이슨 해리슨</td></tr>
<tr><td>**149** 문제는 없었지만 시장님에서 디자인이 구식이라고 느끼셨어요. 우리의 새로운 로고와 더 밝은 색들을 넣은 새롭고 현대적 책자를 의뢰하셨어요.</td><td>오전 9시 48분</td></tr>
<tr><td colspan="2">리사 리</td></tr>
<tr><td>알겠어요. 그럼 제가 가기 전에 신간 책자들을 가져갈게요.</td><td>오전 9시 55분</td></tr>
<tr><td colspan="2">제이슨 해리슨</td></tr>
<tr><td>도와줘서 고마워요, 리사. 회의장에서 곧 봐요!</td><td>오전 9시 56분</td></tr>
</table>

어휘 be about to 막 ~하려고 하다　head straight to ~로 곧장 가다　set up ~을 설치하다　convention 회의　attendee 참석자　unfortunately 안타깝게도, 유감스럽게도　think A through A를 주의 깊게 생각하다　outdated 구식의　CEO 최고 경영 책임자　commission 의뢰하다　incorporate 포함하다　grab 붙잡다, 움켜잡다　appreciate 감사하다

149 이전 서비스 책자들에 관해 언급된 것은 무엇인가?

(A) 틀린 정보를 포함했었다.

(B) 시장님에 의해서 디자인되었다.

(C) 현대적 모습을 갖추지 않았다.

(D) 잘못된 위치로 배달되었다.

해설 9시 48분 내용을 보면, 시장님이 느끼기에 예전 책자는 디자인이 구식이라고 했다. 즉 outdated 표현을 선택지에서는 do not have a modern appearance라는 표현을 이용해서 패러프레이징했다. 따라서 정답은 (C)이다.

150 오전 9시 45분에, 해리슨 씨가 "제가 주의 깊지 못해서"라고 쓴 의미는 무엇인가?

(A) 그는 양을 과소평가했다.

(B) 그는 평가 틀리게 입력했다.

(C) 그는 리 씨를 오해했다.

(D) 그는 서류를 깜빡했다.

해설 해당 문장의 앞과 뒤의 문맥의 내용을 통해 표현의 맥락적 의미를 따져 보자. 해리슨 씨가 업무 외적으로 주의 깊지 못했다고 했으며, 안타깝게도 새 책자가 자기 책상에 있어는 상황이라고 했으므로, 좋의장으로 바로 가기로 한 결정이 잘못된 결정이었음을 알 수 있다. 즉, 회의장으로 바로 가려고 한 결정 때문에 그 사무실을 들러 책자를 찾아오지 못할 것이라는 의미로 정답은 (D)가 된다. through는 'A를 주의 깊게 생각하다'라는 의미로 쓰였다.

노스웨이 비즈니스 뉴스

151 **152** 그린 스카이 커피사는 노스웨이 신성 지역에 새로운 매장을 열 계획이라고 발표했다. 이것은 전국적으로 25번째 그린 스카이 커피 매장이 될 것이며, 주 (州)에서는 첫 번째가 될 것이다. 노스웨이 시장인 젠 브라운은 다음 성명을 발표했다: "노스웨이에도 최근에 활발을 더했던 우리 성업 지역에 그린 스카이 매장을 유치하게 되어 진심 자랑스럽게 생각합니다."

그린 스카이는 미국에서 가장 빠르게 성장하는 커피 회사 중 하나이다. 이 회사는 소매점들과 함께 몇몇 주요 패스트푸드 매장과 국제 항공사 두 곳에 커피를 공급하고 있다. **152** 노스웨이의 매장은 메인 스트리트 옆에 위치할 것이며, 그곳 시내에서 고전분투하는 성업 지역에 더 많은 매장을 유치하기 위한 노력의 일부로 최근에 많은 지원을 받을 것이다.

어휘 release 발표하다　business district 상업 지역　nationwide 전국적으로　welcome 기꺼이 맞이하다. 환영하다　revitalized 새로운 활력을 찾은　along with ~와 함께　retail store 소매점　supply A with B A에게 B를 제공하다　international airline 국제 항공사　attract 국내, 관심 등을 끌다, 유치하다　struggling 분투하는　commercial 상업적인　diversify 다각화하다, 다양화하다

151 기사의 목적은 무엇인가?

(A) 향후 있을 매장의 개장을 발표하기 위해서

(B) 시장 연설의 세부 사항을 설명하기 위해서

(C) 지역에서 지연되고 있는 문제점을 토론하기 위해서

(D) 제품의 변화를 늘리고자 하는 회사의 계획을 설명하기 위해서

해설 기사문은 다게 지문 서두 부분에 글의 목적이 나타나 있음을 확실히 늘 수 있다. 노스웨이 성업 지역에 새 매장을 열 계획이라고 했다. 이와 관련된 세부 사항이 계속 이어지므로 글의 목적은 (A)라고 볼 수 있다. (C)는 지문에 언급된 struggling 표현을 이용하여 만든 함정이다. (B)는 시장의 성업 내용이 나오기는 하나 일부 내용일 뿐 전체 글의 목적으로 보기는 어렵기에 오답이다.

152 노스웨이 상업 지역에 관해 언급된 것은 무엇인가?

(A) 그린 스카이 본사가 있는 곳이다.

(B) 몇몇 패스트푸드 식당들이 가까에 개장했다.

(C) 그곳을 개선하려는 시도가 계속되고 있다.

(D) 메인 스트리트 옆의 많은 가게들이 성업 중이다.

252

어휘 confirmation 확인 place an order 주문하다 overall 전반적인 be willing to 기꺼이 ~하다 related to ~와 관련된 cooperation 협력 survey-taker 설문 응답자 good for ~에 유효한 upon ~하자마자 retailer 소매 업체 elect 선택하다 resubmit 다시 제출하다 transaction 거래 complimentary 무료의(= free)

156 사용자에 관해 알 수 있는 것은 무엇인가?
(A) 사용자는 사이트에서 처음 구매를 했다.
(B) 사용자는 요청받은 정보를 모두 제공하지 못했다.
(C) 사용자는 사이트에 대한 항의 편지를 제출했다.
(D) 사용자는 회사의 계정을 삭제하기로 선택했다.

해설 조번에 이 계정으로 처음 주문했다고 했으므로 정답은 (A)이다.

157 사용자는 어떻게 하라는 요청을 받는가?
(A) 몇몇 개인 정보 다시 제출하기
(B) 의견에 대한 이유 설명하기
(C) 거래에 대한 질문에 답하기
(D) 주어진 배송지 주소 확인하기

해설 구매와 관련하여 간단한 설문지를 작성하려면, 하단의 "계속" 버튼을 클릭하라고 했다. 따라서 정답은 (C)이다. 지문에 short survey related to your purchase를 설문지에서는 questions about a transaction으로 바꾸어 표현하였다.

158 사용자에게 제공될 것은 무엇인가?
(A) 이번 구매 시에 10% 할인
(B) 무료 스포츠 의류 제품
(C) 파손된 제품에 대한 전액 환불
(D) 다음 주문 시에 무료 배송

해설 감사의 표현으로 다음 구매 시에 이용 가능한 온라인 무료 배송 쿠폰을 제공해 주겠다고 했다. 따라서 정답은 (D)이다. 지문의 free를 complimentary로, next purchase를 future order로 패러프레이징하였다.

[156-158]

http://www.blackriver.com

블랙 리버 온라인

홈	검색	배송	구매	도움말

블랙 리버 스포츠웨어에 주문을 완료해 주셔서 감사드립니다. 구매 확인서는 귀하가 제공해 주신 이메일 주소로 처음 주문하신 것이기 때문에 저희 사이트에 대한 귀하의 전반적인 체험 후기를 듣고자 합니다. **157** 귀하의 구매와 관련하여 간단한 설문지를 작성해 주시려면, 이 페이지 하단에 있는 "계속" 버튼을 클릭해 주세요. 설문지는 단 8개의 질문과 마지막에 의견을 적는 부분으로 구성되어 있습니다. 설문을 작성하는 데 10분 이상 걸리지 않을 것입니다.

158 귀하의 피드백과 협조에 대한 감사의 표현으로, 저희는 설문에 응답해 주신 모든 분께 블랙 리버 스포츠웨어에서 다음 구매 시에 사용하실 수 있는 온라인 무료 배송 쿠폰을 제공할 것입니다. 설문지 작성 완료 후 화면에 뜰 링크를 클릭해 주세요.

저희가 계속 미국 최고의 온라인 스포츠 의류 소매 업체가 되도록 도와주셔서 감사합니다.

블랙 리버 스포츠웨어 고객 서비스팀

[계속]

해설 그런 스카이 커내시가 노스쇼어 상권 지역에 새 매장을 개점할 것이라고 했었다. 고전부득는 성권 지역에 매장을 유지하기 위한 노력의 하나로 최근에 다시 문을 연 노스쇼어 매장이라는 것이라고 했다. 따라서 이 두 내용을 종합해 보면, 노스쇼어 상권 지역에 개선하려는 시도가 계속되고 있음을 알 수 있다. 따라서 정답은 (C)이다.

[153-155]

리사 커배너
1140 이스트 15번가; 12B호
포레스트 힐스, 뉴욕

커배너 씨에게,

저희 웹 사이트를 통해 3월 3일에 주문하신 상품들을 동봉합니다. 그런데 예상치 못하게 생품 중 두 개의 재고가 없어서, **153** 일부 제품만 동봉되어 있습니다.

이 소포 안에는 다음 제품들이 동봉되어 있습니다:
- 포마 ZX 14인치 노트북 한 개
- 노트북 전용 가죽 가방 한 개
- 무선 마우스와 마우스 패드 한 개

154 빠진 물품은 레드게이트 요장 하도 드라이브와 포마 여행용 충전기입니다. - [1] -. 저희는 이 물건들을 해외 공급 업체로 주문했으며 현재 배송을 기다리는 중입니다. 저희는 다음 주 안까지 귀하께서 이 물건들을 받으실 수 있을 거라고 예상합니다. - [2] -. 이것이 귀하에게 혹시 불편함을 끼친다면, 제 진심 어린 사과를 받아주십시오.

만약 기다리지 않으시고 주문의 배송 취소를 원하신다면 더 편하신다면 저에게 알려 주십시오. 그러나 만약 기다리시는 48시간 이내에 귀하의 결정을 저에게 알려 주실 것을 요청합니다. - [3] -. **155** 그렇지 않다면 저희는 주문의 나머지 배송을 진행할 것입니다. - [4] -. 다시 한번 예상치 못한 지연에 대해 사과드리며, 그것 때문에 저희 사이트를 계속 애용하는 것을 그만두지 않으셨으면 하는 바람입니다.

진심으로
재스민 조 드림
디스카운트 사이버톤

153 편지의 목적은 무엇인가?
(A) 노트북 액세서리를 주문하라고
(B) 자세한 주문 사항에 대한 설명을 요청하라고
(C) 배송비 지불을 요청하라고
(D) 고객에게 부분적인 주문 지연을 알려 주라고

해설 일부 제품만 배송하게 되어 유감이라고 표현했으므로 정답은 (D)이다.

어휘 enclosed 동봉된 via ~을 거쳐, ~을 통해 partial 부분적인 shipment 배송, 선적 unexpectedly 예상치 못하게 out of stock 재고가 없는 missing 모자란; 분실된 external 외부의, 바깥의 charger 충전기 supplier 공급 업체 currently 현재 undelivered 배송이 안 된 portion 부분, 비율 proceed with ~을 진행하다 remainder 나머지 prevent 막다; 예방하다 patronage 애용 waive 철회하다 clarification 설명 (규칙 등을) 적용하지 않다

브라이터 월드사 (제품 번호 3351A)

159 **단계별 조립법**

1. 비닐 포장에서 모든 부품을 꺼내세요.

2. 동봉된 나사를 이용하여 전등대에 전등갓을 단단히 고정하세요.

3. **161** 플라스틱 덮개를 (전구) 꼭지 꼭대기 위에 놓고, 그것이 딱 들어맞을 때까지 압력을 가해 주세요.

4. **161** 전등대를 전구 꼭지 위에 있는 홈에 미끄러지듯 넣으세요.

5. 전등대를 시계 방향으로 돌려 단단히 조이세요.

주의

· 책상용 전등은 반드시 완전히 조립되기 전까지 플러그를 꽂으면 안 됩니다.

· 이 제품의 작은 부품들은 삼킬 위험이 있습니다. 어린아이들의 손이 닿지 않는 곳에 두세요.

· 이 제품은 항상 건조하고 편평한 표면 위에 두세요.

· **162** 책상용 전등갓은 장시간 사용한 후에는 뜨거워질 수 있습니다. 전등대를 잡고 전등을 조절하세요.

메모

· **160** 브라이터 월드 백열전구는 별도 판매합니다.

· 온/오프 스위치는 전구 꼭지 옆에 있습니다.

어휘 step-by-step 단계적인, 점진적인   assembly 조립   remove A from B A를 B에서 빼내다   affix 붙이다   lampshade 전등갓   firmly 단단히   lamp arm 전등대   enclosed 동봉된   screw 나사   covering 덮개   atop 꼭대기에   base 꼭지   exert (힘 등을) 내다, 쓰다   click into place 딱 미끄러져맞다   slide A into B A를 B로 미끄러뜨리다   slot 홈, 통로; 투입구   rotate 회전시키다   clockwise 시계 방향으로   tighten 단단히 죄다   plug in ∼에 플러그를 꽂다   present 보이다, 나타내다   swallowing 삼키는   hazard 위험   flat 편평한   extended 길어진, 장기간에 걸친   adjust 조절하다   grip 잡다   light bulb 백열전구   separately 분리하여, 따로따로   put together 조립하다   socket 콘센트

159 무엇에 관한 사용 설명서인가?

(A) 배송을 위한 전등 포장하기

(B) 전등의 백열전구 교체하기

(C) 파손된 탁상용 전등 수리하기

(D) 전등 부품 조립하기

해설 제목에 해당하는 Step-by-step Assembly(단계별 조립법)에서 조립 방법을 알려 주는 설명서임을 알 수 있고, 이어지는 단계별 조립법에서 전등을 조립하는 내용임을 확인할 수 있다. 따라서 정답은 (D)이다.

160 포장된 제품 안에 포함되지 않은 것은 무엇인가?

(A) 나사

(B) 백열전구

(C) 전구 꼭지

(D) 전등갓

해설 백열전구는 별도로 판매된다고 했으므로, 백열전구는 제품 안에는 들어 있지 않다는 것을 알 수 있다. 따라서 정답은 (B)이다.

161 전등대를 전구 꼭지에 넣기 전에 해야 하는 일은 무엇인가?

(A) 전등을 전기 콘센트에 꽂아야 한다.

(B) 스위치를 '켜짐' 위치로 밀어야 한다.

(C) 전등대를 감아서 단단히 고정해야 한다.

(D) 플라스틱 덮개를 전구 꼭지에 고정해야 한다.

해설 전등대를 전구 꼭지에 넣는 과정은 단계별 조립 과정 중 4단계에 해당한다. 3단계에서 해야 할 일을 묻는 문제임을 파악할 수 있어야 한다. 3단계에서는 플라스틱 덮개를 (전구) 꼭지 꼭대기 위에 놓고, 그것이 딱 들어맞을 때까지 압력을 가하라고 했다. 따라서 정답은 (D)이다.

162 사용자들에게 전등대로 전등을 조절하도록 조언하는 이유는 무엇인가?

(A) 화상을 입지 않게 하기 위해서

(B) 백열전구를 깨뜨리지 않기 위해서

(C) 전등갓이 반드시 단단히 고정되어 있도록 하기 위해서

(D) 반드시 편평한 표면에 놓도록 하기 위해서

해설 장시간 사용하면 전등갓이 뜨거워질 수 있으니 전등대로 전등을 조절하라고 했다. 따라서 정답은 (A)이다.

현지 예술가가 무료 전시회로 돌아오다

로리머 미술관에서는 레밍턴 출신 예술가인 찰스 라미레스의 다가오는 작품 전시회에 대해 발표했다. **164** 전시회는 8월 14일부터 20일까지 일주일 동안 계속될 것이며, 라미레스 씨의 50점 이상의 수채화와 원작 스케치를 선보일 것이다. 게다가 미술관의 발표에 따르면 이번 특별 전시회는 무료 입장이라고 한다.

163 라미레스 씨는 레밍턴의 힐사이드 지역에서 자랐고, 레밍턴 주립 대학에서 상업 디자인 학위를 받았다. 베를린으로 이사한 후, 그는 수채화 그림물감을 써서 도시의 경치를 그리기 시작했다. 팰릿 매거진에 의해 유럽의 "유망한 젊은 예술가들" 중 한 사람으로 선정된 라미레스 씨는 이제 전 세계 25개 이상의 주요 미술관에 그림을 전시하고 있다. 그의 작품 중 하나는 최근에 익명의 입찰자에게 35만 달러에 판매되었다. 다음 달에 열릴 전시회의 특징은 2014년에 고향을 떠난 이후 처음 돌아와 여는 전시회라는 것이다.

"저를 키워준 지역 공동체에 뭔가를 되돌려 드리고 싶었습니다."라고 라미레스 씨는 WRTV와의 최근 인터뷰에서 말했다. "그래서 저는 로리머 미술관의 사람들과 제 그림에 대한 무료 전시회를 준비했습니다." **164** 그 예술가는 전시회 개막식에 참석하여, 환영사를 하고 한정판 프린트에 사인해 줄 것이다.

어휘 exhibition 전시(회)   upcoming 다가오는   watercolor painting 수채화   admission fee 입장료   commercial design 상업 디자인   name 명명하다, 부르다   promising 유망한   anonymous 익명의   bidder 입찰자   mark 특징짓다   hometown 고향, 고국   community 지역 공동체   arrange 준비하다   showing 전시(회)   folk 사람들   on hand 출석한   limited-edition 한정판의   auction off ∼을 경매에 부치다

163 레밍턴 주립 대학에 대해 알 수 있는 것은 무엇인가?

(A) 로리머 미술관을 소유하고 있다.

(B) 미술 전시회 장소이다.

(C) 라미레스 씨가 다녔던 학교이다.

(D) 레밍턴과 베를린에 분교가 있다.

해설 질문의 핵심어인 레밍턴 주립 대학은 두 번째 문단에서 등장한다. 라미레스 씨가 레밍턴 주립 대학에서 상업 디자인 학위를 받았다고 했으므로 정답은 (C)가 된다. (B)의 경우, 전시회는 로리머 미술관에서 열릴 예정이므로 오답이다.

164 라미레스 씨가 8월 14일에 할 일은 무엇인가?

(A) 잡지사에서 상 받기

(B) 수채화를 경매에 부치기

(C) 예술 학교에서 강의하기

(D) 자신의 작품 사본에 사인해 주기

해설 나눠서 등장하는 두 부분의 단서를 종합해야 하는 문제이다. 첫 번째 문단에서 전시회가 8월 14일에 열릴 것을 알 수 있으며, 마지막 문장에서 라미레스 씨가 개막식에 참석해서 한정판 프린트에 사인해 줄 것을 알 수 있다. 두 내용을 종합하면 정답은 (D)이다.

공지

165 지난여름의 홍수 피해로 인해, 리버 밀 빌딩의 거주자 주차장이 4월 3일에서 7일 동안 다시 포장될 것입니다. 재포장됨과 함께 **166** 주차장은 세 곳의 장애인 공간을 추가 제공하기 위해서 새로 선이 그어질 것입니다.

165 공사는 두 단계로 진행될 것입니다: 월요일과 화요일인 4월 3일과 4일에는 주차장 북쪽 끝(1번부터 34번 공간)이 거주자들에게 폐쇄될 것입니다. ― [1] ―. 이때는 모든 차를 반드시 이 공간에서 방문객 주차장으로 옮기거나 길가에 주차해야 합니다. ― [2] ―. 만약 길가에 주차한다면, 주차 위반 딱지를 끊지 않도록 모든 표지판에 유의하십시오. ― [3] ―. 주차장 남쪽 끝(35번부터 50번 공간)은 수요일에 재포장될 것이며, 목요일에 선이 새로 그어질 것입니다. 그러므로 모든 차는 반드시 그 이틀 동안 이 구역에서 치워져야 합니다. ― [4] ―. 이번 공사로 불편을 끼쳐 죄송합니다. 문의 사항이나 우려되는 점이 있으시면 아파트 관리인 사무실로 연락해 주십시오.

어휘 flooding 홍수   repave (도로 등을) 다시 포장하다   reline 선을 새로 긋다   accommodate 공간을 제공하다, 수용하다   additional 추가적인   handicapped 장애인의, 장애가 있는   space 공간   take place 일어나다, 발생하다   pay attention to ∼에 유의하다   signage (교통) 표지판, 신호판   apologize for ∼에 대해 사과하다

165 공지의 목적은 무엇인가?

(A) 개선된 시설을 재개장한다는 것을 발표하려고

(B) 운전자들에게 미납된 주차 위반 딱지에 관해 경고하려고

(C) 아파트 주민들에게 프로젝트에 대해 알려 주려고

(D) 건물에 대한 홍수 피해에 대해 사과하려고

[168-171]

해설 공지문의 경우 서두 부분에 주제나 목적이 나타나 있는 경우가 많다. 주차장을 재포장하고 셀은 다시 긋는다는 내용이 나와 있으며, 이어진 단락에서 이 프로젝트는 두 가지 단계로 나누어 진행된다고 설명하고 있다. 따라서 주민들에게 주차장 공사에 대해 알려 주려는 공지문임을 알 수 있으므로 정답은 (C)이다. (A)는 아직 공사가 시작된 상황이 아니라 공사로 인해 발생할 불편함에 대해 사과하고 있으므로 (D)도 오답이다.

166 장애인 주차장에 대해 언급된 것은 무엇인가?
(A) 사람들이 불법적으로 사용하고 있다.
(B) 주차장에 더 추가될 것이다.
(C) 4월에는 이용할 수 없을 것이다.
(D) 주차장의 새로운 구역으로 옮겨졌다.

해설 주차장에는 선이 새로 그어질 것인데 이것은 세 개의 장애인 공간을 추가하기 위한 것이라고 언급되어 있다. 따라서 정답은 (B)이다.

167 [1], [2], [3], [4]로 표시된 곳 중 다음 문장이 들어가기에 가장 적절한 곳은 어디인가?

"주차장은 금요일 이후에 완전히 운영될 것입니다."

(A) [1]
(B) [2]
(C) [3]
(D) [4]

해설 [4] 앞의 내용에서는 주차장 공사에 대한 구체적인 내용이 나오고, [4] 이후부터는 이로 인한 불편에 대한 사과 및 추가 전달 사항이 나온 점으로 미루어, 운영 재개에 관해 설명하는 해당 문장은 [4]에 들어가야 문맥상 가장 적절하다. 따라서 정답은 (D)이다.

덴젤 스미스 [오후 3시 13분]	확장 가능성에 관한 토론을 시작할게요. 모두 하루쯤 잘 일고 계시죠?
설리 쿠니 [오후 3시 13분]	15번 고속도로에 있는 거요, 그렇죠? 저는 지난해에 그쪽 개발에 관한 것을 읽었었지만, 벌써 영업을 시작했다는 것은 몰랐네요.
에릴 김 [오후 3시 14분]	사실, 아직 시작 안 했어요. 건축은 완료되었지만 개인이 몇 번 미뤄졌죠. 판매 세입자를 확보하는 데 어려움을 겪고 있는 거로 보여요. 항간의 소문에 의하면 50%의 공실률이라고 하네요.
설리 쿠니 [오후 3시 16분]	그러면 당신도 새로운 지점을 거기에 열기를 원하시는 건가요? 위험 부담이 크지 않을까요?
덴젤 스미스 [오후 3시 17분]	위험 부담이 크죠. 168 169 또한 대단한 기회가 될 수도 있을 거예요. 169 그 부동산 관리팀이 점점 더 절박해지고 있거든요. 168 거의 30%까지 임대료를 낮췄게, 어떻게 생각해요, 에릴?
에릴 김 [오후 3시 19분]	170 그것은 실패를 만해요. 그들이 왜 세입자들을 찾지 못하는지 아시나요?
덴젤 스미스 [오후 3시 20분]	글쎄요. 171 경기 침체와 관련이 있을지도 있겠네요.
에릴 김 [오후 3시 21분]	우리가 행동을 취하기 전에 이유를 확인해 아겠어요. 171 위치나 건축물과 관련해 문제가 있을 수도 있어요.
설리 쿠니 [오후 3시 22분]	제가 부동산 관리자에게 연락해서 몇몇 판매 공간들을 살펴봐 달라고 부탁할게요.
에릴 김 [오후 3시 22분]	훌륭하네요. 알아보시고 우리와 공유해 주세요.

168 스미스 씨가 종사할 것 같은 업종은 무엇인가?
(A) 소매 판매
(B) 건설
(C) 부동산 관리
(D) 위험 평가

해설 오후 3시 16분문의 설리 쿠니는 3시 17분의 덴젤 스미스의 대화에서 당 장소에서 지점을 여는 것이 한 상황에서 큰 기회가 될 수 있다는 것을 말했다고 있으므로, 스미스 씨는 소매 판매 업종에 있다고 추론할 수 있다. 따라서 정답은 (A)가 정답이다.

169 스미스 씨가 히츠빌 몰에 지점을 여는 것을 제안하는 이유는 무엇인가?
(A) 몰이 주 고속도로와 가까이 있어서
(B) 임대 조건이 좋아져서
(C) 그 지역에 거의 새로운 몰이 없어서
(D) 예상치 못한 공실이 있어서

해설 오후 3시 17분의 덴젤 스미스의 대화에서 임대료를 30%나 낮춘 상황임을 명시하고 있으므로 정답은 (B)가 된다. 본문에 lowered their rental fees라는 부분의 내용을 선택지에서는 improved라고 요약한 것이다.

170 오후 3시 19분에 김 씨가 "그것은 실패를 만해요"라고 쓴 의미는 무엇인가?
(A) 덤은 미리 개발을 세울 필요가 있다.
(B) 몰은 완성이 보이지만이 않은 문제가 있다.
(C) 사업은 위태로워 되기에는 너무나 위험하다.
(D) 제안된 고려해보기에 충분히 괜찮다.

해설 김 씨의 의견을 묻는 스미스 씨의 앞은 문맥상 투자하는 것을 고민해볼 여지가 있다는 의미가 있다. 따라서 제안을 고려해볼 가치가 있다는 (D)가 정답이다.

171 몰의 문제에 대한 가능한 이유로 언급되지 않은 것은 무엇인가?
(A) 경기 침체
(B) 온라인 몰의 경쟁
(C) 서투르게 선택된 장소
(D) 건물의 구조상 결함

해설 오후 3시 20분에서 경기 침체가 언급되고, 또한 오후 3시 21분에 위치와 구조상의 문제가 언급되었다. 따라서 언급되지 않은 것은 (B)가 정답이다.

어휘 expansion 확장 opportunity 기회 locate 위치시키다 complete 완성된 성된 grand opening 개장 push back 미루다 apparently 보이 하니 secure (노력으로) 잡다 have difficulty (in) -ing ~하는 데 어려움을 겪다 retail tenant (소매) 판매 세입자 word on the street 길거리 소 보하다 문제에 의하면 struggle with ~에 애먹다 vacancy rate 공실률 risk 위험 property 부동산 desperate 절박한 lower 낮추다 rental fee 임대료 be worth -ing ~할 가치가 있다 look into ~을 살펴보다 be related to ~와 관련이 있다 slowdown 침체, 감속 ascertain 확인하다 make a move 행동을 시작하다, 조치를 하다

[172-175]

간추린 시 뉴스

목요일에 172 해당 미드우즈 주택 개발 건설이 7개 4의 표결로 시 위원회에 의해 폐쇄되었다 승인되었다. 177 건설 공사는 지난해 말 표결을 받아 문제 때문에 시에 의해 폐쇄되었던 리버뷰 파크의 예전 부지에 있을 것이다.

지난 몇 주에 걸쳐서 시 위원회는 173 공영물 저소득자 주택으로 교체하자는 제안을 논의해 왔었다. 몇몇 지역 주민들은 그들의 공영을 잃었던 것에 붙임으로 라며 했다. "저는 이 결정이 왜 이뤄진 것인지 않어요신할 수 없습니다."라고 에러 머리라는 예전 공영의 길 건너에 있는 세 아이의 아버지가 말했다. "꽁영은 언제라도 시 집에서 거기에 거주하고 있는 세대가 위해서 소위을 피웠습니다. 저 편은 안전하지 않았습니다. 때때로 십 대들이 거기 모여서 소란을 피웠습니다. 그러나 근처에 녹지 공간을 가질 수 있다는 점이 좋았습니다."

그러나 시 위원회는 다른 견해를 가졌고, (지금은) 사용하지 않는 공영을 '불법 활동들을 끄는 자석'으로 불렀다. 시 위원회장이 오래 미루어된 주택 프로젝트를 청찬했는데, 174 그녀는 그것을 녹색의 주택 개발이 주택 씨엄에서가 승인되고 이름다운 설계를 본 다음, 그곳도 우리만큼 홍분할 것입니다. 그녀는 176 "일단 근처에 사람들이 주택 개발이 이름다운 건축가의 이름다운 설계를 본 다음, 그곳도 우리만큼 홍분할 것입니다."라고 설명했다. 시장은 논쟁이 않았지만, 시장실에서 시 위원회에 대한 그의 지지를 재표명하는 성명을 175 발표했다. 해당 미드우즈 주택개발에 대한 그의 지지를 재표명하는 성명을 5월에 완공될 예정이다.

어휘 housing development (민간) 주택 단지 개발 approve 승인하다 council 위원회 site 부지, 현장 debate 논의하다 replace A with B A를 B로 바꾸다 low-income 저소득자의 make a noise 소란을 피우다. 시끄럽게 하다 green space 녹지 공간 view 견해, 의견 defunct (지금은) 사용하지 않는 magnet (매력으로) 사람의 마음을 끄는 장소, 사람 illegal 불법의 chairperson 의장 architect 건축가 statement 성명 reaffirm 재확인하다 continued 지속적인 complain about ~에 관해 불평하다 invite ~하도록 요청하다 describe 설명하다 wilderness 황무지 residence 주택 approval 승인 urban 도시의 crime rate 범죄율 shut down ~을 폐쇄하다

172 이 기사가 쓰인 이유는 무엇인가?
(A) 시 위원회의 결정에 대해 불평하기 위해서
(B) 왜 인기 있는 공원이 폐쇄되었는지 설명하기 위해서
(C) 시민들에게 다음번의 시 위원회 회의에 참석하도록 요청하기 위해서
(D) **주택 개발 프로젝트의 승인을 발표하기 위해서**

해설 주택을 나타내는 기사의 첫 번째 문장에서 해당 미드우즈 주택 개발 건설이 7개 4의 표결로 시 위원회에 의해 공식적으로 승인되었다는 내용을 알 수 있다. 따라서 정답은 (D)이다. (A는 기사의 내용 자체라가 불평하는 것이라고 보기 어렵고, (B는 공원에 관한 지엽적인 내용이므로 정답이 될 수 없다.

173 다음 중 해당 미드우즈를 가장 잘 설명하는 것은 무엇인가?
(A) 시 공원 근처의 황무지 지역
(B) **저소득 세입자를을 위해 계획된 주택**
(C) 시 위원회에 의해 지명된 새로운 공원
(D) 범죄율이 높은 도시 지역

해설 해당 미드우즈 건설은 공영을 저소득자 주택으로 바꾸는 것이다. 따라서 정답은 (B)이다. housing은 residence로 패러프레이즈되었다.

174 리버뷰 파크에 대해 알 수 있는 것은 무엇인가?
(A) 해당 미드우즈 근처에 있다.
(B) 현재 보수 중이다.
(C) 휴의의 장소였었다.
(D) **폐쇄되었다.**

해설 리버뷰 파크란 단어는 지문에서 딱 한 번 등장한다. 이 공원이 문이 문제 때문에 지어난어 폐쇄되었다는 점을 알 수 있다. 따라서 정답은 (D)이다.

175 세 번째 문단에서, 첫 번째 줄의 released와 의미상 가까운 것은 무엇인가?
(A) 요청했다
(B) **발표했다**
(C) 거절했다
(D) 수락했다

해설 해당 단어가 들어간 문장 내의 문맥을 잘 확인하고 정답을 찾아보자. '시장실에서 시 위원회에 대한 그의 지속적인 지지를 재표언하는 성명을 발표했다'라는 내용이므로 정답은 (B)이다.

[176-180]

주택 임대 - 로즈힐 하이츠

176 시내의 고급 주택가인 로즈힐 하이츠 지역에 있는 이름다운 2층짜리 주택을 세들습니다. 높은 수요 때문에 이 지역의 주택들은 거의 나오는 적이 없으니, 이번 기회를 놓치지 마세요.

177 방 3개, 화장실 2개짜리의 이 집은 작은 뜰뜰과 차고로 사용하기에 적합한 지하실을 갖추고 있습니다. 집은 6월 1일부터 사용할 수 있고, 집은 2년 이상의 임대 계약을 맺고 있습니다. 모든 신청자는 반드시 이전 집주인으로부터 추천서를 갖고 오셔야 합니다.

임대료는 한 달에 2천 4백 달러이며 수도, 전기 쓰레기 처리 그리고 177 두 대 차량에 대한 노외 주차를 포함합니다. 세입자는 전기요 가스비를 부담해야 합니다. 178 동물을 한 마리당 500달러의 환불 보증금을 내면 실내 애완동물이 허용됩니다.

179 집은 가구가 없는 채로 임대될 것이지만, 현재 세입자가 몇몇 가구를 팔려고 합니다. 177 5월 14일에 집을 (돌려볼 수 있도록) 공개할 것입니다. 그 날짜 전에 개인적으로 둘러볼 약속을 잡으시려면, 부동산 관리자인 에드 마리노에게 marinohomes@freenet.com으로 연락 주세요.

어휘 story (건물의) 층 available ~할 수 있는 exclusive 상류층의, 고급의 feature 특징으로 하다 unfinished basement 미완성 베이스먼트, 방으로 남겨 지하실 suitable for ~에 적합한 storage 창고, 저장고 landlord 주인 임대 applicant 신청자 reference 추천서 off-street parking 노외 주차(도로의 노면 밖에 있는 주차 공간) tenant 세입자 be responsible for ~을 책임지다 indoor 실내의 permit 허락하다 refundable 환불할 수 있는 deposit 보증금, 예치금 unfurnished 가구가 비치되지 않은 open house (입주 둘러볼 수 있게 하는) 공개 주택 showing 구경, 설명회 arrange 준비하다, 마련하다 outdoor 실외의 in response to ~에 응하여

176 로즈힐 하이츠에 대해 알 수 있는 것은 무엇인가?
(A) 넓은 마당이 있는 집으로 알려져 있다.
(B) 저소득층 지역에 있다.
(C) **많은 사람이 살고 싶어 하는 장소이다.**
(D) 대부분의 사람이 가기 어렵다.

해설 로즈힐 하이츠는 높은 수요 때문에 거의 세가 나오는 적이 없이 이번 기회를 놓치지 말라고 했다. 따라서 정답은 (C)이다. rarely는 '거의 ~하지 않는'이라는 부정의 의미를 담고 있음을 유의하자.

177 셋집에 대해 알 수 없는 것은 무엇인가?
(A) 집에 두 대의 차를 주차할 공간이 있다.
(B) 화장실보다 침실이 더 많다.
(C) 물건들을 저장할 수 있는 이층증이 있다.
(D) **현재 집 안에 아무 가구도 비치되어 있지 않다.**

해설 광고의 마지막 단락을 보면, 가구가 비치되어 있지 않은 채로 임대될 것이지만 현재 세입자가 가구를 팔려고 한다고 했으므로 현재 가구가 비치되어 있지 않았다고 볼 수는 없다. 따라서 정답은 (D)이다. (A는 노외주차장 2개가 있다고 했으므로 맞는 내용이고, (B는 방이 3개고 화장실이 2개이므로 직접한 지상심이 있다고 했으므로 역시 맞는 내용이다.

수신: 다라 웨스트우드 <soccermom33@fastmail.com>
발신: 에드 마리노 <marinohomes@freenet.com>
날짜: 5월 20일
제목: 회신: 로즈힐 하이츠 주택

이메일 주셔서 감사합니다. 179 저는 5월 14일에 구하보로 남편을 만나셨던 것을 기억합니다. 아쉽게서 가구는 애완동물에 관해 질문하셨는데 180 집을 보셨으니, 비 전화 허락해 드릴 수 없다고 알려드리는 것을 담당이 이해하실 겁니다. 제가 집에서 가구도 개세에게 마음이 너무 좋다는 것을 분명히 이해하실 겁니다. 180 그 저렴 분명히 밝히지 못했던 점 죄송합니다. 만약 여전히 집에 관심이 있으시면 다면, 일러 주세요.

에드 마리노

178 보증금이 필요한 경우는 무엇인가?
(A) 짐의 가구 임대
(B) 전기 서비스 설치
(C) 녹음 주차
(D) 실내에서 애완동물 기우기

해설 deposit이란 문제 키워드가 나오는 부분은 첫 번째 지문에서 막 한 번 뿐이다. 동물 한 마리당 500달러의 환불 보증금을 내면 실내 애완동물이 하용된다고 했으므로 정답은 (D)이다.

179 마리노 씨는 어떻게 웨스트우드 씨를 알 것인가?
(A) 그가 그녀에게 개인적으로 짐 구경을 시켜주었다.
(B) 그도 그녀의 이전에 바로 옆집에 산다.
(C) 그도 그녀를 짐 공개일 행사에서 만났다.
(D) 그도 그녀 남편의 이전 직장 동료이다.

해설 두 지문의 내용을 연계해서 풀어야 하는 추론 문제 유형이다. 첫 번째 지문에서 집을 둘러보는 공개일은 5월 14일이라고 했고, 두 번째 지문에서도 마리노 씨가 웨스트우드 씨를 5월 14일 공개일에 넘겨와 함께 만났던 것을 기억한다고 했다. 따라서 정답은 (C)이다. (A)의 경우 5월 14일 짐 공개일 이전에 개인적으로 짐 구경을 원한면 연락 달라고 한 부분을 연상시킬 함정이다.

180 마리노 씨와 웨스트우드 씨 사이에서 명확하게 공유되지 않은 정보는 무엇이 있는가?
(A) 짐 마당의 크기
(B) 이숙 날짜
(C) 중개인 수수료
(D) 동네의 위치

해설 애완동물과 관련된 규정을 분명히 밝히지 못했다는 점이 미안하다고 했다. 따라서 명확하게 공유되지 않은 정보는 (A)이다.

[181-185]

사라 노스트롬
채용 담당자
밴 부런 출판사
카운트 플라자, 113호
커넥티, 뉴욕

노스트롬 씨에게:

커크빌 데일리 저널의 9월 1일 지에 광고하신 편집 보조자 자리에 지원하고자 자기소개서와 첨부된 이력서를 보냅니다. 저는 최근에 올림픽 비즈니스 대학을 졸업했으며, 경영을 준학사 학위를 가지고 있는데 존경받는 기업의 신입 사원 자리를 찾고 있습니다. 저는 밴 부런 출판사에 관해 많은 이야기들을 들었으며 귀사에 들어가기를 간절히 바라고 있습니다.

181 저는 정식 업무 경력은 없지만, **182** 2017년도에 사이버셀사의 사무실에서 하계 인턴사원으로 근무했습니다. **183** 저는 또한 2016년에는 뉴든 노숙자 보호소에서 주방 관리자로 자원봉사도 했습니다. **183** 저는 노숙자 보호소의 상사로부터 받은 추천서를 첨부했으며, 참고할 만한 경력을 보러 가서 자신에 대해서도 제출할 수 있습니다. 만약 가능하다면, 제가 면접을 보러 연락 주시길 고대하겠습니다. 당장 주시길 고대하겠습니다.

레베카 윌슨

수신: 레베카 윌슨 (RBW1993@amerimail.net)
발신: 사라 노스트롬 (humanresources@vbp.com)
날짜: 9월 20일
제목: 취업 면접

레베카 씨에게:

면접을 보러 저희주 우리 사무실을 방문해 주셔서 감사했습니다. 이 업종에서 장비가 유명한 젊고 독립한 젊은 여성들을 만나게 되어 기뻤습니다. **183** 우리는 또한 귀하의 조직 능력을 칭찬한 뉴든을 칭찬한 편지에도 감동하 였습니다.

안타깝게도, 우리는 이 자리에 다른 지원자를 채용하기로 했습니다. 이 분야에 서 근무한 그의 이전 경력에 근거하여 이렇게 결정했습니다. **184** 우리는 귀하의 이력서를 보관할 것이고, 만약 향후 귀하의 능력에 적합한 공석이 생긴다면 연락할 것입니다. 시간을 내주셔서 감사하고 지속적인 구직 활동에 행운이 있기 를 기원합니다.

사라 노스트롬

어휘 cover letter 자기소개서 application 지원(서) attached 첨부된 editorial assistant 편집 보조자 edition 호, 판 graduate 졸업생 학사 associate degree 준학사(전문대 졸업 학위) business administration 경영학 entry-level 하급자의, 급단의, 초보의 respected 존경받는 be eager to ~하기를 간절히 바라다 formal 공식의, 정식의 a letter of reference 추천서 supervisor 상사 transcript 성적표 promising 유망한 be impressed by ~에 감 shelter 보호 시설 enthusiastic 열정적인 praise 칭찬하다 organizational 조직 동의하다 candidate 지원자, 후보자 be based on ~에 근거하다 field 분

---

181 편지에 따르면, 윌슨 씨의 현재 직업 상황은 어떠한가?
(A) 그녀는 무직 상태이다.
(B) 그녀는 경영 대학에서 강의한다.
(C) 그녀는 사이버셀사에서 일한다.
(D) 그녀는 최근 밴 부런 출판사에서 해고되었다.

해설 윌슨 씨는 현재 정식 업무 경력이 없다고 밝히고 있다. 현재 취업 준비 를 하는 상황이므로 정답은 (A)이다. 사이버셀사에서는 2017년 여름에 인턴으로 근무한 적이 있지만, 현재 상황은 아니므로 (C)는 오답이 다.

182 윌슨 씨가 사무 업무 일을 했던 곳은 어디인가?
(A) 밴 부런 출판사
(B) 사이버셀사
(C) 올림픽 비즈니스 대학
(D) 뉴든 노숙자 보호소

해설 윌슨 씨는 정식 업무 경력은 없지만, 참고할 만한 경력이고 있으므로 다. 2017년도에 사이버셀사의 사무실에서 하계 인턴사원으로 근무했 다고 했다. (D)의 경우, 주방 관리자로 자원봉사 를 한 것이므로 사무 업무 일이라고 보기는 어려우므로 오답이다.

183 로버트 밀러는 누구일 것 같은가?
(A) 사이버셀사의 인턴사원
(B) 올림픽 비즈니스 대학의 교수
(C) 뉴든 노숙자 보호소에서의 상사
(D) 밴 부런 출판사의 인사 팀장

해설 연계 문제이다. 첫 번째 지문에서 뉴든 노숙자 보호소에서 주방 관리자 로 자원봉사했고, 노숙자 보호소의 상사로부터 받은 추천서를 첨부했 다고 했고, 또한 두 번째 지문에서 구직자에 조직 능력을 칭찬하는 로 버트 밀러 씨의 편지에 감동하였다고 했다. 따라서 두 내용을 함께인 로버트 밀러 씨는 뉴든 노숙자 보호소에서 함께 근무했던 상사 라는 것임으로 사무 읽이라고 보기는 어려우므로 오답으로 오답이다.

184 노스트롬 씨가 윌슨 씨의 이력서에 대해 언급한 것은 무엇인가?
(A) 전문가답지 못했다.
(B) 제때에 받지 못했다.
(C) 회사에서 보관하고 있을 것이다.
(D) 채용 담당자에게 전달되었다.

해설 노스트롬 씨는 윌슨 씨의 이력서를 보관하고 있을 것이라고 했다. 따 라서 정답은 (C)이다. 지문의 keep your resume on file을 선택지에 서는 retain으로 패러프레이징했다.

185 이메일에서, 두 번째 단락 세 번째 줄의 suit와 의미상 가장 가까운 것은 무엇 인가?
(A) 공무하다
(B) 아울리다
(C) 개선하다
(D) 간과하다

해설 suit은 '적합하다'라는 의미로 쓰였으므로, (B) match와 바꿔 쓸 수 있다.

[186-190]

수신: customerservice@zenithcorp.com
발신: marcy777@usemail.com
날짜: 4월 10일
주제: 주문 번호 0022176

안녕하세요,

저는 4월 5일 제가 주문한 것에 대해 귀하께 알리고 싶습니다. 저는 봄 흥미진진한 인테리어에서 저의 상의와 세 벌의 반바지를 주문했어요. **187** 제 신용 카드로 봄 지급되실 경우의 무료 배송이 적용되었고, 제 물품을 무료로 배송해 주셨어요. **188** 이것은 저희가 판매하는 모든 서츠와 바지가 포함된, 실용성 향상을 위해 최근에 새 단장을 한 제니스 온라인 웹 사이트를 통해서만 이용 가능합니다. 세 벌 월말까지만 지속되므로 마음껏 www.shopzenith.com으로 방문하셔서 다가오는 여름을 위한 반짝이와 여름을 상의를 사두세요.

http://www.shopzenith.com

제니스 온라인

남성복	여성복	개주얼복	위시리스트	**쇼핑 카트**

제니스 온라인

날짜: 2017년 4월 5일   주문 번호: 0022176   고객 아이디: Marcy777

물품	크기	개수	물품 당 가격
반소매 단추 블라우스, 흰색	대	1	30달러
개버딘 V넥 티셔츠, 진한 주황색	대	1	15달러
190 개버딘 V넥 티셔츠, 진한 남색	소	1	15달러
무릎 길이의 서퍼 반바지, 빨간색	소	1	20달러
주름 접힌 바뮤다 반바지, 카키색	대/대	2	15달러

종액: 110달러
할인: (27달러 50센트)
판매세: 11달러
배송비: 없음
주문 총액: 93달러 50센트

어휘 savings 절약, 저축 wardrobe 옷장, 의상실 (just) around corner 아주 가까운 get ready for ~을 준비하다 sizzling 아주 흥미진진한, 타는 듯이 더운 (줄눈 소리) 지글거리는 mix and match 짜 맞추다 top 상의 entire 전체의 shipping 배송 available 판매 가능한 exclusively 오로지, 독점적 renovate 개조[수리]하다, 새롭게 하다 enhanced 향상된 usability 유용성, 편리성 last 지속하다 stock up on ~을 사들이다, 사재기하다 summery 여름의, 여름같은 short-sleeved 반소매의 button-up 단추로 잠그는 V-neck V자 목의 lightweight 가벼운, 경량의 burnt 보통보다 진한; 탄 navy blue 진한 남색 knee-length (길이가) 무릎까지 오는 surfer 서퍼(파도타기를 즐기는 사람) pleated 주름 접힌 Bermuda shorts 버뮤다 반바지(무릎이 보일 정도의 반바지), 휴양지의 바뮤다에서 유래) mix-up 혼동 in error 실수로 longtime 장기의

186 제니스 패션 웹 사이트에 대해서 언급된 것은 무엇인가?
(A) 제한된 선택을 제공한다.
(B) 최근에 업데이트되었다.
(C) 회원만을 위한 것이다.
(D) 샹을 받는다.

해설 첫 번째 지문 중간 부분에서 웹 사이트가 실용성을 위해 재단장되었다는 내용으로부터 (B)가 정답임을 알 수 있다. 지문의 renovated를 요청 탁지에서는 updated로 패러프레이징했고, 웹 사이트는 판매하는 모든 옷을 포함하고 있다고 했으므로 (A)는 오답이다.

187 메인 씨의 주문에 관해 알 수 있는 것은 무엇인가?
(A) 4월 마지막 주에 주문되었다.
(B) 몇몇 재고가 없는 물품을 포함했다.
(C) 제니스 신용 카드로 지급했다.
(D) 그것에 실수로 판매되었다.

해설 연계 문제이다. 첫 번째 광고 지문에서 제니스 신용 카드를 이용하면 25% 할인에 무료 배송을 해준다고 했는데, 세 번째 지문에서 지문에서 25% 할인이 적용되었고 무료로 배송되었으므로 이 두 내용을 종합하면 마 린 씨는 제니스 신용 카드로 물건을 주문했음을 4월 5일에 주 문했다고 했으므로 (C)이다. (A)는 이메일 지문 시작 부분에서 4월 5일에 주 문했다고 했으므로 오답이고, (A)는 이메일 지문 시작 부분에서 주문에서 판매되지는 하나 실수가 error)로 추가된 것인지는 알 수 없다.

188 주문에 관한 메인는 씨의 물품은 무엇인가?
(A) 물품 중 하나가 늦게 배송되었다.
(B) 물품 중 하나가 마분되었다.
(C) 물품 중 하나가 포함되지 않았다.
(D) 물품 중 하나의 크기가 틀렸다.

해설 이메일에서 주문에 관해서 할인이나 무료 배송에는 문제가 없었으나, 크기에 혼동이 있었다고 했으므로 정답은 (D)이다.

189 메인스 씨에 관해 암시된 것은 무엇인가?
(A) 컴퓨터 기술이 서투르다.
(B) 제니스의 장기 고객이다.
(C) 봄 할인에 대해 모르고 있다.
(D) 고객 서비스 분야에서 일한 경험이 있다.

해설 이메일에서 자신도 이러한 종류의 실수를 정정했던 개인적인 경험이 있다는 내용이 나온다. 이것을 통해서 Mason 씨 역시 고객 서비스 관련 일을 했었던 적이 있었음을 알 수 있다. 따라서 정답은 (D)이다. (그는 이 메일 시작 부분에서 봄 할인을 이용했다고 명백히 언급되었으므로 오답이다.

190 메인스 씨가 선물로 구매한 물품은 무엇인가?
(A) 하얀색 블라우스
(B) 남색 티셔츠
(C) 주황색 티셔츠
(D) 카키색 반바지

해설 연계 문제이다. 세 번째 이메일에서 메인스 씨는 대(大) 크기의 반소매 블라우스, 대(大) 크기의 티셔츠, 그리고 소(小) 크기의 티셔츠를 요청 했으나, 대(大) 크기 두 벌의 티셔츠와 한 벌의 대(大) 크기 블라우스를 받았다고 했으며, 크기가 틀린 물건이 물건이 성의 선물이라고 했다. 이 부분을 토대로 두 번째 지문의 표에서 티셔츠 중 소(小) 크기의 티셔츠 는 남색 V넥 티셔츠임을 알 수 있으므로 정답은 (B)이다.

음식과 미소를 노인들에게 전달하기

메리 오노

(셸리의 등급 매김: ★★★☆)

☆ 많은 브리지필드의 노인 거주자처럼 마찬가지로 박토리아도 근처에 사는 가족이 전혀 없습니다. 191 그래서 그녀는 5년 전 더 이상 도로 표지판을 수월하게 읽을 수 없게 되자, 운전하는 것을 그만두었습니다. 그로 인해 식료품점에 가는 것이 어려워졌습니다. 그녀는 "저는 매우 월요일에 길을 따라 슈퍼마켓으로 걸어 내려가곤 했어요"라고 말했습니다. "그러나 저는 다는 기력이 없어요."

해서 재빨리 도움의 손길(HHE)이 참여하게 될 것입니다. 그것은 가정이 불편한 노인들에게 배달해 주는 비영리 단체입니다. 박토리아는 일주일에 한 번씩 배달되는 지역에서 재배한 신선한 농산물과 필수적인 식료품을 받고 있으며, 제가 함께 동등 취향되었습니다.

음식과 다른 필수 물품들은 주 단위로 지역 업체들로부터 기부됩니다. 192 지역 재배 업체가 조금씩 보태고 있습니다. "언제까지 모두에게 그것이 정말 보람된 경험이 되고 있습니다."

가정식 요리가 브리지필드로 새로 왔습니다

처음에 블룸스 다이너는 너무 시내 중심가에 최근에 연 새로운 식당ㅡ는 별로 특별해 보이지 않았습니다. 그러나 일단 메뉴를 열면 화려하지 않은 외관과 너무 흔한 실내 장식은 곧 잊어버릴 것입니다. 주인이자 수석 요리사이 도미니크 파멜은 다른 경쟁 식당 숙에서 블룸스 다이너를 돋보이게 하는 통찰력을 가지고 있습니다. 193 메뉴에 있는 모든 것은 야였을 때 영감이 만들어 주었을 것 같은 위안이 되는 음식입니다. 저는 함 명어리가 든 마카로니앤치즈, 토마토 수프 한 그릇, 그리고 사이드로 볶은 경질을 주문했지만, 결국은 평범하지만. 토마토 수프이도 음식으로 볶은 경질을 주문했습니다. 다른 음식은 조금 과해 주문했습니다. 194 그의 사과 파이는 후추 통의 다양한 종류의 디저트입니다. 195 이는 올해 조 근해) 품평회에서 일등 상을 받았고, 도미니크와 호두 브라우니도 역시 맛있습니다.

셸리 매뉴는 브리지필드도 텔레그램의 음식과 와인 편집자이다.

2017년 3월 16일

드리스 잉그램
재빠른 도움의 손길
2801 이스트 플레즌트 스트리트
브리지필드, 캘리포니아 90087

잉그램 씨에게:

193 요청하지 않은 편지를 보내는 것을 용서하십시오, 저는 브리지필드 텔레그램에서 귀하에 관한 기사를 쓴 기자에게서 당신의 주소를 받았습니다.

194 저는 사실 귀하에서 다른 할머니를 읽고 있습니다, 아니 최소한 제가 야었을 때 그분을 알았었지요. 그분은 저에게 방과 후 피아노를 가르쳐주고 했습니다. 저는 그분의 귀하의 단체가 그분을 도와주고 있다는 기사를 읽고 나서, 우리 지역 공동체가 직면한 어려움에 눈을 뜨게 되었으며, 제가 함 등을 취하게 되었습니다.

작은 지역 식당의 주인으로서, 저는 참여하고 싶습니다. 다저트 195 디저트는 제 특기이 며, 저는 매주 배달할 수 있는 것 저도 저도 가능 가 는 식사를 디저트를 기부할 수 있습니다. 우리는 모두 가끔 담콤한 대접을 받을 만한 가치가 있습니다.

만약 관심이 있으시다면 넙부 시내 중심가의 블룸스 다이너에 저에게 들러 주세요, 귀하에게 저녁을 무료로 대접할 것이며, 우리는 구체적인 사항에 관해 얘기를 나눌 수 있을 것입니다.

진심으로
도미니크 파멜

---

191 멀진 씨에 관해 알 수 있는 것은 무엇인가?
(A) 시력이 떨어지고 있다.
(B) 아무 돈이 없다.
(C) 교육을 받지 않는다.
(D) 그녀의 가족이 그녀를 자주 방문한다.

해설 첫 번째 지문 앞부분에서 5년 전 도로 표지판을 제대로 읽을 수 없자 운전을 그만두었다는 내용이 나온다. 따라서 정답은 (A)이다. (D는 주변에 사는 가족이 없다고 했으므로 오답이다.

192 드리스 잉그램에 대해 암시된 것은 무엇인가?
(A) 예전에 반죽사였다.
(B) 요리를 돕는다.
(C) 자원봉사 문제를 겪고 있다.
(D) 지역 슈퍼마켓을 소유하고 있다.

해설 드리스는 젤리의 지배이며, 지난해 HHE 단체를 설립하기 위해서 반죽을 맡았다는 내용이 나오므로 정답은 (A)임을 알 수 있다. (B)는 두 사람이 지배 관계라는 점을 이용한 연상 오답이다.

193 편지에서 첫 번째 줄의 첫 번째 줄의 unsolicited와 의미상 가장 가까운 것은 무엇인가?
(A) 짧지 않은
(B) 예의 바르지 않은
(C) 흥미 있지 않은
(D) 요청하지 않은

해설 unsolicited가 언급된 문장의 다음 문장에서 당사자에게 직접 연락처를 받은 것이 아니라 기사를 통해서 받았음을 알 수 있다. 따라서 '요청하지 않은' 편지를 보내는 것에 대해 사과하는 내용으로 볼 수 있다. 따라서 정답은 (D)이다.

194 요리사 파멜 씨가 아이였을 때 누구로부터 피아노를 배웠는가?
(A) 메리 오노
(B) 빅토리아 엣진
(C) 드리스 잉그램
(D) 켈리 오노

해설 연계문제이다. 첫 번째 기사에서 빅토리아 엣진이라는 노인이 다뤄지고 있는데, 요리사 파멜 씨가 쓴 3 메일에서 기사에서 가르쳐준 다음 함께 나온 내용을 읽고 있고, 그분은 자신에게 방과 후 피아노를 가르쳐주신다고 했으므로... 정답은 (B)가 된다. (A는 기사를 쓴 기자의 이름, (C)와 (D)는 재빠른 도움의 손길(HHE) 조직처럼 시작된 지배들의 이름이다.)

195 요리사 파멜이 HHE에 기부하고 싶어 하는 것은 무엇인가?
(A) 마카로니치즈
(B) 사과 파이
(C) 마운드 케이크
(D) 호두 브라우니

해설 두 번째 지문 마지막에서 요리사가 사과 파이가 품평회에서 일등 상을 받았다는 내용이 나오는데, 세 번째 지문에서 디저트는 자신의 특기이 며 상을 받은 디저트를 기부하고 싶다고 했다. 이 두 내용을 종합하면 정답은 (B)가 된다.

어휘 senior citizen 노인 | elderly resident 노인 거주자 | 지반 grocery 식료품 | come in 참여하다, 도입하다 | nonprofit 비영리(의) | organization 단체 | produce 농산물; 생산하다 | for oneself 혼자 힘으로 | mobility 이동성 | issue 문제 | promising 유망한 | legal 법조계의, 법의 | essential 필수적인 | on a weekly basis 매주, 주 단위로 | contribute to ~에 이바지하다 | donate 기부하다 | whole 전체의 | community 지역 공동체 | chip in (돈을 조금씩) 보태다 | budget 예산 | inspired 영감을 받은 | rewarding 보람 있는 | sauté (기름에 살짝) 볶다, 튀기다 | chunk 덩어리 | comfort food 위안을 주는 음식 | uninspired 영감없는, 감흥 없는 | eatery 식당 | involve 관련시키다 | at first glance 처음에는 | overly 지나치게 | peppery 후추 맛이 나는 | transport 수송 | decor 실내 장식, 인테리어 | unassuming 겸손한 | exterior 외관 | head chef 수석 요리사 | definitely 틀림없이 | pack with ~로 가득한 | specialty 특기 | vision 통찰력, 선견 | set A apart from B A를 B와 다르게 하다 | award-winning 상을 받은, 수상한 | elderly 연세가 지긋한; 노인 | feature 특징으로 하다 | unsolicited 요청받지 않은 | face 직면하다 | take action 행동을 취하다, 조치하다 | get involved 참여하다 | donate 기부하다 | essential 필수적인 | deserve ~할 만한 가치가 있다 | treat A to B A에게 B를 대접하다 | stop by ~에 들르다 | once in a while 가끔, 이따금 | complimentary 무료의

[196-200]

https://www.visitgreenisland.com

그린 아일랜드: 바다 옆 당신의 별장!

숙박

호텔 파라디조 – 그린 아일랜드 빌리지의 가장 오래된 호텔인 파라디조는 방에서 볼 수 있는 아름다운 고풍적 가구로 유명합니다. 호텔의 인기 있는 레스토랑은 사람들이 알맞은 가격에 맛있는 음식을 제공합니다.

래핑 래빗 호텔 – 그린 아일랜드 빌리지의 비치 로드 14번가 – 이런 저렴한 가격의 옵션은 넓은 수영장과 친절한 직원들로 인해 방문하는 가족들에게 인기가 있습니다. 197 건물의 동쪽 방들은 바다 전망을 감상할 수 있습니다.

선셋 리조트 – 포트 웨스트의 클리프사이드 비치 로드 719번가 – 섬 서쪽의 고급 휴양지인, 선셋은 조용한 포트 웨스트의 바로 북쪽에 있습니다. 199 호화 로운 방과 미사가 낭만적인 환경의 숙에서 제공됩니다.

오션 뷰 인 – 그린 아일랜드 빌리지의 비치 로드 13번가 – 마을의 남쪽 끝에 있는, 197 래핑 래빗 바로 맞은편에 있는 이 중간급의 옵션은 낭만적인 전망으로 유명합니다. 꼭대기 층이 좋이 방을 요청해 보세요.

확인해 보세요! 진짜 사람들, 진짜 후기

래핑 래빗 호텔

저는 지난 7월에 그린 아일랜드에 주말 동안 방문하면서 이 호텔에서 3일 동안 머물렀습니다. 196 저는 원래 맞은편 장소에 밤을 예약했지만, 제 남째가 닿지 않 물렀습니다. 그들도 저에게 숙박을 제공할 수 없었습니다. 저는 그의 제안으로 래핑 래빗에 예약했고, 정반함이 있었습니다. 감사하게도 대부분 바다가 보이는 제 방은 넓었습니다. 그리고 200 프론트 데스크 직원은 매우 협조적이었 습니다. 그녀는 기까이 제가 어디에 갈지, 어디서 먹을지 결정하는 데 도움을 주었 습니다. 아쉽게도, 호텔은 소리 지르는 아이들로 가득했습니다. 저는 수영장 옆에서 휴식을 기대했지만, 소음이 참을 수 없는 수준이었습니다. 기겁을 적막했습니다. 그래서 만약 당신이 예산이 제한적이라면 이것을 예약하는 것은 물론이 한 가지 방법이 될 수 있습니다. 그러나 만약 예약할 것이라면 반드시 꾸마개를 준비해 오는 것이 좋을 것입니다.

루이스 개래로

수신: luisg47@fabco.com
발신: manager@lrh.net
날짜: 8월 5일
회신: 당신의 호텔에서의 숙박

개래로 씨에게:

후기 감사합니다. 저희들 당신이 199 저희 래핑 래빗 직원으로 감사드립니다. 대해 따뜻한 얌용을 해 준 것에 관해 고맙습니다. 그녀는 저희 호텔에 수년간 근무해 오고 있으며, 훌륭한 직원입니다. 불편에 관해서 호텔을 대표해서 제가 진심으로 사과드립니다. 200 고객님의 숙박 기간에 호텔에서 다른 가족 모임이 있었는데 안타깝게도 몇몇 아이들은 제 어리기 어려웠습니다. 고객님의 후기 중에 겪었던 불편함에 대한 보상으로, 하룻 밤 무료 숙박을 할 수 있는 쿠폰을 보내드렸었습니다. 바라건대, 저희의 작은 성의로 조만간 다시 오셔서 래핑 래빗에 두 번째 기회를 주셨으면 좋겠습니다.

진심으로

케이라 루소지 드림
호텔 매니저

어휘 vacation home 별장 accommodation 숙박 antique 고풍의, 전통 적인 affordable (가격이) 알맞은 budget 저가의; 예산 option 선택 due to ~ 때문에 feature 특징으로 하다 view 전망, 경치 sleepy (장소가) 생기 없고 조용한 resort 휴양지 high-end 고급의 mid-range 중급의 dining 식사(하기) setting 배경, 환경 originally 원래 accommodate 숙박을 제공하다; 수용하다 gourmet 미식가, 식도락가 unexpectedly 예상치 못하게 mixed 뒤섞인, 혼 합된 screaming 소리 지르는 look forward to ~을 고대하다 spacious 널따란 suggestion 제안 on a budget 한정된 예 산으로 unbearable 참을[견딜] 수 없는 earplug 귀마개 regarding ~에 관해서 appreciate 감사하다 extend an apology 사과하다 on behalf of ~ 대신 complaint 불평 entire 전체의 reunion (오랫동안 못 본 친척, 친구 등의) 모임 a bit 약간 unruly 제어[통제]하기 어려운 compensation for ~에 대한 보 상 inconvenience 불편(함) attached 첨부된 hopefully 바라건대

196 선셋 리조트에 관해 알 수 있는 것은 무엇인가?
(A) 도심에 있다.
(B) 새로 지어졌다.
(C) 인기가 있다.
(D) 비쌌다.
해설 선셋 리조트를 구체적으로 설명하고 있는 첫 번째 지문에서 high-end resort(고급 휴양지), luxury rooms(호화로운 객실)로 받아 같은 표현으로부 터 고급 리조트임을 알 수 있다. 따라서 정답은 (D)이다.

197 개래로 씨가 원래 머물려고 계획했던 장소는 어디인가?
(A) 호텔 파라디조
(B) 래핑 래빗 호텔
(C) 선셋 리조트
(D) 오션 뷰 인
해설 연계 문제이다. 래핑 래빗에 대한 후기가 쓰인 두 번째 지문에서 개래로 씨는 원래 맞은편 업체의 방을 예약하려고 했었다는 내용이 나온다. 그 런데 첫 번째 지문에서 래핑 래빗의 맞은편에 있는 것은 오션 뷰 인 임을 알 수 있다. 따라서 정답은 (D)이다.

198 개래로 씨의 방은 어느 방향을 향해 있는가?
(A) 북쪽
(B) 남쪽
(C) 동쪽
(D) 서쪽
해설 두 번째 지문에서 개래로 씨가 머물렀던 방은 바다가 보인다고 했는데 첫 번째 지문에서 래핑 래빗 동쪽에 있는 방들이 바다 전망을 특징으로 한다고 했다. 따라서 정답은 (C)이다.

199 위기 씨가 개래로 씨를 위해 해 주었던 일은 무엇인가?
(A) 그에게 호텔 쿠폰을 주었다.
(B) 그를 더 조용한 방으로 옮겨주었다.
(C) 그가 일정을 계획하는 것을 도왔다.
(D) 예약을 바꾸었다.
해설 문제를 풀기 위해 프론트 데스크 직원의 이름이 위키임을 찾아내야 한 다. 두 번째 지문에서 프론트 데스크 직원이 했다는데, 세 번째 지문에서 메리 위키가 프론트 데스크 직원임을 명시하였다. 두 내용을 종합하면, 정답은 (C) 가 된다. 본문의 which sites to visit and where to eat을 선택지 에서는 itinerary로 표현했다.

200 개래로 씨의 숙박 기간 중의 소음의 원인으로 언급된 것은 무엇인가?
(A) 건설 공사
(B) 가족 모임
(C) 현지 공휴일
(D) 음악 콘서트
해설 이메일에서 소음의 원인은 가족 모임이 있었다고 했으므로 정답은 (B)가 된다. 본문의 family reunion을 선택지에서나 family gathering으로 패러프 레이징했다.

Actual Test
02

저자 박선영

카카오톡 ID로 찾기(ID: matrix20)
≫ 친구 추가 후 1:1 채팅

본책 P34

Reading Comprehension

PART 7

147 (B)	148 (D)	149 (D)	150 (B)	151 (C)	152 (C)	153 (D)	154 (C)	155 (D)
156 (C)	157 (A)	158 (C)	159 (B)	160 (B)	161 (A)	162 (C)	163 (D)	164 (D)
165 (C)	166 (B)	167 (B)	168 (D)	169 (B)	170 (D)	171 (C)	172 (B)	173 (C)
174 (B)	175 (D)	176 (D)	177 (C)	178 (C)	179 (B)	180 (D)	181 (C)	182 (A)
183 (D)	184 (D)	185 (D)	186 (C)	187 (B)	188 (B)	189 (C)	190 (C)	191 (A)
192 (A)	193 (B)	194 (C)	195 (B)	196 (C)	197 (B)	198 (C)	199 (A)	200 (C)

[147-148]

겨울이 다가오고 있습니다!

겨울마다 기온 강하와 폭설로 많은 곤란을 겪습니다.

⁴⁷⁰ 겨울을 따뜻하고 편안하게 보내기 위해서 점검해야 할 몇 가지 사항이 여기 있습니다:

- 온도가 영하 7도 이하로 떨어지면, 냉방을 꼭 틀어 놓으시오. 외출 시 난방을 최소한으로 틀어 놓으세요, 이것은 파이프의 동파를 막아줄 것입니다.
- **⁴⁸⁰** 물이 똑똑 떨어지게 해서 수도꼭지가 어는 것을 막으세요.
- 수도 계량기를 따뜻한 담요로 덮으세요.
- 눈이 온 후에는, 가능한 한 빨리 현관 주변에서 치우는 것이 가장 좋습니다. 시간이 지나면 눈이 얼음이 될 수도 있습니다.

신중하고 빠르게 행동하면 수리를 기다리며 추위에 떨 필요가 없습니다. 따뜻하게 지내시고 즐거운 휴일 되세요!

어휘 temperature drop 기온 강하 | Celsius 섭씨의 | prevent ~을 방지하다 | freeze 얼다 | burst 파열하다, 터지다 | faucet 수도꼭지 | drip 똑똑 떨어지다 | block 막다 | water meter 수도 계량기 | blanket 담요 | cautious 신중한 | escape 피하다 | avalanche 눈사태

147 제공되는 정보는 무엇인가?
(A) 눈사태에 탈출하는 법
(B) 추운 겨울을 나는 법
(C) 물이 흐름을 개선하는 법
(D) 새 파이프를 설치하는 법

해설 지문의 첫 부분에서도 알 수 있듯이 추운 겨울을 나는 법에 대해서 정보를 제공하는 내용이므로 정답은 (B)이다.

148 공지에 의하면, 가주자들에게 요구되는 것은 무엇인가?
(A) 온도를 7시간마다 확인하는 것
(B) 모든 창문과 문을 닫는 것
(C) 외출 시 난방을 끄는 것
(D) 수도꼭지 물을 계속 흐르게 유지하는 것

해설 선택지 중 지문에서 언급된 내용은 (D)로 두 번째 당부 사항에 언급되어 있다.

[149-150]

수신: 고든 셔크스 (shirks76@hotmail.uk)
발신: 고객서비스 (customerservice@topsneakers.com)
날짜: 8월 3일
제목: 오리지널 캔버스 1961

셔크스 씨께,

⁴⁹⁰ 홀리스 브랜드의 "오리지널 캔버스 1961"이 저희 매장에 있다는 정보를 알려 드리래 매우 기쁩니다. 제가 예전에 이 모델이 단종되어 저희 매장 어디서도 찾기 어려울 것이라고 알씀드린 적이 있었습니다. 하지만 홀리스에서 이 오리지널 모델을 40주년 기념으로 한정 판매를 하기로 했습니다 그때, 고객님께서 주의 깊게 이메일 주소를 남기신 것이 기억이 났습니다. 그래서 고객님께서 오래 기다리시던 "오리지널 캔버스 1961"이 현재 구매 가능하다는 것을 알려 드리게 되어 기쁩니다. **¹⁵⁰** 이 모델 구매에 관심이 있으시면 이메일로 답장을 주시거나 021-555-6751로 저희 매장의 연락을 취해 주세요. **⁵⁰** 상품을 정상 판매가로 내놓기 전에 고객님의 연락을 일주일간 기다리겠습니다. 연락 기다리겠습니다.

밥 트루먼

어휘 in possession of ~를 소유한 | particular 특정한 | discontinue (생산을)중단하다 | limited 한정의 | original 고유의, 최초의 | anniversary 기념일 | in case ~의 경우를 대비하여 | in stock 재고가 있는 | available 이용 가능한 | be willing to 기꺼이 ~하다

149 셔크스 씨에게 이메일이 발송된 이유는 무엇인가?
(A) 그가 구매한 것을 가져갈 수 있다는 것을 알리기 위해
(B) 기념일을 맞이해서 그에게 운동화 디자인을 부탁하기 위해
(C) 경매를 위해 그의 운동화를 포기할 건지 묻어보기 위해
(D) 그에게 결정하라고 요청하기 위해

해설 첫 번째 문장에서 단종되었던 모델을 다시 한정 판매하기로 결정했다고 알리고 있고 또한, 지문 중반에 아직도 이 모델을 구매하고 싶은지 묻고 있으므로 정답은 (D)이다.

150 트루먼 씨가 셔크스 씨에게 제안하는 것은 무엇인가?
(A) 다음 구매에 사용할 할인 쿠폰을 제공하는 것
(B) 일정 기간 상품을 판매하지 않고 기다리는 것
(C) 더 오랜 기다림을 보상하기 위해 무료로 배달해 주는 것
(D) 홀리스 모델 전부가 있는 포스터를 보내 주는 것

해설 지문 후반부에 운동화를 일주일간 판매하지 않고 기다리겠다고 제안하고 있으므로 정답은 (B)다.

[151-152]

겨울에 하는 퀼팅

강사: 낸시 기번스, 엘리자 무어니
첫 번째 강의 등록: 9월 1일, 15명
두 번째 강의 등록: 10월 1일, 15명
장소: 나나와 멜의 전통 퀼트, 15 오크우드 가

¹⁵¹ 저희 퀼팅 매장에서 계절 수업을 개설합니다. **¹⁵²** 참가자는 수준에 관계없이 모두 환영합니다. 초보자들은 지칩과 컵받침을 만드는 것을 배울 수 있습니다. 경험이 조금 있는 분들은 인증, 가방, 그리고 다 많은 것을 만드는 것을 배울 수 있습니다. 그음 실력을 갖춘 분들은 가죽을 위한 퀼트를 배울 수 있습니다. 뛰어난 퀼팅 실력을 갖춘 분들은 그냥 오셔서 장소와 재료를 사용해도 됩니다.

재료비는 전재 단추의 종류와 크기에 따라 다릅니다. 하지만 이 동네에서 가장 낮은 가격이라는 것을 보장할 수 있습니다. **¹⁵²** 직접 옷감을 가지고 오셔도 요금을 받지 않습니다.

일단 등록하시면 영업시간(오전 10시 - 오후 5시) 이무 때나 오시고 싶은 대로 오시면 됩니다. 저희 가게에 업주일에 몇 번 오실지는 스스로 정하시면 됩니다. **¹⁵²** 하지만 인원수를 15명으로 제한하기 때문에 등록 날짜를 놓치시면 안 됩니다.

어휘 quilting 퀼팅 누비기 | instructor 강사 | session 학기 | registration 등록 | seasonal lesson 계절학기 | beginner 조급자 | purse 지갑 | coaster 컵받침 | advanced 진보한,고등의 | talented 재능이 있는 | material 재료 | once 일단 ~하면 | waive 포기하다, 생략하다 | business hours 영업 시간

151 정보의 목적은 무엇인가?
(A) 매장이 재단장했다는 것을 알리려고
(B) 공예품 판매를 홍보하려고
(C) 수업 개설을 알리려고
(D) 매장의 새로운 위치를 요청하려고

해설 지문 첫 번째 문장에서 계절 수업이 열린다고 했으므로 정답은 (C)이다.

152 퀼팅 매장에 관해 알려진 것이 아닌 것은 무엇인가?
(A) 어떤 수준의 학생이든 환영받는다.
(B) 직접 재료를 가지고 오는 학생은 돈을 내지 않는다.
(C) 최고 품질의 재료만을 제공한다.
(D) 수업에는 인원수 제한이 있다.

해설 지문 초반에 수준에 관계없이 모든 참가자를 가져오면 모두 환영한다는 내용으로부터 (A를 참가자가 옷감을 가져오면 재료비를 받지 않는다는 내용에서 (B)를, 15명으로 참가자 수를 제한한다는 내용에서 (D)를 확인할 수 있다. (C)에 관한 내용은 언급되어 있지 않으므로 정답은 (C)이다.

매튜 구드 오전 9:10
안녕하세요, 리지. 전 아직도 인쇄소에 있는데 소책자가 완성되어 있는 것 같아요. 전부 다 해야 할 것 같아요. 153 지금이면 테이블과 의자가 설치되어야 할 시간이에요. 저 대신 좀 해주세요. 제 책상 위에 평면도가 있을 거예요.

리지 캐롤런 오전 9:11
153 물론이죠, 저에게 맡기세요.

매튜 구드 오전 9:12
좋아요. 신입사원 오리엔테이션은 2시 30분이지만, 154 저는 응접실 먼저 준비되었으면 해요.

리지 캐롤런 오전 9:14
154 로비 먼저 말씀하시는 거죠?

매튜 구드 오전 9:15
네, 오리엔테이션은 강당에서 하고요. 그렇지만 제가 도착할 때까지 가까이에 음향 시스템까지 설치할 필요는 없어요.

리지 캐롤런 오전 9:17
알겠습니다. 그럼 직접 시작할게요.

매튜 구드 오전 9:20
고마워요, 곧 봐요.

어휘 printing office 인쇄소 booklet 소책자, 팸플릿 set up 설치하다
floor plan 평면도 leave up to ~에게 맡기다 reception 접대, 환영회
auditorium 강당

153 오전 9시 11분에 캐롤런 씨가 "저에게 맡기세요"라고 쓴 의도는 무엇인가?
(A) 그녀는 소책자가 각 테이블에 놓여 있는지 확인한다.
(B) 그녀는 구드 씨가 작성한 팸플릿을 선택하겠다고 확신한다.
(C) 그녀는 테이블 주문을 확정하고 있다.
(D) 그녀는 구드 씨를 도울 것이다.

해설 이 메시지 바로 앞에 구드 씨가 자신은 지금 인쇄소에 있으므로 캐롤런 씨에게 자신을 대신해 테이블과 의자를 설치해 달라고 부탁하고 있다. 따라서 캐롤런 씨가 "저에게 맡기세요"라고 대답한 것은 구드 씨에 부탁을 할 것이라는 뜻이므로 정답은 (D)이다.

154 캐롤런 씨가 다음에 갈 곳은 어디인가?
(A) 접견실
(B) 인쇄소
(C) 로비
(D) 비품실

해설 구드 씨는 캐롤런 씨에게 응접실이 로비에 먼저 의자와 테이블을 설치해 달라고 부탁하고 있다. 따라서 캐롤런 씨가 마지막 캐롤런 씨가 마지막 메시지에서 작업을 시작하겠다고 말한 것은 로비에 의자와 테이블을 설치하겠다는 말이므로 정답은 (C)이다.

미쓰이사가 5월에 새로운 스마트폰을 출시할 예정

156 157 모든 최첨단 전화 경쟁사들이 스마트폰을 출시하려고 노력하고 있는데, — [1] —. 157 미쓰이사는 이 첨단 기술 경쟁에서 포기한 것 같이 보였다. — [2] —. 미쓰이사는 단숨한 경쟁 성공 2개월 이상의 스마트폰을 곧 출시한다고 발표했다.

미쓰이사의 새로운 스마트폰 모델명은 성공한 시간 동안 그 산업에서 지지되지 않는 다른 희망을 담은 "인버시블"이다. — [2] —. 155 미쓰이사는 이 모델이 컴퓨터 보다 인터넷 접속이 빠르다는 것을 약속했다. 후면 이중 카메라의 생성된 오차마다 공연처럼 고품질의 음향을 위한 쿼드 카드 DAC 칩도 장착되어 있다.

에이스우 노틱스와 같은 다른 스마트폰 회사들이 반응을 기대할 뿐이니 무서워 있었다. — [3] —. 타 스마트폰 회사 직원들이 출시일을 보자 긴장감이 돌았다. 소비자들도 새로운 모델에 들떠 있지만, 스마트폰 가격이 너무 높아지는 데에 대한 우려도 있다. — [4] —.

어휘 launch 출시하다 cutting-edge 최첨단의 strive 노력하다, 힘쓰다 competitor 경쟁 상품 invincible 언으려고 undefeated 무패의 dual 이중의 rear 후면의 high-quality 고품질의 anticipatory 예상한 anxious 불안한 tense 긴장한 hasty 너무 성급한 yet-to-be-launched 아직 출시되지 않은

155 "인버시블"에 대해 언급된 것은 무엇인가?
(A) 1,200만 화소의 카메라를 가지고 있다.
(B) MP3 플레이어 기능을 갖고 있다.
(C) 회사의 좌우명을 따라 이름이 지어졌다.
(D) 훌륭한 인터넷 속도를 가졌다.

해설 "인버시블"은 곧 출시될 신제품을 말하며, 지문 중반에 이 제품이 컴퓨터보다 인터넷 속도가 빠르다고 했으므로 정답은 (D)이다.

156 첫 번째 단락 두 번째 줄의 "strived"와 의미상 가장 가까운 것은 무엇인가?
(A) 출발했다
(B) 멈췄었다
(C) 노력했다
(D) 결정했다

해설 strived는 '노력했다'라는 의미가 있으므로 정답은 (C) attempted이다.

157 [1], [2], [3], [4]로 표시된 곳 중 다음 문장이 위치로 가장 적절한 곳은 어디인가?

"하지만 지금 이는 성급한 결론으로 보인다."

(A) [1]
(B) [2]
(C) [3]
(D) [4]

해설 삽입문장의 역접의 접속사 But을을 고려해 볼 때, 이 문장이 삽입되는 부분 내용상 대조를 이룰 수 있어야 한다; 지문 초반에 미쓰이사는 최첨단 스마트폰 경쟁을 포기한 것 같이 보였다는 내용과, 단숨한 경쟁 성공 그 이상의 뛰어난 제품을 출시한다고 발표했다는 내용이 사이에 삽입문장이 필요하므로 정답은 (A)이다.

사랑하는 이와
휴일을 보낼 기회를 놓치지 마세요!

158 레저전스 리조트는 여러분에게 거절할 수 없는 제안을 합니다! 저희의 리조트는 가장 아름다운 하와이의 한 섬에 있습니다. 그러나 158 이 이름다운 섬에 오셔서 남기지 않는 가격에 품격 휴가를 즐기세요.

이번 주 내로 다음 달 사용을 예약하시면, 159 고객님은 무료로 다른 분야의 한 분야 동행할 수 있습니다! 그러나 여러분과 동행에게 바During에 있는 리조트에서의 휴식을 선물하세요. 그러나 표 구매자는 신용 카드 소지자와 동일이어야 하며, 구매를 동시에 완료하셔야 합니다.

해택은 여기서 끝나지 않습니다. 이 행사에는 1층 트리어엄프 식당에서의 2인 부페가 포함되어 있습니다. 160 그러나 환상적인 다음 달이 예약하셔서 주에 예약하세요!

주의 사항: 이 해택은 주중 예약에만 적용됩니다.

16675 피오르컬러니가
호텔블루, 하와이 98615
미국

어휘 refuse 거절하다 gorgeous 호화로운, 매력적인 accompany 동반하다 treat 다루다, 대우하다 match 걸맞다, 어울리다

158 광고되는 것은 무엇인가?
(A) 호텔에서의 점심
(B) 가족 여행
(C) 리조트 체험
(D) 주말 운전

해설 레저런스 리조트의 할인 행사를 광고하고 있으므로 정답은 (C)이다.

159 광고에서 해택에 관해 언급된 것은 무엇인가?
(A) 예약은 다음 달에 이루어져야 한다.
(B) 동행하는 사람은 무료로 머물 수 있다.
(C) 이원 부페가 빠짐없이 제공될 것이다.
(D) 바During가 전망이 있는 방을 이용할 수 있다.

해설 지문 중반에서 동행하는 사람은 무료임을 알 수 있다. 따라서 정답은 (B)이다.

160 해택을 받으려면 언제까지 하는가?
(A) 오늘
(B) 이번 주
(C) 다음 달
(D) 여름에

해설 지문 마지막 부분에서 다음 달에 해택을 누릴 수 있으려면 이번 주에 예약해야 한다고 강조하므로 정답은 (B)이다.

[161-163]

(icon) 주민 헬스 센터
새로운 곳으로 이사했어요!

아래 주소로 저희를 방문하세요:
(icon) 824 메디나가
스토니브룩 가운티

체육관 시간:
월-금: 오전 7:00 - 오후 10:00
토·일요일: 오전 9:00 - 오후 6:00

* 사우나는 체육관과 같은 시간에 문을 열고 닫습니다. 사우나를 사용하는 데 추가 비용이 발생하지 않습니다. 즉, 사우나를 이용하려면 체육관을 이용해야 합니다.
(사우나는 체육관과 같은 시간을 사용하는 사람들을 위한 것입니다.)
* 국경일에는 쉽니다.

더 많은 장소로 이전한 것을 기념하기 위해, 이번 주까지는 누구나 무료로 우리 체육관을 월요일(4월 1일)부터 일요일(4월 7일)까지 누구나 오셔서 장비와 시설을 체험해 보실 수 있습니다. 신분증을 가져오셔서 시설에 사시는 것을 확인하시면 됩니다.

회원권이 있으신 분들도 세 시설을 확인해 볼 수 있습니다. 그리고 나서, 다음 주부터 새로운 회원권을 판매할 것입니다.

3개월 회비: 120,000달러
6개월 회비: 220,000달러
1년 회비: 410,000달러

무료로 체육관을 체험해 보신 후 회원 가입을 결정하세요!

어휘 gym 체육관 additional 추가적인 sauna 목욕탕 patron 고객 national holiday 국경일 facility 시설 bring 가져오다 incur (비용을) 발생시키다 spacious 넓은

161 공지의 목적은 무엇인가?
(A) 변경 사항을 알리려고
(B) 무료 쿠폰을 나눠주려고
(C) 회원 등록비 인상을 알리려고
(D) 기주민에게 무료 회원권에 대해 알리려고

해설 새로운 지역으로 이전했다는 내용을 체육관에서도 알 수 있으므로 체육관이 위치 변경을 알리는 공지이다. 따라서 정답은 (A)이다.

162 헬스 센터에 관해 사실이 아닌 것은 무엇인가?
(A) 메디나가 기에 있다.
(B) 사우나가 있다.
(C) **다음 주에 다시 문을 열 것이다.**
(D) 국경일에는 문을 닫는다.

해설 지문 중반에 이번 주까지는 누구나 무료로 체육관을 체험해 볼 수 있고 연급되어 있으므로 현재 운영 중인 것으로 짐작할 수 있다. 따라서 다음 주에 다시 문을 열 것이라는 내용은 사실이 아니므로 정답은 (C)이다.

163 센터에 관해 추측할 수 있는 것은 무엇인가?
(A) 사우나는 매일 만문 연다.
(B) 회비 할인이 없다.
(C) 사우나 이용은 추가 비용을 지급해야 한다.
(D) **원래 건물은 지금보다 공간이 더 작았다.**

해설 지문 중반에 이 센터는 규정에에 몸을 만든다고 하였으므로 (A)는 오답. 지문 초반부에 회원 오래 유지할수록 비용이 좋아드는 것을 이용하므로 (B)도 오답, 지문 초반에서 체육권을 이용하는 사람만 사우나를 무료로 이용할 수 있다는 내용이 나오므로 (C)도 오답이다. 지문 중반에 센터 건물이 더 큰 장소로 이전한 것을 기념한다는 내용에서 예전의 센터 건물이 공간이 작았다는 것을 알 수 있으므로 정답은 (D)이다.

[164-167]

수신: 전 직원
발신: 마리오 판조니즈
날짜: 1월 12일
제목: 사브리나 걸리건

임원들이 사브리나 걸리건 씨를 마케팅 매니저로 임명했음을 알리게 되어 기쁩니다. - [1] -. 그녀는 직원들을 감독하고 마케팅 팀의 새로운 전략을 짜는 일을 하게 될 것입니다. 이 변화는 내일부터 적용됩니다.

- [2] -. 그녀는 추천을 받아 시카고에 있는 본사로 전근되었습니다. 그녀는 시간을 지키고 정정하기로 정평이 나 있습니다. 그녀는 자신에게는 엄격하고 다른 직원에게는 따뜻한 마음을 대합니다. 그녀는 모든 직원의 물론 임원에게도 모범이 되어 왔습니다. - [3] -. 그러나 마케팅 매니저는 그녀가 이미 해왔던 일에 대한 새로운 직함일 뿐입니다.

저는 그녀의 훌륭한 경험과 뛰어난 지도력이 우리 회사에 좋은 새로운 토대가 될 것이라고 믿습니다. - [4] -. 여러분 모두 그녀를 따뜻하게 축하해 주시기 바랍니다. 우리 회사의 밝아진 발전하는 것인 만큼, 이 변화로 인해서 우리가 앞으로 한 발자국 더 나아가게 해줄 것이라고 믿습니다. 계속 수고해 주세요!

마리오 판조니즈,
대표이사

어휘 delight 기쁨을 주다 board of directors 임원 appoint 임명하다 be in charge of ~을 담당하다, 책임지다 direct 감독하다, 지시하다 punctual 시간을 지키는 strict 엄격한 executive 임원 splendid 훌륭한 outstanding 뛰어난 foundation 토대 title 직함 keep up 유지하다, 지속하다 promote 승진하다 forward 앞으로

164 메모가 쓰인 이유는 무엇인가?
(A) 직원들에게 직원 파티를 알리려고
(B) 새로운 위원들을 지명하려고
(C) 올해의 전략을 공유하려고
(D) **인사 이동을 발표하려고**

해설 지문 첫 부분에서 사브리나 걸리건이 마케팅 매니저로 임명되었음을 발표하고 있으므로 인사 이동에 관한 내용임을 알 수 있다. 따라서 정답은 (D)이다.

165 걸리건 씨의 업무는 무엇인가?
(A) 실력 있는 직원 추천하기
(B) 전 지점을 감독하기
(C) **자신의 팀을 위해 새로운 전략을 짜기**
(D) 직원들에게 지도력을 보여주기

해설 지문 초반에 걸리건 씨의 업무는 담당 마케팅 부서의 새로운 마케팅 전략을 계획하는 것이라고 나와 있으므로 정답은 (C)이다.

166 걸리건 씨가 시카고로 떠나기 전에 일하고 있던 도시는 어디인가?
(A) 뉴욕
(B) **시카고**
(C) 보스턴
(D) 워싱턴

해설 지문 중반에 걸리건 씨가 시카고에 있는 본사로 전근했다는 사실이 나와 있으므로 이를 토대로 걸리건 씨는 시카고에서 일했음을 알 수 있다. 따라서 정답은 (B)이다.

167 [1], [2], [3], [4]로 표시된 곳 중 다음 문장이 위치로 가장 적절한 곳은 어디인가?

"걸리건 씨는 2012년 보스턴에 있는 우리 회사에 입사했고 2016년에 주어 마케팅 매니저로 승진했습니다."

(A) [1]
(B) **[2]**
(C) [3]
(D) [4]

해설 삽입문장에서 걸리건 씨의 입사 내용이 연급되어 있으므로 그녀가 그동안 회사에서 쌓아 온 평판과 업적이 나온 두 번째 단락을 이끄는 것이 적절하다. 그러므로 정답은 (B)이다.

[168-171]

줄리엣 원크 [오전 9:50]	루퍼트, 지금 우리 회사 웹 사이트를 보고 있나요? 168 신제품 홍보가 저 컴퓨터에서는 보이지 않아요. 당신은 어떤가요?
루퍼트 센더스 [오전 9:52]	잠깐만요.
루퍼트 센더스 [오전 9:55]	저도 찾을 수가 없네요. 이게 언제부터 이런 건가요?
줄리엣 원크 [오전 9:56]	그렇게 오래되진 않은 거 같아요. 169 저도 오늘 아침에 영업부에서 연락을 받고 알았거든요. 당신도 아시다시피, 내일 그 상품이 출시돼야 해서 우리는 당장 그것을 해결해야 해요. 기술 지원팀에 연락 좀 해주실래요?
루퍼트 센더스 [오전 9:58]	팀. 우리 웹 사이트에 신제품 홍보가 생겼나요?
팀 다카시 [오전 10:00]	네, 알고 있어요. 저도 메시지 받았거든요. 170 삭제되었던 것 같아요.
루퍼트 센더스 [오전 10:01]	오, 정말요? 그러면 예비 파일이 있어야 할 텐데요.
팀 다카시 [오전 10:02]	170 걱정하지 마세요. 우리는 만약을 대비해 여 항상 그렇게 하고 있습니다. 제가 즉시 처리하겠습니다.
루퍼트 센더스 [오전 10:03]	171 좋아요. 그런 우리는 영업부에 알릴 필요가 있을 겁니다.
줄리엣 원크 [오전 10:04]	그것은 제가 처리할게요.

어휘 promotion 홍보 right after 직후에 technical support 기술 지원 remove 지우다, 삭제하다 just in case 만약을 대비해서 backup 예비, 백업 inform 알리다 take care of ~을 처리하다 handle 처리하다

168 원크 씨가 보는 것은 무엇인가?
(A) 상점에서 주문을 진행할 수 있다.
(B) 잘못된 연락처가 온라인에 기재되었다.
(C) 회사의 웹 사이트가 열리지 않는다.
(D) 몇몇 정보가 온라인에 게시되지 않는다.

해설 원크 씨는 첫 번째 메시지에서 신제품 홍보가 자신의 컴퓨터에서 보이지 않는다고 보고하고 있다. 따라서 정답은 (D)이다.

169 원크 씨에게 문제를 알려준 사람은 누구인가?
(A) 고객
(B) 동료 영업직원
(C) 기술 지원자
(D) 매장 관리자

해설 원크 씨는 9시 56분 메시지에서 영업부서로부터 연락을 받고 문제를 알게 되었다고 말하고 있다. 따라서 정답은 (B)이다.

170 오전 10시 1분에 센더스 씨가 "그러면 예비 파일이 있어야 할 텐데요"라고 쓴 의미는 무엇인가?
(A) 그는 성격 홍보에 대해 걱정한다.
(B) 그는 다카시 씨가 절차를 설명해 주길 바란다.
(C) 그는 온라인 상점에 대한 접근을 제한하길 원한다.
(D) 그는 어떤 정보를 온라인으로 되돌리길 바란다.

해설 다카시 씨가 신제품 홍보가 삭제된 것 같다고 하자, 센더스 씨가 예비 파일이 있는지 묻고 있다. 이는 삭제되었던 신제품 홍보를 다시 게시할 수 있는 예비 파일이 있는지 묻고 있는 것이므로 정답은 (D)이다.

171 원크 씨가 다음에 할 일은 무엇인가?
(A) 회사 정책을 갱신한다.
(B) 게시판에 공지를 게시한다.
(C) 영업부서에 연락한다.
(D) 신제품을 홍보한다.

해설 오전 10시 3분 메시지에서 센더스 씨가 영업부서에 알려야 한다고 말하자, 원크 씨가 그것을 처리하겠다고 말하므로 정답은 (C)이다.

[172-175]

176 수신: 엘리 타벤바움 (ellitan@fxmotors.com)
발신: 인사과 〈human@fxmotors.com〉
날짜: 3월 22일
제목: 평가

타벤바움 씨에게,

본 이메일은 인사팀에서 발송되었을 것이며, 귀하는 이에 대한 비밀을 지킬 의무가 있습니다. 172 175 직원들을 공정하게 평가하기 위해, 우리 인사팀에서는 상대적으로 낮은 직급의 직원들을 무작위로 선택하여 같은 담에서 높은 직급까지 직원을 평가하게 합니다. 이래 기재된 안내에 따라 평가서를 이번 주말까지 이메일로 제출해 주시면 됩니다.

- 당신이 평가하는 것을 아무에게 보여주지 마세요.
- 되도 편안한 곳에서 평가하셔도 됩니다.
- 173 이 양식을 아무에게도 보내서는 안 됩니다.
- 173 평가서는 총 7페이지이고 5개의 영역입니다.
- 174 어떤 문제도 빼놓지 말고 답변하세요.
- 사용항 항목이 질문들에 대한 답은 갖지 않아도 됩니다. 하지만 특정 174 사건을 묘사해 주시기 바랍니다.

우리는 당신의 진솔한 평가를 할 정직성을 갖추고 있다고 믿습니다. 우리는 평가자의 비밀을 지킬 것을 약속합니다. 또한, 귀하가 평가에 들이는 시간 노력에 대해 감사드리며, 지혜로운 판단을 현명하게 사용하겠습니다. 이 평가에 대해 궁금하신 점이 있으시면 이메일을 보내시거나 인사팀에 전화를 주세요.

협조 감사합니다.
인사과

어휘 evaluation 평가 human resources team 인사부 be obliged to do ~해야 한다 adhere 고수하다 confidentiality 기밀성 fair 공정한 randomly 무작위로 relatively 비교적 follow (규칙 따위를 따르다 convenient 편안한 authorize 허가하다 criteria 평가 기준 기준이다 incident 사건 incidentally 제한하듯이 원하다 진솔한 secrecy 비밀 honesty 성실 fairness 공정함 truthful 진솔한 wisely 비밀하게 regarding ~에 관하여 unanswered 답을 안 한

172 이메일의 목적은 무엇인가?
(A) 엘리에게 다가오는 평가를 상기시키려고
(B) 평가에 협조를 부탁하려고
(C) 양식을 만드는 데에 제안을 물어보려고
(D) 엘리의 승진을 제안하려고

해설 이메일의 목적은 모든 문제이므로 지문 초반부에서 지문 초반부에서 정답의 힌트를 찾는다. 지문 상단에서 직원들을 평가하라는 데 협조를 부탁한다고 했으므로 정답은 (B)이다.

173 평가에 관해 언급된 것이 아닌 것은 무엇인가?
(A) 답변을 넣지 않은 질문은 개도 있으면 안 된다.
(B) 5개의 영역으로 되어 있다.
(C) 참가자들은 평가 후에 상품권을 받게 된다.
(D) 참가자들은 양식을 다른 사람에게 보내서는 안 된다.

해설 지문 중반에 어떤 질문도 그냥 넘어가지 않는 부분에서 (A)를, 평가서는 5가지 평가 기준으로 이루어져 있다는 부분에서 (B)를, 평가양식은 아무에게도 보내면 안 되는 부분에서 (D)를 확인할 수 있지만, 상품권에 관한 내용은 없으므로, 정답은 (C)이다.

174 두 번째 단락 다섯 번째 줄의 "incidents"와 의미상 가장 가까운 것은 무엇인가?
(A) 정신적 외상
(B) 사건
(C) 혼란
(D) 소멸

해설 지문 중반에 평가와 관련해서 특정 사건을 묘사해 달라고 부탁하고 있다. 그러므로 "incidents"는 "사건"이라는 뜻이므로 가장 가까운 것은 "happenings"와 가장 가까운 의미이다. 따라서 정답은 (B)이다.

175 엘리에 대해 알 수 있는 것은 무엇인가?
(A) 그녀의 업체에서 높은 직급을 가졌다.
(B) 평가를 완성했다고 자부했다.
(C) 인사과 직원이다.
(D) 선임 직원을 평가해야 한다.

해설 이 이메일을 받는 사람이 엘리인데, 이 이메일은 직급이 낮은 직원들에 게만 보내는 것이라고 했으며, 직급이 낮은 직원들이 선임 상사를 평가할 것이라고 했으므로, 엘리도 선임 상사를 평가해야 한다는 것을 알 수 있다. 따라서 정답은 (D)이다.

[176-180]

가장 중요한 것은 좋은 관계를 형성하는 것입니다.

176 여러분은 자신의 업체의 첫 번째 문장에서 업체를 잘 이끌 방법을 찾고 계신가요? 그렇다면 여러분에게 필요한 것은 이끌 방법을 찾고 게시나요? 우리 릴레이션룹은 10년이 넘게 우리 지역 업체들의 반영을 위해 일해 오고 있습니다. 우리는 여러분이 필요한 전문적인 반영을 위해 일해 왔습니다.

177 우리는 가시가 교체 그리고 지역 직원들과 좋은 관계를 형성할 수 있도록 컨설팅 서비스와 교육을 제공하고 있습니다. 양성하지 않고 지금 바로 경험해 보세요. 우리는 여러분의 사업 파트너가 될 것입니다. 우리 웹 사이트에 방문하셔서 큰 성공을 경축하세요!

www.relationloop.com

178 행크 서먼
릴레이션룹 컨설팅
339 윌스 가
179 토론토 온타리오 주
서먼 씨에게,

177 우리 회사가 원활하게 돌아갈 수 있도록 도와주셔서 다시 한번 감사드립니다. 직장 내의 관계에 대한 컨설팅을 우리 직원들이 서로를 더 잘 이해하고 효율적으로 의사소통하게 하는 것을 도와주었습니다. 또한 이제까지 동아가신 후 회사를 책임지게 되었습니다. 아버지가 회사 전체 경영까지 도맡아 했었습니다. 덕분에 직원들이 자신보다 저를 더 신뢰하게 되었습니다. 그리고 그들을 쉽게 배웠습니다. 직원들이 새로운 사정을 맞이하면 붙이며 하는다는 것을 알게 되었습니다. 이러한 붙이와 새로운 환경에서 자신을 보증하기 위한 직대인으로 변한다는 것을 알게 되었습니다. 이제 저는 이 세대들을 장기적으로 보는 것입니다. 이제 직원들은 제가 근처에 있어도 편하게 저의 진실 어린 불평을 하기도 합니다. **180** 정말 감사드립니다. 당신은 우리 회사뿐 아니라, 우리 모두를 구해주었습니다. 혹시 우리에게서 추천서가 필요하시면 언제라도, 기꺼이 제공해 드리겠습니다.

하시는 모든 일에 행운이 있기를 바랍니다.

179 대릴 이사, 릴스맥킨 시럽스
윌헬미나 우티에어

176 광고의 대상은 누구인가?

(A) 컨설팅 회사들
(B) 직원들
(C) 교육기관
(D) 지역 사업체들의 소유주들

어휘 lead 이끌다　smoothly 원활하게　effectively 효율적으로　prosperity 번영　local 지역의　decade 10년　hesitate 주저하다　achieve 성취하다　massive 큰　run 경영하다　pass away 사망하다　rough 거친　loss 상실　faith 신뢰　anxiety 걱정　hostility 적의　endeavor 노력　comfortable 편안한　honest 정직한

해설 첫 번째 지문의 첫 번째 문장에서 업체를 잘 이끌 방법을 찾고 있는지 묻고 있는 점, 지문 중반에 이 이끌 방법을 찾고 이렇게 10년 넘게 일해 오고 있다고 연급한 점을 종합하면, 지역 사업체의 반영을 위해 일해 왔으므로 이 연급한 점을 종합하면, 지역 사업체의 반영을 위해 10년 넘게 일해 오고 있다는 것을 알 수 있다. 따라서 정답은 (D)이다.

177 편지의 목적은 무엇인가?

(A) 환불을 요청하는 것
(B) 일자리에 지원하는 것
(C) 일에 대한 감사를 표하는 것
(D) 사업 계획을 제안하는 것

해설 두 번째 지문 초반에 업체를 원활하게 경영할 수 있도록 도와줘서 감사하다고 말하고 있으므로 정답은 (C)이다.

178 릴레이션룹을 컨설팅에 관해 추측할 수 있는 것은 무엇인가?

(A) 이 회사는 20년 전에 운영을 시작하였다.
(B) 서먼 씨는 여러 번 이 회사에 의뢰하였다.
(C) 이 회사와 릴스맥킨 시럽스는 토론토에 있다.
(D) 이 회사는 광고 회사이다.

해설 첫 번째 지문 중반에 회사가 10년 넘게 운영되고 있다고 연급되어 있으므로 (A)는 오답이고, 이 회사에 의뢰한 사람은 윌헬미나이며 세 번에 걸쳐 이 회사에 의뢰했다는 내용이 없으므로 (B)도 오답이다. 또, 첫 지문 중반에 이 회사는 컨설팅 서비스를 제공한다고 했으므로 (D)도 오답이다. 두 번째 지문에 주소 정보에서 릴레이션룹을 컨설팅이 토론토에 있다는 것을 알 수 있는데, 첫 번째 지문에서 이 회사는 같은 지역에 있는 회사들이 서로를 잘 이해하고 효율적으로 의사소통하도록 돕는다는 내용이 있다. 그런데, 릴스맥킨이 이 건설업에 서비스를 제공한다고 나와 있다. 이 두 회사가 같은 토론토 지역에 있다는 것을 알 수 있으므로 정답은 (C)이다.

179 편지에 의하면, 서먼 씨 노력의 결과는 무엇인가?

(A) 제품의 품질이 나아진 것
(B) 직원들 간의 효과적인 의사소통
(C) 직원들 수의 증가
(D) 효율적인 업무

해설 두 번째 지문 초반에 서먼 씨 사이의 컨설팅 덕분에 직원들 간의 효과적인 의사소통이 가능해졌다고 했으므로 정답은 (B)이다.

180 윌헬미나 씨가 서먼 씨에게 제안하는 것은 무엇인가?

(A) 회의 개최
(B) 일자리 제공
(C) 토론토에서의 식사
(D) 추천서 제공

해설 두 번째 지문 후반부에서 윌헬미나 씨는 서먼 씨에게 씨가 필요하다면 추천서를 써 주겠다고 제안하고 있으므로 정답은 (D)이다.

[181-185]

사람들로 가득 찬 강당에서 연기와 춤, 노래를 할 수 있나요?

못 하시더라도 한번 시도해 보세요. 전혀 몰랐던 재능을 발견하게 될지도 모르잖아요.

181 스테이스 포인트 청소년 연기자 클럽이 오는 13주년을 맞을 준비를 하고 있습니다. **176** 기울과 분위기 맞을과 참여할 세 구성원들을 찾고 있습니다.

이 단체는 열정적인 클럽으로, 올해기 참여할 이 단체는 열정적인 클럽으로, 자선에는 〈한여름 밤의 꿈〉, 〈에니의 총을 잡아라〉, 〈라이언 킹〉, 〈맘마미아〉, 〈웨스트사이드 스토리〉를 무대에 올렸습니다. 무대에 오를 자신이 없다면 보조 역할을 할 수도 있습니다. 무대 보조, 티켓 접수를 관리나 기술 보조 등 다양한 기술이 필요한 일도 있습니다. **185** 18세 이하라면 전부 스테이스 포인트 청소년 연기자 클럽에 가입하는 것을 환영합니다.

인생에 한 번 만 있는 소중한 경험을 통해 이런 작품들을 들수 있습니다. 저희가 공연하는 것을 도울수 있습니다.

다음 주 수요일 오후 5시 30분에 클럽의 첫 모임이 열릴 것입니다. 자세한 정보를 원하시면 177 메인 가, 137호에 있는 지원 봉사자이자 후원자인 티나 존스에게 연락해 주세요.

9월 3일

티나 존스
177 메인 가 137호
스테이스 포인트, 위스콘신 주
존스 씨에게,

어제 당신의 클럽 소식을 접하고 **183** 흥미를 갖게 되었습니다. 저는 이 도시에 새로 이사 왔지만, 약간 수줍음이 있는 성격지만, 함께 도움을 드릴 수 있을 것 같습니다.

185 지난 2년간 학생 신문으로 가족과 함께 콜드웰에서 살았을 때, 연기를 좀 경험했습니다. 두 분의 연극(오페라)의 유정과 〈빌리 에리엇〉에게 춤을 경험했습니다. 또한 11살 때부터 사설 댄스 수업을 수강해 왔지만 이주 작은 역할이었습니다. **184 185** 저는 청소년 연기자 클럽의 공연에서 춤도 좋을 것 같습니다. 독소리가 좋고 노래도 잘 하는 편입니다. 지난 몇 년간 교회 성가대에서 노래를 해 왔습니다. 제가 스테이스 포인트 청소년 연기자 클럽에 참여할 수 있다고 생각하시나요?

사라 맥도널드

어휘 thespian 연기자　ambitious 야심 찬　tentative 잠정적인　tragedy 비극　stage 무대에 올리다, 상연하다　serve 일하다, 봉사하다　stagehand 무대 보조　operator 조작자, 기술자　lifetime 생애　production (연극, 영화 등)의 공연　hold 개최하다　intrigue 흥미를 갖게 하다　play 연극　private 개인적인, 사적인　choir 향창단　self-confident 자신 있는

181 기사의 목적은 무엇인가?

(A) 클럽의 기부금을 모으기 위해
(B) 클럽의 연례행사를 기념하기 위해
(C) 클럽의 새 회원을 모집하기 위해
(D) 〈에니의 총을 잡아라〉의 표 가격을 공지하려고

[186-190]

수신: 맥스 오웰 (maxpw@officesupplies.com)
발신: 스테파니 체이스 <dreamchaser@mochinosh.com>
날짜: 7월 11일
제목: 당신 요청

190 첨부해 주신 샘플들을 보니 더 좋습니다. 로고도 선명하고 190 전화 통화한 대로 가장자리에 188 번짐도 없는 것 같네요.
189 그런데 당신이 요청한 내용이 맞지만, 저는 캔버스 가방 수를 4천개로 약간 바꾸고 싶습니다. 그러면 주문은 다 됐습니다.
한 가지 더요, 190 그 제품들이 제작되고 출고될 때 알려주실 수 있나요? 또, 배송 번호와 배송 서비스 업체의 이름도 알았으면 감사합니다.
스테파니 체이스
모기노시 테크놀로지
뉴욕 브루클린

어휘 order form 주문서 manufacture 제조하다 attached 첨부된 confirm 확정하다, 확실히 하다 refund 환불 charge 부과하다 immediately 즉시 adjust 조정하다 feel free to do 자유롭게 ~하다 contact information 연락 정보 vivid 생생한 seem ~처럼 보이다 smudge 번짐 logo 로고 edge 테두리

186 첫 번째 이메일의 목적은 무엇인가?
(A) 체이스 씨에게 가능하지 않은 서비스를 알리는 것
(B) 체이스 씨에게 가격표그룹 보냈다고 알리는 것
(C) 주문 확인을 요청하는 것
(D) 샘플을 보내달라고 하는 것
해설 첫 번째 이메일에서 첨부된 사진과 주문서를 통해 주문한 품목과 샘플을 확인하라고 요청하고 있다. 따라서 정답은 (C)이다.

187 첫 번째 이메일에서 첨부물에 대해 알 수 있는 것은 무엇인가?
(A) 마손된 물품은 부분적으로 환불을 받는다.
(B) 확인된 부분에 대해서는 환불이 불가능하다.
(C) 엄은 환불이 불가능하다.
(D) 환불을 일주일 정도 걸린다.
해설 첫 번째 이메일 주문이 확정된 부분에 대해서는 환불이 불가능함을 알 수 있다. 따라서 정답은 (B)이다.

188 두 번째 이메일에서 첫 번째 단락 두 번째 줄의 "smudges"와 의미상 가장 가까운 것은 무엇인가?
(A) 느 검박가림
(B) 얼룩
(C) 웃음
(D) 반짝임
해설 이 어휘가 쓰인 문제를 살펴보면, 주문서의 로고가 선명해서 만족스러워하고 있다. 그러므로 로고의 가장자리에는 '번짐'이 없다고 고 하는 것이 문맥상 어울린다. 따라서 정답은 (B)이다.

수신: 스테파니 체이스 <dreamchaser@mochinosh.com>
발신: 맥스 오웰 <maxpw@officesupplies.com>
날짜: 7월 10일
제목: 요청
첨부: 샘플 사진들과 주문서.zip

체이스 씨에게,

서비스 사무용품을 이용해 주셔서 감사합니다. 188 제품이 생산에 들어가기 전에 첨부된 사진과 주문서에서 주문하신 품목과 샘플을 확인해 주세요. 187 그 이후에는 확인되거나 변경될 수 없습니다. 하지만 배송 도중에 파손되거나 샘플과 다르다면 전액 환불을 받으실 수 있습니다.

생산과 배송까지는 5~7일 걸립니다. 제품이 배송을 위해 공장을 따나면 신용 카드로 청구될 것입니다. 공장에 주문이 들어가면 취소나 변경은 불가능하므로 급하신 사항이 있으면 전화나 이메일로 즉시 연락해 주세요.

궁금하신 사항이 있으시면 전화나 이메일로 연락을 주시면 감사하겠습니다.
맥스 오웰
서비스 사무용품

서비스 사무용품 주문서

이름: 모기노시의 스테파니 체이스
주문 날짜: 7월 9일

품목	개수
189 회사 로고가 있는 캔버스 가방	189 2,500
회사 로고가 있는 볼펜	3,000
회사 로고가 있는 커피 머그잔	3,000

*이 양식에 문제가 있거나 질문이 있으시면, 자유롭게 우리에게 전화나 이메일을 즉시 보내주세요. 주문해 주셔서 감사드립니다.

*연락처
821-555-8678
customerservice@officesupplies.com

해설 첫 지문의 초반에서 클럽에서 새 회원을 모집하고 있음을 알 수 있다. 따라서 정답은 (C)이다.

182 스티븐스 포인트 청소년 연기자 클럽에 관해 언급된 것은?
(A) 10년보다 더 이전에 활동을 시작했었다.
(B) 18명의 학생으로 제한한다.
(C) 검증된 배우들만 회영받는다.
(D) 새로운 교수 감독진을 찾고 있다.
해설 첫 번째 지문 초반에서 클럽이 13주년을 맞이한다고 했으므로 10년 이전부터 활동을 해왔음을 알 수 있다. 따라서 정답은 (A)이다.

183 편지에서 첫 번째 단락 첫 번째 줄의 "intrigued"와 의미상 가장 가까운 것은 무엇인가?
(A) 선호되는
(B) 계획된
(C) 참가한
(D) 관심 있는
해설 이 단어가 쓰인 앞뒤 맥락을 실펴보면, 사라가 이 클럽에 지원하며 도움을 주고 싶다고 한 이유는 이 클럽이 '흥미'가 있기 때문이므로 선택지 중 적절한 어휘는 (D) interested이다.

184 사라가 클럽에 참여한다면 할 수 있는 일은 무엇인가?
(A) 무대 보조 역할을 한다.
(B) 클럽의 홍보를 돕는다.
(C) 클럽의 비서가 된다.
(D) 무대에서 노래하고 춤춘다.
해설 두 번째 지문 중반에 사라는 연기 경험이 있고 댄스를 배운 적이 있고 성가대에서 노래도 부른 경험이 있기에 클럽에 참여하면 무대에서 노래하고 춤추고 연기를 할 것이다. 따라서 정답은 (D)이다.

185 사라에 관해 알 수 있는 것은 무엇인가?
(A) 자신감에 차 있다.
(B) 연극이 어떻게 만들어지는지 거의 알지 못한다.
(C) 그녀의 나이는 아마도 18세 이상일 것이다.
(D) 연극과 관련된 경험이 좀 있다.
해설 두 번째 지문 중반에서 연극과 관련된 다양한 경험을 이야기하므로 정답은 (D)이다. 첫 지문 중반에 이 클럽은 18세 이하로 나이를 제한하고 있으므로 여기에 가입을 원하는 사라는 역시 18세 미만일 것이므로 여어 짐작해 볼 수 있다. 따라서 (C)는 오답이다.

189 체이스 씨가 이메일을 보낸 이유는 무엇인가?

(A) 몇몇 품목들을 취소하려고
(B) 빠른 배송을 요청하려고
(C) **한 품목의 수를 늘리려고**
(D) 회사 로고의 위치를 바꾸려고

해설 세 번째 지문 중반에 캔버스 가방의 주문 수를 4천 개로 바꾸고 싶다고 주문량을 늘린 것을 확인할 수 있다. 따라서 한 품목(캔버스 가방)의 수를 증가시키기 위해서 이메일을 보냈음을 알 수 있으므로 정답은 (C)이다.

190 두 번째 이메일에 따르면, 체이스 씨에 대해 언급되지 않은 것은 무엇인가?

(A) 그녀는 주문품의 배송비 지불에 대해 연락받기를 바란다.
(B) 그녀는 샘플을 보냈다.
(C) **그녀는 배송 회사를 추천하고 싶다.**
(D) 그녀는 오월에 전화로 대화했다.

해설 세 번째 지문에서 주문품의 제작을 마치고 공장에서 배송이 시작될 때 배송 관련해서 연락을 해 달라고 하는 부분에서 (A)를, 정부터 샘플을 확인해 봤다는 부분을 수 있다. (B)를, 전화상으로 오월 씨와 시를, 정부에 대화했다는 내용에서 (D)가 정답이 된다. 지문에서 언급되지 않은 것은 (C)가 정답이다.

[191-195]

191 취업 기회

타이쿤 은행은 현지 사무소에서 일할 야심 있고 의욕이 넘치는 사람을 찾습니다.

우리가 채우고자 하는 자리는 사람을 좋아하는 뛰어난 의사소통 능력을 갖춘 지원자가 필요합니다. **192 193** 또한, 우리는 종합적인 훈련 프로그램을 통해 금융 서비스 업계 전반에 대해 배우고자 하는 의욕이 넘치는 사람을 찾습니다. **191 192** 영업 담당자는 높은 급여와 큰 판매 수수료를 받습니다. **195** 판매 경험이 있는 지원자들을 우대가 되겠지만, 필요조건은 아닙니다.

업계 최고의 회사에서 일하는 데 관심 있으시다면, 지원해 주세요. 저력 있는 지원자들을 이력서를 인사부장인 클라라 해밀턴 씨에게 clarahamilton@tycoonbanks.co.ca로 보내 주세요.

수신: 클라라 해밀턴 (clarahamilton@tycoonbanks.co.ca)
발신: 다니엘 킨슬리 (dkinsley@mail.net)
날짜: 2월 10일
제목: 영업 담당자에 지원합니다
첨부: 이력서_다니엘 킨슬리.doc

해밀턴 씨에게,

194 저는 광고되고 있는 자리에 지원하려고 자신합니다. 이 이메일과 함께 제 이력서를 첨부합니다.

저는 이 일에 맞는 자격요건들을 다 가지고 있다고 자신합니다. **195** 저는 남자 형제가 두 명, 여자 형제가 세 명이 있는 가정에서 자랐기에 지원에서 저는 자연스럽게 사람들과 잘 어울립니다. 저는 틱월한 팀 플레이어이며 주위에는 팀으로를 주인 센터에서 지원봉사를 합니다.

저는 제가 귀사에 영업을 불러줄 것이라고 믿습니다. 면접 기회를 주신다면 감사하겠습니다.

감사합니다.

다니엘 킨슬리

이력서

1. 개인정보
- 이름: 다니엘 킨슬리
- 주소: 2030 영가, 4514호, 몬트리올, 퀘벡
- 전화: 821-555-8521
- 이메일: dkinsley@mail.net

2. 희망 직책
판매 부서에서 직원으로서의 직책

3. 교육
2010년 3월 - 2015년 2월 몬트리올 대학
경영학 학사, 심리학 부전공

4. 경력
- 채용 날짜: 2015년 2월 - 2017년 1월
- 이름: ABC 보험사
- **195** 직책: 판매사원

어휘 ambitious 야심이 있는   motivated 동기 부여된   individual 개인   fill a vacancy 빈자리를 채우다   outstanding 뛰어난   eager to ~을 간절히 바라는   comprehensive 종합적인   competitive (급여 등이) 돋보이는   qualified 자격을 갖춘   confident 자신 있는   incentive 장려금   representative 직원   enthusiasm 열정   sibling 형제자매

191 광고에 따르면 채용되는 일자리는 무엇인가?

(A) **영업 담당자**
(B) 인사부 매니저
(C) 금융 상담사
(D) 교육 보조

해설 첫 번째 지문의 두 번째 단락 마지막에서 영업 사원의 근무 조건이 언급되고, 세 번째 단락에서 판매 경험은 필수적인 지원 조건이 아니라고 언급한 부분에서 영업 담당자를 찾고 있음을 알 수 있다. 따라서 정답은 (A)이다.

192 회사에서 제공되는 혜택 중 언급되지 않은 것은 무엇인가?

(A) **정기 휴가**
(B) 높은 급여
(C) 성과 관련 보수
(D) 훈련 프로그램

해설 첫 지문이 광고의 초반에서 좋은 급여, 성과금 훈련 프로그램은 언급되어 있지만 정기 휴가에 대한 언급은 없다. 따라서 정답은 (A)이다.

193 타이쿤 은행에서 요구하는 자격 조건은 무엇인가?

(A) 개인적인 인재
(B) **배우고자 하는 열정**
(C) 대표이사를 보조할 능력
(D) 경력

해설 첫 지문 중반에 훈련 프로그램을 통해 금융업계에 모든 측면을 배우는 데 열정이 있는 사람을 찾고 있다고 언급되어 있다. 따라서 정답은 (B)이다. 판매 경험이 있는 지원자들을 우대하지만 필요조건은 아니라고 했으므로 (D)는 오답이다.

194 다니엘이 이메일을 보낸 이유는 무엇인가?

(A) 일자리에 대한 세부 사항을 물어보려고
(B) 감사를 표현하려고
(C) **지원서를 보내려고**
(D) 인터뷰를 확정 지으려고

해설 두 번째 지문의 첫 번째 문장에서 광고된 직책에 지원하려고 지원서를 낸 금을 쓴다. 따라서 지문에 드러나 있으므로 지원서를 보냄을 알 수 있다. 따라서 정답은 (C)이다.

195 다니엘에 대해 암시된 것은 무엇인가?

(A) 그는 회사 근처에 산다.
(B) **그는 취업에 우대될 것이다.**
(C) 그는 혼자서만가 거의 없다.
(D) 그는 임으로 직원에 지원하는 것이다.

해설 첫 번째 지문이 이력서에 경력을 보면 보험 회사에서 판매 사원으로 2년간 근무했던 경력을 볼 수 있다. 그러므로 첫 번째 지문에 언급된 것처럼 다니엘은 이전의 판매 경험을 통해 채용에 우대될 것을 알 수 있다. 따라서 (B)가 정답이다. 다니엘은 이메일에서 남자 형제 2명, 여자 형제가 3명이 있다고 했으므로 (C)는 틀린 내용이다.

엘라시오소의 딜라이트
398 피트 가
콘월 온 하드슨, 뉴욕 12520

엘라시오소 베이커리와 펄티 박사님께,

귀하의 광고를 처음 봤을 때는 매우 회의적이었습니다. 어떻게 쿠키와 케이크가 다이어트식이 될 수 있었어요? ⁽¹⁹⁶⁾ 그래서 귀하가 틀렸다는 것을 증명하기 위해 엘라시오소의 쿠키와 빵을 몇 개 샀습니다. 하지만 당신들이 맞았어요!

⁽²⁰⁰⁾ 쿠키도 맛있었어요. 하지만 섬유질 때문에 3번째 쿠키부터는 배가 부르더라고요. 이럴때는 마른빵을 먹었습니다. 보통 사람들 듯보 친 팬케이크 4장과 베이컨을 먹었어요. 하지만 귀하의 매빵이면 이렇으로 하나로 충분합니다. 그것은 제 큰 머리이고 맛도 있습니다. 그래서 귀하의 쿠키와 제품이 정말 효과가 있다는 것을 인정해야겠고, 고마움을 느낍니다.

아무튼, 저는 한 달 안에 15 파운드가 빠졌어요, 전 제 무게가 나가기에 아직 갈 길이 멀지만, 귀하의 제품으로 가능할 것 같습니다.

정말 감사합니다.

켄 에릭슨

어휘 dieting 다이어트하는 것 part with ~과 헤어지다 refuse 거절하다 come up with 고안하다 diabetes 당뇨병 nibble 조금씩 물어뜯다 diabetic 당뇨병의 bite into ~을 먹다 put aside 따로 떼어두다 cure 치료(법) considerable 상당한 hormonal 호르몬 이상 fiber 섬유질 fill up 채우다, 포만감을 주다 overeating 과식 skeptical 회의적 prove 증명하다 replacement 대체물 joint 공동의

196 광고되는 것은 무엇인가?
(A) 당뇨병 알약
(B) 집에서 만든 디저트
(C) **다이어트 음식**
(D) 설탕 대체품
해설 첫 지문이 광고문에서 다이어트가 이처럼 쉬운 적이 없었음을 먼저 말한 후 엘라시오소의 다이어트 음식에 대해 광고하고 있으므로 정답은 (C)이다.

197 광고에서 세 번째 단락 세 번째 줄의 "considerable"과 의미상 가장 가까운 것은 무엇인가?
(A) 조심스러운
(B) **큰**
(C) 부족한
(D) 배려심 있는
해설 이 단어가 문맥을 고려하면, 이 제품이 다이어트 효과 효과 실험 결과, 몸무게가 좋았다는 내용이 언급되는데, '상당량의' 살이 빠졌다는 듯이 직접하므로 정답은 (B)이다.

198 광고에 의하면, 엘라시오소 베이커리에 관해 사실이 아닌 것은 무엇인가?
(A) 공동의 연구를 했다.
(B) 유명한 업체이다.
(C) **25년 전에 설립되었다.**
(D) 설탕사와 함께 디저트 다이어트 식사를 판다.
해설 첫 지문에서 펄티 박사가 엘라시오소 베이커리와 함께 다이어트 식품을 고안했다고 한 내용에서 (A)를, 엘라시오소 베이커리가 인기 있는 디저트 회사라고 한 내용에서 (B)를, "다이어트 하는 법"이라는 설명 사가 동봉되어 있다고 언급된 부분에서 (D)를 확인할 수 있다. 하지만 박사가 25년간 다이어트 연구를 한 것이지 엘라시오소 베이커리가 25년 전에 설립된 것은 아니므로 정답은 (C)이다.

199 편지가 쓰인 목적은 무엇인가?
(A) **감사를 표하기 위해**
(B) 불만을 나타내기 위해
(C) 새로운 메뉴를 요청하기 위해
(D) 제품을 주문하기 위해
해설 세 번째 지문 상에서 에릭슨 씨가 다이어트 음식을 먹고 실제 살을 뺄 수 있게 된 것에 대해 감사하다고 언급하고 있으므로 정답은 (A)이다.

200 설명서 3번을 포함하고 있는 것은 어떤 제품인가?
(A) 팬케이크
(B) 베이컨
(C) **쿠키**
(D) 샌드위치
해설 두 번째 지문에서 엘라시오소의 딜라이트 제품은 식이섬유가 풍부하여 쉽게 포만감을 준다는 세 번째 먹은 후에 포만감을 느낄 수 있다는 내용을 종합해 볼 때, 설명서 3번을 가진 쿠키 제품에 동일되는 것을 묘사할 수 있다. 따라서 쿠키 제품이 살이 빠졌다는 듯이 직접하므로 정답은 (C)이다.

⁽¹⁹⁸⁾ **다이어트가 이처럼 쉬운 적이 없었습니다!**

우리가 사랑하는 음식과 작별하기는 쉽지가 않습니다. 네, 우리 모두 건강하게 먹는 것이 훌륭한 다이어트로 가는 길이라고 알고 있습니다. 하지만 디저트에 대한 생각이 사라지지 않습니다. 하지만 이제는 ⁽¹⁹⁶⁾⁽¹⁹⁸⁾ 그러지 않아도 됩니다! 펄티 박사와 엘라시오소 베이커리의 디저트로 된 다이어트 식사를 고안했습니다. 다 사실일리가 없다고요? 하지만 사실입니다!

⁽¹⁹⁸⁾ 펄티 박사는 25년간 당뇨를 연구해 왔습니다, 그 또한, 오래전부터 당뇨 병력이 있는 집안 출신입니다. 평생 그는 디저트를 마다하거나 다른 친구들이 생일 케이크를 먹을 때 멀건 음료를 집으로만 섞어야 했습니다. ⁽¹⁹⁸⁾ 그러다가 3년 전 당뇨 치료 연구도 잠시 접고, 당뇨병 환자를 위한 디저트를 만들기로 합니다. 엘라시오소 베이커리에 문의합니다. 엘라시오소 베이커리는 1972년에 청림한 이래, 시에서 디저트 분야의 최고 자리를 지켜 왔습니다.

그래서 펄티 박사와 엘라시오소 베이커리의 설립과 바탕과 있지 않은 다양한 쿠키, 케이크, 그리고 머핀을 만들어 냈습니다. 이 디저트는 당뇨병 환자를 위한 것이지만, ⁽¹⁹⁷⁾ 당뇨를 앓는 설탕 집단 모두 병을 빨리 엘라시오소의 다이어트 제품으로 바꾸만 하면 되는 건강한 방법입니다.

저희 제품은 배가 부르고 건강할 뿐 아니라 맛도 있습니다!

다이어트 하는 법 3

여러분은 정말로 배가 고프요?
먹기 전에 곰곰이 생각해 보세요.

사람들은 실제로 배가 고프지 않을때도 스트레스나 흐르로 이성과 같은 다양한 이유로 계속 먹습니다. 그러므로 무언가를 먹기 전에, 언제 그리고 얼마나 먹었는지를 고려하여 정말 배가 고픈지 반드시 확인해야 합니다.

⁽²⁰⁰⁾ 엘라시오소의 다이어트 제품은 식이섬유가 풍부하여 쉽게 포만감을 주어 과식을 예방할 수 있습니다. 이제 다이어트는 어렵지 않습니다.

다음 다이어트 팁도 기대하세요.

Actual Test

03

저자 이미영

📖 Reading Comprehension

본책 P56

PART 7

147 (D)	148 (C)	149 (A)	150 (D)	151 (C)	152 (B)	153 (B)	154 (D)	155 (A)
156 (D)	157 (B)	158 (C)	159 (A)	160 (D)	161 (C)	162 (C)	163 (A)	164 (B)
165 (D)	166 (D)	167 (A)	168 (D)	169 (A)	170 (D)	171 (B)	172 (C)	173 (D)
174 (A)	175 (B)	176 (D)	177 (D)	178 (B)	179 (D)	180 (D)	181 (C)	182 (C)
183 (B)	184 (D)	185 (D)	186 (D)	187 (C)	188 (C)	189 (C)	190 (B)	191 (D)
192 (C)	193 (C)	194 (A)	195 (B)	196 (D)	197 (A)	198 (A)	199 (D)	200 (B)

메모

147 전 사원들에게 이달 앞에 있을 사들과의 크리스마스 연휴로 인해 우리의 표준 월급 일정을 조정해야 할 것을 알려드리는 메모입니다. 148 우리 월급일이 [3일 앞당겨져서 23일 화요일이 될 것입니다]. 게다가, 중례의 연말 보너스도 1번 월급에 포함될 것입니다. 일정이 이렇게 변경됨으로 인해, 초과 근무 수당과 경비 청구 요청에 대한 마감 기한도 앞으로 당겨집니다. 보통 이러한 요청들을 월요일 오후까지 받았지만, 이번 달 마감 시한은 19일 금요일 퇴근 전 까지입니다. 여러분이 전 부서들에게 이러한 변경된 일정을 확실히 인지하도록 해 주시고, 질문이나 염려 사항들이 있는 직원들은 제 사무실로 새로운 보내주십시오.

어휘 reminder 상기시키는 것 supervisor 상사, 감독자 adjustment 조정, 조절 payroll 급여 payday 봉급날, 봉급일 fall on (날짜 등이) ~에 해당하다 push forward 앞으로 당기다 traditional 전통적인 관습적인 paycheck 월급, 봉급 shift 변경, 변화 deadline 마감 기한 overtime 초과 근무 아는 것 move ahead 앞으로 당기다 be aware of ~을 인지하다 apologize for ~에 대해 사과하다 mix-up 착오, 혼동 modified 변경된 altered 변경된

147 메모의 목적은 무엇인가?
(A) 월급 착오에 대해 사과하기 위해서
(B) 휴일 일정을 변경하기 위해서
(C) 새로운 연말 보너스를 공지하기 위해서
(D) **변경된 일정의 세부 사항을 알려 주기 위해서**

해설 보통 메모 앞부분에 This is a reminder to do ~라는 표현이 나와 면 해당 메모의 주제이 주재하는 부분을 읽어 두자. 크리스마스 휴 일로 인해 표준 월급 일정을 조정을 것임을 명시하고 있으므로 정답은 (D)이다. (A)는 아직 월급 지급 부분에서 문제가 있었던 것은 아니므로 오답이고, (C)의 경우 연말 보너스는 종례에 지급되었던 것으로 새로운 보너스라고 볼 수 없으므로 오답이다.

148 직원들은 언제 보너스를 받을 것인가?
(A) 19일 금요일
(B) 22일 월요일
(C) **23일 화요일**
(D) 26일 금요일

해설 원래의 월급 지급일인 26래에서 23일로 시틀 앞당겨질하며, 1번 월급 에 연말 보너스도 포함될 것이다고 했으므로 정답은 (C)이다. (D)는 일 반적인 월급 지급일이다.

클리프 애런	**오후 4시 39분**
안녕하세요, 제러미 씨! 오타와에 도착하셨나요?	
제러미 코헨	**오후 5시 15분**
늦게 답해서 죄송해요. 세관을 통과하는 데 오래 걸렸어요. 그렇지만 지금은 택시를 타고 호텔로 가는 길이에요.	
클리프 애런	**오후 5시 18분**
잘됐네요. 어디에서 숙박하시나요?	
제러미 코헨	**오후 5시 19분**
램코 본사에서 코너를 돌면 바로 있는 콜린 호텔의 스위트룸을 예약했어요. 내일 오전에서 코너에서 걸어서 갈 수 있는 거리예요.	
클리프 애런	**오후 5시 21분**
149 아, 안됐네요. 우리가 장소를 바꿨어요. 물이 새는 파이프 때문에 우리 회의실에 약간 물이 넘쳤어요. 그래서 우리는 마신에 시 외곽에 있는 사무실에서 회의할 거예요.	
제러미 코헨	**오후 5시 28분**
알았어요. 그게 어디에 있는지 잘 모르겠는데요.	
클리프 애런	**오후 5시 30분**
제 비서한테 시켜서 가는 길과 주소를 보내도록 할게요. 클린에서부터 약 10분 운전하면 가면 돼요. 만약 원하신다면, 우리가 이쪽에 당신을 데리러 가도록 차를 보내드릴 수 있어요.	
제러미 코헨	**오후 5시 35분**
150 괜찮아요. 제가 할 수 있어요. 제가 그냥 호텔 안내원에게 택시를 준비해 달라고 요청할게요. 그렇지만 그렇게 해주신다고 하다니 감사합니다.	

어휘 delayed 지연된 response 응답, 반응 forever 오랫동안: 반응 ~을 통과하다, 빠져나가다 customs 세관 on one's way ~로 가는 중인 book 예약하다 suite 스위트룸(거실과 침실이 이어 져 있는 방) headquarters 본사, 본부 venue 장소 leaky 물이 새는 minor (크기, 범위 등이) 작은(작은) flood 범람, 홍수 uptown 도시 외곽의 instead 대신에 secretary 비서 direction 방향 pick up ~을 데리러 가다 manage 관리하다 concierge (호텔의) 안내원 arrange (미 리) 준비하다

149 램코에 관해서 알 수 있는 것은 무엇인가?
(A) **한 개 이상의 사무실을 갖고 있다.**
(B) 자동차 제조업체이다.
(C) 많은 직원을 고용하고 있지 않다.
(D) 이제는 콜린 호텔 근처에 위치하고 있지 않다.

해설 오후 5시 21분에 클리프 애런이 사이 대화에서 익숙했던 사무실에 물 이 새서 다른 사무실로 장소가 변경되었다고 했다. 이 부분을 통해서

해당 회사는 사무실을 한 개 이상 보유하고 있음을 알 수 있다. 따라서 정답은 (A)이다.

150 오후 5시 35분에, 크렌 씨가 ~할 것으로 추론 무엇인가?
(A) 그는 사무실 관리자가 곧 올 것으로 생각한다.
(B) 그는 혼자 상사와 이야기를 나눌 수 있다.
(C) 그는 컴퓨터 제안의 수익을 만회코 만든다.
(D) **그도 도움 없이 상황을 해결할 수 있다.**

해설 해당 표현 바로 앞에 애런이 시가 크렌에 씨를 위해 이쪽에 차로 데리러 가셨다고 하자 크렌 씨가 괜찮다며 호텔 안내원에게 택시를 준비시기 겠다고 했으므로 스스로 상황을 해결할 수 있다는 의미다. 따라서 정답은 (D)이다.

제11회 연례 트리브로 국제 영화 축제

웨스트 가 영화관 일정

웨스트 가 영화관은 처음으로 트리브로 국제 영화 축제에 참여하게 된 것을 자 랑스럽게 생각합니다. 151 온라인에서 30달러에 구매 가능한 축제 통행권을 소 지하신 분들은 무료로 모든 영화를 관람하실 수 있습니다. 다음의 경우, 성인 입장권은 10달러이고 12세 이하의 어린이 입장권은 5달러입니다. 다음의 성영 시간을 참고하세요.

영화	날짜	상영 시간
사일랜드 모드 (드라마, 독립)	3월 7일 금요일	오후 5시, 오후 9시
콤덱왕 맘 (다큐멘터리, 미국)	3월 7일 금요일	오후 7시, 오후 11시
152 경찰 (드라마, 폴란드)	3월 8일 토요일	오후 2시, 오후 6시
아웃 오브 라이트 (코미디, 한국)	3월 8일 토요일	오후 4시, 오후 8시, 지정
너의 운에서 (코미디, 캐나다)	3월 9일 일요일	정오, 오후 5시
뉴욕을 찾아서 (드라마, 러시아)	3월 9일 일요일	오후 8시

어휘 annual 연례의 international 국제의 cinema 영화관 take part in ~ 에 참여하다 for the first time 처음으로 holder 소지자 pass 통행(권) admit (장소로 들어가는 것을 허용하다, 입장 시키는 주다 at no charge 무 료로 show time 상영 시간 admittance 입장 be entitled to ~의 자 격이 있다 entry 입장 view 보다

151 축제 통행권에 대해 알 수 있는 것은 무엇인가?
(A) 성인 요금은 아동 요금의 두 배이다.
(B) 금요일에 토요일 입장만 사용할 수 있다.
(C) **통행권 소지자들은 무료로 관람할 수 있을 것이다.**
(D) 웨스트 가 영화관에서 구매할 수 있다.

해설 축제 통행권 소지자들은 무료로 모든 영화를 관람할 수 있다고 했으므 로 정답은 (C)이다.

어휘 overcharge 과잉 청구하다 be aware of ~을 알아차리다 complaint 불만, 불평 regarding ~에 관한 specifically 구체적으로, 특히 full refund 전액 환불 vary 다르다, 차이가 있다 circumstance 상황, 사정 authorize 허락하다 compensate A for B A에게 B를 보상하다 specific 구체적인 considering ~을 고려하면 apologize for ~에 대해 사과하다 bill 청구서 complaint about ~에 관해 불평하다 satisfied with ~에 만족하다 condition 조건

155 이메일을 쓴 이유는 무엇인가?
(A) 전액 환불 요청을 거절하기 위해서
(B) 청구서에 있는 실수에 대해 사과하기 위해서
(C) 레스토랑이 가격에 대해 변명하려고
(D) 주문이 늦게 배송된 이유를 설명하려고

해설 라거세 씨는 식사비 전액 환불을 요청했으나, 이런 요청은 가능하지 않다고 했으므로 거절을 하기 위해서 이메일을 쓰셨던 것으로 볼 수 있다. 따라서 정답은 (A)이다.

156 체임스턴에 대해 알 수 있는 것은 무엇인가?
(A) 고객들로부터 몇 통을 불평을 받았다.
(B) 직원들이 근로 조건에 만족하지 않는다.
(C) 10월 첫 주까지 운영되지 않을 것이다.
(D) 가격이 리뷰어 프랜차이즈보다 더 저렴하다.

해설 라거세 씨가 26달러가 아니라 32달러를 청구받은 것은 체임스턴은 레스토랑의 메뉴를 가지고 리뷰바 레스토랑으로 주문했기 때문이라고 한 것이 내용을 종합하면 리뷰바 레스토랑의 가격이 체임스턴 레스토랑 가격보다 높음을 알 수 있다. 이 내용을 질문의 의도에 맞게 선택지에서는 체임스턴은 레스토랑의 가격 기준으로 이해한 정답은 (D)가 된다.

157 [1], [2], [3], [4]로 표시된 곳 중 다음 문장이 위치로 가장 적절한 곳은 어디인가?
"안타깝게도, 저희는 이것이 레스토랑 측의 실수였다고 보다는 귀하의 실수였다고 말씀드리겠습니다."
(A) [1]
(B) [2]
(C) [3]
(D) [4]

해설 삽입될 문장에서 축의 가리키는 것을 파악해 보자. 문장이 이것(this)이 레스토랑 측의 실수가 아니라 고객의 실수라고 했으므로 '26달러가 아니라 32달러를 낸 것을 의미한다고 볼 수 있다. 또한 이 이후에 이어지는 내용은 체임스턴 레스토랑에서 주문하면 가격이 서로 다를 수 있다는 내용으로 자연스럽게 이어지므로 정답은 (B)가 된다.

---

152 토요일 오후에 볼 수 있는 드라마는 무엇인가?
(A) 사일런트 모드
(B) 경향
(C) 이웃 오브 라이트
(D) 누욕을 찾아서

해설 토요일에 상영하는 것은 〈경향〉과 〈오후 2시, 6시, 10시에 상영한다. 이 중 드라마 장르인 것은 〈경향〉으로 오후 2시, 6시, 10시에 코미디이므로 오답이다. (C)는 장편가 드라마가 아닌 코미디이므로 오답이다.

[153-154]

애니 로페즈 [오후 4시 52분]	어제 회의가 잘 되었던 것 같네요, 제 생각에 우리 고객들이 우리가 제안했던 디자인에 만족했던 것 같아요.
헨리 린 [오후 4시 53분]	그래요? 그들이 안 좋게 말하진 않았지만, 검토할 것 같지도 않았어요. [154] 제 생각엔 우리가 기회를 날린 것 같아요.
폴 그린 [오후 4시 55분]	이 점에 대해서는 저는 헨리에 동의해야겠어요. 저는 그들이 침묵을 실망으로 해석했거든요. 하지만 우리가 무엇을 잘못했는지는 잘 모르겠어요.
헨리 린 [오후 4시 56분]	제가 보기에 그들에게 기술적인 세부 사항들을 충분히 제공하지 못해서 발표를 계속 건강하게 하려고 해서, 우리는 중요한 정보를 너무 빨리 넘겼어요.
폴 그린 [오후 4시 58분]	내용을 추가해서 발표를 그들에게 다시 보내야 한다고 생각하세요?
애니 로페즈 [오후 4시 59분]	잠깐만요, 여러분! 너무 성급하게 결론을 내리려고 하고 있어요, 고객들은 우리가 보여준 것에 대해 매우 만족했을 수도 있으니까요.
폴 그린 [오후 5시 02분]	우리가 그들에게 연락해서 알아보면 될 것 같은데요.
애니 로페즈 [오후 5시 03분]	[154] 만약 그들이 더 많은 정보가 필요하다면 우리에게 연락할 거예요. 그냥 기다리죠.
폴 그린 [오후 5시 05분]	알았어요. 그렇지만 저는 발표 결과 수정할을 시작할게요. 만일을 대비해서 말이에요.
헨리 린 [오후 5시 06분]	좋은 생각이네요. 풀, 훌륭하는 것보다는 안전한 게 낫잖아요. 만약 그들이 우리의 첫 발표가 부족하다 느꼈다면, 우리는 개선된 버전을 보낼 수 있도록 준비해 둘을 수 있겠네요.

---

153 오후 4시 53분에, 린 씨가 "제 생각엔 우리가 기회를 날린 것 같아요"라고 썼을 때 의미한 것은 무엇인가?
(A) 그는 그들이 발표를 너무 빨리했다고 느낀다.
(B) 그는 그들의 실패했다고 믿는다.
(C) 그는 그들의 고객과 전화를 못 받았다고 생각한다.
(D) 그는 자기 팀이 최적 을 노력했다고 생각한다.

해설 해당 표현 앞의 애니 로페즈의 대화에서 고객들이 자신들이 디자인에 만족한 것 같다는 말에, 헨리 린은 반대로 고객들이 감동받은 것 같다는 것 같다며 이일을 제기하므로, I think we blew it! 이란 표현을 통해 고객들이 실패했다는 의미로 파악할 수 있다. 따라서 정답은 (B)이다.

154 로페즈 씨가 제안하는 것은 무엇인가?
(A) 발표를 조정하기
(B) 휴식 기간 줄이기
(C) 디자인에 세부 사항 더 추가하기
(D) 고객들이 먼저 연락하도록 하기

해설 대화의 마지막 부분에서 로페즈 씨는 고객들이 더 많은 정보가 필요하다면 우리에게 연락할 것이므로 기다리자고 했다. 따라서 고객이 먼저 연락한다면 자신들에게 make contact라고 제안하므로 정답은 (D)이다. 대화에서는 make contact라고 표현했지만, 지문에서는 get in touch with를 선택지에서는 make contactla고 패러프레이되었다.

[155-157]

수신: 브리트니 라거세 〈brit88@memail.com〉
발신: 월더엄 알버트 〈walbert@familyfeast.com〉
날짜: 10월 6일
제목: 과잉 청구

라거세 씨에게,

저는 최근에 귀하가 올해 10월 3일 패밀리 피스트의 리뷰바 레스토랑에 배달 주문한 것에 대해 청구된 비용과 관련된 불만 사항을 알게 되었습니다. – [1] –. [155] 귀하께서는 구체적으로 귀하가 26달러가 아니라 32달러를 청구받으셨습니다. – [2] –. [156] 귀하께서는 체임스턴 레스토랑의 메뉴를 가지고 리뷰바 레스토랑에서 주문하셨습니다. – [3] –. 식당 가 명칭으로 저희의 음식 가격은 리뷰바에서는 프랜차이즈에 따라 6달러를 변성해 다. – [4] –. 저는 리뷰바 레스토랑의 상황에서 매니저에게 귀하께 귀하의 구체적인 요청 사항을 주로록 하기했습니다만, 상황을 고려했을 때 귀하의 구체적인 요청 사항은 가능하지 않습니다.

진심으로,
윌리엄 알버트
고객 관리 부장
패밀리 피스트 레스토랑

어휘 go well 잘 되다 proposed 제안된 unimpressed 감명받지 못하는 실망한 blow 기회를 날리다 interpret 해석[이해]하다 disappointment 실망

고객 만족 설문 조사

호스피탈리티 스위트에 투숙하신데 주셔서 감사합니다. 체크아웃하시기 전에 잠깐 시간을 내주셔서 다음 고객 만족 설문지를 작성해 주시기 바랍니다. **158** 이 설문지를 작성해 주시는 모든 고객에 자동으로 전국에 있는 저희 호텔 어디서든 하룻밤 무료로 투숙하실 수 있는 월례 추첨에 응모하시게 될 것입니다.

1. 투숙하신 장소를 알려 주세요.

2. 투숙하신 목적은 무엇이었나요?

3. "불만족"을 의미하는 1과 "완전히 만족함"을 의미하는 5점으로, 만족도를 표시해 주세요.

체크인 과정	1	2	3	4	5
159 객실 청결도	1	2	3	4	5
직원 친절도	1	2	3	4	5
159 직원 유용성	1	2	3	4	5
159 조식 뷔페	1	2	3	4	5

아래의 박스에 의견을 작성해 주십시오.

귀하의 이름과 이메일 주소, 혹은 휴대 전화 번호를 여기에 적어 주세요. 이것을 **159** 이 매달 당첨자를 뽑고 알려 주는 목적으로만 사용될 것입니다. **160** 이 설문지의 정보는 엄격히 익명으로 처리될 것입니다.

어휘 questionnaire 설문지 | fill out ~에 기재하다 | complete 작성하다 | automatically 자동으로 | satisfaction 만족 | monthly 월 간의, 월례의 | drawing 추첨 | nationwide 전국적으로 | enter 참가하다 | represent 나타내다 | notify 알리다, 통보하다 | strictly 엄격히 | anonymous 익명의 | preferred 우대되는, 선호되는 | win 얻다 | make a reservation 예약하다 | serve (음식을) 제공하다 | confirm 확인하다 | promote 홍보하다 | be linked to ~와 연결되다 | head doctor 정신과 의사

158 고객 설문지를 작성하는 대가로 무엇을 받을 것인가?
(A) 우대 고객 VIP 카드
(B) 일 할인서 할인
(C) **호텔에서의 무료 1박 기회**
(D) 호텔 매니저로부터의 감사 편지

해설 설문지를 작성해 주시는 전국에 있는 해당 호텔에서 하룻밤을 투숙할 수 있는 추첨에 자동으로 응모된다고 했으므로 정답은 (C)이다.

159 양식에 정보가 포함되지 않는 것은 무엇인가?
(A) **얼마나 쉽게 예약을 했는가**
(B) 객실이 얼마나 깨끗했는가
(C) 직원들이 얼마나 도움이 되었는가
(D) 조식으로 제공된 음식이 얼마나 훌륭했는가

160 설문지의 정보에 대해 연급된 것은 무엇인가?
(A) 전화나 이메일로 반드시 확인해야 한다.
(B) 체크아웃 이후에 제출해야 한다.
(C) 온라인에서 호텔을 홍보하기 위해서 사용될 수 있다.
(D) **고객의 이름과 연결되지 않을 것이다.**

해설 마지막에 이 설문지의 정보는 엄격히 익명으로 처리될 것이라고 했고, 따라서 정답은 (D)이다. 지문의 anonymous의 표현은 '익명이란 뜻으로 선택지(A)에서는 not be linked to the guest's name으로 패러프레이징되었다.

[161-164]

공지

9월에 게임즈 가의 시원이 화제로 마손되 이후에, 하먼 프리 클리닉을 임시로 문을 닫았습니다. **161** 두 달의 중단 후에 진료소는 새로운 곳에서 다시 문을 열 것입니다. **159** 새로운 시설은 세 블록도 떨어지지 않은 곳에 있는데, 센트럴 블러자 맞은편에 프레시 마켓 쇼핑센터 내에 있습니다. 래노소에 있는 뉴 시티 메디컬 센터로 방향을 돌렸던 환자들은 편리한 곳에 저희 새로운 진료소를 이용하실 수 있습니다. 진료소는 공식적으로 11월 19일 월요일에 다시 문을 열 것입니다. **164** 뛰어난 지역을 찾은 의사들과 간호사들로 구성된 모든 직원들이 새로운 추가 인력과 함께 돌아올 것입니다. 이동 영상 문제나 전화인 마다라이브 박사를 새로 영입했습니다. 오시는 길 또는 더 자세한 정보를 원하시거나 저희 새 사무실과 사진들을 둘러보시려면 저희 웹 사이트인 www.harmon-fc. org를 방문하세요.

어휘 temporarily 임시로 | hiatus 중단 | redirect 새 방향으로 돌리다 | nutrition 영양 | sneak peek 미리 맛보기 | partnership 협력, 제휴 | circumstances 상황, 환경 | behind 이면의, 뒤에 | closure 폐업 | around the corner 길모퉁이를 돈 곳에 | lecturer 강연자 | ~을 담당하는, 책임지는 | head doctor 정신과 의사 | in charge of

161 공지의 목적은 무엇인가?
(A) 환자들을 새 사무실로 가게 하기 위해서
(B) 두 회사 간의 제휴를 발표하기 위해서
(C) **사람들에게 문을 닫았던 영업점이 재개될 것을 알려 주기 위해서**
(D) 진료소 폐업 이면의 상황을 설명하기 위해서

해설 공지 내용은 지문의 특성상 서두 부분에 주제문과 목적이 등장한다. 진료소가 두 달간의 중단 이후에 문을 열 것을 알려 주고 있으므로 정답은 (C)이다.

162 하먼 프리 클리닉의 새로운 위치는 어디인가?
(A) 아파티의 제임스 가
(B) 센트럴 플라자의 주차장이 있는 도 곳에
(C) **프레시 마켓 쇼핑센터 내**

해설 이전하는 장소는 센트럴 플라자 맞은편에 프레시 마켓 쇼핑센터에 있다고 했으므로 정답은 (C)이다.

163 고객들이 11월 14일까지 할 수 있는 것은 무엇인가?
(A) **전화로 예약 일정 잡기**
(B) 새로운 사무실 사진 보기
(C) 하먼 프리 클리닉 방문하기
(D) 새로운 의료 시설 고르기

해설 날짜가 등장하는 지문의 내용 중, 해당 질문에서 묻고 있는 14일을 찾으면 빠르게 전문 일정을 잡기 위한 전화 개통할 것이라고 했으므로 정답은 (A)이다.

164 마다라이브는 누구인가?
(A) 의료 전문의료 행사의 초청 강연자
(B) **하먼 프리 클리닉의의 새 직원**
(C) 예약 일정 담당자
(D) 뉴 시티 메디컬 센터의 정신과 의사

해설 고객 명사인 마다의 벨을 카드에 걸고 지문에서 찾으면 마다의 벨을 추가로 새로 영입한 의사임을 알 수 있다. 따라서 정답은 (B)이다.

[165-168]

여러분을 파티에 초대합니다!

장소: 이스트 사이드 공원
시간: 5월 11일 토요일 오후 2시부터 7시까지
이유: GSBA에 대해 더 많이 알기 위해서

그런프로 소개가 경합(GSBA)는 비버큐 바베큐 파티를 열 것입니다. [1] ~ 여러분은 개인적인 비즈니스 네트워크를 넓히고 유용한 관계를 **165** 형성하기 위해서 **165** 현재 구성원들과 만날 기회를 얻게 될 것입니다. [2] ~.

이 회원장으로 5명의 가족 구성원까지 참가하실 수 있으며, 어린 자녀들도 환영합니다. 맛있는 음식과 함께 공연, **165** 재미있는 게임과 라이브 음악도 **165** 있을 것입니다. 파티 참석자들은 GSBA에 가입한 즐거워 무언도 얻을 것입니다. 그냥 오셔서 여러분들의 이웃과 이웃과 함께 지내세요. [3] ~.

회원 요청: **166** GSBA의 행사 담당자인 헤리엇 러네게 555-1132번으로 전화 주시고, 그녀에게 참석 인원을 알려 주세요. ~ [4] ~. 우리는 여러분을 만나길 고대하고 있습니다!

어휘 host 개최하다 | current 현재의 | expand 넓히다 | establish 확립하다 | connection 관계 | performance 공연 | attendee 참석자 | obligation 의무 | RSVP 회답 요망 | privilege 특권

165 파티에서의 활동이 아닌 것은 무엇인가?
(A) GSBA 구성원들 만나기
(B) 재미있는 게임 즐기기
(C) 라이브 음악 듣기
(D) **재미있는 상 받기**

해설 배버큐 파티를 통해 현재 구성원들과 만날 기회를 얻게 될 것이라고 했고, 재미있는 게임과 라이브 음악이 있을 것을 명시했다. 따라서 언급되지 않은 (D)가 정답이다.

166 첫 번째 단락 세 번째 줄의 단어 establish와 의미상 가장 가까운 것은 무엇인가?
(A) 꺼다
(B) 제출하다
(C) 연기하다
(D) **확립하다**

해설 해당 단어 뒤의 목적어인 useful connections와 문맥상 어울리는 동사여야 옳은 말이 되는데, establish의 목적어도 '(관계 등)을 확립하다, 맺다'라는 의미로 사용되었다.

167 [1], [2], [3], [4]로 표시된 곳 중 다음 문장이 위치로 가장 적절한 곳은 어디인가?

"그것의 목표는 현좌에 아직 가입하지 않은 소기업 사업주들에게 회원의 혜택과 특전에 관해 더 많이 알 수 있게 해주는 것입니다."

(A) [1]
(B) [2]
(C) [3]
(D) [4]

해설 삽입 문장의 소유격 Its가 앞에 나온 barbecue party의 소유격을 받아주는 것이 관건이다. 삽입 문장은 배버큐 파티의 목적을 설명하고 있는데, [1] 바로 뒤의 You will also have a chance to ~라는 문장에서 also라는 표현을 통해 배버큐 모임의 또 다른 목적을 추가 설명하고 있음을 알 수 있다. 따라서 삽입 문장이 들어갈 자리는 (A)가 가장 적절하다.

168 린 씨가 요청받는 정보는 무엇인가?
(A) 소기업 이름
(B) GSBA 회원 이름
(C) 사업주의 회원 번호
(D) **파티에 오는 사람들의 인원수**

해설 RSVP(회답 요망)가 등장하는 지문의 마지막 부분에서 해리엇 린이 이 모임 나온다. 그에게 몇 명이 사람이 참석할 것인지를 전화해서 알려 주라고 했으므로 이를 요약한 (D)가 정답이 된다.

[169-171]

온라인 구직 사이트에 계속해서 광고를 게시하는 것에 지치셨습니까? 귀하의 IT 부서의 높은 이직률이 걱정되십니까? 수백 명의 이력서를 살펴보고하는 시간과 지원 너비에 신물이 나셨나요? IT 스태핑 솔루션이 도움을 드리기 위해 여기 있습니다!

169 저희는 다트로이트 대도시 지역에 소재한 기업에 우수한 지격 요건을 갖춘 정보통신 전문 인력들을 임시로 공급해 드립니다. 다음의 혜택들을 살펴보세요:

- 자회사 주의 깊게 각각의 지원자를 연장하기 때문에 여러분들은 그러실 필 요가 없습니다.

170 • 여러분의 복지 혜택 제도되어 ISS 직원들을 추가할 필요가 없습니다.
• 저희 직원들은 6개월 동안이든 단 하루 정규직 직원으로 간에 이쪽 직원들을 대신할 수 있습니다.
• 여러분은 아무런 부대조건 없이 저희 직원을 정규직 직원으로 채용할 수 있습니다.

171 그뿐만 아니라 저희가 모든 월급 문제들을 처리합니다. 일단 여러분의 회사가 ISS에 계약한다면, 여러분은 단순히 매달 서비스 요금이 나온 청구서 한 장만 받게 됩니다. 저희가 직원 채용에 관해 더 알고 싶으시면, 882-555-9014번으로 전화 주셔서 저희 직원과 만날 약속 일정을 잡으세요.

어휘 turnover rate 이직률　sick of ~에 신물이 난　pore over ~을 심사 숙고하다　supply A with B A에게 B를 제공하다　metropolitan 대도 시의　qualified 자격을 갖춘　on a temporary basis 임시로　take a look at ~을 보다　candidate 지원자, 후보자　add A to B A를 B에 더하다　fill in for ~을 대신하다　single 단 하나의　permanent employee 정규직 직원　no strings 부대조건 없는, 무조건의　attach 첨부 하다　take care of ~을 처리하다, 책임지다　payroll 월급 지급　issue 문 제　representative 직원, 대표　telecommute (통신 시설 등을 이용해) 재 택근무하다　go through (절차 등을) 가치다　rigorous 엄격한　handle 처 리하다　payment 지급　deduction 공제　weekly 1주에 한 번의

169 광고되고 있는 것은 무엇인가?
(A) 임시직 직원들을 제공하는 서비스
(B) IT 전문 직원을 위한 직업을 찾아 주는 웹 사이트
(C) 기술 서비스를 제공하라는 회사
(D) 한 회사의 IT 부서에 있는 자리

해설 해당 지문은 채용, 인력 공급을 대행해 주는 서비스 회사를 광고하고 있다. 이 업체는 지격 요건을 갖춘 정보통신 분야의 전문가들을 임시 로 제공해 주는 일을 하는 용역 공급 회사라는 것을 알 수 있다. 따라서 정답은 (A)이다. 지문의 supply는 provide로, professionals는 employees로 패러프레이징되었다.

170 다음 중 ISS 직원들에 언급된 것은 무엇인가?
(A) 그들은 집에서 재택근무를 한다.
(B) 그들은 정규직 직원들보다 적은 임금을 받는다.
(C) 그들은 엄격한 교육 프로그램을 통과했다.

해설 배버큐 파티를 통해 현재 구성원들과 만날 기회를 얻게 될 것이라고 했고, 재미있는 게임과 라이브 음악이 있을 것을 명시했다. 따라서 언급되지 않은 (D)가 정답이다.

171 ISS와 계약할 때 추가 이점은 무엇인가?
(A) 적은 비용으로 정규직 직원을 구할 수 있다.
(B) **서비스에 직원 임금 처리비용 포함되는 것이 포함된다.**
(C) 회사가 세금 공제로 경비를 절감할 수 있다.
(D) ISS 대표와 주기 회의를 한다.

해설 해당 업체는 채용뿐만 아니라 임금 지급 문제도 같이 처리해 준다고 했다. 따라서 정답은 (B)이다. 지문의 take care of는 handling으로, payroll은 payment로 각각 패러프레이징되었다.

[172-175]

코어벡스 LCD 텔레비전 한정 품질 보증

보상 범위 구매일로부터 12개월 동안 코어벡스는 소비자에게 텔레비전 결함이로 인한 수리를 위해 필요한 모든 부품과 인건비를 전부 배상할 것입니다. 이 수 리는 반드시 코어벡스 공인 서비스 센터에서만 해야 합니다. **172** 텔레비전이 수 리를 수 없는 경우, 코어벡스는 소비자들에게 같거나 혹은 더 나은 모델을 무료 로 제공할 것입니다. 코어벡스는 공인되지 않은 기술자에 의해 행해진 수리는 책 임지지 않을 것입니다.

지원: 미국에 있는 코어벡스 공인 서비스 센터를 찾는 데 도움이 필요하시다면 무료 장거리 전화 1-888-555-2923 번으로 저화에게 전화 주세요. **173** 미국 이 아닌 해외에 있는 코어벡스 공인 서비스 센터의 목록을 찾으시려면 저희 웹 사이트 www.convex.com을 방문하셔서 "국제 수리"를 클릭해 주세요.

예외 조항: 이 한정 품질 보증은 다음 사항을 보장하지 않습니다.

- 사용자 장치 또는 오용으로 인한 파손
- 습기나 열에 노출로 인한 파손
- 흥수나 지진을 포함한 자연재해로 인한 파손
- 장기간 스크린에 남아 있는 음모이지 않는 이미지로 야기된 파손

174 175 이 보증은 개인적 용도로 구매된 제품에만 작용하며 적용 제품이 상업 적 용도로 사용된다면 자동으로 무효 처리될 것입니다.

어휘 warranty 보증　coverage 보상 (범위)　reimburse 배상하다　in full 전 부　labor 노동, 인건비　defect 결함　certified 공인된　in the event (that) ~할 때를 대비해서　provide A with B A에게 B를 제공하다　equal 동등한　at no charge 무료로, 무료 없이　be responsible for ~을 책임지다　technician 기술자　locate 찾다　toll-free 무료 장거리 전 화　exception 예외　cover 보장하다　neglect 방치, 등한시　misuse 남용, 오용　exposure 노출　moisture 습기　unmoving 움직이지 않 는, 정지된　prolonged 장기적인, 오래 계속되는　apply to ~에 적용되다　automatically 자동으로　void 무효로 하다, 취소하다　commercial 상업 적　retailer 소매 업체　specialize in ~을 전문으로 하다　defective 결함이 있는　agent 대리업체, 대리인　ship 배송하다　carrier 운송업체

[176-180]

172 이 보증서의 대상은 누구일 것 같은가?

(B) 가전제품을 전문으로 하는 소매 업체들
(C) LCD 스크린을 생산하는 제조업체들
(D) 가정용 텔레비전을 구매하는 소비자들

해설 제목에서 특정 업체의 텔레비전 품질 보증서임을 알 수 있다. 또한 진술 마지막 문장에서 해당 업체의 상품의 개인적 용도로 구매했을 때만 보증서의 내용이 적용된다고 했으므로 정답은 (C)이다.

173 경험이 있는 제품을 수리할 수 없다면 무슨 일이 있을 것인가?

(A) 해외의 비영리 기술자들에게 보내질 것이다.
(B) 고객이 그것을 구매한 매장에 반송해야 한다.
(C) 공인 서비스 센터에서 전액 환불해 줄 것이다.
(D) 동일 모델이나 더 나은 모델로 교체해 줄 것이다.

해설 만약 수리할 수 없을 경우에는 소비자들에게 같거나 더 나은 모델로 무료로 제공해 줄 것이라고 했다. 따라서 정답은 (D)이다. 지문의 replace with or same으로, provide ~ at no charge는 replaced by 패러프레이징되었다.

174 캐나다에 있는 소비자는 공인 서비스 센터를 어떻게 찾을 것인가?

(A) 웹 사이트를 방문해서
(B) 서비스 대리점에 이메일을 보내서
(C) 무료 장거리 전화를 걸어서
(D) 지역의 코어박스 소매 업체에 물어봐서

해설 서비스 센터를 찾는 방법은 두 가지인데 미국 외에서 서비스 센터를 찾기 위해서는 웹 사이트를 방문하라고 하면서 웹 사이트 주소를 알려 주고 있다. 따라서 정답은 (A)이다. (C)는 미국 내 서비스 센터를 찾을 때 쓸 방법이므로 오답이다.

175 다음 중 보증서가 무효일 수 있는 경우는 무엇인가?

(A) 미국 국외로 텔레비전을 옮길 경우
(B) 상업적 기능으로 텔레비전을 이용하면
(C) 비공인 운송 업체를 통해 텔레비전을 배송하면
(D) 제조업체로부터 직접 텔레비전을 구매하면

해설 마지막 문장에서 만약 제품이 상업적 용도로 사용된다면 자동으로 보증서가 무효가 된다고 했으므로 정답은 (B)이다.

개리 리
경리부장
프로그레스 인더스트리
301 소콜가
뉴어크, 뉴저지

리 씨에게,

176 이 편지를 2주 전에 예고를 드리는 것이니, 제가 프로그레스 인더스트리에서 마지막으로 근무하는 날짜는 10월 22일 금요일이 될 것입니다.

이전에 논의했던 바와 같이, 가장 큰 문제는 회사에서 탄력적 근무 시간제를 제공해 줄 수 없다는 것에 있습니다. **177** 2월에 두 번째 아이가 태어날 예정인 저는 단순히 9시에 출근해서 6시에 퇴근해야 하는 근무 조건을 일반적으로 충족시킬 수 없습니다. 저는 프로그레스 인더스트리와 함께 4년간의 너무 즐거웠던 진심으로 이 상황이 안타깝습니다. **177** 저는 제 기족을 우선으로 두고 싶습니다. 제 사임에 대한 세부 상황을 만나서 논의하고 싶으시다면, 제게 연락해 알려 주십시오.

브래들리 슐린저

수신: 브래들리 슐린저 (bsullinger@progress.net)
발신: 개리 리 <glee@progress.net>
날짜: 10월 15일
제목: 당신의 결정

179 사직을 재고하라고 우리 회사에서 시간제로 계속 일하기로 했던 것들이 니까, 저는 진심으로 이것이 관련된 모든 사람에게 최고의 결정이라고 니 기쁩니다. 덧붙여, 저는 인사부서와 이야기를 나눴고, **179** 인사부에서 없으로 다 기꺼운 인사부에 들려주게 다른 서류 작업을 준비해 놨습니다. 기회가 이을 때, 8 층의 인사부에 들러주시기 바랍니다. 또한, 제 생각에 당신과 이달 18 일에 인사부가 당신에 당신의 새로운 역할에 대해 예상되는 바를 검토해 할 것 같습니다. 그걸 한가한 시간이 있는지 제게 알려 주세요.

개리

---

176 슐린저 씨가 쓴 편지의 목적은 무엇인가?

(A) 회사의 일자리를 수락하려고
(B) 초과 근무에 관해 불평하려고
(C) 사임 건에 대해 응답하려고
(D) 회사를 그만두겠다는 것을 알리려고

해설 첫 번째 지문의 첫 문장이 주제로 등장했으므로, 이 편지를 공식적인 사직으로 받아들이라고 했으므로, 이 편지는 회사를 그만두겠다는 것을 알리려는 것임을 알 수 있다. 따라서 정답은 (D)이다.

177 슐린저 씨가 그의 가족에 대해 언급한 이유는 무엇인가?

(A) 그의 일급의 중요성을 강조하기 위해서
(B) 그의 자신의 직업 선택을 보여 주기 위해서
(C) 그의 답변이 늦어진 이유를 설명하기 위해서
(D) 그의 결정에 대한 이유를 제시하기 위해서

해설 슐린저 씨는 두 아이와 앞으로 태어날 아이를 위해서 회사에서 요구하는 출퇴근 시간을 충족시킬 수 없음을 받으고 있다. 따라서 가족에 대해 언급한 것은 사직하는 이유를 받히기 위한 것임을 알 수 있다. 따라서 정답은 (D)이다.

178 슐린저 씨가 휴가를 낼 가능성이 있는 때는 언제인가?

(A) 2주 후에
(B) 1월 언젠가
(C) 10월 초 전에
(D) 10월 18일부터 22일까지

해설 두 번째 지문의 내용을 연계해서 풀어야 하는 추론 문제이다. 첫 번째 지문에서 슐린저 씨의 셋째가 1월에 태어날 예정이라고 했고, 두 번째 지문에서는 인사부서에서 그의 묶이 후가에 대한 서류 작업을 준비해 봤다고 했다. 결국 슐린저 씨는 아이가 태어나는 1월에 후가를 갈 것을 알 수 있다. 따라서 정답은 (B)이다.

179 리 씨가 슐린저 씨가 이메일을 보내기 전에 있을 법한 일은 무엇인가?

(A) 리 씨는 슐린저 씨가 인사부로 전근 가는 것을 허락했다.
(B) 슐린저 씨가 경리부 일을 그만두었다.
(C) 리 씨가 건물 8층에 있는 새 사무실로 옮겨갔다.
(D) 슐린저 씨가 정규직에서 시간제로 처리를 바꿨다.

해설 두 번째 지문에서 슐린저 씨는 퇴직을 결심했으나, 두 번째 지문의 첫 번째 문장에서 이런 결정을 번복하고 시간제 계속 근무하게 되었음을 알 수 있다. 따라서 리 씨가 이메일을 보내기 전에 슐린저 씨가 시간제로 처리를 바꿨음을 알 수 있다. 따라서 정답은 (D)이다.

180 리 씨가 10월 18일에 하고 싶어 하는 것은 무엇인가?

(A) 새로운 회사 규정
(B) 높은 직원 이직률 문제
(C) 인사부의 인력 부족
(D) 슐린저 씨의 새로운 직무

해설 두 번째 지문에서 슐린저 씨는 10월 18일이라는 날짜 키워드를 두 번째 지문에서 찾으면 슐린저 씨의 새로운 역할에 대해서 논의하자고 했다는 것을 알 수 있다. 따라서 슐린저 씨의 10월 18일의 새로운 업무에 대해서 논의하자고 했다는 것을 이 새로운 역할에 대한 논의라고 패러프레이징한 (D)가 정답이다.

어휘 official 공식적인 resignation 사직, 사임 credit coordinator 크레디트 코디네이터(채권 조정자) as per (결정 등에) 따라 center on ~에 집중하다 inability 불능, 무능 flexible (시간을) 바꿀 수 있는, 융통성 있는 due 예정인 meet 충족시키다 requirement 조건, 요건 consistent 일관적 인 sincerely 진심으로 put A first A를 가장 중시하다 involved 관련된 furthermore 게다가 Human Resources 인사부서 prepare A for B A를 B를 위해 준비하다 paperwork 서류 작업 upcoming 앞으로 있을 다가오는 paternity leave 아버지 묶이 후가(출산 시 아버지에게 주어지는 휴가) stop by ~에 들르다 go over ~을 검토하다, 살펴보다 overtime 초과 근무의 respond to ~에 응답하다 stress 강조하다 delay 지연 take time off 후가를 내다 transfer to ~로 옮기다 resign 퇴직하다 full-time 전일제 part-time 시간제 regulation 규정 employee turnover 이직률 shortage 부족, 결핍

[181-185]

헤디 백, 비즈니스 리포터

재활용 논쟁

지역 음료 회사인 앰버트 소다는 **181** 최근 이스트 포츠빌에 새로운 제조 공장을 연 후에 예상치 못한 반대에 직면하고 있다. 국제 환경 단체인 비 그린이 바로 그 반대로, 새로운 이스트 포츠빌 공장이 앰버트사의 인기 제품인 소다 병을 만드는 데 있어서 재활용 유리를 사용하지 않을 것이라고 했다. **183** 비 그린 지부 대변인의 카라 페이지는 단체에서는 자신들이 요구가 충족될 때까지 소비자들에게 앰버트 소다의 모든 음료 제품을 불매하도록 촉구하고 있다고 한다. **182** 특히 비 그린은 앰버트 소다에 모든 음료 제품에 재활용 유리를 사용하도록 공개적으로 요구한 것이다. 그들의 공장들 독립된 환경 조사관이 앰버트 소다 사장이 캐빈 가디가 성명서를 공식 발표했는데, 이스트 포츠빌 공장의 상황을 현재 검토 중이라고 설명하고 있다.

뉴바그 스탠더드
편지부
사서함 1172
뉴바그, 네브라스카
편집자에게:

183 저는 앰버트 소다 불매 운동에 관한 한 기사와 관련해 편지를 쓰고 있습니다. 저는 귀하께서 경제 단신 섹션에 이 사설에 관한 기사를 포함하기로 선택한 것에 정말 기뻤다. 저가 느끼기에 반드시 수정해야 하는 리포터가 사실과 달리 보도한 몇 가지 오류들이 있었습니다. **184** 실은 제가 비 그린 지부의 대변인입니다. 귀하께서 잘못 보도한 사람은 국제단체의 홍보담당자였습니다. 또한 저는 앰버트사의 전 제품에 대한 불매 운동을 요청하고 있는 것이 아니라, 팜 콜라라 불매 운동을 요청하고 있습니다. 회사에서 재활용 정책을 다시 고려 중이라고 들었지만, **185** 현재 시점까지 아무것도 행해지지 않았습니다. 그러므로 저희는 모든 소비자에게 팜 콜라를 구매하지 않음으로써 우리의 환경 보호를 도와달라고 요청하는 것입니다.

진심으로
케라 이야기와

어휘 controversy 논쟁　beverage 음료　face 직면하다　unexpected 예상치 못한　manufacturing 제조　environmental 환경의　organization 조직(체)　chapter 대변인　spokesperson 대변인　urge 촉구하다　specifically 구체적으로, 특히　boycott 불매하다　practice 관습　independent 독립적인　inspector 조사관　issue 발표하다　press release 공식 발표, 보도 자료　statement 성명서　under review 검토 중인　in reference to ~와 관련하여　factual 사실의 기반을 둔　misidentify 오인하다, 잘못 확인하다　media relations 홍보 부서　call for ~을 요청하다　protest 항의　aim at ~을 목표로 하다　environmentalist 환경주의자　export 수출하다　praise 칭찬하다　journalist 기자　point out ~을 지적하다　accuse A of B A를 B에 대해 비난하다　threat 위협　get worse 악화되다　misrepresent 잘못 전하다

181 새로운 제조 공정에 대한 설명으로 옳은 것은 무엇인가?
　(A) 재활용 센터 옆에 있다.
　(B) 항의로 인해 문을 닫았다.
　(C) 이스트 포츠빌에 있다.
　(D) 수질 오염을 발생시키고 있다.

해설 질문의 핵심 키워드는 new manufacturing center인데 표현을 찾아야 한다. 기사 앞부분에서 이스트 포츠빌에 새로운 제조 공장을 열었다고 한다. 따라서 정답은 (C)이다.

182 팜 콜라에 언급된 것은 무엇인가?
　(A) 환경운동가들을 목표로 하는 브랜드이다.
　(B) 전 세계 국가에 수출될 것이다.
　(C) 이전에는 재활용 유리병에 담겼었다.
　(D) 국내에서 가장 유명한 콜라 제품이다.

해설 기사에서 앰버트 소다는 예전에 모든 제품에 대해서 재활용 유리병을 사용했다고 했으므로 (C)가 정답이다.

183 편지의 목적은 무엇인가?
　(A) 기자를 앰버트 보내기 위해서
　(B) 기사에 있는 몇몇 오류를 지적하기 위해서
　(C) 회사 사장이 거짓말을 한 것에 대해 비난하기 위해서
　(D) 환경 위험에 관해 불만을 표현하려고

해설 두 번째 지문인 편지는 첫 번째 지문에 대한 오류들을 지적하기 위해서 쓴 것이다. 기사에 대해 편지를 쓰고 있으며 독적을 밝히고 있으며, 사실과 다른 내용에 대해 것임을 구체화하고 있다. 따라서 정답은 (B)이다. (A)의 경우 해당 내용이 기사를 싫어해서 보기는 언급이 없기 때문에 하지만 이것을 일반화시켜 편지의 독적이라고 보기는 어려우므로 오답이다.

184 비 그린의 홍보담당은 누구인가?
　(A) 헤디 백
　(B) 케라 이야기와
　(C) 케빈 가디
　(D) 카라 페이지

해설 연결 문제이다. 첫 번째 지문에서 카라 페이지가 비 그린 지부의 대변인이라는 언급이 나오지만, 사설을 정정하는 두 번째 지문에서 에티 아는 이가와 자신이 대변인이고, 대변인으로 착각했던 사람이 국제 지문인 첫 페이지가 홍보담당임을 알리고 있다. 따라서 정답은 (D)가 된다. (A)는 첫 번째 지문인 기사를 쓴 기자의 이름이다. (C)는 앰버트사의 사장이다.

185 이야기와 쓰는 현재 상황에 대해 무엇이라고 말하는가?
　(A) 정점이 악화되고 있다.
　(B) 잘못 전해졌다.
　(C) 천천히 개선되고 있다.
　(D) 바뀌지 않았다.

해설 편지에서 현재 아무것도 행해지지 않았다는 내용으로 보아 정답은 (D)이다. 질문으로 current situation은 this point를 패러프레이징했다고 볼 수 있다.

[186-190]

수신: 로렌스 미크위즈 〈awrencem@plainview.gov〉
발신: 매슈 딕스터 〈matthewd@plainview.gov〉
날짜: 3월 5일
주제: 마을 축제

안녕하세요, 로렌스 씨,

올해도 다시 찾아왔군요! 우리는 연례 마을 축제 계획을 모으는 책임을 당신에게 맡기다. 부상님께서 지역에 저희 사람들의 후원과 참여를 모으는 것을 알고 있습니다. 저는 당신이 이런 일에 어떤 경험도 없는 것을 알고 있습니다. **189** 당신의 지난해 축제 장비 임대 준비를 너무나 잘해 주셔서 이 일을 잘 처리할 수 있을 거라 믿습니다. 우리는 기업체들이 100달러를 우리의 일 반 지금에 기부하거나 계획된 행사 중 하나를 후원하도록 독려해야 합니다. 500 달러를 기부한 후원업체들은 모든 축제 마케팅 자료에 무료 광고를 얻을 수 있습니다. 그리고 **188** 만약 2,000달러를 기부하면 회사 이름이 행사 이름에 포함될 것입니다. 우리는 또한 10,000달러를 기부하면 제안을 받아들이 사람이 전체에 언전후 후 연을 제공할 것이지만, 아직 누구도 이 제안을 받아들이 사람이 없었습니다. 조만간 모여서 실수를 피할 수 있도록 기부를 요청하는 시의 규정에 관해서 얼려드리겠습니다.

매트

2017년 3월 16일

팻 월드
32 이스트 메인 가
플레인뷰, 캔자스 71203

메가 싸에게,

올해 마을 축제에 이벤트 후원자로서 참여에 대해 진심으로 감사를 표하고 싶습니다. 3월 13일 우리의 전화 논의에 따라서, **188** 햇 월드는 팻 월드 프라이즈 한드리고 새 이름을 붙인 아이들의 물건 찾기 게임의 유명한 후원체가 될 것입니다. 이것은 가장 인기 있는 행사 중 하나로 귀하의 기게에 많은 호의적인 관심을 끌어낼 것이라고 확신합니다. 우리는 현재 마케팅 자료를 모으고 있으므로 귀하께서 포함했으면 하는 자료로 사본과 함께 귀하의 회사 로고 (GIF 이미지를 kdaniels@plainview.gov로 보도록 빨리 보내 주신다면 감사하겠습니다. 후원 기부의 송금에 관해서는, 555-8101번으로 재무부서의 매리 브래들리에게 연락 주시면 협의하시면 됩니다.

진심으로
로렌스 미크위즈 드림
행사 계획자
플레인뷰 타운 의회

[191-195]

수신: 수잔 팔란디노 <suziep@mymail.com>
발신: 다니엘 라샤펠 <lachapelle@prodigylabs.com>
날짜: 6월 15일
주제: 여름 인턴 훈련 기간

여름 인턴 프로그램에 관심을 가져주셔서 감사합니다. 귀하의 이력서를 실제보고 나서, 191 저는 귀하가 관심을 표현하신 세 가지로 자격조건으로 프로그램에 정식으로 지원해 달라고 요청하고자 합니다. 저의 요건을 갖춘 지원자를 직고 들었을 때 제가 설레는 바처럼, 저의 요건을 갖춘 지원자를 직성하도록 요청받을 것입니다. 192 귀하가 이력서를 제출하려고 이것으로 귀하께서 프로그램에 받이름에었다고 확실히 말씀드릴 수는 없지만 갖는 과정 동안 부정적인 정후가 보이지 않는 한, 정식 지원자들에게 모두 인턴 훈련 기간 제의를 제공할 것이라고 예상합니다. 작성된 양식을 추천서와 함께 이 이메일 주소로 보내 주시면 됩니다. 193 그러나 양식을 작성하기 전에, 제가 추천서에 대한 모든 요구 조건을 귀하에게 자세히 알려줄 수 있도록 전화를 주십시오

다니엘 라샤펠
인사팀 직원
847-555-0228

---

193 **전재 실험실(Prodigy Laboratories) – 인턴 훈련 기간 지원서**

이름: 수잔 팔란디노
성별: 여성
나이: 23세

현재 직업: 시간제 프로그래머
194 **프로그래밍 경력:** 파이어스톰 게임스 2년
능숙한 프로그래밍 언어에 표시하시오:

Java ☑   C ☐   C++ ☑

지원 동기(50 단어 이하): 저는 현재 작은 게임 회사에 시간제로 일하고 있습니다. 대학원에 지원할 계획은 없습니다. 그전에 젊은 기간이나마 전체 설명 같은 큰 회사에서 능력을 맡을 기회를 얻고 싶습니다.

195 **추천서 작성인:** 스티브 제이콥스

어휘 seek 찾다 intern 인턴(교육 실습생) research 연구, 조사 technological 기술적인 innovation 혁신 apply 지원하다 workplace 직장 applicant 지원자 proficient in ~에 능숙한 qualified 자격 요건을 갖춘 submit 제출하다 reference 추천서 supervisor 상사 personal 사적인, 개인의 acquaintance 지인, 친지 coworker 동료 accept 받아들이다 internship 인턴 기간(실습 훈련 기간) in person 직접 stipend 봉급, 급료 party 일행 resume 이력서 corporate 회사의 headquarters 본사 invite 요청하다 officially 공식적으로 apply for ~을 지원하다 fill out ~을 작성하다 attached 첨부된 stop by ~에 들르다 submit 제출하다 qualified 자격 요건을 갖춘 assure 보증하다, 확신하다 anticipate 예상하다 barring ~이 없다면, ~을 제외하고 red flag 위험한 징후, 경고 표시 come up 나오다, 발생하다

주목해 주세요!

전재 실험실(Prodigy Laboratories)이 시카고와 독두 시카고 컴퓨터 연구 센터에서 일할 여름 인턴을 찾고 있습니다. 기술적인 혁신과 관심과 컴퓨터 프로그래밍 경력이 있는 분은 모두 지원하실 수 있습니다. 업무 경험, 교육 경험 다 상관없지만, 지원자들은 C와 C++이나 Java 중 하나에 반드시 능숙해야 합니다. 195 자격 요건을 갖춘 지원자들은 현재 교수님이나 상사로부터 받은 추천서를 제출해야 합니다. —사적인 지인, 동료나 급우의 추천서는 받지 않을 것입니다. 인턴 훈련 기간은 7월 초부터 8월 말까지 운영될 것이며 주당 봉급이 포함될 것입니다. 192 관심 있는 분들은 12번까지 행정실로 직접 이력서를 제출하시거나 1번지에 타라에 있는 우리 회사 본사에 이력서를 우편으로 보내 주십시오.

186 로런스 마코위츠 씨에 대해서 알 수 있는 것은 무엇인가?
(A) 그는 몇 월드의 주인과 친구이다.
(B) 시 정부에 의해 최근 고용되었다.
(C) 축제 행사를 후원했던 경험이 있다.
(D) 지난해의 축제 준비에 참여했었다.

해설 이메일에서 수신인인 로런스 마코위츠에게 지난해 축제 준비 임대 준비를 너무나 잘했다고 일한 점으로 미루어 보아, 로런스 마코위츠는 지난해 축제 준비에 참여했었음을 간접적으로 알 수 있다. 따라서 정답은 (D)이다.

187 이메일에서 첫 번째 단락 마지막 줄의 protocol과 의미상 가장 가까운 것은 무엇인가?
(A) 협력
(B) 승인
(C) 의례
(D) 분위기

해설 protocol은 '행동 규범', '의례'라는 의미가 있으므로 정답은 (C)이다.

188 팻 월드가 축제에 기부했던 금액은 얼마인가?
(A) 100달러
(B) 500달러
(C) 2,000달러
(D) 10,000달러

27주년 연례 플레이뷰 마을 축제

행사	위치	시작 시간
개막 퍼레이드	메인 가	오전 10시
플레이뷰 타임스 5-K 편 경주	시작 타운 홀 도착 플레이뷰 고등학교	정오
오후 콘서트 – 더 블루 스 카이 밴드	위쪽 축제 마당	오후 2시
팻 월드 상 찾기	아래쪽 축제 마당	오후 3시
저녁 콘서트의 춤	위쪽 축제 마당	오후 5시

어휘 annual 연례의 director 부장, 이사 in charge of ~을 책임지는 support 후원 participation 참여 local 지역의 organize 준비하다, 조직하다 equipment 장비 rental 임대 handle 처리하다, 지료 처리 격려하다, 독촉하다 donate 기부하다 fund 지금 material 지료 take ~ up on (~의 제의를) 받아들이다 protocol 규정, 협약 solicit 간청하다 avoid 피하다 make a mistake 실수하다 sincere 진실 어 appreciation 감사 participation 참여, 참가 as per ~에 따라 discussion 토론, 논의 sole scavenger hunt 물건 찾기 게임 favorable 호의적인, 찬성하는 rename 새 이름을 붙이다, 개명하다 put together ~을 모으다 material 지료 GIF 이미지 압축 저장 방식 중 하나 along with ~와 함께 currently 현재 convenience 편의 as for ~에 관해 remittance 송금 (역) make an arrangement 준비하다 annual 연례의 opening 시작, 개시 parade 행렬, 행진 run 경주, 달리기 fairground 축제 마당

해설 (188) 첫 번째 지문에서, 2,000달러를 기부했다 했는데, 두 번째 지문에서 기업제 이름이 행사 이름에 포함될 것이라고 했고, 두 번째 지문에서 물건 찾기 게임의 유일한 후원이 될 것이라고 했다. 제가 될 것이라고 했다. 이 두 정보를 종합하면, 팻 월드는 2,000달러를 기부했을 것을 추론할 수 있다. 따라서 정답은 (C)이다.

189 축제 참석자들이 낮 동안 음악 공연을 즐길 수 있을 장소는 어디인가?
(A) 플레이뷰 고등학교
(B) 타운 홀
(C) 위쪽 축제 마당
(D) 아래쪽 축제 마당

해설 질문의 핵심어는 daytime musical performance다. 이 핵심어를 표에서 찾으면 Afternoon Concert에 해당한다. 따라서 오후의 콘서트 장소인 (C)가 정답이 된다.

190 축제 행사에 포함되지 않은 것은 무엇인가?
(A) 도보 경주
(B) 마을 소풍
(C) 아이들의 게임
(D) 두 건의 콘서트

해설 (A)는 오전 10시 개막 퍼레이드 ... (이는 두 번째 지문에서 the children's scavenger hunt라고 언급된 부분에서 확인할 수 있다. (C)는 오후 2시이나 더 블루 스카이 밴드 콘서트와 오후 5시의 저녁 콘서트를 가리키므로 축제 행사에 포함되지 않는 것은 (B)이다.

해설 연계 문제이다. 마지막 양식에서 팔린다노 씨가 일하는 회사가 피아어스툼 게임스라는 것을 알 수 있으며, 또한 추천서 작성인 이름으로 슈티븐 제이콥스를 확인할 수 있다. 그리고 첫 번째 지문에서 추천인 자격에 관해 확인해 보면 현재 교수님이나 상사로부터의 추천서만 가능하다는 것도 알 수 있다. 따라서 정답은 (B)가 된다.

다 process 과정 completed 작성된 a letter of reference 추천서 fill A in on B A에게 B에 대해 자세히 알려주다 requirement 요구 조건 female 여성 part-time 시간제의 proficient 익숙한 currently 현재 graduate school 대학원 language 언어 expand 확장하다 skill 기량 기능 on a short-time basis 짧은 기간에

191 라사렐 씨의 이메일 목적은 무엇인가?
(A) 인턴 훈련 기간 프로그램에 지원자를 수락하기 위해서
(B) 양식에 대한 지원자의 질문에 답해주기 위해서
(C) 지원자에게 추천서를 요청하기 위해서
(D) 지원자에게 지원서를 제출하기 위해서

해설 이메일의 앞부분에서 첨부된 양식을 작성해서 프로그램에 정식으로 지원해 달라고 요청하고 있다. 따라서 정답은 (D)이다.

192 팔린다노 씨가 이력서를 제출했던 장소는 어디인가?
(A) 시카고 컴퓨터 연구 센터
(B) 동부 시카고 컴퓨터 연구 센터
(C) 회사의 행정실
(D) 회사의 이사

해설 연계문제이다. 첫 번째 공고의 지원 방법을 설명하는 부분에서 관심 있는 사람들은 12부가의 행정실로 직접 이력서를 제출하거나 문서 보내 달라고 했다. 또한, 팔린다노 씨에게 보내는 두 번째 이메일에서 '당신이 이력서를 제출하려고 왔을 때라고 말한 부분을 통해 팔린다노 씨가 직접 행정실에 찾아왔음을 알 수 있다. 따라서 정답은 (C)가 된다.

193 이메일에 따르면 팔린다노 씨가 다음에 할 일은 무엇인가?
(A) 추천서 요청하기
(B) 지원서 작성하기
(C) 라사렐 씨에게 전화로 연락하기
(D) 행정실 들르기

해설 이메일 마지막 부분에서 '양식을 작성하기 전에, 주전사에 대한 요구 조건에 대해서도 알려드릴 수 있도록 전화를 달라는 내용이 나온다. 따라서 건을 자체에도 알려드릴 수 있도록 연락을 달라는 내용이 나온다. 따라서 정답은 (C)가 된다.

194 양식에 따르면 팔린다노 씨에 관해 사실이 가능성이 있는 것은 무엇인가?
(A) 석사 학위를 따는 데 관심이 있다.
(B) 전에 심핸실(Prodigy Laboratories)에서 전에 일한 적이 있다.
(C) 어떤 프로그래밍 언어도 알지 못한다.
(D) 이력서를 잘못된 주소로 보냈다.

해설 양식에 지원 동기 팔린다노 씨는 대학원에 지원을 계획이 있다고 했으므로 정답은 (A)이다. 본문에 graduate school을 정답에서 master's degree라고 표현했다. (C)의 경우 Java, C, C++ 모두에 master's degree에 있으므로 오답이다.

195 제이콥스 씨는 누구일 것 같은가?
(A) 전체 심핸실(Prodigy Laboratories) 직원
(B) 파이어스툼 게임스 직원
(C) 팔린다노 씨의 친구
(D) 대학교 교수님

2017년 3월 16일

엘리스 노스럼
이사회 의장
모비우스 컴퓨터
사서함 1182
로스앤젤레스, 캘리포니아 90011

노스럼 씨에게,

즉시 귀사 운영 부사장으로서의 퇴직을 수락해 주십시오.

[196-200]

새로운 방향을 위한 모비우스 컴퓨터

196 어려움을 겪고 있는 독립 컴퓨터 제조업체 모비우스 컴퓨터가 시장 계획에 있어서 극적이 변화를 발표할 것이다.

http://you-review.com

사용자: 미들서 코레이
회사: 모비우스 온라인
구매한 것: 모비우스 프로페르 2000
내 등급: 별 1개

어휘 struggle 분투하다, 노력하다 independent 독립의 manufacturer 제조업체 turn to ~로 바꾸다, ~에 의지하다 purely 순수하게, 완전히 dramatic 극적인 entire 전체의 startling 놀랍게, 깜짝 놀라게 하는 coincide with ~와 동시에 일어나다, 일치하다 former 이전의, 과거의 successful 성공적인 startup 신규 업체 vice-president 부사장 운영 replace 대신하다, 교체하다 much-admired 매우 존경받는 shed 버리다, 포기하다 unneeded 불필요한 brick-and-mortar 오프라인 거래의, 소매의 asset 자산 streamline 합리화 equip 갖추다, 마련하다 meet 충족시키다 efficient 효율적인 manner 방식, 방법 cutting-edge 최첨단의 previously 이전에 in an effort to ~하려는 노력으로 ease 쉽게 하다 transition 변화 process 과정 catch 문제점, 애로점 apparently 명백히, 외관상 physical 물리적인 respond to ~에 응답하다 query 질문 cutting-and-pasting 자르고 붙이기(의) template 본보기 hardware 기계 strongpoint 강점 middle-of-the-road 그저 그런, 평범한 resignation 퇴사 immediately 즉시 sincerely 진심으로 be determined to ~하기로 결정하다 stick with ~을 계속하다 inevitable 필수 불가결한 period 기간 board of directors 이사회 confer with ~와 의논하다 esteemed 존경받는 predecessor 전임자, 선배 step down 사임하다 engage in ~에 관여하다 prolonged 오래가는, 장기적인 battle 전투 clearly 분명하게 away from ~에서 멀어져 philosophy 사고방식, 철학 overstaffed 직원이 너무 많은 major 주요한 one's fair share of ~의 응당한 몫 detractor 비방하는 사람, 깎아내리는 사람 apparel 의류, 복장 prove 증명하다

진성으로

오주릴도 브라운

convince 확신시키다 hold true 유효하다 manufacturing 제조 make an arrangement for ~을 준비하다 severance 퇴직, 해고 departure 떠남, 출발

196 기사는 무엇에 관한 것인가?
(A) 컴퓨터 제조업체의 새로운 종업 고용
(B) 두 분투하는 회사 사이의 갑작스러운 합병
(C) 컴퓨터 산업이 직면한 재정적 어려움
(D) 예상치 못한 회사 모델 변경

해설 기사 지문의 경우 첫 부분에 주제문이 있을 확률이 높다. 지문 앞부분에서 컴퓨터 제조업체인 모비우스가 모든 매장의 문을 닫고 온라인 사업 모델로 바꾸는 극적인 변경을 발표했다고 했다. 따라서 정답은 (D)이다. 모비우스 컴퓨터가 어려움을 겪고 있다는 내용은 나오지만, 컴퓨터 업체 전체가 재정적인 어려움을 겪고 있다는 것은 아니므로 (C)는 정답이 아니다.

197 코웨이 씨의 주요한 불평은 무엇인가?
(A) 형편없는 고객 서비스
(B) 함입반는 데 실패
(C) 가게 찾는 데 어려움
(D) 질이 낮은 하드웨어

해설 기존에는 훌륭한 고객 서비스와 지원을 받았지만, 지금은 온라인 가게만 운영함으로써 친절하고 도움이 되었던 영업 사원들도 모두 사라졌다는 점을 불평하고 있다. 따라서 정답은 (A)이다.

198 코웨이 씨에 관해서 암시된 것은 무엇인가?
(A) 그녀는 모비우스 매장에서 컴퓨터를 이전에 구매했었다.
(B) 그녀는 가장 최근 모델보다 이전 프로페를 선호한다.
(C) 그녀는 모비우스 매장의 직원들에게 나쁜 경험이 있다.
(D) 그녀는 프로페도 2000이 낮은 가격에 감동하였다.

해설 연계문제이다. 첫 번째 기사의 마지막 부분에서 이전에 모비우스 매장에서 구매했던 고객들은 온라인 구매에서 특별 20%의 할인을 받는다고 했는데, 두 번째 리뷰의 앞부분에서 코웨이 씨가 20% 할인 이메일을 받았다고 했다. 따라서 정답은 (A)임을 알 수 있다.

199 패스트플로우가 팔렸을 것 같은 제품은 무엇인가?
(A) 컴퓨터
(C) 소프트웨어
(D) 옷

해설 패스트플로우라는 회사 이름은 첫 번째 지문에서 한 번 등장한다. 성공을 거둔 신규 업체의 이름이 패스트플로우고, 그 회사의 이전 최고 경영 책임자의 이름이 오즈월드 브라운임을 알 수 있지만, 이 부분으로만은 답이 나올 수 없다. 세 번째 지문의 편지를 쓴 사람이 오즈월드 브라운인데, 내용 중 의류 업계에서 성공을 거둔다는 내용을 찾을 수 있다. 두 내용을 종합하면 정답은 (D)이다.

200 브라운 씨가 퇴직을 결정하기 전에 논의했던 사람은 누구인가?
(A) 에릭스 노스럽
(B) 세스 문
(C) 마르시아 콘웨이
(D) 엘베르토 크루즈

해설 세 번째 지문에서 브라운 씨가 전임자와 논의를 한 후에, 퇴직을 결정했다고 했다. 또한, 첫 번째 지문에서는 세스 문의 후임자로 브라운 씨를 고용했다고 했다. 따라서 브라운 씨가 퇴직을 결정할 때 논의한 사람은 그의 전임자인 (B) 세스 문임을 알 수 있다.

Actual Test

04

저자 박선영

카카오톡 ID로 찾기(ID: matrix20)
>> 친구 추가 후 1:1 채팅

본책 P78

Reading Comprehension

PART 7

147 (B)	148 (A)	149 (B)	150 (B)	151 (C)	152 (B)	153 (D)	154 (C)	155 (C)
156 (A)	157 (B)	158 (A)	159 (B)	160 (A)	161 (B)	162 (C)	163 (A)	164 (D)
165 (C)	166 (C)	167 (B)	168 (A)	169 (D)	170 (D)	171 (C)	172 (A)	173 (B)
174 (C)	175 (D)	176 (A)	177 (C)	178 (B)	179 (D)	180 (C)	181 (C)	182 (C)
183 (D)	184 (C)	185 (A)	186 (D)	187 (A)	188 (C)	189 (C)	190 (A)	191 (C)
192 (A)	193 (B)	194 (C)	195 (A)	196 (A)	197 (D)	198 (C)	199 (D)	200 (C)

소기업을 위한 세미나가 11월 3일에 열릴 예정입니다!

저명한 저자인 지미 톰슨 씨가 자신의 소기업을 창업하는 방법"이라는 제목의 세미나를 여기 새드 오션스 호텔에서 개최하는 것에 동의하였습니다. 이 행사는 11월 3일 수요일 오후 7시부터 9시까지 열릴 예정입니다. ¹⁴⁷ 여러분의 경영주가 되길 오랫동안 원해 왔다면 이 세미나는 여러분의 계획을 행동으로 바꾸는 데 필요한 모든 것을 말해 줄 것입니다.

캘리포니아 출신인 톰슨 씨는 이 주제에 관한 3권의 베스트셀러를 썼는데, 여기에서 소기업 과정 전체에 대해 안내할 것입니다. 그의 가르침을 따르면 여러분은 소규모 사업가로 성공할 수 있습니다. 그는 주의 깊게 자신의 지식 그리고 이익을 포함한 수많은 사업이 그렇게 해서 인상적인 결과를 달성했습니다. 그녀는 2015년에 톰슨 씨의 세미나에 참석했던 사람들 순이어 3만 5천 달러에 달합니다. 지금은 1년에 몇백만은 순이어 시작했는데, 지금은 1년에 몇백만을

세미나의 비용은 75달러로, 35페이지의 유인물을 포함하였기 때문에 충분히 그럴만한 가치가 있습니다. 여러분의 이름을 새긴 수료증을 여러분이 진으로 나중에 보내드릴 것입니다. 여러분의 세미나는 보통 매진되므로, 일찍 신청하시는 게 좋으리라 생각합니다.

어휘 slate for ~할 예정이다 noted 저명한 author 저자 entitled 제목 붙여진 guide 안내하다 through 처음부터 끝까지 follow 따르다 precept 가르침 numerous 수많은 impressive 인상적인 earn 벌다 net income 순이익 well worth 상당한 가치가 있는 handout 유인물 completion 완결 engrave 새기다 sell out 매진되다 sign up 신청하다

147 공지의 대상은 누구인가?
(A) 저자
(B) 미래의 기업체 소유주
(C) 정부 공무원
(D) 여행객
해설 지문 초반에 경영주가 되길 원해 왔다면 세미나를 통해 준비하라고 언급되어 있으므로 정답은 (B)이다.

148 공지를 읽은 사람들은 무엇을 해야 하는가?
(A) 빨리 세미나에 등록하는 것
(B) 새드 오션 호텔의 방을 예약하는 것
(C) 지미 톰슨의 저서 중인 한 권을 사는 것
(D) 톰슨 씨의 재단에 기부하는 것
해설 지문 후반에 톰슨 씨의 세미나는 보통 매진되므로 서둘러 신청해야 한다고 말하고 있다. 따라서 정답은 (A)이다.

1월 24일

토마스 울름, 대표이사
캘리포니아 하이텍스사
팔로알토, 캘리포니아

울름 씨에게,

저는 태레사 스미스 씨가 재너럴모터스사의 디자인 부서에서 회계 담당 비서로 일해 왔던 2년 동안 그녀를 알고 지내 왔습니다. 저는 태라사의 자신의 업무에 대한 태도뿐만 아니라 수행 능력에 항상 감동해 왔습니다. 그녀는 대인관계 및 의사소통 능력이 뛰어났는데 이로 인해 우리 직원의 긍정적인 업무관계를 형성해 왔습니다.

태레사 스미스 씨는 재정적인 평가를 수행하면서 고객으로부터 정보를 얻는 데 필요한 분석적 능력 기술을 소유하고 있습니다. 또한, 태레사 스미스는 품격 있는 업무 환경과 인터뷰 진행의 기술을 소유하고 있습니다. ¹⁵⁰ 그녀는 문제없이 진단하고 실행 가능한 해결책을 생각해내는 분석 기술이 있습니다. ¹⁵⁰ 경영자로 임을 갖게 되었을 때 압착함을 유지하는 그녀의 능력은 그녀가 스트레스를 받는 상황에서 업무를 잘 수행할 수 있음을 보여줍니다.

저는 그녀가 회계 업무에 있어서 미래가 밝다는 것을 의심하지 않습니다. 저는 그녀가 자신의 부서를 책임질 자격이 충분하다고 생각합니다. ¹⁴⁹ 저는 주저함 없이 이 그녀를 채용하는 것을 추천합니다. 추가적인 정보가 필요하시면 알려주세요.

루프라잇 존스
제너럴모터스사
디트로이트, 미시간
(896) 555-9532
rj@gm.com

어휘 corporation 회사 accounting 회계(학) impressed 감동한 attitude 태도 performance 수행 interpersonal 사람 간의 superb 훌륭한 clientele 의뢰인, 고객 assessment 평가 possess 소유하다 quality 고품질의 analytical 분석적인 diagnose 진단하다 viable 실행 가능한 frenzied 광적인 under pressure 압박 하에서 doubt 의심하다 profession 직업 deserve to ~할 가치가 있다 in charge of ~를 책임지는 without hesitation 주저함 없이

149 편지의 목적은 무엇인가?
(A) 재너럴 모터스가 만든 차에 대해 불만을 제기하기 위해서
(B) 한 사람의 채용을 추천하기 위해서
(C) 자동차 대형 구매에 대한 할인을 요청하기 위해서
(D) 재능 있는 사람을 찾기 위해서
해설 지문 후반에 스미스 씨의 채용을 추천한다고 언급되어 있으므로 정답은 (B)이다.

150 다음 중 스미스 씨의 능력으로 언급되지 않은 것은 무엇인가?
(A) 대인관계 및 의사소통 능력
(B) 자동차를 디자인하는 능력
(C) 문제 해결 능력
(D) 스트레스 하에서 침착함을 유지하는 능력
해설 지문 후반에 스미스 씨의 대인관계 및 의사소통에 관한 내용을 언급하고 있으므로

구구 마티로 ¹⁵¹ 스탠리, 당신이 지래에 요청했던 도서관 평면도 3D 프린트의 수정 사항에 관해 얘록 봐도 될까요?	오전 11:12
스탠리 투키 물론이조. 무슨 일입니까?	오전 11:13
구구 마티로 작업이 다 끝나서, 당신에게 보내 줄게요. 제가 직업물 전체를 보내 드릴까요, 아니면 수정된 12페이지만 보내 드릴까요?	오전 11:14
스탠리 투키 지금은 제가 이메일을 열어 볼 수가 없어요. 여기는 인터넷이 연결되어 있지 않거든요.	오전 11:16
구구 마티로 제 생각에 서류를 필요가 없을 것 같아요. 의뢰인라 미팅이 내일 있조. 그렇조?	오전 11:16
스탠리 투키 기다릴 필요가 뭐 있나요? ¹⁵² 지래에 빼스로 변경된 부분만 보내 주실래요?	오전 11:17
구구 마티로 얼마델까요, 번호가 어떻게 되나요?	오전 11:18
스탠리 투키 555-0417번이요.	오전 11:19
구구 마티로 네, 됐어요, 확인해 보세요.	오전 11:25
스탠리 투키 도착했네요, 고마워요, 구구. 회아서 봐요.	오전 11:26

어휘 revision 수정 floor plan 평면도 now that ~이기 때문에 connection 접속 rush 서두르다
해설 첫 메시지에서 도서관 평면도의 수정에 관한 내용을 언급하고 있으므로

151 마티로 씨는 누구인가?
(A) 접수원
(B) 컴퓨터 기술자
(C) 건축가
(D) 도서관 직원

152 오전 11시 17분에 투지 씨가 "기다릴 필요가 뭐 있나요?"라고 쓴 의미는 무엇인가?

(A) 전화하고 싶어 한다.
(B) 즉시 예약을 받고 싶다.
(C) 즉시 그의 팀을 만나고 싶다.
(D) 회의를 미루려고 한다.

해설 오전 11시 17분에 투지 씨가 있는 곳은 인터넷 연결이 안 되지만 팩스를 통해서라도 그 서류를 받으려고 하고 있다. 따라서 정답은 (B)이다.

[153-154]

몬트리올에서 기회!

캐나다 몬트리올에 있는 중간 정도로, 적절히 꾸며진 우리 사립학교는 7월에 올름 시작할 영어 교사를 찾고 있습니다. 여러분은 입을 만하고도 증명된 우리의 교육 과정을 통해서 초중등 학생을 가르칠 것입니다. 여러분은 금세는 동일 직책의 평균치를 훨씬 넘어서 월 1천 800달러가 될 것입니다. 여러분은 잃으랍부터 금요일까지 오후 2시에서 8시까지 주 30시간을 기준할 것입니다. 여러분은 우리 학교에서 고작 10분 거리에 떨어진, 가구를 갖춘 아파트를 받을 것입니다. 우리는 몬트리올이 프랑스어를 대부분 사용하는 도시라는 것을 알고 있는 원어민 영어 교사를 찾고 있습니다.

여기에 고용되시려면, 최소한 인기 받은 대학에서 어떤 분야에서 학사 학위가 있어야 합니다. 여러분이 교수 경험이 있다면 그것은 가산점으로 작용할 수 있지만, 그것은 계획에서 필요조건은 아닙니다. 그러나 여러분은 범죄의 이력이 없음을 증명해야 합니다.

우리 학교의 모든 교사는 친근하고 여러분이 요령을 배울 수 있도록 가까이 도울 것입니다. 때때로 우리는 학생의 영어 학습을 촉진하도록 두 명의 교사가 수업을 계획하며 학생들을 가르칩니다. 우리 또한 함께 전반적인 학생을 신중히 선발하여, 시끄럽고 공격적인 아이가 여러분의 교육적인 노력을 방해하지 않도록 하고 있습니다.

82-2-555-3371로 장 모랑수에게 연락하세요.

어휘 moderately 중간 정도로, 적절히 private school 사립학교 opening 공석 tried-and-true 입을 만하고도 증명된 well above the average 평균을 훨씬 넘어선 furnished 가구가 있는 at least 적어도 accredited 인기 받은 plus 가산점 prove 증명하다 criminal 범죄의 learn the ropes 요령을 배우다 facilitate 촉진하다 screen 선발하다 assure 보장하다 belligerent 적대적인 disrupt 방해하다 publicize 광고하다 whatsoever 무엇이든

153 광고의 목적은 무엇인가?

(A) 캐나다 지역 전체에 교육 기관을 광고하기 위해서
(B) 영어에 해외 학생을 선발하기 위해서
(C) 영어의 중요성을 강조하기 위해서
(D) 영어학원에서 가르치는 사람을 고용하기 위해서

해설 지문 첫 문장에 영어 교사를 찾고 있다고 언급하고 있으므로 정답은 (D)이다.

154 학생들의 면에 대해 언급된 것은 무엇인가?

(A) 그들은 시끄럽고 무례하다.
(B) 그들은 영어를 배우는 데 전혀 관심이 없다.
(C) 그들은 교사를 존경한다.
(D) 그들은 가난한 저소득층에 속해 있다.

해설 지문 후반부에 이 학교는 학생들 신중히 선발하여 시끄럽고 공격적인 아이가 부족한 교육적인 노력을 방해하지 않도록 하고 있다고 언급하고 있다. 따라서 정답은 (C)이다.

[155-157]

샌안토니오(7월 3일)

샌안토니오 익스프레스는 부채 증가와 광고 수익 감소를 해결하는 데 어려움을 겪었기 때문에 월요일에 붕노에게 파산 보호를 신청했다. — [1] —.

2008년에 미디어 투자자 지미 패트리의 인수한 익스프레스는 채권자와의 협상 문제로 최근 몇 달간 파산 지분기와 발을해내를 고용했었다.

그것은 최근의에서만 나타난 미국 신문 업계 문제의 징후일 뿐이다. — [2] —. 패트리의 지주 회사인 샌안토니오 익스프레스는 그 회사의 많은 신문 편집실을 줄였고, 그중이 일부는 완전히 폐고하였다.

패트릭은 "작년에 우리는 재정 문제에 대한 해결책을 찾으려고 노력해 왔고 계속 그렇게 할 것이다. 우리는 여전히 1930년대에 처럼 출판하기 시작한 이 지랑스러운 신문사를 부활시키기 희망하고 있다. 그러나 채권자는 일부 요인이 우리의 통제력을 넘어서는 사실을 깨달을 필요가 있다."라고 성명을 발표했다.

법원 서류에 따르면, 샌안토니오 익스프레스는 자산이 16억 달러인데 비해 부채가 거의 40억 달러에 달했다고 밝히고 있다. — [3] —. 이 부채는 대부분 패트리의 신문사를 인수하기 위해서 돈을 빌려서 거래를 성사시기면서 발생한 것이다.

법원 기록에 샌안토니오 익스프레스가 기록한 주요 채권자는 JP 모건 체이스와 메릴 린치와 같은 대형 은행을 포함하고 있다. — [4] —. 일부 분석가는 이 회사가 올해 3분기까지 부채 상환 불이행을 면할 수 있을 것이라고 주장하고 있다.

어휘 file for bankruptcy 파산 신청을 하다 struggle 애쓰다 cope with ~을 처리하다 debt 부채 federal 연방의 acquire 인수하다 investor 투자자 creditor 채권자 holding company 지주 회사 newsroom 뉴스 편집실 court 법원 asset 자산 filing 서류 기록 strike a deal 거래를 하다 analyst 분석가 contend 주장하다 defaulting 불이행 take out loans 대출하다 inheritance 유산 declining 감소하는 mounting 증가하는

155 기사의 주제는 무엇인가?

(A) 신문 수석 편집장의 사직
(B) 새로운 부문을 추가하는 신문사의 계획
(C) 파산 신청을 하는 신문사
(D) 미디어 산업에서 은퇴하겠다는 지미 패트리의 결정

해설 지문 초반에서 부채 증가와 광고 수익의 감소로 어려움을 겪고 있는 샌안토니오 익스프레스가 붕노에 파산 보호 신청을 했다고 언급하고 있으므로 정답은 (C)이다.

156 패트리 씨는 샌안토니오 익스프레스를 어떻게 소유하게 되었는가?

(A) 구매하기 위해 대출을 함으로써
(B) 다른 자산 일부를 매각함으로써
(C) 그의 방대한 유산을 이용해서
(D) 샌안토니오 지역의 다른 신문사와 합병하여

해설 다섯 번째 단락에서 패트리 씨가 신문사를 인수하는 데 쓰인 돈이 부채가 대부분으로 이었다고 하므로 정답은 (A)이다.

157 [1], [2], [3], [4]로 표시된 곳 중 다음 문장이 위치로 가장 적절한 곳은 어디인가?

"몇몇 신문사는 수익의 감소와 재무 증가에 대처하고 있다."

(A) [1]
(B) [2]
(C) [3]
(D) [4]

해설 삽입문장은 몇몇 신문사가 수익 감소와 재무 증가를 대처하고 있는 내용으로, 미국 신문업계의 최근 불거진 문제를 언급한 이후에 나오는 것이 적절하다. 따라서 정답은 (B)이다.

[158-160]

수신: 테리 리투라다 (terry@hotmail.com)
발신: 셀리나 마운즈 (celinamounts@gmail.com)
날짜: 12월 13일
제목: 우리 상점에서 쇼핑하는 동안 생긴 일

리투라다 씨에게:

158 이 글은 12월 12일 귀하의 이메일에 대한 답장입니다. 우리 상점 종리이 부티크에서 귀하에게 잘못된 것을 교육하셨다고 연급하셨습니다. 실제가 판매 직원이 손 제안에서 고객님 주변을 따라다녔고 그것에게서 마치 가게 물건을 훔치는 사람인 것처럼 행동했다면, 진심으로 사과드립니다. 고객님은 스테인버그 씨가 "와이너 담긴 눈조리"로 바라봤다고 언급하셨지만, 저는 그것이 무엇을 의미하는지 모르겠습니다. **159** 그가 고객님을 빨히 쳐다보고 있었나요, 혹은 도움 준비를 하려고 서서 고객님을 바라보셨나요? 그것은 제가 졸리에 부티크의 모든 직원을 교육하는 방법이기에 저는 후자의 경우였길 바랍니다.

159 제가 스테인버그 씨와 이야기를 해 보았는데, 그는 그런 일이 있었음을 부인하였습니다. 그는 고객님을 불쾌하게 할 의도는 절대 아니었다고 주장하고 있습니다. 어쩌면 고객님이 그의의 의도를 오해한 것 같습니다.

160 우리 직원은 가게 물건을 훔치는 사람을 정체할 의무를 가지다는 것을 고객님께 맹세드리고 싶습니다. 저의 상점은 2016년에 절도 사건으로 2500달러가 넘게 손해를 겪었고, 실제로 절도를 용인할 여력도 없습니다. 그러나 우리가 그것을 위해 고객님을 불편하게 오셨서 부티크에 오시도록 만들게 넘이 감사드리고 싶지도 보여줄 수 없다는 취지로 해 주세요.

진심으로
셀리나 마운즈, 매장 매니저

어휘 sales associate 판매 직원 boutique 고급 여성복 판매장 shoplifter 가게에서 물건을 슬쩍 훔치는 사람 latter 후자의 deny 부인하다 incident 사건 insist 주장하다 misunderstand 오해하다 remind 상기시키다 watch out 경계하다 loss 손실 afford to ~할 여유가 있다 appreciate 감사하다 resemble 닮다 suspected 의심쩍은

158 리트라다 씨가 마운즈 씨에게 글을 쓴 이유는 무엇인가?
(A) 상점의 직원에 대해 불평하기 위해서
(B) 출입구 부근에서 판매하는 옷의 품질을 칭찬하기 위해서
(C) 어떤 물품을 세일을 왜 하지 않는지 묻기 위해서
(D) 상점의 영업시간에 관해 문의하기 위해서
해설 지문 초반에서 마운즈 씨가 겪었던 불쾌한 사항에 대한 담당인을 받는다고 있다. 따라서 그가 그런에 리트라다 씨가 상점 직원에게 불쾌했던 점을 이메일로 보냈던 것을 추측할 수 있으므로 정답은 (A)이다.

159 마운즈 씨에 따르면 문제는 무엇인가?
(A) 스테인버그 씨가 나쁜 하루를 보내고 있었다.
(B) 스테인버그 씨는 단지 리트라다 씨를 바라본 것이고 도와주고 싶어 했다.
(C) 리트라다 씨는 의심 받고 있는 상점 좀도둑과 닮았다.
(D) 리트라다 씨는 상점에서 옷 함으로 받는 방법으로 이웃을 이용하려 있다.
해설 지문 중반에 스테인버그 씨가 리트라다 씨에게 불쾌감을 주려고 했던 것은 아니었고, 마운즈 씨는 매장 직원이 고객에 주변에서 도움을 제공할 수 있도록 교육하고 있다고 말하므로 정답은 (B)이다.

160 마운즈 씨에 관해 암시된 것은 무엇인가?
(A) 직원과 고객 사이의 문제를 해결하려고 노력하는 중이다.
(B) 스테인버그 씨의 해명을 받아들이지 않는다.
(C) 출입하 부근의 새로운 판매 직원을 고용해야 한다.
(D) 리트라다 씨가 너무 과하게 불평한다고 생각한다.
해설 지문이 중후반에 걸쳐 리트라다 씨는 고객과 직원 사이에 있었던 불미스러운 일을 중재하려 하고 있다. 따라서 정답은 (A)이다.

[161-163]
발신: 맥스 기븐즈
타운 레이크 31번가
캔자스 시티, 미주리 66421
이메일: maxieg@email.com

수신: 신디 프로브스트
대표이사
프로브스트 스튜디오
브라켄리지 88번가
캔자스 시티, 미주리 66432
프로브스트 씨에게,

이 편지는 프로브스트 디자인 스튜디오에서 저의 사직을 알리는 정식 통지서이니 받아주시기 바랍니다. 161 저는 블루리더에 있는 신규 회사에서 일자리를 제안받았습니다. 이렇게 훌륭한 일이 일생에 직장을 떠나는 것이 상당히 슬픔니다. 저는 진심으로 귀하의 회사에서 다양한 프로젝트에 도전을 즐겼고 패션 업계에 관해 많은 것을 배웠습니다.

162 저의 고용 계약서의 규정대로, 저는 한 달 전에 통보를 드립니다. 이것은 PDS사에서의 저의 마지막 날이 8월 3일이라는 뜻이죠. 저는 아직 두 건의 주요한 프로젝트를 - 쟝상시 1건과 경이 나머지 건 - 맡고 있는데 그걸 전까지 완료하겠다고 약속드립니다.

귀하, 그리고 매니스 양튼은 존스, 트로이 맥 에 매 없으나 나머지 경영진에게 지난 4년 동안 저에게 베풀어 주신 모든 것에 감사를 표하고 싶습니다. 163 귀하께서는 저에게 실 대를 위한 매객차이고 적절한 기회을 웃을 디자인하는 방법을 기르치 주시고 제 경력 내내 유지할 기술을 갖추도록 도와주셨습니다.

제가 떠난 후 필요한 정보가 있으시면 편하게 연락해 주십시오.

안녕히 계세요.

맥스 기븐즈

어휘 accept 수락하다 formal 정식의 notification 통지 resignation 사직 start-up 이제 막 활동을 시작한 considerable 상당한 sorrow 슬픔 challenge 도전 call for ~을 요청하다 employment contract 고용 계약서 ensure 보장하다 attractive 매력적인 affordable (값이) 알맞은 retain 유지하다 get in touch 연락하다 ailing 병든

161 맥스 기븐즈가 프로브스트 디자인 스튜디오를 떠나는 이유는 무엇인가?
(A) 자신의 사업을 경영할 계획이다.
(B) 다른 직장을 찾았다.
(C) 가족과 함께 해외로 이사할 예정이다.
(D) 병든 어머니를 보살피면서 집에 있어야 한다.
해설 지문 상단에 맥스는 블루리더에 있는 신규 회사의 일자리 제안을 받아 사직을 통보한다고 언급하고 있다. 따라서 정답은 (B)이다.

162 기븐즈 씨에 관해 암시된 것은 무엇인가?
(A) 그는 인턴으로 시작했다.
(B) 그는 보잘것없는 급여를 받는다.
(C) 그는 젊은 사람을 위한 옷을 디자인했다.
(D) 그는 현재 트로이 맥 매니슨와 갈등이 있었다.
해설 지문 후반에 직장 동료에 대한 감사를 표현하면서 심대를 위한 옷을 디자인하고 있다고 언급하는 부분을 잘 배열하고 있다. 따라서 정답은 (C)이다.

163 편지가 쓰인 때는 언제인가?
(A) 7월
(B) 8월
(C) 9월
(D) 10월
해설 지문 중반에 이 편지는 고용 계약서에 따라 퇴직하기 1한 달 전에 보내는 통지라고 언급한 뒤, 마지막 근무일이 8월 3일이라고 했으므로 이 편지가 작성되는 것은 그로부터 한 달 전인 7월 초인 것을 알 수 있다. 따라서 정답은 (A)이다.

[164-167]
6월 22일
캔 하우스맨
이음스톤 보험사
시애틀, 워싱턴

하우스맨 씨에게,

저는 저의 생명보험증권(번호 339-478992)에 관해서 이 편지를 씁니다. 이것은 이 마감 애덤스라는 다른 직원이 2015년에 발행해 주었습니다. - [1] -. 저는 애덤스 씨는 제가 등기로 그 이후 이음스톤 보험사를 퇴사하였고, 그 자리를 당신이 맡았다고 알고 있습니다.

제 생명보험증권의 보험료는 매달 제 은행 계좌에서 자동으로 공제됩니다. 하지만 지난 최근에 제 계좌 명세서를 받는데요. 164 보험료가 매달 34달러에서 88달러로 올랐다는 것을 알고 직잖이 놀랐습니다. - [2] -. 게다가, 이런 인상에 대해 저는 왜 통보받지 못했을까요? 솔직히 보험료가 이렇게 급격히 인상될 줄 알았었더면, 이 보험증권을 계속 유지했을 것이란 확신이 없습니다.

저는 저의 타임스에서 한 달에 생명보험으로 47달러만 내고, 적어도 5년 동안 그 가격을 인상하지 않고 보장해 주는 회사에 관한 기사를 읽었습니다. - [3] - . 165 만약 당신이 급격한 보험료 인상에 대해 이해가 갈 만한 설명을 제공하지 않는다면 저는 그 회사로 바꾸는 것을 진지하게 고려하고 있습니다.

제가 화가 난 것은 아니지만 왜 생명보험이 생활비용을 위해 현지 그렇게 많이 지급되고 있는지 알고 싶을 뿐입니다. 당신도 제가 이 보험증권을 유지해야 한다고 생각하신다면? - [4] -.

진심으로
제니 리버스

어휘 in reference to ~에 관해 life insurance policy 생명보험증권 issue 발행하다 premium 보험료 deduct 공제하다 statement 명세서 somewhat 어느 정도 honestly 솔직히 guarantee 보장하다 beneficiary 수혜자 track down 추적하다 predecessor 전임자 jump 급등

164 리바스 씨가 하우스맨 씨에게 글을 쓴 이유는 무엇인가?
(A) 생명보험증권의 수령인을 변경하기 위해서
(B) 또 다른 보험증권을 얻으려는 것을 알리기 위해서
(C) 한 에이전스를 추천하기 위해서
(D) 월별 생명 보험료 인상에 관해 물어보기 위해서

해설 지문 후반에 급격한 보험료 인상에 대한 민츠스러운 설명을 제공해 달라는 요청이고 있으므로 정답은 (D)이다.

165 마고 에임스는 누구인가?
(A) 리바스 씨의 옛집 이웃
(B) 시애틀 타임스의 논설위원
(C) 이글스톤 보험사의 하우스맨 씨의 전임자
(D) 이글스톤 보험사의 이사

해설 지문 상단에 리바스 씨와 보험증권을 발행해 준 에임스 씨가 퇴사하고 단 후, 그 뒤를 하우스맨이 이어받았다고 언급하고 있다. 따라서 정답은 (C)이다.

166 편지에서 세 번째 단락 세 번째 줄의 "switching"과 의미가 가장 가까운 것은 무엇인가?
(A) 단추를 채우는 것
(B) 돌리는 것
(C) 변경하는 것
(D) 조사하는 것

해설 앞의 배다른 고객에서 보면, 이글스톤 보험사보다 더 저렴하고 일정한 보험료 서비스를 제공하는 회사가 있으므로, 민츠스러운 배달을 모지 못할 경우는 보험사를 '바꾸겠다'라는 의미가 가장 적절하므로 정답은 (C)이다.

167 [1], [2], [3], [4]로 표시된 곳 중 다음 문장이 위치로 적절한 것은 어디인가?
"이것은 매우 큰 인상이며 왜 그런 건지 알고 싶습니다."
(A) [1]
(B) [2]
(C) [3]
(D) [4]

해설 문맥상 상위문장은 보험료의 대폭적인 인상이 인상이 언급된 후에 나오는 것이 논리적이다. 그러므로 34달러에서 88달러로 보험료가 인상되었음을 알리는 문장 뒷자리가 가장 적절하다. 따라서 정답은 (B)이다.

어휘 inventory status 재고 현황 indicate 나타내다 sign up with ~와 계약하다 supplier 공급업체 be aware of ~을 알고 있다

168 오전 11시 30분에 파슨스 씨가 "물론이지"라고 쓴 것이는 무엇인가?
(A) 그는 모내에게 보고하고 있다.
(B) 그는 모내 씨가 주문했던 것을 알지 않았다.
(C) 그는 모내 씨와 함께 있는 것에 동의한다.
(D) 그는 모내 씨가 프로젝트를 맡는 것을 원한다.

해설 바로 앞 메시지에서 모내 씨가 참고의 재고 현황을 말해 줄 시간이 있는 나고 질문하고 있으므로 여기서 "물론이지"라는 답은 매달을 할 시간이 있다는 의미로 볼 수 있다. 따라서 정답은 (A)이다.

169 모내 씨에 관해 암시되는 것은 무엇인가?
(A) 데이터베이스를 구축했다.
(B) 오늘 주문을 받았다.
(C) 내일 주문을 할 것이다.
(D) 최근에 출장을 다녀왔다.

해설 오전 11시 32분에 파슨스 씨와 메시지에서 모내 씨가 부재중이었던 지난주 예 공급업체를 변경하여 주문을 처리한 사실이 언급되어 있다, 이를 미루어 보아 모내 씨는 자리를 비우고 출장을 점차해 볼 수 있다. 따라서 정답은 (D)이다.

170 파슨스 씨와 모내 씨는 어떤 업체에서 일하는가?
(A) 인쇄 가게
(B) 소매상

(C) 제조업체
(D) 유통업체

해설 새로운 공급업체에서 토너를 주문하여 인쇄 가게에 배달한다는 내용 등 미루어 보아 두 사람이 일하는 회사는 유통업체임을 알 수 있다. 따라서 정답은 (D)이다.

171 파슨스 씨가 주 후반에 한 일은 무엇인가?
(A) 주문서를 수정했었다.
(B) 새로운 직원을 교육했었다.
(C) 새로운 상품에 대해 그에게 일었다.
(D) 모내 씨를 재조사보기 도왔다.

해설 대화 후반에 파슨스 씨가 윌요일에 새로운 공급업체에서 받은 저렴한 제품을 납품받게 될 것이라고 인쇄점에 통보하고 있으므로 정답은 (C)이다.

청구서 번호 T987246   ITE 10월 14일

[172-175]

수신: 이치 드레이슨
다이내믹 소프트웨어사
15 매디슨 가
시카고, 일리노이 44293

발신: 베스트 웨스턴 호텔
154 그랜드 가
마이애미, 플로리다 73401

이 청구서는 아래와 같은 서비스에 대해 발행됩니다:

172 숙박 서비스:
1개 1인실 150달러(10% 세금 포함) / 1박당 * 3회   ITE 450달러

173 룸서비스:
조식 뷔페 35달러(10% 세금 포함) / 식사당 * 2명   70달러
미니 바: 소량의 술(25달러/ 병당) * 2병   50달러
　소량 포장의 스낵(15달러 / 봉지당) * 3봉   45달러
─────────────────────────────
합계 :   615달러

이 청구서를 확인하시고 귀하의 수표와 함께 동봉하여 주세요. ITA 청구서는 발행된 날짜로부터 15일까지 지급해야 합니다. 귀하의 회사에 제출물을 추가적으로 영수증이 필요하시면 ITB 본인이 직접 오시거나 혹은 이메일이나 전화로 저에게 연락해 주시기 바랍니다. 곧 다시 만나요!

귀하가 우리와 함께 즐겨져 지내셨기를 바랍니다. 곧 다시 만나요!

제니퍼 트루디
호텔 프런트 매니저
이메일: jennifer_t@bestwestern.com
전화: 412-555-5280

[168-171]

저넬 모내 [오전 11:29]	안녕, 짐. ITB 재고 현황을 알고 싶어. 시간 있니?
짐 파슨스 [오전 11:30]	물론이지!
저넬 모내 [오전 11:31]	데이터베이스 상으로는 ADFC 컬러 토너가 지장 30개의 잉크 카트리지가 겨우 4상자 밖에 없는 것을으 보여. ITD 최근에 배달을 많이 했어, 더 주문해야 하지 않을까?
짐 파슨스 [오전 11:32]	아니, 그럴 필요 없어. ITD 우리 고객에게 더 싼 브랜드를 제공하기 위해서, 이미 또 다른 공급업체와 계약했어, ITE 내가 부재중이었던 지난주에, 내가 그 공급업체에서 50상자를 주문했어. 그것들이 아직 배달되지 않았어.
저넬 모내 [오전 11:33]	잘했네!
짐 파슨스 [오전 11:35]	ITD 그리고 또, 윌요일에 내가 그 변경에 관해 인쇄업체에 통보했어, 인쇄점도 이미 그것에 대해 알고 있어.
저넬 모내 [오전 11:37]	다시 한번 고마워!

어휘 invoice 청구서 issue 발행하다 check 수표 payable 지불해야 하는 additional 추가적인 receipt 영수증 in person 본인이 직접

172 청구서는 무엇에 관한 것인가?
(A) 음식과 숙소
(B) 국제 전화
(C) 드라이클리닝 서비스
(D) 객실 등급 향상
해설 청구 내용을 보면 숙박 사항과 식사 등이 언급되어 있으므로 정답은 (A)이다.

173 지불 기한은 언제인가?
(A) 10월 14일
(B) 10월 29일
(C) 11월 3일
(D) 11월 8일
해설 이 청구서가 작성된 날짜는 10월 14일이고, 지문 중반에 이 청구서가 발행된 날짜로부터 15일까지 지불해야 한다고 명시되어 있으므로 정답은 (C)이다.

174 숙박비는 총 얼마인가?
(A) 45달러
(B) 70달러
(C) 450달러
(D) 615달러
해설 지문 중반에 드러나 있는 상세 청구 내용을 보면 1박당 150달러로 총 3일 머물러서 450달러가 청구될 것을 확인할 수 있다. 따라서 정답은 (C)이다.

175 제니퍼 트루디에게 연락하는 방법으로 제시되지 않은 것은?
(A) 본인이 직접
(B) 인터넷으로
(C) 전화로
(D) 팩스로
해설 지문 하단에 본인이 직접 찾아오거나, 이메일이나, 전화로 연락해 달라고 하고 있으므로 언급되지 않은 (D)가 정답이다.

[176-180]

메모

수신: 전 직원
발신: 윌리스 저드슨
날짜: 1월 3일
제목: 긴급 조치

여러분도 알다시피, **180** 국내외의 경기 침체로 윌리스 저드슨 별품회사의 재정 실적이 영향을 받고 있습니다. 이러한 **177** 과도한 사업을 보장하기 위해서 몇몇 비용 절감 조치가 필수적이라는 것을 알게 되었습니다.

이 조치와 관련된 정보는 우리의 최신 온라인 사보에서 찾아보실 수 있습니다.

저드슨 모든 직원이 이 조치의 필요성을 이해하고 그것을 수행하는 것을 돕는 데 최선을 다해 주기를 희망합니다. 부장들(특히, 제리 로버슨, 도 메리디스와 **180** 부정할도록 지켜야도록 신경 써야 할 책임이 있습니다.

윌리스 저드슨 별품회사
비용 절감 조치

1. 에어컨은 여름 달(6, 7, 8월)에 오전 8시 30분부터 오후 5시 30분까지만 동작시켜 주세요. 그 시간 이후에는 반드시 꺼 주세요.

2. 급한 일을 끝낼때 하는 것이 아니라면 **179** 전 직원은 늦어도 오후 8시까지는 퇴근해야 합니다. 만약에 늦은 시간까지 회사에 있어야 한다면, 그 사람들은 그들의 직속 상사 또는 제 비서인, 마리조 구에레로에게 반드시 알려야 합니다.

3. 저는 여러분에게 사무용품을 절약하여 사용해 주기를 요청합니다. **180** 새로운 사무용품이 필요하다면, 로버슨 씨, 메리디스 씨 혹은 브랜드버리 씨에게 알려주시고 **178** 모니터링을 위해 일지에 서명하여 주십시오.

어휘 urgent 긴급한 measure 조치 given ~을 고려하면 recession 침체 law firm 법률회사 distressing 고통스러운 implement 실행하다 cost-cutting 비용 절감이 viability 생존 action 조치 available 이용 가능한 latest 최신의 newsletter 사보 cooperate 협조하다 department head 부장 responsibility 책임 operate 작동시키다 at the latest 늦어도 immediate supervisor 직속 상사 office supplies 사무용품 sparingly 절약하여 sign in 서명하다 logbook 일지 solicit 간청하다 cubicle 칸막이로 된 공간 stationery 문구류

176 메모가 쓰인 이유는 무엇인가?
(A) 새로운 정책에 관해 전 직원에게 알리기 위해서
(B) 경기 침체를 알리기 위해서
(C) 직원들에게 도움을 기부해 달라고 요청하기 위해서
(D) 회사 확장에 관한 의견을 구하기 위해서
해설 첫 지문 상단에서 경기 침체 상황에서 회사의 생존을 위해 새로운 비용 절감 조치를 실행해야 한다고 언급하고 있으므로 정답은 (A)이다.

177 메모에서 첫 번째 단락 두 번째 줄의 "distressing"과 의미상 가장 가까운 것은 무엇인가?
(A) 주의가 산만한
(B) 안도하는
(C) 고통스러운
(D) 놀라운
해설 앞서 매도를 고려해 보면 회사가 국내외의 경기 침체로 재정적인 영향을 받는 것은 '괴로운' 상황이라고 볼 수 있다. 따라서 정답은 (C)이다.

178 사무용품에 관하여 언급된 것은 무엇인가?
(B) 직원들은 사용 기록을 해야 한다.
(C) 사무용품을 받기 위해 새로운 공급업체를 고용했다.
(D) 사무용품은 소모품 캐비넷에 저장될 것이다.
해설 두 번째 지문의 마지막 항목에서 사무용품 사용에 관해 일지를 작성해 달라고 명령하고 있다. 따라서 정답은 (B)이다.

179 직원들에게 오후 8시까지 요청하는 것은 무엇인가?
(A) 에어컨을 켜둘 것
(B) 간부에게 공간을 청소하고 쓰레기통을 비울 것
(C) 해로운 팩스나 이메일을 보내는 것을 중단하는 것
(D) 사무실 밖으로 나갈 것
해설 두 번째 지문의 두 번째 항목에서 전 직원은 늦어도 오후 8시까지는 퇴근하라고 언급하고 있다. 따라서 정답은 (D)이다.

180 이 별품회사에 관해 암시된 것은 무엇인가?
(A) 직원들은 보상 근무를 해야 한다.
(B) 이 회사는 재정적으로 계속 어려울 것이다.
(C) 사무용품의 사용은 부정적이 보고되어야 한다.
(D) 감사 소프트웨어가 가능한 한 빨리 도입될 것이다.
해설 첫 번째 지문 마지막에서 저드 로버슨, 도 메리디스, 제니스 브랜드버리 이 직원이 부정인 것을 알 수 있는데, 두 번째 지문 세 번째 항목에서 사무용품 사용과 관련된 정보를 이들에게 보고하라고 요청하고 있다. 따라서 정답은 (C)이다. 흔면, 이 회사가 경기 침체의 영향을 절감 정책을 내놓았지만 이 재정적 어려움이 앞으로도 지속할 것이라는 내용은 없으므로 (B)는 오답이다.

[181-185]

수신: 엘리엇 이브람스 (eliot@gmail.com)
발신: 엘리너 무어 (emoore@tri-state.com)
날짜: 2월 3일
제목: 우리에게 고객을 위탁하는 것

이브람스 씨에게,

당신은 기업 중개인이기 때문에 기업을 매도하고 매입할 때 해마다 수백 개의 만 매자 출자 기업 어음이 쓰여서 나온다는 것을 알고 있을 것입니다. 이는 추가적인 소득을 얻을 절호의 기회입니다.

181 트라이 스테이트 투자사는 엘라배마에서 가장 큰 기업 어음 매입 회사입니다. 우리 회사는 귀하와 같은 기업 중개인에게 매주 소개료를 지급합니다. 이러한 분들은 의뢰인을 우리에게 위탁함으로써, 그 의뢰인의 기업 182 어음을 일시 급의 현금으로 받도록 돕습니다. 귀하는 귀하의 고객에게 자산들이 현금을 마련하는 방법을 보여줌에, 유용한 서비스를 제공할 수 있습니다. 이 과정에서, 현금 마련에 관해 의심스러웠던 판매를 촉진함으로써 귀하는 소개료를 받고 귀하의 수수료를 올릴 수 있습니다.

다른 회사와는 달리, 우리는 오직 기업 어음만 매입합니다. 우리는 미국 기업 중 개인 협회의 회원입니다. 귀하는 귀하의 고객에게 자산들이 현금을 마련하는 방법을 보여줄 수 있도록 돕습니다. 저는 귀하와의 대화를 보여 드리고 싶고 또 우리가 함께 일할 방법을 찾아보고 싶 하네서에서 가장 가능성 수도 있는 어떤 질문에도 받길래 답변할 것입니다. 183 바영에 메 인 스트리트 115번가에 있는 우리 사무실에 개인적으로 방문하는 것에 대해 184 응을 받지 않으실 경우 저는 특정한 기업 어음 상황에 이용할 수 있는 선택 사항이 온택을 보여 드리고 싶고 또 우리가 함께 일할 방법을 찾아보고 싶 습니다. 답변을 기다리겠습니다.

진심으로

엘리너 무어, 직원
트라이 스테이트 투자사

수신: 엘리너 무어 (emoore@tri-state.com)
발신: 엘리엇 이브람스 (eliot@gmail.com)
날짜: 2월 4일
제목: 답장: 우리에게 고객을 위탁하는 것

무어 씨에게,

2월 3일 자의 귀하의 이메일을 읽었습니다. 지난 10년간 저는 기업의 중개업으로 일해 왔습니다. 그 시간 동안 귀하께서 설명한 것이 매우 독특한 상황에 있는 많은 의뢰인을 돕기 위해 애써 왔습니다. 그들이 자산들의 매자 출자 기업 어음을 일시금으로 연금 받도록 한다는 것을, 이로 미루어 보 니 notes의 적절한 의미는 "어음"이다. 따라서 선택지 중 이에 적절한 의미를 가진다 것은 (C)가 정답이다.

저는 귀하와 함께 일할 수 있음을 의심하지 않습니다. 184 이러한 서비스가 은 필요하지도 모르고 의뢰인에 대해 말씀드려 볼게요. 그리운 투수공루사에 있는 갑스 오토 크레디이라는 이름의 중고차 매매상입니다. 저는 그것의 소유권 이 곧 변경될 것이라고 예상합니다. 그리고 앞으로 소유주가 될 사람으로 말해 대 리점이 소유주가 바뀌 뒤에 지금 부족을 겪을 것이 빠를나다. 귀하께서 이 작은 업체에 대한 일시금 규모를 지금 규모를 어떻게 측정할 것인지 저에게 말씀해 주세요. 두 번째 의뢰인 아브람스 씨는 지속적인 사업 관계를 맺을 기회를 논 의하고 싶다고 했다. 즉, 논의하기 위해서 바영에 사무실을 찾을 것임을 알 수 있으므로 (D)가 정답이다.

185 귀하께서 갑스 오토 크레디을 위한 소개료를 제공 할 수 있는지 저는 궁금합니다. 저는 5천 달러 이하는 아니길 바랍니다.

185 저는 지속적인 사업 관계를 맺을 기회를 논의하고 싶습니다. 저는 그러한 추천을 받을 만한 다른 고객이 현재 몇 명이 있습니다.

진심으로

엘리엇 아브람스

어휘 refer 위탁하다 broker 중개인 realize 깨닫다 hundreds of 수백 의 note 어음 come into existence 나타나다 annually 해마다 investment 투자 referral fee 소개료 a lump sum 일시금 cash 현 금 commission 수수료 facilitate 촉진하다 be in doubt 의심하다 receipt 수령 decade 10년 seek 추구하다 used-car dealership 중 고차 매매상 anticipate 예상하다 ownership 소유권 prospective 장래의 be short of ~이 부족하다 change hands 손에 넘어가다 quantify 양을 재다 fairly 꽤 typical 전형적인 furthermore 더욱이 ongoing 진행 중인 legitimacy 합법성

---

181 첫 번째 이메일의 목적은 무엇인가?
(A) 연체된 지급금에 관해 통보하기 위해서
(B) 사무용품을 주문하기 위해서
(C) 기업 서비스를 제공하기 위해서
(D) 새로운 상품에 대해 광고하기 위해서
해설 첫 번째 지문 두 번째 문단에서 기업 어음을 매입하여 일시금으로 지급 하는 서비스를 제공하는 업체라고 소개하고 있다. 따라서 정답은 (C)이다.

---

182 첫 번째 이메일에서 첫 번째 단락 두 번째 줄의 "notes"와 의미상 가장 가까 운 것은 무엇인가?
(A) 기록
(B) 증명서
(C) 어음
(D) 화폐
해설 첫 번째 지문 전반에 이 단어가 여러 번 등장하는데, 이것은 기업을 매 도하거나 매입할 때 수백 개가 쓰여서 나온다는 것이며, 트라이 스테이트 투자사는 이것 을 매입하여 일시금으로 받도록 한다고 연급하고 있다. 이로 미루어 보 니 notes의 적절한 의미는 "어음"이다. 따라서 선택지 중 이에 적절한 의미를 가진다 것은 (C)가 정답이다.

---

183 아브람스 씨에 대해 암시된 것은 무엇인가?
(A) 무어 씨의 상사이다.
(B) 최근에 중고차를 구매했다.
(C) 기업 중개인 협회 회원이다.
(D) 조만간 바영에 갈 것이다.
해설 첫 번째 지문에 질문이 있으면 바영에는 있는 사무실에 오라고 하고 있는데 두 번째 지문에서 아브람스 씨는 지속적인 사업 관계를 맺을 기회를 논 의하고 싶다고 했다. 즉, 논의하기 위해서 바영에 사무실을 찾을 것임을 알 수 있으므로 (D)가 정답이다.

---

184 아브람스 씨가 무어 씨에게 위탁할 회사는 어떤 종류의 회사인가?
(A) 종이 제품 판매 회사
(B) 배달 회사
(C) 중고차 판매 회사
(D) 여행사
해설 두 번째 지문 중반에 위탁 서비스가 필요할지도 모르는 중고차 매매상 을 소개하고 있다. 따라서 정답은 (C)이다.

---

185 두 번째 이메일에서 아브람스 씨는 무어 씨가 어떤 문제를 다루어 주길 원하 는가?
(A) 소개료 약수
(B) 트라이 스테이트 투자회사의 합병성
(C) 투수공루사에서 바영일까지의 거리
(D) 계약 체결을 위해 필요한 법적 서류
해설 두 번째 문단 마지막 부분에서 자신이 소개하고 있느지 묻고 있 다. 따라서 정답은 (A)이다.

공지

수신: 모든 거주자
발신: 제파슨 플레이스 건물의 유지관리 부서
제목: 건물 개선 프로젝트

아시다시피, 이 건물은 피닉스에 있는 우리 지구에서 가장 오래된 건물 중 하나입니다. **186** 그 결과 엘리베이터는 낡고 다소 느립니다. 우리는 최근 몇 년 동안 엘리베이터와 관련하여 수많은 불만 사항을 접수해 왔습니다.

물론, 우리도 우리의 건물을 가능한 한 최신의 상태로 유지하고 싶습니다. 그러나 엘리베이터에 대해 우리가 선택할 수 있는 것은 다소 제한되어 있습니다. **187** 새로운 것을 설치하는 것은 비용이 많이 들 것 같고, **188** 거의 모든 거주자에게 엘리베이터 교체 비용을 끼쳐 드려 죄송합니다.

그런 후에 한동안은 기존 엘리베이터를 계속 사용해 주세요. **190** 6개월이 지나면 서쪽 동까지에서 각각 1대의 엘리베이터가 최신 모델로 교체될 것입니다.

이 건물을 개선하기 위한 귀하의 제안에 감사드립니다. 앞으로도, 우리는 더 좋은 시설과 환경을 제공하기 위해 노력할 것입니다.

그러므로 제파슨 플레이스 빌딩 거주자의 근무자에게 이 문제에 관해 글을 써서 우리에게 보내 달라고 요청합니다. 저 척 힐리라는 시간을 내어 아래에 쓰인 주소로 편지를 보내 주십시오. 문제가 무엇이라고 생각하든지 솔직하게 저에게 말씀해 주시고, 그것을 바로잡는 방법에 관해 편하게 제안해 주세요. 저는 귀하의 피드백을 신중히 검토하겠다고 약속드립니다.

척 힐리
건물 감독자
제파슨 플레이스 빌딩, 100호
피닉스, 애리조나

척 힐리
제파슨 플레이스 빌딩, 100호
피닉스, 애리조나

힐리 씨에게,

저는 제파슨 플레이스 건물의 7층에 있는 씨엔씨 커뮤니케이션에서 근무하고 있습니다. 이 회사에서 3년 전에 근무하기 시작했는데, 저는 엘리베이터 문제가 그 어느 때보다 심각하고 악화되었다고 말하고 싶습니다. 5분 동안 엘리베이터를 기다려야만 한다면서 1층 로비에서 서 있다니까, 우리는 모두 매 바쁘고, 소중한 시간을 허비하고 있습니다. 아시다시피, **189** 또한 엘리베이터는 안정적이지 않습니다. 엘리베이터 중 하나가 바로 지난주에 고장이 났고, 우리에게는 남들 수 있습니다. 언제 수리를 예정일까요? 그것은 멈출 때까지, 우리집에는 단지 3대(서쪽 1대 그리고 동쪽 2대)밖에 없습니다. 우리 건물 중앙에 새 엘리베이터를 설치하는 것이 작동 중인 엘리베이터라는 단지 3대밖에 없습니다.

귀하께서 제안을 요청하셨으므로 제 의견을 알려드립니다. 저는 정말로 제파슨 플레이스 빌딩이 다음 엘리베이터가 최신식 고속 엘리베이터로 바꿔야야 한다고 생각합니다. (현재 작동되고 있지 않지 있는 방향이 되고 있을 저렴하지 않을 수도 있었던, 새로운 엘리베이터를 추가합니다. 더욱 방해가 되고 있을 곳으로 있는 2대의 엘리베이터를 추가하면 모든 것이 좋지 않지 않는 엘리베이터가 서쪽에 있는 2대의 엘리베이터를 교체하는 것을 추천합니다. 즉, 기존의 동쪽에 나머지 2대의 엘리베이터도 신경을 설치해 주세요. 설치가 끝난 후에 거주자도 이 변화를 반길 것이고 결국 이 건물의 수명도 보장할 것입니다.

진심으로
태미 조지프슨
씨엔씨 커뮤니케이션즈

186 of 348

어휘 district (행정구역) 지구 rather 다소 numerous 수많은 up to date 최신의 somewhat 다소 disrupt 피해를 주다 occupant 거주자 dependable 신뢰할 수 있는 honestly 솔직하게 break down 고장 나다 out of order 고장 난 functioning 작동하는 replace 교체하다 disruption 혼란 tenant 거주인 in the long run 결국에는 viability 생존력 improvement 개선 major part 주요 부분 inconvenience 불편함 existing 기존의 for a while 한동안 state-of-the-art 최신식의 permanently 영구적으로 partially 부분적으로 desperate 절실하게 prestigious 명망 높은, 일류의

186 엘리베이터에 대해 언급된 것은 무엇인가?
(A) 다섯 대의 엘리베이터가 있다.
(B) 또 다른 엘리베이터가 설치되는 중이다.
(C) 최근에 개조되었다.
(D) 느리고 안심하고 이용할 수 있다.

해설 첫 번째 지문 상단에 건물이 오래되어 엘리베이터가 낡고 다소 느리다고 언급되어 있고, 두 번째 지문 첫 번째 문단에서 엘리베이터를 언급하고 있으므로 정답은 (D)이다.

187 힐리 씨가 피하고 싶어 하는 것은 무엇인가?
(A) 낡은 엘리베이터를 새것으로 교체하는 것
(B) 현재 엘리베이터의 개조
(C) 작동하지 않는 엘리베이터 수리
(D) 영구적으로 엘리베이터 폐쇄

해설 첫 번째 지문 중반에 새 엘리베이터 설치는 비싸서 거주인을 불편하게 하고 공사에 긴 시간이 필요하다고 주장하며 엘리베이터 교체에 대해 회의적이라 부정적인 반응을 보이고 있다. 따라서 정답은 (A)이다.

188 새 엘리베이터 설치 시 발생 가능한 문제로 언급되지 않은 것은 무엇인가?
(A) 신속하게 끝나지 않을 것이다.
(B) 큰 비용이 들어갈 것이다.
(C) 지역 정책 위반이 될 수 있다.
(D) 거주인에게 많은 문제를 일으킬 수도 있다.

해설 첫 지문 중앙에 새로운 엘리베이터 설치에 긴 시간이 소요될 수 있다는 내용에서 (A)를, 설치 비용이 비쌀 것이라는 내용에서 (B)를, 거주인에게 피해를 가져다 줄 수 있다는 내용에서 (D)를 확인할 수 있다. 따라서 언급되지 않은 내용에서 (C)가 정답이다.

189 조지프슨 씨에 관해 언급된 것은 무엇인가?
(A) 5년 동안 제파슨 플레이스 건물에서 거주했다.
(B) 힐리 씨의 제안에 동의하고 있다.
(C) **사람들이 엘리베이터 때문에 가끔씩 시간을 낭비한다고 여긴다.**
(D) 거주인들이 한 명도 건물을 떠나지 않을 것이라고 장담한다.

해설 두 번째 지문의 중반에 많은 사람이 1층에서 엘리베이터를 기다리느라 소중한 시간을 낭비하고 있다고 언급하므로 정답은 (C)이다.

190 제파슨 플레이스 빌딩에 관해 추정할 수 있는 것은 무엇인가?
(A) **한 가구인의 제안이 부분적으로 받아들여졌다.**
(B) 새로운 거주인을 위해 엘리베이터를 설치했다.
(C) 몇몇 거주인은 이미 떠났다.
(D) 피닉스에서 가장 명성 높은 건물이다.

해설 두 번째 지문 중반에서 거주인인 조지프슨 씨가 고장 난 1대를 포함한 여 서쪽 엘리베이터의 2대를 교체해 달라고 제안하고 있는데, 세 번째 지문 후반부에 6개월 후 서쪽과 동쪽 각각 1대씩 교체될 예정이라고 밝히고 있다. 이는 그녀의 제안 중 일부가 수용된 것이므로 정답은 (A)이다.

[191-195]

제10회 국내 회계 감사 공개 토론 총회

7월 10일, 하얏트 호텔
모즈 하퍼, 프로그램 담당자

191 총회의 일정은 다음과 같습니다:

◇ 9:00	개막 연설(사무엘 뱅크스, 감사 협회 회장)
◇ 9:30	회계 감사를 강화하기 위한 새로운 정책 발표 (타나 콜스, 하이테크사의 마케팅 관리자)
◇ 11:00	회계 감사 구성의 변경 사항 통보 (마크 호번슨, 감사 협회 후임 회원)
◇ 12:00	점심
◇ 14:00	개선된 회계 감사 소프트웨어 발표 (찰스 아이젠버그, 테크룬사의 판매부장)
◇ **192** 16:00	새로운 기술에 대한 소그룹 체험 및 웟즈 몬드 직접으로 답변
◇ **193** 17:00	폐회 연설(사무엘 뱅크스, 감사 협회 회장)

피드백 양식

성명: 힐러리 스펜서

어느 시간이 가장 유익하다고 생각하셨습니까? 그 이유가 무엇입니까?

193 아이젠버그 씨의 발표가 가장 유익했었습니다. 그의 소프트웨어는 매우 혁신적이었고, 이 상품은 실제의 업무 환경을 개선했습니다. 또한, 발표자가 그 프로그램을 사용법을 자세한 예시와 함께 제시한 것은 유용하고 인상 깊었습니다.

총회를 어떻게 개선할 수 있을까요?

제 생각에 그룹 활동 시간이 너무 짧았던 것 같습니다. 새롭게 소개된 상품에 대해 체험하고 토론할 수 있는 충분한 시간이 있었으면 좋았을 것 같습니다.

수신: 촛스 아이젠버그 <charles@hotmail.com>
발신: 힐러리 스펜서 <HS@hotmail.com>
날짜: 7월 15일
제목: 회계 감사 소프트웨어

아이젠버그 씨에게,

제10회 국내 회계 감사 공개 토론 총회에서 귀하의 발표는 매우 인상 깊었습니다.

저는 귀하의 소프트웨어를 우리 회사 중역에게 소개했습니다. 그들은 귀하의 회계 감사 소프트웨어에 큰 관심을 보였으며 귀하에게 연락해 보라고 요청하였습니다.

194 그래서 저는 추후의 사업을 논의하기 위한 회의 일정을 잡고 싶습니다. **195** 귀하가 편한 시간을 알려 주세요. 저는 귀하로부터 곧 답변을 듣길 기대합니다.

진심으로,
힐러리 스펜서
린더의 회계 감사 위원

어휘 national 국내의 auditing 회계 감사 forum 공개 토론회 convention 총회 president 회장 association 협회 enhance 강화하다 regulation 규정 innovative 혁신적인 actual 실제의 impressive 인상 깊은 in detail 자세하게 executive 중역 matter 사안 convenient 편안한 commissioner 위원 위원

191 공지의 목적은 무엇인가?
(A) 연설자의 프로필을 알리기 위해서
(B) 손님에게 메뉴를 알리기 위해서
(C) 자세한 일정을 알리기 위해서
(D) 행사에 사람들을 초대하기 위해서
해설 지문 전체에 회계 감사 장기 총회에 대한 상세한 일정이 나와 있으므로 정답은 (C)이다.

[196-200]

4월 27일
안녕시 샌도우
WV 운송사
태평양 87번가
햇필드, 웨스트버지니아 08065
샌도우 씨께,

196 저는 햇필드 조합에 광고된 프로그래머 직책에 지원하고 싶습니다. 이 편지에 동봉된 저의 이력서와 4명의 추천인과 그들의 추천서를 확인할 수 있을 것입니다.

이 목록에 기재된 직무는 매우 흥미로우며, 저의 강력한 배경과 교육을 통해 제가 분명히 경쟁력 있는 지원자라고 생각합니다. 이 직책에 제가 가진 가장 큰 강점은 애플리케이션을 성공적으로 설계, 개발 및 지원해 왔다는 점입니다. 제 이력서에 명시된 것처럼, 저는 웨스트버지니아 대학의 컴퓨터 프로그래밍 학사 학위를 가지고 있습니다. 또한, 저는 소프트웨어 개발 프로젝트의 라이프 사이클을 완벽히 이해하고 있습니다. 저는 신기술 습득과 개발에 4년간의 경험이 있습니다.

이메일 pc@email.com과 214-555-9842번의 휴대전화로 언제든 저에게 연락하실 수 있습니다. 시간을 내서 고려해 주셔서 감사합니다.

진심으로
펩 컨트럴

300 입에 드라이브
찰스턴, 웨스트버지니아 08642

안녕시 샌도우	**오전 10:05**
안녕하세요, 피트 씨. 컨트럴 씨의 이력서를 검토해 보셨어요? 그에게 대해 저희에게 간단히 설명해 주시겠어요?	
마이클 피트	**오전 10:06**
물론이죠. 제 생각에 그는 적합한 지원자일 것 같습니다. 그의 이력서에 여러 정보가 빠져 있어요.	
안녕시 샌도우	**오전 10:07**
어떤 것이요?	
마이클 피트	**오전 10:09**
197 그에 대해 확장해 1년 반 정도의 경력이 없었어요. 당신이 원하신다면 그의 추천인에게 연락하여 확인해 보세요.	
안녕시 샌도우	**오전 10:10**
좋은 생각이네요. 감사합니다.	

192 공지에 따르면, 16시 50분에 일어난 일은 무엇인가?
(A) 참여자가 질문을 했다.
(B) 간단한 간식이 전달되었다.
(C) 새로운 소프트웨어에 관한 발표가 있었다.
(D) 참가자는 폐막 연설을 들었다.
해설 첫 지문에 드러난 16시의 일정을 보면 소그룹 체험과 질의응답 시간이 연결되어 있고, 그 이후의 마지막 순서는 17시에 폐막 연설이 진행된다. 그러므로 16시 50분경에는 질의응답이 이루어졌으므로 정답은 (A)이다.

193 스펜서 씨의 마음에 들었던 연설자는 누구인가?
(A) 감사 협회 회장
(B) 테크론사의 판매부장
(C) 하이테크사의 마케팅 관리자
(D) 린더의 회계 감사 위원
해설 두 번째 지문에서 스펜서 씨는 아이젠버그 씨의 발표를 가장 유익하다고 평가했다. 이 아이젠버그 씨의 직함은 첫 지문의 일정에 테크론사의 판매부장으로 나와 있으므로 이를 종합하면 정답은 (B)이다.

194 이메일을 보낸 이유는 무엇인가?
(A) 견본을 요청하기 위해서
(B) 또 다른 발표를 준비하기 위해서
(C) 회의를 요청하기 위해서
(D) 회사의 위치에 대해 한 사람에게 일러기 위해서
해설 세 번째 지문 중반에 아이젠버그 씨와 논의를 위해 회의 일정을 잡고 싶다고 말하고 있으므로 정답은 (C)이다.

195 힐러리 스펜서는 촛스 아이젠버그에게 그가 언제 시간이 되는지 알려 주는 것은?
(A) 그녀에게 그가 언제 시간이 되는지 알려 주는 것
(B) 그의 사무실을 방문하는 새로운 장치를 설치하는 것
(C) 그의 중역들을 위한 프로젝트 제안서를 준비하는 것
(D) 회계 감사에 관한 활동 연구를 위한 계좌를 수립하는 것
해설 세 번째 지문 후반에 회의하기 편한 시간을 알려 달라고 요청하고 있으므로 정답은 (A)이다.

수신: 팸 컨트렐 (pc@email.com)
발신: 앤서니 샌드우 (Anthony@wvtransport.com)
날짜: 5월 25일
제목: 귀하의 지원에 관하여

컨트렐 씨에게,

우선, 귀하의 편지에 대한 답변이 늦어서 죄송합니다. [198]저는 사우스캐롤라이나의 나의 긴급한 사업 문제 때문에 3주 동안 출장을 가 있었습니다. 그리고 햄릿을 오고오자마자, 우리는 근무일 5일 동안 계속되는 [197]경영진 세미나가 있었습니다. 그러나 귀하에게 관심이 없었다고 [197]오해하진 않길 바랍니다.

저는 귀하의 이력서를 신중히 검토하였는데, 몇 가지 의문점이 있습니다. 우선 웨스트버지니아 대학 재학 중 평균 학점을 기재하지 않았더군요. 우리는 적어도 평균 점수 3.5(4.0 만점)를 취득한 졸업생이 아니면 고용하지 않습니다. 둘째, 졸업과 첫 직장 이후에 18개월의 공백이 있는 것으로 보입니다. 그 시기에 무엇을 하셨나요?

제 동료가 귀하의 4명의 추천인에게 모두 연락을 시도했었지만, 그중 3명(산세티어와 엔더슨, 퍼킨스)은 연락이 되지 않았습니다. [199]4번째 사람인 로날드 존스는 귀하가 또 다른 직장으로 이직하기 전 2일 동안만 자신의 회사에 있었다고 말했습니다. [200]솔직히 말해서, 이러한 상황을 그리 바람직하지 않습니다. 이에도 귀하께서 이 다음 문제에 관해 설명을 할 수 있어야 할 것입니다. 저는 그래도 기회를 가까이 제공하겠습니다. 6월 2일 화요일 오후 3시에 저의 사무실로 연락하러 오세요.

진심으로
앤서니 샌드우

어휘 enclosed 동봉된 reference 추천인 recommendation 추천서 listing 목록 competitive 경쟁력 있는 primary 주요한 a variety of 다양한 reach 연락이 닿다 brief 간단하게 주다 말하는 suitable 적합한 applicant 지원자 university 대학 credit 대한 학점 disclose 밝히다 apologize 사과하다 delay 지연 business day 영업일, 영업일 misconstrue 오해하다 on the contrary 오히려 grade point 학점 GPA 평균 점수 attempt 시도하는 frankly speaking 솔직히 말해 encouraging 장려하는 dubious 미심쩍어 하는

196 컨트렐 씨가 지원한 직책은 무엇인가?
(A) 컴퓨터 프로그래머
(B) 비서
(C) 고객 서비스 직원
(D) 인사부서의 비서

해설 첫 지문 초반에 컨트렐 씨는 프로그래머의 직책에 지원하고 싶다고 밝히고 있다. 따라서 정답은 (A)이다.

197 이메일에서 첫 번째 지문의 단락 세 번째 줄의 "misconstrue"와 의미상 가장 가까운 것은 무엇인가?
(A) 비난하다
(B) 유지하다
(C) 기민하다
(D) 오해하다

198 샌드우 씨가 컨트렐 씨에게 답장하는 데 한 달 가까이 걸린 이유는 무엇인가?
(A) 그녀의 지원서가 그의 책상에서 없어졌었다.
(B) 그는 가족의 긴급한 일을 처리해야만 했다.
(C) **그는 다른 급한 용무가 있었다.**
(D) 그는 다른 지원자를 인터뷰하였다.

해설 첫 번째 지문 샌드우 씨는 급한 사업무 용무를 처리하기 위해 3주 동안 출장 가 있었고 근무일 5일 동안 계속될 경영진 세미나가 있었다고 말하므로 정답은 (C)이다.

199 피트 씨는 컨트렐 씨에 대한 정보를 누구로부터 들었는가?
(A) 조지 앤더슨
(B) 아놀린 브라운
(C) 이블린 퍼킨스
(D) **로날드 존스**

해설 두 번째 지문에서 피트 씨가 컨트렐 씨의 추천인에게 연락해 보겠다고 했고 세 번째 지문에서 샌드우 씨가 자신의 동료가 추천인에게 연락해 봤지만 로날드 존스 씨만 연락이 되었다고 했다. 로날드 존스 씨는 컨트렐 씨에 대해 불리한 정보를 제공한 것을 알 수 있으므로 정답은 (D)이다.

200 샌드우 씨에 대해서 언급된 것은 무엇인가?
(A) 컨트렐 씨에 추천인으로부터 빠르게 정보를 전해 들었다.
(B) 어떤 상황에서도 컨트렐 씨에게 세를 고용하지 않을 것이다.
(C) **미심쩍어 하지만 컨트렐 씨에게 기회를 주려고 한다.**
(D) 컨트렐 씨가 좋은 지원자라고 생각하지만 다른 사람을 고용할 것이다.

해설 세 번째 지문 마지막에 샌드우 씨는 컨트렐 씨의 지원서에 누락된 정보가 있는 것은 바람직스럽지는 않지만 충분히 설명할 기회를 주겠다며 연결을 요청하고 있다. 따라서 정답은 (C)이다.

Actual Test

05

저자 이미영

다음 카페(http://cafe.daum.net/speedytoeic)
» [나토토 1:1 코칭] 게시판 이용

본책 P.102

📁 **Reading Comprehension**

PART 7

147 (C)	148 (A)	149 (C)	150 (D)	151 (D)	152 (A)	153 (D)	154 (D)	155 (B)
156 (B)	157 (C)	158 (A)	159 (B)	160 (D)	161 (D)	162 (B)	163 (A)	164 (C)
165 (C)	166 (B)	167 (A)	168 (A)	169 (C)	170 (C)	171 (A)	172 (C)	173 (A)
174 (B)	175 (A)	176 (C)	177 (D)	178 (B)	179 (D)	180 (C)	181 (C)	182 (D)
183 (B)	184 (B)	185 (B)	186 (B)	187 (B)	188 (D)	189 (D)	190 (C)	191 (D)
192 (B)	193 (D)	194 (D)	195 (C)	196 (B)	197 (C)	198 (A)	199 (A)	200 (D)

[147-148]

http://www.speedyon.com

스피디 오피스 온라인

홈	사무 장비	종이 용품	잉크와 토너	도움말

제품 가격 업데이트

알려 드립니다! 그 이후에나 그 이전에 주문하시는 모든 주문품에 대하여 다음과 같은 가격 변동이 있을 것입니다. 저희 오랜 공급 업체 중 한 곳이 폐업해서 이 2017년 12월 16일이나 그 이후에 적용될 것입니다. 저희 오랜 공급 업체 중 한 곳이 폐업해서 이 번 가격 변동은 불가피했습니다. 아래 목록에 열거된 제품만 가격이 인상됩니다. 따라서 이 목록에 포함되어 있지 않은 제품들은 이전처럼 저렴한 가격으로 구매하실 수 있으며, **147** 저렴한 저희 배송 요금에는 변동 사항이 없습니다.

물품	인상 전 가격	신규 가격
A4 복사 용지 (낱장)	25달러 50센트/상자당	28달러/상자당
146 팩스 용지 (두루마리)*	16달러/상자당	36달러/상자당
팩스 토너 카트리지	85달러/개당	99달러/개당
볼펜	2달러 50센트/packet당	3달러/packet당
일반 사무 봉투	29달러/상자당	32달러 50센트/상자당

*두루마리 6개짜리 상자 포장만이 팩스 용지는 더 이상 판매되지 않습니다. 모든 상자에는 두루마리 12개가 들어 있습니다. 만약 문의 사항이나 우려 사항이 있으시면, 언제든지 저희에게 연락해 주세요.

어휘 equipment 장비 pricing 가격 책정 effective 시행되는 place an order 주문하다 unavoidable 불가피한 go out of business 폐업하다 pertain to ~에 관련된 affordable 저렴한, 구입할 만한 delivery fee 배송 요금 carton 상자 roll 두루마리 plain 보통의, 평범한 contact 연락하다 undergo 겪다 affect ~에게 영향을 주다 outsource (업무를) 외주에 위탁하다, 절단 double 두 배가 되다

147 회사의 배송 서비스에 관해 언급된 것은 무엇인가?
(A) 더 이상 제공되지 않는다.
(B) 요금이 인상되었다.
(C) 가격 변동의 영향을 받지 않는다.
(D) 다른 회사로 외주를 주었다.

해설 delivery와 관련된 내용을 보면, 저렴한 배송 요금에는 변동 사항이 없다고 했으므로 정답은 (C)가 된다. (B)는 일부 제품 가격이 인상된 것이지, 배송비가 인상된 것은 아니므로 오답이다.

148 웹페이지에서 팩스 용지에 대해 알 수 있는 것은 무엇인가?
(A) 상자당 가격이 두 배 이상 올랐다.
(B) 스피디 오피스 온라인에서 더 이상 판매되지 않는다.
(C) 낱장이나 두루마리로 구매할 수 있다.
(D) 현재 두루마리 6개짜리 상자 포장된 것으로 구매할 수 있다.

해설 두루마리 6개짜리 상자 포장만이 팩스 용지는 더 이상 판매되지 않는다. 36달러로 인상되었으므로 정답은 (A)이다. (A)는

[149-151]

수신: 올리버 이오 (oyao@redhouse.com)
발신: 줄리아 우든 (jwooden@redhouse.com)
날짜: 2월 2일
제목: 모니터

안녕하세요, 올리버.

IT부 줄리아입니다. 저희는 월요일에 27인치 새 데스크톱 모니터를 배송받았는데, 사정상께서 현재 사용하고 있는 23인치 모니터를 전부 교체하라고 지시하셨습니다. 당신의 IT부에서 연구개발팀의 탐과이나, 오늘 해 주실 필요는 없지만, 금요일까지 의 **149** 기회가 있을 때 당신 팀에게 신속한 조사를 해 주시기를 부탁드립니다. 더 작은 모니터를 사용하고 있는 사람은 누구이며, 그들이 더 큰 모니터를 원하는지도 알려 주십시오. 그리고 저장 **151** 할 필요 없습니다 — **150** 팀 일정에 방해가 되지 않게 하려고, 제하도 주말까지 모니터를 교체하지 않을 것입니다. 곧 답변 주시기를 기다리겠습니다.

줄리아

어휘 shipment 배송(품) instruct A to do A에게 ~하도록 지시하다 replace 교체하다 currently 현재 in use 사용되는 head 부장 survey (설문) 조사 whether or not ~인지 아닌지 prevent 막다, 예방하다 disruption 방해 coworker 직장 동료 apologize for ~에 대해 사과하다 interfere with ~을 방해하다 outdated 오래된

149 이메일의 목적은 무엇인가?
(A) 사무기기를 주문하려고
(B) 고객에게 배송 지연에 대해 알리려고
(C) 동료에게 정보를 요청하려고
(D) 일정 변경에 대해 사과하려고

해설 편지 수신자에게 신속한 조사를 해 주기를 요청하고 있다. 따라서 정답은 (C)이다. (A)는 두 번째 문장에서 모니터는 이미 주문을 해서 배송받은 상황임을 알 수 있으므로 오답이다.

150 IT 팀이 새 모니터를 주말까지 설치하지 않는 이유는 무엇인가?
(A) 일정이 꽉 찼다.
(B) 모니터 배송이 지연되었다.
(C) 사장이 교체를 승인해 주어야 한다.
(D) 업무를 방해하지 않기 원한다.

해설 '팀 일정에 방해가 되지 않도록 주말까지는 모니터를 교체하지 않을 것이라고 했으므로 정답은 (D)이다. 지문의 disruption of team schedule을 선택지에서는 interfere with work라고 패러프레이징 했다.

---

151 이오 씨는 이 이메일을 받은 후에 무슨 일을 할 것인가?
(A) 몇몇 오래된 컴퓨터를 교체한다.
(B) 사장에게 컴퓨터 문제에 대해 설명한다.
(C) 27인치 컴퓨터 모니터를 주문한다.
(D) 자신의 팀에 있는 직원들에게 질문한다.

해설 줄리아는 이오 씨에게 팀원 중의 더 작은 모니터를 쓰고 있는 사람은 누구인지에 대해 조사해 달라고 요청했다. 따라서 정답은 (D)이다.

[152-153]

제17회 연례 윤리 저널리즘 총회

6월 3일 토요일 - 연설자 일정

주 강당	A실	B실
오전 11시 ~ 오후 1시 젠 캐링턴, 사장, 윤리 저널리즘 협회	예정된 행사 없음	예정된 행사 없음
협회 개회사와 환영 활동		
점심 휴식	점심 휴식	점심 휴식
오후 2시 ~ 3시 알리스 믹스, 기자, 뉴욕 타임	오후 2시 ~ 3시 은진 김, 저널리즘 교수, 펜실베이니아 대학	오후 2시 ~ 3시 **152** 젠 캐링턴 사장, 윤리 저널리즘 협회 공개 토론회
153 전영 사진: 책임감 있는 포토저널리즘	**153** 교실에서의 저널리 즘: 다음 세대 교육하기	
오후 3시 ~ 4시 프랭크 오라일리, 최고 경영자, 우니 뉴스사 무료 뉴스: 인터넷으로부 터 신문 보호하기	오후 3시 ~ 4시 개런 수아레스, 수석 편 집자, 몬트리올 프레스 **153** 정치적 위험: 뉴스 에서 편견을 갖지 않기	예정된 행사 없음

어휘 annual 연례의 ethical 윤리적인 journalism 저널리즘, 신문 잡 지 conference 총회, 협의 remark 발언, 말 responsible 책임감 있는 organization 조직, 협회 opening photojournalism 보도 사진 educate 교육하다 generation 세대 open forum 공개 토론회 protect 보호하다 peril 위험 bias 편견 free discussion 자유 토론 neutral 중립의 battlefield 전쟁터

152 누가 자유 토론 행사를 진행할 것인가?
(A) 젠 캐링턴
(B) 알리스 믹스
(C) 프랭크 오라일리
(D) 유진 김

해설 질문의 free discussion(자유 토론)은 지문의 open forum(공개 토론회)과 같은 표현으로 볼 수 있다. 따라서 이 행사의 진행자는 (A) 젠 캐링턴임을 알 수 있다.

153 총회에서 강의 주제로 언급되지 않은 것은 무엇인가?

(A) 학생들에게 자발심을 기르도록 하기
(B) 정치 문제에 대해 중립을 유지하기
(C) 전쟁터에서 사진 찍기
(D) 온라인 신문 홍보하기

해설 총회에 여러 가지 주제가 등장한다. 교실에서의 자발심, 정치적 위험을 뉴스에서 편견을 갖지 않기가 등장하였으므로 (A). (B)는 모두 강의에 표현이 주제이다. (C) 또한 전쟁 위험 사진: 책임이 있는 보도 사진이라는 표현이 지문에서 나오므로 모임이다. 따라서 언급되지 않은 정답은 (D)가 된다.

154 오후 2시 04분에, 스미스 씨가 "제가 이유를 알아봐야겠어요"라고 쓴 의미는 무엇인가?

(A) 그녀는 실수에 대한 책임을 질 것이다.
(B) 그녀는 그녀가 직업을 잃을 거라고 걱정한다.
(C) 그녀는 일을 더 좋게 만들려고 열심히 일한다.
(D) 그녀는 문제의 원인을 밝힐 것이다.

해설 get to the bottom of는 ~의 원인을 밝히다, 진상을 규명하다란 뜻이 숙어 표현이다. 또한 문맥상 해당 문장 뒤의 내용을 읽어보면 택배 회사에 전화해서 답변을 들어보겠다고 했으므로 정답은 (D)이다.

155 배달 지연의 원인으로 나타난 것은 무엇인가?

(A) 고장 난 팩스 기계
(B) 정지된 자동차
(C) 잘못된 주소
(D) 못 받은 전화

해설 오후 2시 15분 대화에서, 배달 트럭이 고장이 났다는 것 같다고 했다. 따라서 정답은 (B)이다. truck이나 broke down을 선택지에서는 vehicle이나 stalled(정지된)으로 각각 패러프레이징되었다.

[154-155]

[156-157]

패터슨 고등학교는 4월 3일 토요일에 학교의 연속 체육관에서 연례 직업의 날을 개최할 예정입니다. 졸업반 학생들은 이 행사에 의무적으로 참석해야 하며, 우리 졸업 예정자들이 현명하게 직업 선택하도록 안내하는 것을 목표로 하고 있습니다. 매번 행사의 일부로 패터슨 고등학교는 학생들의 부모님들이 자발적으로 자신들의 경력에 관한 짧은 강연을 해 주십니다. 만약 자원 학생들과 시간을 가지며 전문적인 직업 자신을 함께 공유하고 싶으시다면 학교의 직업 상담가인 킴 그레이슨에게 kgrayson@phs.ok.edu로 간단한 이메일을 보내 주세요. 여러분의 직업에 관한 간단한 설명과 낮에 지원을 드릴 수 있는 전화번호도 포함해 주세요. 협조해 주셔서 감사합니다.

어휘 hold 개최[주최]하다 annual 연례의 gymnasium 체육관 mandatory 의무적인 senior 졸업반 학생 graduating student 졸업 예정자 make a choice 선택하다 volunteer 자원하다 share 공유하다 brief 간단한 description 설명 occupation 직업 daytime phone number 낮에 연락받을 수 있는 전화번호 solicit 요청하다 cooperation 협조 협력 간청하다

156 공지문의 목적은 무엇인가?

(A) 졸업반 학생들에게 행사에 참여하도록 권장하려고
(B) 자원자들에게 짧은 연설을 해 달라고 요청하려고
(C) 부모들에게 일정 변경을 알리려고
(D) 학교의 부서 이전을 공고하려고

해설 학부모들에게 하교 행사인 직업의 날에 자발적으로 짧은 강연을 해 달라고 요청하는 공지문이다. 학생들과 전문적인 직업 지식을 함께 공유 할 수 있다며 이메일을 보내라고 했으므로, 이 글의 목적으로는 (B)가 가장 적절하다.

157 이 이메일에 포함되어야 하는 정보는 무엇인가?

(A) 학생 직원 목록에 대한 설명
(B) 행사 참석에 관한 확인
(C) 부모들의 직업에 대한 간단한 요약
(D) 졸업 예정자들의 이름 목록

해설 직업에 관한 간단한 설명과 낮에 연락할 수 있는 전화번호를 포함하는 문장이 마지막 부분에 나온다. 따라서 정답은 (C)이다. 지문의 brief description이 선택지에서는 short summary로, occupation이 profession으로 각각 패러프레이징되었다.

[158-160]

그린 리버 내추럴 시리얼사

로고 디자인 대회
공식 지원서

그린 리버는 새 얼굴이 필요하며, 지원은 새 로고를 디자인하는 데 고객 여러분께서 도와주시기를 요청하려고 합니다. 지원는 다음과 같이 얻을 만기가 필요합니다: "그린 리버 시리얼은 건강에 좋고, 전연 식품이며 정말 맛있습니다!" 지원 이사회에서 최고 디자인 10점을 선정하여 그린 리버 웹 사이트에 게재할 것이며, 저희 고객들이 가장 좋아하는 것에 투표를 하게 될 것입니다. 우승한 로고의 디자이너는 10,000달러의 수표를 받게 될 것이고, 나머지 9명의 입상자는 1년간 맛있는 그린 리버 제품을 받게 될 것입니다.

참가하시려면, 이래의 정보를 기재하신 후, 여러분의 로고 디자인을 제공된 공간에 첨부해 주세요. 로고는 손으로 그리거나 컴퓨터로 정작된 이미지이면 됩니다.

이름	
성명	
주소	

지는 위의 디자인이 저 자신의 창작물이며 현존하는 어떤 저작권도 위반 하지 않았음을 확인합니다. 지는 또한 현재 그린 리버 내추럴 시리얼사 (GRNCC)나 어떤 자회사에서도 근무하고 있지 않으며, 예전에 근무한 적도 없습니다. 또 제 직계 가족들도 역시 그러하다는 것을 확인합니다. 지는 이 대회 예 참가함으로써 GRNCC가 홍보용 자료나 포장에 제 디자인을 사용할 수 있도록 완전히 허락합니다.

이름 (인쇄체로 또박 쓰시오)	
서명	
날짜	

어휘 submission 제출 turn to ~에 의지하다 board of directors 이사회 post 게시하다 vote 투표하다 check 수표 runner-up (1위 외의) 입상자 supply 공급 fill in ~을 기입하다. 작성하다 attach 첨부하다 provide 공급하다 hand-drawn 손으로 그린 certify 확인[보증]하다 violate 위 반하다, 어기다 existing 현존하는, 현재의 copyright 저작권 further 게 다가, 더구나 subsidiary 자회사 immediate family member 직계 가 족 grant 승인하다, 허락 permission 허가, 허락 promotional 홍보의, 판촉의 packaging 포장 random drawing 제비뽑기 entrant 참가자

어휘 hard copy 인쇄 출력물 contract 계약서 courier 택배(사) guarantee 보장하다 drop off ~을 갖다 놓다[내려주다] get to the bottom of ~ 의 원인을 밝혀내다, 진상을 규명하다 apparently 분명 이, 외관상 pick up ~을 찾으러다 parcel 소포 fax 팩스를 보내다 go over ~을 검토하다 stalled 정지된

[오후 1:52]
매디슨 오노
거의 오후 2시가 다 되어 가는데, 계약서 인쇄 출력물들이 아직 도착하지 않았네요.

[오후 1:56]
에밀리 스미스
정말이에요? 택배 회사에서 오늘 정오까지 배달될 거라고 장담했어요.

[오후 2:03]
매디슨 오노
제가 프런트 데스크에 방금 다시 확인해 봤어요. 모든 접물 가기에 가져다 놓거나, 아무것도 들어오지 않았어요.

[오후 2:04]
에밀리 스미스
제가 이유를 알아봐야겠어요. 택배 회사에 전화해서 답변은 듣는 동안 기다려 주세요.

[오후 2:15]
에밀리 스미스
문제가 있어요, 듣자 하니 그들의 배달 트럭이 고장이 난 것 같아요. 그들이 소포를 가지러 기기 위해 다른 트럭을 보내셨지만, 한 시간 후에나 계약서가 당신에게 도착할 것이라고 하네요.

[오후 2:18]
매디슨 오노
반기운 소식은 아니네요. 라이트먼사의 동업자들은 계약서에 서명하기 위해 15분 후 여기에 올 거예요.

[오후 2:19]
에밀리 스미스
제가 당신한테 당장 사본을 팩스로 보내드릴 수 있어요. 라이트먼 사람들에 게 먼저 사본을 검토하라고 하죠. 그럼이 확인으면 원본이 도착할 거예요.

[오후 2:21]
매디슨 오노
그러면 될 것 같아요.

[161-163]

발신자	내용
리치 쿠마 [오전 11:01]	영업직 공석에 대한 면접은 어떻게 되어가고 있나요?
앨리슨 에이지 [오전 11:02]	사실, 저스틴이 그것들을 처리하고 있어요. 쿠마 씨, 제가 이력서를 걸러서 최고의 후보들을 찾았어요, 제가 저스틴에게 다섯 정을 잡고 진행하도록 맡겼죠.
리치 쿠마 [오전 11:04]	알겠어요, 저스틴, 거기 있나요?
저스틴 패널 [오전 11:07]	네, 있어요, 그렇지만 ⑯① 저는 면접 일정을 잡는 것을 아직 해결하지 못했어요, 제가 지금 너무 할 일이 많아서요.
앨리슨 에이지 [오전 11:08]	정말이에요, 저스틴? 저는 그 면접들이 지금 쯤 진행 중일 거라고 예상했어요.
리치 쿠마 [오전 11:09]	솔직히, ⑯② 저는 채용 관리자는 당신이라고 생각해요, 알레슨. 제품을 관리하는 당신이잖아요. 이런 면접은 당신의 책임이에요.
앨리슨 에이지 [오전 11:11]	맞습니다, 쿠마 씨, 제가 그 일을 맡기는 것을 더 잘 해야 했습니다.
리치 쿠마 [오전 11:13]	걱정하지 마세요, 아직 시간은 충분해요. 그렇지만 ⑯③ 누군가는 그 면접 일정을 가능한 한 빨리 잡아야 해요.
저스틴 패널 [오전 11:14]	⑯③ 제가 오늘 오후에 할 수 있어요. 그렇지만 이제 당신이 다른 누군가에게 실제 면접을 진행하도록 해야 할 거예요.
앨리슨 에이지 [오전 11:15]	좋아요, 그냥 저한테 오늘 끝날 때까지 일정을 잡아 주세요, 거기서부터 제가 그것을 처리할게요.

어휘 handle 처리하다 screen (적정)전자, 거르다, 가려내다 identify 찾다, 발견하다 candidate 후보자 conduct an interview 면접을 하다 get too much on my plate 너무 많은 일을 맡다 underway 진행 중인 by now 지금쯤 supervisor 상관, 상사 responsibility 책임, 책무 delegate (업무 등을) 위임하다 plenty of 많은 get 시키다 take care of ~을 처리하다 drop the ball 실수하다 help-wanted ad 구인 광고

158 로고를 선정하는 과정이 한 부분으로 제시된 것은 무엇인가?
(A) 온라인 투표
(B) 공개 토론회
(C) 채택뽑기
(D) 라이브 프레젠테이션
해설 최고 디자인 10개를 선발하여 웹 사이트에 게재할 것이며, 거기서 고객들이 가장 마음에 드는 디자인에 투표할 수 있게 된다고 했다. 따라서 정답은 (A)이다.

159 대화 참가자들이 반드시 확인해야 하는 것이 아닌 것은 무엇인가?
(A) 다른 사람의 작품을 모방하지 않았다.
(B) 다른 사람들의 도움 없이 로고를 디자인했다.
(C) GRNCC에서 근무한 적이 한 번도 없다.
(D) 회사에서 자신의 디자인을 사용할 수 있도록 허락한다.
해설 이탈릭체로 표시된 부분에 단서가 나열돼 있다. 위의 디자인이 자신의 창작물이며 원본이어야 하며 어떤 저작권도 위반하지 않았는지 확인한다고 했으며, 현재 그린 리뷰 내부용 시립새(GRNCC)나 어떤 자회사에서도 근무하고 있지 않으며, 예전에도 근무한 적도 없어야 한다. 마지막으로 GRNCC가 홍보용 자료나 포장에 디자인을 사용할 수 있도록 허락한다고 했으므로, 언급되지 않은 (B)가 정답이다.

160 대화 우승자는 무엇을 받을 것인가?
(A) 그린 리뷰 공장 견학
(B) 12개월 동안 무료 제품 받기
(C) 이사회 자리
(D) 특정 금액의 상금
해설 로고 대회 우승자가 받게 될 상품을 설명한 부분을 보면, 우승한 로고 디자이너는 10,000달러의 수표를 받을 거라고 했다. 따라서 정답은 (D)이다. (B)의 경우 우승자를 제외한 나머지 9명의 입상자가 1년간 맛 있는 그린 리뷰 제품을 무료로 받게 될 것이라고 했으므로, 정답으로 혼동하지 않도록 유의하자.

161 패널 씨가 면접 일정을 잡지 않은 이유는 무엇인가?
(A) 지원자들을 면접할 자격이 되지 않아서
(B) 면접 일정을 잡도록 요청받지 않아서
(C) 지원자들이 자격 요건을 갖추지 않았다고 생각하지 않아서
(D) 다른 일들로 인해 너무 바빠서
해설 면접 일정을 잡지 못한 이유는 지금 할 일이 너무 많기 때문이라고 말하고 있으므로 정답은 (D)이다. too much on one's plate는 '너무 많은 일이 많다'라는 뜻이다.

162 오전 11시 09분에 쿠마 씨가 "저는 그 문제는 당신이라고 생각해요"라고 쓴 의미는 무엇인가?
(A) 그는 에이지 씨가 해당 직업을 걱정한다.
(B) 그는 그 문제가 에이지 씨의 실수라고 느낀다.
(C) 그는 에이지 씨가 진급을 얻었다고 믿는다.
(D) 그는 에이지 씨가 해결책을 찾았다고 생각한다.
해설 해당 대화 바로 앞의 오전 11시 08분 대화에서 에이지 씨가 저스틴에게 이 면접 일정을 잡아놓았을 줄 알았다고 말하자, 이에 쿠마 씨가 면접 일정은 본인이 채용자가 될 일이라면서 당신은 잘못은 에이지 씨에게 있다는 의미로 이해될 수 있다. 따라서 정답은 (B)이다. drop the ball은 '일을 망치다'라는 뜻이다.

163 패널 씨가 다음에 할 일은 무엇인가?
(A) 가장 자격 요건을 갖춘 지원자들에게 연락하기
(B) 앞으로 있을 면접 일정 다시 잡기
(C) 제출된 이력서들을 검토하기
(D) 새로운 구인광고 내기
해설 11시 13분 대화에서 면접 일정을 가능한 한 빨리 잡아야 한다는 말에, 11시 14분 패널이 자신이 오늘 오후에 할 수 있다고 하였으므로 정답은 (A)이다.

[164-167]

우리와 함께 하시겠어요?

과거에 20kg 이상을 감량한 경험이 있는 18세에서 36세 사이의 여성이신가요? - [1] -. 그렇다면 터코마 대학교의 건강 영양센터에서 진행하는 유료 연구에 참여하실 자격을 갖추신 것인지도 모릅니다. 반드시 건강한 상태여야 하고 ⑯④ 광역 터코마 지역 내에서 거주하고 있어야 하며, 하루에 대략 30분을 연구에 시간을 들여야 하는데, 이는 총 4개월간 지속될 것입니다. 이는 주 단위로 하는데, ⑯⑤ 매일 섭취한 음식을 기록해야 하고, 주 단위로 제출의 변화를 기록하셔야 합니다. - [2] -. ⑯⑤ 매일 섭취한 음식을 기록해야 하고, 주 단위로 제출의 변화를 기록하셔야 합니다. - [3] -.

⑯⑥ 참가자들은 연구 기간 내내 주당 35달러를 받을 수 있고 총 4개월간의 프로그램을 성공적으로 완수하게 되면 250달러를 보너스로 받게도 받게 될 것입니다. ⑯⑦ 참여 가능한 지원자들은 일요일부터 금요일 오전 10시부터 오후 4시 사이에 건강 영양센터의 주 행정실을 방문해 주세요 - [4] -.

⑯⑧ **어휘** qualified 자격이 있는 take part in ~에 참여하다 paid 유료의 devote A to B A를 B에 헌신[전념]하다 approximately 대략 a total of 전부 ~ responsibility 책임 책무 intake 섭취 record 기록하다 on a weekly basis 주 단위로 participant 참가자 completion 완료, 완성 entire 전체의 prospective 미래의, 가망이 있는 applicant 지원자 administrative office 행정실 compensation 보상 party 사람, 단체, 일행 fill out ~을 작성하다, 기재하다 in person 직접, 몸소

164 연구에 참여할 수 있는 요구 조건으로 언급되지 않은 것은 무엇인가?
(A) 여성이어야 함
(B) 특정 지역에서 살아야 함
(C) 특정 몸무게가 나가야 함
(D) 특정 연령 범위에 들어야 함

[168-171]

초과 근무

168 168 최근 신입 사원 중에서 초과 근무 보고에 관한 적절한 관련한 여 중에서 좀 있었는 것을 알게 되었습니다. 모든 초과 근무는 우선 반드시 여러 분의 직속상관이나 부서장의 승인을 받아야 합니다. 초과 근무를 할 때는 그 다 나서 여러분들이 승인받은 초과 근무의 총 근무 시간은 공식 초과 근무 보고 양식에 한 달에 두 번 기록되어야 합니다. **171** 이 양식은 이제 인사팀 사무실에 없습니다. 반드시 회사의 웹 사이트에서 출력해야 합니다. 이 양식이 제출 기간은 매월 14일과 28일 되는 전까지입니다. 일단 이 양식들은 여러분 상 관이 수리해서 급여 지급 부서에게 처리되면. (초과 근무 수당이) 다음 달 급여에 포함되어 지급될 것입니다. 문의 사항이 있으면 인사팀으로 연락 주세요. 감사합니다.

어휘 it has come to one's attention that ~라는 것을 알게 되다 confusion 혼란, 혼동 regarding ~에 관 hire (회사의) 신입 사원 either A or B A 또는 B 하나 immediate supervisor 직속상 관 no longer 더 이상 ~하지 않다 due 예정인 close of business 업무 종 료 payroll department 급여 지급 부서 paycheck 급여, 봉급 clarify 명확하게 하다 procedure 절차 policy 정책, 방침 job opening 공석

166 참가자들에 대한 보상으로 언급된 것은 무엇인가?
(A) 임금
(B) 주급
(C) 월별 보너스
(D) 여유

해설 참가자들은 연구 기간 중, This는 온라인으로 함수 있어야 한다. This 는 문제상 [3] 앞에서 성취 염량을 매일 기록하고 제중 변화를 매주 기록해야 하는 것을 가리키는 것이 가장 자연스러우므로 (C)가 정답이다. 또 [3] 뒤의 문장에서 주당 지급받아 언급되어 있으므로 답에 앞에 한 달에 두 번 반문하면 언급되는 내용과 자연스럽게 이어진다.

167 관심 있는 사람들은 연구에 참여하려면 어떻게 지원해야 하는가?
(A) 직접 센터에 가서
(B) 센터의 웹 사이트를 방문해서
(C) 센터에 이메일을 보내서
(D) 신청서를 기재해서

해설 지원 마지막 문장에서 관심 있는 지원자는 건강 영양센터의 주 행정 실을 방문하라고 했으므로 정답은 (A)가 된다. in person은 '직접'이라 는 뜻으로 지문의 visit과 의미가 통한다.

[168-171]

165 [1]. [2]. [3]. [4]로 표시된 곳 중, 다음 문장이 위치로 가장 적절한 곳은 어디인 가?

"이것은 온라인으로 할 수 있지만 건강 영양센터로 한 달에 두 번 전화해 야 합니다."

(A) [1]
(B) [2]
(C) [3]
(D) [4]

해설 연구에 참여할 수 있는 대상자의 조건으로 18세와 36세 사이의 여성 이어야 하고, 공역 티코더 지역 내에서 거주해야 한다고 했다. 따라서 연금대지 낳은 공역을 보고 (C)가 정답이다. 지문에서 '과거에 20kg 이상을 감량한 사람'이라는 낳은 내용을 보고 (D)와 혼동해서는 안 된다. weight는 '무게'가 나가다라는 의미로 특정 몸무게가 나가야 한다는 의미이다.

---

171 초과 근무 양식을 얻을 수 있는 곳은 어디인가?
(A) 인터넷에서
(B) 부서장님으로부터
(C) 급여 부서에서
(D) 인사팀 사무실에서

해설 초과 근무 양식은 인사팀 사무실에 없고, 회사의 웹 사이트에서 출력할 수 있다고 했다. 따라서 정답은 (A)이다. 지문의 Web site를 선택지에 서는 Internet으로 패러프레이징했다.

[172-175]

172 해리스빌 시 정부가 영화 촬영을 위원하는 해리슨 재슨 감독이 그의 최신 영화의 몇몇 장면을 시의 경계 내에서 촬영하도록 (승리의 끝)이라는 스튜디오 와 합의했다고 한 세 명의 직 군인들의 이야기를 제로하다. [1] –.

정확한 촬영 장소는 아직 공개되지 않았고, 출연자들의 이름도 아직 공개되지 않았다. 그러나 전직 레슬링 전설인 폴 앵글레톤이 주연을 제안받았다는 소문이 있다. [2] –. **170** 이것은 지역 경기를 활성화하는 수단으로 해리스빌에 거의 6개월에 걸쳐 노 영화 프로젝트를 유치하려는 새로 임명된 영화 위원회의 거의 6개월에 걸쳐 노 력의 완성이다. – [3] –.

지역 시민 단체인 해리스빌 시민 네트워크는 시 도로에서 차 추격 장면을 촬영 하는 것에 대해 공공의 안전을 우려했지만 해리스빌 경찰 대변인은 어릴 제작팀이 수준 엄격한 안전 지침을 준수하도록 **175** 조치들이 취해질 것이라고 대중들이 심사했다. – [4] –.

어휘 commission 위원회 reach an agreement 협의하다 allow A to do A가 ~하도록 허락하다 scene 장면 press release 언론 보도 former 전임의 rob 강도질 하다 exact 정확한 shooting 촬영 release 공개 하다 legend 전설 rumor 소문을 내다 starring role 주연 culmination 완성, 최고조 newly 최근에 appointed 임명된 attract 유인하다, 끌다 means 수단, 조치 boost 끌어올리다 local 지역 civic 시민의 public 공중, 대중 safety 안전 spokesperson 대변인 assure 보장하다, 확신히 하다 take a measure 조치를 하다 strict 엄격 한 observe 준수하다, 지키다 feature 특징으로 하다 celebrity 유명 인 사, 스타

172 이 기사를 작성한 이유는 무엇인가?
(A) 영화 세트장에서 일어난 사고를 설명하려고
(B) 새 영화 위원회의 설립을 발표하려고
(C) 영화 일부가 지역에서 촬영될 것임을 설명하려고
(D) 팬들에게 개봉을 앞둔 영화 감독의 경력에 대해 알려 주려고

해설 기사의 목적은 주로 서두 부분에 제시되는 경우가 많다. 해리스빌 시 정부 위원회가 시의 경계 내에서 촬영할 수 있도록 영화사와 합 의를 보았다는 내용을 설명하고 있다. 따라서 정답은 (C)이다. [D]의 경우 영화 촬영이 지역 경기를 활성화하려는 수단으로 이해했다는 내 용이 나오므로 단순히 유명 감독의 영화를 팬들에게 소개하려는 기사로 으로 볼 수는 없다.

---

168 공지의 목적은 무엇인가?
(A) 절차를 명확히 하려고
(B) 정책 변경을 제안하려고
(C) 초과 근무를 요청하려고
(D) 공석을 발표하려고

해설 공지의 목적은 지문 서두 부분에 등장하는 경우가 많다. 최근 신입 사 원 중에서 초과 근무 보고에 관한 적절한 관련에서 혼동이 좀 있었다고 했으므로 초과 근무 보고와 관련된 절차를 명확히 설명하기 위 한 공지문임을 알 수 있다. 따라서 정답은 (A)이다.

169 공지의 대상은 누구인가?
(A) 부서장들
(B) 회사 고객들
(C) 신입 사원들
(D) 급여 관련 직원들

해설 특히 최근 신입 사원 중에서 초과 근무 관련 절차를 이었다고 했 다. 따라서 정답은 (C)이다. 지문의 recent hires와 훈동이 있다는 (회사의) 신입 사원들을 의미한데, hires를 선택지에서는 new employees 로 패러프레이징했다.

170 초과 근무 양식은 얼마나 자주 접수되는가?
(A) 일주일에 한 번
(B) 매월 (말에만)
(C) 한 달에 두 번
(D) 두 달에 한 번

해설 초과 근무의 기록 단어를 설명하고 있는 부분을 보면, 승인받은 총 초 과 근무 시간은 공식 초과 근무 보고 양식에 한 달에 두 번 기 록되어야 한다고 했다. 따라서 정답은 (C)이다. 지문이 a month로 패러프레이징 한 내용을 선택지에서는 Two times a month로 표현했다. 초과 근무 양식은 인사팀 사무실에 on a twice-monthly basis로 패러프레이징 되었다.

173 [1], [2], [3], [4]로 표시된 곳 중 다음 문장의 위치로 가장 적절한 곳은 어디인가?

"은행 강도 장면과 함께 자동차 추격전과 주연 배우와 경찰 사이의 카페 안에서 싸우는 장면이 해리스빌에서 촬영될 것이다."

(A) [1]
(B) [2]
(C) [3]
(D) [4]

해설 삽입 문장에서 '은행 강도 장면과 함께(Along with the bank robbery scene)'라는 내용이 나오는데, [1] 앞에서 은행 강도 장면과 관련된 설명이 나오고 있다. 따라서 삽입 문장의 가장 자연스러운 위치는 [1]로 정답은 (A)이다.

174 해리스빌에서 영화를 촬영하는 것의 주요 이점으로 제시된 것은 무엇인가?
(A) 지역 기업들을 특집으로 다룰 것이다.
(B) 시가 재정적으로 이익을 얻게 될 것이다.
(C) 시에 관광객들을 유치할 것이다.
(D) 시민들이 유명 인사들을 만날 수 있다.

해설 영화 촬영은 지역의 경기를 활성화하려는 수단이라고 언급되어 있다. 따라서 정답은 (B)이다. (C)는 연상할 수도 있는 부분이지만, 지문에서 관광객(tourists)이라는 부분이 언급된 바 없으므로 오답이다.

175 세 번째 단락 여섯 번째 줄의 measures와 의미상 가장 가까운 것은 무엇인가?
(A) 조치
(B) 제안
(C) 항의
(D) 분석

해설 해당 단어가 들어가 있는 문장의 앞뒤 문맥을 살펴보면, 해리스빌 경찰 대변인인 에릭 제이콥슨이 엄격한 안전 지침을 준수할 수 있도록 '조치(measures)'가 취해질 것이라고 대중을 안심시켰다는 내용이 되어야 자연스럽다. 따라서 정답은 (A)이다.

[176-180]

〈마드리드로의 귀환〉이 발매되었습니다!

블루 호라이즌 출판은 호평받는 작가인 미셸 박의 최신 작품인 〈마드리드로의 귀환〉의 발매를 발표하게 되어서 기쁩니다. 176 실화 작품인 이 책은 박 씨가 언어 교환 학생으로서 거의 20년 전에 처음 방문했던 도시로 돌아오는 이야기를 해 줍니다. 그녀는 자기가 가장 좋아하는 장소를 방문하고 현재 인기 있는 음반 녹음 예술가인 현지 민요 가수를 포함해서 그녀가 학생 시절 동안 알았던 사람들을 만납니다. 책의 많은 부분은 앞으로 있을 앨범에 관한 그의 작업을 자세히 설명합니다. 177 유머와 통찰력으로 쓰인 그 책은 읽는 즐거움이 있습니다. 지역의 라디오 방송국인 WEZD는 178 방송국 매니저가 첫 장(章)을 읽으면서 그 책을 특집으로 할 것입니다. 만약 여러분이 스페인에 관심이 있거나 그냥 일반적으로 좋은 글을 좋아하신다면, 4월 11일 일요일 오전 10시에 오전 DJ 마르셀라 로즈의 프로에 채널을 맞추세요. 그 책은 현재 판매 중이며, 온라인이나 어느 주요 서점에서도 구매할 수 있습니다.

수신: 미셸 박 <mpark83@umail.com>
발신: 마르셀라 로즈 <djmarci@ezd.net>
날짜: 4월 13일
제목: 마드리드로의 귀환

박 씨에게,

제 프로그램에 나오시는 데 동의해 주셔서 너무나 감사합니다. 귀하의 대리인이 아마 귀하에게 말씀드렸겠지만, 178 첫 장(章)을 톰 헤르난데스가 읽어준 것에 대한 관객 반응은 압도적이었습니다. 180 저희는 귀하께서 인터뷰를 위해 방송에 나와 달라는 너무나 많은 요청을 받아서 그저 안 된다고 할 수 없었습니다. 저는 알렉스 크루즈의 앨범으로부터 나온 곡들을 또한 틀어줄 것입니다. 방송 자체는 25일 일요일 오전 9시에 할 것이지만, 저희는 180 우리가 토론할 주제 몇몇을 검토하기 위해 귀하께서 1시간 일찍 와 주신다면 감사하겠습니다. 귀하께서는 또한 계약서에 서명하셔야 하며, 179 대회에서 저희가 나눠줘야 할 두세 권의 책들에 자필 서명을 해 주셔야 할 것입니다. 방송국은 3번 가 1273번지에 있습니다.

당신을 만나 뵙기를 고대합니다!

마르셀라 로즈

어휘 release (책의) 발매; (제품의) 출시 acclaimed 호평을 받는 non-fiction 실화, 비소설 exchange student 교환 학생 nearly 거의 detail 자세히 설명하다[말하다] upcoming 다가오는 author 저자 insight 통찰력 do a feature on ~을 특집[특종]으로 하다 tune in to ~에 채널을 맞추다 agent 대리인 response 반응 overwhelming 압도적인 request 요청 broadcast 방송 appreciate 감사하다 go over 검토하다 contract 계약(서) autograph 자필로 서명하다 give away ~을 나눠주다 Spanish 스페인어 autographed 자필 서명된 auction 경매에 팔다 donate 기부하다 charity 자선 단체 review 검토하다

176 박 씨가 20년 전에 마드리드를 방문했던 이유는 무엇인가?
(A) 책을 조사하기 위해서
(B) 앨범을 녹음하기 위해서
(C) 스페인어를 공부하기 위해서
(D) 친구들을 방문하기 위해서

해설 해당 책은 박 씨가 예전에 언어 교환 학생으로 20년 전 방문했던 도시인 마드리드에 관한 이야기를 담고 있다는 내용이 나온다. 따라서 박 씨는 스페인의 수도인 마드리드에 언어(스페인어)를 공부하러 갔음을 알 수 있다. 따라서 정답은 (C)이다. (B)의 경우 앨범 녹음 참여는 20년 전이 아닌 두 번째 방문했을 때 한 일이므로 정답이 될 수 없다.

177 책에 관해 언급된 것은 무엇인가?
(A) 저자의 첫 번째 소설이다.
(B) 소설(허구) 작품이다.
(C) 조만간 발매될 것이다.
(D) 읽기 재미있다.

해설 유머와 통찰력으로 쓰인 그 책은 읽는 즐거움이 있다는 내용이 나온다. 따라서 정답은 (D)이다. 단서의 delight라는 표현은 정답에서 amusing으로 패러프레이징되었다. 책은 실화(non-fiction)라고 했기 때문에 (A), (B)는 오답이며, (C)의 경우 책은 이미 발매가 되어서 주요 서점에서 판매 중이므로 오답이다.

178 톰 헤르난데스는 누구인가?
(A) 박 씨의 대리인
(B) 방송국 매니저
(C) 스페인 민요 가수
(D) 오전 디제이

해설 두 지문에 나눠서 등장한 단서를 종합해서 정답을 찾아보자. 첫 번째 지문을 통해서 방송국 매니저가 책의 첫 장(章)을 읽는다는 것을 알 수 있으며, 두 번째 지문에서는 톰 헤르난데스가 첫 장(章)을 읽었다는 내용을 통해 톰 헤르난데스가 곧 방송국 매니저임을 알 수 있다. 따라서 정답은 (B)이다.

179 자필 서명된 책으로 할 일은 무엇인가?
(A) 청취자들에게 경매로 팔릴 것이다.
(B) 자선 단체에 기부될 것이다.
(C) 디제이들에게 주어질 것이다.
(D) 대회 상(품)으로 이용될 것이다.

해설 대회에서 나눠줘야 할 두세 권의 책들에 자필 서명을 해 달라는 내용이 나온다. 따라서 대회가 있을 예정이고, 그 대회에서 자필 서명된 책을 상품으로 나눠줄 것을 알 수 있다. 따라서 정답은 (D)이다.

180 박 씨가 방송 당일에 할 일이 아닌 것은 무엇인가?
(A) 인터뷰 받기
(B) 계약서에 서명하기
(C) 몇몇 곡을 노래하기
(D) 토론 주제 검토하기

해설 박 씨가 출연하는 방송 당일에 할 일은 두 번째 지문에서 나온다. 박 씨는 인터뷰를 위해 방송에 나오며, 계약서에 서명하고, 토론할 주제 몇몇을 검토해야 한다는 내용을 찾을 수 있다. 따라서 (C)가 정답이다.

[181-185]

배송 실패 통지

우편 고객에게:

182 지역 집배원이 2017년 4월 14일 오전 10시에 하버스톤 도로 40번지로 소포를 배송하려고 했습니다. 이것은 소포를 배송하려는 저희의 두 번째 시도였습니다. 그러나 위의 주소에는 아무도 없었습니다. 발송인이 이 소포를 "서명 요망"이라고 표시해 두었으므로, 저희는 그것을 문간에 놔두고 갈 수가 없습니다. 저희는 내일 오전 대략 비슷한 시간에 다시 배송할 것입니다. 181 만약 소포에 서명할 사람이 없을 것으로 예상하면, 아래 상자 중 하나에 표시해 주시고 문에 이 통지문을 다시 붙여 주세요.

감사합니다.

미국 우편 서비스

☐ 저는 제 소포를 74번 가에 있는 우체국에서 찾아가겠습니다.

☑ 183 제 소포를 하버스톤 도로 42번지에 있는 제 이웃에게 남겨 주세요.

우체국장
사우스 레이크 우체국
사우스 레이크, 미네소타 55924

담당자에게,

저는 최근에 로스엔젤레스에 있는 제 남동생으로부터 소포를 받았습니다. 귀중한 서류가 들어 있었기 때문에 저는 그것에 서명하는 요청을 받았습니다. 안타깝게도, 저는 그때 사무실에 있었습니다. **182** 다음 날도 또한 제가 사무실에 있어야 했기 때문에, 저는 우체부가 남긴 양식에 길 건너에 사는 제 이웃에게 그 소포를 남겨 달라고 표시를 했는데, 그 이웃은 친한 친구이기도 합니다. **183** 다음 날, 제 친구가 사무실로 전화해서 그가 소포를 받지 못했다고 말했습니다. 제가 우체국에 전화했을 때, 저는 소포가 수령되었고 그 메모리트는 서명이 되어 있다는 것을 알게 되었습니다. 아주 검사 후에 저는 그 서명이 제 이웃의 것이 아니라는 걸 알게 되었지만, 담당했던 우체부 부주의로 인해 저는 큰 어려움을 겪었습니다. 설상가상으로, 그는 아직 사과를 **185** 하지 않았습니다. **184** 저는 다시는 이런 상황이 발생하지 않을 것이라는 확인을 받고 싶습니다.

진심으로,

오스카 알바레스 드림

어휘 postal 우편의 mail carrier 집배원 present 있는, 존재하는 signature 서명 sign for ~에 서명하다 reattach 다시 붙이다 valuable 귀중한 unfortunately 안타깝게도 indicate 나타내다 recognize 알다, 본 간하다 graciously 감사하게 carelessness 부주의 involve 관련되다 distress 괴로움, 비통 to make matters worse 설상가상으로 have yet to 아직 ~하지 않았다 extend an apology 사과하다 assurance 확신, 보증 accuse 고소하다 reimbursement 배상, 변제, 상환

181 이 공지는 어디에서 발견되었을 것 같은가?
(A) 서류가 들어 있는 소포 위에서
(B) 알바레스 씨의 새 이웃집에서
(C) **알바레스 씨의 집 문 앞에서**
(D) 74번지 우체국에서

해설 소포에 서명할 사람이 없을 것으로 예상하면, 아래 박스 중 하나에 표시해 주고 문에 이 통지문을 다시 붙여 달라고 했다. 이 부분을 통해서 해당 공지는 소포 수신인의 집 문 앞에 붙어 있음을 알 수 있다. 그 러니 소포 수신인으로 두 번째 지문인 발신인 알바레스이므로 정답은 (C)이다.

182 알바레스 씨에 관한 설명으로 올바른 것은 무엇인가?
(A) 그는 우체국에서 근무한다.
(B) 그는 최근 새로운 주소로 이사했다.
(C) 그는 배송비 지급하기를 거부했다.
(D) **그는 낮에 일한다.**

해설 소포를 배송했던 오전 10시 경에 사무실에 있었고 다음 날도 역시 사무실에 있어야 했다는 내용을 통해서 알바레스 씨는 낮에는 일하고 있음을 알 수 있다. 따라서 정답은 (D)이다.

---

183 하베스토 도로 42번가에 사는 사람은 누구인가?
(A) 지역 우체부
(B) **알바레스 씨의 친구**
(C) 알바레스 씨의 남동생
(D) 존 머레이

해설 첫 번째 지문에서 소포를 하베스토 도로 42번지의 이웃에게 남겨 달라 표현이 나온다. 또한, 두 번째 지문에서는 알바레스 씨가 우체부가 남긴 양식에 자신의 친한 친구 중 한 사람에게 소포를 남겨 달라고 했다는 것을 알 수 있다. 이 두 내용을 종합하면 해당 주소에는 알바레스 씨의 친구가 살고 있음을 알 수 있으므로 정답은 (B)이다.

184 편지의 목적은 무엇인가?
(A) 분실한 소포를 신고하려고
(B) **배송 오류에 관해 불평하려고**
(C) 이웃을 우편 절도로 고소하려고
(D) 잃어버린 서류에 대해 배상받으려고

해설 두 번째 지문은 알바레스 씨가 요청했던 사람에게 소포가 전달되지 않고 다른 사람에게 전달되었다는 것을 설명하면서, 다시는 이런 일이 발생하지 않기를 요청하는 글이다. 따라서 (B)가 정답임을 알 수 있다.

185 편지에서 세 번째 단락 두 번째 줄의 extend와 의미상 가장 가까운 것은 무엇인가?
(A) 강조하다
(B) **제공하다**
(C) 확장하다
(D) 철회하다

해설 To make matters worse, he has yet to extend an apology란 문장을 보면, extend an apology란 표현은 '사과하다'라는 의미 로 해석함을 알 수 있다. 따라서 extend는 (B) offer의 의미임을 알 수 있다.

[186-190]

수신: 아놀드 호킨스 (ahawkins@ari.net)
발신: 제시카 이스턴 (jeaston@ari.net)
날짜: 10월 22일
주제: 온라인 교육 총회

아놀드에게,

저는 당신이 보낸 시드니에서 진행되는 온라인 교육 총회 자료들을 살펴보고 있는데, **186** 유감스럽지만 우려되는 점이 몇 가지 있습니다. 제가 전에 언급드렸듯 이, **187** 저는 원격 교육 기술 워크숍을 진행하게 되어 매우 기쁩니다. 그러나 총 회의 강연자가 되는 것을 수락하기 전에 **188** 이미 저는 참석자가 되기로 계획 했었습니다. 특히, 저는 슈미트 박사님의 특수 요구 학습자들을 위한 기술 강의 에 참석하려고 총회에 등록했었습니다. 그러나 제 워크숍 시간을 변경하지 않는 이 상 변경하고 그의 강의와 겹치게 될 것입니다. 다른 문제는 제 워크숍의 규모와 상 부분에 그로의 강의와 겹치게 될 것입니다. 다른 문제는 제 워크숍의 규모와 정 했던 재용을 초래합니다. 일정표에 실린 최대 참가자 수가 제가 영향이 정 했던 재용을 초래합니다. 이 문제를 총회 주최자들과 의논해 해결해 주시겠 습니까? 저는 정말로 제 워크숍을 취소하고 싶지 않습니다.

제시카

2017년 10월 22일
교육 기술 총회 위원회
사서함 7091
뱅크스타운, 뉴 사우스 웨일스 2200

위원회 구성원에게,

189 저는 이가레미 리세샤의 제 부정에 대한 인상과 제시가 이스턴 씨를 대신해서 글을 쓰고 있습니다. 귀하가 잘 알고 있다시피, 제시가 씨는 앞으로 있을 총회에서 제 워크숍 진행에 동의했습니다. 그러나 그녀는 귀하가 보낸 홍보 자료를 살펴본 후에, 귀하가 교재에 주길 바라는 두 가지 요청 사항이 있습니다. 첫 번째는 그녀가 다른 워크숍 참여자들과 함께~ **187** 슈미트 박사님의 워크샵 인기 때 문에 명명히 총회의 하이라이트 중 하나가 될 거라 예상되는 그 강의에 참석 할 수 있도록 그녀의 워크숍을 한 시간 일찍 시작하자는 것입니다. **189** 두 번째 는 현재 일정표에 실린 그녀의 워크숍 참석자의 최대 인원을 20명까지 줄이는 것입니다. 그렇게 할 수 없는 경우 그녀는 참가자들과 제대로 상호작용하지 못 하는 상황을 걱정하고 있습니다.

만약 이 요청들을 들어줄 수 없거나 들어줄 의향이 없으시다면, 차이가 되도록 일찍 편리함때 연락을 주셔서 이 문제를 추후로 이논했으면 합니다.

진심으로

아놀드 호킨스
보조 사무실 관리인
아카데미 리세샤서

어휘 e-education 온라인 교육　conference 총회, 회의　look over ~을 살 펴보다 materials 자료 regarding ~에 관해 thrilled (너무 좋아서) 아 주 흥분한 workshop 워크숍 lead 진행하다 distance-learning 원격 교육 attendee 참석자 sign up for ~을 등록하다 overlap 겹치다 maximum 최대 special-needs (장애인들의) 특수 요구

2017년도 교육 기술 회의
수정된 일정

워크숍 주제	워크숍		메인 홀	
	시간	최대 크기	행사	시간
교실에서의 가상현실	신규 오전 9시~11시	참가자 50명	강연자: 에이미 찬 박사 주제:	오전 10시 30분 ~
원격 교육 기술	신규 오전 11시~오후1시	**188** 신규 참가자 30명	교사들에게 기술 가 르치기	11시 30분
하드웨어 문 제 해결	오후 2시~4시	참가자 40명	강연자: 오토 슈미트 박사	오후 1시
190 온라인 수업 계획	오후 4시~6시	참가자 50명	주제: 특수 요구 학습자들을 위한 기술	30분 ~ 2시 30분

이름: 조쉬 피자
주소: 46 일 가, 플리전트, 노스캐롤라이나 27013
전화: 704-555-2018
이메일: fizz97@allonline.com
[188] **요청 금액:** 500달러

요청 이유:
저는 제 연례 버스 승차권에 대한 부분 환불을 요청하고 있습니다. 귀하가 49-1번 버스 노선을 변경했기 때문에 이 승차권을 사용할 수 없습니다. [189] 저는 이전에 이 상황에 대해서 제 요청을 참고하라고 엘레나 앤더슨과 이논했습니다. 그러기 22914년 사본을 참고하라고 이논했습니다.

이 양식을 빠짐없이 작성하셔서 다음 주소로 보내 주시기 바랍니다:

선호되는 환급 방법 (승인 시에 한함)
☒ 개인 수표
☐ 자기앞 수표
☐ 현금
☐ 계좌 입금 (양식서 뒤에 은행 정보를 포함하세요)

벨뷰 교통부
392 레이크 사이드 공정지대
벨뷰, 노스캐롤라이나 83212

어휘 public transportation 대중교통 route 노선 intersection 교차로 take place 열리다, 발생하다 forward 앞으로 in place 제자리에, 준비 된 express shuttle 직행 버스 it has come to one's attention ~을 알게 되다 arcade 상가 건물 salesclerk 영업사원 annual 연례의 pass 승차권 commute 통근(하다) completely 완벽히 useless 쓸모없는 normally 보통 mark 표시하다 aforementioned 앞서 언급한 non-refundable 환불받을 수 없는 exception 예외 policy 정책 dilemma 딜레마, 진퇴양난 full refund 전액 환불 prorated 비례 배분된 reimbursement 환급 partial 부분적 previously 이전에 reference 참고하다 case 사례 preferred 선호되는 method 방법 personal check 개인 수표 cashier's check 자기앞 수표 direct deposit 계좌 입금 fill out ~을 작성하다

191 공지의 목적은 무엇인가?
(A) 버스 지연에 대한 이유 설명하기
(B) 시(市) 버스 서비스에 대한 의견 요청하기
(C) 교통 문제에 관해 거주자들에게 주의 주기
(D) 노선 변경에 대해 승객들에게 알려주기

해설 공지들은 대중 교통부에서 발표한 것으로, 버스 노선 변경 시행을 설명하고 있다. 따라서 정답은 (D)이다. (C)는 버스 노선이 바뀐 것이지 교통들이 문제가 생겼다고 볼 수는 없으므로 오답이다.

192 피자 씨에 대해 알 수 있는 것은 무엇인가?
(A) 버스 운전사라고 논쟁했다.
(B) 소매 판매업에 고용되어 있다.
(C) 공항 근처에서 산다.

[어휘 목록]
[최고의] participant 참가자 exceed 초과하다 limit 제한 invitation 초대 straighten out 해결하다 organizer 주최자 back out of ~을 취소하다 on behalf of ~대신에 incorporated 반영한, 반영 하 고 있는 conduct 수행하다 upcoming 앞으로 오는 promotional 홍보의 stature 위상 anticipate 예상하다 highlight 하이라이트, 중요점 fear 두려워하다 adverse effect 역효과, 부작용 effectively 효과적으로 be unwilling to do ~하는 것을 꺼리다 at one's earliest (possible) convenience (가능한 한) 되도록 일찍 편리할 때 virtual 가상의 reality 현실 deal with ~을 해결하다, 다루다 issue 문제 esteemed 존경받는 figure 인물

186 이메일의 목적은 무엇인가?
(A) 일정 승인하기
(B) 도움 요청하기
(C) 워크숍 제안하기
(D) 총회 칭찬하기

해설 이메일 시작 부분에서 몇 가지 걱정이 있다고 했으며, 마지막 부분에서 문제들을 해결해 달라고 도움을 요청하고 있다. 따라서 정답은 (B)이다.

187 슈미트 박사에 대해 암시된 것은 무엇인가?
(A) 아카데미 리서치사의 직원이다.
(B) 자신의 분야에서 존경받는 인물이다.
(C) 이스트 씨의 워크숍에 참석할 것이다.
(D) 총회의 총회를 책임지고 있다.

해설 두 번째 지문을 실펴보면, 슈미트 박사의 강연은 인기 때문에 총회의 하이라이트 중 하나가 될 거라고 예상한다고 했다. 따라서 정답은 (B)이다. (C)는 이스트 씨가 슈미트 박사의 강연에 참석할 것인지는 정답이 될 수 없다.

188 이스트 씨에 관해 맞지 않는 것은 무엇인가?
(A) 그녀는 호킨스 씨의 부장이다.
(B) 그녀는 워크숍을 진행할 것이다.
(C) 그녀는 강의에 참석할 것이다.
(D) 그녀는 총회를 책임지고 있다.

해설 (A)는 두 번째 지문 첫 문장에서 제시가 이스트는 자신의 부장임을 명시하고 있으므로 맞는 내용이다. (B)는 첫 번째 지문에서 원격 교육 기술 워크숍을 진행하게 되어 매우 기쁘다고 했으므로 역시 맞는 내용이다. (C)도 첫 번째 지문에서 워크숍에 참석하기로 계획했다고 했으므로 맞는 내용이다. 언급되지 않은 내용은 (D)이다.

189 이스트 씨에 관해 맞지 않는 것은 인원수로 일정표에 처음 실린 것은 무엇인가?
(A) 20명
(B) 30명
(C) 40명
(D) 50명

해설 두 번째 지문에서 참가자 수를 최대 20명 줄여달라고 요청했는데 수정된 일정표의 세 번째 지문에서, 이스트 씨의 워크숍에 참여 하 있는 최대 참석자 수는 30명이라고 되어 있다. 이 두 내용을 종합하면, 최대 20명

[다른 칼럼]

을 줄여 30명이 된 것이므로 현재 일정표에는 50명이 최대 참가자 수였음을 추론할 수 있다. 따라서 정답은 (D)이다.

190 교육 기술 총회의 마지막 행사는 무엇인가?
(A) 고장 난 기계 수리에 관한 워크숍
(B) 학습 능력이 부족한 학생들에 관한 강의
(C) 인터넷 수업 계획에 대한 워크숍
(D) 기술과 관련한 교사 연수 강의

해설 총회를 시간대별로 열거하고 있는 세 번째 지문을 보면, 마지막 시간대의 행사는 온라인 수업 계획(Online lesson planning)이다. 따라서 이름 패러프레이징한 (C)가 정답이다. 지문의 online을 선택지에서는 Internet으로, planning을 creating으로 각각 바꿔 쓴 점에 유의하자.

[191-195]

7월 28일부터 효력 발생

이것은 플리전트 대중교통 시스템을 이용하는 모든 분을 위한 공지입니다. [191] 시(市) 버스 노선의 조정 때문에 49-1번 버스는 다음 두 교차로에서 더 이상 정차하지 않을 것입니다: 45번 거리와 2번가가 만나는 교차로와 45번 거리의 4번가가 만나는 교차로입니다. 이러한 변경은 2017년 7월 28일부터 적용될 것입니다. 그럼 이후부터 앞서 언급된 두 정거장 중 하나이기 때문에 이 결정을 이해하기 어렵습니다. [192] 제 경우에 저는 대형 상가 건물 안에 있는 이글 스테이크하우스에서 근무하는데 매일 통근을 위해 49-1번 버스를 이용하기 위해서였습니다. 그러나 지금은 600달러 이상 옛내가 49-1번 쓸모가 없어졌습니다. 보통 저는 기차를 타고 도시에 오셔 옛내서 이해해 주셔서 감사합니다. 시(市) 버스를 이용해 주시라 감사합니다.

수신: 고객서비스 (customerservice@bellevuedpt.gov)
발신: 조쉬 피자 (fizz97@allonline.com)
날짜: 7월 29일
주제: 버스 노선 변경

저는 최근에 49-1번 버스가 45번 거리와 4번가가 만나는 지점에서 정차하지 않는다는 것을 알게 되었습니다. 그것이 그 노선에서는 사람들이 가장 많이 타는 정거장 중 하나이기 때문에 이 결정을 이해하기 어렵습니다. [192] 제 경우에 저는 대형 상가 건물 안에 있는 이글 스테이크하우스에서 근무하는데 매일 통근을 위해 49-1번 버스를 이용하기 위해서였습니다. 그러나 지금은 600달러 이상 옛내가 49-1번 쓸모가 없어졌습니다. 보통 저는 기차를 타고 도시에 오셔 옛내서 [194] 62-1번과 84번 버스도 그 역에서 탈 수 있지만, 둘 다 쇼핑 상가 근처에서 정차하지 않습니다. 현재 공항버스만 정차하는데, 그 버스가 역 근처에 정차하는 것은 한 군데도 없습니다. 그래서 이제 저는 출근할 수 있다고 명시되어 있을지라도, 제가 지원 관련한 상황이 노선을 바꾼 귀하 부서의 결정 때문에 아기되었으므로 오답이다. 이 정책을 예외를 요청하고 싶습니다. [195] 만약 전액 환불이 불가능하다면, 저는 승차권에 남아 있는 요금만큼 환불을 요청하고 싶습니다.

조쉬 피자

(D) 일자리를 찾고 있다.

해설 두 번째 지문에서 대령 상기 건물 내에서 영업 시업을 하고 있다(I'm a salesclerk)고 했으므로 정답은 (B)이다.

193 멜라니 앤더슨은 누구인가?

(A) 버스 기사
(B) 피자 씨의 친구
(C) 피자 씨의 상사
(D) 시(市) 직원

해설 마지막 지문에서 조리 피처는 멜라니 앤더슨과 환불 과정에 대해 이는 첫을 그러나 그것을 수락했음을 알 수 있다. 따라서 멜라니 앤더슨은 공무원임을 알 수 있다. 따라서 정답은 (D)이다.

194 기차역에서 정차하지 않는 버스는 무엇인가?

(A) 49-1번
(B) 62-1번
(C) 84번
(D) 323-A번

해설 두 번째 지문에서 49-1번, 62-1번, 84번이 기차역에서 정차한다는 것을 알 수 있다. 하지만 이 공항 버스는 기차역에서 정차를 안 한다고 했는데 첫 번째 지문에서 공항 버스가 323-A번을 알 수 있다. 따라서 정답은 (D)가 정답이다.

195 피자 씨는 연 버스 승차권에 남아 있는 달이 수도 얼마인가?

(A) 6개월
(B) 8개월
(C) 10개월
(D) 12개월

해설 두 번째 지문에서 승차권 가격이 거의 600달러라고 했는데, 세 번째 지문에 서 부분 환불로 500달러를 요청하고 있다. 이 내용을 토대로 계산해 보면 승차권에 남아 있는 달이 수도 12개월이므로 정답은 (C)이다.

[196-200]

중요한 항공사 정책 업데이트

노스 퍼시픽 항공사의 국제 항공기 위탁 수화물 정책 업데이트 즉시 발효됩니다. 특히 국제 여행객 1인당 위탁 수화물 무게 제한도 20kg에서 두 개로 늘어됩니다. 게다가 각 가방에 대한 무게 제한도 20kg에서 25kg으로 상향 조정했고, 중량 초과 가방에 대한 벌금을 100달러에서 50달러로 낮췄습니다. 그러나 두 개의 가방에 대한 벌금은 가방 기방에 대한 청구 요금은 4개의 추가 가방까지 가방을 25달러로 유지하고 했습니다. 이러한 변경 사항은 국내 항공기 정책에는 전혀 중량을 마지지 않을 것입니다. 그 개당 무료 기방 20kg 제한. 그리고 중량 초과 가방에 대한 벌금의 정책은 현재도 계속 독리이 남아 있습니다. 만약 여러분이 질문이 있으시다면, 저희 탑승 수속 청구 직원에게 말해주세요.

감사합니다.

Wings.com 항공사 여행객 온라인 후기

저는 최근에 도쿄에서 제 고향 샌프란시스코로 가는 노스 퍼시픽 항공의 새 직항편 중 하나를 이용했으며, 전반적으로 비행은 만족스러웠습니다. 노스 퍼시픽 항공은 저가 항공사의 표준 국제 항공사의 중간급 또는 수준이었습니다. 즉 가격은 저렴하고, 기껏해야 늘릴 수 있었습니다. 그런데 저는 두 번째 위탁 수화물에 대해서 요금을 받지 않는다는 것을 알고 매우 기뻤습니다. 이것은 새로 도입된 변화인 것 같으니, 매우 환영할 만했습니다.

그러나 최근 LA에서 조리 피처는 멜라니 앤더슨과 환불 과정에 대해 이는 간 친구가 저에게 국내 여행에 대해서는 기존의 한 가방 정책이 유지된다는 말을 들었는데, 이는 매우 실망스러웠습니다. 저는 항공사가 새 항공편이 세 항공사가 새 항공이 모든 항공편을 확대하는 것을 그래해 주시길 바랍니다.

수신: 에릭 린드스트롬 〈travelguy@jazzco.com〉
발신: 카이리 로페즈 〈lopezk@npa.com〉
날짜: 12월 10일
주제: 귀하의 후기

고객님께서 Wings.com 웹 사이트에서 노스 퍼시픽 항공을 최근 이용해 주신 경험에 대해서 시간을 내어 평가해 주셔서 감사합니다. 저희는 여행객께서 우리 요금 정책에 대해 우리만큼 그래님께서서 반가워하시는 것을 들으니 기쁩니다. 소비자 반응이 압도적으로 긍정적이었고 그 것은 매우 기분 일이었습니다. 국내 항공편까지 정책을 확장하는 것에 대한 고객님의 제안은 미국 연방 항공국이 요구하는 제한 때문에 불가능하다는 점을 알려드리게 되어 유감입니다. 그렇지만, 저희는 2018년을 시작으로 국내 승객에게 중량 초과 수화물 벌금을 25%까지 줄일 것입니다. 저희는 또한 저희의 국제 여행객들이 기대하는 수준까지 국내 서비스의 질을 올림 방법을 계속 찾을 것입니다.

진심으로

카이리 로페즈
노스 퍼시픽 항공

어휘 initiate 시작하다, 개시하다 checked-baggage 위탁 수화물 effective (법, 규정 등이) 발효되는, 유효한 specifically 특히 allowance 허용량 additionally 추가로, 게다가 weight 무게 penalty 벌금 overweight 중량 초과의 lower 낮추다 charge 요금 수수료 domestic 국내의 in effect 사실상[실질] 상의 check-in counter 탑승 수속 청구 take advantage of ~을 이용하다 direct flight 직항편 overall 전반적으로 satisfactory 만족스러운 budget airline 저가 항공사 standard 표준의 carrier 항공사 charge for ~에 대한 청구를 하다 apparently 명백히 disappointing 실망스러운 expand 확장하다 cover 포함하다 consumer 소비자 response 반응 overwhelmingly 압도적으로 positive 긍정적인 extremely 매우 gratifying 기쁜 as for ~에 관한 suggestion 제안 regarding ~에 관한 be unable to do ~할 수 없다 restriction 제한 impose 부과하다 Federal Aviation Administration 미국 연방 항공국

196 국제 항공기에서 승객 1인당 무료로 딸릴 수 있는 현재의 가방이 수도 몇 개인가?

(A) 한 개
(B) 두 개
(C) 세 개
(D) 네 개

해설 첫 번째 지문의 앞부분에서 국제 여행객 1인당 위탁 수화물 허용량을 한 개에서 두 개로 늘렸다는 내용이 나오므로 정답은 (B)이다. (A)는 국 내 항공기에서 무료로 위탁할 수 있는 가방 개수이므로 오답이다.

197 항공사에 대한 린드스트롬 씨의 전반적인 의견은 무엇인가?

(A) 저렴하지만 승객들을 환영하지 않았다.
(B) 대부분의 국제 항공사들보다 더 좋다.
(C) 낮은 가격을 고려하면 품질이 좋다.
(D) 빠르고 편리하나 값이 너무 비싸다.

해설 두 번째 지문에서 린드스트롬 씨는 해당 항공사의 서비스는 제돈값을 한다, 두 번째 수화물에 대해 요금을 청구하지 않는다는 점에 만족하고 있다. 따라서 (C)가 정답이다.

198 이메일에서 첫 번째 단락 네 번째 줄의 gratifying과 의미상 가장 가까운 것은 무엇인가?

(A) 기쁘게 만드는
(B) 무사안
(C) 당황스러운
(D) 깜짝 놀라게 하는

해설 해당 단어 이 문장에서 변경된 수화물 정책에 대해 소비자들의 반응이 압도적으로 긍정적이라고 했으므로 문맥상 '기쁘게 만드는'이란 의미 의 (A)가 가장 적절하다.

199 새로운 정책 덕분에 린드스트롬 씨가 절약했던 금액은 얼마인가?

(A) 25달러
(B) 50달러
(C) 75달러
(D) 100달러

해설 첫 번째 지문에서 국제 여행객 두 개의 기방에서 두 개의 기방에서 두 개 가방까지 금액을 받지 않으며, 두 개가 초과할 경우 기방당 추가 요금 은 25달러의 국제 항공기를 이용했다고 했다. 또한, 두 번째 지문에서 린드스트롬 씨가 국제 항공기를 이용했다는 내용이 나오므로 정답은 (A)가 된다.

200 2018년도에 국내 승객에 대한 중량 초과 가방 벌금은 얼마인가?

(A) 없음
(B) 10달러
(C) 50달러
(D) 75달러

해설 첫 번째 지문에서 국내 항공기 이용 시 중량 초과 가방에 대한 벌금이 현재 100달러라고 했으며, 세 번째 지문에서 2018년부터 국내 승 객들의 중량 초과 수화물 벌금이 25% 줄어든다고 했다. 이 두 가지 정 보를 종합하면, 2018년도부터 중량 초과 수화물 벌금은 100달러에서 25% 줄어든 75달러이므로 정답은 (D)이다.

Actual Test

06

저자 박선영

카카오톡 ID로 찾기(ID: matrix20)
>> 친구 추가 후 1:1 채팅

본책 P124

Reading Comprehension

PART 7

147 (A)	148 (C)	149 (A)	150 (D)	151 (B)	152 (C)	153 (C)	154 (B)	155 (C)
156 (D)	157 (B)	158 (A)	159 (B)	160 (A)	161 (A)	162 (C)	163 (C)	164 (D)
165 (B)	166 (A)	167 (A)	168 (C)	169 (D)	170 (B)	171 (B)	172 (A)	173 (B)
174 (B)	175 (A)	176 (C)	177 (B)	178 (A)	179 (D)	180 (C)	181 (B)	182 (D)
183 (C)	184 (C)	185 (D)	186 (D)	187 (C)	188 (A)	189 (D)	190 (D)	191 (C)
192 (A)	193 (D)	194 (B)	195 (A)	196 (D)	197 (D)	198 (D)	199 (C)	200 (D)

[147-148]

짜릿한 새로운 경험을 찾고 계십니까?

147 판매 제안서를 만들고 유지하신 경력이 있으십니까? 마케팅 자료의 제작을 감독한 경험이 있으십니까? 당신이 있으신 체계적인 사람입니까? 당신은 전략적인 사고교정인 사람입니까?

당신이 이런 질문에 그렇다고 대답하면 당신은 새미 데이터베이스사의 새로운 마케팅 책임자가 될 만한 자격을 가지실 것입니다. 이 새로운 직책은 광범위한 마케팅 프로젝트 관리를 수반합니다. 이것들은 판매, 제품 개발과 고객서비스 부서와의 소통이 포함됩니다. 마케팅 책임자의 직무는 작무는 부서 간의 협력을 책임을 지는 것입니다.

이 직책의 자격요건은 다음을 포함합니다.

- 마이크로스프트 오피스와 웹 디자인 등의 컴퓨터 활용 능력
- **148** 압박 아래서 일하고 빠르게 마감일을 맞추는 능력
- 마케팅 이론에 대한 독실한 이해
- 경영 마케팅 혹은 조직 개발 분야의 학사 하위

어휘 supervise 감독하다 people person 사교성이 있는 사람 qualification 자격 coordinator 책임자, 조정자 position 직책 entail 수반하다 interaction 상호작용 ensure 보장하다 collaboration 협력 requirement 자격 요건 computer proficiency 컴퓨터 활용 능력 operate 일하다 under pressure 압박 하에서 meet 맞추다 solid 확실한 principle 원리, 이론 a letter of interest 이력서

147 이 일자리의 지격 요건이 아닌 것은 무엇인가?
(A) 석사 학위
(B) 압박 속에서 일하는 능력
(C) 마케팅 원리에 대한 지식
(D) 이전의 근무 경력

해설 지문 중반에 압박 속에서 마감일을 맞추는 능력이 연급되어서(B)를, 지문 상단에 마케팅에 대한 확실한 이해가 연급되어서(C)를, 지문 상단에 판매 제안서를 만들고 마케팅 자료를 제작한 적이 있는지를 묻는 부분에서(D)를 확인할 수 있다. 이 일자리에는 석사 학위가 아닌 학사 하위를 요구하므로 정답은 (A)이다.

148 지원자가 이 직업에 관해 회사와 연락을 취할 수 있는 방법은 무엇인가?
(A) 전화로
(B) 편지로
(C) 이메일로
(D) 개인이 직접 방문해서

해설 지문 후반에 이력서를 이메일로 보내라고 언급하므로 정답은 (C)이다.

[149-150]

공지

제목: 제48회 연례 수련회
수신: 전 직원

제48회 연례 브레드베드 출판부 수련회에 오신 여러분을 환영합니다. 저는 여러분 모두가 이름다운 캐스킬 산에서 수련회들을 알 수 있게 해주신 우리의 훌륭한 대표이사인 존 브레드베드 씨께 특별히 감사드리길 바랍니다. 저는 모든 분이 별 볼 수 있 여기에 오셔서 작업하면서 긴장을 푸실 수 있도록 계획하면 주는 바라는 준비가 되어 있음을 알지도. **149** 주말에 관해 몇 가지를 말씀드리도록 하겠습니다. 독회에 올라와 있는 첫 번째 사항으로, **150** 내일 아침 오전 9시에 수 있 금 선택에 낮은 봉우리로 4시간의 신행을 갈 예정입니다. 산행에 참여를 원하시 지 않는다면, 다른 많은 선택을 할 수 있습니다 — 이 멋진 리조트에 대해 직원 중 한 명에게 물어보세요. 8시에 저녁 식사를 먹은 후에 새로운 경영에서 우리는 연 말 판매 보고와 연례 시상식을 개최할 예정입니다.

어휘 annual 연례의 retreat 수련회 settle in (새 환경에) 적응하다 properly 적절히 hold 개최하다 peak 봉우리 ridge 산맥 hike 도보여행 fabulous 멋진 year-end 연말의 yearly 연례의 awards 시상식 auditorium 강당

149 공지의 주제는 무엇인가?
(A) 주말에 받아질 일
(B) 고객의 전화를 다루는 방법
(C) 판매상을 받을 사람
(D) 존 브레드베드의 일생

해설 지문 중반에 주말 일정을 발표하겠다고 연급되어 있으므로 정답은 (A)이다.

150 수 이튿에 관해 암시된 것은 무엇인가?
(A) 그녀는 신행을 포함할 것이다.
(B) 그녀는 판매상을 나눠 줄 것이다.
(C) 그녀는 고객서비스를 나눠 줄 것이다.
(D) 그녀는 고객서비스 부서에서 일한다.

해설 지문 중반에 주말 일정 중 오전에 고객 전화를 다루는 방법에 대해서 강연을 하다고 연급된 내용에서 그녀는 고객서비스 관련 부서에 속해 있는 것을 알 수 있다. 따라서 정답은 (D)이다.

[151-152]

레베카 파커스 **오전 10:23**
바가레 씨, 전략 인더스트리스의 사장인 에스피노사 씨에게 막 전화 왔었습니다. **151** 그는 자신의 회사를 위한 광고를 촬영을 원하고 있는 중이고, 우리의 서비스에 대해 논의하기 위해 내일 오후 2시에 여기에 오고 싶다고 했습니다.

아리온 바가레 **오전 10:25**
좋은 소식이네요! 전략 인더스트리스는 규모가 커서 우리 회사의 좋은 사업 마 트너가 될 것 같습니다. 그러면, 그를 위해서 가장 좋은 회의실로 예약해 주 실래요? 507호 회의실 508호가 제일 좋을 겁니다.

레베카 파커스 **오전 10:26**
네, 제가 해보는데, 다른 누군가가 이미 그것을 예약했더라고요.

아리온 바가레 **오전 10:26**
정말요? 제가 확인해 볼게요.

아리온 바가레 **오전 10:28**
당신이 많이 맞았어요. **152** 로드리게스 씨가 예약했어요. 그가 507호 회의실을 쓸 수 있으면 좋을 텐데요.

레베카 파커스 **오전 10:29**
152 그건 괜찮을 거예요. 제가 그에게 변경할 수 있는지 물어볼게요.

어휘 huge 거대한 book 예약하다 reserve 예약하다 conference room 회의실

151 바가레 씨와 파커스 씨가 일하는 곳은 어디인가?
(A) 법률 사무소
(B) 광고 회사
(C) 연락 기획사
(D) 출판사

해설 광고사를 찾고 있던 전략 인더스트리스의 사장이 서비스를 논의하기 위해 방문하고 싶다고 했으므로 광고 회사에서 일한다는 것을 짐작해 볼 수 있다. 따라서 정답은 (B)이다.

152 오전 10시 29분에, 파커스 씨가 "그건 괜찮을 거예요"라고 쓴 의미는 무엇인가?
(A) 그녀는 바가레 씨가 그 장소를 예약하길 원한다.
(B) 그녀는 자기 동료에게 전화할 필요가 있다.
(C) 그녀는 로드리게스 씨가 그 변화를 받아들이길 원한다.
(D) 그녀는 회의의 일정을 변경을 필요가 없다.

해설 이 메시지 바로 이전에 바가레 씨는 로드리게스 씨가 507호 회의실을 사용하면 좋을 것 같다고 의견을 제시한다. 따라서 문맥상 로드리게스 씨가 그 변경의 제안을 받아들이길 바라는 것을 짐작할 수 있으므로 정답은 (C)이다.

한 해 더 구독 신청을 하시면 귀하는 1년 내내 과학계에서 해낸 경이로운 발견을 지속해서 누릴 수 있습니다. [153] 귀하가 구독을 갱신하면, [154] 평범한 일상 장치에서 찾아볼 수 없는 통찰력 있는 정보를 얻을 것입니다. [153] 〈새로운 과학 세계〉는 최고의 과학 뉴스를 매달 여러분의 현관 앞으로 배달할 것입니다. 이 기회에 [153] 만약 귀하가 이번 달에 구독을 갱신한다면 세 가지의 다른 할인 방식을 선택할 수 있습니다.

1년	1년 → 29.99달러
2년	5년달러 → 49.99달러
5년	145달러 → 129.99달러

계다가, 귀하는 매년 수정이 나올 때 수집앱을 놓치고 싶지 않을 겁니다. 올해의 집판은 현재 물리학과 수학의 경이로운 이야기들 이외에 뉴턴을 다룰 것입니다. 우리는 그가 현대 과학자들에게 아직 알려지지 않아 많이 연구되지 않았던 것이 있는지 보여줄 것입니다. 그가 현대에 어전히 과학에 영향을 주고 있는지를 읽어 보세요.

어휘 subscription 구독(예약) enjoy 누리다 wonder 경이로움 discovery 발견 renew 갱신하다 insightful 통찰력 있는 leave out 빠뜨리다 in addition 게다가 edition 판 feature ~을 특집기사로 다루다 mathematics 수학 influence 영향을 주다

153 광고의 목적은 무엇인가?

(A) 독자에게 새로운 정책을 알려 주기 위해서
(B) 독자에게 잡지에 관해 알려 주기 위해서
(C) 독자에게 잡지 구독을 이번 달에 신청하라고 독려하기 위해서
(D) 추가의 수정판에 관해 독자에게 보고하기 위해서

해설 첫 번째 문단에서 이번 달에 구독을 갱신하면 기간 매월 할인을 누릴 수 있다고 했으므로 정답은 (C)이다.

154 잡지에 관해 암시되지 않은 것은 무엇인가?

(A) 잡지의 독자는 이미 구독을 하고 있다.
(B) 수집판은 오직 5년 구독을 신청하는 것만을 위한 것이다.
(C) 잡지는 매달 발행된다.
(D) 잡지에서 새로운 소식을 찾아볼 수 있다.

해설 첫 번째 문단 전체에 걸쳐 잡지 구독을 갱신할 것을 요청하는 내용에서 (A) 와 (C), 평범한 장치에선 얻을 수 없는 통찰력 있는 정보를 얻게 될 것이라는 내용에서 (D)를 확인할 수 있다. 수집판이 5년 구독자에게만 해당된다는 내용은 없으므로 정답은 (B)이다.

메모

수신: 마케팅과 홍보팀
발신: 마이클 존스
날짜: 2017년 11월 14일
제목: 새로운 제안

2017년도 새로운 시장과 조사 분석이 완료되었습니다. [155] - . 새로운 정보는 새로운 인구통계를 새롭게 조사해야 할 필요성을 보여줍니다. 계다가, 마케팅의 고객의 인구통계를 새롭게 조사하는 것을 보여줍니다. 지난 2년간 이용되었던 마케팅 전략은 우리 기준에 못 미치고 있습니다. 계다가, [156] [157] 판매량은 지난 4개월 동안 매출의 약 2.1%까지 떨어졌다고 말을 끼쳤습니다. - [2] - .

저는 새로운 여름옷 제품군을 위해 고객 인구통를 새로 조사하는 것을 먼저 제안하고자 합니다. 새롭게 획득한 정보를 이용해서 정확한 마케팅으로 다른 인구 집단을 개선할 수 있습니다. 둘째, 마케팅팀은 광고를 늘릴 필요가 있습니다. - [3] -. 새로운 정보통신 시대는 마케팅을 위한 광고의 많은 가능성을 열어놓았습니다. 마케팅팀은 오직 인터넷을 통해서만 광고를 시작했었지만, [156] 마케팅은 더욱 확장을 통해서 할 수 있다고 믿습니다.

[155] 1월에 마케팅팀을 회의를 개최할 예정입니다. 남쪽은 아직 확정되지 않았습니다. - [4] -. 이 회의에서 모두 직접적인 방식으로 우리의 인구 집단을 개발할 것인지에 관한 의견과 광고를 위한 새로운 의견을 가질 것을 요청합니다.

마이클 존스
경영진

어휘 publicity 홍보 proposal 제안 research 조사 analysis 분석 complete 완료하다 perform 수행하다 demographics 인구 통계, (공통적인 특성을 가진) 인구 집단 strategy 전략 standards 기준 suggest 암을 깨내다, 시사하다 figure 수치 swift 신속한 action 조치 line 제품군 attain 획득하다 precise 정확한 expand 늘이다, 확장하다 expansive 확장하는 encourage 격려하다 via ~을 통하여 bring forth 내놓다

155 1월에 있어날 일은 무엇인가?

(A) 새로운 마케팅 계획이 시작할 것이다.
(B) 광고는 새로운 인구 집단으로 확장되어야 한다.
(C) 마케팅팀은 토론을 할 것이다.
(D) 인터넷을 통한 광고가 시작될 것이다.

해설 지문 하단에 1월에 마케팅팀은 회의를 개최하여 여러 가지를 논의하겠다고 밝히고 있다. 따라서 정답은 (C)이다.

156 메모에서 추측할 수 있는 것은 무엇인가?

(A) 조사는 많은 회사가 마케팅 정책을 구축하도록 돕는다.
(B) 마케팅팀은 다양한 광고 방법을 사용한다.
(C) 마케팅팀은 직접적 방법을 선호한다.
(D) 구독 광고로 판매가 감소했다.

해설 이 회사는 지난 4개월 동안 판매가 감소했는데, 그동안 인터넷 광고만 감소을 이용했으나 내용이 언급되어 있다. 그러므로 구독 광고로 판매가 감소하였음을 미루어 짐작할 수 있다. 따라서 정답은 (D)이다.

157 [1], [2], [3], [4]로 표시된 곳 중 다음 문장이 위치로 가장 적절한 곳은 어디인가?

"이 수치가 시사하는 바는 신속한 조치가 취해져야 한다는 것입니다."

(A) [1]
(B) [2]
(C) [3]
(D) [4]

해설 삽입문장에서 언급된 '이 수치'는 바로 앞에 언급된 구체적인 수치를 가리켜야 한다. 매출의 2.1% 하락했다는 내용 뒤인 [2]에 나오는 것이 자연스러우므로 정답은 (B)이다.

수신: 스티브 존스 (SJones187@abc.com)
발신: 스콧 윌리엄스 (ScottWilliams87@abc.com)
날짜: 4월 10일
제목: 판매 보고서

안녕하세요, 스티브. 저는 영부서 소콧입니다. [158] 당신에게 지난달 회사 영업에 대해서 알려 드리고자 편지를 씁니다. 저는 보고서 작성을 끝내고 그것을 당신 사무실로 보냈어요. 제가 이 이메일을 보낸 것은 단지 보고서에서 몇 부분을 [160] 강조하기 위해서입니다.

[159] 우선 우리 회사 판매가 지난달에 2.1% 오르면서 우리 회사가 지역 경쟁에서 한 발짝 앞서 있다는 것을 보여줍니다. 올해 마지막 분기는 수익률이 이 단계에 판매가 증가했습니다.

당신이 보고서를 볼 때, 판매 도표에 오류가 있는지 검토해 주시기 바랍니다. 또한, 저는 보고서에 하나의 항목을 첨가했으니 그것은 영업 사원이 더 많은 조을 얻을 수 있는 제안문입니다. 이것이 가까운 미래에 판매를 개선하는 데 도움이 되었으면 좋겠습니다. 좋은 하루 되십시오.

스콧 윌리엄스

어휘 highlight 강조하다 ahead of ~보다 앞서서 margin 판매수익 appreciate 감사하다 review 검토하다 chart 도표 section 부분

158 이메일의 목적은 무엇인가?

(A) 지난달 실적 결과를 보고하기 위해서
(B) 보고서의 오류를 지적하기 위해서
(C) 테이블 세트의 판매를 촉진하기 위해서
(D) 월리엄스 씨가 이메일을 보낸 것을 직원에게 알리기 위해서

해설 지문이 상단에 지난달 회사의 영업에 대해 알리고자 편지를 썼으므로 정답은 (A)이다.

159 지난달에 증가한 것은 무엇인가?

(A) 보고서의 오류
(B) 지난달의 판매량
(C) 고객 서비스 부서의 직원을 위한 제안
(D) 식량 테이블 세트의 크기

해설 월리엄스 씨가 이메일에 언급하는 것은 무엇인가? 그중인 인터넷 광고만 감소했으니 내용이 언급되어 있다. 그러므로 구독 광고로 판매가 감소하였음을 미루어 짐작할 수 있으므로 정답은 (D)이다.

해설 지문 중반에 지난달의 판매가 2.1% 올랐다고 언급하고 있으므로 정답은 (B)이다.

160 첫 단락 세 번째 줄의 "highlight"와 의미상 가장 가까운 것은 무엇인가?
(A) 강조하다
(B) 강화하다
(C) 숨기다
(D) 증가하다

해설 highlight는 '강조하다'라는 의미가 있으므로 정답은 (B)이다.

[161-163]

공지

한솔 전화 회사 직원 여러분께 인사드립니다. 이번 주에 회사는 다가오는 공휴일인 금요일에 문을 닫을 것입니다. 이 공지와 함께 행복한 공휴일이 되시길 바랍니다.

회사는 휴일이 다가옴에 따라 주간 일정을 조정할 것입니다. 이번 주 수요일과 목요일에 회사는 한 시간 일찍 문을 닫을 것입니다. 둘째, 회사는 공장 직원과 영업사원이 이번 주에 추가로 2시간을 더 근무하기 원합니다. 어느 날에 업무를 하고 싶은지 선택권이 주어질 것입니다. 이번 주 새로운 일정을 검토해 주십시오.

로버트 조든
관리자

161 공지의 목적은 무엇인가?
(A) 새로운 업무 일정을 발표하기 위해서
(B) 신상품을 홍보하기 위해서
(C) 직원을 격려하기 위해서
(D) 판매를 올리기 위해서

해설 지문 상단에서 다가오는 공휴일로 인한 업무 일정 변화를 발표하고 있다. 따라서 정답은 (A)이다.

	월요일	화요일	수요일	목요일	금요일
	시작: 9:00	시작: 9:00	시작: 9:00	시작: 9:00	
	점심: 12:00-12:50	점심: 12:00-12:50	점심: 12:00-12:30	점심: 12:00-12:30	공휴일
	종료: 17:00	종료: 17:00	종료: 16:00	종료: 16:00	

162 회사가 한 시간 일찍 문을 닫는 때는 언제인가?
(A) 월요일과 화요일
(B) 화요일과 수요일
(C) 수요일과 목요일
(D) 화요일과 목요일

해설 지문 중간에 공휴일 때문에 이번 주 수요일과 목요일에 한 시간 일찍 문을 닫는다고 언급하고 있고, 표에서도 같은 내용을 확인할 수 있다. 따라서 정답은 (C)이다.

163 공지에 언급된 것은 무엇인가?
(A) 전 직원은 평소보다 더 많은 시간을 일해야만 한다.
(B) 점심시간이 변경이 없다.
(C) 특정 직원들만 추가로 2시간을 더 근무해야 한다.
(D) 회사는 공휴일에 문을 닫지 않을 것이다.

해설 지문 중반에 공장 직원과 영업사원만 추가시간 2시간을 더 근무해야 한다고 하므로 특정 직원만 표를 보면 월·화요일에 비해 수·목요일에 점심시간이 20분이 짧으므로 (B)는 오답이며, 지문 상단에 다가오는 공휴일에 문을 닫는다고 했으므로 (D)도 오답이다.

[164-167]

메모

수신: 펜사슈즈 전 직원
발신: 경영진
제목: 의무 연수

회사는 다음 3주간 매주 토요일에 의무 연수를 개최할 예정입니다. 신입 인턴을 위해 이 연수에 반드시 참석해야 합니다. 최근에 있었던 시안은 경영진의 시선을 끌었습니다. 일부 직원이 배송을 받고 재고를 조사하는 절차와 직장 내 안전 수칙 등을 명확히 이해하지 못하는 것으로 보입니다.

첫 번째 연수는 배송을 받는 절차에 대해 다룰 것입니다. 두 번째 연수는 어떻게 적절히 재고를 조사할 수 있는지를 다룰 것입니다. 이 연수에서 정확한 절차를 시연해 줄 것이며, 직원들은 재고를 조사하는 두 가지 방식을 연습해 볼 것입니다. 세 번째 연수는 직장 내에서의 안전을 다룰 것입니다. 직장 내의 안전은 이 회사를 위해 매우 중요합니다. 경영진은 모든 직원이 이 연수에 진지하기에 임해 주기를 바랍니다. 직장 내에서의 안전은 일상 업무의 많은 측면을 포함합니다.

이 연수는 의무적이며, 9월 3일, 10일, 그리고 17일 토요일에 열리는 것을 기억해 주세요. 각 연수는 오전 9시에 시작하오니 정시에 참여하도록 하세요.

로버트 브라운
경영진

어휘 mandatory 의무적인 workshop 연수 occupational safety 산업 안전 take inventory 재고를 조사하다 procedure 절차 shipment 배송(품) deal with ~을 다루다 properly 적절하게 demonstrate 시연하다 method 방식 extremely 극도로, 몹시 seriously 진지하게 encompass 포함하다 on time 정시에

164 메모의 목적은 무엇인가?
(A) 연수의 중요성을 강조하기 위해서
(B) 직원에게 연설하기 위해서
(C) 연수에 대한 반응을 표현하기 위해서
(D) 여러 연수에 대해 직원에게 알리기 위해서

해설 지문 상단에 앞으로 있을 연수의 개요를 알리는 내용이 있으므로 정답은 (D)이다.

165 회사가 연수를 개최하는 이유는 무엇인가?
(A) 사고가 있었기 때문에
(B) 경영진은 직원의 안전에 관심을 기울이기 때문에
(C) 직원이 재고 관리하는 법을 시연해야 하므로
(D) 직원과의 대화가 중요하기 때문에

해설 지문 상단에서 직원의 안전을 위해 반드시 연수에 참석하라고 밝히고 있다. 그러므로 이 연수의 최종 목적은 직원의 안전임을 알 수 있다. 따라서 정답은 (B)이다.

166 연수는 며칠에 걸쳐 열리는가?
(A) 3일
(B) 3주
(C) 주말마다
(D) 이번 주 토요일 온종일

해설 지문 조반과 마지막에 이 연수는 9월의 3주간 토요일에들 즉, 3일간 진행되는 연수라고 언급되어 있다. 따라서 정답은 (A)이다.

167 첫 번째 단락 첫 번째 줄의 "mandatory"와 의미상 가장 가까운 것은 무엇인가?
(A) 의무적인
(B) 고정된
(C) 중요한
(D) 심각한

해설 이 연수는 직원의 안전을 위해 개최하는 것이므로 '의무적으로 참석해야 한다는 것이 의미상 적절하다. 따라서 정답은 (A)이다.

Actual Test 06   052 · 053

[168-171]

존 위커 [오후 3:31]	안녕하세요. **168** 구조조정 발표 이후 여러분 지사의 직원 의견에 맞춤해 주길 바랍니다.
로즈 샌버그 [오후 3:33]	처음 발표가 난 직후에는, 힘들어 했었는데, 점차 안정되어 가는 것처럼 보여습니다. 그들은 춘후의 변화에 대해 자세히 추시하고 있습니다.
룬다 블레 [오후 3:34]	여기 직원들은 구조조정으로 일부 이동이 대량 해고로 예상됩니다. 심지어 경기 침체 때문에 일부로 발생할지도 모르는 변화에 대해 걱정하고 있습니다.
성 강 [오후 3:35]	저는 저의 직원들에게 이 문제에 대해 무언 기틀 말하는 게 조심스럽습니다. **169** 추가적인 정보 없이는 그들에게 말해 줄 게 없습니다.
존 위커 [오후 3:36]	우리는 그것을 환한 작업 중입니다. **170** 6월 부장 회의를 거쳐 대략적인 결정이 난 후에 여러분과 자세히 상의하도록 하겠습니다.
룬다 블레 [오후 3:37]	7월에 우리 사무실 일부가 이상되다 가득 참에도 모르겠어요. 만감이 협조가 구조조정이 끝날 때까지, 여러분의 협조가 매우 절실합니다.
존 위커 [오후 3:38]	**170** 그 외에 다른 질문이 있으시면, 편하게 저에게 연락해 주세요.

어휘 branch 지사, 지점 announcement 발표 restructuring 구조조정 uncomfortable 불편한, 편하지 않은 gradually 점차 keep a close eye on ~에 자세히 주시하다 involve 수반하다 arrangement 조정 massive 대량의 layoff 해고 severe 독독한 recession 경기 침체 roughly 대략 share 공유하다 be filled with ~로 가득 차다 have mixed feeling 만감이 교차하다

168 위커 씨가 글을 쓴 이유는 무엇인가?
(A) 회의 일정을 잡기 위해서
(B) 가능한 계획을 발표하기 위해서
(C) 직원의 의견을 알아내기 위해서
(D) 사무실 이전 일정을 확정하기 위해서

해설 위커 씨의 첫 메시지에 구조조정 발표 이후 각 지사에 있는 직원의 의견을 알아 달라고 요청하고 있다. 따라서 정답은 (C)이다.

169 오후 3시 36분에 위커 씨가 "우리는 그것을 환한 작업 중입니다."라고 쓴 의미는 무엇인가?
(A) 업무 시간이 상당히 연장되었다.
(B) 여러 사무실이 문 운을 닫게 될 것이다.
(C) 그는 대표이사들을 장기적으로 만난다.

170 지사들은 언제 최신 정보를 얻게 될 것인가?
(A) 5월에
(B) 6월에
(C) 7월에
(D) 8월에

해설 위커 씨가 6월 부장 회의를 거쳐 구조조정에 관해 대략적인 나눔이 걸 둘이 나면 이에 대해 다 상의한다고 했다. 따라서 정답은 (B)이다.

171 지사장들은 무엇을 하도록 요구되는가?
(A) 새로운 작업을 고르기
(B) 연제든 질문하기
(C) 새로운 신문을 제공하기
(D) 사무 장비를 주문하기

해설 위커 씨의 마지막 메시지에 그 외에 다른 질문이 있으면 편하게 자신에게 연락해 줄 것을 당부하고 있다. 따라서 정답은 (B)이다.

[172-175]

짐 토마스
980 엘름 가
덴버, 콜로라도 80247
토마스 씨에게,

172 175 저는 콜로라도 노바 공장에 도착될 납재를 예약해 두셨는지요. - [1] -. 저는 10월 24일 일요일 오후 4시에 덴버 국제공항에 도착할 예정입니다. 귀하는 제가 묵을 장소에 대해 걱정하지 않으셔도 됩니다. 그 지역의 호텔에 모든에 방을 예약했습니다.

저는 공장 현장을 직접 다녀 보기를 학수고대하고 있습니다. **173** 우리는 내 방 직원 건강 기 독과 안전 프로그램을 보는 것에 관심이 있습니다. - [2] -. **173 172** 우리는 내 방 공장의 새로운 행동을 제품군을 생각에 달게 있습니다. - [3] -. 저는 또 한, 공장의 새로운 안전 프로그램을 시행될 예정입니다. 저 는 이것이 국가가 발전함에 따라 내게에 열리게 될 새로운 시장을 위한 교양한 제품이라고 믿고 있습니다.

항상 그렇게, 저는 당신을 다시 볼 것을 학수고대하고 있습니다. 24일에 봅시다. - [4] -.

진심으로
아서 클라라

어휘 arrival 도착 look forward to ~하기를 학수고대하다 instigate 실시한 게 하다 fluorescent light 형광등 be in need of ~이 필요하다

172 편지의 주제는 무엇인가?
(A) 콜로라도 씨의 콜로라도 노바 공장 방문
(B) 콜로라도 씨의 본사 방문
(C) 행광등의 새로운 생산
(D) 해외로 열리는 새로운 시장

해설 집문 상단에 콜로라도 씨가 콜로라도 공장에 방문할 날짜를 예약해 두었 다고 하며 공장에 방문할 것을 알리고 있다. 따라서 정답은 (A)이다.

173 회사는 내부 춘에 무엇을 할 것인가?
(A) 건강 기록을 확인한다.
(B) 직업장에서 안전 프로그램을 시작한다.
(C) 행광등을 생산한다.
(D) 일부 직원을 해고한다.

해설 집문 중간에 작업장의 새로운 안전 프로그램을 내 춘에 시작할 것이 라고 언급하고 있다. 따라서 정답은 (B)이다.

174 [1], [2], [3], [4]로 표시된 곳 중 다음 문장이 위치로 가장 적절한 곳은 어디인 가?

"문서에서 작업장의 안전을 개선해야 한다는 우려가 있었습니다."

(A) [1]
(B) [2]
(C) [3]
(D) [4]

해설 작업장의 안전 프로그램 시행 개월이 드러나 있는 바로 앞자리에 삼입 문장이 들어가기 가장 적절하므로 정답은 (B)이다.

175 편지에서 언급되지 않은 것은 무엇인가?
(A) 콜로라도 씨가 얼마 동안 머무를 예정인지
(B) 콜로라도 씨가 언제 도착할 예정인지
(C) 해외로 열리는 새로운 시장
(D) 콜로라도 씨가 어디에 머물 예정인지

해설 콜라다 씨는 10월 24일 일요일 오후 4시에 도착한다는 내용에서 (B) 를, 내게의 해외에서 열릴 새로운 시장에 대한 언급에서 (C)를, 콜로라 씨가 한 모텔에서 머물 것이라는 내용에서 (D)를 확인할 수 있다. 따라 서 언급되지 않은 (A)가 정답이다.

[176-180]

판매: 2016년식 편의래리같 4문형 승용차

저는 1년 전에 이 승용차를 구매해서 사고 없이 지금까지 이 차를 타고 있습니다. 그러나 우리 아이들 때문에 제 처럼 SUV로 바꿀 예정입니다. **180** 관심 있으시 다면 아래 휴대전화번호로 연락 주시면 차를 보러 오실 수 있게 시간을 잡겠습 니다.

사무엘 데이비스
023-555-8403

판매자 정보

명: ⓘⓦⓦ 사무엘 데이비스
소: 3544 메인 가
도시: ⓘⓦⓦ 제임스타운
주: 버지니아
우편번호: 32095

ⓘⓦⓦ 거래 차량 특징

연식: 2016   색상: 진회색
차체 스타일: 4문형 승용차   차량번호: 39470662394
(2문형, 4문형 등등)

주행거리 표시: 18,000마일

공시 및 보증

판매자는 그가 알고 본 차량의 주행거리 표시가 정확함을 증명하고, 판매 자가 주행거리계를 조작하거나, 전력을 끄거나 혹은 소유 기간에 주행 거리를 낮추지 않았음을 증명한다.

본 차량은 "있는 그대로" 매매되고 있기에 어떠한 결함에도 보증이 없다. 모든 수리는 판매자가 여기에서 지급을 수락을 하며 혹은 한, 구매자가 책임질 의무가 있다:

다른 나머지 수리는 판매자에 의해 지급되지 않는다. 구매자는 이에 의하여 모든 재정적 책임을 맡는다.

지급

판매자는 판매자가 본 차량을 판매할 권한과 구매자에게 명의를 이전할 권한 이 있음을 구매자에게 보증한다. 판매자는 더욱이 그 명의가 담보권이 없음을 보증한다.

서명

판매자와 구매자는 이 판매 명세서의 모든 정보가 그들이 아는 한 정확하다는 것에 동의한다. ⓘⓦⓦ 판매자는 구매자로부터 대금을 받았고 이로써 본 차량의 소유권을 구매자에게 양도한다.

176 계약서가 쓰인 이유는 무엇인가?
(A) 서비스에 대해 불만을 제기하기 위해서
(B) 매매 차량을 개선하기 위해서
(C) 차량 판매를 설명하기 위해서
(D) 정보의 변경을 보고하기 위해서

어휘 sedan 승용차 accident 사고 arrange 정하다, 준비하다 zip code 우편번호 odometer 주행거리계 reading 표시 disclosure 공시 warranty 보증 certify 증명하다 modify 수정하다 disconnect 전원 을 차단하다 roll back 낮추다 mileage 주행 거리 ownership 소유권 as is 있는 그대로 defect 결함 hereby 이로써 assume (책임을) 맡다 title 명의 담보 bill 명세서 lien 담보

ⓘⓦⓦ 구매자 정보

성명: 밥 스쿠필드
주소: 257 뉴먼 가
도시: 뉴먼
주: 버지니아
우편번호: 32083

제조업체: 판아메리칸

차량 판매가: 5,350,00달러

해설 두 번째 지문의 판매자와 구매자의 정보, 거래 차량 특징 등을 미루어 보 아 차량 판매 계약서임을 알 수 있다. 따라서 정답은 (C)이다.

177 계약서에 따르면, 차를 파는 사람은 누구인가?
(A) 아이작 뉴턴
(B) 사무엘 데이비스
(C) 밥 스쿠필드
(D) 판아메리칸

해설 두 번째 지문의 계약서에서 판매자는 사무엘 데이비스인 것을 알 수 있 다. 따라서 정답은 (B)이다.

178 어떤 차에게 차가 구매되었는가?
(A) 2016년식 판아메리칸 진파런스, 4문형 차
(B) 2016년식 판아메리칸 파런스, 2문형 차
(C) 2017년식 진파런스, 4문형 차
(D) 2017년식 파런스 차

해설 두 번째 지문의 거래 차량 특징을 보면, 2016년에 출시된 판아메리칸 진파런스 4문형 차량인 것을 알 수 있다. 따라서 정답은 (A)이다.

179 계약서에 관해 사실이 아닌 것은 무엇인가?
(A) 구매자는 판매자에 의해 표시되지 않은 모든 수리에 책임이 없다.
(B) 판매 가격은 표시되어 있다.
(C) 구매자는 계약을 통해 소유권을 가진다.
(D) 판매자는 좋은 가격으로 팔기 위해 차를 개조하였다.

해설 두 번째 지문의 공시 및 보증 사항에 모든 수리는 판매자가 책임진다는 지급을 수락을 하거나 혹은 한, 구매자가 책임진다고 언급되어 있으 므로 (A)는 맞고, 지급란에 판매가가 명시되어 있으므로 (B)도 맞다. 마 지막 서명란에 구매자는 대금을 지급하고 소유권을 양도받음이 기술 되어 있으므로 (C)도 맞다. 따라서 사실이 아닌 것은 (D)가 정답이다.

180 차량에 관해 암시된 것은 무엇인가?
(A) 사고 이력이 있다.
(B) 두 명의 사람들을 위한 것이다.
(C) 스쿠필드 씨는 제임스타운에서 시험 운행을 하였다.
(D) 데이비스 씨는 그 차의 두 번째 주인이다.

해설 첫 번째 지문에서 데이비스 데이비스는 예비 구매자에게 차를 직접 보러 올 수 있도록 시간에 연락을 주면 약속을 잡겠다고 하고 있다. 그러므로 두 번 째 지문에서 이 차를 구매한 사람으로 밝혀진 스쿠필드 씨는 데이비스 씨가 사는 제임스타운으로 시험 운행을 하러 갔을 수도 있음을 미루어 짐작해 볼 수 있다. 따라서 정답은 (C)이다.

수신: 벤위이 박사 (BenWy@hotmail.com)
발신: 랜디 스미스 (RandyS@hotmail.com)
날짜: 2월 1일
제목: 대학원 연구 요청

벤위이 박사님께

저는 조지아 대학교의 대학원생입니다. 저는 현재 박사 학위 논문을 쓰 지 조사를 진행 중입니다. 저는 이 유저지에서 나오는 굴 껍데기가와 등의 표본을 조지아와 사우스캐롤라이나 해안을 따라 있는 다른 유저지의 것과 비교해서 조 사하는 것에 관심이 있습니다. ⓘⓦⓦ ⓘⓦⓦ 저는 넓은 조게나데미 대략적인 연령대 추정을 돕기 위해 많은 유저지에서 자료를 수집하는 것을 희망합니다.

저는 그고학 연구실의 이음 시간에 관하여 ⓘⓦⓦ 연구실 책임자인 수 존스와 연락 을 한 적이 있습니다. 수는 2월에 1주일 연구를 할 수 있게 저에게 시간을 좀 수 있을지 모른다고 했다네, 그녀는 제가 당신과 저의 연구가들로서 저의 연구에 도움이 될 수 있기를 희망합니다.

ⓘⓦⓦ ⓘⓦⓦ 저는 당신이 발굴 작업에 주요 연구가들과 저의 연구에 도움이 될 수 있기를 희망합니다.

ⓘⓦⓦ 만약 당신이 2월 20일부터 25일까지 시간이 된다면, 저는 그 시간 동안 연 구를 하고 싶습니다만, 필요하다면 날짜를 변경할 수도 있습니다. ⓘⓦⓦ 저는 제 가 다른 유저지에서 수집했던 자료에 대해 당신과 함께 논의해 보고 싶습니다. 저는 제가 수집한 자료에 대해 당신이 도와주기를 바랍니다. 제가 조게나데미 연 령대를 추정하는 데 주시는 어떠한 도움도 감사할 것입니다. 저 이메일 주소인 RandyS@hotmail.com으로 연락해 주세요. 당신으로부터 온 답변을 듣기 바랍니다.

진심으로
랜디 스미스

수신: 랜디 스미스 (RandyS@hotmail.com)
발신: 벤위이 박사 (BenWy@hotmail.com)
날짜: 2월 2일
제목: 회신: 대학원 연구 요청

스미스 씨에게,

저에게 연락해 주셔서 감사합니다. 제가 메릴랜드 대학에서 박사 학위 논문을 쓰 던 당시에 그 지역에서 유사한 연구를 해 봤기 때문에 도움이 될 수 있을 것 같 습니다. ⓘⓦⓦ 조게나데미 연령 연구는 우리 과학 분야에 매우 관련성이 높은 사안 이기 때문에 이것을 주제로 선택하는 것을 축하드립니다.

ⓘⓦⓦ 제가 2월 20일을 보스턴에서 2갱이 있어서 시간이 나지 않습니다. 하지만 그날을 제외하고는 괜찮을 겁니다. 당신이 지금까지 수집해 온 정보를 검토하고 당신과 자세히 논의하고 싶습니다. 특히, 제가 당신의 연구 방법론에 대해 더 많 은 것을 알고 있었으면 좋겠네요. 아마도 같이 연구를 함으로써 우리는 공동 연구를 마치 면, 아주 같이 있는 연구들로서 우리는 공동 연구를 할 수 있을 것입니다.

더욱 2월 21일에 당신과 만나길 기대합니다.

진심으로
벤위이 박사 올림

수신: 샘 데이비스 (bluechateauresort@netmail.com)
발신: 존 브래드퍼드 (JohnBradford908@bradfordpublishing.com)
날짜: 3월 5일
제목: 블루 샤토 리조트 정보

데이비스 씨에게,

안녕하십니까. 저는 브래드퍼드 출판사의 대표이사 존 브래드퍼드입니다. **[189]** 저는 저희 직원들을 위해 강당을 갖춘 멋진 휴양지를 찾던 중이었습니다. 블루 샤토 리조트가 어느 정도 가능할 것 같은데, 몇 가지 질문을 좀 하겠습니다.

[188] 일주일 동안의 회사를 위한 패키지 가격이 있는지 알고 싶습니다. 또한, 리조트의 시간을 가격 할인을 제공하시죠? **[189]** 저의 마지막 질문은 4월에 객실이 이용 가능한지에 관한 것입니다. 시간 내주셔서 감사합니다.

진심으로
존 브래드퍼드

어휘 chateau 성 amid 한가운데 majestic 웅장한 get-away 휴양지 congestion 혼잡함 hiking trail 등산로 relieve 덜어주다, 덜어 주다 year-round 연중 내내 brand-new 아주 새로운 auditorium 강당 top-of-the-line 최신식의 hence 그러므로 wilderness 황무지, 대자연 as for ~에 관해서는 kitchenette 간이 주방 accommodation 숙박(시설) up to 최대 audiovisual 시청각의 free of charge 무료로 promise 가망성 seasonal 계절적인 retreat 휴양지

186 광고된 무엇에 관한 것인가?
(A) 출판사
(B) 여행사
(C) 새로운 강당
(D) 회사 휴양지

해설 첫 지문 상단에서 리조트가 회사 직원에게 탁 트인 공간과 신선한 공기 속에서 이용할 수 있는 휴양지를 제공한다고 언급하고 있다. 그러므로 회사 휴양지를 위한 리조트 광고라고 볼 수 있다. 따라서 정답은 (D)이다.

187 블루 샤토 리조트에 대해 암시된 것은 무엇인가?
(A) 사전에 금액을 지불해야 한다.
(B) 식당으로 유명하다.
(C) 개조될 선정에 있다.
(D) 전에 데이비스가 씨가 소유했었다.

해설 첫 지문 상단에서 웅장한 개스킬 산맥에 안락함 속에 위치한다고 언급하고 있다. 따라서 정답은 (C)이다.

188 이 이메일의 지문 하단에 쓰는 어떤 종류의 정보를 찾고 있는가?
(A) 할인될 가격과 객실 이용 가능성
(B) 제공되는 음료
(C) 리조트로 가는 방법
(D) 스포츠 단지에 관한 세부 사항

해설 세 번째 지문 하단에 가격이 할인되는지, 객실을 이용할 수 있는지 묻고 있다. 따라서 정답은 (A)이다.

어휘 graduate student 대학원생 conduct research 연구하다 archaeological 고고학의 remain 유적(지) oyster shell 굴 껍데기 mound 더미, 무더기 laboratory 실험실 principal investigator 책임 연구자 excavation 발굴 be of help 도움이 되다 if need of assistance 도움이 되는 relevance 관련성 methodology 방법론 collaborate 공동연구하다 in-depth 심층의

랜딩가 다른 유적지에서 수집했던 자료에 대해 벤제이 박사와 논의하고 싶다고 밝힌 부분에서 (C)를 확인할 수 있다. 반대로 벤제이 박사는 메리랜드 대학에서 박사학위를 땄다고 했다기보다는 대학에서 교수라는 점은 알 수 없으므로 (D)가 정답이다.

[186-190]

블루 샤토 리조트

[187] 웅장한 개스킬 산맥의 안락함 속에 위치한 저희 집은 우리 휴양지는 사무실의 혼잡으로부터 완벽한 안식처를 제공합니다. **[186]** 귀사의 직원은 이곳 블루 샤토 리조트의 탁 트인 공간과 신선한 공기 속에서 휴식을 취할 수 있습니다. 개스킬 산책로의 웅장한 광경과 더불어 다양한 스트레스 해소 방법을 제공하는 많은 등산로, 스포츠 단지와 온천이 있습니다.

[189] 블루 샤토 리조트는 크고 작은 업무 회의를 위한 서비스를 많이 제공하고 있습니다. 우리는 연중 내내 이용할 수 있는 4개의 회의실과 **[188]** 최신 오디오 시스템, 비디오 프로젝터와 새롭게 설치된 자연 속에 있는 주요 도시와 연결하는 2 강의이 있습니다. 따라서 당신은 인터넷 서비스를 갖춘 새로운 식사 통나무집이 있습니다! 수소가 적정하려면, 우리 리조트는 케이블 TV, 고속 인터넷 서비스, 간이 부엌이 개스킬의 이름다운 경관을 갖춘 1인실에서 2인실까지 있습니다.

더 많은 정보를 원하신다면, 다음을 통하여 연락해 주세요.

전화: 740-555-0356
새로운 웹 사이트: http://www.bluechateauresort.com
이메일: bluechateauresort@netmail.com (샘 데이비스가 볼 수 있도록)

오늘 주저하지 말고 당신 회사의 예약을 하세요!

http://www.bluechateauresort.com/services/prices

회의 및 행사	숙박	서비스	질문과 응답

회의실
- 기본: 주중 하루에 280달러 / 주말 하루에 350달러
- 강당: 주중 하루에 600달러 / 주말 하루에 680달러
[190] (한 번에 최대 100명 수용 가능)

장비
- 오디오 시스템: 하루에 30달러
- 비디오 프로젝터: 하루에 45달러
(강당은 모든 시청각 장비를 갖추고 있으며, 무료로 이용할 수 있음. 또한, 리조트 어디에서도 무선 인터넷 사용 가능)

숙박
- 통나무집: 1인실 주중 하룻밤에 45달러 / 주말 하룻밤에 50달러
2인실 주중 하룻밤에 50달러 / 주말 하룻밤에 55달러

질문이 있으시면, 장안도 주저 말고 전화 혹은 이메일 주세요.
감사합니다.

이메일: bluechateauresort@netmail.com

---

181 첫 번째 이메일의 목적은 무엇인가?
(A) 조게디미 연맹체를 추천하기 위해서
(B) 연구에 도움을 요청하기 위해서
(C) 프로도 유적지를 연구하기 위해서
(D) 존스 씨로부터 자료를 얻기 위해서

해설 이메일의 첫머리에 '대학원 연구 요청'이라고 명시하고 있고, 지문 중반에 벤제이 박사에게 연구에 도움이 되어주었으면 한다고 이메일을 쓴 목적을 밝히고 있다. 따라서 정답은 (B)이다.

182 첫 번째 이메일에서 첫 번째 단락 네 번째 줄의 "estimation"과 의미상 가장 가까운 것은 무엇인가?
(A) 수치
(B) 결정
(C) 측정
(D) 추정

해설 바로 앞에 '대략적인'을 뜻하는 general이 왔으므로 '대략적인 추정'이 되는 것이 한다. 따라서 '가장 추정'을 뜻하는 (D)가 정답이다.

183 스미스 씨는 벤제이 박사와 언제 함께할 것인가?
(A) 3월 20일에서 25일까지
(B) 2월 20일에서 25일까지
(C) 2월 21일에서 25일까지
(D) 2월 19일

해설 첫 번째 지문에 2월 20일부터 25일까지 시간이 되는지 물었는데 두 번째 지문에서 20일은 안 되고 그날 이후에는 가능하다고 했다. 따라서 21일부터 25일까지라는 (C)가 정답이다.

184 스미스 씨의 연구 주제는 무엇인가?
(A) 프로도 지역
(B) 굴 껍데기
(C) 조게디미 연맹대
(D) 고고학

해설 첫 지문의 첫 번째 문단 마지막에서 조게디미 연맹체를 추구하고 싶다고 했으므로 정답은 (C)이다.

185 두 개의 이메일에 따르면, 다음 중 사실이 아닌 것은 무엇인가?
(A) 존스 씨는 연구실 책임자이다.
(B) 벤제이 박사는 전문인이 고고학자이다.
(C) 스미스 씨는 그의 연구를 높이길 원한다.
(D) 벤제이 박사는 메리랜드 대학 교수이다.

해설 첫 이메일에 연구실 책임자인 존스 씨와 연락을 했다는 내용에서 (A)를, 발굴 작업의 주요 전문인 벤제이 박사라고 박사를 설명한 부분에서 (B)를

189 광고에서 언급되지 않은 것은 무엇인가?

(A) 비디오 프로젝트를 찾은 경험 경험
(B) 웅장한 경치가 보이는 통나무집
(C) 업무 회의를 위한 회의실
(D) 계절 가격 할인

해설 첫 번째 지문에서 비디오 프로젝터를 갖춘 새로운 경험이 언급된 부분에서 (A)를, 아름다운 경관을 볼 수 있는 전통 산 통나무집이 언급된 부분에서 (B)를, 크고 작은 사업 모임을 위한 서비스가 제공된다는 부분에서 (C)를 확인할 수 있다. 계절별 가격 할인은 언급되지 않았으므로 정답은 (D)이다.

190 브레드패드 씨에 관해 추측할 수 있는 것은 무엇인가?

(A) 그는 최근에 회사를 설립했다.
(B) 그는 새로운 직원과 경험을 훈련할 필요가 있다.
(C) 그는 리조트에 투자하는 것에 관심이 있다.
(D) 그는 곧 있을 행사에 최대 100명의 직원을 참여시킬 수 있다.

해설 세 번째 지문에서 브레드패드 씨는 경우 멋진 휴양지를 찾고 있다고 언급하고 있고, 그가 찾는 가장 큰 규모의 공간이 정당은 두 번째 지문에서 100명을 수용할 수 있다고 받고 있다. 그러므로 그는 지문에서 최대 100명의 직원을 참여하게 할 수도 있다고 미루어 짐작해 볼 수 있다. 따라서 정답은 (D)이다.

[191-195]

수신: 데이비드 브라운 (DBrown@ProCinema.com)
발신: 킴벌리 존슨 (KJohnson@ProCinema.com)
제목: 7채널 홈시어터 SKS-3020
첨부 파일: 프로시네마의 새로운 홈시어터 시스템에 문제가 계속 이어지다.doc

데이비드에게,

영국 소비자 보고서에 발췌해서 동봉한 기사를 봐주세요. 그 기사가 가슴 아플 정도로 분명히 밝히듯, 우리의 주력 상품인 7채널 홈시어터 SKS-3020에 심각한 문제가 있습니다. 당신이 프로시네마에서 품질 관리를 담당하기 때문에 최고의 인력을 동원하여 이 사안을 즉시 처리할 필요가 있습니다. 배선 문제가 깨끗하게 해결되지 않는다면 우리는 회수를 발표해야 할 것입니다. 그것은 근래의 홍보 측면에 있어 손해를 끼치 하고 싶은 회사는 없을 것입니다.

프로시네마의 이사회 의장인 통 이봇스은 이미 회수 조치를 옹호하는 것을 당신에게 말씀드립니다. 회사 사장인 개슬린 모튼는 당신의 답변을 들을 때까지 이 개념을 막을 예정입니다. 늦어도 금요일까지 7채널 홈시어터 SKS-3020의 배선 문제에 관한 최종 답변이 필요합니다.

진심으로
킴 존슨
경영진

영국 소비자 보고서 2017년 8월호
프로시네마의 새로운 홈시어터 시스템에 문제가 계속 이어지다

소비자들을 빌보고 싶어가는 프로시네마의 7채널 홈시어터 제품이 결함이 있다는 것에 동의하는 것 같다. 그 시스템은 지난해에 대대적인 홍보를 받고 출시되었다. 그 제품은 지난 4년에 걸쳐 프로시네마의 효자 상품이었던 5채널 홈시어터 SKS-2020을 대신해서 상당 기간 이어가기로 되어 있었다.

후면 스피커에 배선 문제에 신제품과 그것을 구매한 사람들을 괴롭혔다. 많은 수의 SKS-3020이 소리 높여 불평했고, 주가 가득날수록 판매는 하락했다. 5채널 홈시어터 SKS-2020과 비교하여 판매가 현재 40% 감소하였으나, 심지어 일부 사람은 이전 모델을 되돌리고 7채널 홈시어터 SKS-3020을 폐기하라고 요청하고 있다.

이것은 고품질 제품으로 고객을 만족하게 하며 평판을 쌓아 왔던 프로시네마사에게는 특히 달갑지 못한 사안이다. 새로운 시스템의 배선 문제가 신속하게 해결되지 않는다면, 리베를에 본사들은 두 이 회사는 시장 점유율을 잃을 것이고 그것은 결국 회복하기 힘든 상황일 것이다.

프로시네마는 SKS-3020을 회수할 것입니다.

이 제품의 후면 스피커에서 섬각한 배선 문제 때문에 우리는 7채널 홈시어터 SKS-3020의 회수를 결정하였습니다.

최근에 이 신제품을 구매하신 모든 고객은 7월 21일부터 3개월 동안 우리 가전 제품 매장으로 상품을 보낼 수 있습니다. 우리가 신속하고 안전히 처리해 드리겠습니다.

우리 프로시네마는 고객님께 불편을 끼쳐 대단히 죄송하다는 말씀을 올립니다. 앞으로 우리는 더 좋은 제품과 서비스를 제공하겠다고 약속드립니다.

어휘 issue 통 consumer report 소비자 보고서 persist with 개슬리다 be in agreement 동의하다 be put on the market 출시하다 fanfare 팡파르 rear 뒤 bedevil 괴롭히다 bring back 선전, 홍보 (엿것을) 회복하다 junk (폐기물을) 버리다 unwelcome 달갑지 않은 reputation 평판 make up 보상하다, 만회하다 painfully 고통스럽게 key 중요한 clear up 깨끗하게 해결하다 in terms of ~한 면에서 advocate 옹호하다 hold off 막다 definitive 최종의 at the latest 늦어도 appliance 가전제품 immediately 즉시 completely 완벽히

191 기사에 요지는 무엇인가?

(A) 프로시네마의 시장이 은퇴할 예정이다.
(B) 5채널 홈시어터 SKS-2020이 판매되었다.
(C) 7채널 홈시어터 SKS-3020에 배선 문제가 있다.
(D) 블루스 작가는 7채널 홈시어터 SKS-3020을 극찬하였다.

해설 첫 번째 지문에 제목과 상단에 신제품에 문제가 있음이 드러나 있고, 이 문제는 지문 중반에 7채널 홈시어터 SKS-3020모델의 후면 스피커 배선 문제라고 했으므로 정답은 (C)이다.

192 일부 고객이 주장하는 것은 무엇인가?

(A) 7채널 홈시어터 SKS-3020을 이전 모델로 대체하는 것
(B) 7채널 홈시어터 SKS-3020은 아저도 프로시네마의 가장 훌륭한 작동이라는 것
(C) 프로시네마의 평판은 그 어느 때문에 좋다는 것
(D) 프로시네마는 새로운 시스템으로 많은 돈을 벌고 있다는 것

해설 첫 번째 지문 중간에 예전 모델을 되돌리고 신제품을 폐기하라고 일부이 사람들이 요청하고 있다고 언급하고 있다. 따라서 정답은 (A)이다.

193 브랜드 씨에 대해 사실인 것은 무엇인가?

(A) 리베를에 산다.
(B) 최근에 존슨 씨를 고용했다.
(C) 7월 21일에 출장을 갈 것이다.
(D) 품질 관리를 담당하고 있다.

해설 두 번째 지문 중반에서 품질 관리를 담당하고 있다고 했으므로 (D)가 정답이다. 본사가 리베를에 있다고 했지만 브랜드 씨가 리베를에 사는 것은 알 수 없으므로 (A)는 오답이다.

194 통 이봇스이 하기 원하는 것은 무엇인가?

(A) 이사회의 회의를 소집하는 것
(B) 7채널 홈시어터 SKS-3020을 회수하는 것
(C) 5채널 홈시어터 SKS-2020으로 되돌리는 것
(D) 데이비드 브라운을 해고하는 것

해설 두 번째 지문 하단에 이사회 의장인 통 이봇스은 제품 회수 조치를 옹호하고 있다고 밝히고 있다. 따라서 정답은 (B)이다.

195 프로시네마에 관해 암시된 것은 무엇인가?

(A) 개슬린 모튼이 사장을 정했다.
(B) 존슨 씨는 금요일까지 고객의 답변이 필요하다.
(C) 프로시네마의 수익은 얼마 상승하지도 모른다.
(D) 5채널 홈시어터 SKS-2020은 폐기 처분될 것이다.

해설 두 번째 지문에서 사장이 개슬린 모튼는 데이비드의 답변을 들을 때까지 회수를 막을 예정이라고 언급하고 있지만, 세 번째 지문이 상단에서 회수를 회수한다는 것을 알 수 있다. 이로 미루어 보아 사장인 개슬린 모튼는 결국 회수 조치를 받아들인 것으로 볼 수 있다. 따라서 정답은 (A)이다.

수신: 리차드 데버서 〈Richard_D@southeastelectrical.com〉
발신: 셸리 오스틴 〈S_Austin@hotmail.com〉
날짜: 4월 5일
제목: hotjobs.com의 구인광고에 응답

데버서 씨에게,

196 남동부 전기회사를 대신해서 귀하께서 hotjobs.com의 취업 검색 엔진에 올린 광고를 보고 이 글을 씁니다. 우선, 전기공학 분야에서의 저의 경력을 설명해 보겠습니다. 저는 노스캐롤라이나 기술대학에서 전기공학 석사 학위를 취득했습니다. 199 대학원생 시절에는 캐서린 포브스 박사님 연구실에서 연구를 조교로 일했습니다.

저는 2017년에 듀크 대학에서 박사 학위를 취득했습니다. 199 그 당시에 노스캐롤라이나 전력 회사의 연구 개발 부서에서 인턴사원으로 근무했습니다. 박사 학위 취득 이후에도 그곳에서 확실한 기여를 해왔지만, 저는 새로운 기회에 대해서 열린 자세를 가지고 있습니다. - 그래서 저는 남동부 전기회사에서 일하는 것에 관심이 있습니다. 저는 주로 대형 전력 발전기를 위한 전기 회로 기판을 제작하는 데 주력하고 있습니다. 197 199 저는 주로 대형 전력 발전기를 위한 전기 회로 기판을 제작하는 데 주력하고 있습니다. 첨부된 이력서에 추천서 3통이 증명하듯, 저는 엄숙하고 활동적인 직원입니다.

제가 구직 신청서를 진지하게 고려해 주시기 바랍니다. 곧 소식 듣길 바랍니다.

진심으로
셸리 오스틴

수신: 셸리 오스틴 〈S_Austin@hotmail.com〉
발신: 리차드 데버서 〈Richard_D@southeastelectrical.com〉
날짜: 199 4월 15일
제목: 회신: hotjobs.com의 구인광고에 응답

오스틴 씨에게,

198 199 남동부 전기회사에 관심을 가져 주셔서 감사합니다. 3통의 추천서와 함께 당신의 이력서를 검토해 보았습니다. 당신이 강력한 교육적 배경을 가지고 있다는 것에는 의심의 여지가 없습니다. 당신은 전기기사로 우리가 찾고 있는 모든 자격을 명백히 갖추고 있습니다.

그러나 당신의 이력서 중 제가 확실히 했으면 하는 부분이 하나 있습니다. 당신은 대형 전력 발전기의 전기 회로 기판을 제작한 경험이 있다고 하셨네요. 198 하지만 당신이 맡았었던 것이 정확히 어떤 종류의 발전기인가요? 증기 터빈 발전기, 방사성 동위 원소 발전기, 핵전지, 기타 종류도 있습니다.

199 당신의 경력 중에 설계에 설계한 다양한 발전기에 관한 더욱 구체적인 정보를 이메일로 보내 주시길 바랍니다. 일단 우리가 이와 관련된 사실을 확보하고 있다면, 당신을 면접에 부를 것인지 결정할 수 있을 것입니다. 시간 내 주셔서 감사합니다.

진심으로
리차드 데버서

발신: 남동부 전기회사
043-555-1029

안녕하세요, 오스틴 씨는 남동부 전기회사의 리차드 데버서입니다.

우리는 귀하가 보낸 서류를 신중하게 검토하였습니다. 199 무엇보다도, 귀하가 만든 방사성 동위 원소 발전기가 특히 인상적이었습니다. 그러므로 저는 만나서 더 많은 이야기를 나누고 싶습니다. 200 방사선 지방 시설에 방문할 시기가 오늘 오후쯤 전화해 주실 것에요. 그러면 이번 주 안에 가능한 시간을 선택하시고, 저의 사무실을 방문하도록 또 다른 질문이 있으시면 그에게 질문해 주세요. 곧 뵙니다.

오후 5:38 메시지

어휘 on behalf of ~을 대신해서 electrical engineering 전기공학 master 석사 doctoral degree 박사 하위 research and development 연구 개발 solid 견고한, 충실한 contribution 공헌 specialize in ~을 전문으로 다루다 circuit board 회로 기판 generator 발전기 attest 증명하다 energetic 활동적인 pedigree 계통 quality 자격 steam turbine 증기 터빈 radioisotope 방사성 동위 원소 thermoelectric 열전기의 nuclear 핵의 pertinent 관련된, 적절한 core business 주력 사업 dissertation 논문

196 리차드 데버서는 누구인가?
(A) 노스캐롤라이나 기술대학 학생
(B) 노스캐롤라이나 전력 회사의 직원
(C) hotjobs.com의 직원
(D) 남동부 전기회사의 직원

해설 첫 지문의 상단에 오스틴 박사는 데버서 씨가 남동부 전기회사를 대표해서 올린 구인광고를 보고 글을 쓴다고 언급하고 있으므로 데버서 씨는 남동부 전기회사의 직원임을 알 수 있다. 따라서 정답은 (D)이다.

197 오스틴 씨가 전문적으로 다루는 것은 무엇인가?
(A) 홍보
(B) 모바스 박사를 돕는 것
(C) 대학원생을 가르치는 것
(D) 전기 회로 기판을 제작하는 것

해설 첫 지문 중반에 오스틴 박사는 대형 전력 발전기를 위한 전기 회로 기판을 제작하는 데 주력한다고 언급하고 있으므로 정답은 (D)이다.

198 데버서 씨가 구체적으로 요청하는 정보는 무엇인가?
(A) 오스틴 박사가 언제 인터뷰가 올 수 있을 건지
(B) 오스틴 박사의 박사 하위 취득하고 있다
(C) 오스틴 박사의 하력
(D) 전력 발전기에 대한 정보

해설 두 번째 지문 하단에 데버서 씨는 오스틴 박사에게 그녀가 설계한 발전기에 대한 구체적인 정보를 보내 달라고 요청하고 있으므로 정답은 (D)이다.

199 문자 메시지에서 알 수 있는 것은 무엇인가?
(A) 데버서 씨는 오스틴 박사와 여러 번 일했다.
(B) 남동부 전기회사는 4월에 신제품을 출시할 것이다.
(C) 오스틴 박사는 4월 15일에 데버서 씨에게 이메일을 보냈다.
(D) 데버서 씨는 최근에 매니저로 고용되었다.

해설 두 번째 이메일에서 데버서 씨가 발전기에 관한 더욱 구체적인 정보를 이메일로 보내 달라고 했다. 문자 메시지에서 데버서 씨는 오스틴 씨는 오스틴 박사가 만든 방사성 동위 원소 발전기가 인상적이었다고 했으므로 데버서 씨는 오스틴 박사와 이메일을 보냈음을 알 수 있다. 두 번째 이메일을 보낸 날짜가 4월 15일이고 문자 메시지를 보낸 날짜도 4월 15일이므로 같은 날에 이메일을 보낸 것이므로 정답은 (C)가 정답이다.

200 오스틴 박사에 관해 추측할 수 있는 것은 무엇인가?
(A) 그녀는 노스캐롤라이나 전력 회사에서 정규직으로 근무한다.
(B) 그녀는 hotjobs.com에 이력서를 정규적으로 제출하였다.
(C) 그녀는 항목 광고에서 매우 큰 도움을 받았다.
(D) 그녀는 전화상으로 포브스 씨와 대화할 것이다.

해설 세 번째 지문에서 박사인 포브스 씨가 전화할 것이라고 했으므로 (D)가 정답이다.

Actual Test

07

저자 이미영

다음 카페(http://cafe.daum.net/speedytoeic)

» [나훈토 1:1 코칭] 게시판 이용

본책 P148

Reading Comprehension

PART 7

147 (C)	148 (D)	149 (B)	150 (D)	151 (D)	152 (B)	153 (A)	154 (A)	155 (B)
156 (D)	157 (C)	158 (B)	159 (A)	160 (C)	161 (A)	162 (B)	163 (A)	164 (D)
165 (A)	166 (D)	167 (C)	168 (B)	169 (B)	170 (A)	171 (D)	172 (C)	173 (D)
174 (B)	175 (A)	176 (D)	177 (D)	178 (D)	179 (B)	180 (A)	181 (A)	182 (D)
183 (C)	184 (C)	185 (C)	186 (D)	187 (C)	188 (B)	189 (C)	190 (C)	191 (C)
192 (D)	193 (D)	194 (C)	195 (C)	196 (D)	197 (D)	198 (B)	199 (C)	200 (D)

수신: 전 직원
발신: 해롤드 칸 <Kahnh@krontel.com>
날짜: 7월 4일

안녕하십니까, 여러분.

지난 몇 달 동안 크론텔 산업에 다사다난한 일들이 있었습니다. 이 소식을 여러분 모두와 현 상황에 대해 궁금해 할 것을 알고 있기에 이 소식을 **[147]** 저는 여러분 전체에 드리겠습니다. 예정했던 HVC사와의 합병은 최근 몇 차례의 협상 동안 몇 조건에 동의하지 못했기 때문에 완전히 수포로 돌아갈 수 있을 것 **[148]** 안 이었습니다. 또 다른 변경 사항은 이제 외부 전화를 걸기 전에 반드시 9번을 눌러야 리 이사회에서 투표로 정해진 것입니다. 또한, 여러분은 이미 우리 회사와 힐러리 트 한다는 점입니다. 그리고 동료에게 전화를 걸기 위해선, 1번을 누른 후에 내선 서 아무것도 정해진 것은 없습니다. 저는 새로운 시스템으로 변경하게 되어 아주 순조로울 롱 부사장이 퇴사하는 것으로 정해진 것도 아닙니다. 저는 여러분에게 이 소식을 전하며 오 것이라고 예상합니다. IT팀은 여러분들이 직접적인 모든 것을 철저하게 모든 문제에 도 읽은 HVC 상황과 아무런 관련이 없다는 것을 확실히 하고자 합니다. 그녀는 개 움을 드릴 수 있을 것입니다.

이것이 이유로 인해 크론텔을 영원히 떠날 것입니다. 마지막으로 저는 여러분 모두에게 지속적 인 그린 업무 크론텔을 일하기 위한 좋은 회사로 만들어 준 것에 감사를 드리 고 싶습니다.

해롤드 칸
대표 이사, 크론텔 산업

어휘 eventful 사건이 많은, 다사다난한 status 상태, 상황 merger 합병 fall through (성공; 예상 등이) 안 되다 무너지다 inability 무능력 terms (계약) 조건 round 차례 negotiation 협상 board of directors 이사회 resume 재개하다 retire 퇴직하다 assure 장담하다 elect 선출하다 demand 요구하다 resign 퇴직하다

147 간 씨가 이 이메일을 보낸 이유는 무엇인가?
(A) 두 회사 간의 합병을 제안하기 위해서
(B) 신임 부사장을 발표하기 위해서
(C) **직원들에게 최근 일들에 대해 알려 주기 위해서**
(D) 그가 퇴직하는 이유를 설명하기 위해서

해설 이메일의 목적은 주로 앞부분에 제시되는 경우가 많다. 여러분 모두 회 사의 상황에 대해 궁금해할 것이나 간단히 최신 소식을 전하겠다고 했으므로 정답은 (C)이다. (A)는 합병 관련 내용이 나오지만 씨가 씨가 제안하는 사람은 아니므로 함병을 진행 중인 상황이며, 퇴직하는 간 씨가 아니고 부사장 (힐러리 트롱)이므로 (D)도 오답이다.

148 크론텔 이사회에 관해 언급된 것은 무엇인가?
(A) 새로운 이장을 선출했다.
(B) HVC사의 제안을 수락했다.
(C) 간 씨에게 퇴직하라고 요구했다.
(D) **계속 협상하기로 했다.**

해설 이사회 투표를 통해 사내에 HVC사와 대화를 재개하기로 했다는 내용 이 나온다. 따라서 결국 이사회는 협상을 지속하는 것을 원한다는 걸 알 수 있으므로 정답은 (D)이다.

메모

수신: 전 리드위크 빌딩 직원들
발신: 조너던 페이스, IT 부장

[149] 다음 월요일부터 건물에 새로운 전화 시스템이 완전히 가동될 것입니다. 이 전 시스템과 다른 주요 변경 사항은 각 개인에게 개인 음성 사서함이 추가될 것이라는 점입니다. **[150]** 여러분은 월요일에 단순히 따르면 새로운 사서함에 접속할 수 있을 것 입니다. 또 다른 변경 사항은 이제 외부 전화를 걸기 전에 반드시 9번을 눌러야 한다는 점입니다. 그리고 동료에게 전화를 걸기 위해선, 1번을 누른 후에 내선 번호를 눌러야 합니다. 저는 새로운 시스템으로 변경하게 되어 아주 순조로울 것이라고 예상합니다. IT팀은 여러분들이 직접적인 모든 것을 철저하게 모든 문제에 도 움을 드릴 수 있을 것입니다.

어휘 operational 가동의 운영 primary 주요한 addition 추가 individual 개인(적인), 개별(적인) voice mailbox 음성 사서함 pound key (전화기의) 우물 정(#)자 step-by-step 단계적인 instruction 지시, 명령 external 외부의 coworker 동료 extension number 내선 번호 transition 변화 seamless 아주 매끄러운, 순조로운 encounter 맞닥뜨리다 remind A of B A에게 B를 상기시키다 passcode 비밀번호 stoppage 중지, 정지 enforce 시행하다 policy 정책, 방침 initiate 시작하다

149 메모의 목적은 무엇인가?
(A) 직원들에게 사무실 비밀번호를 상기시키려고
(B) **새로운 시스템으로 인한 변경 사항을 설명하려고**
(C) 직원들에게 서비스 중단에 대해 알려 주려고
(D) 사적인 전화에 관한 방침을 시행하려고

해설 해당 메모는 전 직원들에게 다음 주 월요일부터 건물에 새로운 전화 시 스템이 가동된다는 사실을 알려 주기 위한 것이다. 따라서 정답은 (B) 이다. 새로운 전화 시스템의 변경 사항으로 음성 사서함의 추가와 외부 전화 사용과 관련된 것 등이 있다.

150 직원이 우물 정(#)자를 눌러야 하는 이유로 언급된 것은 무엇인가?
(A) 메시지를 삭제하기 위해서
(B) IT팀과 연락하기 위해서
(C) 전화를 끊기 위해서
(D) **과정을 시작하기 위해서**

해설 새로운 시스템에 접속하기 위해서는 우물 정(#)자를 누르고 단계적 지시 사항을 따르라고 했다. 즉, 우물 정자를 누르면 다음 지시 사항 과정이 시작된다는 의미이므로 정답은 (D)이다.

제메인 바리아	오후 7:15
이봐요! 우리 월요일 열차표를 사용했나요?	
스테판 윌리엄스	오후 7:21
물론이죠. 목요일에 돌아오는 **[151]** 웰링턴 행 10시 20분 고속 왕복표 2장 사 놓았어요.	
제메인 바리아	오후 7:26
오, 안됐어! 안타깝게 됐네요!	
스테판 윌리엄스	오후 7:27
무슨 일이죠? 제가 표를 잘못 샀어요?	
제메인 바리아	오후 7:30
아니요, 그렇지만, 제가 여행사 콤드 신용 카드로 표를 샀으면 10% 할인을 받 았을 수 있었다는 걸 몇 분 전에 안 거예요.	
스테판 윌리엄스	오후 7:35
아, 그랬군요, **[152]** 별일 아니에요. 그 표가 값이 꽤 싸요. **[151]** 제가 온라인으로 각각 40달러에 샀거든요	
제메인 바리아	오후 7:38
생각보다 싸네요. 오전 10시 20분이요, 아니면 오후인가요?	
스테판 윌리엄스	오후 7:44
오전 10시 20분이에요. **[151]** 웰링턴에 도착하는 건 오후 4시쯤이에요. 그러면 우리는 Michael을 만나 저녁을 먹기 전에 호텔을 찾고 느긋하게 쉴 시간이 충분할 거예요.	

어휘 round-trip 왕복 여행의 express 급행열차 it's no big deal 별일 아니다 settle in 쉬다, 휴식하다

151 바리아 씨와 윌리엄스 씨에 관해 암시되지 **않는** 것은 무엇인가?
(A) 열차표 비용은 대해서 80달러를 썼다.
(B) 목적지는 웰링턴이다.
(C) 오후에 도착할 것이다.
(D) **한 주 동안 머무를 것이다.**

해설 7시 15분의 첫 대화에서 열차는 월요일에 떠남을 알 수 있으며, 7시 21분 대화에서 목요일에 돌아온다는 것을 알 수 있다. 따라서 머무르 는 시간은 일주일이 되지 않으므로 (D)가 정답이다. 총 2장의 표를 각 각 40달러에 샀으므로, 총액은 80달러로 (A)는 맞는 내용이다. (B)도 웰링턴으로 가는 왕복표를 샀다고 했으므로 맞는 내용이다. (C)도 오후 4시경에 도착한다고 했으므로 맞는 내용이다.

152 오후 7시 35분에 윌리엄스 씨가 "별일 아니에요"라고 쓴 의미는 무엇인가?
(A) 표가 너무 비쌌던 것 같다.
(B) **그 문제는 중요하지 않다.**
(C) 신용 카드는 승인되지 않았다.
(D) 여행은 중요하지 않다.

해설 해당 표현 앞에서 흠잡을 받을 기회를 놓치지 하겠고, 해당 표현 뒤에 이어지는 문맥에서는 표이 가격이 꽤 썼다고 했다. 따라서 사이에 들어갈 만한 내용은 (B)이다. It's no big deal은 '별로 아니다'라는 뜻으로 읽어두자.

[153-155]

자동 사용 설명서

웨스트랜드 다큐프로 2000

1. 전력 스위치를 " 기호로 표시되는 켬 위치로 미세요. **154** 기계가 제대로 작동할 때는 기계 뒷면에 있는 초록색 LED 등불이 들어올 것입니다. 만약 초록색 불이 들어오지 않으면 기계의 문이 단단히 닫혀 있는지 확인하세요.

2. 용지 공급 간에 원지 않는 문서들을 놓으시고 그것을 부드럽게 안쪽으로 누르세요. **155** 종이가 일단 용지 공급 감지 센서를 지나가면, 기계는 자동으로 그 종이들을 처리가 시작할 것입니다.

3. 끝나면, 기계가 자동으로 작동을 멈추기를 기다리십시오. 마지막 문서가 완전히 처리된 후, 대략 5초 후에 멈출 것입니다. 초록색 LED 등불이 꺼질 것이고, 빨간색 불이 지속적으로 빛날 것입니다.

4. **155** 빨간색 불이 깜빡이면, 종이 걸림 현상이 발생한 것입니다. 눈에 보이는 모든 서류를 용지 공급 간에서 부드럽게 꺼내십시오. 칼날이 작동하지 않는 동안에도 심한 부상을 유발할 수 있으니, 절대 기계 안에 손가락을 넣지 않도록 유의하세요.

5. 앞문을 열고 쓰레기 비닐봉지를 확인하십시오. 만약 가득 차 있으면, 기계에서 전체 틀을 빼내 가벼 꺼낸 후에 봉지를 제거해 폐기하세요.

어휘 slide 미끄러뜨리다 power 전력 on 켜진 position 위치(시키다) indicate 나타내다, 가리키다 illuminate 불이 들어오다 properly 적절히 activate 활성화하다 firmly 단단히, 굳게 paper feeder 용지 공급기 tray 칸막이 상자, 접시, 정리 상자 automatically 자동으로 deactivate 비활성화하다 occur 일어나다, 발생하다 approximately 대략 go off (불이 나가다) glow 빛나다 steadily 지속적, 꾸준히 blinking 깜빡이는 paper jam 종이 걸림 visible 눈에 보이는 blade 칼날 plastic bag 비닐봉지 frame 틀 disposal 처리 shredder 파쇄기 scanner 스캐너 flashing 번쩍이는

153 다큐프로 2000은 무엇일 것인가?
(A) 종이 파쇄기
(B) 컴퓨터 프린터
(C) 복사기
(D) 디지털 스캐너

해설 전체적인 상황을 종합해서 해당 기계의 용도를 찾아야 하는 문제이다. 기계가 작동하는 내용에서 일단 용지 감지 센서를 지나갈 것이라고 했다. 따라서 이 기계의 사용 목적은 종이를 파쇄하는 것임을 알 수 있으므로 정답은 (A)이다.

154 다음 중 기계 작동을 막는 것은 무엇인가?
(A) 문을 제대로 닫지 않기
(B) 용지 공급 센서를 활성화하기
(C) 비닐봉지 설치하기
(D) 용지 공급 간에 서류 넣기

해설 기계가 제대로 작동되는 표시인 초록색 LED 등불이 들어오지 않는다면 문이 단단히 닫혀 있는지 확인하라고 했으므로, 정답은 (A)이다. 지문의 shut을 선택지에서는 close으로 표현했다.

155 사용 설명서에 따르면, 깜빡이는 불이 나타내는 것은 무엇인가?
(A) 기계가 제대로 작동 중이다.
(B) 종이가 걸렸다.
(C) 문이 열려 있다.
(D) 쓰레기봉투가 가득 차 있다.

해설 질문에 등장하는 키워드 flashing light(깜빡이는 불)는 문의 blinking red light(깜빡이는 빨간 불)을 패러프레이징한 것이다. 단 사이 내용에서 만약 깜빡는 빨간색 불이 나타내면 종이 걸림이 발생한 것이라고 언급되어 있으므로 정답은 (B)이다. 지문의 paper jam을 선택지에서는 The paper is stuck으로 패러프레이징했다.

[156-158]

http://www.LCU.ac.uk

런던 시립 대학교

홈	학생	생활	연락처

올여름에 머물 장소를 찾고 계신가요? 캠퍼스에서 2km 이내에 있는 방 두 개짜리 아파트가 있는데, 6월 초부터 8월 말까지 다시 세를 놓을 계획입니다. **157** 이것은 함께하으로 다시 세를 놓는 것이므로, 계약서에 서명할 필요는 없지만 집 주인의 허가를 받아야 합니다. 하지만 현재 주인으로 꽤 느긋한 사람입니다! **156** 저는 그 3개월 동안 교통 프로그램의 일원으로 해외에서 공부할 것이기 때문에 당장 이사 오실 수 있으며 제 물건을 쓸 수도 있으니, 가구, **158** 주방용품이나 수건을 챙겨 오실 필요가 없습니다! 방문 학생 장소를 찾고 있는 사람에게는 바로 완벽한 곳입니다. 여분에는 **158** 20용 침대가 있습니다. 욕실에는 **158** 세탁기와 건조기 간 있으니, 편리이 쓰는 다른 방에는 1인용 침대가 있습니다. 목실에는 20용 침대가 있습니다. 관심이 있으시면 저에게 직접 재해 자산들을 간 단히 소개하는 이메일을 보내 주시면, 가능한 한 빨리 답변드리도록 하겠습니다.

어휘 sublet 다시 임대주다 easygoing 편안한, 느긋한 landlord 주인 visiting student 방문 학생 kitchenware 주방용품 situation 상황 real estate 부동산 signed 서명된 bathtub 욕조 separate 분리된 별도의 dishwasher 식기 세척기 clothes washer 세탁기 strict 엄격한 시기 세탁기

156 이 웹 페이지에 공지문을 게시한 사람은 누구인가?
(A) 부동산 중개인
(B) 건물 주인
(C) 교수
(D) 학생

해설 공지를 올린 사람은 3개월 동안 교통 프로그램의 일부로 해외에서 공부할 것이라고 밝혔다. 따라서 학생임을 알 수 있으므로 정답은 (D)이다.

157 집주인에 관해 언급된 것은 무엇인가?
(A) 그는 자동차에 관해 걸치 못한다.
(B) 그는 서명된 계약서가 필요하다.
(C) 그는 엄격한 사람이 아니다.
(D) 그는 그 건물에 산다.

해설 landlord(집주인)가 등장하는 문맥을 보면, 바로 앞 문장에서 pretty easygoing이 선택지에서 표현된 strict person이라는 표현을 통해서 정답을 파악할 수 있다. 그는 편안한(느긋한) 사람이다라는 것은 곧 엄격한 사람이 아니라는 것이므로 정답은 (C)이다. 지문의 pretty easygoing이 선택지에서는 not a strict person이라고 패러프레이징되었다.

158 아파트에 포함된 것으로 언급되지 않은 것은 무엇인가?
(A) 두 개의 침대
(B) 식기 세척기
(C) 냄비와 팬
(D) 세탁기

해설 아파트에 포함된 것으로 언급된 것을 하나씩 대조하면서 소거해 보자. 20용 침대와 1인용 침대, 총 2개의 침대가 있다고 했으며, 주방용품, 세탁기와 건조기뿐만 아니라 욕조와 별도의 샤워기가 있습니다. 관심이 있으시면, 관계 채택 주방용품 세탁기가 언급되지 않은 (B)가 정답이다.

존 로즈 [오후 4:41]	안녕하세요, 여러분. **160** 저를 도와줄 사람이 필요해요. 제 일정이 갑작스럽게 변경되어서, 내일 오후에 반 다이크 박사님을 공항에 데 태우러 갈 자원봉사자가 필요해요.
브랜든 조 [오후 4:42]	제가 기꺼이 그분을 데려올게요. 로즈 씨. 저는 내일 일정이 여유로워요.
데비 웨이드 [오후 4:42]	제가 할 수 있어요. 회사 차를 빌릴 수 있을까요?
존 로즈 [오후 4:47]	그게 문제예요. 제가 내일 도시 외곽 회의에 가는데 회사 차가 필요하거든요. 여러분 중 한 분이 개인 차량을 갖고 있지 않나요?
데비 웨이드 [오후 4:48]	죄송하지만, 저는 없어요.
브랜든 조 [오후 4:49]	저는 SUV를 가지고 있어요. 그렇지만, 만약 데비가 그분을 태우러 가는 것이 낫다고 생각하시면, 제가 차를 빌려드릴 수 있어요.
존 로즈 [오후 4:51]	고마워요, 브랜든. 그렇지만 당신은 혼자서 그 일을 처리할 수 있을 거예요.
브랜든 조 [오후 4:53]	물론이죠, 문제없어요. 몇 시에 그분이 도착하죠? **159** 그분의 항공편 번호를 아시나요?
존 로즈 [오후 4:54]	제가 검색해봤어요. 제 비서한테 가서 그 이브 세르, 비서가 모든 세부 사항에 대해 알려줄 거예요.
브랜든 조 [오후 4:55]	알겠어요. **160** 제가 그녀와 얘기해 볼게요.

어휘 get A out of B A를 B로부터 구하다 · unexpected 예상치 못한 · volunteer 자원자 · pick up ~을 태우다 · out-of-town 도시 외곽의 · conference 회의 · vehicle 차량 · SUV 스포츠 유틸리티 차량 = sport utility vehicle · on one's own 스스로 · slip one's mind 깜박 잊다 · fill A in on B A에게 B에 대해 모든 일을 알려주다

159 조 씨가 다음에 할 일은 무엇인가?

(A) 항공기 정보 얻기
(B) 공항으로 SUV 운전해 가기
(C) 반 다이크 박사에게 연락하기
(D) 집으로 귀가하기

해설 로즈 씨는 반 다이크 박사의 항공편 번호를 묻는 조에게 비서가 관련 세부 사항을 알려줄 거라고 했다. 이에 조 씨가 그녀와 얘기하겠다고 했으므로 정답은 (A)가 된다.

---

160 오후 4시 41분에 로즈 씨가 '저를 도와줄 사람이 필요해요'라고 쓴 의미는 무엇인가?

(A) 그는 교통 체증으로 꼼짝 못 하고 있다.
(B) 그는 약간의 자료를 원한다.
(C) 그는 도움이 필요하다.
(D) 그는 프로젝트를 걱정한다.

해설 로즈 씨가 갑작스러운 일정 변경 때문에 반 다이크 박사를 공항으로 태우러 가거나 그분을 대려올게요, 로즈 씨. 저 우리 가지 못하게 되자, 자기 대신 갈 사람을 구하고 있으므로 정답은 (C)가 된다.

[161-164]

조셉 기드먼
인수부
레인골드 도회사
19188 6번가
디트로이트, 미시간 48207
기드먼 씨에게,

지난 금요일에 디트로이트 사무실에서 귀하와 직원들을 만나서 기뻤습니다. **161** 귀사에 보안 장비와 모니터링 서비스를 제공하는 것에 관해 논의했던 대로, 저희 대표이사의 승인을 받은 정식 가격 견적서를 보내드립니다. - [1] -. 저희 가 귀사에 제공하는 서비스가 이 할인의 한계 기준을 충족시키지 못하지 만, 저희 대표이사가 귀사의 성장을 기대하여 할인을 제공하는 데에 동의하셨습 니다. - [2] -. 이 계약 조건에 동의하신다면, 계약서에 서명한 시점부터 1년 동 안 이 할인이 유지될 것입니다. - [3] -. **164** 이 기간이 만료되면, 저희는 귀사 가 요청하신 서비스가 저희의 표준 최소 기준을 충족시키거나 그 이상의 메일까 대량 구매 할인을 계속 제공해 드릴 것입니다. - [4] -. 첨부된 견적서를 검토 하시고 거래를 계속하도록 빨리 연락주세요.

진심으로
패트릭 챈센
하우스맨 보안 서비스

어휘 acquisition 인수 · as per ~에 따라 · security 보안, 안전 · equipment 장비 · monitoring 감시, 감독 · formal 정식의, 형식의 · estimate 견적(서) · in anticipation of ~을 예상하고, ~에 대비하여 · forecasted 예상된 · meet the threshold (한계) 수준을 충족하다 · scale 규모 · surpass 능가하다 · in place 제자리에 · expire 만료되다 · minimum 최소 · attached 첨부된 · at one's earliest convenience 되도록 빨 리 · follow up 후속 조치를 하다 · confirmation 확인 · proposal 제안 · approximation 견적, 추정 · revised 개정된, 수정된 · reflect 반영하 다 · bulk discount 대량 구매 시 할인 · large customer 대량 매매 고객 · reassess 다시 평가하다

---

161 이 편지의 목적은 무엇인가?

(A) 회의 후속 조치를 하라고
(B) 새로운 서비스를 소개하려고
(C) 제안을 거절하려고
(D) 할인을 요청하려고

해설 글의 목적이 등장하는 서두 부분에서 논의한 대로, 정식 가격 견적서를 보낸다고 했다. 따라서 이 편지는 회의 이후에 관련된 후속 조치를 위한 내용임을 알 수 있다. 따라서 정답은 (A)이다.

---

162 이 편지와 동봉될 것으로 암시된 것은 무엇인가?

(A) 소개 편지
(B) 비용 견적서
(C) 수정된 계약서
(D) 제품 목록

해설 대표이사의 승인을 받은 정식 가격 견적서를 보낸다고 했다. 따라서 이 편지는 비용 견적서임을 알 수 있으므로, 정답은 (B)이 다. 지문의 price estimate를 선택지(에서는 cost approximation으 로 패러프레이징했다.

---

163 [1], [2], [3], [4]로 표시된 곳 중 다음 문장이 위치로 가장 적절한 곳은 어디인 가?

이 가격은 대량 구매 고객들에게 제공하는 15%의 대량 구매 할인이 반영된 것입니다.

(A) [1]
(B) [2]
(C) [3]
(D) [4]

해설 [1] 앞에서 대표이사의 승인을 받은 정식 가격 견적서를 보내드린다고 했는 데, 뒷부분에는 저희 서비스가 사실상 대량 할인의 기준을 충족시키 지는 못했지만 앞으로의 성장을 기대하며 대량 할인을 승인해 주었다 는 내용이 나오므로 이 사이에 15%의 대량 구매 할인이 반영되었다는 삽입 문장이 들어가야 가장 적절하다. 따라서 정답은 (A)이다.

---

164 만약 할인이 도입된다면 1년 후에 무슨 일이 있을 것인가?

(A) 대량 구매 할인이 증가될 것이다.
(B) 계약이 자동으로 갱신될 것이다.
(C) 대표이사가 또 다른 회의를 요청할 것이다.
(D) 계약 조건이 다시 평가될 것이다.

해설 해당 계약 기간이 1년이 만료되면, 회사의 요청 서비스가 최소 기준을 충족시키거나 그 이상인 경우에만 대량 구매 할인을 계속 제공해줄 것 이라고 했으므로 정답은 (D)가 된다. (B는 현재의 계약 조건이 지속되 는 것이 아니라 다시 한번 서비스 유형 평가에서 해당 평가대로 계약을 유지할지 정할 것이므로 오답이다.)

JL 미스테이기

JL 미스테이기는 운영이 건조한 사무실에 통과하여 있는 사람들에게 완벽한 탁상용 친구입니다. 이 최신식의 초음파 가습기는 여러분에게 10시간 이상 지속해서 수분을 제공할 수 있는 1.5리터의 물탱크를 특징으로 합니다. 작은 크기와 거의 소리가 나지 않는 초음파 모터 덕분에, 미스테이기는 전국 각지의 사무실 근로자들이 1순위로 선택하는 제품입니다.

물탱크는 쉽게 물을 보충할 수 있도록 뺄 수 있으며, 청소해야 할 불편한 필터도 없습니다. (170) 그리고 만약 여러분이 바쁜 일과를 끝내고 퇴근할 때 미스테이기를 끄는 것을 잊어버리셨다고 해도, 걱정하지 마세요! 일단 물탱크가 비면 시스템이 자동으로 꺼집니다.

이상들은 인후를 가라앉고 코 막힘을 포함하여 (170) 감기나 독감 증상을 완화하는 데 도움이 되므로 가습기를 사용하길 추천합니다. 그것들은 또한 (170) 피부가 건조하고 가려운 눈을 진정시키는 데 훌륭한 방법이기도 합니다.

JL 미스테이기는 47가지 선명한 색상으로 출시되는데, 아무 가게에서나 구매할 수 없으니! (171) 오늘 저렴한 가격인 39달러 99센트로 주문을 하시려면 JL 일 렉트로닉스 무료 전화인 1-888-555-7822번으로 전화해 주세요.

어휘 desktop 탁상용의 companion 친구, 벗 confine 가두다 {정의} (에) humidifier 가습기 state-of-the-art 최신식의 ultrasonic 초음파의 특징(으로 하다) provide A with B A에게 B를 제공하다 continuous 지속적인 moisture 습기 compact 작고 경제적인 removable 제거할 수 있는 refilling 같이 채우기, 다시 보충하기 inconvenient 불편한 ease 완화하다 sore throat 인후통 nasal congestion 코 막힘 soothe 진정시키다, 누그러뜨리다 itchy 가려운, 근질근질한 vibrant 선명한 toll-free (수신자) 무료의 automated 자동화된 shutdown 중지, 멈춤 regulation 조절 waterproof 방수의 moisten 촉촉하게 하다 comfort 편안하게 하다 wholesaler 도매상 department store 백화점

169 JL 미스테이기의 안전한 기능으로 언급된 것은 무엇인가?

(A) 이중 여과
(B) 자동 중지
(C) 온도 조절
(D) 방수 케이스

해설 만약 제품을 끄는 것을 잊어버렸다고 하더라도 일단 물탱크가 비면 시스템이 자동으로 꺼진다고 했다. 따라서 정답은 (B)이다. 지문의 automatically switches off라는 표현을 선택지에서는 Automated shutdown으로 패러프레이징했다.

170 가습기가 증상을 완화하는 것으로 언급되지 않은 것은 무엇인가?

(A) 스트레스 줄이기
(B) 피부를 촉촉하게 하기
(C) 눈을 편안하게 하기
(D) 기침 완화하기

해설 가습기가 질병들을 세 번째 단락에 언급되어 있다, 피부가 건조해지는

스마트 스티프 주문 제작 전화 케이스
온라인 주문 양식

성명	
배송 주소	
전화번호	

(165) 케이스 종류 선택하기:
☐ 딱딱한 케이스 14달러 99센트
☐ 부드러운 케이스(플라스틱) 9달러 99센트
☐ 부드러운 케이스(가죽) 29달러 99센트

(165) 케이스 색상 고르기:
☐ 흰색 ☐ 검정 ☐ 초록 ☐ 빨강 ☐ 진한 파랑 ☐ 밝은 파랑

(165) 질감 선택하기:
☐ 부드러운 것 ☐ 거친 것

각인을 추가하세요. (166) 각인은 (띄어쓰기 포함) 공간을 포함해 30자를 초과하면 안 되고, 글자와 숫자, 그리고 구두점만을 포함해야 합니다. (5달러 추가)

사진을 추가하세요. 사진들은 반드시 JPG 이미지로 되어야 하며, 크기가 2.5MB를 초과하지는 안 됩니다. (15달러 추가)

(167) 19달러 99센트 초과 주문 시에 무료 국내 배송 기능됩니다. (167) 3달러짜리 빠른 배송을 원하신면 7일당거 추가되고, 일반 배송을 원하신면 3달러 가 추가됩니다. (168) 15개 이상 주문 시에 할인이 요금이 적용됩니다. 주문 총액의 10%의 할인이 제공될 것입니다. 문의 사항이 있으시면 516-555-9927로 저희에게 연락해 주세요.

어휘 customized 맞춤제작된 mailing 우편 배송 texture 질감, 감촉 rough 거친 inscription 각인 exceed 초과하다 character 문자 punctuation 구두점 express shipping 빠른 배송 domestic 국내의 rate 요금, 가격 provide 제공하다 customizable 맞춤 제작할 수 있는 option 선택(권) free of charge 무료로 limit 제한 waive 적용하지 않다, 철회하다 qualify for ~에 자격을 갖추다 charge for ~에 대한 지불 particular 특정의 inscribed (이름, 문자 등이) 새겨진, 각인된

165 맞춤 제작 시 선택권으로 언급되지 않은 것은 무엇인가?

(A) 크기
(B) 색깔
(C) 질감
(D) 재료

해설 해당 지문은 전화 케이스 주문서로, 다양한 맞춤 제작 상품에 관한 것이다. 선택지 각각을 대조해서 등장한 것을 소개하는 방식으로 문제를 풀어보자. 케이스 종류, 색상. 질감은 선택할 수 있지만 크기에 대해서는 언급되어 있지 않다. 따라서 (A)가 정답이다.

---

166 각인에 관해 언급된 것은 무엇인가?

(A) 다양한 서체로 출력된다.
(B) 서체를 선택할 수 있다.
(C) 무료이다.
(D) 길이 제한이 있다.

해설 각인은 공간을 포함해서 반드시 30자를 초과하면 안 된다고 했다. 따라서 정답은 (D)이다. 지문의 must not exceed 30 characters in length를 선택지에서 length limit(길이 제한)이 든다고 표현했으므로 정답은 (D)이다.

---

167 고객들은 어떻게 하면 배송비를 감면받을 수 있는가?

(A) 전화로 주문함으로써
(B) 느린 배송을 선택함으로써
(C) 특정 달러 금액을 초과함으로써
(D) 많은 양의 케이스를 주문함으로써

해설 19달러 99센트 초과 주문 시에 무료 국내 배송이 가능하다는 내용을 통해 19달러 99센트 초과하면 배송비를 받지 않는다는 것을 알 수 있다. 따라서 정답은 (C)이다. 지문의 free(무료)이라는 표현은 보기 waived와 의미상 일맥상통한다. 또한, 지문의 19달러 99센트는 보기 의 a certain amount(특정 달러 금액)을 의미한다고 볼 수 있다.

---

168 다음 중 특별 할인율을 받을 수 있는 것은 무엇인가?

(A) 빠른 배송
(B) 특정 수량의 주문들
(C) 특정일 이전에 구매한 물품
(D) 각인 케이스 한 개 구매

해설 15개 이상 주문 시에 할인이 요금이 적용된다고 했다. 따라서 정답은 (B) 이다. 질문의 special discount는 지문의 special rate와 같은 의미이며, 지문의 15 cases or more라는 구체적인 주문 수량은 선택지에서 particular number로 패러프레이징되었다.

[176-180]

공지

자택가 최인데 웨스트 코스트 선샘을 인수한 것이 일환으로, **175** **176** 전 직원자 직원들이 모든 웨스트 코스트 헬스 월드 피트니스 센터 회원권을 50% 할인받을 수 있다는 것을 알려 드리게 되어 기쁩니다. 헬스클럽에 등록할 때, 온라인이나 혹은 직접 방문하는 다음 코드를 사용하기만 하면 됩니다: 그 코드는 BVC115 입니다. 여러분들은 신청서 하단에 코드를 기재할 것임을 칠을 수 있을 것입니다.

176 직계 가족 또한 이 할인을 받을 수 있는데, 직원 본인을 가족 3명으로 제한됩니다. 가족들은 약간 다른 코드를 사용해야 합니다: 코드는 BVC115F입니다.

시간제 직원들은 BVC112 코드를 사용해서 20% 할인을 받으실 수 있으며, 계약직 직원들은 BVC111 코드를 써서 회원권 10% 할인을 받을 수 있습니다. 그러나 시간제 직원들과 계약직 직원들의 가족들은 할인을 받을 수 없습니다. **177** 코드들을 사용하는 모든 신청서는 경리부에서 검토한 후 승인될 것이며, 이 코드를 남용하지 말 것을 권고합니다. 또한, 할인은 기존 회원권에는 적용되지 않지만, 갱신권에는 적용이 가능합니다.

웨스트 코스트 헬스 월드
등록 신청서

이름: 나탈리 린
성별: 여성
나이: 27세

179 **이메일 주소:** soccerfan97@goldpro.com
(업데이트나 홍보 자료를 위해서만 요청함; 제3자 누구에게도 양도하거나 공유하지 않을 것)

☑ 신규 회원
☐ 갱신

회원권 종류를 고르세요.

☐ 골드 회원권(한 달에 90달러): **180** 메일 개인 트레이너와의 상담 및 지역할인 VIP 라운지를 모두 이용할 수 있는 권리와 더불어 풀 회원권의 특전들을 모두 제공합니다.

☐ **179** 풀 회원권(한 달에 50달러): 무료 주차 스티커, 채용권 사용함과 무료 해스트 코스트 운동복(티셔츠와 반바지)과 더불어 저희의 사설을 모두 이용하실 수 있는 것을 특징으로 합니다.

☐ 이코노미 회원권(한 달에 30달러): 수영장과 사우나를 제외한 모든 시설을 이용할 수 있는 저렴한 회원권 입니다. 주차 스티커와 그릴 렌탈 열악실은 운동복 또는 수영장과 수영장과 그래 렌탈 열악실 비용은 포함되지 않습니다.

178 할인 코드 (해당하는 경우): BVC115F
날짜: 2017년 9월 8일
서명: 나탈리 린

어휘 acquisition 인수　full-time employee 전일제(전일근무) 직원 eligible for ~에 대한 자격이 있다　membership 회원(권)　register 등 be

---

잃을 예약하거나, 피곤하고 기력을 눈을 진정시킨다고 했고, 감기나 독감 증상을 완화시키는 데 도움이 된다고 했다, 따라서 언급되지 않은 (A)가 정답이 된다.

171 JL 미스트메이크는 어떻게 구매할 수 있는가?
(A) 인터넷에서
(B) 도매업자로부터
(C) 박물관에서
(D) 전화로

해설 오늘 저렴한 가격인 39달러 99센트로 주문을 하려면 JL 인텔레크닉 스 무료 전화인 1-888-555-7822로 전화를 걸면 됐으므로 정답은 (D)이다. 단서의 toll-free란 표현은 수신자 무료 전화를 의미하는 표현이다.

[172-175]

중요한 공지

172 폴크-메시이스 은행(PMB)은 3월 2일 금요일 오후 10시부터 3월 4일 일요일 오후 2시까지 정기 주말 시스템 점검을 할 것입니다. 이 시간 동안 저희 ATM은 작동을 멈추게 될 것지만, 모든 기능을 다 이용할 수는 없을 것입니다. - [1] -. **176** 점검 기간 내내 ATM 입금은 불가능할 것이며, ATM 잔액 문의는 추가적으로 불 가능하지도 모릅니다. - [2] - PMB 사이버뱅킹 웹 사이트는 3월 3일 토요일 새벽 시간이 지정부터 새벽 3시까지 온라인 상태가 될 것입니다. 모든 토요일 이용 할 수 없을 것입니다. 마지막으로, 모든 종류의 직불 카드와 신용 카드 거래 는 점심시와 마찬가지로 이용할 수 있을 것이지만, 마감된 입금도 되지 않을 것 입니다. 폴크-메시이스 은행은 저희 고객들이 가장 안전하게 전자 서비스를 이 용하실 수 있도록 하기 위하여 정기적으로 시스템 점검 일정을 잡습니다. - [4] - 이로 인해 불편을 끼쳐 드려 사과드립니다. 만약 문의 사항이 있으시면 정규 은행 근무 시간에 602-555-9542번으로 저희에게 연락해 주십시오.

어휘 undertake 수행하다　maintenance 보수　function 작동(하다) deposit 예금, 입금　balance (은행) 잔액; (지급) 잔액　inquiry 질 문　periodically 정기적으로　briefly 일시적으로　debit card 직불(현 금) 카드　credit card 신용 카드　transaction 거래　secure 안전한　electronic 전자(전기)의　apologize for ~에 사과하다　inconvenience 불편(함)　unexpected 예상치 못한　pace 속도　accelerate 가속하다　withdrawal 인출　affect 영향을 미치다

172 점검에 관해서 암시된 것은 무엇인가?
(A) 예상치 못했던 일이다.
(B) 점검 속도가 빨라질 것이다.
(C) 정해진 일정으로 진행된다.
(D) 시작 날짜가 지연된다.

해설 폴크-메시이스 은행은 예정된 정기 주말 시스템 점검을 할 것이라고 했 다. 일정이 정해져 나오고 있으므로 정답은 (C)이다.

173 ATM을 통한 입금에 대해 언급된 것은 무엇인가?
(A) 점검으로 인한 영향을 받지 않을 것이다.
(B) 3월 2일에 잠깐만 허용될 것이다.
(C) 주말 동안 이용 가능할 수도 있고 가능하지 않을 수도 있다.
(D) 점검 기간에는 되지 않을 것이다.

해설 점검 기간 내내 ATM 입금은 불가능할 것이라고 했으므로 정답은 (D) 이다. It will not be possible을 선택지에서는 It cannot be done으로 패러프레이징했다.

174 [1], [2], [3], [4]로 표시된 곳 중 다음 문장이 위치로 가장 적절한 것은 어디인 가?

"그러나 ATM 인출은 점검의 영향을 받지 않을 것입니다."

(A) [1]
(B) [2]
(C) [3]
(D) [4]

해설 [2] 앞부분에서 ATM 이용은 가능하지만 모든 것들이 기능이 기능한 것은 아 니라는 설명이 구체적으로 예로 ATM 입금과 전체 문의는 이용할 수 없 다는 내용이 나온다. 설명 문장이 However 뒤에는 이와 반대로 ATM 에서 이용할 수 있는 기능이 나오고 나오고 있으므로 적절한 위치는 (B)이다.

175 신용 카드 사용자들에게 제한 사항으로 언급된 것은 무엇인가?
(A) 요금을 낼 수 없다.
(B) 구매를 할 수 없다.
(C) 잔액을 확인할 수 없다.
(D) 고객 서비스에 전화할 수 없다.

해설 모든 종류의 직불 카드와 신용 카드 거래는 평소대로 이용할 수 있을 것이지만, 마감된 입금은 되지 않을 것이라는 내용을 통해서 정답은 (A)가 된다. 지문의 balance payments will not be accepted가 선택지에서는 can't pay their bills로 표현되었다.

고객 만족 조사

아래 양식을 작성하셔서 저희에게 여러분이 경험하신 올드햄 스미스, 패튼, 드 산토스에 관해 알려 주세요. 이름을 기재할 필요가 없으니, 하셨든하고 솔직하게 작성해 주세요. 이 카드는 우리 사무실로 우편으로 보내 주시거나 대기실에 있는 의견함에 넣어 주시면 됩니다.

185 첫 상담에서 변호사는 신속하고, 전문적이고, 예의가 있었나요?
네. 변호사와의 제 첫 만남은 아주 좋았습니다. 저는 사실 예약이 10분 늦어지는데, 그가 저에게 괜찮다고 안심시켜 주었습니다.

183 모든 질문에 답변을 받았나요?
네. 저는 과세 연도 기간 중에 여기에 왔는데, 본국에서의 소득을 어떻게 신고해야 할지 몰랐습니다. 변호사님은 상황을 명확하게 설명해 주었고, 제게 직접 양식들을 제공해 주었습니다.

저희 사후 상담 서비스에 대한 경험은 어땠나요?
182 저는 그가 제공한 정보를 얻기 위해 귀사의 사무실에 두 번 전화를 걸었습니다만, 통화할 했던 여직원으로 변호사님은 도움이 되지 못했습니다.

185 앞으로도 저희 서비스를 이용하시겠습니까?
이미도 이용하지 않을 것 같습니다. 저는 이제는 저 혼자서 세금 신고를 처리할 수 있을 거라는 자신감이 있기 때문입니다. 그러나 저는 친구나 직장 동료에게 귀사의 서비스를 추천할 것입니다.

어휘 blues 우울(증)   circumstances 상황; 환경   file tax 세금을 신고하다   one-on-one 일대일(의)   attorney 변호사   consultation 상담   unlimited 무제한의   qualified 자격을 갖춘   delinquency 체납   rectify 바로잡다; 수정하다   minimum 최소   penalty 처벌   strict 엄격한   confidentiality 비밀   guarantee 보증하다   one's own 자신의   hands 처리 부담을 지는   efficiently 효율적으로   immigration 이민; 이주   issue 문제   when it comes to ~에 관한 한   translation 번역   dependent 부양가족   prompt 즉각적인 초기의   midway 중간쯤   tax year 과세 연도   earnings 소득; 수입   proper 적절한   subsequently 그 후에, 그다음에   additional 추가의   engage 고용하다   confident 자신 있는   handle 처리하다; 다루다   on one's own 혼자   colleague 동료   partial 부분적인   total 절대적인   promptness 신속   procurement 조달; 획득   follow-up 뒤따르는 행위를; overall 전반적인   demeanor 태도   query 질문   likelihood 가능성

181
서비스의 특징으로 언급된 것은 무엇인가?

(A) 단 한 번 지급
(B) 24시간 전화
(C) 온라인 회의
(D) 회원 카드

해설 서비스에 대한 전문적인 설명은 첫 번째 지문 첫 단락에서 등장한다. 이 부분 중에서 '1회의 전문적인 상담을 비용으로 변호사와 직접 일대일 상담을 받을 수 있다'고 했다. 따라서 one-time(single로, fee를 payment로 바꾸어 표현했다. 정답은 (A)이다. 지문의 one-time을 single로, fee를 payment로 바꾸어 표현했다.

어휘 entitle ~할 권리를 주다   in person 직접   immediate family 직계 가족   contract worker 계약직 근로자   slightly 약간   payroll 급여, 임금   approval 승인   urge 권고하다   abuse 남용   apply to ~에 적용되다   existing 기존의   renewal 갱신   gender 성   female 여성   promotional 홍보의   third party 제삼자   feature 특징점   consultation 상담; 면담   access 이용 권리, 접근 가능성   unlimited 무제한의   complimentary 무료의   workout 운동   budget 예산을 쓴   clarify 명확히 하다   attached 첨부된   changing room 탈의실   merger 합병   open (job) position 공석   registration 등록   verify 확인하다

176
공지의 목적은 무엇인가?

(A) 피트니스 센터를 광고하려고
(B) 등록 절차를 명확히 하려고
(C) 회사 합병을 설명하려고
(D) **직업 공석을 제공하려고**

해설 공지문의 목적은 주로 지문 앞에서 등장한다. 전 정규직 직원들이 모두 웨스트 코스트 센터를 떠날 때 피트니스 센터 회원연봉을 50% 할인받는다는 것을 공지하게 되어 기쁘다고 말하고 있어서는 내용에서는 할인 내용을 상세히 설명하고 있다. 이것이 내용에서 지문 앞부분에서 할인을 제공하는 이유인 할인율을 차지했다고 해서 첫 번째 단락으로 작성하도록 유의하자.

177
경리부에 관해 언급된 것은 무엇인가?

(A) 더 많은 정보를 제공할 수 있다.
(B) 공석이 있다.
(C) 새로운 장소로 이전할 것이다.
(D) **등록 양식을 확인할 것이다.**

해설 코드를 사용한 모든 신청서는 경리부에서 검토한 후 승인될 것이라고 했으므로, (D)가 정답이다. 지문의 review를 선택지에서는 check으로 바꾸어 표현했다.

178
린 씨가 회원권에 대해 한 달에 내야 할 금액은?

(A) 50달러
(B) 45달러
(C) 30달러
(D) **25달러**

해설 두 지문을 연계해야 하는 주로 문제이다. 두 번째 등록 신청서를 보면 린 씨는 50달러짜리인 풀 회원권을 신청했고, 여기에 할인 코드 BVC115F를 기록했음을 알 수 있다. 또한 첫 번째 지문에서 보면, 해당 기록인 BVC115F가 정규직 직원의 직계 가족의 할인 코드라는 점과 가족 역시 직원과 마찬가지로 50%를 할인받는 것을 알 수 있다. 따라서 정답은 50달러의 50%인 (D) 25달러가 된다.

179
지원자의 이메일 주소에 관해 언급된 것은 무엇인가?

(A) 반드시 작성해야 하는 부분은 아니다.
(B) **피트니스 센터에서 사용할 것이다.**
(C) 반드시 회원임을 받아야 한다.
(D) 휴대 전화번호로 바뀔 수 있다.

해설 엄데이트나 홍보 자료를 위해서만 요청되고, 제삼자 누구에게도 양도하거나 공유하지 않는다고 명시되어 있으므로 정답은 (B)이다.

180
골드 회원만의 혜택으로 언급된 것은 무엇인가?

(A) **임대물 할인 조건**
(B) 제휴업체 제품에 대한 특별 할인
(C) 24시간 센터 이용 권리
(D) 주차장의 VIP 공간

해설 골드 멤버십 혜택인 매월 개인 트레이너와의 상담을 받을 수 있다. 따라서 정답은 (A)이다. 지문의 personal을 one-on-one으로, consultations를 advice로 각각 패러프레이즈했다.

[181-185]

세금 때문에 우울하십니까?

심지어 가장 좋은 상황에서도, 세금 신고는 어려울 수 있습니다. 그러나 때때로 그것은 출구가 없는 미로처럼 불가능처럼 보일 수도 있습니다. 이것이 올드햄, 스미스, 패튼 그리고 드산토스가 현재 특별 상담 서비스를 제공하고 있는 이유입니다. **181** 여러분은 1회의 전문적인 비용으로, 저희 세금 변호사와 직접 일대일로 상담을 받으실 수 있으며, 상담 후에는 전화나 이메일을 통해 이주 우수한 저희 직원의 조언도 무제한으로 받으실 수 있습니다.

올드햄 – 세금 체납 전문
182 세금을 내지 않고 계산인가요? 저희는 여러분이 최소한도로 벌금을 내는 상황으로 조정할 수 있도록 도와 드릴 수 있습니다. **182** 완전히 비밀이 보장됩니다.

디산토스 – 중소기업 전문
신생 업체 소유자들은 이미 충분한 많은 부담을 안고 있습니다. 저희가 여러분에게 어떻게 세금을 빠르고 효율적으로 신고할 수 있는지 보여 드리겠습니다.

패튼 – 이민 문제 전문
183 우리 나라에 새로 오신 분들은 세금에 관한 한 특별한 도전에 직면하시게 됩니다. 저희는 스페인어, 프랑스어, 한국어와 일본어 번역 서비스를 제공합니다.

스미스 – 최근 대학 졸업자 전문
이제는 부모님의 부양가족이 아니신가요? 저희에게 오시면 여러분에게 세금 신고 방법에 관해 명확하고 간단하게 안내해 드리겠습니다.

상담을 원하신다면, 오늘 저희 웹 사이트 www.osftd-law.com을 방문하세요.

[186-190]

모든 직원은 주목해 주세요

188 경영진이 지난주 구매했던 프로젝트의 마감일 연장이 불가피해졌음을 알리면서, 지난 2주 동안 인사팀에 의한 휴가 중인에 예외를 신청하고 있습니다.

표준에서, 지난 2주 동안 인사팀에 의한 휴가 중인에 예외를 신청하고 있습니다. 감사합니다.

된 프로젝트 일정에 따르면 3월 1일까지 연료될 것입니다. 우리는 일정을 또다시 지연시킬 여유가 없으므로, 이 중요한 기간에 우리는 회사의 모든 인력이 필요합니다. 휴련된 경로를 통해 정상적으로 휴가 일정을 잡는 것은 3월에 재개될 것입니다. 이로 인한 불편에 대해 사과드리면서, 우리가 성공적으로 이 중요한 프로젝트를 완료하려고 노력하기 때문에 경영진에게서 개인적으로 모두의 노고에 감사하는 마음을 전하길 원하십니다. 만약 문의 사항이 있다면 직접 인사팀장인 해롤드 보르지에게 habor@JIVC.org으로 문의해 주세요.

수신: 프랭크 위성턴 (frwas@JIVC.org)
발신: 해롤드 보르지아 (habor@JIVC.org)
날짜: 2월 15일
주제: 회신: 사전 계획된 휴가

프랭크 씨, 안녕하세요

당신의 상황을 저에게 알려주셔서 감사합니다. 당신이 상사와 기 이는 문에, 저는 구매베르그 프로젝트와 관련해 권리가 불필요한 인제라는 주장에 동의할 수 없습니다.

189 귀하의 프로그래밍 기술은 웹 플랫폼의 최종 검사 단계에서 해심적인 역할을 담당할 것으로 예상합니다. **190** 저는 또한 귀하가 꽤 오래 전에 휴가를 계획했고, 이미 여행과 숙박에 대해 상당의 환불 불가 금액을 지급했다고 알고 있습니다.

그러므로 만약 검사팀에서 귀하를 가까이 대신해 줄 동료 한 명을 찾을 수 있다면, 저는 휴가 중인에 대한 당신에게 예외를 승인할 것입니다. **190** 일단 귀하가 제안했던 대체 인력이 이에게 귀하 승인을 받으면 귀하는 휴가 신청을 다시 제안하는 것을 **187** 알아두시기 바랍니다. 이 접층에서 귀하가 만족하길 바랍니다.

해롤드 보르지아
인사팀장 JIVC

---

182 회사에서 세금을 내지 않은 사람들에게 익숙한 것은 무엇인가?
(A) 법률 연체
(B) 무료 조건
(C) 일부 환급
(D) 절대 비밀

해설 질문에서는 세금을 내지 않은 사람을 대상으로 하는 서비스에 관해 묻고 있다. 세금 체납이라는 언급이 나오며, 이에 완전한 비밀이 보장된다는 점을 설명하고 있다. 따라서 정답은 (D)이다. 지문이 strict confidentiality을 선택지에서 total privacy로 패러프레이징했다.

183 설문을 작성한 고객이 만나을 사람은 누구인가?
(A) 웨인 올드햄
(B) 리사 스미스
(C) 참소 제룸
(D) 에리 드신토스

해설 두 지문을 연계해서 풀어야 하는 추론 문제이다. 두 번째 지문에서 그 고객은 과세 연도 기간 동안에 다른 나라로부터 읽기 때문에 본국으로부터의 소득 신고에 양상했음을 알 수 있다. 이 부분을 담당하는 번호를 첫 번째 지문에서 찾아보니 이민 전문 담당자는 참소 제룸임을 알 수 있다. 따라서 정답은 (C)이다.

184 고객의 서비스 중 불만이었던 점은 무엇인가?
(A) 변호사의 신속함
(B) 필요한 서류 조립
(C) 사후 질문에 대한 응답
(D) 전반적인 서비스의 비용

해설 고객은 추가적인 정보를 얻기 위해 사무실에 두 번 전화를 걸었으나, 고객 상담을 해준 직원은 변호사만큼 도움이 되지 못했다고 불평했다. 즉 사후 질문에 대한 응답이 미흡했으므로 정답은 (C)이다.

185 다음 중 양식에서 요청한 정보가 아닌 것은 무엇인가?
(A) 변호사의 태도
(B) 질문에 대한 답변을 받았는가
(C) 고객은 서비스에 관해 어떻게 들었는가
(D) 향후 서비스를 제외

해설 변호사의 신속성, 전문성, 예의에 관해 물었으며, 모든 질문에 답변을 받았는지, 그리고 나중에 다시 서비스를 이용할지를 물었다. 따라서 이 중 언급되지 않은 항목인 (C)가 정답이다.

JIVC 휴가 신청서

직원 이름: 프랭크 위성턴
직책과 부서: 부(副) 프로그래머, IT부서.
내선 번호: 62번
이메일: frwas@JIVC.org
요청된 날짜: 2월 17일 - 21일

아래에 적절한 박스에 표시하세요:
☑ 유급 휴가
☐ 무급 휴가
☐ 정체 휴가
☐ (자) 출산 휴가/(남자) 출산 휴가

추가 의견

저는 보르지아 씨와 의논한 내용에 따라 휴가 중인에 예외를 신청하고 있습니다.

다. **190** 제 대체 인력으로 미드시아 로페즈에 의해 승인되었습니다.

직무 사항: 프랭크 위성턴

이 양식을 출력해서 인사팀에 직접 다시 가져주세요.

어휘 unavoidable 피할 수 없는 extension 연장 Human Resources 인사부(= HR) implement 실행(시행)하다 blackout (일시적인) 중단 revamp 수정(개정)하다 afford ~할 여유가 있다 vital 필수적인 established 확립된, 기정의 channel 경로, 접근 수단 resume 재개하다 convey 전달하다 strive 노력하다, 애쓰다 address A to B A를 B에게 말하다 bring A to one's attention A를 ~의 시선을 끌게 하다 lengthy 긴 disagree with ~에 동의하지 않다 assertion 주장 non-essential 필수적이지 않은 personnel 인력 in regards to ~에 관해 play a (key) part in ~에 (핵심적인) 부분(일을) 담당하다 platform 플랫폼 (소프트웨어) substantial 상당한 non-refundable 환불할 수 없는 be willing to 기꺼이 ~하다 take one's place ~를 대신 하다 grant 승인하다, 주다 exception 예외 resubmit 다시 제출하다 leave 휴가 replacement 대인 approve 승인(하다) compromise 접층, 타협 title 직함 extension 내선 번호(= ext) paid leave 유급 휴가 bereavement leave 장례 휴가 maternity leave (여자가 가는) 출산 휴가 paternity leave (남자가 가는) 출산 휴가 comment 의견, 논평 in person 직접 procurement 조달 exemption 면제

186 휴가 중단에 원인으로서 언급된 것은 무엇인가?
(A) 재정적인 위기
(B) 새로운 제품
(C) 의사소통 오류
(D) 예상치 못한 지연

해설 vacation blackout이 질문의 주문을 키워드다. 첫 번째 지문에서 프로젝트 마감일 연장 때문에 휴가가 중단되었다고 했으므로 정답은 (D)이다.

187 이메일에서 세 번째 단락 두 번째 줄의 "note"와 의미상 가장 가까운 것은 무엇인가?
(A) 받아 적다
(B) 읽다, 확신하다

(C) 인지하다
(D) 끄다

해설 해당 표현이 들어간 문장을 보면, '휴가에 대한 요청을 다시 고려해야 한다'는 점을 읽어두세요라는 내용이 되어야 자연스러우므로 정답은 (C)이다.

188. 구데베르크 프로젝트에서 위스턴 씨의 역할은 무엇인가?
(A) 데이터 입력
(B) 온라인 검사
(C) 마감일 일정 조정
(D) 소프트웨어 조정

해설 두 번째 지문인 이메일을 보면, 위스턴의 프로그래밍 기술은 웹 플랫폼의 최종 검사 부분에서 핵심적인 부분을 담당할 것이라고 했다. 따라서 내용을 종합하면 정답은 (B)이다.

189. 위스턴 씨가 휴가 중단 통지에 먼저를 요청한 이유는 무엇인가?
(A) 그가 프로젝트 일부를 완료했다.
(B) 그가 휴가 중단에 대해 들어온 적이 없다.
(C) 계획된 휴가에 대해 이미 지불했다.
(D) 집에서 재택 근무를 하기를 원한다.

해설 두 번째 지문에서 위스턴 씨가 휴가를 미리 계획했었고, 이에 대해서 환불 불가한 여행과 숙박 비용을 이미 지불한 점이 언급되므로 정답은 (C)이다.

190. 마르시아 로페즈는 누구일 것 같은가?
(A) 인사팀 직원
(B) 위스턴 씨의 후임자
(C) 위스턴 씨의 상사
(D) 회사의 최고 경영자

해설 연계형 문제이다. 두 번째 지문에서 제안된 대체 안건 인데이터 진상으로부터 승인을 받아야 한다고 했다. 그러며, 마지막 지문인 이건 부분에서 대체 인력이 마르시아에 의해 승인받았다고 했다. 이 두 부분의 내용을 종합하면 정답은 (C)이다.

[191-195]

그렌트 자동차의 라이사와의 계약 체결

현지 부품 제조업체인 그렌트 자동차는 오늘 이탈리아 자동차 제조업체 라이사 모터스에게 기존 정화 장치 채결을 제공한다는 회기사의 계약을 발표했다. 이 장치는 최신의 라강 세단과 인기 있는 고급 SUV 제품군의 최신상 제품인 SX5 중 다섯 제품을 잇는 고급 세단 제품군에도 들어갈 것이다. 계약의 가치는 기록될 만큼 수백억 달러가 되는 것으로 평가되며, 새로운 일자리와 하청 일자리를 만들 것이다. 최초 계약은 5년간이며, 6개월 연장 선택권인 3개월 선택권이 달려있었다. 1965년에 설립된 그렌트 자동차는 연속 급속 부품들을 제조회사에 제공했는다 이후에 유럽에서 5번째로 큰 자동차 부품 제조업체로 성장했습니다. 라이사는 유럽에서 신망까지 신경 쓰는다는 것으로 알려져 있습니다.

191. 기사의 주제는 무엇인가?
(A) 새로운 제조 부품 공장의 개시
(B) 대형 자동차 구매
(C) 현지 회사의 수익성 좋은 거래
(D) 국제 기업 합병

해설 한 자동차 부품 업체가 개발한 정화 장치를 라이사 모터스에 납품하는 거래에 관한 글이다. 이 거래가 수백 달러의 가치로 평가된다며, 정체에 좋은 영향을 줄 것이라고 했으므로 정답은 (C)이다.

192. L5 현가장치를 사용한 첫 번째 모델은 무엇인가?
(A) SX5
(B) V15
(C) 리갈
(D) 스타라이온

해설 연계 문제이다. 첫 번째 지문에서 최신 상품인 SX5는 기존의 인기 모델인 스타라온의 뒤를 잇는다고 했는데, 두 번째 지문에서 SX5의 이전 모델에서 처음 도입할 것이 L5 현가장치라고 했으므로, 이 두 내용을 종합하면 정답은 (D)가 된다.

193. 평가에서 SX5의 비판 내용이 아닌 것은 무엇인가?
(A) 너무 비싸다.
(B) 신뢰성 면에서 시동이 켜지지 않는다.
(C) 매끄럽게 운전이 되지 않는다.
(D) 연료가 너무나 많이 소비된다.

해설 두 번째 지문의 마지막 부분에서, (A) SX5의 높은 가격표, (B) 시동을 켜는 것을 여러 번 시도해야 하는 점, (C) 울퉁불퉁한 주행이 각각 언급되었다. SX5의 연비는 좋다고 했으므로 (D)가 틀린 내용이다.

194. 편지에 따르면 라이사의 불만의 원인으로 나타난 것은 무엇인가?
(A) 원료 계약의 조건
(B) 배송과 처리 비용
(C) 구매된 부품의 질
(D) 제품된 부품의 개수

해설 제품 성능이 완전히 만족하지 않았다고 정확히 이야기했으므로 정답은 (C)이다.

자동차 세계 – 간단한 자동차 평가

제조사: 라이사
모델: SX5
결론: 고급스러우나 문제가 많다

SX5는 라이사의 최신 고급 SUV이며, 화려한 고급스러움에 대한 명성을 가진 회사에서 기대하는 바대로, 자동차는 연비는 연료 판촉을 뿐만 아니라, 편리한 기계 장치와 운전을 특별한 경험을 주는 방법을 가득 차 있습니다. 빠르고 날렵한 V15 모델을 마찬가지로 음성 인식 온도 조절 장치와 조정할 수 있는 컵받이를 특징으로 하는 SX5는 멤버의 운전자의 승객을 고려하서 설계되었습니다. 그렇지만 결함이 없음을 수 없죠. SX5의 이전 차세대 지난해 처음 도입된 독특한 L5 현가장치는 울퉁불퉁한 주행을 일으키고, 전기 점화 장치는 기대보다 신뢰도가 낮아. 엔진이 실제 켜지기 전에 여러 번 시도해야 하는 경우가 자주 있습니다. SX5의 높은 가격표를 고려할 때, 여러분이 기대하지 못할 것입니다.

리차드 루이스
최고경영자, 그렌트 자동차
1771 공방로
워터타운, 위스콘신 53094

루이스 씨에게,

이 편지는 전기 점화 장치 제공에 대한 두 번째에 세 번째 연장을 공식적으로 거절한다는 라이사 모터스의 결정에 대해 귀하에게 알려 주기 위한 것입니다. 요전데, 우리는 귀사 제품의 성능에 완전히 만족하지 않았으며, 철저한 고객 조사의 결과를 보면 소비자들 역시 만족하지 않았습니다. 이 정보는 귀사의 영업 사원들과 가졌던 가장 최근의 비디오 총회 때 귀사의 직원들에게 계속해서 전달되었으며, 귀사 측에서 저희의 걱정을 해소하기 위한 시정이 이뤄졌다고 볼 만한 징후를 찾을 수 없었습니다. 저희가 원래의 계약의 연장이지는 유지를 계속할 것이지만, 우리의 정비 조달 부서에 새로운 계약이 물색을 시작하도록 지시했습니다.

진심으로

메리앤 펠레그리노
최고경영자
라이사 모터스

어휘 strike (계약을) 체결하다 | part 부품 | manufacturer 제조업체 | landmark 획기적 사건 | keyless 열쇠가 없는 | ignition 점화 장치 | sedan 세단(자동차) | contract 계약 | estimate 추정하다, 어림잡아 계산하다 | value (가치, 가격을) 평가하다 | favorable 이로운 | generate 발생시키다 | subcontract 하청 계약 | initial 최초의, 처음의 | option 선택(권) | extension 연장 | establish 설립하다 | originally 원래, 처음에 | branch out 가지를 치다 | electronics 전자 장치 | in brief 간단히 말해 | reputation 명성 | unbridled 억제되지 않은 | be packed with ~로 가득하다 | nifty 멋진 | gadget 기구 | high-end 고급의 | gas mileage 연비(燃比) | decent (수준, 질이) 괜찮은 | feature 특징으로 삼다

특징(특징)으로 하다 | voice-activated 음성 인식의 | adjustable 조정할 수 있는 | sporty 빠르고 날렵한 | design 설계하다 | in mind 염두에 두고 | flaw 결함 | unconventional 관습적이지 않은, 독특한 | suspension system 현가장치(충격 등 중격 등을 완화시켜 승차감을 좋게 하는 장치) | predecessor 이전의 것 | make for ~을 야기하다 | bumpy 울퉁불퉁한 | electronic 전기[전자]의 | dependable 신뢰할 만한 믿을 수 있는 | considering ~을 고려했을 때 | eyebrow-raising 놀라운 | officially 공식적으로 | Ltd. (회사명 뒤에 붙여서) 유한 책임의(=Limited) | extend 연장하다 | provision 제공, 지급 | performance 성능 | based on ~에 토대를 둔, intensive 집중적인 | survey 조사, 검사 | repeatedly 반복적으로 | convey 전달하다 | call on one's end 대표 | representative 직원, 대표 | indication 지표, 표시 | uphold 유지하다 | address 해결하다 | remainder 나머 지 | procurement 정비[물품] 조달 | supplier 공급업체

195 계약이 종료될 때까지 그렌트와 라이시의 계약이 지속하는 기간은 얼마인가?

(A) 6개월
(B) 12개월
(C) 18개월
(D) 24개월

해설 연기 문제이다. 첫 번째 지문에서 최초 계약 기간이 1년이며, 6월씩 세 차례 연장할 수 있는 선택권이 있다고 했다. 또한, 세 번째 지문에서 점화 장치의 품질 때문에 두 번째와 세 번째 연장을 공사업자으로 가 진한다고 했다. 이는 최초의 1년째의 계약이와 첫 번째 계약 연장 기간인 6개월을 마지막으로 계약을 종료하겠다는 의미이므로 총 18개월 동안 계약이 유지된다는 것을 알 수 있다. 따라서 정답은 (C)이다.

[196~200]

수신: 랭스턴 쿰 〈langston@alpine.net〉
발신: 이안 맥도날드 〈ian_mcdonald@chc.com〉
날짜: 11월 12일
주제: 제안된 일정

안녕하세요, 랭스턴 씨.

우리가 난관에 봉착한 것 같습니다. 우리는 페어뷰 주택 단지 개발에 관한 건 관리인과 상세하게 정식으로 연락을 취할 것입니다만, **[199]** 저는 귀하에게 구체적인 문제들에 관한 주의를 드리려고 합니다.

첫 번째로도 배관과 배선 부품이 예정된 배송 날짜와 설치 시작 날짜 사이에 10일 동안의 저장이 있 지연이 있습니다. **[198]** 그들은 배송과 설치 시작 사이에 10일 동안에 건자재의 오 랜 기상 파해를 막을 어떤 저장고가 준비될 것인지를 알고 싶어 합니다. 두 번째 **[197]** 우리 프로젝트 중간에 끼어 있는 일주일의 휴일이 있습니다. 그것은 이전의 연준일 바로 앞에 승인되 바로 없었음으로 인해, 그리고 마지막으로 개장식을 8월 1일에 하기로 예정되어 있지만, 귀하의 건축 종료인은 더 늦게 잡혀 있습니다. 저는 우리가 몇 몇 적종은 창문 수 있도록 협사가 일정에 대해 탄력적으로 움직일 수 있기를 바랍니다.

이안

[197] 페어뷰 주택 단지 개발에 관련 귀하의 11월 13일 자 편지에 대한 응답으로 저는 다음의 해결책을 제시할 수 있습니다. 우선, **[200]** 귀하의 8월 1일 개장식 계 획을 받아들이는 것은 문제가 되지 않습니다. 저희가 최종 검사 과정을 6월에서 3일로 단축하면 될 것입니다. 배관과 배선 부품에 대해서는 현장 저장 시설이 없습니다—사실 우리 대기열 자재들을 단순히 방수포로 덮을 것입니다. **[199]** 우리가 3월로 단축하는 것은 문제가 되지 않습니다. 저희가 포함합니다. **[199]** 예정된 부품 설치 시작일인 7월 11일을 방수 포로 덮을 수 있었다. 귀하가 허럽하신다면 우리

---

195 계약이 종료될 때까지 그렌트와 라이시의 계약이 지속하는 기간은 얼마인가?

196 이메일의 목적은 무엇인가?

(A) 일정 지연에 대해 사과하기
(B) 누군가에게 앞으로 있을 행사에 대해 알려 주기
(C) 잘못된 건설에 대해 불평하기
(D) 누군가에게 잠재적인 문제에 대해 주의 주기

해설 이메일의 첫 번째 단락에서 공사 일정의 문제에 대해 알리려고 하고 있 으므로 정답은 (D)이다. (A)는 건설 완료 일정이 예정된 개장식 개장식이나처럼 뒷 여겨 수 있다고 언급된 내용을 이용한 영상 오답이다. (B)는 opening ceremony를 이용한 오답으로 유도한 선택지이다. (C)는 건설이 아직 완료되지 않았으므로 정답이 아니므로 정답이 될 수 없다.

페어뷰 주택 단지 개발 – 최종 건축 일정

날짜	업무	날짜	업무
3/18 ~ 4/19	현장의 수평화와 준비	6/28	배관과 배선 부품 배송
4/20 ~ 4/22	토대를 위한 콘크리트 도포	7/1 ~ 7/15	배관과 배선 부품 설치
4/23 ~ 4/30	휴식 기간	7/15~ 7/28	내부와 외부 마무리 작업
5/1 ~ 6/30	**[200]** 건물 뼈대의 전체적인 건축	**[200]** 7/29 ~ 7/31	**[200]** 최종 검사

어휘 run into (곤경 등을) 만나다 snag (뜻하지 않은) 문제 formally 정식으로 or so 쯤[정도] heads-up 주의, 경고 plumbing 배관 (공사) wiring 배선 component 부품 installation 설치 storage 저장고 in place ~을 위한 준비가 되어 있는 prevent 예방 하다, 막다 potential 잠재적인 weeklong 일주일에 걸친 approve 승인하다 opening ceremony 개장식 be meant to ~할 의도이다, ~하 기로 되어 있다 occur 일어나다, 발생하다 flexible (시간을 조정할 수 있 는) 유연한 middle ground 중용, 타협안 in response to ~에 응답하 여 regarding ~에 관한 solution 해결책 accommodate (요구 등 을) 받아들이다 hold 개최하다 condense 단축하다 inspection 검사, 조사 as for ~에 관해 on-site 현지의 facility 시설 materials 자재 waterproof 방수하다 approval 승인 non-negotiable 협상할 수 없는 union 노동조합 mandated 규정된 coincide with 부합[일치] 하다 foundation 토대, 하부 구조 set (시멘트 등이) 굳어지다, 응고하다 leveling 수평화, 균등화 application 도포, 바르기 frame (건물 등의) 뼈 대 finishing touch 마무리 작업[손질]

---

197 캠빌리 이담스 씨는 누구일 것 같은가?

(A) 이안 맥도날드 씨의 관리자
(B) 톰 거스틴 씨의 상사
(C) 건물 검사관
(D) 프로젝트 조정자

해설 첫 번째 지문에서 일정 문제와 관련해 관리자인 톰 거스틴 씨에 프로젝 트 조정자 중 하나가 연락을 할 것이라고 했고, 두 번째 지문에서는 건 설 문제 해결 방면에 관한 담당을 이안이 아닌 캠빌리 이담스에게 쓰고 있다. 이 상황을 종합해 보았을 때, 캠빌리 이담스 씨는 이안 사이 첫 번째 이메일 이후 건설 회사에서 연락한 프로젝트 조정자임을 알 수 있다. 따라 서 정답은 (D)이다.

198 원래 일정에서 배관과 배선 부품 배송 날짜는?

(A) 6월 1일
(B) 6월 21일
(C) 6월 30일
(D) 7월 1일

해설 첫 번째 지문에서 배송과 설치 사이에 10일 동안의 기간이 있다고 했 는데, 해당 표에서 배관과 배선 부품은 6/28에 배송으로 되어 있다. 두 번째 지문에서 배송 날짜는 변경할 수 있다고 했다. 따라 서 원래 부품 배송 날짜는 7월 1일보다 10일 이전임을 알 수 있다. 따 라서 정답은 (B)이다.

199 언제누드 씨가 입주자간의 휴식에 대해 언급한 것은 무엇인가?

(A) 짧아질 것이다.
(B) 미뤄질 것이다.
(C) 바뀔 수 없다.
(D) 이 프로젝트에는 적용되지 않는다.

해설 두 번째 지문에서 다른 것들은 해결책을 제시하고 있지만, 휴식에 대해 서는 현상이 불가하다고 했으므로 정답은 (C)이다.

200 원래 일정에서 마지막 건설 날짜는 언제였는가?

(A) 7월 29일
(B) 7월 30일
(C) 8월 2일
(D) 8월 3일

해설 두 번째 지문에서 8월 1일 개장식 날짜를 맞추기 위해 검사 과정을 6 일에서 3일로 단축하겠다고 했다. 세 번째 지문의 일정표를 보면 7월 29일부터 31일까지 검사 날짜가 잡혀 있다. 이 두 내용을 종합하면 원래 일정에 따르면 6일간 검사를 한 후 건축이 종료되기 때문에 건설 마지막 날짜는 8월 3일로 추론할 수 있다. 따라서 정답은 (D)이다.

Actual Test

08

저자 박선영

카카오톡 ID로 찾기 (ID: matrix20)
≫ 친구 추가 후 1:1 채팅

Reading Comprehension

본책 P170

PART 7

147 (C)	148 (D)	149 (D)	150 (C)	151 (B)	152 (A)	153 (A)	154 (C)	155 (D)
156 (C)	157 (B)	158 (C)	159 (C)	160 (D)	161 (B)	162 (A)	163 (D)	164 (A)
165 (B)	166 (D)	167 (C)	168 (B)	169 (A)	170 (D)	171 (B)	172 (D)	173 (B)
174 (D)	175 (D)	176 (C)	177 (A)	178 (D)	179 (C)	180 (A)	181 (C)	182 (C)
183 (A)	184 (B)	185 (C)	186 (D)	187 (B)	188 (A)	189 (C)	190 (C)	191 (A)
192 (B)	193 (D)	194 (D)	195 (B)	196 (D)	197 (C)	198 (A)	199 (D)	200 (B)

http://www.realtimeedu.com

홈	교육과정	공지	등록

147 청각 장애인을 위한 실시간 강의가 현재 온라인상에서 이용 가능합니다. 듣기가 힘든 사람들이 자신들이 노트북 컴퓨터에서 공부하는 것에 맞춘 장시를 만들 수 있을 것입니다. 여러분이 교수님의 말을 읽을 수 있도록 수업 도우미들이 강의 중에 교수님이 말하는 것을 입력할 것입니다. 더욱이, 실제 강의 장면으로 실시간 강의 읽고 옆에서 보이기 때문에 여러분은 다른 급우들과 같은 강의를 들을 수 있을 것입니다. 수업 노트를 이용하시려면 아래 지시 사항을 따라주세요.

1. 대화 대표 웹 사이트에 접속하세요.
2. "실시간 강의"를 클릭하세요.
3. **148** 우리의 온라인 강의 저장 목록에 접근하려면 아래처럼 로그인해야 합니다.
   a. 여러분의 학생 ID를 입력하세요.
   b. 여러분의 특정 암호를 입력하세요.
4. 여러분의 과목 이름을 클릭하면 당신의 급우들과 학습을 즐기세요.

어휘 hearing-impaired 청각 장애인 available 이용 가능한 hard of hearing 청각 장애가 있는 actual 실제의 scene 장면 script 원고, 대본 access ~에 접근하다 archive 기록 보관소, 많은 파일을 하나로 저장하는 것 specified 특정한

147 이 정보는 누구를 위한 것인가?
(A) 수업 도우미 지원자
(B) 웹 디자이너
(C) 장애 학생
(D) 온라인강의를 통해 가르치는 교수

해설 이 글은 듣는 데 어려움이 있는 청각 장애인들을 위한 실시간 강의에 대한 내용이므로 정답은 (C)이다.

148 "실시간 강의"에 관하여 암시된 것은 무엇인가?
(A) 컴퓨터용 파일 음식
(B) 컴퓨터에 저장할 수 있다.
(C) 인쇄된 원고는 강의 직후에 나누어진다.
(D) 로그인하는 것은 이용을 위해 필수적이다.

해설 지문 중반의 3번 지시 사항에서 실시간 강의를 이용하려면 로그인을 해야 한다고 언급하고 있으므로 정답은 (D)이다.

파티 매니악스!
오늘의 마지막인 것처럼 파티하세요!

149 파티 매니악스는 여러분이 꿈꿔왔던 꿈처럼 딱 알맞은 환경에 더불어 우리 고객들에게 모든 종류의 기쁨일을 위한 최상의 환경을 제공하는 것에 자부심을 느낍니다. 우리는 여러분을 위한 최상의 적합한 환경과 고객의 요구에 맞춘 장시를 만들고 꾸며하는 것을 전문으로 하고 있습니다. 행사가 가족의 일원, 친구 혹은 동료를 위한 것이든, 혹은 실제어 단지 자유한 낮을 즐거운 낮을 만들기 위한 것이든, 우리는 알맞은 분위기를 조성하기 위해 있겠어나.

그뿐만이 아닙니다! **150** 우리는 우아한 행사를 여는 것을 잘하고 그러한 행사에서 훌륭함을 빼고 고객의 요구에 맞춘 얼음 조각을 제대로 개발할 수 있습니다. 파티에 빠뜨나 천사 조각을 놓는 것은 흔합니다. 우리는 여러분의 선택에 따라 어떤 모양이든 좋게 만들어 드릴 수 있습니다.

우리와 함께 얼음 파티를 준비하시려면, 201-555-9645로 연락하세요. 우리는 월요일부터 금요일까지 오전 9시부터 오후 7시까지 영업을 합니다. 토요일에는 오전 9시에서 오후 3시까지 문을 엽니다.

어휘 take pride in ~ing ~하는 데 자부심을 느끼다 atmosphere 분위기 specialize in ~을 전문적으로 하다 customized 고객의 요구에 맞춘 suit ~에 적합하다 for the sake of ~을 위해서 set the tone 분위기를 조성하다 be capable of ~을 할 수 있다 put on 개최하다 sculpture 조각상 class 우아함; 품위 organize 조직하다, 준비하다 veterinary hospital 동물병원

149 파티 매니악스는 어떤 회사인가?
(A) 호텔
(B) 동물병원
(C) 출장요리 서비스
(D) 행사 대행 업체

해설 지문 초반에 고객들이 꿈꿔왔던 모든 종류의 행사를 제공하는 대 자부심을 느낀다고 하고 있으므로 정답은 (D)이다.

150 광고에 따르면, 고객들이 받을 수 있는 것은 무엇인가?
(A) 애완동물용 파티 음식
(B) 전통적인 음식
(C) 개인 요구에 맞춘 물건들
(D) 단체 할인기

해설 지문 중반에 어떤 행사든 빼든나 고객 요구에 맞춘 얼음 조각을 추가될 수 있다고 언급하고 있으므로 정답은 (C)이다.

시티 바이커즈
패달을 밟고 우시선을 참단하세요!

151 시티 바이커즈는 11회 연례 크로스 스테이트 자전거 경주를 4월 17일에 시작하기로 하셨음을 발표하게 돼서 기쁩니다. 출발점은 시애틀, **152** 도착 지점은 물롤먼이 될 것입니다.

- 참가자들은 4월 1일까지 신청량를 지급해야 주세요.
- 패 긴 경주이기 때문에 건강 증명서가 필요합니다.
- 호응 차량마다 안전 요원들이 배치될 것입니다.
- 임시 숙소가 미칠 제저 여분, 수수와 간식 등도 모두 이용 가능할 것입니다.
- 참가비는 200달러입니다. **152** 숙소 비용뿐만 아니라 참간, 수수와 간식 등도 포함됩니다.
- 지난해에 이어 재등록하는 참가자들에게 경기 후에 35달러를 돌려드립니다.
- 가장 먼저 도착하는 5명의 참가자들에게 상을 중 것입니다. 나머지 참가자들은 메달을 받을 것입니다.

시티 바이커즈는 지난 10년간 대회에서 큰 사고가 없었음을 알릴 수 있습니다. 우리는 이 기록을 유지하길 원합니다. 더욱이, **152** 참가비의 11%가 하루 투하트 어린이 재단에 기부될 것이오니, 좋은 취지를 위해 상쾌한 봄 자전거 경주에 참가하세요.

어휘 annual 연례의 escorting 호송하는 safety agent 안전 요원 temporary 임시의 entrance fee 참가비 eligible 자격을 갖춘 rebate 환불, 환불금 accident 사고 decade 10년 refreshing 상쾌한 cause 원인, 동기

151 이 공지의 주제는 무엇인가?
(A) 자동차 보험
(B) 연례 대회
(C) 후원자 모집
(D) 자전거 판매

해설 지문 초반에 11회 연례 자전거 경주 대회가 있음을 알린다는 내용이 있으므로 정답은 (B)이다.

152 행사에 관련 언급되지 않은 것은 무엇인가?
(A) 등록 후 환불이 불가능하다.
(B) 최종 목적지는 물롤먼이다.
(C) 수익금 일부는 자선단체에 기부될 예정이다.
(D) 수수와 간식은 비용에 포함되어 있다.

해설 지문 중간에 참가비의 11%가 어린이 재단에 기부된다고 했으며, 참가비에 포함된다고 했다. 환불이 불가능하다는 내용은 없으므로 (A)가 정답이다.

[153-154]

에이미 에먼스	오후 2:44
안녕, 제레미. 우리의 새 서쪽 건물의 설계도를 검토했어?	

제레미 마저라	오후 2:45
응. 했어. 그런데 그렇게 큰 공간이 대기실로 필요할 것인지는 의문이야.	

에이미 에먼스	오후 2:47
맞아. 하지만 우리가 성장함에 따라 더 많은 환자가 우리를 찾아올 거야.	

제레미 마저라	오후 2:48
그렇기는 하지만 내 생각엔 가까운 시일 내에 그렇게 될 것 같진 않아.	

에이미 에먼스	오후 2:50
잠. 단기적인 요구를 지지하게 고민하는 것이 좋겠네. 이 건물의 의료 서비스 확장을 위한 최신의 공간을 제공한다고.	

제레미 마저라	오후 2:52
네 말이 맞아. 우리는 특히 최신 의료시설을 사용하기 시작할 때 바뀔 수도 있으니까.	

어휘 blueprint 청사진, 설계도 reception room 대기실 wing 부속 건물 property 소유물, 건물 alternative 대체의, 대안의 though 그렇긴 하지만 expansion 확장 especially 특히 up-to-date 최신의 facility 시설

153 에먼스 씨가 중사람을 것 같은 사람은 어떤 분야인가?
(A) 병원
(B) 건축회사
(C) 부동산
(D) 지역 제조업체

해설 오후 2시 47분에 에먼스 씨가 더 많은 환자가 찾아올 수 있다고 한 점으로 보아 에먼스 씨는 병원 직원임을 알 수 있으므로 정답은 (A)이다.

154 오후 2시 50분에 마저라 씨가 "네 말이 맞아"라고 썼을 때 무엇을 의미하는 것 같은가?
(A) 의료 장비가 대체되어야 한다.
(B) 새로운 서비스가 너무 비쌀 것이다.
(C) 그 건물은 앞으로의 요구에 적합할지도 모른다.
(D) 그 건물은 구조적인 개조가 필요하다.

해설 2시 50분에 에먼스 씨가 장: 단기적으로 의료 서비스 확장에 따른 넓은 대기실이 필요할 수도 있음이 언급되었으므로 정답은 (C)이다.

[155-157]

파멜라 리브즈
298 이스트우드 가
캔자스 시티, 캔자스 66104
리브즈 씨께,

앞으로 24개월간 올베이즈 텔레콤의 휴대전화 서비스를 이용해 주시기로 한 것에 대해 고객님께 감사드립니다. 우리는 고객님께 국내에서 가장 깨끗한 음질과 최고 최신의 기술을 제공할 것을 약속드립니다. 이 편지는 우리와 고객님과의 계약을 유효하게 만들기 위한 것입니다. — [1] —. 개인 식별번호와 계약서 사본을 이 편지에 동봉하여 드립니다.

올베이즈 텔레콤 회원의 일부로, 우리는 고객님께 회원카드를 제공해 드립니다. [2] —. 고객님은 회원카드를 좀 더 빨리 받고 싶으시면 온라인으로 신청하시고 우리 매장 어디에서든 받으실 수 있습니다. 회원카드의 혜택은 이 편지 뒷면에 자세히 나와 있습니다.

고객님은 회원 혜택과 함께 **155** 추가 비용 없이 발신자 번호 표시, 스팸 메시지 보고 그리고 길든 다양한 편의 기능을 누릴 수 있습니다. — [3] —. 우리는 또한 실시간 교통정보가 나오는 내비게이션 벨 소리, 그리고 인터넷 접속과 같은 프리미엄 서비스를 제공합니다.

우리는 고객님께 언제, 어디서도 최상의 서비스를 제공하는 데 최선을 다합니다. **156** 24시간 고객 서비스 부서에 연락하시려면, 1-800-555-0058번으로 전화해 주세요. — [4] —. 고객님의 정보를 수정하시려면 온라인 서비스를 이용하시거나 서비스 전화 상담원에 전화하시면 됩니다.

톰 브레즈
고객 관리 부장

어휘 appreciation 감사 mobile telephone 휴대전화 be meant to ~할 예정이다 validate 유효하게 하다 personal identification number 개인 식별번호 issue 발행하다 a variety of 다양한 caller ID 발신자 번호 표시 장치 ringtone 벨 소리 be committed to -ing ~하는 데 헌신하다 customer relations 고객관리 process 처리하다 adjustment 조정

155 올베이즈 텔레콤에서 제공하는 혜택으로 언급된 것은 무엇인가?
(A) 전화비용을 바꿀 때 비용을 지원한다.
(B) 초기 3개월 동안 인터넷 접속이 무료다.
(C) 고객은 회원카드로 할인을 받을 수 있다.
(D) 발신자 번호 표시 서비스는 무료다.

해설 지문 중간에 회원 혜택과 함께 발신자 번호 표시 서비스를 무료로 누릴 수 있다고 연급되고 있으므로 정답은 (D)이다.

156 고객 서비스 전화 상담원에 관해 암시된 것은 무엇인가?
(A) 다른 나라에서 오는 전화는 무료다.
(B) 실시간 교통정보를 제공한다.
(C) 항상 열려 있다.
(D) 오프라인 매장에 있다.

해설 지문 하단에 고객 서비스 부서가 24시간 운영된다고 했으므로 정답은 (C)이다.

157 [1], [2], [3], [4]로 표시된 곳 중 다음 문장이 위치로 가장 적절한 곳은 어디인가?

"하지만 처리되려면 약 2주의 시간이 걸리고, 우편으로 방송될 것입니다."
(A) [1]
(B) [2]
(C) [3]
(D) [4]

해설 설문조사의 접속부 However(그러나)와 it(회원카드)를 그리킴 매 회 먼 지라는 자동(automatically)으로 발송된다는 문장 뒤에 위치하는 것이 적절하다. 그 뒤로 더욱 빨리(more quickly) 회원카드를 받기 위 하는 경우 취할 방법이 나오므로 정답은 (B)이다. 세마나의 정보는 아래와 같습니다. 세마나는 또한 인터넷을 위한 정보와 신상서를 제공합니다.

[158-160]

웨스트사이드 미디어 협회
국제 전시 센터
산 호세

날짜: 12월 20일
장소: 재머슨 홀
시간: 오전 10시 - 오후 4시

앨리스 쿠퍼	**158** 무엇이 부서를 유명하게 하는가?
산 호세 뉴스	앨리스 쿠퍼는 3년 동안 산 호세에서 아침 뉴스 진행자를 해 왔다. 또, 뉴스 진행자가 되기 전 5년 동안 산 호세 뉴스에서 리포터로 근무했다.

샘 클레드웰	**159** "그 사람이 되는 것"
CNC 10 라디오	샘 클레드웰은 **160** 10년 동안 CNC의 인기 아침 프로그램 "레라몬 오늘 아침 어때요?"의 프로듀서를 하기 전인 2007년에 CBC 10 라디오에 입사했었다. 그는 현재 국내에서 가장 유명한 라디오 방송국의 총괄 관리자이다.

니클 박	**159** TV에 아이디어를 올리는 방법
ABN 미디어	니클 박은 작가이자 **160** ABN 미디어의 대표 프로듀서로 승진해왔다. 그녀는 영화 프로그램을 만들어 전 세계에 그것들을 파는 획신적 프로듀서로 알려져 있다.

샌드라 페르난데스	**159** 여론이 불물린 더 많은 형태의 직업
몬테레이 미디어	샌드라 페르난데스는 몬테레이 미디어의 대표 이사고 최고의 인기를 누리는 지역 라디오 방송국 중 하나인 Party FM 106.9를 여는 데 도움을 주었다.

어휘 association 협회 anchor 뉴스 진행자 serve as ~로서 근무하다 general manager 총괄 관리자 innovative 획기적인 launch 출시하다

158 지문에서 언급된 것은 무엇인가?
(A) 제퍼슨 홀의 수용량
(B) 선생샤가 있는 장소
(C) 세미나 주제
(D) 신 호버 뉴스의 대표 프로그램

해설 지문 중반에 앞으로 진행될 세미나의 주제가 표로 제시되어 있으므로 정답은 (C)이다.

159 작가 경험이 있는 강사는 누구인가?
(A) 엘리스 쿠퍼
(B) 셈 클래드웰
(C) 니콜 박
(D) 센드라 페드너빅스

해설 지문 첫 부분에서 니콜 박이 ABN 미디어의 대표 프로듀서로 승진했다고 언급되어 있으므로 정답은 (C)이다.

160 셈과 니콜의 공통적인 직책은 무엇인가?
(A) 뉴스 진행자
(B) 대표이사
(C) 프로모터
(D) 프로듀서

해설 셈은 10년 전부터 프로듀서로 일해 왔다고 언급되어 있고, 니콜은 막 ABN 미디어의 대표 프로듀서로 승진했다고 나타나 있다. 따라서 이들의 공통 직책은 프로듀서라는 것을 알 수 있으므로 정답은 (D)이다.

[161-163]

헤르메스의 배송 서비스(HDS)

(161)(162) 헤르메스의 배송 서비스는 현재 전국적인 네트워크를 갖추고 있습니다. 우리는 이들 항공사와 글로벌 항공사와 계약을 체결하여 하루 안에 모든 국가에 도달하는 것을 가능하게 했습니다. 이 계약으로 HDS는 미래세관에 아니라 세계적인 경쟁에서도 명백히 우위를 점하게 될 것입니다. 우리는 속도를 중가시켜 왔지만, (162)전산화된 시스템, 그리고 믿을 만한 배송 서비스는 여전히 우리의 강점입니다. 더욱이, 우리는 모든 서비스를 빨리 토 저렴하게 드립니다.

우리 서비스를 이용하려면, 대표번호 1-800-555-8767로 전화해 주세요. 우리의 상담원이 가장 가까운 지점으로 여러분을 연결해 줄 것입니다. (162)여러분은 또한 우리의 웹 사이트, www.hds.com로 온라인 주문을 할 수 있습니다. 전화하시든 혹은 온라인으로 하시든, 정오 이전에 접수된 주문은 당일 배송을 보장해 드립니다. 오후 5시 이후에 접수된 주문은 당일 접수하여 다음 날 배송됩니다.

보상 정책 (163)HDS는 24시간 내에 모든 배송을 할 것을 약속합니다. 더욱이, 우리 서비스가 여러분의 기대에 미치지 못한다면, 기꺼이 어떤 불편에도 보상해 드릴 것입니다. 그러나 지연게로 인한 물품의 손상은 보상 대상에서 제외됩니다.

어휘 nationwide 전국적인 be equipped with ~을 갖추다 reach 도달하다 reliable 믿을만한 outcome 성과 definitely 명백히 computerized 전산화되다 willingly 기꺼이 operator 전화 교환원, 상담원 fulfill 이행하다 bankruptcy 파산 compensate 보상하다 be subject to ~의 대상이 되다

161 이 공지가 쓰인 목적은 무엇인가?
(A) 파산을 선언하기 위해서
(B) 고객들에게 새로운 서비스를 알리기 위해서
(C) 새로운 계약을 알리기 위해서
(D) 사용 과정을 설명하기 위해서

해설 지문 첫 부분에서 전국적인 네트워크를 갖추게 되었다고 이루어질 수 있는 서세로 나가는 모든 배송이 이제는 24시간 내로 이루어질 수 있게 됐다고 있다. 전국적인 네트워크 구축을 통한 빠른 배송 서비스가 새로 생겼음을 알리고 있으므로 정답은 (B)이다.

162 HDS사의 정책 중 하나로 언급되지 않은 것은 무엇인가?
(A) 온라인 주문 할인
(B) 전국적인 네트워크
(C) 최첨단 시스템
(D) 안전한 포장

해설 온라인 주문이 가능하다고 언급되어 있지만, 할인에 관한 내용은 없으므로 정답은 (A)이다.

163 HDS사의 보상 정책에 관하여 언급된 것은 무엇인가?
(A) 북물으로 인한 소포의 손상은 전혀 환불된다.
(B) 보상은 24시간 이내에 이루어져야 한다.
(C) 불법 사항은 오직 온라인으로만 접수된다.
(D) 배송 지연은 보상 대상이 될 것이다.

해설 지문의 보상 정책을 살펴보면, 24시간 내에 배송을 약속하며 최선을 다할 것이며, 그렇지 못한 경우 기꺼이 보상하겠다고 언급되어 있다. 따라서 정답은 (D)이다.

[164-167]

더 데일리 이코노미스트

SLU 스틸즈 분기별 재정 보고서

런던(4월 19일) - (164) (167) SLU 스틸즈의 최고 재무 책임자인 로 피셔 씨는 오늘 줄에 첫 분기의 회사 수익이 지난해 재무 책임자보다 7% 앞섰다고 보고하였다. 이것은 시장의 현재 상황을 고려할 때 총격적인 성과이다. - [1] -. 또, 피셔 씨는 붉은 화살표가 느리지만 꾸준히 올라가는 그래프를 보여주는 회사의 대차대조표를 덧붙였다. (165) (166) 이 결과는 지난 12월 마다 기업의 럭포트 스틸즈와 SLU 스틸즈의 제휴로부터 예측된 것이다. - [2] -. 더욱 긴밀한 제휴를 통해 두 회사는 자동차 제조업체에 우수한 제품을 공급하는 그룹의 사업을 강화하는 것을 목표로 한다.

피셔 씨는 기자회견에서 SLU 스틸즈의 많은 화살표가 허락하는 것을 막을 수 있도록 다른 방안을 마련할 것이라고 밝혔다. (167) SLU 스틸즈는 기간산업의 중요한 공급업체로서 1970년대에 이래로 영국의 경제 성장에 원동력이 되어왔다. - [3] -. 기반을 강화하는 것을 넘어서 이 회사는 급속하게 변하는 세계 철강업계를 선도하기 위해 새로운 기술 성공을 옮겨 한 발짝 더 나이가고 있다.

피셔 씨는 향후 몇 년간 이 회사가 기술과 기술의 제품의 다양화에 집중할 것임을 밝혔다. SLU 스틸즈를 포함하여 세계에는 철강회사들이 몇 개 안 되지만 그렇다고 다른 시장에 비해 경쟁이 더 약한 것은 아니다. - [4] -. 피셔 씨는 SLU 스틸즈가 여전한 철강업계에서 우위를 차지하려고 노력하고, 국가의 경제를 끌어 올릴 것이라고 언급했다.

어휘 CFO (= chief financial officer) 최고 재무 책임자 precede 앞서다 apply 적용하다 balance sheet 대차대조표 alliance 제휴, 동맹 strengthen 강화하다 automaker 자동차 제조업체 driving force 추진력 shift 옮기다 diversification 다양화 steelmaker 철강업체 pull up 끌어 올리다 accuse 고소하다 share 주식 counterbalance ~을 균형 잡히게 하다 stem from ~에서 기인하다 consolidation 통합 steel industry 철강산업 boost 촉진시키다 union 결합

164 이 기사의 목적은 무엇인가?
(A) 회사의 재정 성과를 공표하기 위해서
(B) 행병을 발표하기 위해서
(C) 회사의 신제품을 소개하기 위해서
(D) 법명으로 한 회사를 고소하기 위해서

해설 이 기사의 지문은 "SLU 스틸즈 분기별 재정 보고서"와 기사 초반에 로 피셔 씨가 올해 첫 분기의 회사 수익이 지난해의 수익률보다 7% 앞섰다고 언급한 내용에서, 이 글의 목적은 회사의 재정 성과를 보고하려는 것임을 알 수 있다. 따라서 정답은 (A)이다.

165 [1], [2], [3], [4]로 표시된 곳 중 다음 문장이 위치로 가장 적절한 것은 어디인가?

"이 두 회사 모두는 청양광계에서의 통합에서 기인하는 난제들을 상세하기기 위하여 서로에게 부가적인 주식을 매입하는 거래를 해 왔다."

(A) [1]
(B) [2]
(C) [3]
(D) [4]

해설 삽입 문장에 연급된 Both companies가 나오라면 이전 문장이 이 두 회사가 연급되어 있어야 한다. 따라서 SLU 스틸즈와 라포트 스틸즈의 합병이 연급된 문장의 뒤자리인 [2]에 위치해야 한다. 따라서 정답은 (B)이다.

166 SLU 스틸즈의 성장을 촉진한 것은 무엇인가?

(A) 새로운 자료의 개발
(B) 시장 점유율 증가
(C) 주식에 올바른 투자
(D) 또 다른 회사와의 결합

해설 첫 단락에서 첫 분기에 이래적인 성과를 올린 이유로 라포트 스틸즈와의 제휴를 연급하고 있으므로 정답은 (D)이다.

167 SLU 스틸즈에 관해 암시되지 않은 것은 무엇인가?

(A) 회사의 수익률이 올르라고 있다.
(B) 신설 변화에 대응할 계획이다.
(C) 현재 세계에서 가장 강력한 철강회사이다.
(D) 1970년대 이래로 경제 성장을 선도하는 역할을 해왔다.

해설 첫 분기의 회사 수익이 지난해의 수익률보다 7% 앞섰다고 했으므로 (A)는 맞는 내용이다. 급속하게 변하는 청양업계를 선도하기 위해 새로운 기술 방식으로 초점을 옮겼다는 내용에서 (B)도 맞는 내용이다. 두 번째 단락에서 SLU 스틸즈는 1970년대 이래로 영국 경제 성장에 역동이 되어 왔다고 언급하고 있으므로 (D)도 맞는 내용이다. 따라서 연급되지 않는 (C)가 정답이다.

[168-171]

나틸리 티블트 [오전 11:15]	모두 안녕하세요. 온라인 토론에 참여해 주셔서 감사합니다. 우리의 다음 회의 전에 행사 준비가 어떻게 되어가고 있는지를 공유하고 싶습니다. 마이클, 새로운 소식 좀 있나요?
마이크 스톨버그 [오전 11:16]	네, 평장한 소식이 있습니다. **[169]** 현지의 상공회의소에서 마침내 우리 회사가 시 청에서 직접 박람회를 얻는 것을 승인했습니다.
보희 박 [오전 11:17]	놀랍네요!
캐비스 발라드 [오전 11:18]	평장한 소식이네요! **[169]** 저는 그것 때문에 걱정했었습니다.
마이클 스톨버그 [오전 11:19]	제가 그들에게 우리가 현지 회사에 행사에 참가 우선권을 좀 계획었으요. 그 것이 그들을 납득시킨거죠.
나틸리 티블트 [오전 11:20]	오, 평장해요! 다른 소식은?
보희 박 [오전 11:21]	킹 컹장사는 이미 그 박람회에서 부스 3개를 설치하는 데 동의를 했으습니다. **[170]** 또 저는 나머지 현지 업체들에 여러 차례 연락을 취하고 있습니다. 늦어도 금요일까지 다른 참 가자들로부터 응답을 받도록 노력할 것입니다.
캐비스 발라드 [오전 11:22]	저는 이것 이 행사를 위해 우리가 계획 중인 강습회를 위한 더 적합한 강연자를 찾고 있 는 중입니다. **[170]** 손 레배 씨는 방 받이라는 강연을 진행하는 것에 잠정적으로 동의했습니다.
나틸리 티블트 [오전 11:23]	그가 괜찮을 것 같습니다. 저도 그가 이 분야에서 유명한 전문가라고 알고 있습니다.

어휘 preparation 준비　chamber of commerce 상공회의소　hold 개최하다　job fair 직업 박람회　priority 우선권　convince 납득시키다　at the latest 늦어도　suitable 적합한　tentatively 잠정적으로　lead 이끌다

168 글쓴이들이 논의하는 것은 무엇인가?

(A) 지역 회사
(B) 박람회
(C) 강연
(D) 공공기관

해설 나틸리가 첫 메시지에서 행사의 진행 상황을 묻자 마이클이 상공회의소의 소로부터 직접 박람회 개최 승인을 받았다고 말하고 있으므로 정답은 (B)이다.

---

169 오전 11시 18분에 발라드 씨가 "저는 그것 때문에 걱정했었습니다."라고 쓴 의미는 무엇인가?

(A) 그 제안이 승인될 것으로 생각하지 않았다.
(B) 그 기관에 행사에 참여할 것으로 생각했다.
(C) 그 회의가 취소될 것으로 생각했다.
(D) 현지 사업체가 제외될 수도 생각했다.

해설 이전 메시지에서나 마이클이 상공회의소를 설득하여 결국 승인을 얻어냈다고 하고 있으므로 발라드 씨의 메시지는 승인이 안 될 가능성을 걱정했던 것을 알 수 있다. 따라서 정답은 (A)이다.

170 박 씨가 기다리는 것은 무엇인가?

(A) 승인에 관한 공지
(B) 강연자로부터의 응답
(C) 계획의 변경
(D) 여러 업체로부터의 응답

해설 오전 11시 21분에 박 씨가 늦어도 금요일까지 나머지 현지 업체들에게 계속 응답을 확보하기 위해 노력하겠다고 말하고 있으므로 정답은 (D) 이다.

171 레배 씨는 누구인가?

(A) 시청 공무원
(B) 강연자
(C) 행사 조직자
(D) 심사위원단

해설 오전 11시 22분에 캐비스 씨가 행사를 위한 적합한 강연자를 찾고 있고 이미 한 강의 진행에 동의한 사람으로 레배 씨를 소개하고 있으므로 정답은 (B)이다.

에밀리 일즈
대표이사
PSI 인터내셔널사

일즈 씨에게,

172 우리는 귀사가 지난 여러 해 동안에 걸쳐 꾸준히 올렸던, 도덕적으로 후원해 주셨던 것에 대해 진심으로 감사를 표하고 싶습니다.

모금 초기에 **175** 우리 회사는 모두 직원으로 목표로 세운 뱃돈 달러가 너무 높다고 느꼈습니다. 하지만 그런 전에 제가 당신에게 말씀드렸다시피, 이 목표로 제 마음속에 떠오른 단순한 숫자가 아니라 **176** 미슈이들과 그들이 어머니에게 식량과 예방 접종과 모금 기본적인 요구 사항을 충족시키는 것과 함께 그들을 위한 병원 건축비는 데 필요한 실질적인 금액의 액수입니다. 놀랍게도, 많은 분이 우리의 명분에 관심을 가져주셨고, 그 목표치에 도달하도록 도와주셨습니다.

더욱 감사를 드리고 싶은 부분은 귀사 직원들이 열정입니다. **175** 우리는 귀사의 직원들이 손수로 부분을 써서 모자를 보고 같이 모자를 보고 2천 개의 모자를 선하는 일에 감동했습니다. 우리는 귀사에 아무리 감사해도 지나치지 않을 것입니다. 다음이, 귀사가 자체적으로 개최한 자선 박람회에서 우리를 위해 수집한 웃과 운동화는 에티오피아의 아이들에게 보내고 있습니다. 우리는 에티오피아 아이들이 이 선물에 기뻐하는 사진과 동영상을 받았습니다. 곧 이것을 이메일로 당신에게 보내드리겠습니다.

175 50개가 넘는 회사들이 이 모금 행사에 그들의 시간과 자원을 쓴 지 벌써 4년이 목표치 이상에 도달할 수 있게 되었습니다. 이는 우리가 더 밝은 미래를 꿈꿀 수 있음을 보여주셨습니다.

우리는 귀사가 더 나은 세상을 만들기 위해 도왔는지 새 소식을 꾸준히 전할 것입니다.

사무엘 타커
모금 박람회
두 번째 눈물 흘리지 않는 아프리카(NMTA)

어휘 chief executive officer 대표이사 sincere 진실 어린 gratitude 감사 generous 관대한가. organization 단체 regularly 정기적으로 materially 물질적으로 fundraising 모금 come up 나타나다 premature 미성숙의 nutrition 영양분 음식 vaccination 예방접종 enthusiasm 열정 hand-knitted 손으로 직접 짠 charity fair 자선 박람회 fundraiser 모금 행사· projection 예상

172 타커 씨가 일즈 씨에게 이 편지를 보낸 이유는 무엇인가?
(A) 모금 행사를 요청하기 위해서
(B) 매출을 신청하기 위해서
(C) 기부를 요청하기 위해서
(D) 후원에 감사함을 표현하기 위해서

해설 지문 첫 부분에서 후원에 대해 진심으로 감사를 표하고 싶다고 했으므로 정답은 (D)이다.

---

173 NMTA는 무엇을 위해 지금을 사용할 것인가?
(A) 아이들에게 장학금을 주는 것
(B) 시설을 짓는 것
(C) 모자를 사는 것
(D) 모금 행사를 위해 장소를 대여하는 것

해설 지문 중반에 지금의 사용처 중 미슈이와 그들이 어머니를 위한 병원 건축이 언급되었으므로 정답은 (B)이다.

---

174 에티오피아의 아이들에게 보낸 것은 무엇인가?
(A) 책가방
(B) 배지
(C) 야구모자
(D) 신발

해설 지문 중반에 PSI 인터내셔널사가 자선 행사로 모은 웃과 운동화를 에티오피아 아이들에게 보내고 있다고 했으므로 정답은 (D)이다.

---

175 모금 운동에 관해 사실이 아닌 것은 무엇인가?
(A) 50개가 넘는 회사가 참여하였다.
(B) 뱃돈 달러의 기부가 이루어졌다.
(C) PSI 인터내셔널사로부터 물품을 받았다.
(D) 처음 예상에 부응하는 지금을 모을 수 없었다.

해설 지문 하단에 50개가 넘는 회사가 이 모금 행사에 참여하여 뱃돈 달러라는 목표치 4년이 가능했다고 했으므로 정답은 (D)이다.

---

www.dreamwebsdesign.com/news/jobopening

홈	서비스	뉴스	직의응답

우리 회사는 함께 일할 뛰어난 분을 찾고 있습니다.

직책의 업무는 다음을 포함하지만, 거기에 제한되지 않습니다:
- **176** 고객의 선배을 위한 포트폴리오와 디자인을 고민하기
- **176** 큰 프로젝트의 팀원으로서 작업하기
- 고객의 요구를 엄격히 지키고 전문적인 웹 사이트를 개설하기
- 고객과 대화를 하고 고객과 디자이너 자신을 만족하게 하는 최상의 디자인을 제출하기
- 미래의 사업 프로젝트를 위한 새로운 디자인 아이디어를 과감히 실험하기

이 직책은 컴퓨터 디자인 혹은 관련 분야에서 마슈 하일을 소유한 사람이 연 누구에게나 열려 있습니다. 적어도 3년의 경력은 우대하지만, 특히 재능이 있다고 믿는 사람들도 역시 지원합니다. 관심 있는 지원자들은 **176** 정당한 시간 안에 개요를 생각해 낼 수 있어야 하고 일정표를 계획할 수 있어야 하며 그 개요를 최종 디자인으로 실행하는 데 있어서 **176** 그 일정을 유지할 수 있어야 한데 합니다. 훌륭한 대화의 기술 또한, 고객이 당신의 의욕을 볼 수 있게 하는 데 필요합니다.

추가로 정보를 원하시면 고용부장인 그레이 씨에게 403-555-0132로 연락하시면 됩니다.

어휘 emerging 최근에 만들어진 rising 증가하는 experienced 숙련된 talented 유능한 competent 유능한 sensitive 인접한 be willing to 기까이 ~하다 party 당사자 forward 전송하다 portfolio 모음집 직 품집 cover letter 자기소개서 screening 선발 approximately 대략 outstanding 뛰어난 limited 제한된 close adherence 엄격한 고 수 venture 과감히 시도하다 bachelor 학사 prefer 우대하다 come up 나타나다 sketch 개요 reasonable 합리적인 vision 전망 execute 실행하다 uphold 유지하다

176 드림웹스에 관해서 언급된 것은 무엇인가?
(A) 업계 최고의 디자인 회사이다.
(B) 새로운 곳으로 이전할 것이다.
(C) 고객 층이 늘어나고 있다.
(D) 최근에 디자이너들만 옳았다.

해설 첫 번째 지문 조반에 회사의 서비스 수요가 증가하는 것에 맞춰 사무실을 응확장하고 있다고 언급하고 있으므로 정답은 (C)이다.

---

177 이 직책에 관심 있는 사람이 해야 할 일로 안내받는 것은 무엇인가?
(A) 경력을 강조한 자기소개서를 제출하는 것
(B) 홈페이지에 이력서를 올리는 것
(C) 회사를 위한 웹디자인을 고안하고 게재하는 것
(D) 회사 일정이 정해질 때까지 좀 더 기다리는 것

해설 첫 번째 지문 하단에서 웹 디자인의 경력을 강조한 자기소개서를 보내라고 했으므로 정답은 (A)이다.

드림웹스에서 웹 디자이너 직책 채용

6월 23일

드림웹스는 새로 설립되었지만 빠르게 성장한 회사입니다. 우리는 다양한 종류의 전문 웹 디자인을 제공하고 있습니다. 우리의 역사는 짧지만 만족한 고객을 많이 확보하고 있고, 우리 고객에게 개선 최선의 노력을 다할 것입니다.

176 우리는 현재 증가하는 서비스의 수요를 맞추기 위하여 웹 디자이너를 찾고 있습니다. 그 결과, 우리는 숙련되거나 유망한 웹 디자이너를 찾고 있습니다. 웹 디자이너의 주요 업무는 고품질의 웹 사이트를 제공함으로써 고객들을 만족하게 하는 것입니다. 그래서 웹 디자이너는 고객의 요구에 잘 응해야 할 뿐만 아니라 고객에게 인정받아 하고 고객의 소리를 기까이 들을 수 있어야 합니다. **180** 직책에 관한 더 자세한 정보를 위해서 우리 웹 사이트를 방문해 주세요.

177 **180** 관심 있는 분들은 포트폴리오, 이력서, 그리고 자신의 관심사를 설명하고 웹 디자인 경력을 강조하도, 희망하는 직무 조건을 간략하게 기술한 자기소개서를 이메일로 보내 주시기 바랍니다. 온라인 홈페이지 역시 포트폴리오로 인정할 것입니다. 하지만 우리는 제출된 모든 지원서에 대해 일일이 응대할 수 없습니다. 최초 선발 과정을 통과한 사람들은 대략 인터뷰 1주일 전에 연락을 받을 것입니다. **180** 독시 질문이 있으면 우리 인사부로 연락해 주세요

해설 지문 첫 부분에서 후원에 대해 진심으로 감사를 표하고 싶다고 했으므로 정답은 (D)이다.

178 광고된 직책의 업무가 아닌 것은 무엇인가?

(A) 동료들과 함께 협업하는 것
(B) 자사간에 업무를 판매하는 것
(C) 다양한 디자인 초안을 작성하는 것
(D) 고객 정보를 관리하는 것

해설 두 번째 지문의 업무 설명 중. 큰 프로젝트의 팀원으로 참여해야 한다는 내용으로부터 (A)는 맞는 내용이다. 두 번째 지문 중간에 일정을 유지할 수 있어야 한다고 했으므로 (B)도 맞는 내용이다. 고객에 선택을 포트폴리오와 디자인을 고려해야 한다고 했으므로 (C)도 맞는 내용이다. 고객 정보 관리는 언급되지 않았으므로 정답은 (D)이다.

179 웹 페이지에서 두 번째 단락 네 번째 줄의 "reasonable"과 의미상 가장 가까운 것은 무엇인가?

(A) 올림리한
(B) 만족시킬
(C) 실질적인
(D) 불공평한

해설 이 단어가 들어간 앞뒤 맥락을 살펴보면, 최종 디자인이 나오기까지 다양한 과정들이 사전의 시간 간격을 맞춰 진행되어야 함을 강조하고 있다. 그러므로 그 개념에 적합한 즉, 실질적인 시간 안에 디자인의 개요를 제출할 것을 당부하고 있으므로 정답은 (C)이다.

180 다음 중 지원자가 직책에 지원하기 위해 사용할 수 없는 것은 무엇인가?

(A) 우편
(B) 이메일
(C) 웹 사이트
(D) 전화

해설 첫 번째 지문 중반에 지세한 정보를 알고 싶으면 웹 사이트를 자기소개서와 이력서를 보내라고 했으므로 (C)는 맞는 내용이다. 그 이후에 이력서나 자기소개서는 이메일을 통해 회사로 보내라고 했으므로 (B)도 맞는 내용이다. 또한 첫 번째 지문 하단에 질문이 있으면 인사부서에 연락하라고 나와 있는데 이는 두 번째 지문 하단에 고용 담당자 씨의 전화번호가 지세어 있으므로 (D)도 맞는 내용이다. 따라서 언급되지 않은 (A)가 정답이다.

181 마우스의 가격이 인하된 이유는 무엇인가?

(A) 그 모델이 개선되었다.
(B) 재조화시가 가격을 내렸다.
(C) 마우스가 회사에 큰 수익을 가져다주었다.
(D) 공급업체는 새로운 기술력을 홍보해 왔다.

해설 첫 번째 글에서 이 마우스가 판매가 잘돼서 낮은 가격으로 고객에 시장에 보급하겠다고 했으므로 정답은 (C)이다.

182 광고에서 첫 번째 단락, 다섯 번째 줄의 "available"과 의미상 가장 가까운 것은 무엇인가?

(A) 유용한
(B) 자유로운
(C) 이용 가능한
(D) 익숙한

해설 판매에서 그 상품의 다양한 색상으로 '이용할 수 있다'는 의미로 이와 일치하는 (C)가 정답이다.

183 편지의 목적은 무엇인가?

(A) 정보를 요청하기 위해서
(B) 대량 구매에 대해 문의하기 위해서
(C) 빠른 서비스에 감사를 표현하기 위해서
(D) 직원에 관해 물어보기 위해서

해설 두 번째 지문 마지막에서 잘못 청구된 배송비에 대해 해명해 달라고 요청하고 있으므로 정답은 (A)이다.

184 페리 씨에게 얼마가 청구되었는가?

(A) 36.99달러
(B) 43.99달러
(C) 79.99달러
(D) 86.99달러

해설 첫 번째 지문에서 할인된 가격이 36.99달러이고 이에 추가 해택으로 배송비가 청구되지 않는다고 언급되어 있다. 그리고 두 번째 지문에서 배송비가 청구되지 않는다고 광고된 배송비가 청구되었다고 언급되어 있으므로 이 물건을 주문한 페리 씨가 그녀에 배송비를 합친 43.99달러가 된다. 따라서 정답은 (B)이다.

185 페리 씨에 관해 추측할 수 있는 것은 무엇인가?

(A) 배달된 날짜가 전화를 직원에게 연락되었다.
(B) 그는 예전에 그 제품에 관한 광고를 본 적이 있다.
(C) 세금이 그에게 청구되었다.
(D) 그는 9월 10일에 그 센터로 다시 전화했다.

해설 페리 씨가 선 두 번째 지문에서 그가 물건을 받은 날짜와 배송비가 잘 못 청구되었음을 알고 전화에 남짜가 모두 9월 8일로 같음을 알 수 있으므로 (A)는 맞는 내용이다. (B)는 광고에서 모든 세금과 배송비 그리고 취급 비용이 부과되지 않는다는 내용을 보냈다고 했으므로 이것도 맞는 내용이다. 또한 처음 서비스 센터에 연락한 날은 물건을 받았던 9월 8일이었고, 다시 전화한 것이 그 다음날인 9월 10일임을 알 수 있으므로 (D)도 맞는 내용이다. 세금이 청구되었다는 내용은 언급되지 않았으므로 정답은 (C)이다.

[181-185]

댄의 사무용품

이번 기회를 놓치지 마세요!
다른 사람들보다 더 쉽게 작업하세요!
네오타크 EZ77 마우스를 써보세요!
③ 지금 할인 중입니다.
79.99달러 → 36.99달러

지금 주문하시면 여러분이 어디에 있든 배송해 드립니다.
③ 더불어, 세금, 배송 그리고 취급 비용 모두 지불하실 필요가 없습니다.

재대로 "일할 시간"을 가질 기회 기회입니다. ③ 특별한 제안은 단 한 번뿐인 행사입니다. 우리 회사는 이러한 관심에 매우 낮은 가격으로 여러분의 사랑이 보답하고 있습니다. 이 획신적인 상품은 전형적이 재료처럼 만들어지고 사람 손에 자연스럽게 잡히도록 고객에게 맞춤 제작되었습니다. 다양한 색상으로도 이용 가능하니, 여러분이 원하는 색을 선택하시려면 서둘러 주세요. 주문하시려면 1-558-555-1346으로 전화하시거나, 웹 사이트 http://www. dansofficesupplies.com으로 방문해 등록하면 10%의 포인트를 적립할 수 있습니다.

관계자분께,

안녕하세요, 제 이름은 브랜든 페리이며, 저는 최근에 네오타크 EZ77 마우스를 샀습니다(구매: 9월 6일 / ③ 수령: 9월 8일). ③ 저는 구매 비용에 대해 질문이 있습니다. ③ 광고에 따르면, 세금, 배송비, 취급비 모두 도착했을 때, 그 영수증에는 모든이 언급되어 있었습니다. ③ 그러나 제품(7길러를 포함하고 있었습니다.

그래서 9월 8일에 서비스 센터로 전화했습니다. 15분가 다가 미침 내 한 서비스 직원에 연결되었습니다. 저는 그 직원에게 제 문제를 말했고, 그녀는 그것을 살펴보겠다고 다시 전화해 주겠습니다. 그래서 저의 연락처를 그에게 남겼지만, 그러나 저는 가사의 어떤 직원으로부터 답변을 받지 못하였습니다. ③ 그래서 이틀 후에 또다시 전화를 했지만, 똑같은 일이 벌어졌습니다. 저는 전에 통화한 직원이 전화를 다시 주겠다고 한 것을 잊어버렸다고 그 서비스 직원에게 말했습니다.

③ 저는 이런 상황이 어떻게 일어날 수 있으며, 또한 어떻게 배송비가 붙었는지에 관해 청구되었는지 설명을 매우 듣고 싶습니다. 3일 안에 이 문제가 해결되지 않는다면, 지역 소비자 센터에 당신 업체를 신고할 작정입니다. 그뿐 아니라, 가사의 웹 사이트에 이 편지를 게재할 것입니다.

브랜든 페리

어휘 office supplies 사무용품 handling cost 취급 비용 sell like hot cakes 불티나게 팔리다 overwhelm 압도하다 revolutionary 획신적인 customized 맞춤 제작되는 available 이용 가능한 accumulated 축적되는 charge 청구하다 definitely 명백하게 put on hold 대기하다 representative 직원 specifically 분명히, 명확하게 unreasonably 함당하지 못하게 bulk purchase 대량 구매

[186-190]

수신: 유니버설 가든 온천

발신: 에이미 베이츠, 레저 타운사

날짜: 12월 7일

186 레저 타운사는 유니버설 가든 온천을 인수했다는 것을 발표하게 되어 기쁩니다. 우리는 이미 경영을 인수받았고 지금은 유니버설 가든 온천의 관련된 모든 일을 책임지고 있습니다. 우리는 우리 직원 모두와 생산적인 시업 관계가 유지될 것을 기대하고 있습니다. **187** 만약 도움이 필요하시면, 동봉된 사람의 목록에 있는 직원들에게 연락하실 수 있습니다.

다음은 우리 회사의 중요 직책의 사람들의 연락처 목록입니다.

인사 부서

인사 담당자, 스텔라 스톤 (stellastone@leisuretown.com)

서비스 유지 관리 부서

유지 관리 감독자, 놀린 딘 (n_dean@leisuretown.com)

시설 관리부서

188 시설 서비스 담당자, 루카스 반즈 (lucasrepairs@leisuretown.com)

기술 유지관리 부서

기술 서비스 담당자, 딜런 웨스트 (techdylan@leisuretown.com)

업무 관리 부서

행정 업무 담당자, 에이미 베이츠 (abates@leisuretown.com)

레저 타운사

1-555-8520

188 수신: 루카스 반즈 (lucasrepairs@leisuretown.com)

발신: 클라라 하트 (clara_h@leisuretown.com)

날짜: 12월 11일

제목: 샤우나 문제

안녕하세요, 제 이름은 클라라 하트입니다. **189** 저는 유니버설 가든 온천의 일반적 노천탕의 접수대에서 일하고 있습니다. 최근에 온천 사우나 중 하나에 관한 불만 사항을 접수하였습니다. 그 고객은 온도가 충분히 높지 않았는데 습도가 너무 높다고 말했습니다. 그녀는 그 사우나를 확인했는데 온도가 **190** 화씨 77도라고 표시되어 있었지만 실제로는 섭씨 60도를 넘지 못했습니다. 제 생각에 이것이 높은 습도를 일으키 원인으로 보입니다. 그 사우나는 현재 폐쇄되었으며 온천의 많은 시설이므로 빨리 수리되어야 합니다. 언제 수리될 수 있는지 알려 주십시오.

클라라 하트

어휘 spa 온천 acquisition 인수 take over 인수하다, 인계하다 look forward to -ing 경험짓다 ~할 것을 학수고대하다 business relationship 시업 관계 representative 직원 personnel department 인사부 human resource 인적자원 maintenance 유지 관리 supervisor 감독자, 관리자 facility 시설 coordinator 조정자 office operations 행정 업무 lately 최근에

complaint 불만 사항 temperature 온도 humidity 습도 celsius 섭씨 ventilating 환기의 density 밀도 dense 밀도가 높은 put up for auction 경매에 부치다

186 레저 타운사는 어떤 사업체에 속하는가?

(A) 전문적인 마사지 치료사를 훈련한다.

(B) 기업체에 전문적인 조언을 해준다.

(C) 공식에 적절한 시험을 소개한다.

(D) 온천 시설을 관리한다.

해설 첫 지문에서 이 회사가 유니버설 가든 온천을 인수하여 경영하고 있다는 정보가 연급되어 있으므로 정답은 (D)이다.

187 메모에서 연급되는 것은 무엇인가?

(A) 유니버설 가든 온천은 화제를 올릴 것이다.

(B) 도움을 위해 전문가들과 연락할 수도 있다.

(C) 유니버설 가든 온천은 경매에 부쳐질 것이다.

(D) 인력 감축은 곧 시행될 것이다.

해설 첫 지문 마지막 부분에 도움이 필요하다면 동봉된 목록에 기재되어 있는 각 부서의 직원들에게 연락할 수 있다고 언급하고 있으므로 정답은 (B)이다.

188 하트 씨는 어느 부서에 연락하고 있는가?

(A) 시설관리 부서

(B) 인사 부서

(C) 업무 관리 부서

(D) 기술 유지관리 부서

해설 첫 지문 하단에 도움이 필요하면 동물된 목록에 얼맞던 직원에게 연락하라고 언급하고 있고, 세 번째 지문 상단에 하트 씨가 문의 번즈 씨에게 이 메일로 연락하고 있음을 알 수 있다. 이에 따라 첫 번째 지문에 번즈 씨는 시설 관리부에 근무하는 것을 알 수 있으므로 정답은 (A)이다.

189 하트 씨가 이메일을 쓴 목적은 무엇인가?

(A) 직책에 지원하기 위해서

(B) 온천 이용 방법에 관해 문의하기 위해서

(C) 문제를 보고하기 위해서

(D) 검사를 실행하기 위해서

해설 세 번째 지문 첫 부분에서 고객의 불만 사항으로 접수된 온천의 문제점을 언급하고 있으므로 정답은 (C)이다.

190 이메일에서 첫 단락 네 번째 줄의 "dense"와 의미상 가장 가까운 것은 무엇인가?

(A) 가벼운

(B) 거친

(C) 진한, 밀집한

(D) 향기로운

해설 메일을 고려해 보면 사우나의 문제가 높은 밀도의 습기이므로 이것의 동의어로 농도가 진한'이라는 의미의 (C)가 정답이다.

[191-195]

수신: 리디아 홍즈 (lydiah@smithandgrant.com)

발신: 잭 그랜트 (jg1970@smithandgrant.com)

191 날짜: 6월 8일

제목: 이메일 사용

리디아에게,

저는 지금의 직원들에게 우리 회사의 이메일 사용 규정을 상기시킬 때라고 생각합니다. 저는 직원들이 대부분 시간에 이메일을 올바르게 사용하고 있다고 믿지만, 이 이메일의 업무 목적으로만 쓰이고 있지 않은 것 같습니다.

그래서 기존의 직원들에게 기억을 되살리고 신입 직원들에게 **192** 분명히 알리기 위해서, 이메일 규정에 관한 발표가 필요합니다. 스미스앤그랜트는 이메일 사용이 업무를 위한 필수 수단이라는 것을 인정합니다. 그래서 이 도구를 남용하는 것은 우리 업체의 명성에 영향을 줄 수 있습니다.

저는 우리 직원들이 어떤 종류의 이메일이 적절한지 아닌지를 명확히이 이해하도록 확실한 조치를 취하고 싶지만, 그들이 엄격하게 통제되고 느끼길 원하는 것은 아닙니다. 그러니 **197** 당신이 저 대신 직원들이 읽어 볼 메모를 작성해 주신다면 감사하겠습니다. 되도록 빨리 작성하셔서 **193** 이 업무일 후에 정책이 발표되었으면 합니다.

미리 감사드립니다.

잭 그랜트

스미스앤그랜트

메모

직원들에게,

이 글은 현행 이메일 사용 정책에 관한 것입니다. 우리 회사와 여러분의 안전을 위해 이메일 사용 규정을 읽고 숙지하는 시간을 가지십시오.

이 메모를 경고로 오해하지 마십시오. 이메일의 사용은 이러한 이메일의 이용 이 업무의 이용을 위한 목적이었으면 하는 하나의 정책이 있습니다만, 그러니 나 우리는 직원들이 엄격하게 하는 하나의 정책이 있으며, 즉 리 웹 사이트에 있는 정책에 대한 안내 지침을 다음을 받으시고, 여러분의 책상에 붙어 놓고 계속 확인해 주세요.

193 리디아 홍즈

이메일 사용 정책

이메일 사용 시 다음 사항에 유념해 주세요:

- 현재의 규정을 지키세요
- 용인되는 방식으로 사용하세요
- 인터넷을 남용하지 마세요

응답될 수 없는 사용

194 음란하거나 불법성이 있는 사진, 급소 등의 자료를 유포하거나 저장한 는 것

2. 회사 통신망의 어떠한 형식의 컴퓨터 바이러스도 침투시키는 것

일정

날짜	7월 2일			
기차 번호	X214 (XAT)	S5678 (일반)	A9521 (일반)	**200** X271 (XAT)
출발: 메인	오전 10:15	오후 12:05	오후 2:30	오후 4:50
도착: 뉴욕	오후 12:35	오후 3:35	오후 6:00	오후 7:10

날짜	7월 6일			
기차 번호	A7412 (일반)	X214 (XAT)	A5641 (일반)	X804 (XAT)
출발: 뉴욕	오전 9:20	오전 11:55	오후 3:45	오후 6:20
도착: 메인	오후 12:50	오후 2:15	오후 7:15	오후 8:50

수신: 댄 파커 (d_parker@quadtech.com)
발신: 루시 모리스 〈lucym@quadtech.com〉
날짜: 6월 19일
제목: **195** 기차 예약
첨부: 일정.doc

댄 씨에게,

당신은 오늘 일찍 저에게 기차표 예매를 요청하러 갈 것이라고 말했습니다. 그래서 7월 2일에 메인에서 출발하는 뉴욕행 기차의 일정표를 첨부해 드립니다. 고속기차와 일반기차를 선택할 수 있습니다. **196** 기차의 일정을 첨부해 드립니다. 고속기차와 일반기차를 선택할 수 있습니다. **197** "XAT"는 제가 줄 수 바에 따르면 조선 사이에 공간이 조금 더 있는 빠르고 안락한 기차입니다. **200** 그러나 "XAT"의 좌석의 절반은 거꾸로 배치되어 있고 좌석은 무작위로 배정되기 때문에 당신이 어느 방향에 앉았는지 미리 알 수 없습니다. 그러니 생각해 보시고 출발 시간을 확인하셔서 필요 수 있는 대로 빨리 당신의 결정을 저에게 알려 주십시오. 그러면 그때 당신을 위해 준비를 준비해 두겠습니다.

한 가지 더 있습니다. **200** 터너 씨도 뉴욕에 갈 예정입니다? **198** 저는 그녀가 당신의 첨부하는 "세계 교통 모형"에 갈 것을 고려 중이라고 들었습니다만 그녀가 현재 인도로 출장을 가서 연락받지 않습니다. 그래서 그녀가 당신에게 어떤 말을 했는지 궁금합니다. **200** 그녀를 위해 복습은 날짜와 시간에 기차표를 예매해야 할까요?

루시 모리스

* 문의 사항이 있으면 언제든 이메일을 보내 주세요.

[196-200]

3. **194** 개인적인 용무를 위해 이메일과 인터넷을 사용하는 것
4. 허가되지 않는 비밀번호와 우편함을 사용하는 것
5. 저작권법을 위반하는 것
6. 직원들의 업무나 통신 지원을 낼비할 수 있는 고의적인 행동을 하는 것
7. 불필요한 생성 · 광고성 자료를 보내는 것
8. **194** 불쾌하거나, 차별적이거나 혹은 하대하는 글을 보냄으로써, 인신공격하거나 협박을 하는 것

감시

회사 이메일 자원은 단지 업무 목적을 위해서만 제공된다는 것을 알아두십시오. 그러므로 회사는 시스템에 기록된 어떠한 정보도 조사하고 감시할 수 있는 권한을 가집니다. 이 정책을 수행하기 위해서, 회사는 이메일 내용과 쓰임을 검토하기 위한 감시 소프트웨어를 사용할 권한을 가집니다. 이러한 감시 활동은 도하기 위한 감시 목적을 위한 것이고 직원들이 동의한 정책을 준수하게 생활될 것임을 단지 정당하 목적을 위한 것입니다.

어휘 usage 사용(법) ｜ remind 상기시키다 ｜ protocol 규약 ｜ enlighten 일깨우다, 계몽하다 ｜ acknowledge 인정하다 ｜ misuse 남용 ｜ impact 영향 ｜ on ~에 영향을 ｜ reputation 평판 ｜ regulate 규정하다, 통제하다 ｜ on one's behalf ~을 대신해서 ｜ in advance 사전에 ｜ familiarize A with B A를 B에 익숙하게 하다 ｜ affirmatively 적극적으로 ｜ warning 경고 ｜ unacceptable 용납될 수 없는 ｜ tolerable 용납할 수 있는 ｜ legislation 법률, 규정 ｜ indecent 음란한 ｜ spread 퍼뜨리다 ｜ in possession 소유하고 있는 ｜ illegal 불법의 ｜ personal business 개인적인 용무 ｜ copyright 저작권 ｜ undertake 착수하다 ｜ deliberate 고의적인 ｜ squander 낭비하다 ｜ threat 협박 ｜ unsolicited 필요치 않은 ｜ commercial 상업적인 ｜ attack 공격 ｜ offensive 불쾌한 ｜ discriminatory 차별적인 ｜ abusive 하대하는 ｜ inspect 조사하다 ｜ in accordance with ~에 따라서 ｜ legitimate 정당한 ｜ compliance with ~을 준수하기 ｜ implement 실행하다 ｜ carry out 수행하다

191 이메일에 따르면 그랜트 씨가 홈즈 씨에게 하길 바라는 것은 무엇인가?
(A) 안내 지침을 보내는 것
(B) 이메일을 감사하는 소프트웨어를 찾는 것
(C) 정책을 위한 제안을 하는 것
(D) 정책을 준수하는지 감사하는 것

해설 첫 번째 지문 후반에서 그랜트 씨가 자신을 대신해서 이메일 사용에 관한 규정을 메모로 작성해 달라고 부탁하고 있으므로 정답은 (A)이다.

192 이메일에서 두 번째 단락 첫 번째 줄에 단어 "enlighten"과 의미상 가장 가까운 것은 무엇인가?
(A) 채용하다
(B) 가르치다
(C) 돕다
(D) 비추다

해설 첫 번째 지문에서 신입직원들에게 이메일 사용 규정을 정확히 알려야 한다고 언급하고 있다. 따라서 정확히 알려야 한다는 의미와 유사한 단다고 연급하고 있다. 따라서 정확히 알려야 한다는 의미와 유사한 (B)가 정답이다.

193 이메일 사용 정책에 관해 암시된 것은 무엇인가?
(A) 홈즈 씨가 보낸 메모에 첨부되어 있다.
(B) 갱신될 필요가 있다.
(C) 첨부된 특정 문양으로 제출될 것이다.
(D) 6월 중순쯤에 발표되었을 것이다.

해설 첫 지문이 이메일은 6월 8일에 작성된 것인데, 그랜트 씨가 하단에 이 메일 정책에 대한 발표가 이르부터 약 1주일 후에 있었으면 좋겠다고 언부하고 있으므로 정책 발표는 이마도 6월 중순쯤에 있었음을 짐작해 볼 수 있다. 따라서 정답은 (D)이다. 홈즈 씨가 보낸 메모에서가 아니라 정책은 회사 웹 사이트에서 다운받았을 수 있다고 했으므로 (A)는 정답이 될 수 없다.

194 이메일 사용 위반으로 판단되는 것이 아닌 것은 무엇인가?
(A) 개인적 목적으로 이메일을 사용하는 것
(B) 인증서류의 글을 보내는 것
(C) 불법 사진을 유포하는 것
(D) 직장 동료들 사이에 파일을 교환하는 것

해설 이메일 사용 목적으로 용납될 수 없는 것으로 개인적인 용무로 이메일을 사용하는 것, 인신공격성의 메시지를 쓰는 것, 불법적인 글이나 사진 등을 유포하는 것이 포함되어 있으므로 (A), (B), (C)는 맞는 내용이다. 이메일 사용 규정에 위반되지 않는 것은 (D)이다.

195 이메일 감사에 관해 언급된 것은 무엇인가?
(A) 회사는 불법 업체를 감사할 것이다.
(B) 회사는 이메일 감시 권한을 가진다.
(C) 검사 절차는 대표이사에 의해 이루어질 것이다.
(D) 부적절한 정보를 가진 직원만 조사할 것이다.

해설 세 번째 지문 하단에서 회사는 시스템에 기록된 정보는 무엇이든 조사하고 감시할 수 있는 권한이 있음을 언급하고 있다. 따라서 정답은 (B)이다.

해설 모리스 씨가 쓴 첫 번째 이메일에서 그녀는 티나 씨가 파커 씨와 함께 포럼 참석을 위해 누워페 갈 것을 고려 중이라는 말을 듣는데 그녀가 현재 출장 가 있어 연락이 되지 않는다고 말하므로 정답은 (A)이다. 티나 씨가 누워페 갈 것이라는 아직 확답을 듣지 못하였으므로 (D)는 오답이다.

199 파커 씨는 모리스 씨가 무엇을 하길 원하는가?

(A) 포럼에서 연설할 것
(B) 역에서 호텔로 가는 택시 라인에 마련할 것
(C) 그에게 제때에 컨벤션 센터로 가는 지도를 보낼 것
(D) 교통수단과 숙박시설을 예약할 것

해설 파커 씨가 쓴 두 번째 이메일에 자신과 티나 씨의 기차표를 예약하고 숙박할 호텔 예약을 부탁하고 있다. 따라서 정답은 (D)이다.

200 모리스 씨는 티나 씨를 위해 7월 2일의 어떤 기차를 예약할 것인가?

(A) A5678
(B) X271
(C) X214
(D) A9521

해설 세 번째 지문에서 파커 씨는 말미 편정이 없어 마지막 기차를 타길 원한다고 했고, 소개중에서 마지막 기차는 X271인데 세 번째 지문에서 파커 씨가 티나 씨도 자신과 같은 기차표를 예매해 달라고 했으므로 (B)가 정답이다.

수신: 루시 모리스 (lucym@quadtech.com)
발신: 댄 파커 (d_parker@quadtech.com)
날짜: 6월 21일
제목: 최소 기차 예약

첨부 문서 고맙습니다. 포럼이 7월 3일 시작하기 때문에 저는 7월 2일에 누워으로 출발해야 합니다. **200** 그래서 저는 마지막 기차를 타야겠다는 생각이 듭니다. 저는 멀미 걱정이 없으므로 방향은 관계없습니다. 7월 6일 포럼 폐막 행사가 오후 2시에 끝나기 때문에 제때에 제일 나은 선택은 이어도 오후 3시 45분 A5641(일반) 기차일 것입니다. 그리고 티나 씨는 자료 함께 포럼에 참석할 예정이어서 당신이 그녀의 표도 예약해야 합니다. **200** 제 것과 같은 표로 예약해 주세요.

그리고 한 가지 부탁이 더 있습니다. **199** 저와 티나를 위해 호텔 객실 예약도 해 좋을 수 있습니까? 우리는 포럼이 개최되는 컨벤션 센터 인근에 있는 라치 몬드 호텔에 묵고 싶습니다. 1인실 2개를, 4박으로 예약해 주세요. 그리고 또한 우리가 7월 2일 늦은 시간에 체크인할 것이므로 호텔 측에 알려 주세요.

매우 감사합니다. 당신의 수고에 진심으로 감사드립니다.

댄 파커

어휘 attach 첨부하다 option 선택 사항 express 고속의 comfortable 안 락한 reversed 거꾸로 된 randomly 무작위로 assign 배정하다 at one's earliest convenience 될 수 있는 대로 빨리 reach 연락이 닿다 attachment 첨부물 carsickness 멀미 ceremony 행사 reserve 예 약하다 appreciate 감사하다 effort 수고

---

196 모리스 씨가 파커 씨에게 이메일을 보낸 이유는 무엇인가?

(A) 그의 출장에 그를 동반할 것을 제안하기 위해서
(B) 변경된 일정을 요청하기 위해서
(C) 더욱 편안한 기차를 소개하기 위해서
(D) 교통수단 일정을 알려 주기 위해서

해설 첫 이메일을 쓴 목적은 "기차 예약"이라는 주어진 제목과 지문 초반에 기차 일정을 첨부한다는 내용을 통해 기차의 운행 일정을 알리기 위한 글이라는 것을 알 수 있다. 따라서 정답은 (D)이다.

197 "XAT" 기차에 관해 언급된 것은 무엇인가?

(A) 좌석은 모두 역방향이다.
(B) 표 가격은 비싸다.
(C) 여분의 공간을 제공한다.
(D) 좌석은 승객들이 선택한다.

해설 첫 번째 이메일에서 XAT 기차는 좌석 사이에 공간이 조금 더 있다고 언급하고 있으므로 정답은 (C)이다.

198 모리스 씨가 파커 씨에게 티나 씨에 관해 묻는 이유는 무엇인가?

(A) 티나 씨에게 연락할 수 없다.
(B) 티나 씨는 파커 씨의 비서이다.
(C) 파커 씨는 티나 씨로부터 메시지를 받았다.
(D) 티나 씨는 파커 씨와 함께 누워으로 갈 것이다.

Actual Test

09

Reading Comprehension

본책 P194

PART 7

147 (D)	148 (C)	149 (C)	150 (D)	151 (A)	152 (B)	153 (A)	154 (C)	155 (C)
156 (D)	157 (C)	158 (C)	159 (A)	160 (A)	161 (B)	162 (D)	163 (B)	164 (C)
165 (D)	166 (B)	167 (B)	168 (A)	169 (D)	170 (A)	171 (B)	172 (C)	173 (A)
174 (C)	175 (A)	176 (A)	177 (C)	178 (A)	179 (B)	180 (A)	181 (C)	182 (B)
183 (C)	184 (A)	185 (D)	186 (C)	187 (A)	188 (D)	189 (B)	190 (D)	191 (A)
192 (C)	193 (C)	194 (C)	195 (B)	196 (C)	197 (A)	198 (B)	199 (A)	200 (A)

달라스 공공 도서관
도서관 상호 대출 신청서

만약 찾으시는 책이 저희 소장 도서가 아니라면, 주州)에 소재한 다른 공공 도서관으로부터 대출을 요청하실 수도 있습니다. 최근 발간된 신간 도서와 잔내 참고 도서를 제외한 도서를 도서관 상호 대출 시스템을 통해 이용하실 수 있습니다. 개인은 한 달에 네 번으로 대출을 신청하실 제한됩니다.

이름: 카밀 로프트

제출일: 2월 2일

🔴**148 연락 가능한 전화번호 또는 이메일:** 469-555-7301

도서관 카드 번호: 8882156a

🔴**148 책을 찾아가실 지점:** 5번가 도서관

🔴**148 도서명:** 코너 오브리의 연익 삶과 시대

저자명: 짐

요청하신 책을 지점에서 날짜에 제공해 드리지 못할 수도 있습니다. 대부분의 신청 도서는 입수하는 데 대략 2주에서 3주 정도 소요됩니다. 🔴**147 이 신청서가 접수된 이후에, 예상 날짜와 함께 연락을 드릴 것입니다.**

어휘 public library 공공 도서관 interlibrary loan 도서관 상호 대출 collection 소장품 수집품 state 주州(의) note 주의하다 release 발간(발매)하다 reference book 참고 도서, 잔내 열람 도서 loan 대출 individual 개인(의) be limited to ~으로 제한되다 submission 제출 branch 지점 pick up ~을 찾아오다 guarantee 견적하다 approximately 대략 estimated 예상되는 submit 제출하다

147 이 신청서가 제출된 후에 도서관은 무엇을 할 것인가?
(A) 로프트 씨에게 책의 위치 알려 주기
(B) 다른 도서관에 책 전달하기
(C) 서관에서 도서 구매하기
(D) 로프트 씨에게 언제 책을 받을 수 있을지 알려 주기

해설 질문에 this form is submitted라는 표현이 지문 마지막 문장에서 this form is received라는 표현으로 등장한다. 이 부분의 내용을 살펴보면, 신청서가 접수된 후 예상 도착 날짜와 함께 연락을 주겠다고 했다. 따라서 정답은 (D)이다.

148 신청서에 요청된 정보에 포함되지 않은 것은 무엇인가?
(A) 개인에게 어떻게 책이 연락을 수 있는지
(B) 책을 어디로 보내야 하는가
(C) 책이 언제까지 필요한가
(D) 도서명은 무엇인가

해설 NOT이 들어간 문제는 선택지를 하나씩 지문과 대조하면서 풀어야 한다. 연락 가능한 전화번호 또는 이메일, 책을 찾아갈 수 있는 지점 그리고 도서명이 언급되어 있다. 따라서 지문에 언급되지 않은 (C)가 정답이다.

태드 존스 **오후 10:05**
브리짓, 이렇게 늦은 시간에 귀찮게 해서 정말 죄송해요. 하지만 지금 곤란한 상황이에요 아직 아직 자고 있죠?

브리짓 가터 **오후 10:11**
네, 그냥 책 좀 보고 있었어요, 무슨 일이에요, 태드? 제발 아직 사무실에 있는 게 아니라고 말해줘요

태드 존스 **오후 10:12**
유감이지만, 사무실에 있어요, 상사가 이용에 제일 먼저 이번 판매 발표 준비를 해 놓으라고 하거든요 🔴**149 혹시 텍사스 지난해 판매 수치가 어디 있는지 아세요?**

브리짓 가터 **오후 10:14**
그 자료는 모두 온라인에 "Sales Archives"라는 이름의 공유 폴더에 있어요. 비밀번호로 보호되지만, 당신은 접근할 수 있어요.

태드 존스 **오후 10:15**
네, 거기 봤어요, 텍사스 없고 다른 지점들 자료만 있어요.

브리짓 가터 **오후 10:16**
아, 맞아요! 우리가 5월에 대부모 감사 기간 동안에 그 자료를 옮겼어요. 그것은 모두 "Legal"로 표시된 폴더 안에 있어요.

태드 존스 **오후 10:20**
아하! 🔴**150 찾았어요 당신이 일한 대로 바로 거기 있었네요, 감사해요, 브리짓. 당신은 구세주예요!**

브리짓 가터 **오후 10:21**
천만에요. 당신이 곧 끝냈으면 해봐요, 아침에 봅시다.

어휘 bother 귀찮게 하다, 방해하다 a bit of 약간의 ~ have a crisis 곤경에 빠지다, 위기를 겪다 first thing 무엇보다도 먼저, 처음에 push back ~을 미루다 sales figure 판매 수치 shared 공유된 protect 보호(하다) access 접근(하다) audit 감사 marked 표시된 lifesaver 곤경(위기)에서 구해주는 사람(것)

149 존스 씨의 문제는 무엇인가?
(A) 그는 감사를 받는 중이다.
(B) 그는 발표를을 완성했다.
(C) 그는 어떤 자료를 찾을 수 없다.
(D) 그는 텍사스로 전근을 갈 것이다.

해설 존스 씨는 늦은 시간에 귀터 씨에게 문자를 보내서 텍사스 지점이 지난 해 판매 수치 자료가 어디에 있는지 묻고 있으므로 정답은 (C)이다.

150 오후 10시 20분에 존스 씨가 "찾았어요"라고 쓴 의미는 무엇인가?
(A) 그는 그녀의 문자 메시지를 받았다.
(B) 그는 그 일을 했던 사람이다.
(C) 그는 상황을 이해한다.
(D) 그는 그가 찾고 있었던 걸 찾았다.

해설 존스 씨는 늦은 시간에 존스 씨가 어디에 있는지를 묻는 메시지에 대한 응답으로 "찾았어요"라고 말했다. 따라서 그가 찾던 자료를 지금에서야 찾았다는 (B)가 정답이다.

수신: 모리스 스티븐슨 <mostevenson14@tsu.edu>
발신: 애나 그린 (agreen@trimoco.com)
날짜: 9월 9일
제목: 트리모코

좋은 오후예요, 모리스.

🔴**152 트리모코의 애나 그린인데 다시 연락드립니다.** 인터강케로, 어제 우리 사무실에 전기적 인재와 작은 화재가 있었습니다. 다행히도, 다친 사람도 없고 피해 미미하이 미했지만, 청소와 수리 작업이 진행 중입니다. 따라서 🔴**151 152 회의일에 예정된 귀하의 면접을 진행할 부서에서 제 연락을 하루 미루어야 할 것 같습니다.** 하지만 귀하의 면접 시간과 장소는 변동이 없습니다. 만약 일정을 하루 조정할 수 있으시다면 우리에게 바로 알려 주십시오. 그러면 예정되 면접 시간을을 다른 지원자와 바꿀 수 있도록 최선을 다할 것입니다. 그러나 새로 정해진 면접 일정에 관하여 일정을 맞추도록 최선을 애써 주시면 감사하겠습니다. 불편을 끼쳐 드려 진심으로 죄송합니다.

애나 그린
인사담당자
트리모코

🔴**152 트리모코의 애나 그린이 모리스에게 연락을 보내온다.**

어휘 minimal 최소의 clean-up 청소, 정리 push back ~을 미루다 executive assistant 비서, 보좌관 remain ~이 자료 있다 adjustment 조정, 조절 switch 바꾸다 fit 맞추다 newly 새로 assigned 할당된 sincerely 진심으로 apologize for ~에 대해 사과하다 inconvenience 불편함 HR 인사팀(= Human Resources) coordinator 담당자, 조정자 reject 거절하다 be aware of ~을 인지하다, 알아차리다 recommendation 추천(사)

151 이메일의 목적은 무엇인가?
(A) 면접 날짜를 변경하려고
(B) 실수에 대해 사과하려고
(C) 새 사무실을 요청하려고
(D) 구직 지원자를 거절하려고

해설 이메일 서두 부분에서 어제 사무실에 화재 사건을 언급하면서, 면 접 일정을 두로 미루고자 보낸 이메일임을 알 수 있다. 따라서 정답은 (A)가 된다. 지문의 to be pushing back the interview를 선택지에서 to change an interview date로 패러프레이징했다.

152 스티븐슨 씨에 대해 알 수 있는 것은 무엇인가?
(A) 전에 트리모코와 일한 적이 있다.
(B) 트리모코에서 누군가를 만나기로 되어 있다.
(C) 트리모코에 직원이다.
(D) 그린 씨의 친척이다.

해설 스티븐슨 씨는 이메일의 수신자로 원래 트리모코에서 면접을 보기로 되어 있었다. 따라서 누군가를 만나기로 되어 있었다는 (B)가 정답이다.

해설 "Sales Archives"라는 공유폴더에 존스 씨가 찾는 자료가 없고 "Legal"이라는 폴더에서 찾게 되자. "I got it."이라는 말이 나왔다. 이 표현은 원하는 자료를 거기에서 찾았다는 의미로 쓰였다. 따라서 정답은 (D)이다.

[153-154]

데미안 앨런 [오후 2:05]	최근에 누가 존 오브라이언과 연락한 적이 있나요?
칼린 렐린 [오후 2:06]	제가 며칠 전에 전화로 그와 통화를 했어요. 무슨 일 있어요?
에이미 마르쿠스키 [오후 2:06]	저는 한 15분 전에 휴게실에서 그를 보기만 했어요. 그가 항상 서류를 검토하고 있던데요. 무가 잘못됐나요?
데미안 앨런 [오후 2:07]	휴게실이요? 이런. 저는 시내 건너에서 고객과 회의를 하고 있어요. 그가 5분 전에 여기에 도착해야 했는데. 전화를 받지 않네요.
칼린 렐린 [오후 2:08]	어머나. 그의 건전지가 다 되었나 봐요. 잠깐만요, 제가 그를 찾을 수 있는지 볼게요.
데미안 앨런 [오후 2:09]	감사해요. 저는 전체 저 혼자서 이 일을 처리하고 싶지 않아요. 이문은 그의 기술적 설명으로 저는 그냥 여기서 몇 가지 기술적 설명을 그를 보조하려고 있을 뿐이거든요.
에이미 마르쿠스키 [오후 2:10]	그가 가는 중이었음 좋겠어요. 당신 존을 알잖아요. 그는 항상 모든 걸 마지막 순간까지 미뤄두죠.
칼린 렐린 [오후 2:13]	그가 이곳도 휴게실에 있었어요. 그는 회의를 완전히 잊어버리고 있었어요. 지금 당장 택시에 올라탈 거예요. 그가 고객한테 사과하고, 15분 내로 자기네 갈 거라고 말했어요.
데미안 앨런 [오후 2:14]	차가 막히지 않아야 할 텐데. 도와주셔서 감사해요, 여러분들.

어휘 breakroom 휴게실 ~ go over ~을 검토하다 be supposed to do ~하기로 되어 있다, 예정이다 die (배터리 수명이) 다 되다 hold on 기다리다 track down 찾아내다 handle 처리하다 on one's own 혼자 힘으로 technical 기술적인 hopefully 바라건대 until the last minute 마지막 순간까지 completely 완전히 hop 타다 ~간신히 hop into 급히 타다

153 채팅 토론 중 앨런 씨가 있는 장소는 어디인가?
(A) 사무실 밖
(B) 휴게실 안
(C) 택시 안
(D) 집

해설 앨런 씨는 시내 건너 고객 회의에 있다고 했다. 오기로 한 존 씨가 나타나지 않자 그를 찾는 것인데, 정답은 (A)이다.

154 오후 2시 10분에 마르쿠스키 씨가 "당신 존을 알잖아요"라고 쓴 의미는 무엇인가?
(A) 당신은 존을 이전에 만나보았다.
(B) 당신은 존처럼 행동해야 한다.
(C) 당신은 존의 성향을 잘 안다.
(D) 당신은 존의 행동에 대한 책임이 있다.

해설 해당 문장의 앞뒤 내용을 보면 휴게실에 지각한 존이 가는 길이기를 바란다면서, 그가 항상 모든 일을 마지막까지 잘 하지 않는다는 사실을 잘 알고 나내는 일을 미루어 볼 때 정답은 (C)이다.

[155-157]

편안하게 페닌술라 셔틀을 타세요

공항에 가는 것은 꿈만큼 정도로 불편합니다. 주차비는 너무 비싸고, 주(州)의 예산 삭감으로 인해 우리는 대중교통 선택권도 빼앗겼었습니다. 그러나 링컨 국 제공항에서는 이제 전문 교통 서비스로 새로운 서비스를 추가하였습니다. 바로 페닌술라 셔틀버스입니다.

페닌술라 셔틀버스는 젠슨, 베이사이드, 북부 팔링턴과 팔링턴 비치를 포함하여 반드시에 있는 전 지역을 운행합니다. 버스는 오전 6시부터 오후 10시까지 매시 정각에 라이트하우스 포인트에서 출발합니다. 첫 셔틀버스는 오전 6시 30분에 공항에서 출발하며, 마지막 버스는 오후 10시 30분에 (라이트하우스 포인트)공항 사이에서 운행합니다. 젠슨 버스 정류장; 베이사이드도 메인 가, 페닌술라 쇼핑몰, 북부 팔링턴 버스 정류장과 팔링턴 비치 우체국에 서 정차합니다.

젠도 표는 8달러에 미리 구매하시거나 운전기사에게 10달러에 구매할 수 있습니다. 카운티 교통카드도 10장 묶음에 노인들과 학생들도 10% 할인됩니다. 문의 사항이 있으시면, 저희 웹 사이트 www.liashuttle.com을 방문해 주세 요.

어휘 in comfort 편안하게 inconvenient 불편한 budget 예산 cut 삭감 take away ~을 빼앗아 가다; 치우다 public transportation 대중교통 private transportation 전용의, 사적인 community 지역 공동체 located on ~에 있는 at the top of each hour 매시 정각에 one-way 편도의 in advance 미리 transit card 교통 카드 senior citizen 노인 urban 도시의

155 링컨 국제공항에 관해 암시된 것은 무엇인가?
(A) 하루에 반드시로 가는 항공편이 몇 대 있다.
(B) 마지막 비행기는 저녁 8시경에 출발한다.
(C) 대중교통으로 갈 수 없다.
(D) 대도시 지역 근처에 있다.

해설 링컨 국제공항을 설명하고 있는 첫 단락을 보면 공항에 가는 것이 불편하다는 것을 설명하므로, 주의 예산 삭감으로 인해 대중교통 선택권들을 빼앗겨 버렸다는 것을 통해 대중교통으로 모든 공항에 갈 수 없음을 추론할 수 있다. 따라서 정답은 (C)이다.

156 마지막 페닌술라 셔틀버스가 공항을 출발하는 때는 언제인가?
(A) 오후 6시
(B) 오후 6시 30분
(C) 오후 10시
(D) 오후 10시 30분

해설 첫 셔틀버스는 오전 6시 30분에 공항에서 출발하며, 마지막 버스는 (출발한다는 내용을 토대로, 정답은 오후 10시, 10 P.M.은 공항이 아니라 라이트하우스 포인트를 출발하는 마지 시간이다.

157 학생이 버스에서 표를 구매하면 얼마를 지급해야 하는가?
(A) 7달러 20센트
(B) 8달러
(C) 9달러
(D) 10달러

해설 버스에서 운전기사에게 표를 구매할 경우 10달러를 지급해야 하는데, 학생들은 10% 할인을 받는다고 했다. 따라서 학생이 버스에서 표를 사면 9달러를 지급해야 하므로, 정답은 (C)이다.

[158-160]

루시 포토웍스
상품 반품 양식

품목에서는 30% 이상 할인받은 제품을 구매한 경우를 제외하고 모든 저희 제품에 대해서 30일 환불 정책을 제공합니다. 모든 파손되거나 반품하는 제품에 대해서는 지회가 배송비를 부담하지만, 다른 이유로 교환하거나 반품하는 제품에 대한 반송 제품 비는 고객이 부담해야 합니다. 모든 반품 제품은 원본 영수증과 송장을 받으셔도 드시 동봉해야 합니다.

| 이름 | 루시 에드워즈 |
| 배송 주소 | 15 마시 레인, 아파트 2B, 대블린, 몬타나 59012 |

요청하는 서비스:
☐ 교환
☑ 현금 환불
☐ 스토어 크레디트
☐ 수리

반품하는 제품명: 마이크로 17mm SLR 줌 렌즈

반품한 이유: 해외에서 업무상 야생 생물 사진을 찍다가 실수로 렌즈 줌 렌즈를 떨어뜨리고 난 후, 이 제품을 구매했습니다. 그러나 이 새로운 렌즈를 첫 사용에 보았는데 화질이 만족스럽지 못했습니다. 저는 대신 렌즈를 수리하기로 결정했습니다.

어휘 merchandise 물품, 제품 policy 정책, 방침 excluding 제외하고 cover (요금, 비용 등을) 부담하다, 지급하다 be responsible for ~을 책임지다 shipping and handling fees (우편료, 운송, 포장료 등) 배송 및 경비 invoice 청구서, 송장 store credit 스토어 크레디트(매장에서 환불 대신 제공하는 물건값의 상응의 표) accidentally 우연히 wildlife 야생 생물 assignment 업무 overseas 해외에서, 해외 on sale 할인 중인 undamaged 손상되지 않은 image quality 화질 meet 충족시키다 improperly 부적절하게 previous 이전의

158 고객이 배송비를 지불해야 하는 이유로 연결된 것은 무엇인가?
(A) 제품은 할인된 가격에 구매되었다.
(B) 고객이 영수증을 가지고 있지 않다.
(C) 반품된 물품이 손상되지 않았다.
(D) 한 달 이상 지났다.
해설 모든 마순품에 대해서는 매장에서 배송비를 부담하지만, 다른 이유로 교환하거나 반품하는 제품에 대한 배송비는 고객이 부담해야 한다고 했으므로 정답은 (C)이다. (A)의 경우 30%나 그 이상 할인된 제품은 환불에서 제외된다고 했으므로 오답이다.

159 에드워즈 씨가 제품을 반품한 이유는 무엇인가?
(A) 그녀의 기대치를 충족시키지 못했다.
(B) 그녀가 주문한 것 중 하나다.
(C) 사고로 파손되었다.
(D) 잘못 수리되었다.
해설 회장이 만족스럽지 못했다고 했으므로 정답은 (A)이다.

160 에드워즈 씨에 관한 설명으로 올바른 것은 무엇인가?
(A) 전문 사진가이다.
(B) 반품 절차에 대해 알지 못한다.
(C) 전에 좀 렌즈를 구매한 적이 없다.
(D) 이전에 품질과 문제가 있었다.
해설 에드워즈 씨가 좀렌즈를 사용한 내용을 보면, 해외에서 업무상 야원 생해 사진을 찍어가 중반으로 찍어야 했던 것을 통해 전문 사진가임을 추론할 수 있다. 따라서 정답은 (A)이다.

[161-164]

온라인이나 도로 위에서

- [1] -. 가장 인기 있는 신기술을 지속해서 살펴보는 가운데, 우리는 자동차 산업에서 최신 경향을 확인할 것이다. 그것은 바로 커넥티드 자동차이다. 커넥티드 자동차는 기본적으로 그들의 이름이 암시하듯이, 인터넷에 연결된 자동차입니다. 기본적으로, 여러분의 자동차는 클라이는 무선 인터넷 접속 기능지역에 될 것이며, 여러분과 승객들은 모든 정보를 자동차의 연결을 통해 인터넷에 연결할 수 있습니다.

그러나 가까에는 이 이상의 뭔가가 있습니다. - [2] -. 예를 들어, 여러분의 자동차가 사고를 당하게 된다면, 여러분의 자동차는 자동으로 교통경찰과 여러분의 보험 회사에 알릴 것입니다. 다른 인전한 기능도 적용될 여러 상황이 나가 기계 문제에 관해 경고하는 것입니다. - [3] -.

이 어디에 자동차가 연결될 때, 얼쇠는 필요 없습니다. - [4] -. 여러분의 자동차에 가까이 있게 되면, 문을 잠글 수 있고 차에 경보가 울리게 할 수도 있습니다. 히터를 켤 수도 있으며, 문을 잠글 수 있고 차에 경보가 울리게 할 수도 있습니다. 이 기술이 진화하는 운전 상황이면, 마지막엔 커넥티드 기능으로 스스로 운전할 수 있게 될 것입니다!

어휘 continuing 지속적인 hot 인기 있는 최신의 trend 경향 automotive industry 자동차 산업 vehicle 자동차, 탈 것 automobile 자동차 basically 기본적으로 link A to B A를 B에 연결하다 automatically 자동으로 alert 경고하다 insurance 보험 feature 특징, 기능 warning 경고 hazardous 위험한 mechanical 기계적인 given 고려하면, 생각하면 enable ~을 할 수 있게 하다 ongoing 진행 중인 evolve 진화하다 expert 전문가 be based on ~을 기반으로 하다 publish 출판하다 source 연원 necessity 필수품

161 기사에 관해 암시하는 것은 무엇인가?
(A) 전문가에 의해 작성되었다.
(B) 진행 중인 시리즈의 일부이다.
(C) 사실을 기반으로 하지 않는다.
(D) 이전에 출판되었다.
해설 해당 기사의 시작 부분에서 계속해서 인기 있는 신기술을 보면서 소개하는 시리즈 기사의 새로운 기술을 일려 주는 시리즈 기사 중 일부임을 추론할 수 있다. 따라서 정답은 (B)이다.

162 커넥티드 카가 강정으로 연급되지 않은 것은 무엇인가?
(A) 사고 후에 도움을 받는다.
(B) 기능한 위험을 경고한다.
(C) 열쇠를 사용할 필요가 없다.
(D) 더 운전을 잘하게 해준다.
해설 NOT 문제 유형으로 선택지의 내용을 하나씩 대조해 기반시를 독도록, 심각한 사고를 당하게 된다면 자동으로 교통경찰과 보험 회사에 알릴 것이라고 했고, 위험한 운전 상황이나 기계 문제에 관해 경고한다고 했으며, 마지막으로 열쇠는 없다고 했다. 따라서 언급되지 않은 (D)가 정답이다.

163 [1], [2], [3], [4]로 표시된 곳 중 다음 문장이 위치로 가장 적합한 것은 어디인가?
"여러분의 자동차가 계속 온라인 상태이기 때문에 중요한 정보를 보내고 전송할 수 있습니다."
(A) [1]
(B) [2]
(C) [3]
(D) [4]
해설 해당 문장은 자동차의 온라인 기능 덕분에 중요한 정보를 송수신할 수 있다는 내용이다. 따라서 해당 문장 뒤에는 보낼 수 있는 상태에서의 정보를 설명하는 내용이다. 따라서 정답은 (B)이다.

164 글쓴이가 휴대전화를 연급한 이유는 무엇인가?
(A) 새로운 기술의 안전을 지적하려고
(B) 이차들 퍼수들의 연결을 암시하려고
(C) 커넥티드 가능 어떻게 조작할 수 있는지 설명하려고
(D) 커넥티드 카가 얼마나 빨리 바뀔 바랄 수 있는지 보여 주려고
해설 어디에 있는지 간에 휴대전화로 자동차 시동을 걸 수 있고, 히터를 켤 수 있으며, 문을 잠글 수 있고 차에 경보가 울리게 할 수도 있다고 했다. 따라서 커넥티드 기능 어떻게 조작할 수 있는지 설명하고 있으므로, 정답은 (C)이다.

[165-168]

만약 문제가 와이파이 연결과 관련이 있다면, 다음 고장 수리에 대한 설명서를 참조하세요.

155 우선 라우터 소프트웨어가 최신인지, 전선이 모두 독실히 플러그에 꽂혀 있는지, 그리고 새로운 라우터의 전원이 켜져 있는지를 확인하세요. 만약 이것으로 문제가 해결되지 않는다면, 구매한 상황을 가장 잘 묘사하는 설명을 선택하셔서 추천된 해결책대로 따라 해 주세요.

(A) 인터넷에 전혀 연결할 수 없습니다.
일반적 네트워크에 접속되고 있는지 확인하십시오. **157** 비슷한 이름을 지닌 이용 가능한 네트워크들이 여러 개 있을 수 있습니다.

(B) 인터넷에 접속할 수도 있지만, 연결이 평소에 느립니다.
1) 스트리밍 영화나 온라인 게임과 같은 양이 대역폭을 사용하는 프로그램을 모두 닫아십시오.
2) 다른 어떤 기기들이 네트워크에 연결되어 있는지 확인하십시오. 불필요은 기기들을 끄면 연결 속도가 개선될 것입니다.

(C) **156** 인터넷이 연결되었으다가 끊어졌다가 합니다.
기기를 라우터 가까이 이동시키십시오. 라우터는 금속만 벗어를 갖고 있으며, 어떤 물건이나 다른 전자 기기에 의해 방해받음을 수 있습니다.

어휘 be related to ~와 관련되다 connection 연결 refer to ~을 참조하다 troubleshooting 고장 수리 router 라우터(인터넷 전달 장치) up to date 최신식의 securely 튼튼하게, 확고히 plug in 플러그를 꽂다 statement 진술 access 접속(하다), 접속(하다) unusually 평소와 달리 bandwidth (송신 전파의) 대역폭 streaming 스트리밍(인터넷상에서 영상 실시간으로 재생됨는 방법) come and go 연결이 되었다 안 되었다 하다 preliminary 사전의, 예비의 wireless 무선의 improperly 부적절하게 mistake 잘못 생각하다 disconnected 연결되지 않은 intermittent 간헐적인, 일시적으로 멈추는 relocate 새 장소로 두다, 재배치하다 close down ~을 닫다

165 이 설명서를 읽을 것 같은 사람은 누구인가?
(A) 컴퓨터가 바이러스에 걸린 사람
(B) 와이파이에 대해 배우고 싶어 하는 사람
(C) 전자 제품 가계를 가진 사람
(D) 최근에 라우터를 구매한 사람
해설 설명서의 시작 부분에서 라우터에 대한 기본 사항을 확인해 보라고 한 후에, 그래도 문제가 해결되지 않으면 해당 사용을 찾이 해결책을 살 펴보라고 했다. 따라서 이 설명서를 읽을 사람은 라우터를 구매자였으을 알 수 있다. 따라서 정답은 (D)이다. (B)는 wi-fi 단어를 반복한 함정이며, (C는 전자 기기(electronic devices) 관련 부분에서 연상할 수 있는 오답이다.

166 사전 문제 해결 단계로 제안되고 있는 것이 아닌 것은 무엇인가?
(A) 가장 최신 소프트웨어를 가졌는지 확인하기
(B) 다른 무선 기기를 모두 끄기
(C) 전선이 제대로 연결된 것인지 확인하기
(D) 라우터 스위치가 켜져 있는지 확인하기

해설 라우터 소프트웨어가 최신이었지만, 전선이 모두 확실히 틀틀그레 꽂혀 있는지, 새로운 라우터의 전원이 켜져 있는지를 확인해 보라고 했고, 따라서 언급되지 않은 (B)가 정답이다.

167 네트워크 이름과 관련된 문제로 연결된 것은 무엇인가?
(A) 네트워크 이름을 잊어버림
(B) 몇몇 비슷한 이름과 혼동함
(C) 너무 긴 이름을 만듦
(D) 다른 사람과 네트워크 이름을 공유함

해설 비슷한 이름을 가진 이웃 이웃 가능한 네트워크들이 여러 개 있을 수 있다고 했으므로 정답은 (B)이다. (D)는 공동통 수 있으나 여러 개의 비슷한 네트워크 이름이 존재한다는 것이지, 한 개의 네트워크 이름이 꼭 언급되는 내용은 아니므로 오답이다.

168 간헐적인 연결에 대한 해결책으로 제시된 것은 무엇인가?
(A) 기기를 라우터로 옮기기
(B) 다른 프로그램 닫기
(C) 네트워크 이름 바꾸기
(D) 모든 소프트웨어 업데이트하기

해설 질문의 intermittent connection이란 '간헐적인 연결'을 의미하는 것으로 지문의 Internet connection comes and goes'를 같은 의미로 이다. 인터넷 연결이 잘 안 될 경우 기기를 라우터 이동시키라고 하고 있다. 따라서 정답은 (A)이다. (B)의 경우는 연결이 끊어질 때 느릴 때 하게 되는 방법이므로 오답이다.

[169-171]

여러분들에게 리앤드 파인스 테니스 테니스 클럽이 9월 1일 자로 폐업할 것을 알 드리게 드림 소세 되어 마음이 무겁습니다. 저희는 10년 이상 주에서 가장 인기 있는 테니스 클럽 중 한 곳이었습니다. 클럽이 있는 부동산을 소유한 신사분이 저희의 임대 계약을 갱신하지 않기로 보이하니 그도 가까운 미래에 이 건물을 외부로 중개를 통제하는 노인 주거 공동체로 개발하니다.

자희가 통제할 수 없는 상황이기는 하지만, 취소된 회원권에 대해서는 납찌를 개선하여 환불받으실 수 있으니 안심하셔오. 대안으로, 감사하게도 리앤드 파인스 이전 회원들을 모두 받아들이겠다고 동의한 근처의 테니스 클럽인 Tennis World로, 남아 있는 회원권을 이전하실 수도 있습니다.

만약 회원권을 이전하길 원하신다면, 8월 31일까지 저희에게 알려 주세요. 저희가 그때까지 연락을 받지 못하면, 환불을 처리해 드릴 것입니다.

이만다 노바치코프

어휘 go out of business 폐업하다 property 부동산 elect 선택하다 renew 갱신하다 lease 임대 apparently 외관상으로 convert A into B A를 B로 전환하다 residential community 주거 공동체 senior citizen 노인 out of one's hands ~을 통제 벗어나 rest assured that ~을 안심하도 되다 be entitled to ~을 자격이 있다 prorated 비례 배분된 portion 부분 alternative 대체(의) transfer 전환

169 편지의 목적은 무엇인가?
(A) 부족한 서비스에 대해 환불해 주기 위해서
(B) 경쟁 클럽으로부터 회원들을 모집하기 위해서
(C) 고객들에게 새로운 혜택을 알려 주기 위해서
(D) 폐업을 발표하기 위해서

해설 글의 목적은 주로 서두 부분에 제시되며, 여기서도 첫 번째 문장을 보면 리앤드 파인스 테니스 클럽이 9월 1일자로 폐업하게 된다는 것을 알려 주는 내용임을 알 수 있다. 따라서 정답은 (D)이다. (A)의 경우 서 비스의 부재가 아닌 질에 대한 언급은 없으므로 오답이다.

170 부동산 소유주에 관해 제시된 것은 무엇인가?
(A) 양로원에 들어가 있다.
(B) 인도 월세를 요구하고 있다.
(C) 다른 일자리를 찾고 있다.
(D) 다른 테니스 클럽 회원이다.

해설 부동산 소유주는 클럽이 있는 곳이 임대 계약을 갱신해 주지 않기로 했다고 했고 이어지는 문장에서 해당 땅을 노인 주거 공동체로 전환 할 예정임을 밝혔다. 따라서 정답은 (A)이다. 지문의 the gentleman who owns the property를 질문에서는 the owner of the property로 패러프레이즈 되었다.

171 글쓴이가 테니스 월드를 언급한 이유는 무엇인가?
(A) 자신의 새 임을 설명하기 위해서
(B) 회원들에게 선택권을 주기 위해서
(C) 클럽의 혜택을 비교하기 위해서
(D) 자신의 문제를 그에 탓으로 돌리기 위해서

해설 테니스 월드는 리앤드 파인스 회원들을 받아들이겠다고 동의한 근거의 테니스 클럽이며, 회원들을 기존 회원권을 테니스 월드로 옮길 수 있다고 했다. 따라서 정답은 (B)이다.

어휘 remainder 나머지 graciously 고맙게, 자비롭게 former 이전의 process 처리하다 inferior (가치 등이) 열어지는 recruit 채용하다 rival 경쟁하는 nursing home 양로원, 요양소 compare 비교하다 blame A for B B를 A의 탓으로 돌리다

[172-175]

스트랫포드 요리 학원
단순한 요리 학교가 아닙니다

대부분의 요리 학교에서 여러분들은 단순히 요리하는지를 배우지만, 저희 스트랫포드에서는 여러분들에게 어떻게 성공할 수 있는지를 가르쳐 드립니다.

스트랫포드 수료증은 레스토랑 업계에서 평가 중요한 의미가 있습니다. — [1] —. 이것은 스트랫포드 졸업생 10명 중 9명이 졸업 직후 전문 식당 주방에서 일하고 있다는 것을 의미합니다.

대부분의 요리 학교들은 단순히 여러분에게 가장 많은 수익 취 업 성과률을 보여주려고 하는 것입니다. — [2] —. 저희의 비결은 전국의 모든 요리 학교 중에서 가장 많은 수의 취 업 성과률을 보유하고 있는 것입니다. 저희는 경력 서비스부도 여러분의 평판 하게 요리 관련 직업에 빨리 받일 수 있도록 졸업 전이나 졸업 후에도 여러분을 위해 대기하고 있을 것입니다. — [3] —. 저희는 또한 여러분이 일단 새로운 일을 시작하면 기꺼이 조언에 좋을 수 있는 헌신적인 졸업생과도 연락망을 갖고 있습니다.

그리고, 물론, 스트랫포드 교육만큼 종합적인 교육은 어디에도 없습니다. 그 유수들은 스트랫포드 졸업생들이 뛰어나게 준비되도록 상태로 온다는 것을 압니다. — [4] —. 여러분은 수상 경력이 있는 저희의 세 가지 프로그램 중 하나를 선택 하실 수 있습니다: 요리별, 각국 요리와 제과 프로그램입니다. 여러분에게 어느 것이 맞는지 확신이 안 서신다고요? 212-555-1172로 전화해 주세요.

어휘 culinary 요리 institute 교육, 시설 diploma 수료증 career counselor 취업 상담사 dedicated 헌신적인 alumni 졸업생 comprehensiveness 종합성, 포괄성 award-winning 상을 받은 respond to ~에 반응하다 numerous 수많은 affordable 저렴한, 가격 이 알맞은 staff (직원들) 배치하다 multiple 다수의 potential 잠재 적인

172 이 광고 전반에 반영할 것 같은 사람은 누구인가?
(A) 주방에서 일하고 있는 사람
(B) 교육 수업을 기르치는 사람
(C) 주방장이 되길 원하는 사람
(D) 레스토랑을 소유하고 있는 사람

해설 스트랫포드 요리 학원을 단순한 요리 방법이 아닌 업계 성공 방법을 알 려 주고 졸업 후에 전문 식당 주방에서 일하게 된다는 내용을 종합할 때 이 광고 전반에 관심을 보일 만한 사람은 주방장이 되고 싶은 사람임을 추론할 수 있다. 따라서 정답은 (C)이다. (A)의 경우 식당에서 일하는 사람의 종류가 다양할 수 있어 정답으로 보기 어렵고, (D) 역시 레스토랑의 소유주가 직접 요리를 할 사람인지 알 수 없으므로 오답이다.

173 요리 학원 졸업생에 관해 알 수 있는 것은 무엇인가?
(A) 대부분의 졸업생이 빨리 일을 찾는다.
(B) 많은 졸업생이 학원을 추천한다.
(C) 일부 졸업생이 해외 유명하다.
(D) 식당에서 일하는 졸업생은 거의 없다.

해설 졸업생 10명 중 9명이 졸업 후 곧 관련된 일을 갖는다고 했으므로 정답은 (A)이다, (D)의 few of them에서 few는 '거의 없음'이라는 부정

의 의미를 나타내는 표현으로, '식당에서 일하는 종업원들이 거의 없다'라는 의미가 되므로 정답으로 혼동하지 않도록 유의한다.

174 요리 학원의 강점으로 언급된 것이 아닌 것은 무엇인가?
(A) 수많은 취업 상담사들
(B) 도움이 되는 과거 졸업생들
(C) 저렴한 수업료
(D) 포괄적인 교육

해설 지문의 내용과 선택지를 비교하면서 문제를 풀어야 하는데 요리 요리학원 중에서 가장 많은 수의 취업 상담사를 보유하고 있다고 했으므로 (A)는 언급된 내용이고, 전국의 요식업계에 종사하는 졸업생들과도 연락망을 갖고 있다고 했고, 마지막으로 교육적으로 종합적인 교육을 갖고 있다고 했다. 따라서 언급되지 않은 내용인 (C)가 정답이다.

175 [1], [2], [3], [4]로 표시된 곳 중 다음 문장이 위치로 가장 적절한 곳은 어디인가?

"저희는 졸업 후 거의 90%의 취업률을 보유하고 있습니다."

(A) [1]
(B) [2]
(C) [3]
(D) [4]

해설 해당 문장은 졸업 후 취업률을 정확히 밝히고 있는 문장으로, [1] 뒤의 졸업생 10명 중 9명이 일을 하고 있다는 부연 설명과 자연스럽게 이어진다. 따라서 정답은 (A)이다.

[176-180]

수신: 이브 커 (hannak@evcorp.net)
발신: 하나 권

11월 15일에 우리는 일본 지배 회사에서 오는 네 분의 방문객을 맞이할 것입니다. 그들의 방문 목적은 우리의 자동화된 주문 처리 시스템에 관한 생각과 정보를 교환하려는 것입니다. 그들이 체류하는 시흘 동안에 주문 처리에 관한 회의를 할 것입니다. 16일에는 자주 저녁 시간을 갖게 될 것입니다. **177**

우리는 특히 일본에서 구사할 줄 알거나 일본 문화에 익숙한 우리 직원들이 그들에게 편안한 저녁 식사를 대접하고 시내 구경을 시켜주었으면 합니다. 내 **178** 방문객들은 우리의 사무부장과 함께 갈 것이지만, 우리는 더 즐겁고 사교적인 방문객을 더 많은 사람이 함께 했으면 합니다. **179** 많이 어려운 들의 팀원들이 그날 저녁에 시간이 있어서 참여하고 싶어 한다면, 그들에게 저의 이메일을 보내라고 하거나 주말 전에 제 사무실에 들러게 해 주세요. 협조해 주셔서 감사합니다!

176 메모의 목적은 무엇인가?
(A) 지원자들을 모집하기 위해서
(B) 방문객들을 환영하기 위해서
(C) 일정을 조정하기 위해서
(D) 아이디어를 요청하기 위해서

해설 일본 지배 회사에서 4명의 방문객이 올 예정이다. 방문객 접대를 함께할 수 있는 사람들을 구하려고 쓴 글임을 알 수 있다. 따라서 정답은 (A)이다.

177 메모에서 첫 번째 줄의 concerning과 의미상 가장 가까운 것은 무엇인가?
(A) 걱정하는
(B) 보우하는
(C) 관련된
(D) 정의하는

해설 meetings concerning order processing은 '주문 처리에 관한 회의'라는 의미이다. 따라서 concerning은 '~에 관한, 에 대하여'라는 의미를 지닌 (C) involving과 바꿔 쓸 수 있다.

178 11월 16일 저녁에 일본인 일본인 방문객들과 함께할 사람은 누구인가?
(A) 조디 쿰
(B) 존 굿윈
(C) 하나 권
(D) 가스 로저스

해설 두 지문을 연계해야 하는 주론 문제이다. 첫 번째 지문에서 일본에서 온 4명의 방문객이 사무부장과 함께 갈 것이라는 내용을 알 수 있으며, 두 번째 지문에서는 발신인이 자신의 방사 내용을 통해서 자신이 조디 쿰이라는 이름이 조디 쿰임을 알 수 있다. 두 내용을 종합하면 결국 일본이 방문객을 만날 사람은 조디 쿰임을 알 수 있다. 따라서 정답 (A)이다.

179 마크위즈 씨에 대해 암시된 것은 무엇인가?
(A) 이제는 이브사에 고용되어 있지 않다.
(B) 이전에 군 복무를 했었다.
(C) 현재 휴가 중이다.
(D) 부장으로 승진했다.

해설 마크위즈는 공군으로 복무했던 3년간 그 곳 근처에서 주둔했다고 했다. 따라서 마크위즈는 이전에 군 복무를 했었던 사람임을 알 수 있으므로, (B)가 정답이다.

180 마크위즈 씨가 16일에 참석할 수 없는 이유는?
(A) 출장을 갈 것이다.
(B) 일본어 실력이 부족하다.
(C) 개인적인 계획을 이미 세웠다.
(D) 그의 부서장이 허가하지 않을 것이다.

해설 마크위즈 씨는 도와주고 싶은 마음은 있으나 프레젠테이션을 위해서 16일에 가스 로저스와 에반스토로 가서 저녁 8시나 저녁 9시나 이후에나 돌아올 수 없을 것이라고 했다. 따라서 정답은 (A)가 된다.

[181-185]

신선한 꽃처럼 "저는 당신을 사랑합니다"라고 말하는 것은 없습니다!

머큐리 꽃 가게는 이스트 코스트 전역에 있는 100곳 이상의 꽃 가게를 보유한 기업입니다. **181** 아주 많은 매장을 보유함으로써 저희는 경쟁 업체보다 더 저렴한 배송비를 유지할 수 있습니다. 더우리 저희는 메인에서부터 플로리다까지 거의 모든 주소에 2시간 배송을 보장할 수 있습니다.

182 머큐리 꽃배달을 주문하는 가장 쉬운 방법은 단순히 저희에게 무료 장거리 전화 1-888-555-3559로 전화하시는 것입니다. 또한 저희 신규 웹 사이트(www.mercuryflowers.com)로 온라인 주문을 하시거나 저희의 매장을 들러 주문하실 수 있습니다.

4월 인타임 특별 할인!

4월 한 달 동안에 저희는 특별 할인 붐이 있습니다. 그리고 저희의 유명한 매주 백화도 들어 있습니다. 꽃다발은 25송이로 구성되며, 각각은 4~5개의 꽃송이가 달려 있습니다. **183** 4월 한 달 동안 온라인으로 꽃다발을 주문하시면, 39달러 99센트에서 19달러 99센트로 할인해 드립니다. 여러분들도 또한 5달러만 추가하시면 장식 꽃병도 받으실 수 있습니다.

어휘 host 접대하다 take up (시간, 공간 등을 차지하다, 쓰다 concerning ~에 관해 especially 특히 familiarity 익숙함, 친밀함 take out ~을 데리고 나가 접대하다 casual 격식 없는 accompany 동반하다 atmosphere 분위기 take part ~에 참여하다 stop by ~에 들르다 colleague 동료 station 배치하다 Air Force 공군 rusty 녹이 슨, 예전 같지 않은 fairly 꽤 be scheduled to do ~하도록 예정되다 recruit 모집하다 adjust 조정하다 employ 고용하다 formerly 이전에 serve in the military 군 복무를 하다 promote 승진시키다

머큐리 꽃 가게
고객 서비스 센터
우편 사서함 77181번
더햄, 노스캐롤라이나 27703

담당자님께,

4월 17일에 저의 조카가 첫째 딸을 낳았습니다. 제 건강상의 문제로 그를 축하해 주러 갈 수 없었습니다. 저는 뉴욕시에 살고 있고, 그녀는 5000리일 떨어진 시골 지역에 살기 때문에 그녀에게 꽃을 배달시키기로 했습니다. 제 친구 중 한 사람이 귀사를 추천했습니다.

저는 귀사의 웹 사이트에 들어가서, 예쁜 백합 특별 할인을 선택했습니다. 온라인으로 주문을 완료했습니다. 제 조카가 꽃을 거리 주소를 잘못 입력했다는 연락받았습니다. 주소는 블루 마운틴가 311번지가 아니라 113번지로 썼던 것입니다. 저 조카에 따르면 귀사의 배달 기사가 누군가 그녀의 이름을 알아낼 때까지 시골에 올라갔다 내려갔다 해야 운전했습니다. 이 마침내 시골스런 초록색 꽃밭에 담긴 아름다운 꽃다발을 배송했습니다.

요즘에 자기 일에 정말 정말 정성하게 노력하는 사람을 보는 것은 드문 일입니다. 저 조카가 그 기사의 이름을 받았는데, 브랜든 웨어라고 합니다. 그래서 자는 잠시 시간을 내어 그의 진심 어린 느낌에 찬사를 보내고 싶다고 싶었습니다. 이 메시지를 그의 상사에게 전달해 주십시오.

진심으로
캐런 킹스베리

어휘 up and down 전체에 outlet 판매점 delivery 배송 competitor 경쟁 업체 guarantee 보장하다 bouquet 꽃다발 toll-free (전화가) 무료인 retail 소매(의) come with ~이 딸려 있다, 같이 오다 stem 줄기 contain 포함하다 bud 봉오리 slash 식감하다 decorative 장식의 give birth to ~을 낳다 issue 문제 celebrate 축하하다 unfortunately 안타깝게도 mistakenly 실수로 recognize 알아보다 sincere 진심인 dedication 현신, 전념 commend 칭찬하다 supervisor 상사 advantage 장점 freshly 신선하게, 생생하게 bulk sale 대량 판매 wide variety of 매우 다양한 place an order 주문하다 in person 직접 praise 칭찬하다 partial 부분적인 point out 지적하다 misread 잘못 읽다

181 회사의 장점으로 언급된 것은 무엇인가?
(A) 방음 자전 꽃들
(B) 편리한 대량 판매
(C) 저렴한 배송비
(D) 아주 다양한 선택권

해설 광고에서 해당 꽃 가게는 많은 판매점을 갖고 있으므로, 다른 경쟁 업체보다 저렴한 배송비를 계속 유지할 수 있다고 했다. 따라서 정답은 (C)가 된다. (A)나 (D)의 경우, 쉽게 연상할 수 있는 부분이나 정확한 단서를 찾을 수 없으므로 답 오답이다.

182 가장 쉬운 주문 방법으로 언급된 것은 무엇인가?
(A) 팩스
(B) 전화
(C) 직접 방문
(D) 인터넷

해설 가장 쉬운 방법은 무료 전화 1-888-555-3559로 전화하는 것이라고 연급했고, 완전히 탈바꿈했다는 암시문이 없음으로. 지문에 the easiest way가 질문에 서는 the simplest way로 패러프라이즈되었다.

183 킹스베리 씨가 백합 비용으로 지급한 것은 얼마인가?
(A) 14달러 99센트
(B) 19달러 99센트
(C) 24달러 99센트
(D) 39달러 99센트

해설 두 지문을 연계해서 풀어야 하는 주목 문제이다. 첫 번째 지문 광고에서 4월 한 달 동안 온라인으로 꽃다발을 주문하면, 19달러 99센트 로 할인해 주고, 또한 5달러만 추가하면 장식 꽃밭도 받을 수 있다고 했다. 두 번째 지문에서는 킹스베리 씨가 백합과 꽃밭을 함께 구매했으 음을 알 수 있다. 따라서 두 개의 가격을 합친 것은 24달러 99센트이므 로 정답은 (C)이다.

184 킹스베리 씨가 편지를 쓴 이유는 무엇인가?
(A) 배달 기사를 칭찬하려고
(B) 부분 환불을 요청하려고
(C) 광고에 오류를 지적하려고
(D) 늦은 배달에 관해 불평하려고

해설 킹스베리 씨는 잠시 시간을 내어 배달 나서 기사의 진심 어린 느낌에 찬사를 보내고 싶다고 편지를 쓴 이유는 명확히 받으고 있다. 따라서 정답은 (A)이다. 지문의 commend를 보기에서는 praise로 바꾸어 표현했다.

185 운전기사에 관하여 암시된 것은 무엇인가?
(A) 그 지역 출신이 아니었다.
(B) 상을 받았다.
(C) 고객의 전화를 잘못 받았다.
(D) 잘못된 정보를 받았다.

해설 킹스베리 씨는 거리 주소를 잘못 입력했다고 했으므로 정답은 (D)가 된다. 지문에 the wrong street address를 선택지에서는 incorrect information이라고 패러프라이즈했다.

[186~190]

에이펙스 은행 고객들을 위한 중요한 업데이트

6번가에 있는 저희 시내 지점은 4월 16일부터 5월 12일까지 보수 공사로 문을 닫을 것입니다. 로비에 있는 두 대의 자동 현금 인출기는 여전히 이용하실 수 있지만, 은행 직원과 상담을 원하는 고객님들은 2번가로 바지니아가 가 교차로에 있는 다른 시내 지점을 방문하셔야 합니다. 불편을 끼쳐 죄송하게 생각하지만, 6번가 지점이 소규모 회의 테이블 그리고 터치스크린 및 모듈을 갖춘 최신식의 고객 친화적인 시설로 개선될 것을 발표하게 되어 기쁩니다. 이 것은 모든 고객에게 은행 업무를 더 빠르고, 더 편하고, 더 즐겁게 해 줄 것입니다. 동시에 지점이 있는 1세기가 된 건물의 전통적인 특징은 유지될 것입니다. 여러분은 에이펙스 은행 웹 사이트에서 보수 공사 개혁에 관한 더 많은 세부 사항들을 찾아볼 수 있습니다.

즉석 고객 평가 - 시애틀 - 은행 업무와 재무

여러분들이 듣지 못했을가 봐서 그런데, 6번가의 에이펙스 은행이 마침내 문을 다시 열었고, 완전히 탈바꿈했다는 얘쯤들일 수 있습니다. 그것은 전통적인 은행이라기보다는 마치 신규 첨단 기술 업체의 휴게실 같은 모습입니다. 새로운 구조가 저에게는 정이 안 갈 수도 있었지만, 저는 순식간에 그것에 반하게 되었습니다. 구식 번호표 기계는 터치스크린으로 교체되었고, 직원들은 이제 큰 가운 티 뒤에 숨어 있지 않습니다. 그들은 바로 앞으로 나와 있고 고객을 맞이고 여러분의 일을 처리해 줍니다. 로비에 있는 ATM도 똑같은 옛날 모델들이지 만, 지점 안에는 3개의 새로운 것들이 있습니다. 실제어 여러분들이 기다리는 동안에 페이스트리 빵과 커피로 즐길 수 있습니다. 저는 보수 공사가 공지됐던 것보다도 몇 주 더 오래 걸려 꽤 실망했었지만, 기다릴만한 가치가 있었습니다!

프레디 니콜스 (nosmo@apex-la.com)

수신: 이사벨 재머슨 (jeff@apex-corporate.com)
발신: 넬슨 오스몬드 (nosmo@apex-corporate.com)
날짜: 6월 15일
주제: 회신: 보수 공사

안녕하세요 이사벨,

저는 단호한 의견을 가진 사람으로서, 제가 틀렸을 때 이를 인정하기가 쉽지 다는 것을 알고 있습니다. 그러나 이번에는 그것을 미말 수 없을 것 같습니다. 저는 도스엔젤레스 지점을 새로운 라운지 스타일을 위한 시험대를 삼으라는 당신이 시도에 대해 강력히 반대했었습니다. 한 번에 모든 걸 시애틀 지점을 방문 하고 요즘응을 개선했으며, 지점장이 쉴레 슈데드가 저에게 보여준 고객 구조가 연속 설문 으로 업체 인성을 남겼습니다. 저희가 여기서 비슷한 보수 공사 실행을 노야를 회의 일정을 잡을 수 있을까요? 편하실 때 저에게 빨리 지예에 알려 주세요.

진심으로
넬슨 오스몬드
지점장
에이펙스 은행 로스앤젤레스

어휘 renovation 보수 수리 accessible 사용할 수 있는 representative 직원 대표 regret 유감으로 여기다 inconvenience 불편(함) state-of-the-art 최신식의 module 모듈(= 장비의) 일을 수행하는 프로그램) result in ~ 결과를 낳다 retain ~인 채로 유지하다 feature 특징점 instant 즉 섹스시의 finance 재무 undergo 겪다 transformation 변화, 변형 breakroom 휴게실 off-putting 정이 안 가는, 좋아하긴 않는 number-ticket dispenser 번호표 자동 발매기 face to face 얼굴을 맞대고 indulge in ~을 탐닉하다 frustrated 실망한, 좌절한 worth 가치가 있는 unavoidable 피할 수 없는 resist 저항하다 serve as ~의 역할을 하다 prototype 프로토타입(= 시제품)(앞서서 미리 제작해 보는 형태) blow A away A에 너무나 반하다 impressive 인상적인 efficiency 효율성 implementation 실행, 시행 annoyance 짜증

뉴질랜드 도착 카드

이름:	리차드 콜린슨
시민권:	캐나다인
동반인:	0명
여권 번호:	001163629
체류 기간:	6일
주요 방문 목적:	총회 참석
뉴질랜드에서의 주소:	**189** 플라자 호텔, 오클랜드
탑승 공항:	몬트리올, 캐나다
비행기 또는 선박 번호:	뉴질랜드 항공 23편 항공기

어휘 annual 연례의 association 협회 conference 총회 represent 대표하다 institution 협회, 단체 a variety of 다양한 related to ~와 관련된 obtain 얻다 round-trip 왕복 air fare 항공 요금 attendee 참석자 compensate for ~을 보상하다 incur (비용이) 발생하다 at the latest (아무리) 늦어도 on behalf of ~ 대신에 catch one's eye 눈길을 끌다 request 요청 affect 영향을 주다 citizenship 시민권 accompany 동반(수반)하다 embarkation 탑승 aircraft 항공기 vessel 선박

주목해 주세요! 대학교 도서관 직원들!

194 제3회의 연례 국제 대학 도서 협회 총회가 11월 4일 뉴질랜드의 오클랜드에서 개최될 것입니다. 우리는 이 행사에 우리 협회를 대표할 세 명의 지원자를 찾고 있습니다. 여러분들은 이틀의 추가 휴일을 포함하여 뉴질랜드에 대해 3일을 지낼 것이며, **189** 총회에서 돌아오자마자 여러분의 플라자 호텔 개별실을 제공할 것입니다. 대학 측은 항공 요금과 2박 동안의 플라자 호텔 개별실을 제공할 것입니다. 그러나 식사와 음료 비용은 참석자들이 부담해야 하며, 발생한 그 어떤 추가 비용도 배상하지 않을 것입니다. 만약 여러분이 참석에 관심이 있거나 더 많은 정보를 알고 싶으시다면, gbronson@uta.edu로 개리 브론슨에게 연락해 주십시오.

수신: 개리 브론슨 (gbronson@uta.edu)
발신: 리차드 콜린슨 (rcollison@uta.edu)
날짜: 10월 20일
주제: ICLA 총회

안녕하세요 브론슨 씨,

저는 대학교 도서관을 대표해 올해 ICLA 총회에 참석하는 데 관심이 있다는 걸 알려드리기 위해 글을 쓰고 있습니다. 귀하가 제 지원서를 받으셨기를 바랍니다. **190** 우리는 바로 셀러니에서 열린 1차 ICLA 총회에 함께 참석했었습니다. **195** 일정 중복 때문에 제가 지난해에 마이애미 총회를 놓쳤다 하더라도, 오클랜드에 제 가족이 있으므로, 올해의 행사가 제 눈길을 끌었습니다. 그러나 몇 가지 특별한 부담이 있습니다. 첫째, 저는 오전보다 몬트리올에서 출발했으면 합니다. 이렇게 하면 해서 표 가격이 덜어질 것으로 생각합니다. 또 **185** 플라자 호텔 대신에 바닷가도 호텔 객실을 하고 싶습니다. 플라자 호텔은 제가 찾아내야 하는 제 조부모님 댁과 꽤 멀기 때문입니다. 마지막으로, 제 가족과 함께 더 많은 시간을 보낼 수 있도록 여행의 발표를 3일이 마지막에 끝이 휴가를 덧붙일 것을 요청합니다. 제 부탁을 고려해 주셔서 감사합니다.

리차드 콜린슨
도서관 인수 전문가

---

191 공지에서 첫 번째 단락 여덟 번째 줄의 compensated와 의미가 가장 가까운 것은 무엇인가?

(A) 되갚아지다
(B) ~에 포함되다
(C) ~에 관해 상담되다
(D) ~에 관해 문의되다

해설 해당 표현 앞의 내용을 보면 식사와 음료비는 각자 지급해야 한다고 했기 때문에 돈이란 표현이 들어가야 부분이 발생한 그 어떤 추가 비용도 보상하지 않는다는 의미가 되어야 문맥상 적절하다. 따라서 배상이 되다라는 의미인 (A)가 정답이다.

192 총회 참석자들의 요구 조건으로 나타난 것은 무엇인가?

(A) 본인이 추가 기간을 써야만 한다.
(B) 호텔 객실을 같이 써야 한다.
(C) **그들이 알게 된 것을 공유해야만 한다.**
(D) 총회에서 발표해야 한다.

해설 첫 번째 지문의 공지를 보면 참석자들은 돌아오자마자 얻은 정보에 대해 다양한 발표를 하도록 요청하고 있다고 했으므로 정답은 (C)이다. 지문의 the information you obtain at the conference를 선택지에서는 what they learn이라고 패러프레이징했다.

193 콜린슨 씨에 관해서 암시된 것은 무엇인가?

(A) 매년 ICLA 총회에 참석한다.
(B) 이제 대학교 도서관에서 일하지 않는다.
(C) 이전에 브론슨 씨를 만난 적이 있다.
(D) 뉴질랜드의 시민권자이다.

---

186 6번가의 에이펙스 은행에 대해 언급되지 않은 것은 무엇인가?

(A) 5월에 재개장하기로 일정이 잡혀 있었다.
(B) 로비에 ATM 2대를 보유하고 있다.
(C) 2번가로 이전할 것이다.
(D) 오래된 건물에 있다.

해설 보수 공사 기간인 4월 16일부터 5월 12일까지이므로 5월에 재개장을 하다는 (A)는 맞는 내용이다. 두 대의 ATM이 로비에 있다고 했으므로 (B)도 맞는 내용이다. 해당 은행이 1세기가 된 건물에 있다는 내용에서 발생한 내용이다. 2번가로 이전한다는 없으므로 정답은 (C)이다.

187 나름스 씨가 제종 난 이유는 무엇인가?

(A) **예상치 못한 장기간의 폐점**
(B) 놀라도록 무례한 은행 직원
(C) 신기술 부족
(D) 불편한 위치

해설 두 번째 지문 마지막 부분에서 보수 공사가 공지했던 것보다도 몇 주 더 오래 걸렸을 때 실망했다고 했으므로 정답은 (A)가 된다.

188 보수 공사 이후에 에이펙스 은행이 보유한 ATM은 몇 개인가?

(A) 없음
(B) 2개
(C) 3개
(D) **5개**

해설 첫 번째 지문에서 로비에 2대의 ATM이 있다고 했고, 두 번째 지문에서 보수 공사 이후 로비에 있는 ATM에 대해서 지점 안에 새 ATM 3대가 더 생긴 것을 알 수 있다. 따라서 전체 ATM은 5대이므로 정답은 (D)이다.

189 새로운 은행으로 바꾸는 것에 대한 오스문드 씨의 원래 의견은 무엇인가?

(A) 그것에 대해 기대했었다.
(B) **너무나 과도하다고 느꼈다.**
(C) 비용이 너무나 많이 든다고 생각했다.
(D) 안전에 대해 염려된다.

해설 세 번째 지문에서 로스앤젤레스 지점을 새로운 라운지 스타일로 바꾸는 것에 대해 한가번에 모든 걸 시도하는 것은 너무나 많은 변화인 것 같다고 했다. 따라서 정답은 (B)이다.

190 오스문드 씨가 제파드 씨에게 원하는 것은 무엇인가?

(A) 그녀의 무례한 행동에 대해 사과하기
(B) 시애틀 지점 둘러보기
(C) 고객 만족 실문 조사하기
(D) **지점을 보수하는 것에 대해 그와 이야기 나누기**

해설 세 번째 지문 마지막에 오스문드 씨는 시애틀 지점과 비슷한 보수 공사 실행에 대한 논의 일정을 잡고 싶어 한다는 걸을 알 수 있다. 따라서 정답은 (D)이다.

해설 콜린스 씨가 쓴 이메일에서, '우리가 바르셀로나에서 열린 1차 ICLA 총회에 함께 참석했었다'고 했으므로 콜린스 씨는 보몬슨 씨를 예전에 만난 적이 있다. 따라서 정답은 (C)이다.

194 두 번째 연례 ICLA 총회가 열린 장소는 어디인가?
(A) 오클랜드
(B) 바르셀로나
(C) 마이애미
(D) 몬트리올

해설 연례 문제이다. 첫 번째 지문의 앞 부분에서 제3회 연례 총회가 오클랜드에서 열릴 것임을 알 수 있다. 또 두 번째 지문에서 지친해의 총회가 마이애미에서 열렸다고 했으므로 두 번째 연례 총회는 (C) 마이애미에서 열렸음을 알 수 있다.

195 콜린스 씨의 요청 중 보몬슨 씨가 거절한 것은 무엇인가?
(A) 회의에 참석하기
(B) 다른 호텔로 바꾸기
(C) 추가 휴일 갖기
(D) 다른 공항에서 떠나기

해설 연계 문제이다. 두 번째 지문에서 보몬슨 씨는 대신 호텔에서 숙박하고 싶다고 요청했지만, 세 번째 지문을 보면 숙소는 여전히 블라자 호텔임을 알 수 있다. 따라서 정답은 (B)이다.

[196-200]

http://www.presidentialprint.com

프레지덴셜 인쇄 서비스

비즈니스 솔루션을 위한 최적 프레지덴셜입니다!

홈	서비스	요금	추천 후기	전문	우리에 관해서

사내에서 만들어진 이류(一流) 마케팅 자료에 의존하는 것에 질리셨나요? 프레지덴셜 인쇄는 소기업에서부터 중간 규모의 업체까지 고객사의 예산에 맞춘 종합 인쇄 서비스를 제공합니다. 저희의 저렴한 가격은 비용 대량 비율 차등제입니다. 인쇄 주문량이 많을수록, 값은 더 저렴하답니다!

인쇄 서비스: 책자, 전단, 그리고 팸플릿
이것은 저희가 고객사를 위해 인쇄를 할 수 있는 것 중 일부분일 뿐입니다. 단일 물품부터 대량 인쇄까지 저희는 모든 것을 할 수 있습니다. 만약 사용자 지정 요청을 하신다면, 저희는 그것들도 해드릴 수 있을 것입니다. kt1@presidentialprint.com 의 크리스틴 린에게 연락만 해 주세요.

디자인 서비스: 로고와 표지
자회에게 가사의 아이덴티티를 갖고 오시면, 저희가 그것을 구현해 드릴 것입니다. 저희는 디자인과 인쇄 두 가지 모두 포함된 작업물에 대해 대폭적인 할인율을 제공합니다. jw2@presidentialprint.com로 제레미 워커에게 연락만 해 주세요.

계약 서비스
프레지덴셜을 귀하의 유일한 공급업체로 만드시고, 지역 최고의 인쇄 서비스를 가진 저희 제휴 혜택을 즐겨보세요. iit1@presidentialprint.com의 이안 리에게 연락만 해 주세요.

수신: 피터 데빌 (pcd@mindset.com)
발신: 프란시스 모리스 (frm@mindset.com)
날짜: 1월 15일
주제: 인쇄 과부하

안녕하세요 피터.

저는 지난 목요일 경영진 회의에서 우리 영업팀이 요청한 인쇄 자료량 때문에 IT 부서의 자원이 소모되는 것에 대해 당신이 염려 계속 생각해 왔습니다. 저는 당신이 IT 부장으로서 인쇄 소프트웨어와 하드웨어에 투자했다는 것을 알지만, 이제는 우리가 인쇄 업무를 외주로 맡기는 것을 고려해야 할 때인 것 같습니다. 우리는 대량의 이메일 주소 이용할 수 있을 것입니다. 모의 대해서는 수신 대량의 정보를 계속 이용할 수 있을 것입니다. 이런 방식으로 이 서비스를 기각가 날 때 실패보십시오: www.presidentialprint.com. 저는 제휴 담당자와 이메일을 주고 받았으며, 그들은 같은 지역에 저렴하므로, 우리 문제에 해결책을 제공해 줄 수 있을 것입니다.

프란시스

인쇄 작업에 관한 공지

이번 다가오는 앞으로를 시작으로, 인쇄 관련 요청은 우리의 새로운 지역 공급업체인 프레지덴셜 인쇄로 외주로 맡길 것입니다. 우리의 사내 출력 장비의 기술은 경영 간부들만 하던이 할 수 있게 지정할 것입니다. 이러한 구조에는 예외가 기동하나, IT 부장님의 하락이 있어야 합니다. 새로운 인쇄 작업 요청 양식은 직원 인트라넷에서 이용 가능합니다—메인 페이지에서 "양식서로 서류"라고 표시된 링크를 따라가시면 됩니다. 양식을 출력하거나 인사부서로 갖고 오지 마세요. 그것들은 반드시 온라인으로 작성해서 printing@mindset.com으로 제이크 영에게 보내셔야 합니다. 만약 이 새로운 서비스에 문제가 있다면, 우리 공급업체에 직접 얘기하지 말고 제이크에게 그것들을 가지고 오세요.

어휘 testimonial 추천 후기 | rate 요금; 비율 | specialty 특기, 특징 | second-rate 이류(二流); 싹 좋지 않은 | in-house (회사) 내부의 | midsized 중간 크기의 | comprehensive 종합적인 | tailor 맞춤제작하다 | budget 예산 | affordable 저렴한 | sliding scale 차등제(급 등을 상황에 따라 조정하는 방법) | bulk 대량의 | custom request 사용자 지정 요청 | mass 대량의 | signage 표지 신호 | deep discount 대폭 할인 | entail 수반하다 | exclusive 유일한 | partnership 제휴 | drain 소모 | resources 자원 | investment 투자 | outsource 외주로 제작하다 | utilize 이용하다 | equipment 장비 | specialized 특정한 | out-of-house 회사 외부의 | responsibility 책임, 책무 | in charge of ~을 책임지는 | upcoming 다가오는 | reserve 따로 두다 | executive 경영 간부 중 | exception 예외 | permission 허락 | intranet 인트라넷(~사내 전산망) | marked 표시된 | fill in ~을 작성하다 | attachment 첨부 (파일)

196 프레지덴셜에 의해 제공되는 서비스가 아닌 것은 무엇인가?
(A) 로고 제작하기
(B) 팸플릿 인쇄하기
(C) 웹 사이트 설계하기
(D) 회사들과 제휴하기

해설 첫 번째 지문을 살펴보면 (A) 로고나 표지 디자인 서비스, (B) 책자, 전단, 그리고 팸플릿에 대한 인쇄 서비스, (D) 제휴(partnership) 서비스가 있음을 각각 알 수 있다. 따라서 지문에 언급되지 않은 (C)가 정답이다.

197 모리스 씨가 프레지덴셜에서 연락했을 것 같은 사람은 누구인가?
(A) 이안 리
(B) 크리스틴 린
(C) 제레미 워커
(D) 제이크 영

해설 연계 문제이다. 첫 번째 지문에서 프레지덴셜에서 제휴를 하기 위해서는 이안 리에게 연락하라고 했다. 또한 두 번째 지문 마지막 부분에서 이 메일 발신인인 프란시스 모리스 씨가 제휴 업무를 위해 이메일을 주고 받으오고 있다고 했다. 따라서 정답은 (A)임을 추론할 수 있다.

198 직원들에게 사내 인쇄 장비를 사용하도록 허락할 수 있는 사람은 누구인가?
(A) 이안 리
(B) 피터 데빌
(C) 프란시스 모리스
(D) 제이크 영

해설 두 번째 지문에서 사내에서 출력기기를 사용하려면 IT 부장의 하락을 받아야 한다고 했고, 세 번째 지문에서 사내에서 지문에서 출력기기는 IT 부장님의 따라서 정답은 (B)이다.

199 영 씨가 일하는 회사 부서는 어디인가?
(A) 행정부서
(B) 인사부서
(C) IT 부서
(D) 영업부서

해설 두 번째 지문에서 인쇄 작업을 외주로 빼냄으로써 인쇄 관련 책임을 행성부서로 옮길 수 있다고 했는데 마지막 지문에서 인쇄 작업 양식을 작성해서 제이크 영에게 보내 주라고 한 내용으로 보아, 제이크 영은 행성부서에서 일한다는 것을 추론할 수 있다. 따라서 정답은 (A)이다.

200 인쇄 요청 양식이 전달되어야 하는 방법은 무엇인가?
(A) 이메일로
(B) 직접
(C) 팩스로
(D) 우편으로

해설 두 번째 지문에서 인쇄 요청 양식이 전달되어야 하는 것에 제이크 영 앞에 첨부 파일의 형태로 이메일로 전달되어야 한다고 했으므로 정답은 (A)이다.

Actual Test

10

저자 **박선영**

카카오톡 ID로 찾기 (ID: matrix20)
≫ 친구 추가 후 1:1 채팅

본책 P216

Reading Comprehension

[147-148]

📢 고객 만족 설문조사

하이 파크 마트는 고객님의 생각을 알고 싶습니다!

하이 파크 마트는 고객님과 같은 분의 여러분의 의견을 더없이 중요하게 생각합니다. 147 그렇기에 고객 만족 설문조사에 대한 그 의견에 대해 정중히 부탁드립니다. 설문조사는 저희 제품과 서비스에 대한 고객님의 생각을 정확히 정중을 전할 수 있는 가장 좋은 방법입니다. 더 많이 여러분이 생각을 들을수록, 저희가 더 드릴 수 있습니다. 저희는 여러분의 요구에 매우 관심 있으며 정확하지 부분을 수정하고 싶습니다.

148 본 설문조사는 매우 간단하여 완성하는 데 1분이면 걸리지 않습니다. 질문은 온 주로 저희 서비스와 제품에 관한 것입니다.

148 고객님에 담긴 응답은 언제나 몇몇 문제들을 담하지 않아도 됩니다.

148 반드시 담해야 할 질문은 있으므로 모든 문제들을 담하지 않아도 됩니다. 고객님의 담은 비밀로 지킬 것입니다. 저희의 질문을 절하는 것을 서슴 지 말아 주세요, 사소한 불편에도 저희는 관심을 기울이겠습니다. 이러한 부담도 느끼지 마시고, 무슨 의견이든지 적어 주세요.

협조에 감사드립니다.

어휘 customer satisfaction 고객 만족 survey 조사 anxious 매우 ~하고 싶어 하는 improve on ~보다 더 발전하다 brief 간단한 mandatory 의무적인 hesitate 주저하다 fault 잘못, 결점 pressure 압박, 부담 honest 정직한, 솔직한 gift certificate 상품권

147 공지의 목적은 무엇인가?
(A) 새로운 직원을 고용하려고
(B) 협조를 부탁하려고
(C) 감사를 표현하려고
(D) 휴업을 알리려고

해설 제목과 지문 초반에 고객에게 설문조사에 응해 달라고 요청하는 것이 드러나 있다. 따라서 공지의 목적을 부탁하기 위함이므로 정답은 (B)이다.

148 설문조사에 관해 언급된 것은 무엇인가?
(A) 완성하는 데 몇 분이 소요된다.
(B) 모든 질문에 답은 해야 한다.
(C) 완성하는 사람에게 상품권을 준다.
(D) 설문 답은 공개되지 않을 것이다.

해설 지문 중반에 설문조사를 끝내는 데 1분이 채 걸리지 않을 것이라고 하고 있으므로 (A)는 틀린 내용이며, 꼭 답해야 할 질문은 없다고 했으므로 (B)도 틀린 내용이며, 상품권에 대한 내용은 지문에 나와 있지 않으므로 (C)도 정답이 될 수 없다. 고객의 응답은 비밀로 유지될 것이라고 하므로 정답은 (D)이다.

[149-150]

메모

수신: 전 직원
발신: 벨라 피어스
날짜: 5월 1일
149 제목: 고객 서비스

149 어머니 날이 곧앞으로 다가왔습니다. 정신없는 주말이 우리를 기다리고 있 네요. 그래도 여러분 모두 자신이 가진 힘을 모아 고객 만족이 가치 최우선이 될 수 150 고객을 만족하게 하는 것이이 우리 매출 목표에 도달할 수 있는 가장 올바른으로 유일한 방법입니다. 또한, 고객 얼굴에 번진 미소 는 우리에게 천번 행복을 전합니다.

이렇기에 고객 서비스를 개선할 방법을 구상한다 경영진이 "최고 서비스상"을 생각해 냈습니다. 우리는 고객들에게 그들이 받은 최고의 서비스에 어느 부서가 가장 친절했는지 물어볼 것입니다. 상을 타는 부서는 정기 보너스에 추가 보너스를 받을 것입니다. 그러니 우리 모두 이번 어머니 날에 넣이 최고의 주문이 될 수 있도록 최선을 다합시다!

감사합니다!

벨라 피어스
150 영업부

어휘 (just) around the corner 아주 가까운 face to face 직면하여 hectic 매우 바쁜 priority 우선(권) contagious 전염성이 있는 improve 개선 하다 management 경영(진) come up with ~을 생각해내다 award-winning 상을 받은

149 메모가 쓰인 목적은 무엇인가?
(A) 고객 서비스를 향상시킬 아이디어를 요청하기 위해서
(B) 고객들에게 더 나은 서비스를 제공하도록 장려하기 위해서
(C) 휴업에 대한 추가 정보를 알리기 위해서
(D) 최고의 부서를 고르기 위한 투표를 요청하기 위해서

해설 메모의 제목과 지문 초반에 모 다가올 어머니 날을 위해 고객 만족을 위해 최선의 노력을 다할 것을 장려하고 있다. 따라서 정답은 (B)이다. 고객 서비스를 개선할 방법을 제안해 달라고 요청하는 것이 아니라 그 방안을 제시하고 있으므로 (A)는 오답이다.

150 벨라에 관해 무엇이 암시되고 있는가?
(A) "최고 서비스상"을 고안해 냈다.
(B) 고객으로부터 불만을 들었다.
(C) 영업 매니저이다.
(D) 오늘 사람들에게 보너스를 지급하였다.

해설 이 메모를 작성한 영업부 소속으로 첫 번째 단락에서 고객을 행복하게 만드는 것이 판매 목표를 달성하는 방법이라고 강조하고 있다. 이를 미루어 보아 벨라인 씨 이를 바탕으로 벨라는 영업부 담당 것임을 알 수 있다. 따라서 정답은 (C)이다.

[151-152]

이안 맥케인	작업에 대해 새로운 정보를 알고 싶습니다. 거기 상황은 어떻습니까?	오후 3:19
브리지 고메즈	대부분 끝났습니다. 151 우리는 온실 뒷벽에 환풍 장치를 설치 중이고 거의 끝났습니다.	오후 3:21
이안 맥케인	152 만약 그 작업이 오후 5시 이전까지 끝나면, 저는 당신이 여기에 와서 우리를 도와주셨으면 해요.	오후 3:23
브리지 고메즈	우리는 그 시스템이 설치 후에 시범 운영도 해 보아야 해요.	오후 3:25
이안 맥케인	흠, 오늘 안으로 해야 하나요?	오후 3:26
브리지 고메즈	네, 고객이 그렇게 해 달라고 요청했어요.	오후 3:28
이안 맥케인	알았어요, 그러면 오후 4시 30분쯤에 전화해 주세요.	오후 3:32

어휘 update 최신 정보 complete 완성하다 ventilation 환풍 장치 green house 온실 almost 거의 conduct 수행하다 client 의뢰인 sanitation 위생 처리

151 고메즈 씨가 일하는 업체는 무엇인가?
(A) 가구회사
(B) 건축회사
(C) 위생업체
(D) 디자인 회사

해설 고메즈 씨가 현재 온실 작업 중 뒷벽에 환풍 장치를 설치하고 있다고 하므로 온실을 건축하는 일을 하고 있음을 알 수 있다. 선택지에서가 가 장 적절한 정답은 (B)이다.

152 오후 3시 23분에 맥케인 씨가 "그게 다예요?"라고로 쓴 의미는 무엇인가?
(A) 그는 작업의 예약을 확인할 필요가 있다.
(B) 그는 작업이 끝나는 데 시간이 얼마나 걸리는지 알고 싶어 한다.
(C) 그는 문제의 원인을 발견하였다.
(D) 그는 다른 서비스가 필요하다.

해설 이 메시지 바로 뒤에서 맥케인 씨는 고메즈 씨에게 하던 일을 마무리하 고 자기 일을 도와달라고 요청하고 있다. 이로 미루어 보아 맥케인 씨 는 현재 하는 일이 언제 끝날 것인지를 물어보고 있음을 알 수 있다. 따 라서 정답은 (B)이다.

[153-154]

🎬 발리우드 영화의 밤

시간: 오후 7:00 - 9:30, 7월 매주 목요일
장소: 국립미술관박물관 옆에 있는 델턴 시민문화회관

🔔 다른 여름철 발리우드 영화를 인도의 정신을 느껴 보세요. 라이브 배경, (립 싱크, (라가)인: 민 엿날 인도에서) 그리고 가장 유명한 (슬램독 밀리어네어를 상영할 예정입니다. 영화뿐만 아니라 일부 티카(인류된 감각적 이집트 쿵, 사모사(쿵을 채운 인도 디저트) 그리고 라씨(인도 요염마 등 또는 우유를 섞은 요그르티와 같은 인도 간식도 맛보실 수 있습니다. 🔔 간식은 할리적인 가격에 판매될 것이며, 모든 수익금은 인도에 학교를 세우는 데 기부될 것입니다.

영화 관람은 무료이지만 🔔 좌석이 한정되어 있으니, 적어도 영화 상영 15분 전에 와 주실 것을 부탁드립니다. 또한, 예로 좌석이 있어도 영화 시작 후에는 추가 입장이 불가합니다.

더 많은 정보를 원하시면 742-555-6502로 연락 주세요.

어휘 Bollywood 인도 영화 산업 spirit 정신 reasonable 할리적인 fund 자금 at least 적어도 donate 기부하다 proceeds 수익금 additional 추가적인 audience 청중 regardless of ~에 관계없이 complimentary 무료의 seating 좌석

153 광고되고 있는 것은 무엇인가?
(A) 곳 있을 영화의 밤
(B) 인도 식당의 개업
(C) 아이들을 위한 자선 단체
(D) 인도 요리 수업 등록

해설 "발리우드 영화의 밤"이라는 제목과 지문 첫 부분에서 여름밤 영화를 함께 누려 보라는 내용에서 영화 행사에 대한 공지임을 알 수 있다. 따라서 정답은 (A)이다.

154 행사에 관해 옳지 않은 것은 무엇인가?
(A) 좌석이 한정되어 있다.
(B) **간식은 무료로 제공된다.**
(C) 행사는 일사적이다.
(D) 영화 중 하나는 (슬램독 밀리어네어)이다.

해설 지문 중간에 간식은 할리적인 가격에 판매된다고 했으므로 정답은 (B)이다.

[155-157]

캐빈 닉스
987 웨스트우드 가
밴쿠버, 브리티시 컬럼비아 주

닉스 씨에게,

🔔 고객님께서 하와이에 머무시는 동안 저희 서머셋 비치 리조트를 방문해 주신 데 대해 감사드립니다. 고객님의 기부을 이메일을 읽고 분실물 보관소를 확인해 보았습니다.

🔔 고객님께서 듀크 카바나모쿠의 포스터를 실수로 두고 가신 당일 날 저희 직원이 물건을 발견하였습니다. 현재 해드되지 않으면 오랫동안 도에있습니다. 그것을 해 드릴 것을 요청하셨습니다. 저희는 당연히 그것을 해 드릴 수 있어 기쁩니다. 🔔 하지만 저희가 보내드리기 전에 확인할 것이 한 가지 있습니다. 리조트가 섬에 있는 관계로 추가적인 배송비가 발생할 것입니다. 배송비는 총 30달러 정도 될 것입니다. 저희의 규정은 금전적인 가치가 15달러보다 작게 나가는 것일수록 전송적인 서비어도, 🔔 고객님께서 구매하신 포스터는 오직 이 섬에서만 판매되므로 그 일을 다 해 드릴 수 있습니다. 하지만 고객님께서 포스터를 보내달라고 하셨을 때 추가 배송비를 염두에 두셨는지를 몰라보아야 했습니다. 어제 되셨든 30달러는 착불이기 때문입니다.

답변으로 이전 주시면 감사하겠습니다.

헌리 플레밍
매니저, 고객 상담실

어휘 urgent 긴급한 lost property 분실물 ruin 망쳐 놓다, 못쓰게 하다 concern 걱정 monetary 금전(상의 legendary 전 설적인 surfer 파도 타는 사람 at any rate 어찌 되었든 due 지불되어야 하는 realize 깨닫다 mythical 신화적인

155 이 편지를 닉스 씨에게 보낸 이유는 무엇인가?
(A) 확인을 요청하기 위해서
(B) 새로운 배송 방침을 알려주기 위해서
(C) 주문하기 위해서
(D) 환불을 요청하기 위해서

해설 지문 중반에서 닉스 씨가 분실한 포스터를 배송을 경우 발생하는 배송비를 지불할지 확인을 요청하고 있으므로 정답은 (A)이다.

156 닉스 씨에게 어떤 문제가 있었는가?
(A) 룸서비스 도중 포스터가 망가졌다.
(B) 편지에 담하는 것을 잊었다.
(C) **방문했던 호텔에 물건을 두고 왔다.**
(D) 듀크 카바나모쿠를 만나지 못했다.

해설 지문 초반에 닉스 씨가 리조트를 방문했었던 닉스 씨가 그곳에 간 포스터를 발견했다고 언급하고 있으므로 정답은 (C)이다.

157 포스터에 관해 언급된 것은 무엇인가?
(A) 하와이에서만 판매된다.
(B) 신화적인 그림이 그려져 있다.
(C) 가격이 20달러 이상이다.
(D) 듀크 카바나모쿠의 사인이 되어 있다.

해설 지문 후반에 그 포스터는 오직 하와이에서만 판매된다고 했으므로 (A)가 정답이다.

[158-160]

빨래하는 날

주목해 주세요, 이웃 여러분. 마침내 따스한 봄이 주요 겨울을 몰리쳤습니다! - [1] -. 그러니 모든 빨랫감을 모으세요. 노튼 씨네 세탁소에서 엄청난 세일을 하거든요. 깔끔하고 말쑥한 노튼 씨네 세탁소가 작업이 이난 가격을 완화하였습니다. 봄맞이 대청소에 딱 좋은 시작입니다? - [2] -.

🔔 다음 주 월요일(3월 25일부터 토요일(3월 30일)까지 드라이클리닝 비용이 50%만큼 없어집니다. 그러니 모든 겨울 코트, 스웨터, 점퍼 등을 가져오세요. 저 희가 엄료을 뺄수 있는 빨랫감은 없답니다. 그리고 이번 할인은 이 도시에서 여 러분이 바믐을 수 있는 해볼 중 가장 큰 해볼입니다! 작은 가격 부분으로 봄을 향한 산뜻한 출발을 하세요. - [3] -. 깔끔하게 세탁이 되어 개어진 겨울옷이 여러분에게 봄옷을 넣을 자리를 마련해 줄 것입니다!

🔔 또한, 신발 세탁비도 30% 할인입니다. - [4] -. 내년에 다시 신을 수 있도록 새것으로 바꿔드릴게요.

이 엄청난 기회를 놓치지 마세요! 여러분의 여러분의 세탁물을 기다리고 있었습니다.

노튼 씨네 세탁소: 20 엘름 가
🔔 영업시간: 오전 8:00 - 오후 7:00 (월-금)   오전 9:00 - 오후 2:00 (토)
전화번호: 033-555-9785

어휘 laundry 세탁물 beat down ~을 쳐서 넘어뜨리다, 억누르다 warmth 따스함 gather up 모으다 neat 깔끔한 tidy 말쑥한 loosen up 완 화하다 stain 얼룩 burden 부담 pocket book 돈지갑 room 공간 moreover 더욱이

158 세일 기간은 얼마 동안인가?
(A) 4일
(B) 5일
(C) **6일**
(D) 7일

해설 지문 초반에 언급된 할인 기간이 3월 25일부터 3월 30일까지 총 6일 이을 앞수 있으므로 정답은 (C)이다.

159 광고에 대해 옳은 것은 무엇인가?
(A) 배달 서비스가 포함되어 있다.
(B) **신발 세탁 비용이 할인된다.**
(C) 노튼 씨네 세탁소는 매일 연다.
(D) 노튼 씨네 세탁소는 항상 아침 8시에 문을 연다.

[164-167]

글로브넷

글로브넷은 위성 서비스 업체로 여러 주요 채널이 150개 그리고 추가로 50개의 특수 채널을 갖추고 있습니다. 2천 명 이상의 케이블 시청자들이 글로브넷 서비스를 사용하고 있습니다. 전 지역에게 인체와 장비와 지원을 제공하고 있는 글로브넷 본사에서 바로 지금 예의 바르고, 시끌 좋아하는 기술자를 찾습니다.

업무 설명

TV 위성 기술자의 주요 업무는 **164 위성 접시를 설치하고 164 케이블을 TV에** 연결하는 것입니다. **164 케이블 채널을 추가하거나** 설치된 위성 접시의 위치를 조정하는 등의 비교적 쉬운 작업도 있습니다. 능력 있는 후보자들은 기술자를 매니저로 승진할 기회가 추가됩니다.

165 자격 요건

* 165 최소 1년 정도의 전기 배선과 취급 경험
* 운전면허증
* 탁월한 의사소통 능력
* 고객을 향한 받은 태도

선발 과정

166 직업 경력이 쓰여 있는 지원서를 아래의 이메일 주소로 3월 21일까지 보내 주세요. 정해진 양식이 없으니, 연락처와 있으면 어떤 형태의 지원서라도 지원 가능합니다. **167 선택된 후보들은 개별적으로 전화로 연락이 갈 것입니다. 그러나 지원서에 연락처를 꼭 적어시기 바랍니다. 167 지원서는 joseph_m@ globenet.com으로 조셉 미첼에게 보내 주세요.**

어휘 satellite 위성 decent 예의 바른 description 서술 earn a promotion 승진을 따내다 handle 다루다 attitude 태도 serve ~을 위해 일하다 fixed 고정된, 일정한 contact number 연락처 individually 개인적으로

164 광고에 의하면 업무가 아닌 것은 무엇인가?

(A) 위성 접시 설치
(B) 새로운 고객 유치
(C) TV에 케이블 선 연결
(D) 케이블 채널에 추가 채널 넣기

해설 업무를 물어보는 질문이므로 업무 설명 부분을 확인해야 한다. 위성 접시 설치와 케이블 선을 TV와 연결하는 것, 그리고 케이블 채널을 추가하는 것이 지문에서 확인할 수 있으나, 새로운 고객 유지는 나와 있지 않다. 따라서 (B)가 정답이다.

165 지원하기 위해 무엇이 요구되는가?

(A) 1년 이상의 기술적 경험
(B) 생명 보험
(C) 대학 학위
(D) 다양한 언어 구사 능력

해설 지문에 제시된 자격 요건에 따르면 적어도 1년 정도의 전기 배선에 관한 경험이 있어야 한다고 했으므로 1년 이상의 기술적 경험을 요구하는 것으로 볼 수 있다. 따라서 정답은 (A)이다.

해설 네 번째 단락에서 신일 세탁기 잘인이 연급되었으므로 (B)가 정답이다. (A는 언급이 없고, 지문 마지막에 토요일에는 오전 9시에 연다고 했으므로 (D)는 오후이고, 토요일까지는 영업 시간이 명시되어 있으므로 (C)도 오답이다.

160 [1], [2], [3], [4]로 표시된 곳 중 다음 문장이 들어가기 가장 적절한 곳은 어디인가?

"부끄러워 마시고 눈과 흙으로 다려워진 부츠와 운동화들을 가져오세요."

(A) [1]
(B) [2]
(C) [3]
(D) [4]

해설 이 문장 바로 앞에 신일 세탁 비용 할인이 연급되고 있으므로 이에 치일이 필요한 부츠나 운동화에 대한 언급이 이어지는 것이 논리적이다. 따라서 정답은 (D)이다.

[161-163]

8월 11일

줄리아 브룩스
153 비트 가

몬트리올 퀘벡 주

브룩스 씨에게,

자료 화사의 새로운 세부 관리 제품 세트를 구매해 주셔서 감사합니다. 고객님께서 자회의 제품과 서비스에 만족하셨기를 바랍니다.

161 고객님께서 구매하신 제품으로 자사의 신제품이라 고객 설문지를 동봉합니다. 고객님의 미드백은 정말로 자사에게 소중합니다. 자회의 서비스와 제품을 고객님의 162 요구에 맞추는 것은 저희에게 중요합니다. 첨부된 본 설문조사는 완료 후 한 장으로 되어 있는 매우 간략한 설문입니다. **163 첨부한 시가로 하셨다면 설문지를 우편으로 보내 주시면 됩니다. 편지를 위해 설문지와 같이 동봉된 자사 주소가 있는 봉투를 사용하시면 됩니다.** 설문지를 우편으로 보내는 명별 대신에 가까운 매장으로 가셔서 직접 제출하실 수 있습니다.

협조에 대한 감사를 위해, 설문지를 받은 후 앞으로 구매하실 때 도움이 될 120 달러의 상품권을 보내드립니다. 매장에 직접 설문지를 제출하시면 즉시 상품권을 받으실 수 있습니다.

제가라싱 불만 사항이 있으시다면 지회에게 우편이 도착할 때까지 기다리지 마시고, 바로 전화로 연락해 주세요.

협조에 감사드립니다.

브룩스 윌

매니저, 고객서비스

어휘 content with ~에 만족하는 valuable 소중한 enclose 동봉하다 in line with ~와 일치하는 consumer 소비자 consist of ~으로 구성되다 convenience 편의 in lieu of ~대신에 appreciation 감사 complaint 불평 file 제기하다 cooperation 협조 recommendation 추천

---

161 편지의 목적은 무엇인가?

(A) 신제품 출시를 소개하려고
(B) 문서의 반납을 요청하려고
(C) 배달 착오에 사과하려고
(D) 추천을 요청하려고

해설 지문 전반에 걸쳐 설문지를 작성하여 동봉된 봉투로 보내 달라고 요청하고 있으므로 정답은 (B)이다.

162 두 번째 단락 세 번째 줄의 "needs"와 의미상 가장 가까운 것은 무엇인가?

(A) 시도
(B) 요구
(C) 수치
(D) 실험

해설 소비자의 '요구에 부응하는 상품과 서비스를 제공하는 것이 중요하다'고 연급하고 있으므로 선택지 중에서 이와 유사한 의미가 있는 것은 (B) demands이다.

163 편지에 동봉된 것은 무엇인가?

(A) 상품권
(B) 회원증
(C) 가까운 매장 지도
(D) 봉투

해설 지문 중반의 설문지와 같이 동봉된 자사 주소가 있는 봉투를 사용하라고 나와 있으므로 정답은 (D)임을 알 수 있다.

166 지원서를 언제까지 지원자를 보내야 하는가?

(A) 이번 주
(B) 다음 주
(C) 3주 이내
(D) 4주 이내

해설 지문 하단에 선발 과정 부분에서 3월 21일까지 지원서가 제출되어야 함을 알 수 있다. 그러므로 이 광고가 작성된 3월 1일을 기준으로 약 3주 후에 지원서를 제출해야 함을 알 수 있다. 따라서 정답은 (C)이다.

167 광고를 통해서 알 수 없는 것은 무엇인가?

(A) 지원자들이 언제 문서를 제출해야 하는지
(B) 지원서에 어떤 정보가 들어가야 하는지
(C) 지원자들에게 언제 연락이 갈 것인지
(D) 지원자들이 지원서를 어디로 보낼지

해설 선발 과정에서 선정된 후보자들은 개별적으로 전화로 연락이 갈 것이라는 내용을 있지만, 구체적으로 언제 연락이 갈 것인지는 나와 있지 않다. 따라서 정답은 (C)이다.

[168-171]

켄 무어 [오전 8:25]	안녕, 브라이언. 지금 어디야?
브라이언 하워드 [오전 8:28]	내 사무실이야, 왜?
켄 무어 [오전 8:30]	**⒳** 우리 지점에 화이트 스노우 케이크를 만드는 설탕이 다 떨어지고 있어. 참고에 엄마 나 남아 있는지 좀 알아봐 줄래? 만약에 없으면, 여기 주변에 아무 가게에서 사야 해.
브라이언 하워드 [오전 8:33]	에이미가 참고에 있어. 흠. 기다려 봐. 여기 이 채팅방에 그를 초대할게. 엄마나 필요한데?
켄 무어 [오전 8:35]	**⒳** 아마도 20봉지 정도면 충분할 것 같아.
에이미 굿윈 [오전 8:38]	운이 좋네요!
에이미 굿윈 [오전 8:39]	잠깐만요, 우리는 늦어도 오전 11시까지 그것이 필요해요.
에이미 굿윈 [오전 8:40]	사실 트럭 한 대에 다른 지점을 위한 몇몇 제품을 실을 거예요. 무어 씨가 요청한 양도 약 시막 맞춤 준비할게요. **⒳ ⒳** 먼저 배달해 줄게요.
켄 무어 [오전 8:42]	모두 감사합니다. 제 이름으로 봉지 수를 업무일지에 올려 주시겠어요?
에이미 굿윈 [오전 8:43]	**⒳** 물론이죠

어휘 run out of ~이 고갈되다 warehouse 참고 cover ~에 충분하다 load 싣다 ~에 맞다 log 업무일지 fit ~에 맞다

168 무어 씨가 근무하는 업체는 어디인가?

(A) 식료품 가게
(B) 배달 업체
(C) 제과 회사
(D) 참고

해설 무어 씨는 자신의 지점에서 화이트 스노우 케이크를 만드는 데 설탕이 부족하다고 말하며 물건을 요청하고 있으므로 제과 회사에 종사하고 있음을 알 수 있다. 따라서 정답은 (C)이다.

169 오전 8시 38분에 굿윈 씨가 "운이 좋네요"라고 쓴 의도는 무엇인가?

(A) 지시사항이 쉽다.
(B) 그녀는 오전 11에 한가하다.
(C) 하워드 씨가 요청한 돈은 이용 가능하다.
(D) 작업을 위한 재료가 충분하다.

해설 이 메시지의 앞의 맥락을 고려해 보면 무어 씨가 케이크를 만들기 위해 20봉지 설탕을 요청하고 있으므로 굿윈 씨가 운이 좋다고 하는 것은 요청한 물량을 충분해 줄 수 있음을 의미한다. 따라서 정답은 (D)이다.

170 굿윈 씨가 간다고 말한 곳은 어디인가?

(A) 참고로
(B) 무어 씨의 가게로
(C) 식료품점으로
(D) 하워드 씨의 사무실로

해설 굿윈 씨는 무어 씨가 요청한 설탕을 싣고 먼저 배달해 주겠다고 하고 있으므로 무어 씨가 있는 제과점으로 갈 것을 알 수 있다. 따라서 정답은 (B)이다.

171 무어 씨는 굿윈 씨에게 무엇을 할 것을 요청하는가?

(A) 도착지로 향하는 길을 알려 줄 것
(B) 그가 했던 요청을 승인해 줄 것
(C) 문서를 작성할 것
(D) 그가 엄마나 필요한지 개산할 것

해설 오전 8시 42분에 무어 씨가 자신의 이름으로 요청했던 설탕 봉지의 수를 업무일지에 기재해 줄 것을 당부하고 있고, 굿윈 씨가 그렇게 하겠다고 하고 있으므로 정답은 (C)이다.

[172-175]

시카고, 일리노이 주 ⒳⒳ 지역 주민들은 르네상스 호텔에서 열린 시카고 아동 병원을 위한 11번째 연례 기금 행사에서 흥겹게 파티를 보냈습니다. – [1] –. 2,100명 이라는 엄청난 인원이 지난밤 행사에 참여했습니다. 행사의 하이라이트는 코미 디언들이 몇몇 유명 시트콤 장면들을 패러디한 연극이었습니다. – [2] –. 행사 **⒳⒳** 마지막에는 기금에서 흥겨운 3명의 어린이의 부모적인 사회로 이루어졌습니다. 이 어린이 사회자들은 무대에 30분 간 있었지만, 관객들에게 비 기분 감동을 주고도 넘은 시간이었습니다.

지역 사업장, 시카고 주민들과 공연자들과 기금 모음을 기부하였습니다. **⒳⒳** 르네상 스 호텔을 무료로 행사를 개최함으로써 기금 모음을 지원했습니다. – [3] –. **⒳⒳** 하지만 가장 큰 기부자는 지난해 마천가지로 시카고 세트은행이었습니다. **⒳⒳** 은행장이신 에드 존슨 씨는 작년보다 넓은 150만 달러를 기부했습니다. 이 기금 행사가 오래지는 않았지만 더욱 더 많은 사람이 지도해서 참여하고 있습니다. – [4] –. 르네상스 호텔은 오랜 시간 내내 이벤트를 주최하기로 지원했습니다. **⒳⒳** 이 호흡한 행사는 5월에 열립니다.

어휘 local 지역의 citizen 시민 fundraiser 기금 모음 amazing 놀라운 parody 풍자 sitcom 상황극 성황극 partially 부분적으로 sponsor 후원자 recover 회복하게 하다 host 주최자 touch 감동하게 하다 performer 공연 자 donation 기부 donor 기부자 voluntarily 자발적으로 generous 관대한 adorable 사랑스러운

172 행사가 열린 곳은 어디인가?

(A) 호텔
(B) 병원
(C) 시청
(D) 은행

해설 지문 초반에서 행사는 르네상스 호텔에서 개최되었음을 알 수 있다. 따라서 정답은 (A)이다.

173 가장 큰 기부자는 누구인가?

(A) 병원
(B) 숙박업체
(C) 공연자들
(D) 금융기관

해설 두 번째 단락에서 가장 큰 기부자는 시카고 세트은행이라고 했으므로 정답은 (D)이다.

174 행사에 대해 알 수 있는 것은 무엇인가?

(A) 매년 겨울에 열린다.
(B) 르네상스 호텔에서 무료로 행사를 개최하였다.
(C) 총 150만 달러를 마련했다.
(D) 어린이들이 행사 전체의 사회자였다.

해설 지문 중반에서 르네상스 호텔이 무료로 이 행사를 개최해 주었다고 했으므로 정답은 (B)이다. 행사는 매년 5월에 열리며, 150만 달러라는 총 기부금이 아니라 시카고 세트은행에서 기부한 금액이다. 또 어린이들의 사회를 본 시간은 행사 후반 30분 정도이므로 나머지 선택지는 답이 되지 않는다.

르네상스 호텔에서 무료로 이 행사를 개최해 주었다고 했으므로 정답은 (B)이다.

175 [1], [2], [3], [4]로 표시된 곳 중 다음 문장이 위치로 가장 적절한 곳은 어디인가?

"또한, 시간과 이동 병 연 아이들이 양쪽만도 있었습니다."

(A) [1]
(B) [2]
(C) [3]
(D) [4]

해설 삽입문장이 also(또한)라는 표현을 고려해 보면 앞서 다른 공연이 언급되어야 함을 알 수 있으며 삽입문장 이후에 마지막 공연이 공연인(The last part of the event)이 이어지는 것이 논리적으로 맞으므로 정답은 (B)이다.

[176-180]

www.oakvilleyouth.com/volunteer/plan

홈	소개	공지	지원	질문과 답변

수업 계획

강사	이안 버틀러
수업 종류	심폐소생술
목표 연령	15~18세 학생들
장소	오크빌 타운 청소년 시민회관 지하 102호
일시	□ 12주 반 (6월 1일 ~ 8월 31일) ■ [180] 1일 발표회: 2017년 7월 23일 수요일

의견

"한 아이를 키우기 위해 사회가 다 동참해야 한다"라는 표현은 이미 잘 아시고 있으실 겁니다. 이 문장이으로도 한 작은 인재에게 단체가 주는 영향과 아이에게 필요한 환경을 제공하는 데 필요에 대해 노래에 담은 생각이 들 수 있습니다. 우리는 모두 그 하지만 우리는 우리 마을 아이들에게 주는 것이 얼마나 될까요? 우리는 어디서 그 어떻게 해야 한다고 생각하고 있지는 않지만, 어떻게 좋은 어디서 해야 하나요?

그 질문들에 대한 답은 우리가 가지고 있습니다. [176] 오크빌 타운 청소년 시민회관에서 이번 여름에 청소년을 기르칠 지원자를 찾고 있습니다. 우리는 청소년들 악력과 폭력과 같은 유해 환경에서 관심을 돌릴 인전 수업이 필요합니다.

어떤 재능을 가지고 계신든 우리는 당신을 위한 교실을 열어 드릴 의사가 있습니다. 우리 웹 사이트인 www.oakvilleyouth.com으로 들어오셔서 목표 연령대와 어떤 종류의 수업인지 적어 주세요. [177] 도자기, 회화, 그리고 모형 비행기 등이 좋은 교실이 될 수 있습니다. 각종 운동 및 독서 클럽도 가능합니다. [178] 사진 수업이나 컴퓨터 프로그래밍과 같이 비싼 장비가 필요한 수업은 하지 않습니다. 시민회관에서 컴퓨터를 구매하기 위해 기금을 모금하는 중이지만, 시간이 조금 걸릴 것 같습니다.

[179] 간략한 12주짜리 수업 계획을 제출하시면 하지만 내용은 제출 후 바꿀 수 있습니다. 우리가 계획을 검토한 뒤 시민회관 직원들이 교육적인 수업이라고 생각되면 연락드리고 교실을 배정해 드릴 것입니다. [180] 12주가 너무 길다고 여겨지신 다면, 건강, 심폐소생술 등 1일 발표회도 지원할 수 있습니다.

또한, 수업을 도와주는 것도 지원성을 수 있습니다. 우리 마을을 더 좋게 굿우 만드는 데에는 너무나도 많은 방법이 있습니다. 그리고 지금이 그때입니다!

오크빌 타운 청소년 시민회관: 617 페리가

전화번호: 612-555-9787

어휘 raise 기르다, 양육하다 familiar 익숙한 impact 영향 in need of ~이 필요한 volunteer 지원(자) youth 청소년 attract 끌어모으다 hazard 위험 요소 drug 약물 violence 폭력 eager 열망하는 craft 수공 예 pottery 도자기 제조법 quilting 퀼트/누비기 discourage 저지하다 draft 초안 go through 검토하다 assign 할당하다 CPR 심폐소생술 instructor 강사 mat 매트 tentative 잠정적인 flexible 융통성 있는

176 무엇에 관해 공지인가?
(A) 자원봉사자가 필요하다는 것
(B) 아이들을 약물 복용으로부터 보호하는 방법
(C) 새로운 학교에 대한 요청
(D) 청소년 센터의 패쇄

해설 첫 지문 중반에 시민회관에서 자원봉사자를 구한다는 말을 한 뒤 상세 내용을 언급하고 있다. 따라서 정답은 (A)이다.

177 시민회관에서 새로운 수업은 언제 열 예정인가?
(A) 봄에
(B) 여름에
(C) 기을에
(D) 겨울에

해설 첫 지문 중반에 이번 여름에 청소년들을 가르칠 자원봉사자가 필요하다 고 했으므로 정답은 (B)이다.

178 이 회관은 수업을 열기 위해서 무엇이 필요한가?
(A) 3명 이상의 도우미
(B) 대략적인 수업 요강
(C) 재료와 운동 기구
(D) 새로운 컴퓨터

해설 첫 지문 중반에 12주짜리 수업 계획을 제출해야 한다고 했으며 그것을 검토한 후에 교육적인 것이라면 교실을 배정해 주겠다고 하였다. 따라서 교실을 열기 위해서는 먼저 대략적인 수업 요강이 필요함을 알 수 있으므로 정답은 (B)이다.

179 추천되지 않는 수업은 무엇인가?
(A) 사진
(B) 도자기
(C) 책 읽기
(D) 야구

해설 첫 지문 중반에서 비싼 장비가 필요한 사진 수업은 하지 않는다고 나와 있으므로 (A)가 정답이다.

180 버틀러에 대해 감지도 옳은 것은 무엇인가?
(A) 오크빌 타운 청소년과 시민회관나 일하는 것은 처음이다.
(B) 항상술 위한 그의 계획은 확정됐다.
(C) 그는 7월 발표회를 위해 어떤 장비도 필요하지 않다.
(D) 그는 12주간의 프로그램이 너무 길다고 여긴다.

해설 지문에서 12주간의 수업이 너무 많은 1일 발표회 가능하다고 했고 그 금요일 이고 두 번째 지문에서 버틀러 씨가 수업 계획서에 1일 발표회를 선택했기 때문에 12주간의 프로그램이 너무 길다고 여겼음을 축측할 수 있다. 따라서 정답은 (D)이다.

[181-185]

수신: 전 직원
발신: 존 김스
10월 4일

동료들에게,

[181] 10월 12일 저녁 팰리스 호텔 그랜드 홀에서 열리는 감 하계를 랄 하계를 위한 파티에 참석해 주세요.

[182] 올는 청가지 만화 제작자가 되는 멋진 기회를 얻게 되어 빈티지 코믹스를 따나게 되었습니다. 올는 드림웍스에서 새로 제작되는 만화 영화의 감독으로 계약을 체결했습니다. 이제 국장에서 가족들과 같이 작품들을 볼 수 있게 됐다 습니다.

이밖은 슬프지만, 행복은 이별이기에 올에게 행복을 받아줍시다. 그동안이 감사 를 표하기 위해 선물로 스크랩북을 준비하려고 합니다. [183] 올의 만화 캐릭 터를 사용하여 떠나는 올에게 메시지를 전하려고 합니다. 전화로 싶은 메시지가 있으시면 저에게 이메일을 주세요. 어떠한 말도 좋습니다. 너무 길게 쓰시는 마세요. 1~2 문장 정도면 괜찮습니다. 또한, 파티 참석 여부도 저에게 알려 주세요.

감사합니다. 파티에 많은 참여 부탁드립니다!

존 김스
부팀장

수신: 존 깁슨 〈john_g@vintagecomics.com〉
발신: 타일러 밀러 〈tylermiller@vintagecomics.com〉
날짜: 10월 8일
제목: 송별 파티

존에게,

[183] 믿을 수 없이 5년을 같이 일한 동료로서 정말 즐거웠습니다. 그간 일하는 시간은 정말 즐거웠고, 그가 떠나서 슬퍼집니다. 그의 성공에 진심으로 기쁩니다. 저는 10월 12일 마지막에 정말 참석해서 얼마나 그가 훌륭했는지 말해주고 싶습니다. 그 주에 출장을 갑니다. **[182]** 누욕에 있는 2017 만화 박람회에 마술 감독으로 가야 합니다. 하지만 10월에 시작해서 13일에 끝나가는 동안에 꼭 오는 모습을 못 볼 것 같네요. 하지만 개인적으로 자네 식사를 하겠습니다. 그러나, 스크랩북 관련해서 자료 메시지를 전하고 싶습니다. **[183]** 〈책 더 머신〉 캐릭터를 사용해 주시고, "어디에 있는 내가 도와줄게요."라고 적어 주세요.

감사합니다.
타일러 밀러

어휘 celebration 축하 in honor of ~에게 경의를 표하여 accept 수락하다 sign a contract 계약서에 서명하다 animation director 만화 감독 put together 합치다; 모으다 character 등장인물 statement 말, 문장 coworker 동료 fair 박람회 personally 스스로 have (got) one's back 도와주다; 보살피다 hospitalize 병원에 입원시키다

181 메모의 목적이 무엇인가?
(A) 퇴사 관련 신문 기사를 알리려고
(B) 사람들에게 선물을 가져오라고 요청하려고
(C) 파티를 위한 장소를 물어보려고
(D) 행사에 사람들을 초대하려고

해설 메모는 동료를 떠나는 동료를 위한 파티에 참석해 달라고 요청하는 글이다. 따라서 정답은 (D)이다.

182 타일러 빈티지 코믹스사를 떠나는 이유는 무엇인가?
(A) 개인 사업을 열어서
(B) 그의 고향으로 돌아가고 싶어서
(C) **다른 회사에 고용돼서**
(D) 병원에 입원해서

해설 첫 지문의 중반에 타일러 씨가 다른 회사인 드림잡스사에서 만화 감독으로 계약을 체결했다고 했으므로 정답은 (C)이다.

183 타일러 씨에 관해 언급된 것은 무엇인가?
(A) 그는 정규직 시험을 치렀다.
(B) 그는 직접이 TV를 방영될 것이다.
(C) 타일러는 지난 5년 동안 그의 친구였다.
(D) 그의 캐릭터 중의 하나는 〈책 더 머신〉이다.

해설 첫 지문의 후반부에 깁슨 씨가 쓴 만화 씨의 캐릭터와 함께 작별의 메시지를 전해달라고 동료들에게 요청하고 있다. 두 번째 지문 마지막에 타일러 씨는 〈책 더 머신〉 캐릭터를 이용하고 싶다고 말에서 〈책 더 머신〉은 타일러 씨의 만화 캐릭터 중 하나임을 짐작할 수 있다. 따라서 정답은 (D)이다.

184 메모에서 세 번째 단락 첫 번째 줄의 "show"와 의미상 가장 가까운 것은 무엇인가?
(A) 표현하다
(B) 수행하다
(C) 발표하다
(D) 전시하다

해설 이 단어의 앞뒤 맥락을 고려해 보면, 화사를 떠나는 동에게 감사함을 표현한다는 의미가 가장 적절하므로 이 의미와 일치는 동의어는 (A)이다.

185 2017 만화 박람회는 며칠 동안 열리는가?
(A) 2일
(B) 3일
(C) 4일
(D) 5일

해설 두 번째 지문 중반에 이 박람회는 10일에 시작해서 13일에 끝난다고 언급되어 있으므로 나흘 동안 열림을 알 수 있다. 따라서 정답은 (C)이다.

[186-190]

앤젤스 가정 음식 제공 서비스

다음 행사 때는 걱정하지 마시고 앤젤스 가정 음식 제공 서비스를 통해 **[187]** 우아하게 처리된 고급 요리를 준비해 보세요.

저희는 다음과 같은 서비스를 제공합니다:
- 행사를 단계별로 준비해 주는 전문 코디네이터
- **[188]** 다양한 메뉴 선택권
- 훈련된 예절 바른 서비스 직원들
- 다양한 식기류
- **[186]** 장식 전문가

대규모의 행사를 계획한다면, 동봉된 특별 쿠폰을 사용할 수 있습니다. 자한된 기간 내에 놀라운 혜택을 누려 보세요!

궁금하신 사항이 있으시면 043-555-8523으로 전화를 주시거나, 043-555-8525로 팩스를 보내 주시거나, 웹 사이트인 www.angelskitchen.com을 방문해 주시기 바랍니다.

앤젤스 가정 음식 제공 서비스
여름 특별 할인 쿠폰
우리는 당신에게 최상의 완벽한 서비스를 제공하고 있습니다. 아래에 있는 쿠폰을 잘라 필요에 따라 자유롭게 사용하세요

[189] 150분 이상을 모실 수 있는 행사를 위한 요즘이 15% 할인 7월 1일 ~ 8월 31일	250분 이상을 모실 수 있는 행사를 위한 요즘이 25% 할인 7월 1일 ~ 8월 31일

수신: 앤젤스 가정 음식 제공 서비스
발신: 엘리 레인
날짜: 6월 20일
제목: 음식 주문 예상 가격

[188] 저는 제 직원들과 그들의 가족을 위해 7월 4일 야유회를 계획하려고 합니다. 제 직원들은 50명이고 그들이 가족을 데리고 오면 **[189]** 160~200명 정도 될 것입니다. 저는 차려진 바비큐나 조그만 샌드위치 그리고 손으로 집어 먹을 만한 음식들이 간단하고 전형적인 독립 기념일 메뉴들이면 좋겠습니다.

정식으로 서비스를 요청하기 전에 제가 계획하고 있는 행사의 대략적인 가격과 메뉴 선택권들을 알고 싶습니다. 그리고 제 선생이 200명이 넘으면 20% 할인을 받을 수 있나요?

[190] 제 휴대전화 014-555-9632로 연락 주셔서 알려 주세요.

감사합니다.
엘리 레인

어휘 catering 출장 음식 서비스업 aside 제쳐놓고 gourmet 미식가를 위한 delicate 섬세한 presentation 제시, 보여주는 방식 expert 숙달된 coordinator 진행자 courteous 예의 바른 tableware 식탁용 식기류 specialist 전문가 huge 대규모의 incredible 놀라운 cut out 자르다 rate 요금 estimate 견적 outing 야유회 formal 정식적인 approximate 대략적인 abundant 풍성한

186 앤젤스 가정 음식 서비스에서 제공하지 않은 것은 무엇인가?
(A) 장식 전문가
(B) 다양한 식기류의 선택
(C) 예절 교육 서비스
(D) 풍부한 메뉴 선택권

해설 첫 지문 중반에 제공되는 목록을 살펴보면, (A) 장식 전문가와 (B) 다양한 식기류, (D) 다양한 메뉴 선택권에서 각각 확인할 수 있지만 예절 교육 서비스는 내용은 없으므로 정답은 (C)이다.

187 전단지에서 첫 번째 단락 두 번째 줄의 "delicate"와 의미상 가장 가까운 것은 무엇인가?
(A) 얇은
(B) 우아한
(C) 바삭
(D) 여린

해설 고급 요리를 우아하게 처리된다는 내용으로 우아한의 의미를 갖는 (B) graceful이 정답이다.

188 레인 씨는 누구를 위한 행사를 계획하고 있는가?
(A) 친구들
(B) 고객들
(C) 조부모님
(D) 동료와 가족들

해설 세 번째 지문의 맨처음 보면 레인 씨는 팩스를 보내 쓰는 사람이다. 이 지문 중반에서는 직원들과 가족을 위한 야유회를 열고 싶다고 했으므로 정답은 (D)이다.

189 라인 씨는 행사에서 얼마만큼의 할인을 받을 수 있는가?
(A) 10%
(B) 15%
(C) 20%
(D) 25%

해설 라인 씨는 손님이 160~200명 정도 될 거라고 했는데, 쿠폰을 보면 150명이 넘는 경우 15%를 할인해 주므로 정답은 (B)이다.

190 라인 씨는 앱솔루 카드 음식 제공 서비스로부터 어떻게 연락받고 싶어 하는가?
(A) 팩스로
(B) 전화로
(C) 그녀의 사무실에 방문해서
(D) 이메일로

해설 세 번째 지문 마지막 부분에서 라인 씨는 자신의 휴대전화 번호로 연락해 달라고 했으므로 정답은 (B)이다.

[191-195]

수신: 모든 지점장
발신: 앱솔 은행 본사
날짜: 2월 1일
제목: 센더 카드 준비

191 센더 카드는 우리 은행이 가장 최신 신용 카드 서비스 중의 하나입니다. 이는 이번 달 15일부터 시장에 출시될 것입니다.

그렇기에, 모든 은행 직원들은 센더 카드와 관련된 계약 조건들을 다 숙지하여야 합니다. 비록 이 세부 사항들이 아직 마련되지 않았지만, 내일 이점까지는 모든 최종적인 관련 정보를 확인할 수 있을 것입니다.

192 194 더불어, 모든 지점장은 센더 카드 제품에 대한 평가 보고서를 제출시 한 달 후에 제출해야만 합니다.

센더 카드
계약 조건

* 모든 은행 직원들은 센더 카드 제품에 관련된 계약 조건을 충분히 이해하고 있어야 합니다.

1) 고객은 최초 예금 300달러를 가지고 있어야 합니다.
2) 고객은 TC 01 양식을 작성해야 합니다.
3) **193** 제품 수혜자는 반드시 최소 한 달에 4,000달러의 같은 수입을 지재해야 합니다.
4) 카드 신용에 운전면허증, 전화 요금 청구서(휴대전화함 가능), 여권 - 사면증, 운전면허증 같은 고객들을 위해 언급된 조정들에 대해 충분히 인지되어 있어야 합니다.

- 서비스 가입에 관심이 있는 고객들은 센더 카드에 신청을 제출해야 합니다.

수신: 지점의 전 직원들
발신: 앱솔 은행 워싱턴 D.C. 지점
날짜: 3월 20일
제목: 센더 카드 업데이트

주의: 참고를 위해 이 메시지의 복사본을 보관하세요. 센더 카드 이후, 다음과 같은 문제들이 있었습니다:

1. **195** 카드가 작동하지 않거나 주요 시스템에 등록되지 않았음.

2. **194** 미성년자들이 운전면허증을 가지고 카드를 요청함. (주의: 운전면허증은 16세에 취득할 수 있습니다. 하지만 신용 카드는 20세 미만의 고객에게 발급될 수 없습니다.)

우리가 지난달에 연 갖진 교훈이 미래에 더 나은 계획들을 세우는 데 도움이 될 것입니다. 우리는 더 철저하고 같은 실수를 반복하지는 않을 것입니다. **195** 그러므로 센더 카드 제품에 대한 세미나를 교육을 하려고 합니다. 이 교육이 고객에게 더 높은 질의 서비스를 제공할 수 있는 방안이 되기를 바랍니다.

메이슨 포터
워싱턴 D.C. 지점

어휘 preparation 준비 launching 출시 personnel 직원 terms and conditions 계약 조건 specific 세부 사항 furthermore 더욱이 be obligated to ~할 의무가 있다 aware 알고 있는 initial 초기의 beneficiary 수혜자 income 수입 recipient 수령인 deposit 예치금 inoperative 효력이 없는 minor 미성년자 secure 확보하다 foundation 토대, 기초 assessment 평가 thorough 철저한 affiliating company 가맹점 brainstorm 생각해 내다, 떠올리다

191 메모의 목적은 무엇인가?
(A) 직원들에게 새로운 카드 제품을 판매하려고 말하려고
(B) 센더 카드에 대한 의견을 요청하려고
(C) 새로운 제품에 대한 고객의 반응을 올리려고
(D) 모든 지점장에게 가까운 미래의 계획에 대해 알리려고

해설 첫 지문 초반에 센더 카드의 출시를 알리면서 그에 대한 정보를 숙지해야 한다고 말하고 있으므로, 이 글이 목적은 앞으로의 계획에 대해 알리는 것임을 알 수 있다. 따라서 (D)이다.

192 지점장들에게 요구되는 것은 무엇인가?
(A) 현장에서 고객들에게 새로운 제품을 판매하기
(B) 새로운 제품에 대한 평가를 제출하기
(C) 이번 달까지 카드 디자인 브레인스토밍하기
(D) 더 많은 기명당 모으기

해설 첫 지문 후반에 센더 카드에 대한 평가 보고서를 제출해야 한다고 하므로 정답은 (B)이다.

193 센더 카드 제품을 받으려는 고객에게 요구되는 것이 아닌 것은 무엇인가?
(A) 신분증 제시
(B) 최초 예금
(C) 정기적 소득
(D) 부동산 자산

해설 두 번째 지문에서 카드를 발급받으려면 사면증 운전면허증 같은 신분증을 지시해야 하고, 통장에 300달러가 있어야 하고, 매달 4,000달러 이상의 정기적인 수입이 있어야 하는 점 등이 언급되었다. 부동산 자산은 언급되어 있지 않으므로 정답은 (D)이다.

194 다음 중 제품 출시에 관해 암시되지 않은 것은 무엇인가?
(A) 몇몇 카드사 후원하고 있었다.
(B) 제품은 3월 중에 출시되었다.
(C) 제품 출시 후 워크숍이 예정되어 있다.
(D) 미성년자들에게 카드를 요구했다.

해설 세 번째 지문 중반에 (A)는 1번 항목, (D)는 2번 항목에서 각각 확인할 수 있다. 모든, 세 번째 지문은 첫 지문 하단에 명시되었듯이 세 번째 지문 발송일이 3월 20일이고 첫 번째 지문 발송일은 2월 15일이라고 했으므로 (B)가 정답이다.

195 포터 씨가 제안하는 것은 무엇인가?
(A) 직원들의 교육에 참여하는 것
(B) 영업 직원의 수를 늘리는 것
(C) 은행 마감 시간을 조정하는 것
(D) 직원들이 가능한 한 많은 경험을 하는 것

해설 포터 씨는 세 번째 지문 후반부에서 센더 카드 제품에 관한 교육을 열 계획이라고 했으므로 정답은 (A)이다.

KDC 일렉트로닉스사

저희 제품을 구매해 주셔서 매우 감사합니다.

저희 KDC 일렉트로닉스는 고객님을 위해 최고 품질의 가전제품을 제공하기 위해 항상 노력하고 있습니다. 저희는 구매일로부터 2년 이내에 어떤 문제가 발생하더라도 상품을 보증해 드립니다.

또한, 저희는 어느 때나 여러분의 의견, 제안 그리고 질문을 받을 준비가 되어 있습니다. 저희가 고객님의 메시지에 응답하기 위해서 저희 헬프 사이트 www.kdcelectronics.com을 방문해 주시고 198 성함, 이메일 주소, 전화번호 그리고 국가명을 남겨 주시기 바랍니다.

www.kdcelectronics.com/contactus

KDC Electronics.com
문의 사항

성함: 클로이 라이스
이메일: chloe1981@topmail.com
전화번호: 312-555-4765
국가: 영국

의견

저는 최근에 귀하의 한 가게에서 냉장고를 구매했습니다. 제품은 제대로 설치되었고 잘 작동하였습니다. 하지만 오늘 아침에 일어나 보니 냉장고에서 약간의 문제가 있다는 걸 발견했습니다. 199 냉장고를 열었을 때 거의 방 안 온도와 비슷할 정도로 실내 온도가 되어 있습니다. 가게에 가서 음식을 버리거나 가게에서 음식을 사용하는지 대부분 음식이 이미 상했거나 점검 안 되었지 일 나도 제 안 냈는데, 그러면 수리 비용을 지급하지 않아도 되는 것이잖요 맞나요?

수신: 클로이 라이스 〈customer@kdcelectronics.com〉
발신: 고객서비스 〈customer@kdcelectronics.com〉
200 날짜: 8월 11일
200 제목: 8월 11일자 고객님 의견

저희 KDC 냉장고로 인한 불편에 사과를 드립니다. 모든 197 기기가 창문을 떠나기 전에 철저한 검사를 받지만, 몇몇 경험이 있는 기기들이 현지 상점에 배치되기도 합니다.

오늘 고객님 댁에 방문하도록 서비스 팀에게 연락하였습니다. 그러니 198 냉장고 안에 있는 모든 내용물을 빼 주시고 코드를 빼지는 말아 주세요.

고객님의 기기는 기본 2년의 보증됩니다. 그렇기에 수리 비용이 청구되지 않을 것입니다. 200 오늘 서비스 직원이 방문하도록 처리하겠습니다. 하지만 서비스 직원이 늦는다 싶으시면 1-800-555-7412로 전화해 주세요.

KDC 냉장고 중에 다음과 같은 문제들이 발견될 수 있다는 것을 알아두세요.

KDC-10은 윙윙거리는 소리가 날 수도 있으며, 문제가 있을 수 있습니다. 199 KDC-GV 제품은 온도 문제가 있을 수 있으며, KDC-R2는 내부 불빛에 문제가 있을 수 있습니다. KDC-Q5는 냉동고가 너무 차가워질 수 있습니다. 이 제품들에 대한 보증 기간은 연장되었습니다.

에반 로이드
고객 서비스 담당 직원
KDC 일렉트로닉스

어휘 supply 제공하다 top-quality 최고 품질의 appliance 가전제품 U.K. 영국 properly 올바르게 liquid 액체 temperature 온도 fridge 냉장고 apologize 사과하다 thoroughly 철저히 defect 결함 residence 거주지, 주택 content 내용물 disconnect 분리하다 power source 전원 cover 보증하다 warranty 보증 buzzing 윙윙 거리는 extend 연장하다 empty 비우다

196 회사에 연락할 때 불필요한 연락 정보는 무엇인가?
(A) 이름
(B) 집 주소
(C) 이메일 주소
(D) 전화번호
해설 첫 지문 후반에 이름, 이메일 주소, 전화번호 국가는 필요하지만 집 주소는 언급되어 있지 않다. 따라서 정답은 (B)이다.

197 이메일에서 첫 번째 단락 두 번째 단어 중 "appliance"와 의미상 가장 가까운 것은 무엇인가?
(A) 기구
(B) 시설
(C) 특권
(D) 자산
해설 문맥상 "appliance"는 KDC 일렉트로닉스에서 출시한 제품, 즉 기기임을 알 수 있다. 이와 유사한 의미가 있는 단어는 (A) device이다.

198 이메일에 따르면, 라이스 씨는 서비스 직원이 오기 전까지 무엇을 하도록 권고받았는가?
(A) 냉장고의 플러그를 빼는 것
(B) 서비스 센터에 확인 전화를 하는 것
(C) 냉장고를 비우는 것
(D) 냉장고의 물을 끄는 것
해설 세 번째 지문 중반에 냉장고에 보관된 모든 내용물을 빼라고 하고 있으므로 정답은 (C)이다.

199 이메일에 따르면, 라이스 씨가 산 냉장고는 무엇인가?
(A) KDC-GV
(B) KDC-10
(C) KDC-R2
(D) KDC-Q5
해설 두 번째 지문에서 라이스 씨의 냉장고 안의 온도가 실온과 거의 비슷하다는 문제가 언급되었는데, 세 번째 지문 하단에서 KDC-GV 제품에 온도 문제가 있다고 명시되어 있다. 따라서 라이스 씨는 KDC-GV 제품을 구매했음을 추측할 수 있으므로 정답은 (A)이다.

200 라이스 씨에 관해 암시된 것은 무엇인가?
(A) 그녀는 12개월보다 이전에 냉장고를 구매하였다.
(B) 그녀는 가전제품 업체에 전액 환불을 요청하였다.
(C) 그녀는 전에 KDC사와 여러 번 거래를 한 적이 있다.
(D) 그녀의 냉장고는 그녀가 요청한 날짜에 수리될 것이다.
해설 두 번째 지문 하단에 고객이 오늘 라이스 씨가 당일 냉장고를 고쳐달라고 요청하고 있다. 세 번째 지문은 수리 의뢰에 대한 답장인데 이 당장은 요 기이 수리를 의뢰한 당일 그날에 쓰겠음을 알 수 있다. 또, 세 번째 지문 중반쯤에 당일 중으로 수리 기사를 보내겠다고 언급한 내용을 종합해 보면 라이스 씨는 수리 요청을 한 그 당일에 수리를 받게 될 것을 알 수 있다. 따라서 정답은 (D)이다.

혼자 공부하는 초급들을 위한 나홀로 끝내는 新 토익

신토익 고득점을 결정하는 PART 7 완벽 대비 실전 모의고사

★ 더욱 까다로워진 신토익 대비 PART 7 실전 모의고사 10회분 수록

★ 저자 직강 PART 7 공략별 음성 강의 제공 >> QR코드 & 홈페이지(www.nexusbook.com)

★ 궁금한 것은 바로바로 해결하는 나만의 1:1 토익 코치 >> 나홀로 1:1 저자 코칭

★ 저자의 핵심 노하우의 패러프레이징 정리한 일제 해설 수록

★ 신토익 빈출 어휘 리스트 & 테스트 제공 >> 홈페이지(www.nexusbook.com)

나홀로 1:1 코칭

저자 이미영
다음 카페(http://cafe.daum.net/speedytoeic)
>> [나홀로 1:1 코칭] 게시판 이용

저자 박서영
카카오톡 ID로 찾기(ID: matrix20)
>> 친구 추가 후 1:1 채팅

COLUM BOOKS

스마트폰으로 저자 음성 강의 듣기
콜롬북스 APP

나혼자 끝내는

新토익 PART 5&6

신토익 실전 12회

저자 직강 무료
음성 강의 제공

토익 고득점을 위해 필히 정복해야 하는 PART 5&6

틀린 문제는 다시는
틀리지 않도록
훈련하는 체계적 구성

스스로 점검하고
보완할 수 있는 나혼토
체크 리스트 제공

저자 직강의
무료 음성 강의 지원

어휘 리스트
& 테스트 제공

신토익 실전 12회 수록 | 박혜원, 전보람 지음 | 2017년 2월 출간 | 257페이지

新토익을 대비하는
가장 현명한 선택!

· 나혼자 끝내는 新토익 실전서 ·

신토익 LC+RC 5회분 + 해설집

신토익 LC+RC 3회분 + 해설집

실제 시험지가
봉투 안에 쏙~

나혼자 끝내는 新토익
LC+RC 1000제

✓ 한 권으로 끝내는 신토익 실전 모의고사 5회분 수록

✓ 해설집을 따로 구매할 필요가 없는
  LC+RC 합본 실전서

✓ 저자의 노하우를 담아 문제의 키워드를
  단숨에 파악하는 알짜 해설 수록

✓ 실전용 · 복습용 · 고사장 버전의 3종 MP3
  무료 다운로드(www.nexusbook.com)

나혼자 끝내는 新토익
실전 모의고사 3회분(봉투형)

✓ 실제 시험지 형태 그대로,
  신토익 실전 모의고사 3회분 수록

✓ 문제의 키워드를 단숨에 파악하는 알짜 해석 · 해설
  무료 다운로드(www.nexusbook.com)

✓ 실전용 · 복습용 · 고사장 버전의 3종 MP3
  무료 다운로드(www.nexusbook.com)

나혼자 끝내는 신토익 LC+RC 1000제 | 홍진걸, 이주은 지음 | 2017년 6월 출간 | 364쪽
나혼자 끝내는 신토익 실전 모의고사 3회분 | 김랑, 박자은, 임철, 넥서스토익연구소 지음 | 2017년 7월 출간 | 144쪽